Adaptive Radiations in Prehistoric Panama

Number 5

PEABODY MUSEUM MONOGRAPHS

HARVARD UNIVERSITY · CAMBRIDGE, MASSACHUSETTS

Adaptive Radiations in Prehistoric Panama

Edited by

Olga F. Linares

Smithsonian Tropical Research Institute

and

Anthony J. Ranere

Temple University

PEABODY MUSEUM OF ARCHAEOLOGY AND ETHNOLOGY
HARVARD UNIVERSITY, CAMBRIDGE, MASSACHUSETTS
1980

ISBN   0-87365-905-8

LIBRARY OF CONGRESS CATALOG CARD NUMBER 79-57108

This book was set in Palatino by the Cold Type Center, Harvard University Printing Office, and was printed and bound by the Halliday Lithograph Corporation. Manufactured in the United States of America.

Contents

REPORTS

ILLUSTRATIONS

REPORTS

TABLES

Acknowledgments

In a project of this scope and duration, with numerous institutions and individuals involved, it may be impossible to thank, or even to remember, everyone who was helpful. The names listed below are only the most important.

The following grants made possible the field and laboratory research.

To Olga F. Linares:

1969 (spring): University of Pennsylvania Junior Faculty Grant; American Philosophical Society (Penrose Fund No. 5090) for a preliminary survey and excavations at Bocas.

1970-1973: National Science Foundation, Grant 2846, for spring and summer field seasons in western Panama.

1970–1973: Ford Foundation Traineeship grants, administered through the University of Pennsylvania Museum, for four to six United States and Panamanian students to participate in the excavations each year.

1974: Smithsonian Tropical Research Institute (STRI) small grants for final surveys of the Aguacate Peninsula and the Chiriqui Gulf.

1975: Fluid Research Fund award, Smithsonian Institution, for palynological work.

1976 to the present: Several STRI grants to help in the analysis of the materials and writing up of the results.

To Anthony J. Ranere:

1970–1972: Ford Foundation Traineeship grant.

1971: National Science Foundation dissertation improvement grant.

1972–1973: Smithsonian Tropical Research Institute, postdoctoral grant.

1975–1978: Several STRI grants for trips to Panama for analysis and writing.

Thanks to the enlightened policies of the official authorities, Panama still remains one of the most hospitable places to do research in the tropics. First we must thank the Directora of Patrimonio Histórico, Reina Torres de Araúz, and the sub-Directora Marcia de Arosemena, for their constant support and faith in the mutual benefits of international cooperative research in anthropology. To Marcela Camargo de Cooke, Directora of what was in the early seventies the Museo Nacional de Panama and is now the proud Museo del Hombre Panameño, goes our gratitude for her interest and actual participation in our project. From Roberto de la Guardia we have always received knowledgeable and disinterested advice on archaeological matters. The *autoridades provinciales* of Bocas and Chiriqui kept a well-informed and cooperative eye on our whereabouts. For a quick understanding of the scientific aims of our project in granting us permission to excavate in their property we are indebted to: H. Gonzáles, F. Gonzáles, and P. Samudio (Casita de Piedra, Trapiche Shelter, Horacio Gonzales Shelter, and Zarsiadero Shelter); J. Baker and family (Cerro Brujo); C. Machuca (Sitio Machuca); M. Díaz (La Pitahaya); D. Pittí and P.E. González (Sitio Pitti-Gonzalez). In addition, the following persons were especially helpful in making local arrangements and in offering us their hospitality: in the upper Rio Chiriqui region, Roberto Carresedo; in Bocas, the late Mrs. Peck and Xenia Peck; in Chiriqui, the whole Linares-Tribaldos clan. Welcome assistance in the analysis was provided by Joan Ranere.

Our colleagues in the Smithsonian Tropical Research Institute (STRI) have always given instructive, and sometimes even critical but always helpful, advice. We must especially thank the director of STRI, Ira Rubinoff, for unwavering financial and intellectual support. Martin H. Moynihan, senior scientist at STRI, has understood better than anyone else the objectives of our work and has contributed sustentative ideas. His editorial suggestions are found in every page of this monograph.

Several of those who participated in the field research in 1970–1973 as students (I. Borgogno, B. Dahlin, A.J. Ranere, E.J. Rosenthal, P.D. Sheets, S. Spang, G.J. West) have made contributions to this volume. Other crew members were not at the time of fieldwork engaged in writing sundry theses. Nevertheless, the success of the work was in great measure due to John Alden, Richard McCarty, Robert McNealy, Máximo Miranda, and Chip Williams. It is impossible to thank by name the dozens of local workers who labored with care and enthusiasm in our excavations. When all is said and done, they are the real heroes in any field research.

In the field laboratory, other experts, besides the authors of different sections, assisted us with solving particular problems. For interpretations of the geology we have relied on William Bishop, James Clary, Allan Gottesfeld, and Robert Stewart; for identifications of the Cerro Brujo mollusks, on Joseph Rosewater; for help with the computers, Richard A. Bartlett and Donald Windsor; for radiocarbon determinations, Robert Stuckenrath and James Buckley; for a preliminary identification of the Cerro Brujo mammals, Donald K. Grayson.

Besides the illustrators acknowledged separately, we would like to thank Muriel Kirkpatrick for preparing many of the artifact figures. The actual typing of much of the manuscript was done by Terry Sparshott; everything else — from preparing the bibliography, several drafts of the final chapters, and some of the drawings — was in the able hands of María Luz de Jiménez.

The publication of this work was financed by a grant from the Smithsonian Institution. We should like to thank Gordon R. Willey and C.C. Lamberg-Karlovsky for advising that it be accepted in the Peabody Museum Monograph Series.

Olga F. Linares and Anthony J. Ranere

Adaptive Radiations in Prehistoric Panama

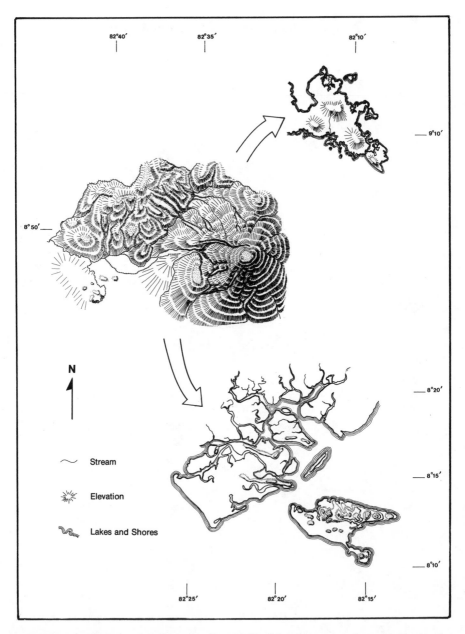

82°40′ 82°35′ 82°10′

9°10′

8°50′

N

Stream

Elevation

Lakes and Shores

8°20′

8°15′

8°10′

82°25′ 82°20′ 82°15′

Figure 1.0-1: Diagram of the biotopes discussed in this volume: top: Aguacate Peninsula; middle, the Talamancan highlands; bottom, the Gulf of Chiriqui.

1.0

Defining the Problem

O.F. LINARES AND A.J. RANERE

Groups moving into new places in the economy of nature do not simply occupy it broadly. They radiate into it; they split into distinct types and populations each of which specializes in the occupation of some part of the new sphere (Simpson 1949, p. 117).

The following study is an attempt to reconstruct a prehistoric example of adaptive radiation among human populations in the New World tropics and to evaluate divergent settlement and subsistence systems resulting from different ecological and social conditions. Ideally, such studies would analyze changes in settlement patterns and subsistence techniques, and in social and political organizations, as a population expands out of one ecological zone into two or more contrasting zones. The role of ecology in the evolution of adaptive strategies could then be kept separate from the particular cultural configuration brought into new areas by migrant groups.

In actuality many studies of human adaptation suffer from a certain looseness of conceptual structure and research design. For example, differences in sociopolitical organization among historically related groups in Madagascar (Kottak 1972), or conversely, similarities in culture between unrelated groups in Amazonia (Meggers 1971) have been attributed to some kind of "adaptive imperative." Perhaps the time has come to discuss adaptive strategies in the light of an actual historical reconstruction, however incomplete and fragmentary the evidence may be.

Western Panama seems to be an appropriate place in which to attempt a controlled comparison of adaptive changes through time. This land of considerable ecological diversity, involving the province of Bocas del Toro facing the Atlantic side and the province of Chiriqui facing the Pacific, has highlands and two coasts only 100 kilometers apart. Furthermore, this area has been settled for at least 7,000 years. The transformation from hunting-gathering, first to root- and tree-crop cultivation, then to seed agriculture, seems to have involved these local populations, despite undeniable influences from the outside.

1.1 PREVIOUS ARCHAEOLOGICAL WORK IN BOCAS DEL TORO AND CHIRIQUI

The dearth of previous archaeological knowledge from Bocas del Toro (henceforth Bocas) reflects the general situation for the Isthmus. From the beginning, archaeological work has concentrated on developments on the Pacific coast, especially in the provinces of Veraguas and Cocle, and in the Azuero Peninsula, particularly Parita Bay (Lothrop 1937, 1942, 1950; Mason 1940; Willey and McGimsey 1954; McGimsey 1956; Ladd 1964; Cooke ms. 1972; Ichon 1974). The Caribbean coast from Costa Rica to Colombia was, archaeologically speaking, practically terra incognita, and the main reason seems to be the unspectacular nature of its remains. Lothrop's statement (1966, p. 193) reflects this attitude: "We should add that, apart from northeastern Costa Rica, no archaeological remains of importance have been reported on the Atlantic slopes of Lower Central America and Panama."

It was not until the 1960s that the numerous shell middens of Bocas were first given any attention, and then by a geographer (Gordon 1969). Even the Stirlings, who in 1953 paid a ten-day visit to Bocas (Stirling and Stirling 1964), ignored the shell middens, devoting their efforts instead to descriptions of other kinds of sites: an open (non-shell) midden site, a cave burial, and an urn burial site. Hence, ours was the first systematic work ever to be done in Bocas del Toro province.

In Chiriqui, archaeological knowledge dates back to the turn of the century with the voluminous descriptions of Holmes (1888) and MacCurdy (1911) of "Classic Chiriqui" ceramics from graveyards in the coastal plains to the north, east, and west of the city of David. For many decades the only work on Chiriqui was Osgood's museum article (1935) and more recently Haberland's (1957, 1960, 1962) sporadic graveyard excavations. In the 1960s, the results of the program on coastal Pacific Panama (Project G: 1961-62), sponsored by the Institute of Andean Research, were published (Linares 1966, 1968a, 1968b). Although the Linares report (1968b) proposed the first chronology for Chiriqui based on stratigraphic excavations of habitation sites, it covered only the very late periods for a small portion of the coast and offshore islands in the Gulf of Chiriqui, ignoring the highlands totally. Its emphasis is on chronology. A reconstruction of subsistence patterns through time was offered, but the limited nature of the test excavations placed serious restrictions on interpretation.

1.2 THE CONCEPTUAL HISTORY OF THE PROJECT

The central idea behind the present project grew out of ethnographic realities in western Panama. Two groups speaking the same dialect variant of Guaymí, a macro-Chibchan language, still occupy the ecologically contrastive provinces of Chiriqui and Bocas. Although both Guaymí groups are swidden cultivators, they differ in some important aspects of settlement and subsistence. These differences seem to be corroborated by the chronicles of the sixteenth century. Previous knowledge of the archaeology of Chiriqui (Linares 1968a, 1968b) also seemed to support to a large degree the ethnohistoric picture. In 1969 we conducted an exploratory archaeological survey of Almirante Bay, in the province of Bocas del Toro, which indeed confirmed our impression that the ancient subsistence adaptations on this coast had been different from those of Chiriqui, despite strong similarities in aspects of the ceramic record (Linares and Ranere 1971). An attempt to document the times when major changes occurred and the processes behind these strikingly different adaptations seemed to us a substantive, if not a theoretic, contribution. Thus, in 1970 we began a two-year research project comparing human adaptations in western Panama.

As work progressed on either coast, we initiated a survey of preceramic rock shelters at the midelevations of the slopes and highlands of Chiriqui. It was becoming apparent that the history of human occupations in western Panama had a greater time span in the interior than on the coast, and that the origin of coastal populations might be found in the interior. For this reason, we expanded our project for a third year, in order to cover the mountainous area of Volcan, midway between the coasts. Our aim was to investigate the evolution of agricultural villages from a preceramic hunting-gathering base and then to document the expansion out of the highlands to the coast, including the adjustments made to different maritime situations. The successes and failures of this attempt will become apparent in the sections that follow.

1.3 ORGANIZATION OF THE BOOK

The first half of this book includes a number of general and interpretative chapters on the ecology, chronology, and prehistory of western Panama. The second part contains the more specific reports and substantive data behind the interpretations. This organization responds to the feeling that archaeology often suffers from either a surfeit of undocumented ideas or a surfeit of data. When these are combined in the same chapters they often result in jarring transitions, from the very abstract to the most concrete discussions all in the same breath. Hence, our design is prompted not only by the desire to maintain continuity in the discussion and presentation of the ideas but also by the desire to make documentation directly accessible. We hope that a separate technical section, which can easily be consulted without losing one's place in the primary text, will ease the assimilation of so much detail.

The division of labor between the editors has followed more or less stereotyped lines. Whereas Ranere did somewhat more of the fieldwork on which the book is based, Linares did more of the writing. The introduction to each of the parts and the conclusions are by her. Both of us, however, have applied an equally strong editorial hand in the contributions by the other authors. We hope that in the process we helped improve what in some instances were very good, but very rough first drafts.

Figure 2.0-1: Study areas: Almirante Bay on the Atlantic coast; Cerro Punta and El Hato in the Volcan highlands; upper drainage of Rio Chiriqui; Gulf of Chiriqui on the Pacific. Courtesy, Instituto Cartográfico Tommy Guardia.

2.0

Introduction

O.F. LINARES

2.1 THE NATURAL SETTING

Tropical communities are remarkably complex in many respects (see MacArthur 1972). Panama in particular shows great variation within a relatively small area. Talking only of its herpatology, Myers (1972, p. 199) remarks: "Few regions of the world support such a diversity of terrestrial life in such a small area as the Isthmus of Panama, illustrated, for example, by my estimate that 4 percent of the world's living species of amphibians and reptiles occur there." This diversity has a long history (Woodring 1966; Simpson Vuilleumier 1971). It is maintained by the existence of closely juxtaposed yet different habitats and climatic regimes.

Our study area in western Panama is a transect roughly 110 kilometers long by 25 kilometers wide, running north-south from the Pacific to the Atlantic coast, bisecting the longer east-west axis of the Isthmus (fig. 2.0-1). It extends from sea level to an altitude of over 2,500 meters along the continental divide. This strip includes portions of two adjacent provinces, separated by the Cordillera de Talamanca, "a narrow rugged highland that is nearly unbroken up to the 1,200-meter contour" (Myers 1969). The highest point, Volcan Baru, with a peak 3,474 meters high, had long been considered an extinct Pleistocene volcano (Terry 1956) until our research showed it to have been active relatively recently.

Although the two provinces are separated by the same mountain range, the topography of Bocas varies considerably from that of Chiriqui. If we refer to the coastal edge, including the plains up to 600 meters, as the lowlands, and to the rest of the land above 600 meters as the highlands, then clearly two-thirds of Chiriqui but only one-third of Bocas, which has a much more broken and hilly relief, lie in the lowlands. In fact, Bocas has a narrower coastal edge, and a much shorter distance from seashore to the 600-meter contour, than Chiriqui. Nonetheless, very short distances separate the coasts. A two-day walk takes a person from the Atlantic to the Pacific slopes. A modern Guaymí Indian who lives on the Bocas side, up the

7

headwaters of any of the major rivers, can start from his village at daybreak and be with his relatives on the Pacific side of the Cordillera at dusk.

The effects of the Cordillera on maritime air masses and rainfall on either side of the Isthmus have been discussed by Holdridge and Budowksi (1956), Bennett (1968), and Myers (1969). Even though Tosi (1971) recognizes the effects of the Talamancan range on the patterns of rainfall, he still characterizes the vegetation on both sides of the mountains as "tropical moist forest," apparently disregarding the fact that a nonseasonal rain forest covers most of the Atlantic slopes, inland as well as on the coast, while a deciduous forest, easily converted into savanna, is found over most of the Pacific slopes (fig. 2.0-2). Indeed, it would be most surprising if the vegetation did not differ in species composition and structure between two areas with such marked differences in topography and rainfall distribution. (Similar difficulties with the Holdridge classification have been voiced before; see Bennett 1968, p. 24; Myers 1969, pp. 9-12.)

Generally speaking, the high mountains of western Panama form a barrier to moisture-laden winds from the northeast, forcing them throughout the year to drop their moisture on the slopes facing the northern or Atlantic side. Hence, the slopes and coastal plains on the Pacific side of western Panama tend to be drier and exhibit greater seasonal differences on the average than those on the Atlantic side. In the highlands above 2,000 meters "ascending air currents throughout the year carry sufficient moisture to produce cloud formation on the higher peaks and ridges" (Myers 1969, p. 7). These rainy, cold regions above 1,800 meters are covered by wet (Cf) tropical montane evergreen forests.

The Bocas coast itself is under an Af (tropical wet) regime. Rainfall averages more than 3,000 mm per year on the coast, and it rains on more than two-thirds of the days in the year (table 1). With the exception of reduced periods of rain in February-March and September-October, there is no severe dry season with less than 50 mm of rain. Not only is the rainfall fairly evenly distributed throughout the year, but nearly half of it falls at night, discouraging rapid evaporation. As a result, dense rain forest covers these areas undisturbed by humans. Since the Talamancan range extends its ridges nearly to the ocean edge, there are no extensive coastal plains and literally no beaches, except on the Valiente Peninsula. The only two large and important rivers flowing into this portion of the Caribbean coast are the Changuinola and the Cricamola, located on opposite ends, east and west, of Bocas province.

In contrast, the province of Chiriqui has wide and extensive coastal lowlands and flat plains bathed by numerous meandering rivers with substantial floodplains. The yearly rainfall is not only less than that of Bocas but it is also differently distributed. In Chiriqui it rains on half, or less than half, of the days in the year, and there are three to five months with less than 50 mm of rain. In addition, three-fourths of the rainfall on these coastal plains tends to fall during the day, encouraging rapid evaporation. Hence Chiriqui has an Aw (tropical wet and dry) regime. Grassland or savanna

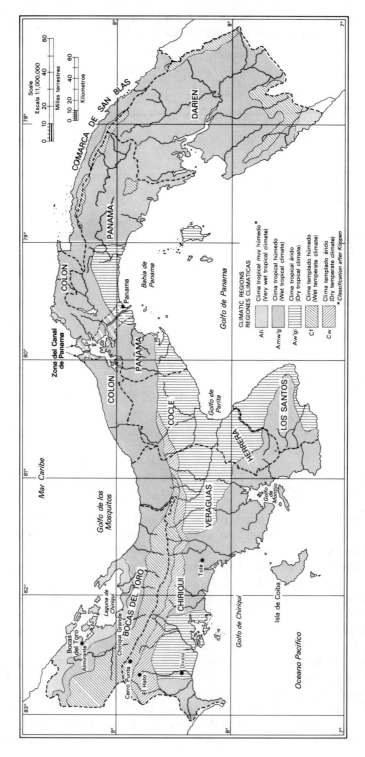

Figure 2.0-2: Climatic map of Panama according to Köppen's classification. Courtesy, Instituto Cartográfico Tommy Guardia.

TABLE 1 AVERAGE RAINFALL FOR THE BOCAS COAST, CHIRIQUI HIGHLANDS, AND CHIRIQUI COAST[1]

	Elevation in meters	Days with rain	Months with < 50 mm	Totals 1973 and 1975	Average for several years	No. of years averaged
BOCAS COAST						
Bahía de Almirante (Af)	2					
1973		247	0	3,987.8	3,387	3
1975		257	0	3,183.2		
CHIRIQUI HIGHLANDS						
Cerro Punta (Cf)	2,000					
1973		252	2	2,515.5	2,260	8
1975		244	3	2,144.0		
Nueva California (Cw)[2]	1,400					
1973		201	3	2,914.3	2,801	9
1975		no data	4	no data		
CHIRIQUI COAST						
Divala (Aw)[3]	8					
1973		169	5	2,858.6	2,490	7
1975		196	3	2,978.3		
David (Aw)	27					
1973		189	3	2,994.3	no data	no data
1975		no data	4	no data		

1. Information from Estadística Panameña: *Meteorología, Años 1973, 1975.* Panamá.

2. Near El Hato (fig. 2.0-2).

3. See fig. 2.0-2.

vegetation, and patches of dry or fire-resistent shrubs and small trees, such as "chumico" (*Curatella americana*), "nance' (*Byrsonima crassifolia*), marañon" (*Anacardium occidentale*), and "malagueto" (*Xylopia* sp.), representing "a culturally disturbed complex" (Bennett 1968), are characteristic of these Pacific coastal lowlands. Nowadays, the few peasants left in Chiriqui who still practice slash-and-burn agriculture prefer the alluvial zones where river resources and groundwater sometimes permit year-round cultivation without the need for irrigation.

The marine inshore geography of the two western Panamanian coasts also differs in parallel fashion, depending on the "coastal geomorphology, the quantitative and qualitative nature of river discharge, and tidal fluctuations" (Collier 1964, p. 136). These differences have been discussed by Glynn (1972). Generally speaking, shallow-water coral formations and marine grass beds are well developed on the Bocas side, while mudflats and beaches are not. This is characteristic of the entire Caribbean coast of

Panama (Porter 1972). Other phenomena affecting the Bocas coastal ecology are strong buffeting northeast winds, few protected harbors, and tides of low amplitude (less than .5 meter). Chiriqui, on the other hand, has a wide continental shelf, extensive mudflats and beach formations, fewer coral reefs except in the Secas and Contreras islands, fewer marine grass beds, and tides of greater amplitude, sometimes reaching 6 meters. These conditions must affect the molluscan and fish biota, though in ways that are not always clear. For example, species diversity of fish may well be greater on the Atlantic side of the Isthmus because of greater coral reef development, but the fish biomass (expressed in the number and size of individuals) appears to be greater on the Pacific coast, at least in the Bay of Panama, which experiences a yearly upwelling. All these factors affected human adaptations in the past, as they indeed still affect the adaptations of traditional groups living today in western Panama.

2.2 THE MODERN PARALLEL: THE GUAYMI INDIANS

Approximately 52,000 Guaymí, practicing a slash-and-burn or swidden-subsistence agriculture, now live in the mountain valleys of eastern Chiriqui, Bocas, and western Veraguas. Accounts by the well-known chroniclers of the Conquest (González Dávila, Oviedo y Valdés, Ruiz de Campos, Pascual de Andagoya, Requejo y Salcedo, and Herrera for the Pacific coast; Fernando Colón and Hernán Porras for the Caribbean coast) leave little doubt that the Guaymí are the direct descendants, or close relatives thereof, of the Indian groups encountered by the Spaniards.

The broad picture of Guaymí social and economic organization is known from a study that Philip Young (1971) carried out in the San Felix highlands of eastern Chiriqui. Several points developed in Young's work are of direct relevance to our archaeological investigations: (1) He argues that the agricultural basis of the modern Guaymí has remained practically unchanged from the sixteenth century (and, by implication, from the immediate pre-Conquest periods). This has encouraged three hundred years of relative social structural stability. (2) He shows how marriage, residence, and descent function together with slash-and-burn agriculture, based (in the San Felix area) on a two-year cultivation/ten-year fallowing cycle, to keep settlement patterns dispersed and composed mainly of single cognatic kin-unit hamlets. (3) In areas of Chiriqui where the carrying capacity of the land has reached a maximum (14 persons per square kilometer calculated by Carneiro's formula), the fissioning process by which households disperse is becoming rare, and multiple-kin hamlets are emerging. (4) These processes of nucleation and emigration are being accelerated by ecological degradation due to overcultivation and cattle raising.

The adaptations of the 12,000 Guaymí and their relatives, the Bogotá, living in Bocas seem to be quite different from those of their Chiriqui relatives. Some Bocas Guaymí still wear barkcloth garments, do most of their hunting with bows and arrows, and have a number of other tools and utensils only slightly modified from the past (Gordon 1969, pp. 35-50). A few households around Rio Caña still make pottery. More important, outside the more densely settled areas along the Cricamola and Changuinola rivers, the rest of the Bocas Guaymí territory is characterized by very low population densities.

These groups live in dispersed hamlets, practicing a long forest-fallow, slash-and-mulch agricultural system, unlike the short-fallow, slash-and-burn system of the Chiriqui Guaymí. Among the crops grown today by the Bocas groups, the *Pejibaye* or peach palm *(Guilielma gasipaes)* is an important staple. In contrast to the Pacific Guaymí, whose diet includes a great deal of maize, the Bocas Guaymí grow little maize, and that which they do grow is apparently a small tropical flint corn (possibly *morocho*). Instead, root crops, especially the "otoe" (*Xanthosoma* sp.), whose tubers are more easily preserved than manioc's, and imported products (plantains and rice) are the important staples. This contrast, maize and beans on the Pacific watershed and root crops plus tree crops on the Caribbean (see Young, section 14.0 and report no. 19; Bort, report no. 20), seems also to have existed in late pre-Hispanic times among groups who were, in turn, the direct ancestors, or close relatives thereof, of the groups encountered by the Spaniards in western Panama.

Early ethnohistorical sources also suggest that at the time of the Conquest basic sociopolitical differences were reflected in the type of societies inhabiting either province. A numerous, but dispersed, population, living in hamlets and mountain enclaves near the headwaters of large rivers, was characteristic of Bocas del Toro (Iglesia 1947; Sauer 1966). On the coastal plains of the Pacific, in Chiriqui, early accounts mention the presence of large politically federated tribes, what we call chiefdoms, located in towns of over 1,000 persons, with political power vested in chiefs and some sort of class differences expressed in wealth, burial customs, and rituals. Best known among these are the Azuero and Parita Bay chiefdoms described by Lothrop (1937, pp. 3-32) from historical sources, but those to the west, in Chiriqui were also fairly impressive (Stirling 1950; Linares 1968b).

2.3 DEVELOPING A HYPOTHESIS

The relationship of subsistence activities to settlement patterns and sociopolitical developments in the humid tropics of the New World has been a source of considerable speculation in American archaeology. During the fifties, emphasis was placed on broad culture-stage typologies (Steward and Faron 1959), with generalizations defining the tropical forest as a macroenvironment with limited evolutionary potential (Meggers 1954). Subsequent studies had a more particularistic focus. For example Lathrap (1968) had emphasized the difference between large horticultural riverine societies and small hinterland groups in the Amazon, and Coe and Flannery (1964) had assessed the role that microenvironments have played in the process of sociopolitical elaboration. A hypothesis based on the unlimited availability of land in the vast Amazonian forest, rather than on the limitations of slash-and-burn agriculture *per se,* was offered by Carneiro (1961) as an explanation for arrested development in some tropical areas of South America. He saw the evolution of the Circum-Caribbean chiefdoms and the lowland Maya as a result of an increase in population density in circumscribed zones of arable land. This connection between population density, resource scarcity, differential access to resources on the one hand, and social stratification and/or complex political organization on the other has been explored with growing sophistication in different parts of the Americas. The most distinguished study to date (Flannery 1976) presents a model of Early Formative Mesoamerican society and casts serious doubt on the assumed causal connections between these variables.

Given the differences that existed by Conquest times in western Panama between societies north and south of the continental divide, and being cognizant of the long-range ecological processes that may have contributed to these contrasts, in 1971-1973 we formulated a number of broad, preliminary questions: What was the nature of the differences in settlement patterns and subsistence activities between Bocas and Chiriqui? How did these change during the whole range of occupation of selected zones? What was the effect of a balanced humidity, as opposed to pronounced seasonal variations, on the types of crops that were grown, on the choice of living areas, and on the importance of additional procurement activities such as hunting and fishing? Were settlement and subsistence practices more similar at earlier than at later periods? Does one area show a longer history of occupation and change through time? Our inability to provide even partial answers to these questions demonstrated the need for a broad and integrated program of archaeological, ethnographic, and ecological research. Only then could explanations for the origin of different sociocultural systems in this part of Panama be advanced with any degree of confidence. Using the method of controlled comparison through time (see Eggan 1954), we set out to investigate the possible effects that ecological variables may have had on the evolution of cultural systems on either side of the Talamancan range.

Two contrastive littoral zones, both outside major river systems, were chosen for investigation: Almirante Bay on the Atlantic side and the Gulf of Chiriqui on the Pacific side. We reasoned that such differences as may have existed in the adaptations of prehistoric societies to either coast would show up more clearly in nonriverine "marginal" environments than in richer, and probably more "permissive," riverine-edge habitats.

However, as we have mentioned before (section 1.2), after Ranere started his survey it became apparent that human occupations were older and had experienced earlier changes, such as the adoption of agriculture, in the interior than on the coast. Furthermore, the highlands also seemed to have harbored the first Formative-period societies associated with regional centers. Again, this situation needed to be explained. Thus, rather than contrasting developments on either coast, we concentrated on a three-way investigation of human adaptations to the highlands, to the Atlantic, and to the Pacific coasts. A preliminary inspection of the ceramic collections from the oldest levels of our test excavations in the three areas had suggested a common origin for these populations. This presented us with a unique opportunity to study human adaptive radiations and the evolution of new cultural systems in three distinct tropical habitats.

It seemed unnecessary at the beginning of our study to embark upon a long discussion of concepts such as "adaptive radiation," "cultural system," and so forth. Suffice it to say that by adaptation we meant the organizational responses made by a population to new and probably stressful conditions. By a cultural system we meant the processes that in human groups regulate the interaction between natural and social phenomena. As will become evident from our discussions, our reconstructions of past cultural systems are very sketchy indeed, and our explanations for them sketchier still. It is in the nature of archaeological inference that to reconstruct what probably happened is difficult, but to know why or how it should have happened may be impossible. This does not mean that one should not try.

PART ONE

FROM PRECERAMIC SHELTERS TO LARGE VILLAGES AND CENTERS

The following sections cover two periods of unequal length. From 4800 B.C. to 300 B.C. pre-pottery-using peoples were living in rock shelters and open habitation sites near the river's edge, on the Rio Chiriqui canyon floor, at elevations below 1,000 meters. Their subsistence-settlement pattern has been termed the Tropical Forest Archaic by Ranere, who believes that they used their simple stone tools to make more sophisticated wooden implements, used directly for securing food and shelter. Changes occurring in the stone tool inventory between the oldest (Talamancan) and more recent (Boquete) preceramic phases are difficult to interpret. Could the sudden appearance of polished stone axes and celts around 2300 B.C. signal the transition from hunting-gathering to root-crop agriculture in this area? If so, what then was the function of the edge-ground cobbles and milling stone bases occurring in *both* preceramic periods? Ranere concludes his section by alerting us to the hazards of reconstructing lifeways in the tropics, where organic remains are preserved only under very special circumstances. He cautions against the idea that such adaptations as "hunting-gathering," or "early agriculture," are mutually exclusive. Especially in the tropics, where many alternatives are possible, hunter-gatherers have always coexisted with shifting cultivators.

While maize was not present, or was of very minor importance, in the diet of the Rio Chiriqui preceramic peoples, it seemed to have been the mainstay of subsequent groups living 35 kilometers to the west, and 1,000 meters higher up, on the foothills of Volcan Baru. According to Linares and Sheets, the occupation of these highlands spanned La Concepción phase (300 B.C. to A.D. 200?) and the Early and Late Bugaba phases, from A.D. 200 to A.D. 600. A hiatus of five hundred years separates these prosperous maize farmers from their preceramic, root-growing (?) predecessors. Was this the time when maize-carrying peoples spread all over the plains and highlands of western Panama? This is a difficult question to answer, but there are indications in that direction. The successful colonization of the highlands seemed to have been related as much to the fertility of the soils as to the presence of hard stone of volcanic origin with which to make tools. Essential to every process of land clearance and agriculture, celt manufacture was in the hands of specialists. Could the growth of a site hierarchy by A.D. 400 have been related in some way to craft specialization? Certainly, the introduction of maize agriculture, the manufacture of stone objects, and the growth of "ceremonial" centers all seem to have been associated in the Volcan area. As with other phenomena in archaeology, however, it is hard to spell out the exact causal connections between these variables.

3.0

Preceramic Shelters in the Talamancan Range

A. J. RANERE

3.1 LOCATING PRECERAMIC SITES IN CHIRIQUI

Preceramic sites were unknown in western Panama at the time our research was initiated in 1970. In fact, the shell midden Cerro Mangote in the Parita Bay region of central Panama was the only preceramic site reported in all of lower Central America (McGimsey 1956). An intensive survey along the Gulf of Chiriqui in 1961 failed to discover a single "early" site, even though this was one of the project's major goals (Linares 1968b). We now know that the existence of preceramic groups in Parita Bay and their absence from the Chiriqui coast is almost certainly related to the occurrence in the first region, but not in the second, of both a dry-season upwelling, which brings a marked enrichment of the marine fauna, and extensive mudflats, which are an excellent habitat for mollusks (Linares and Cooke 1975; Ranere and Hansell 1978).

The earliest evidence of human occupation in western Panama in 1970 consisted of numerous cemeteries and habitation sites, some with large stone carvings and low platform mounds (e.g., Barriles, section 4.3 and report no. 5) dating to more than 2,000 years ago. Thus, the first known inhabitants of the Chiriqui region were there in large numbers and as members of a complex society, quite probably chiefdoms. While it may be true that no one had been looking inland specifically for early sites, the nature of the vegetation (much of lower Central America being tropical forest) and the nature of the preceramic components themselves may have played major roles in preventing discovery of preceramic sites on the one hand and their proper interpretation on the other (Ranere 1972b). For these reasons I chose in 1970 to concentrate my research for preceramic occupations on caves and rock shelters. For thousands of years human populations around the world have taken advantage of these natural shelters, and it seems reasonable to assume that they did so in Panama as well. Besides being easily located, rock shelters and caves seemed the most suitable kinds of sites to examine in our survey since they tend to be occupied over long time spans, and they provide depositional environments for rapid accumulation of sediments and, therefore, for good separation of archaeological materials.

In the dry season of 1970 I spent three weeks in the mountains of western Panama doing a preliminary site survey. Of the four areas examined, three contained preceramic sites, but only one, the Rio Chiriqui canyon, had rock shelters. In fact, I was led to survey this valley because of one well-known shelter named appropriately Casita de Piedra (Little Stone House). This rock shelter is a favorite camping spot for Guaymí Indians and campesinos traveling the Third of November Trail (Camino Tres de Noviembre) across the divide between the Atlantic and Pacific sides of the Isthmus. The remoteness of the area and the time available for the survey limited the testing operations to hand-troweled 1/2 x 1/2-meter pits excavated no deeper than 70 centimeters. While not extensive, the testing did demonstrate that two of the Rio Chiriqui shelters had preceramic components (Casita de Piedra and the Zarsiadero Shelter).

In the upper Rio San Felix region 90 kilometers to the east, and in the India Vieja region 9 kilometers to the west, open air sites were located that appeared to be preceramic. However, the former region produced only open campsites with no apparent depth, while the latter contained an extensive quarry area, which seemed to have been used in ceramic as well as in preceramic times. A later survey along the Pacific coastal plain of Chiriqui failed to locate any caves or rock shelters suitable for human habitation. The evidence for preceramic occupations in Chiriqui appeared to be widespread, but the most complete record discovered still lay in the Rio Chiriqui drainage basin. Hence, four rock shelters and one open campsite, all with preceramic components, were excavated in this region in 1971.

3.2 THE UPPER RIO CHIRIQUI REGION

The Pacific coastal plain of Chiriqui is crossed by a number of rivers that maintain a high volume of water even during the dry season. The largest of these rivers is the Rio Chiriqui (not to be confused with the Rio Chiriqui Viejo), which drains a considerable portion of the continental divide before flowing south past the city of David to the Gulf of Chiriqui. The sites discussed in this chapter are all located within one kilometer of the Rio Chiriqui in an area of high relief (see figs. 3.0-1 and 3.0-2). All sites are located on narrow terraces near the floor of the canyon at elevations between 645 and 900 meters above sea level. The canyon walls rise 600 to 800 vertical meters within a distance of two kilometers on either side of the river (which here runs north-south). The continental divide itself, which is five to eight kilometers to the north of the sites, rises to an average height of 2,000 meters.

Rainfall in the region is seasonally distributed, with a pronounced dry season lasting for about four months (December to April). During the dry season, monthly rainfall averages less than 50 mm, while wet-season monthly rainfall averages around 500 mm, a tenfold increase. Annual rain-

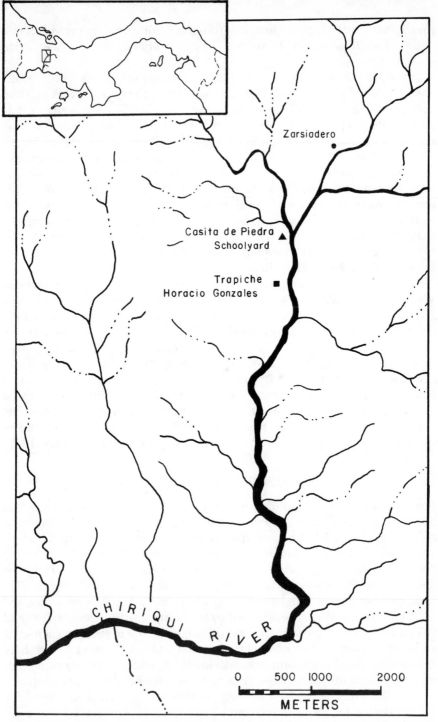

Figure 3.0-1: Site locations in the Chiriqui River drainage basin: The Trapiche Shelter and the Horacio Gonzales Shelter (■), The Casita de Piedra and the Schoolyard Site (▲), and the Zarsiadero Shelter (●).

fall in the region is approximately 4,000 mm (Tosi 1971; Estadística Panameña 1976). However, the canyon floor is in a rain shadow and probably receives somewhat less rain.

Resources from several physiographic zones could have been utilized by the inhabitants of the rock shelters. Most important is the zone of high terraces and gently sloping alluvial fans bordering the Rio Chiriqui and its major tributaries (e.g., Rio Casita de Piedra and Rio Zarsiadero). All of the excavated sites reported on in this section are found in this zone, which today supports a small farming population living in dispersed hamlets. Behind the alluvium are the canyon slopes that have been cleared for agriculture and pasture. Here and there a few patches of the semievergreen seasonal forest that once covered these slopes remain. Along the tributary streams draining the divide, the mountainsides are still covered with lower montane evergreen forest. Downstream, where the canyon broadens, lowland semievergreen seasonal forest would be the natural vegetation, but in this area, strongly modified by human activity, savanna vegetation, maintained by fire, is the dominant formation today.

Figure 3.0-2: Aerial photograph of the terrain in the vicinity of the Chiriqui River sites.

3.3 DESCRIPTION OF THE ROCK SHELTERS

Casita de Piedra is located 175 meters southwest of the confluence of the Rio Chiriqui and its tributary, Rio Casita de Piedra. The site is at the edge of a small terrace ca. 45 meters above the Rio Chiriqui and 25 meters above the Rio Casita de Piedra. The difference in elevation of the site above the two rivers, a height of 20 meters, reflects the fact that the Rio Casita de Piedra literally falls into the Rio Chiriqui for the last 200 meters of its course.

The shelter itself is formed by an overhanging section of a truly enormous granite boulder (fig. 3.0-3). This sheltered area is not large; less than 24 square meters of floor space is beneath the overhang now, and the low ceiling plus large blocks of rock protruding form the floor make the usable space smaller still. However, these partially buried roof-fall blocks suggest that initially the overhang extended out somewhat farther than it does today. Then too, removal of one meter of fill from the shelter makes almost all of the space underneath the overhang usable. Still, 30 square meters seems the maximum protected floor space ever available at the site. We excavated 10 square meters of the site in its central section (fig. 3.0-4), of which approximately 7 square meters fell inside the dripline or underneath the overhang. (For an interpretation of depositional processes at Casita de Piedra and the other excavated rock shelters see report no. 1.)

Figure 3.0-3: Casita de Piedra.

Figure 3.0-4: Plan and section of Casita de Piedra showing the relationship of the excavated blocks and the protected floor space (dripline indicated by dashed line). (Adapted from figure 3, Proceedings of the First Puerto Rican Symposium on Archaeology, Fundación Arqueológica, Antropológica e Histórica de Puerto Rico.)

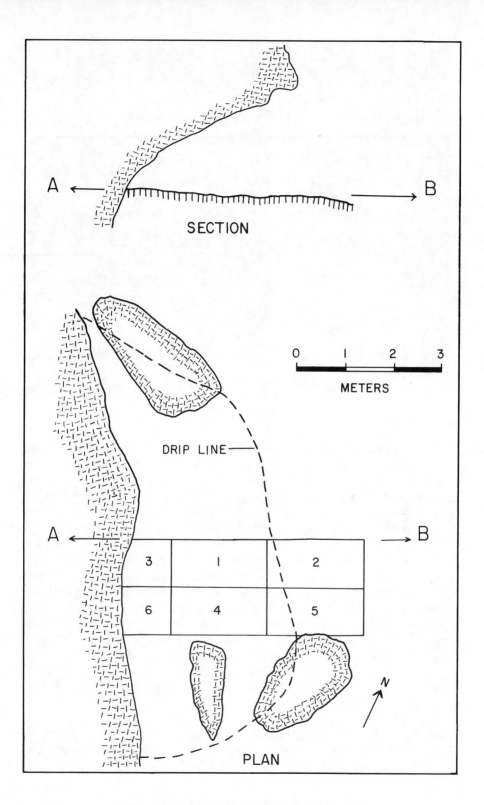

SECTION

DRIP LINE

METERS

N

PLAN

Figure 3.0-5: Trapiche Shelter.

The Trapiche Shelter is one kilometer downstream from Casita de Piedra on the same, or west, bank of the Rio Chiriqui. It sits 250 meters back from the river and 45 meters above it, at an altitude of 645 meters above sea level. The overhang is formed by a huge boulder which is but one of a number outcropping in the immediate vicinity, four of which were shelters yielding evidence of human use (the Horacio Gonzales site among them).

The Trapiche Shelter was the largest and most protected of the four. It is about the same size as Casita de Piedra, holding 22 square meters floor space (fig. 3.0-5), although because of the low ceiling, as much as one third of it would not be usable living space with the floor at its present high level. However, upon excavation we discovered that the rear of the shelter sloped downward only slightly; thus with the floor lowered 80 to 100 centimeters, eight to ten additional square meters of floor space would have been available. Still, the shelter would have to be considered a small one, with less than 30 square meters of protected living space. We excavated 12 square meters of the site, 10 square meters within and 2 square meters beyond the dripline (fig. 3.0-6).

The Horacio Gonzales Shelter is literally around the corner from the Trapiche Shelter, no more than 50 meters downriver. It sits at about the same elevation above sea level (645 meters) and in about the same relationship to the Rio Chiriqui (250 meters back and 45 meters above it) as the

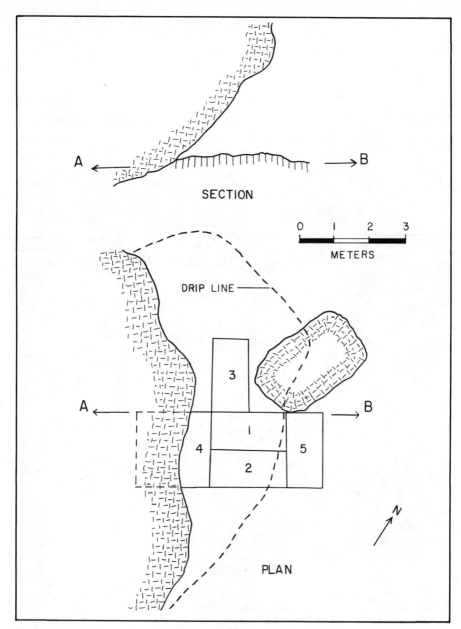

Figure 3.0-6: Plan and section of the Trapiche Shelter showing the relationship of the excavated blocks and the protected floor space (dripline indicated by dashed line). (Adapted from figure 4, Proceedings of the First Puerto Rican Symposium on Archaeology, Fundación Arqueológica, Antropológica e Histórica de Puerto Rico.)

Trapiche Shelter. A spring-fed stream flows 25 meters from the front of the shelter and 4 meters below the level of the shelter floor (fig. 3.0-7). Although the site has considerably less area underneath its overhang than either of the other two shelters upriver, it has a comfortably high ceiling and perhaps

Figure 3.0-7: Horacio Gonzales site.

more usable floor space than is available at the Trapiche site today. Five square meters were excavated at the site with all but the very front of blocks 2 and 3 being within the dripline.

Slightly under a kilometer upstream from the Casita de Piedra the canyon of the Rio Chiriqui makes a right-angle turn and heads due east toward the headwaters of the river. Entering from the north at this point is a major tributary, the Rio Zarsiadero. The Third of November Trail follows the Rio Zarsiadero up toward the continental divide, less than 5 kilometers away, leaving the Rio Chiriqui valley proper. Between 3/4 kilometer and one kilometer above the confluence of these two rivers, a rock unit outcrops on the west slope of the Rio Zarisiadero canyon in such a way as to produce a series of overhangs. Several of these overhangs have been occupied in the past and two are now occupied sporadically by men clearing new fields, planting crops, or harvesting coffee. One of the two has ceramic and preceramic occupations as well as a modern one; this is the Zarsiadero Shelter.

The shelter sits behind what appears to be a high terrace remnant almost 50 meters above the Rio Zarsiadero. The terrain in front of the site at first slopes gently, then more steeply toward the river about 200 meters away. The shelter itself has a width of 5 meters and measures 3.5 meters from front to back. Although a high ceiling makes most of the area underneath the overhang usable, the site is still much smaller than Casita de Piedra, or about the same size as the Horacio Gonzales site. Excavation at the Zarsiadero Shelter was limited to a single 1 by 2-meter pit.

The Schoolyard site was the only open habitation site to be tested in the study area. It also occupies a high terrace of the Rio Chiriqui, 20 meters above Casita de Piedra and directly behind it. A 1 by 2-meter test pit was dug into the flat, exposing a normal soil or weathering profile that could be compared with profiles from the other excavated rock shelters, particularly from the nearby Casita de Piedra. While the pit was not dug in order to test a site, the recovery of flakes, tools, pottery, and charcoal was not unanticipated.

3.4 THE CULTURAL CHRONOLOGY

In the Rio Chiriqui shelters the interplay between natural and cultural factors responsible for the stratigraphy complicates the correlation of the deposits from site to site. However, in the two deeply stratified sites, Casita de Piedra and the Trapiche Shelter, only a single major natural stratigraphic break occurs after the beginning of the occupation. The breaks in each site are similar in character and in time (fig. 3.0-8 and report no. 1). In Casita de Piedra, the break occurs between layers D and E, dividing the upper layers (A, B, C, and D) of silt with relatively little larger rock from the lower layers (E and F) of silty clay with more sand and rock. The break in the Trapiche Shelter between layers B and C is still more distinct. The upper unit (layers A and B) is almost entirely loose light brown silt, while the bottom unit (layers C, D, and E) is a compact brown silt with much sand and rock included.

The entire occupation in the Horacio Gonzales site lies within a zone equivalent to the upper units defined from the two more deeply stratified rock shelters. Upstream at the Zarsiadero Shelter, the deposits appear to span the time of both the upper and lower units. The occupation zone has the physical characteristics of the lower depositional unit (i.e., dark brown silt with large rocks included), but the upper part of the site is highly

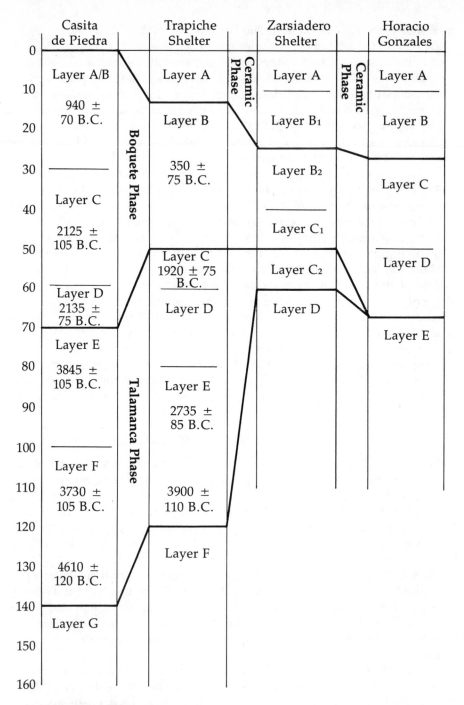

▲ DEPTH IN CENTIMETERS

Figure 3.0-8: Correlation of the stratigraphic sequence in Casita de Piedra, Trapiche Shelter, Zarsiadero Shelter, and the Horacio Gonzales site.

disturbed, to judge from the mixture of cultural remains. Thus, layer C is in part equivalent to the lower unit recognized in Casita de Piedra and Trapiche Shelter, while layers B and A are equivalent to the upper unit, plus the top part of the lower unit.

All undisturbed layers in the Rio Chiriqui shelters, with one exception, contain preceramic occupations. The exception, layer B in the Horacio Gonzales site, contained ceramics which are similar to those that occur elsewhere in western Panama during the late Bugaba phase, dated to A.D. 400-600 (section 5.2). This ceramic phase is also represented in the mixed surface deposits of the Trapiche Shelter. A later ceramic phase, Chiriqui Classic (Linares 1968b), occurs in the disturbed upper layers of the Zarsiadero Shelter.

The preceramic sequence for the Rio Chiriqui region is divided into two phases: the Talamanca phase, named after the mountain range in which the sites are located, and the Boquete phase, named after the local district. The earlier Talamanca phase materials occur in what we called the lower depositional unit in Casita de Piedra (layers E and F), the Trapiche Shelter (layers C, D, and E) and the Zarsiadero Shelter (layer C and the lower part of disturbed layer B). Six radiocarbon determinations, all on charcoal, come from Talamanca phase contexts: (1) 4610 ± 120 B.C. (I-6278), associated with the base of layer F in the Casita de Piedra; (2) 3845 ± 105 B.C. (I-5765), associated with the base of layer E in Casita de Piedra; (3) 3730 ± 105 B.C. (I-5764) associated with a pit dug into layer G at the Casita de Piedra, presumably from layer E; (4) 3900 ± 110 B.C. (I-5613), associated with layer E in the Trapiche Shelter; (5) 2735 ± 85 B.C. (SI-1848), also associated with layer E in the Trapiche Shelter; (6) 1920 ± 75 B.C. (SI-1847), associated with the top of layer C in the Trapiche Shelter. The date of 4610 B.C. came from charcoal collected in disturbances at the top of layer G (but originating from the base of layer F) in Casita de Piedra. It is estimated that the occupation of the site began at this time or perhaps a few hundred years earlier, since there was some mixing of the deposits (report no. 1).

The later Boquete phase has four radiocarbon dates run on charcoal associated with it: (1) 2135 ± 75 B.C. (SI-1845), associated with the base of layer D in Casita de Piedra; (2) 2125 ± 105 B.C. (I-5614), associated with the base of layer C in Casita de Piedra; (3) 940 ± 70 B.C. (SI-1844), associated with the top of layer B in Casita de Piedra; (4) 350 ± 75 B.C. (SI-1846), associated with the top of layer B in the Trapiche Shelter. My interpretation of the C14 dates would place the break between the Talamanca and Boquete phases (i.e., the break between the lower and upper depositional units) at about 2300 B.C. The 1920 ± 75 B.C. date for the end of the Talamanca phase deposits in the Trapiche Shelter can be "explained" by slight contamination of the sample from higher levels. If the break between the two phases is placed at 1900 B.C., then we are compelled to "explain" the two dates of 2135 ± 75 B.C. and 2125 ± 105 B.C. for Boquete phase deposits in Casita de Piedra. Consistent with the principle of parsimony, the fewer dates "explained," the better.

The date of 350 ± 75 B.C. marks the end of the Boquete phase deposits in the Trapiche Shelter. Above the unit that provided the charcoal for this date, a ceramic occupation level occurred. Casita de Piedra was abandoned, in all probability, shortly after 940 ± 70 B.C. or before the end of the Boquete phase. All rock shelters and perhaps the Schoolyard site had occupations dating from the Boquete phase (ca. 2300-300 B.C.): layers A, B, C, and D in Casita de Piedra, layer B in the Trapiche Shelter, layers C and D in the Horacio Gonzales site, the disturbed layers A and B in the Zarsiadero Shelter and perhaps below 60 centimeters in the Schoolyard site.

3.5   DEFINING THE TALAMANCA AND BOQUETE PHASES

The divison of the preceramic period represented in the Rio Chiriqui shelters into two phases was based on differences in the lithic assemblages, the only cultural material to be preserved in the sediments. In both Casita de Piedra and the Trapiche Shelter, abrupt changes in some tool types, changes in tool-type frequencies, and changes in the raw materials used in tool-making occurred at the boundary between the lower and upper strati-graphic units (see report no. 8). A detailed description and interpretation of the stone tools can be found in report number 8 of this volume (see also Ranere 1975). Here I would simply like to summarize the descriptions and present certain conclusions drawn from the analysis of the 45,000 flakes and artifacts recovered from the Rio Chiriqui shelters.

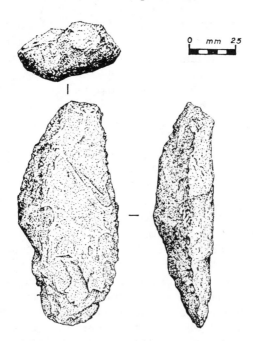

Figure 3.0-9: A bifacial wedge. (Reprinted from Lithic Technology, *edited by Earl H. Swanson.)*

The Talamanca phase, as was pointed out above, lasted for at least 2,300 years, or from 4600 to 2300 B.C. Its most characteristic artifact type is the bifacially flaked wedge (fig. 3.0-9). This celtlike tool appears to have been used in heavy woodworking activities like splitting logs or even felling trees. Other heavy woodworking tools include scraper-planes and perhaps choppers (figs. 3.0-10, 11). The chipped stone assemblage also includes a variety of scrapers, flake knives, burins, and gravers. With the exception of some bifacial wedges, scraper-planes, and cobble tools, implements from the Talamanca phase are made on small flakes, many of them without modification. In fact, most choppers, a number of scraper-planes, and the irregular bifacial wedges are also made on flakes, albeit large ones. More

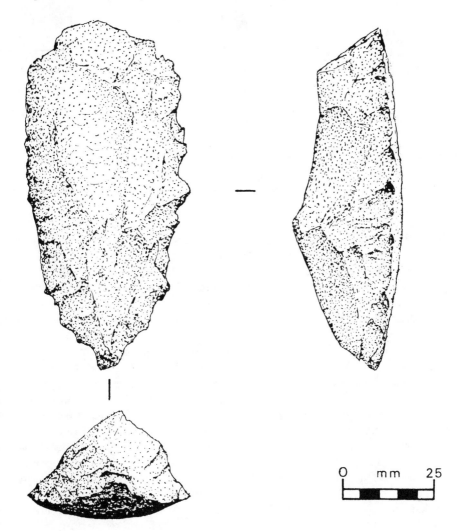

Figure 3.0-10: A scraper plane. (Reprinted from Lithic Technology, *edited by Earl H. Swanson.)*

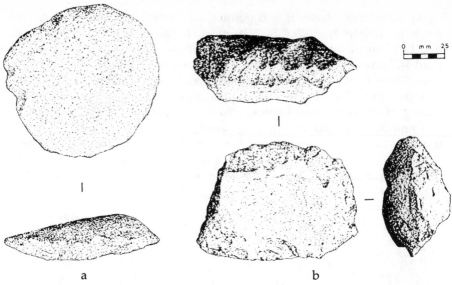

0 mm 25

Figure 3.0-11: a. Cobble spall chopper; b. bifacial chopper. (Reprinted from Lithic Technology, edited by Earl H. Swanson.)

than 90 percent of the Talamanca flakes and tools are andesite; most of the remaining few percent are chalcedony. The techniques employed in making these and the other stone tools described below have been summarized in report number 8.

A large number of cores from Talamanca phase deposits are irregular or multidirectional. Flakes appear to have been struck from these cores from any convenient location. Also numerous were bipolar cores, which have flakes detached at opposite ends as a result of the use of anvil stones in the knapping process. A few cores are conical in shape and have a single platform for flake detachment. Other cores are bifacial; that is, an acute angled edge is used as the striking platform and flakes are removed from both faces.

Hammerstones showing the heaviest use during the Talamanca phase were made from what were probably once choppers. The edge on most specimens has been converted by repeated battering into a smooth, rounded facet completely encircling the tool. Less heavily used were elongated cobbles, light hammering facets occurring on both ends. A number of anvils, cobbles with roughly pitted surfaces, were also recovered.

The only other tools found in any great quantity in the Talamanca deposits were edge-ground cobbles and milling stone bases. The edge-ground cobbles have a smooth working facet on the thin edge rather than on the face of the cobble (fig. 3.0-12). They are used against the milling stone bases which have smoothed, sometimes slightly convex, surfaces. There are, in addition, a few stones with small pecked depressions or nutting stones, so-called because similar stones are still used in the area today for cracking palm nuts.

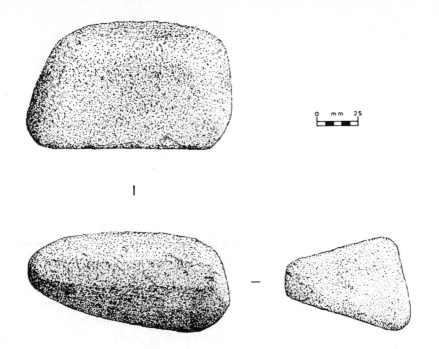

Figure 3.0-12: An edge-ground cobble. (Reprinted from Lithic Technology, *edited by Earl H. Swanson.)*

Figure 3.0-13: A small tabular wedge. (Reprinted from Lithic Technology, *edited by Earl H. Swanson.)*

In the succeeding Boquete phase, dated between 2300 and 300 B.C., a number of tool types continue to be found. Edge-ground cobbles, milling stone bases, nutting stones, hammerstones, anvils, irregular cores, and bifacial cores are equally common in both Talamanca and Boquete phases. Scraper-planes, scrapers, and flake knives are present in the Boquete phase, but occur with less frequency than in the preceding phase. On the other hand, bifacial wedges are completely absent from the Boquete phase. Moreover, a small tabular wedge or chisel (*pièces écaillées,*fig. 3.0-13), which accounts for about 50 percent of the tools recovered from Boquete phase deposits, is either rare or more likely absent from the Talamanca assemblage.

There are a number of other distinctions which can be made between the two preceramic phases. Used quartz crystals, rectangular handstones, handstones with offset grinding facets, and pestles are found only in the Boquete phase. In addition, 25 to 50 percent of the flakes and tools from the

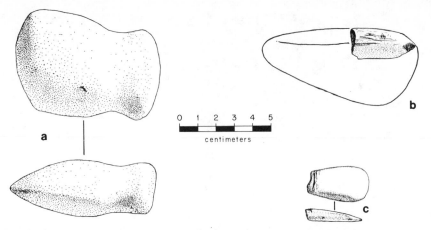

Figure 3.0-14: Ground and polished stone artifacts from Casita de Piedra: a. grooved stone axe; b. celt fragment; c. chisel bit.

Boquete phase were made of nonandesitic material (chalcedony, quartz, and obsidian), whereas less than 10 percent were in the preceding Talamanca phase. Most important perhaps, ground and polished stone axes, celts, and chisels (fig. 3.0-14) were found only in Boquete phase deposits.

Despite these differences, the Boquete phase appears to represent a development out of the Talamanca phase since almost all of the earlier tool types continue to be manufactured in the later phase. What distinguishes the Boquete phase from the earlier Talamanca phase is a number of new elements in the stone inventory. Beginning at about 2300 B.C., a wider variety of material is used in the manufacturing of tools, the technique of shaping tools by grinding and polishing is introduced, and new tool types appear. Since the changes which mark the Boquete phase all appear simultaneously in the Rio Chiriqui canyon, they seem to have evolved into a cultural pattern outside the canyon and to have been introduced as an integrated whole. Once introduced, the pattern remained almost unchanged for 2,000 years and was as stable as the Talamanca pattern which it replaced.

The Boquete pattern was itself succeeded by one which included ceramics. This Bugaba ceramic phase is not well represented in the Rio Chiriqui shelters, being present only in layers A and B of the Horacio Gonzales site and in the disturbed layer A of the Trapiche Shelter. Nonetheless, the Bugaba phase occupation seems totally different from the occupations that preceded it. More extensive excavations of Bugaba phase sites in highland and coastal settings of Chiriqui tended to confirm this difference. Bugaba phase occupations have far fewer types of chipped stone tools but larger numbers of ground and polished stone tools than the preceramic occupations. In addition, the edge-ground cobble and milling stone complex is replaced by the mano and metate complex in the Bugaba phase (reports no. 14 and no. 16).

3.6 INTERPRETING THE LITHIC ASSEMBLAGES

What can lithic assemblages from the Rio Chiriqui canyon tell us about the people who made and used these tools? Most of the stone tools appear to have been used to make other tools, of other materials. Bifacial and tabular wedges, chisels, choppers, whittling knives, scraper-planes, scrapers, burins, and gravers all fit this description. The most elaborate as well as the greatest variety of stone tools were used in woodworking (Ranere 1975 and report no. 8). Hence, rather than being the products of recent immigrants, the Talamancan and Boquete lithic assemblages seem to be the product of peoples well acquainted with tropical forest environments. Knapping techniques are only as complicated as necessary to provide suitable edges for woodworking.

From ethnographic examples of the material culture of modern and historical tropical forest groups we are well aware that projectile points are made of hardwoods, chisels are made from rodent incisors, gouges from shell, and knives from bamboo. What is perhaps surprising is that this reliance on raw materials other than stone can be traced back nearly 7,000 years in western Panama.

The edge-ground cobble and milling stone complex, present from the beginning in the shelters' deposits, appears to represent yet another tropical forest adaptation. Unlike the manos and metates associated with the grinding of maize and other seeds, the narrow working surface of the cobbles seems unsuited for grinding grain, a point made quite clear to me in replicative experiments. On the other hand, these tools are superior to manos in the mashing of starchy roots like manioc (section 5.3 and report no. 8). Since it is the action of stone upon stone that shapes the working facet irrespective of the material being worked, tubers are not the only product whose mashing would produce edge-ground cobbles and milling stone bases. They simply seem the most logical foodstuff because they are at the heart of tropical forest agricultural systems known historically. It is likely and logical that tubers were important in preagricultural exploitation of tropical forest environments as well (see discussions farther on).

The quantity of chipping debris recovered from the Rio Chiriqui shelters makes it clear that one important activity carried on at the sites was the manufacture of stone tools. It would be a mistake, however, to conclude that these sites were nothing but lithic workshops. A large number of both chipped and non-chipped stone tools from the shelters showed evidence of heavy use in the form of resharpening and wear polish. Furthermore, the ratio of flakes to finished tools indicates that most of the tools made at the sites were also used at the sites (section 5.3). The absence of large quantities of preforms and rejects (tools abandoned in manufacturing because of some error in workmanship or flaw in the material) also militates against the sites being only workshops.

I have interpreted most of the chipped stone tools as being woodworking tools (Ranere 1975), and it is possible that these sites are woodworking stations. As Crabtree and Davis (1968) have pointed out, chipped stone tools rapidly wear out when used on wood. Thus, there is a certain advantage in carrying our woodworking tasks near a supply of stone. Andesite, quartz, chalcedony, and obsidian were all readily available to the Rio Chiriqui canyon residents.

The large number of edge-ground cobbles, milling stone bases and other food-preparation tools, such as handstones, mortars, pestles, and nutting stones, supports the contention that these shelters served as domestic living sites for extended periods of time. Quantities of wood charcoal, fire-cracked rock, and carbonized seeds lend further support to the supposition.

The patterning of debris at the sites may indicate long-term (e.g., several consecutive weeks), if not permanent, occupation. In Casita de Piedra, debris was concentrated along the rear wall of the shelter and beyond the dripline, while in the central zone the debris was noticeably less dense. Charcoal was scattered, and most hearthstones (fire-cracked rock), with the exception of two hearths on the periphery of the central living area, were displaced. This evidence seems to imply that debris was continually being swept or otherwise removed from the center of the site to the peripheries.

The only hint we have about the seasonality of occupation comes from charred seeds (section 6.2). Every preceramic layer contained seeds that mature at the end of the dry season and the beginning of the wet season (roughly late March to June). Presumably the shelters were occupied at least during this time of year. Since living surfaces were not preserved, and features were rare (report no. 1), each of the smallest natural units identified, the layers, lasted several hundred years; thus it is impossible to know at this stage if the shelters were occupied on a permanent (i.e., year-round) basis.

To summarize, the Rio Chiriqui shelters are best interpreted as domestic living sites, occupied for weeks if not for months at a time, by tropical forest people. The proximity of lithic sources allowed the inhabitants to carry out their essential tool-making activities at the sites themselves.

3.7 ORIGIN OF THE RIO CHIRIQUI PRECERAMIC ASSEMBLAGES

An increasing number of chipped stone assemblages being identified in the New World tropics are technologically simple (none contain bifacially flaked projectile points). Characteristically, hard hammer percussion is the major or only knapping technique employed. If modified at all after initial detachment, the tools consist of flakes shaped by simple unifacial retouch. Many of the tools seem designed to make other tools from other materials, wood being the most cited (e.g., J.B. Richardson 1973; Hurt et al. 1976; Stothert 1976). Such assemblages range in age from 2,500 to more than 12,000 years old and are found in Ecuador (Stothert 1976), Peru (J.B. Richardson 1978), Colombia (Reichel-Dolmatoff 1965; Hurt et al. 1976), Ven- (Cruxent and Rouse 1958; Roosevelt 1977), Trinidad (Harris 1976), Brazil

(Miller 1969; Laming and Emperaire 1959), as well as in Panama (Bird and Cooke 1974; Ranere and Hansell 1978). The Talamanca and Boquete assemblages belong to this group.

Insofar as they imply intensive use of wood, bone, and shell, these assemblages at some level provide indirect evidence for adaptations to tropical forest resources. Contemporary chipped stone assemblages in temperate latitudes and in drier neotropical highlands include a wide range of stone tools (bifacially flaked projectile points being foremost) that are absent from tropical forest contexts.

There are several ways to account for the presence of these simple assemblages in the tropics. Their ancestry can be traced to the pre (stone)-projectile point industries brought into tropical South America by the earliest migrants (see Bryan 1978). If this were the case, the simple stone industries which persisted in the tropics after the Pleistocene would be interpreted as representing a continuation (and improvement) of the pattern. As it happens, the evidence we have for early occupation in the tropics is invariably associated with the seasonal tropics, rather than the wet tropics where rainfall is evenly distributed throughout the year. Savannas are important components of seasonal tropic vegetation, so one would expect early migrants to take advantage of savanna resources, particularly of their endemic fauna, as they expanded into South America. Nonetheless, the traditional view of early migrants hopping from savanna to savanna on their way from Mexico to South America, avoiding tropical forests at all costs, seems a bit far-fetched (but see Lynch 1976). It seems to me more logical to argue that these generalized hunter-gatherers would have utilized the resources of both savannas and seasonal forests.

In view of the skepticism which early preprojectile point assemblages still evoke (see Lynch 1974, 1976 for recent appraisals), an alternate hypothesis to account for these simple chipped assemblages can be offered. It proposes that complex stone technologies would in time become increasingly simplified as populations became more familiar with, and better adapted to, tropical forest resources. Ultimately, when more efficient and/or expendable tools made of tropical hardwoods, bone, teeth, and so forth replaced stone ones, chipped stone assemblages would be reduced to those simpler tools necessary for shaping these other materials. The skills needed to produce bifacially flaked projectile points and other specialized stone tools would no longer be needed and would in time be forgotten.

Of course, the above hypotheses are not mutually exclusive. The simple assemblages documented from several areas in the seasonal tropics during the Holocene may, in fact, represent the convergence of different cultural traditions as they adapt to similar environments (cf. J.B. Richardson 1978).

In any event, the widespread occurrence of simple assemblages suggests that within a common pattern, which we could perhaps call the "Tropical Forest Archaic," these local assemblages exhibited specialized adaptations to local resources as was the case elsewhere in the New World. Upon close examination, significant differences among some of these simple chipped stone assemblages emerge. For example, bifacial (celtlike) wedges and tabular wedges are diagnostic artifacts for the preceramic assemblages from the Rio Chiriqui canyon, yet these tools are not found in any other preceramic assemblages from the New World tropics, including those from central Panama. Their absence is somewhat surprising in view of the similarities seen in the ground stone or cobble tool assemblages from the Rio Chiriqui canyon and those from Central Panama (Willey and McGimsey 1954; McGimsey 1956; Ranere and McCarty 1976). I refer specifically to the edge-ground cobble and milling stone complex. Edge-ground cobbles ("edge-grinders") and the bases with which they are used were first described by Willey and McGimsey (1954) for the early ceramic Monagrillo site in central Panama. McGimsey (1956) later found them at the preceramic shell midden of Cerro Mangote in the same region. Still later, Ranere and McCarty (1976) encountered them in the nearby preceramic and early ceramic Aguadulce Shelter. These tools, then, are hallmarks of the preceramic and early ceramic periods in Panama, dating from 5000 to 1000 B.C. They do not appear in later contexts (reports no. 14 and no. 15).

To complicate matters, the distribution of the edge-ground cobble and milling stone complex outside of Panama is very patchy. While these tools have *not* been reported from preceramic assemblages in Colombia (Reichel-Dolmatoff 1965; Hurt et al. 1976), or from the north coast of Peru (J.B. Richardson 1978) — although they may be present at Vegas sites in Ecuador (Stothert 1977) — they have, however, been found along the Caribbean coast of Venezuela (Cruxent and Rouse 1958) and in preceramic contexts in Puerto Rico (Alegria et al. 1955).

It is not at all clear whether the distribution of the edge-ground cobble and milling stone complex in the tropics resulted from historical connections or from independent invention. The existence of edge-ground cobbles and "anvil" bases in the Pacific Northwest (Butler 1962; Sims 1971) suggests that the complex has been invented more than once, as the probability of historical contacts between tropical America and the Pacific Northwest is remote. In both regions the function of the tool complex has been interpreted as pounding and mashing of starchy tubers and bulbs. The probability of historical connections within the tropics cannot be so easily dismissed, however. Such a connection seems likely between the Rio Chiriqui canyon and the Parita Bay area of central Panama, only 150 kilometers apart. Moreover, Stothert (1977) has made a convincing case that a preceramic interaction sphere, involving the Parita Bay sites, the Vegas sites on Ecuador's Santa Elena Peninsula, and the Siches and Estero sites on the north coast of Peru was operating by at least the fifth millennium B.C. The nearly identical burial patterns recorded from Cerro Mangote in Panama and from the Vegas site in Ecuador are particularly difficult to explain in the absence of cultural connections.

One can only speculate about the participation of the Talamanca phase peoples in this suggested interaction sphere, nothing more. My personal feeling is that western Panama was for the most part outside this sphere. In fact, it is tempting to project the cultural division between western and central Panama, recognized for the historic and prehistoric ceramic periods, backward into the preceramic to at least the Talamanca phase (i.e., 5000 B.C.). Certainly, by the third millennium B.C., the introduction of ceramics into central Panama (ca. 2500 B.C.) (Ranere and Hansell 1978) and its absence from the Boquete phase (2300–300 B.C.) in western Panama, seem to indicate some sort of separation between these regions.

In short, the Talamanca phase cannot, for the moment, be linked closely to any other known archaeological components. With one exception, the only earlier remains reported from Central America are fluted point assemblages (Gruhn and Bryan 1977; Snarskis 1977), or simply isolated fluted points (e.g., Bird and Cooke 1978). The exception is El Bosque, possibly a very early pre(stone)-projectile point site in Nicaragua (Espinosa 1977). Any relationship between the Talamanca phase assemblage and either the fluted point assemblages or the El Bosque assemblage seems remote indeed. Farther to the south, assemblages which predate and/or are contemporary with the Talamanca phase, such as those from El Abra in highland Colombia (Hurt et al. 1976), the Vegas sites of coastal Ecuador (Stothert 1976), and the Siches, Estero, and Amotape sites of north coastal Peru (J.B. Richardson 1978), are very much like one another, but significantly different from the Talamanca assemblage.

3.8   SUBSISTENCE PATTERNS DURING THE PRECERAMIC PERIOD

3.8.a.   In the Rio Chiriqui Shelters

Reconstructing the total subsistence economy of the preceramic inhabitants of the Rio Chiriqui canyon is a somewhat hazardous undertaking, since bone was not preserved in any of the shelters. However, the following mammals would probably have been available to shelter inhabitants: white-tailed deer *(Odocoileus virginianus)*, brocket deer *(Mazama americana)*, tapir *(Tapirus bairdii)*, collared peccary *(Tayassu tajacu)*, white-lipped peccary *(Tayassu pecari)*, armadillo *(Dasypus novemcinctus)*, opossum *(Didelphis marsupialis)*, rabbit *(Sylvilagus brasiliensis)*, raccoon *(Procyon lotor)*, paca *(Cuniculus paca)*, agouti *(Dasyprocta punctata)*, and a number of small rodents (Adames et al. 1977; Bennett 1968). Some amphibians (particularly *Bufo marinus*), Iguanids, and several bird species would also have been potential food sources. All of the above species, with the exception of the tapir, have been recovered from other archaeological sites in Panama (section 6.4; Cooke 1978).

In the immediate vicinity of the rock shelters the Chiriqui River itself is impoverished, containing no potential food for humans except perhaps for the presence of the small shrimp *Atya dressleri* (Goodyear et al. 1977). However, several edible fish and one large shrimp species range upriver to within 10 kilometers of the shelters and could have been utilized by the occupants. A species of sardine *(Astyanax albeolus)*, plus catfish *(Rhamdia wagneri)*, "sabalo" *(Brycon striatulus)*, "boca chica" *(Agonostomus monticola)*, and a large shrimp *(Macrobrachium americanum)* were the potential food items (ibid.). Nevertheless, I think it unlikely that aquatic resources ever contributed significantly to the protein intake of the shelter inhabitants. Terrestrial fauna, particularly deer and peccary, probably provided the bulk of the meat consumed.

We are on somewhat firmer ground in our discussion of the plant foods utilized during the preceramic period. Over five hundred identifiable seed fragments were preserved through carbonization from Casita de Piedra and the Trapiche Shelter, the overwhelming majority being palm nut fragments (Smith, section 10.2). Two species, "corozo pacora" (*Acrocomia* cf. *vinifera* Oerst) and "corozo gunzo" (*Scheelia zonensis* Bailey) were utilized throughout the preceramic sequence. A third species of palm, not identified, also was represented in the deposits. The only other species commonly encountered throughout the sequence was "nance" (*Byrsonima* sp. — probably *crassifolia*). Three seeds from the "algarrobo" (*Hymenaea courbaril*) were recovered, two from Boquete phase contexts, and one from Talamanca phase contexts, plus a few additional unidentifiable remains (see section 10.2, for a detailed listing of the plant remains by site and layer).

All the species listed above can be found today in the vicinity of the rock shelters, and all are collected by local peoples. Although no species is purposefully cultivated, the "corozo palms" are protected by being left standing when fields are cleared. In Panama as elsewhere these palms are valued not only for their fruit but also for their leaves, which are used for thatching, for their sap, which is fermented to make palm wine, and (less frequently) for their wood, which is used in construction (Standley 1928).

Today, both the corozo palms and nance are conspicuous members of disturbed habitats, that is, of fire-maintained savannas and scrub forests (Bennett 1968; Wagner 1964). It is therefore tempting to interpret their presence in the shelter deposits as an indication of human modification of the Rio Chiriqui canyon environment as far back as 5000 B.C. However, since corozo palms are found elsewhere in apparently undisturbed forest formations (Tosi 1971; Porter 1973; Gomez-Pompa 1973), their presence in the Rio Chiriqui canyon does not constitute unequivocal evidence of disturbed habitats. Nance may have also occurred several thousands years ago as part of the natural vegetation in the canyon. I should add here that nance seeds from the preceramic deposits are similar in size to those from wild plants, suggesting that the archaeological specimens came from wild rather than cultivated plants.

It is interesting to note that corozo palm fruits continue to be utilized in later ceramic phases in Chiriqui. Moreover, Smith (section 10.2) has suggested that they may have been cultivated at this later time. The specimens recovered from Sitio Pitti-Gonzalez in the Cerro Punta basin were either imported from lower elevations where corozo palms occur naturally, in which case they need not have been cultivated, or they came from trees planted in the basin. Smith carefully measured the palm seed and kernel fragments from Casita de Piedra and the Trapiche Shelter and found no indication of selection for fruit size through time. Similarly, the range in seed size remained constant. Thus, there is no evidence for corozo palm cultivation at any time during the preceramic occupation of the Rio Chiriqui canyon. (This is not to say that uniformity in seed size necessarily rules out cultivation. Planting could be done without selection for larger seeds, a distinct possibility if the palms were being valued for their sap or leaves.) Nonetheless, as important as palm nuts were in the diet of the preceramic peoples, I doubt whether they were the major staple any more than they were during the succeeding ceramic phases, when maize was the staple but palm nuts continued being utilized.

Whatever may have been the diet of the Boquete and Talamancan phase peoples, it did not have maize or beans as staples. Despite the quantity of charred plant remains preserved in the preceramic shelters, not one kernel or cob fragment showed up. This fact stands in marked contrast to the later ceramic sites. Maize cobs, kernels, and/or pollen are found in Chiriqui in both highland and lowland sites as early possibly as 300 B.C., but certainly by A.D. 200 (sections 10.3 and 10.4). Similarly, the ceramic sites have manos and metates as their most common grinding implements (reports no. 14 and no. 15). The use of these implements for grinding seeds, especially maize, is widespread throughout tropical America. That the mano and metate grinding complex is entirely absent from both the Talamancan and Boquete preceramic assemblages is a fact that cannot be stressed enough. The dominant food-processing tools at that time were edge-ground cobbles and milling stones. As I have elaborated elsewhere (section 8.3) these tools are ideal for mashing starchy tubers like manioc. Hence, quite late in the Chiriqui sequence, some time after 300 B.C., maize replaced an earlier staple, probably manioc (Ranere 1972). Whether this manioc was cultivated and for how long are questions that I will consider in more detail shortly. But first let me hasten to add that there is not one bit of hard (i.e., botanical) evidence for the use of manioc or any other tuber in the Rio Chiriqui shelters. On the other hand, none can reasonably be expected. Pollen was not preserved in the sediments, and preservation of charred tubers is most unlikely.

In the discussions above I have been careful to mention the presence and absence of maize *as a staple*. I have done so in order to leave open the possibility that maize was used by the occupants of the Rio Chiriqui shelters as a "pot vegetable"; that is, as green or ripe "corn on the cob" rather than being stored and used as grain. It is the multiple uses of maize as grain and as a storable staple which are important in defining a maize agricultural complex. I am reasonably certain that maize was not used in this manner during the preceramic period of western Panama.

To reiterate, an agricultural system based on the cultivation of root crops, particularly manioc, and tree crops seems the most likely predecessor of the maize or seed agricultural system found together with ceramics in Chiriqui a few centuries before or after the Christian era. Given this hypothesis, the questions then become: when did this vegecultural system first appear in the Rio Chiriqui sequence? Does the beginning of the Boquete phase around 2300 B.C. mark the introduction of vegeculture into the region, or did the Talamancan phase peoples that preceded it enter the Rio Chiriqui canyon 2,500 years earlier already cultivating root crops? Alternatively, were the Rio Chiriqui sites occupied by hunter-gatherers throughout the preceramic period?

An examination of the plant remains and stone tool assemblages from the shelters gives somewhat conflicting clues. There is absolutely no way of distinguishing the Talamancan phase from the Boquete phase with respect to the charred plant remains (the relative abundance of nance seed fragments in the earliest layers of the shelters reflects the fact that fine screening and water separation techniques were concentrated in these layers). Similarly, the presumed root crop processing complex, edge-ground cobbles and milling stones, is found associated with both phases. On the other hand, the addition of ground and polished stone axes and celts marks an abrupt change in the stone tool inventory beginning with the Boquete phase. Evidently, then, the question of when root crops began to be cultivated in the Rio Chiriqui area cannot be answered by looking at these data alone.

3.8.b. In Other Panamanian Areas

A dilemma rather similar to that presented by the Rio Chiriqui data confronts us when we consider the contemporary information from seven sites in the Parita Bay region of central Panama. The introduction of ceramics into this area at about 2500 B.C. is the single major innovation in a cultural sequence spanning 4,000 years, from about 5000 B.C. to 1000 B.C. Five of the sites are shell middens located along an old coastline, of which one, Cerro Mangote (McGimsey 1956; McGimsey et al. 1966) is preceramic, and four — Monagrillo, Zapotal, He-12, and He-18 — are ceramic (Willey and McGimsey 1954). The remaining two sites are rock shelters that contain both preceramic and early ceramic components. The Aguadulce Shelter is located in the coastal plains (Ranere and Hansell 1978), while La Cueva de los Ladrones is in the foothills 25 kilometers inland from the coast (Bird and Cooke 1974).

There is one radiocarbon date published for the preceramic phase: 4860 ± 110 B.C. (Y-458-D) from Cerro Mangote (Deevey et al. 1959). There are eight radiocarbon dates securely associated with Monagrillo ceramics, from the Monagrillo site itself, ranging from 2455 ± 75 B.C. to 1295 ± 100 B.C. (Ranere and Hansell 1978). Edge-ground cobbles and milling stones occur in both preceramic and ceramic phases, and no differences are apparent in the simple chipped stone tool industries of these two phases. Thus, like the Rio Chiriqui sequence, strong continuity in the lithic assemblages exists throughout the Central Panama sequence, despite the presence or absence of ceramics and differential treatment of the dead, which serve to separate the phases. Also, as in the Rio Chiriqui sequence, we have little evidence in central Panama that indicates whether agriculture was part of the subsistence strategy during any part of the sequence. Palm nut fragments from both preceramic and ceramic contexts in the Aguadulce Shelter are the only plant macrofossils recovered. Piperno's (ms. 1979) recent examination of phytoliths from the Aguadulce Shelter indicates the presence of cross-shaped phytoliths from maize in the Monagrillo levels, but not in the pre-ceramic levels. However, as Piperno notes, the embryonic stage of phyto-lith research in archaeology dictates that we be cautious in accepting large cross-shaped phytoliths as unequivocal products of the maize plant. The first firmly documented agriculture in the region dates to about 300 B.C., when maize is clearly present; maize kernels, cob fragments, pollen, and manos and metates all appear at this time (Cooke/Camargo 1977; Cooke 1978).

Farther east, in the Canal Zone, pollen cores have indicated clear evi-dence of agriculture at 1200 ± B.C. where maize pollen, finely divided charcoal and increased percentages of Gramineae and Compositae occur together (Bartlett et al. 1969). Bartlett, Barghoorn, and Berger also report maize pollen at levels dated to 5350 ± 130 B.C. and 4280 ± 80 B.C., but these dates have been seriously questioned (Pickersgill and Heiser 1977, p. 806). Besides the maize pollen, no other indication of agricultural activities occurred in the cores at these levels. Although the investigators suggested that this pollen represents wild maize, recent evidence placing this Meso-american domesticate in the Andes by the fifth millennium B.C. (Mac-Neish, Patterson, and Browman 1975). suggests otherwise. Perhaps this early maize was planted as a minor vegetable by tropical forest farmers who placed greater emphasis on root crops.

3.8.c. In Other New World Regions

The presence of root crop cultivation in Panama or elsewhere is notoriously difficult to prove, since the humid tropics seldom permit preservation of vegetal remains other than those which have been carbonized. Unfortu-nately, roots are not likely to be carbonized in such a way as to render them identifiable. The earliest physical remains of manioc come in two arid regions at opposite ends of the natural range for this plant. Starch from coprolites dating from the Santa Maria phase (1000-200 B.C.) in the Tehuacan Valley has been identified as manioc (Callen 1967). Actual re-mains of the plant have been recovered from the coastal desert of Peru at about 1000 B.C. (Towle 1961).

In contrast, in those areas in which manioc occurs naturally, where it is most used today and where presumably it was domesticated, only indirect evidence of its use can be cited. Root crops, including manioc, can be and are cultivated and consumed without the use of any specialized tools that would be preserved in the archaeological record. However, the time-consuming and elaborate process of turning manioc into a storable and transportable starch or staple involves a number of specialized tools, some of which can be recovered in archaeological contexts. Clay griddles, stone insets from graterboards, and, to a lesser extent, juice or "buck" pots (used to catch juice squeezed from manioc) are the indirect evidence most com-monly cited for the presence of domesticated manioc in an archaeological context (Lathrap 1970, 1973). This evidence is not unequivocal, however. As DeBoer (1975) points out, clay griddles are also used ethnographically for roasting maize (tortillas), and graters can be used for other foods besides manioc. Nonetheless, if clay griddles are found without manos and metates, it is more likely that they were used with manioc rather than maize. Moreover, while graterboards may well have been used for foods other than manioc, they were certainly more likely to have been used on root crops than seed crops.

Be that as it may, Rouse and Cruxent (1963) have noted the presence of clay griddles in Rancho Peludo, a ceramic complex dating to the early third millennium B.C. The succeeding Guasare phase, which begins about 1000 B.C. (Wagner 1967), is assumed to have been based on maize agriculture, since the mano and metate complex was present. A rather similar sequence occurs at Momil in Colombia (Reichel-Dolmatoff 1957), where the Momil I assemblages contain griddles and the Momil II assemblages contain manos and metates. Momil II begins sometime during the first millennium B.C. More recent investigations along the Orinoco also suggest that the change from a manioc to a maize staple occurred at about 1000 B.C. (Roosevelt 1977). At that time carbonized maize is first encountered in the carbonized plant remains. The earlier La Gruta phase, beginning at ca. 2200–2000 B.C., contained only wild plants among the charred remains, plus griddles and grater chips, but no manos and metates. Roosevelt thus concludes that cultivated manioc was present, although in the absence of botanical remains, the case is not proved.

Coastal Ecuador, the scene of considerable recent research, appears to represent a rather early instance of intensive maize agriculture beginning well back into the third millennium B.C. (Zevallos et al. 1977). Maize impressions on pottery, maize phytoliths (Pearsall 1978), and the mano and metate complex support the contention that maize was present for most if not all of the Valdivia sequence. However, the earlier pre-Valdivia Vegas sites which are preceramic do not appear to be based on maize. At least, no botanical evidence for maize has been found and the mano and metate complex is absent. Stothert (1977) has suggested that both root crop agriculture and unspecialized hunting and gathering are consistent with the Vegas evidence.

Finally, Davis (1975; see also Lowe 1967) has reviewed the assemblages at Altimira and other lowland sites along the Pacific coast of Guatemala and concluded that the introduction of maize agriculture began around 1300–1000 B.C. The presence of obsidian flakes as possible grater chips in earlier assemblages but not in later assemblage has led both Lowe and Davis to suggest that root crop agriculture probably preceded maize agriculture in the region.

The reasons for the replacement of vegeculture by seed agriculture in the seasonal tropics has been discussed by Harris (1972; see section 16.0). Of course, Sauer (1969) long ago hypothesized that vegetative reproduction was the most ancient planting method since it was the most primitive. Yet, whether root crop agriculture was slightly earlier or slightly later than seed agriculture is perhaps less of an issue here than whether there existed an early agriculture pattern in the lowlands between highland Mesoamerica and the Andes. The hypothesis that tropical forest groups were engaged in some form of cultivation 8,000 to 10,000 years ago has a certain appeal. If such were the case, highland Mesoamerica and the Andes would not be considered as isolated and independent centers of early plant domestication, but as part of a single interaction sphere with the Intermediate area, where peoples, already familiar with cultivation, aided in the spread of early crops between the two highland regions. Phenomena such as the spread of the Mesoamerican domesticated maize to South America at an early date, to be transformed there into an economically valuable plant and be later reintroduced into Mesoamerica, could be better understood in this fashion.

It may, of course, be misleading to talk about "early" agricultural patterns and hunting-gathering patterns as if the two were mutually exclusive, opposing states. The literature is full of examples of "non-agriculturalists" who grow tobacco, irrigate natural grass stands, spare economically valuable plants, pen wild animals for later use, and so forth. There is every reason to believe that such practices were ancient. In fact, human groups have always manipulated their ecosystems; agriculturalists are just more manipulative than some others.

It may also be misleading to assume that because agriculture was early, all tropical forest peoples were farmers. Peoples whose subsistence economies ranged from hunting-gathering to intensive agriculture undoubtedly coexisted (sometimes cooperating, sometimes conflicting) for thousands of years (cf. Turnbull 1965; Peterson 1978).

In short, the business of reconstructing subsistence patterns in tropical America is enormously complicated given the time range involved, the exceedingly poor preservation of botanical remains, and the likely juxtaposition of contemporary peoples with distinctly different subsistence pursuits. For the moment, we had best keep an open mind and be prepared to consider seriously some wildly different hypotheses.

3.9 CLOSING REMARKS

In this chapter we have moved from a straightforward description of the Rio Chiriqui canyon and the excavated sites to the only slightly more problematic discussion of the chronology, definition of the phases, and descriptions of the stone assemblages. Inferences about the activities carried out at the shelters and about the uses of the stone tools, while admittedly more tenuous, are still rooted in the evidence recovered from the excavation and from analysis of the shelters' deposits. However, the attempt to view the preceramic occupation of the Rio Chiriqui region in broader perspective must be considered highly speculative. With the present information, it is simply impossible to reconstruct with precision the exact subsistence system operating in the Rio Chiriqui canyon during the preceramic, nor is it possible to specify the antecedents of the Talamancan phase pattern. Nevertheless, it seems to me that an investigator is obliged to attempt an interpretation of the evidence, even though it may represent no more than a "best guess." One must, of course, be careful to distinguish "best guesses" from established fact or inspired vision.

4.0

Highland Agricultural Villages in the Volcan Baru Region

O.F. LINARES AND P.D. SHEETS

4.1 INTRODUCTION

The Volcan region falls entirely within the zone of upper elevations having the richest agricultural lands in the tropics due to lower rates of humus decomposition associated with cooler soils (Janzen 1973, p. 1215). Parts of the Cerro Punta basin now contain over a meter and a half of rich humic soils. A sustained agricultural system, centered on truck gardening, but with subsistence crops such as maize being important, is practiced in this basin today.

The mammalian fauna of the Panamanian highlands is generally similar to that of the lowlands, including several species of monkeys, squirrels, caviomorph rodents, and, once upon a time, tapir, peccary, and brocket deer. However, it may be assumed that "tropical mountaintops have fewer species than tropical lowlands" (MacArthur 1972, p. 214). Not only may the mammalian fauna be somewhat sparser in the highlands than in the lowlands, but fishing possibilities are also reduced by the incident rivers and the lack of standing water (Linares, Sheets, and Rosenthal 1975). Thus, the limiting factor for early human populations appears to have been the amount of protein available.

Once such protein-rich vegetable resources as beans and palms, together with maize, became the important staples, the Volcan region was converted into one of the most densely settled areas of the Isthmus; until some of the settlers were forced out.

4.2 BIOTOPES IN THE CERRO PUNTA AND EL HATO BASINS

The Rio Chiriqui Viejo has its source in the highlands slightly to the north of Volcan Baru, from where it flows westward along the edge of the small highland valley of Cerro Punta, located at 8°56′ N latitude and 82°35′ W longitude at an elevation from 1,800 meters to 2,375 meters above sea level.

This is known as the "lower montane" ecological zone (Tosi 1971, pp. 67–70).

Within the Cerro Punta basin, the following biotopes played an important role in the past: the flat stream terraces of the Rio Chiriqui Viejo, the river itself and its feeder streams, and the surrounding piedmont spurs.

On the relatively flat stream terraces of Cerro Punta, including most of the basin floor, are found the archaeological sites. This gently sloping land is covered with rich lake and volcanic soils where potato fields and vegetable gardens now prosper (fig. 4.0-1). Given the fertility of these soils, ancient fields and houses would have had to be shifted only if "weedy shrubs and trees became too much of a problem" (section 10.6). To judge from the presence of carbonized plant remains and abundant groundstone tools and from the absence of shell or faunal remains, the first inhabitants we know of in this valley relied primarily on agriculture for their livelihood (sections 10.3 and 10.4).

The piedmont spurs bordering the valley above 2,000 meters are steep and rocky; many spots have recently been cleared of vegetation to produce grazing land. Where vegetation survives, it is typical lower montane evergreen forest with two or three levels. The dominant species in the highest canopy (10 to 25 meters high) are *Quercus* sp. ("roble") and *Cyrilla* sp. ("palo colorado"), whose branches are often covered with epiphytes (La Bastille ms. 1972). Other common evergreen trees found here are *Persea schiedeana* ("coyo avocado"), *Weinmannia pinnata* ("oreganillo"), and *Cedrela tonduzii* ("cedro"). "There are several timber species and trees of large dimensions" (Holdridge and Budowski 1956, p. 102), some of which may have served for housebuilding in the past. In prehistoric times, much of the forest in the hills surrounding Cerro Punta may have been left uncut, providing good hunting grounds.

The basin of El Hato is ecologically somewhat different. Rather than being an evergreen montane valley, El Hato can be classified as semideciduous, with a Pacific type of dry forest, including a number of indicator trees listed by Holdridge (1956, pp. 97-98). The dominant vegetation was probably not unlike that described for the Talamanca shelters (section 3.2) or La Pitahaya (section 6.2).

4.3 A SUMMARY OF SETTLEMENT AND COMMUNITY PATTERNS IN THE VOLCAN REGION

Settlement patterns in the surveyed area have been summarized by Sheets (report no. 2), while Dahlin's posthole survey (report no. 3) and Rosenthal and Spang's excavations (reports no. 4 and no. 5) have helped to define the community patterns and depositional history of the Pitti-Gonzalez (BU-17 a-b) and Barriles (BU-24) sites. Here we will give a brief account of their work as a background to the reconstruction of the Volcan settlement system in the section that follows.

The Cerro Punta basin contains 7 to 8 square kilometers (700 to 800 hectares) of flat, cultivable land, of which about half (roughly 350 hectares)

Figure 4.0-1: Terraces of the Rio Chiriqui Viejo.

was occupied in prehistoric times. All of the 15 sites encountered in the valley were clustered in its lower portion, at elevations from 1,800 meters to a maximum of 2,000 meters (fig. 4.0-2). The 2,000-meter contour seems to represent the uppermost limits of human occupation of the Chiriqui highlands. Settlement farther north was arrested by a cloud forest, uncolonized even today. (For a discussion of settlement patterns vis-à-vis agricultural developments in the Volcan area see Linares, Sheets, and Rosenthal 1975.) Most of the Cerro Punta sites, and certainly all the major ones, were located below 1,900 meters. Of the three groups of sites in Cerro Punta, the cluster in the central portion of the basin consisting of five sites was the largest, with Sitio Pitti-Gonzalez (BU-17) being the largest and most internally differentiated. Thus, the Cerro Punta settlement pattern was one of discontinuous villages, marked by surface refuse (mostly pottery and stone tools) spread over areas ranging in length from 50 meters to 500 meters. The absence of raised middens, plus the evidence from house floors, suggests that refuse simply accumulated naturally under house structures. Most of these dwellings were located near one of the numerous *quebradas* (Graille, Iglesia, Callejon) that traverse the basin from several directions to join the main Rio Chiriqui Viejo channel.

Although much more extensive excavation would be needed in order to reconstruct the community pattern represented by the BU-17 deposits, it is safe to assume, on the basis of the soundings (report no. 3) that dwellings were located on the flatter contours, near but not at the edge of the quebradas. Single dwellings were placed 40 to 50 meters from each other and about the same distance from special features such as the communal (?) hearth found in area 3. Outside of the dwelling area, refuse was much less dense and, in some spots, missing altogether.

To summarize, Sitio Pitti-Gonzalez is located on an ancient lake bed with rich soils, next to a small quebrada. Although above-surface structures were nowhere to be seen, posthole soundings, plus more extensive testing, allowed us to make tentative distinctions between activity areas associated with everyday behavior. The total area within which refuse was found was very large, but it was by no means uniformly covered with dense deposits. In all likelihood, BU-17 was a very large village composed of dispersed dwellings strung out along the banks of Quebrada Callejon. Although BU-17, as well as some of the other large Cerro Punta villages of this period, may have specialized in such activites as celt manufacture and making engraved pottery, few, if any, ceremonial and/or adminstrative functions can be attributed to this or to any other of the Cerro Punta villages.

To the south of Cerro Punta, the Chiriqui Viejo cuts a narrow canyon through Bambito, Los Llanos, and what we call the Intermediate region (i.e., around Paso Ancho and Tisingal). While Bambito harbored numerous but fairly small archaeological sites, only a few sites were encountered in the Intermediate area and none at all in the Los Llanos area. It is only when one reaches the Southwest area around Nueva California and El Hato that one encounters massive zones of habitation at elevations of between 1,200 and 1,340 meters. The five sites encountered here, including Barriles (BU-24), were the largest found in the Volcan Baru region.

Putting together the information found by Stirling (1950) and Ichon (1968) with ours, we are able to postulate at least three activity areas at Barriles (report no. 5): (A) The socioceremonial area includes the central

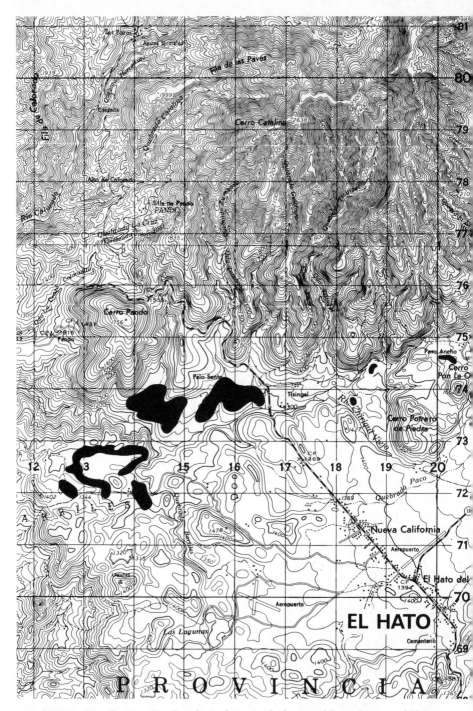

Figure 4.0-2: Distribution of archaeological sites in the basins of Cerro Punta and El Hato.
Reprinted from O.F. Linares, P.D. Sheets, and E.J. Rosenthal, Science, 1975, vol. 187,
fig. 3, p. 140 (© 1975 by the American Association for the Advancement of Science).

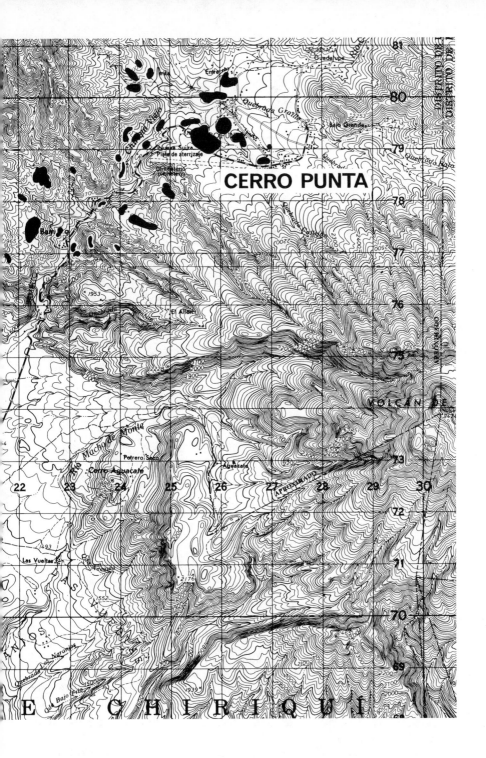

CERRO PUNTA

Figure 4.0-3: Barriles lapidary art: a. "ceremonial" metate and stone seat, Museo del Hombre Panameño; b,c. support figures once attached to some seat or table; location unknown. Reprinted from O.F. Linares, P.D. Sheets, and E.J. Rosenthal, Science, 1975, vol. 187, fig. 6, p. 142 (© 1975 by the American Association for the Advancement of Science).

mound (Stirling's "ceremonial center"), which had a rectangular "floor" of stone slabs and boulders and was flanked by petroglyphs on large boulders; off this area to the east stood once the row of statues mentioned by Stirling. (B) The living or habitation zone seems to have been located immediately to the east of the cermonial mound in the arch following a dip in the quebrada. (C) A cemetery of burials in large, lidded urns was found by Stirling to the south of the mounded area.

These three activity areas reveal a degree of elaboration unknown for the other sites in the Volcan area. Likewise, the iconography of stone carvings is revealing: retainer statues, individuals wielding stone axes, *chicha* jars, and giant metates are all associated (fig. 4.0-3). "Thus, whatever its specific meaning and symbolic function, Barriles sculpture associates symbols of rank and warlike attributes with maize agriculture" (Linares, Sheets, and Rosenthal 1975, p. 141).

4.4 THE VOLCAN SETTLEMENT SYSTEM

In *The Mesoamerican Village,* Flannery (1976, p. 162) distinguishes between a settlement pattern — or the particular distribution of sites over a landscape — and a settlement system, which he defines as "the set of 'rules' that generated the pattern in the first place." Clearly, Flannery is talking not about immutable "laws," but about general principles influencing settlement choices in the past. These principles should be derived from a close scrutiny of the site distributional data, only after consideration of other cultural evidence as well.

In the following discussion of the Volcan settlement "rules" we will be keeping these questions in mind: What types of factors explain most satisfactorily certain aspects of the Volcan site-distribution data? Are some distributions better understood as responses to social forces, rather than as responses to natural features or to subsistence requirements? A discussion of each settlement "rule" follows below, moving from the more specific to the more general.

1. As reconstructed by Sheets (report no. 2) the Volcan settlement pattern was a variant of a linear stream and river system. As he also emphasizes, however, the 45 sites encountered were located, not in the channel of the Rio Chiriqui Viejo itself, but on the high stream terraces or on the basin floor (see fig. 4.0-2). This is the only flat and fertile land available. Both the plant remains (section 10.3) and the stone tools (report no. 14) clearly indicate that the Volcan inhabitants were intensive farmers, with maize and beans predominating. Hence rule number 1 can be stated as follows: the Volcan settlements were placed where the best and flattest agricultural lands were found, without regard to river irrigation. Since these lands occur in the stream terraces along the Rio Chiriqui Viejo, a linear pattern of villages resulted.

2. However, the amount of good flat land available was not everywhere the same. For example, the basins of Cerro Punta and El Hato contained much larger cultivable surfaces than the more hilly region of Bambito. Hence, more sites would be expected to occur in these basins than in Bambito. This expectation is not quite supported by the evidence, however. More, but smaller sites, occurred at Bambito than at Cerro Punta; much larger but fewer sites occurred at El Hato than at Cerro Punta (report no. 2, table 1). The general rule thus seems to be: The flatter the land, the larger the villages; the more hilly the land, the smaller the villages.

3. Another glance at the same table suggests that rule number 2 may not be quite so simple either. In Cerro Punta 64 percent and in Bambito 61 percent of the sites are of medium size (i.e., classes 2 and 3). Hence, the rule

should be modified to read: Regardless of topography, the "ideal" site was somewhere between 200 and 400 meters long.

4.   Among the other size classes, small sites of class 1 occur more often than really large sites of class 5 (1/4th as compared with 1/9th). The rule is thus: Relatively few villages attained a truly big size, and if one did, all of them did, in the Southwest region.

5.   Even in areas where size classes 2 and 3 predominated, there were always one or two sites that were larger (class 4) than the others. In this region, if one or two villages increased in size, the rest did not.

So far we have discussed site classes as if they were purely abstract categories. Let us now attempt a site typology based on inferred site functions.

a.   Nucleated farming villages: Slightly over 50 percent of the sites were medium size (classes 2 and 3) and "nucleated"; that is, the houses were contiguous and not scattered as were those belonging to the Bocas hamlets discussed later on in this volume. This nucleation was a response to the predominant agricultural pattern: possibly a sustained-yield swidden system, but certainly one requiring little fallowing. "The volcanic increment in the soil makes the fertile Cerro Punta soil available for long-term cultivation rather than for the usual pattern of shifting cultivation" (C.E. Smith, section 10.6). A village could grow in size, up to a certain point, without requiring that its inhabitants walk more than 1/2 kilometer to their more distant fields. The immediate area around the dwelling was probably also used for raising crops (i.e., for dooryard gardens).

b.   Craft-specialists villages: In contrast to the crude Volcan chipped-stone industry, which Sheets (1975) calls a "cottage industry" because it seems to have been practiced by all households, the groundstone and polished stone industry was most likely in the hands of specialists (report no. 14). This industry consisted mostly of celt reparation and/or celt manufacture. Only 7 out of the 45 sites found seemed to have been celt repair centers, and all are among the largest sites in the area. Five of these centers (Barriles, BU-1, BU-3-5) are in the Southwest area; the other two (Sitio Pitti-Gonzalez and BU-34) are two of the largest villages in the central Cerro Punta village cluster. An eighth site where some celt flakes were found (BU-18) is one of the two largest sites in the Bambito region. Hence, in addition to having a resident farming population, the largest Volcan villages also seemed to include celt specialists. Celts were the only tools available for land-clearance. (As suggested below, the limiting factor for agriculture was probably not the amount of land available but how much of it could be cleared for planting.)

In addition, it is important to note that the ceramic collections from these same villages (size 4 and above) also had higher percentages of Bugaba Engraved Ware. This may have been a "special-status" ware, as the figure most commonly depicted in the underside or interior of engraved vessels was that of a male personage wearing a conical hat, like the personage being carried on the shoulders of another, in the giant Barriles statues (Linares et al. 1975, cover and fig. 4.0-3).

c.   Regional centers: As we have argued elsewhere (Linares, Sheets, and Rosenthal 1975; Linares 1977), the site of Barriles in the Southwest region was most likely a socioceremonial center of some sort. However, it was only one of five large villages in this region. Whether the other sites at one time contained monumental sculptures, "plaza" floors, and "high status" burials is a moot point, however. Hence Barriles may have served as the center of a federation of large villages, or simply as one of several large and important villages. Be that as it may, the iconography at the site seems to indicate a connection between maize-farming, warfare, and chiefly status.

Concerning the few and small villages of the Intermediate region, Sheets has suggested (report no. 2) that this area functioned as a "buffer zone," a no man's land between the two above-mentioned regions. If this interpretation is correct, then the paucity and smallness of the sites near Tisingal and Paso Ancho may be due to social rather than natural "causes"; either to an effort on the part of the Southwest villages to keep villages in the immediate vicinity from growing large and strong, or to the desire on the part of the groups in Bambito and Cerro Punta to keep a certain distance from the villages in the Southwest. Which of these two explanations — if either — is correct, we shall never know for certain.

4.5   CONCLUSIONS

As Flannery (1976, p. 165) remarks of other efforts to estimate prehistoric populations, it is preferable "to light one small candle rather than curse the darkness." Hence we will hazard some *very* tentative estimates of the number of people that may have lived in the Volcan region. Let us begin with the evidence from Sitio Pitti-Gonzalez (BU-17) and assume that the dwelling excavated here, which measured 7 meters x 6 meters (or 42 m²), housed five persons (this is a conservative estimate for a modern Guaymí household). The average distance between one dwelling and another was about 50 meters. If we assume an equal spacing for all households, then each household (which included gardens, unused areas, and so forth) covered an area approximately 2,500 square meters (50 meters x 50 meters) which we will assume included the house structure itself. Now, the BU-17 site measured roughly 600 meters x 300 meters, or 180,000 square meters. Hence, the total number of households that it could accommodate at any one time was 72. Assuming that new households were built every twenty-five years or so, when old ones decayed and/or new families were formed, then only about one-fourth of the BU-17 households were occupied simultaneously. This gives us 18 households of 5 persons each, or a population for the site of 90 persons; that is 15 persons per 100 linear meters of site. Now, if we extrapolate from this figure to the other site-size classes (report no. 2, table 1) we can suggest the following figures: Class 1 sites had less than 30 persons; class 2, 31 to 40 persons; class 3, 41 to 60 persons; class 4, 61 to 105 persons; and class 5, 106 to 150 persons. (These figures were arrived at by using the total lengths of the sites and comparing these with BU-17.) By taking the mean population for each size-class we can also suggest the following populations for each region at any one time: 653 for Cerro Punta, 983 for Bambito, 158 for the Intermediate region, and 638 for the Southwest region. Going out on a limb even farther, we can offer a maximum population for the Volcan region surveyed: about 2,432 persons at the time it was abandoned in A.D. 600. Again, assuming that the people were evenly spread over the 62 square kilometers area (which we know could not be true), we can offer a population density figure of 39 persons per square kilometer. We need not add that these figures represent the roughest of approximations, to be taken with extreme caution; yet they are within reasonable limits, given the carrying capacity of these kinds of habitats.

To conclude, we offer a tentative reconstruction of the process of colonization and expansion in the Volcan region based on all available evidence. The area occupied first, sometime around 200 B.C. during the Concepción phase (section 7.4), was the Southwest. It was settled by groups moving up from the Chiriqui coastal plains, carrying a developed maize-growing culture. Not only was the Southwest area nearer to the midaltitude plains, but it also had a coastal dry-wet (Aw) climatic regime, with several months of dry season, optimal for growing maize. Sometime in the first few centuries of the Christian era, during the Barriles phase, the area of El Hato received new migrants, or at least new influences, from the nearby neighboring zone of Agua Buena in Costa Rica, thirty five kilometers away. The elaborate pottery being made in these two areas around A.D. 200 was virtually identical. At this point in time, during the Early Bugaba phase (A.D. 200-400), groups "fissioned off" from the Southwest region and began moving up, following the stream-terraces along the Rio Chiriqui Viejo. Whether they first settled in the Cerro Punta basin and from there spilled over to the Bambito region (as we believe but cannot prove they did), or whether they first settled in Bambito and then Cerro Punta, is not yet clear. During this same period, some villages may have developed craft specialists and special services and as a consequence (or, possibly, as a prerequisite) grew larger in size. Meanwhile, Barriles (and possibly some other large villages of the Southwest) evolved into a regional "ceremonial" center. Just how this center was articulated with the "daughter" communities farther north is not quite clear either; but the relationship probably involved some use of force. In Barriles lapidary art, giant metates are encircled by trophy heads and are found in enormous graves; the people are carried on the shoulders of others; personages depicted on the pottery carry staffs and wear conical hats; celts are hung around the necks of prominent individuals and figures of men wielding axes (or celts?) are carved on the legs of giant grinding-stones (some of them possibly functioning as seats or "thrones"). Now, if both Bambito and Cerro Punta had larger populations than the Southwest region, we may assume that perhaps the inhabitants of the latter region kept their ascendancy by offering craft and socioceremonial services, possibly extracting labor or a share of the maize crop in return. This hypothesis is at least worthy of being tested in the future. What seems a safe conclusion is that by A.D. 400 and possibly before, the germ of a site hierarchy (Flannery 1976, pp. 168–171) existed in western Panama. This may have been the oldest such hierarchy in the Isthmus, and, interestingly enough, it was tied to a seed culture, whose long-term ecological effects have been discussed by Harris (1972).

At the time Baru made its last eruption (around A.D. 600–700) only half of the Cerro Punta habitable area was occupied, in contrast to most of El Hato, which seemed "filled in" with sites. The limiting factor for population growth and migration into the Volcan region may well have been the difficulty of clearing new land in these evergreen forests, rather than the availability of land itself. For populations moving upriver from the mid-elevation coastal plains, the lure of these fertile lands may have been counteracted by the year-round humidity and the excessive coldness of these tropical mountain regions.

PART TWO

COASTAL SETTLEMENTS ON THE
ATLANTIC AND PACIFIC SIDES

S ections 5.0 and 6.0 summarize the settlement system of two "marginal" (i.e., nonriverine) coastal communities on either side of the Isthmus. The time span is A.D. 600 to A.D. 900; the exact location, two peninsulas (one of them semidetached) in the midst of fairly calm embayments. Discussion will center on Cerro Brujo, a site on the Aguacate Peninsula of Bocas province, and La Pitahaya on the Palenque-Boca Brava "islands" of the Gulf of Chiriqui. These are by no means the only two sites found on either coast, but they are certainly among the largest, if not the largest. Thus they represent the maximum possibilities for settlement size in each of these environments. One or both of the sites were also initially populated by migrants from the highlands (section 7.9).

The contrast between these two coastal adaptations could not be more striking. Dispersed and fairly undifferentiated hamlets, marked by shellfish middens located on ridgetops, and separated from each other by large, uninhabited territories, occur in the Aguacate Peninsula. We have calculated that each hamlet was occupied by approximately 30 persons, giving an overall population density for the peninsula at A.D. 900 of 3 to 4 persons per square kilometer. On the Pacific shore, in this same period, one large nucleated village, probably the seat of a paramount chief like the ones described for the Chiriqui Gulf at contact times (Linares 1968b), held a preeminent position. La Pitahaya was organized into clearly differentiated utility and special purpose areas, where a population estimated at several hundred lived in an area of less than one square kilometer. Although it was a "center" of some kind, there are few indications that La Pitahaya exerted a coercive influence over the surrounding villages. Its influence seemed, instead, to have been tied in with trade and with special socioceremonial functions.

Although few hard and fast explanations can be given for the denser and more complex organization of La Pitahaya, as compared with Cerro Brujo, certain subsistence practices do seem to have allowed, if not "caused," nucleation in one instance and not the other. Intensive agriculture of house gardens and palm plantations near the site, and shifting agriculture of maize fields in nearby places like Boca Brava, were practiced at La Pitahaya, whose inhabitants also utilized two protein resources, the white-tailed deer and marine catfishes. Extensive agriculture, based on crops other than maize, was the system practice by the Cerro Brujo inhabitants, who exploited many patchily distributed protein resources, including mollusks, several reef-dwelling fishes, and several species of terrestrial mammals.

5.0

Ecology and Prehistory of the
Aguacate Peninsula in Bocas del Toro

O. F. LINARES

5.1 INTRODUCTION

A recent article discussing human adaptations in the Amazonian area (Ross 1978) presents yet another version of the old argument that among horticultural-hunting groups living in interfluvial areas small group-size and impermanence of settlement are related to the low protein productivity of these areas (see also Carneiro 1970; Lathrap 1968; Morey 1970; Meggers 1971).

In the following section I try to demonstrate that the prehistoric groups inhabitating the Aguacate Peninsula were indeed organized into small and highly mobile groups. However, it is difficult to conceive of these groups as "protein-limited," given the garden-hunting system they probably practiced (Linares 1976 and section 12.5), the abundant marine resources available to them (sections 13.0 and 14.0), and the possibility that they were also supplementing their diet with protein-rich vegetable resources like the peach palm.

Both the Cerro Brujo data and the present-day Guaymí practices tend to disprove the common belief (Ross 1978, p. 15) that increased dependence on fishing is correlated with increased sedentariness. In fact the groups that moved from the highlands to the Bocas coast around A.D. 600 must have experienced a marked increase in availability of animal protein, becoming much more, rather than less, mobile. (For another criticism of Ross's hypothesis, published after completion of this chapter, see Chagnon and Hames 1979.)

Hence, we must look to other factors, not just availability of animal protein, to explain the settlement strategy of a group. Among relevant factors are the type of agriculture employed, the methods of defense against predators, the influence of diseases, and so forth. A dispersed settlement pattern can, in turn, be considered successful and adaptive, not just limiting as many advocates of the protein-scarcity hypothesis seem to believe.

5.2 TERRESTRIAL AND MARINE HABITATS
IN THE AGUACATE PENINSULA

The more general aspects of the Bocas del Toro environment have been discussed in section 2.1. Here we will focus on the location, size, distribution, and potential productivity of the marine and terrestrial habitats utilized in the past (fig. 5.0-1). The embayment formed by Almirante Bay and the Chiriqui Lagoon in the northwest sector of the province is divided by a small peninsula we will call Aguacate, borrowing the name from a village on its southern side. By settling on the Aguacate point, the prehistoric inhabitants could, at least in theory, partake of the slightly different resources of either bay.

Of the two bays, Almirante is the smaller (19 km x 8 km, as the crow flies), as well as the shallower (average depth is 5 fathoms) (fig. 5.0-2). It is also better protected from offshore action by large, steep islands (Cristobal, Bastimentos, Isla Popa, Cayo Agua), as well as by numerous tiny flat islands covered by pure stands of mangrove barely projecting above the water. By way of contrast, the Chiriqui Lagoon (which is in Bocas, despite the name) is larger (28 km by 12 km), deeper (average depth is 10 to 15 fathoms), and more exposed to tidal action. It is also bordered by numerous beaches and, on its eastern half, by a "swampy alluvial coastal plain five to six miles wide" (Terry 1956, p. 9). No such broad coastal plains or beaches exist in Almirante where the hilly slopes made up of "sediments and andesite" extend to the water's edge. Several rivers (Robalo, Guarumo, Cricamola,

Figure 5.0-1: A view of Almirante Bay from the Aguacate Peninsula.

Guaivira) flow into the Chiriqui Lagoon, while Almirante Bay receives only minor streams referred to locally as "creeks." Generally speaking, Almirante Bay resembles a shallow oceanic lagoon, while the Chiriqui Lagoon is more like a tropical estuary system, subject to the influx of considerable fresh water.

The Aguacate Peninsula itself is small, measuring roughly 9 kilometers by 6 kilometers along each of the longer T-shaped axes (fig. 5.0-3). It is located at 9°10' N latitude and 82°15' W longitude in the district of Bocas, corregimiento of Cauchero. Although connected to the mainland, this juncture is so narrow (slightly more than one kilometer) that Aguacate may well be considered as just another of the inshore islands found in the Bocas embayment. Like them, it is fairly hilly, with a ridge averaging 80 meters to 100 meters above sea level traversing it from west to east, and the rest of the land in rolling slopes that fall directly into the mangrove-fringed coast. The principal biotopes utilized prehistorically were: ridge tops, slopes, streams, swamps, shore, and inshore and offshore marine substrates.

Above the 60-meter contour line, usually on the ridge tops, are found the larger prehistoric middens; these flat-topped ridges with a view of either bay were the preferred dwelling localities. Nowadays, these spots are uninhabited because the modern Antillean settlers of Aguacate prefer to live on the shore as a by-product of cash-cropping and the outboard motor (Linares 1970). Four ridges, 40 to 120 meters above sea level, occur within the peninsula; the Cerro Brujo ridge itself is 2.5 x 1.0 kilometers. An overall rough estimate of the ridged area available for settlements here is thus 250 hectares, of which less than .5 hectare was covered with settlements in pre-Spanish days.

Common large trees growing on or near the Cerro Brujo ridge include the following genera: *Spondias* ("jobo"), *Ficus* ("higuerón"), *Ceiba* sp. (the "bongo"), *Ochroma* sp. ("balsa"), *Cedrela* sp. ("cedro"), *Cordia* sp. ("laurel"), and *Carapa* sp. ("bateo"). Most of these species are suitable for canoe building and/or house building. Important trees and shrubs, tended or protected now and probably in the past, are the edible "ramon" tree (*Brosimum* sp.), the edible wild papaya with its small apple-sized fruits (*Carica* sp.), the "chingongo" or latex tree (*Achras zapote*), and the "pita" (*Aechemea* sp.) which is used for cordage. (For a more complete description of the Bocas vegetation, see Gordon 1969.)

On the slopes between the 20- and 40-meter contours are occasionally found secondary small middens marking the locality of at most a single prehistoric dwelling, perched on the edge of a slope. The main use of these slopes was probably for shifting cultivation, as they are the only land available for this purpose. Wherever the modern Guaymí have recolonized, they have cultivated on the slopes. I have calculated the absolute amount of slope land below the 80-meter contour available for cultivation within Aguacate as being roughly 19 square kilometers (1,900 hectares).

Typical regrowth vegetation of the slopes includes species thriving on cleared areas and quickly invading abandoned fields such as the broad-

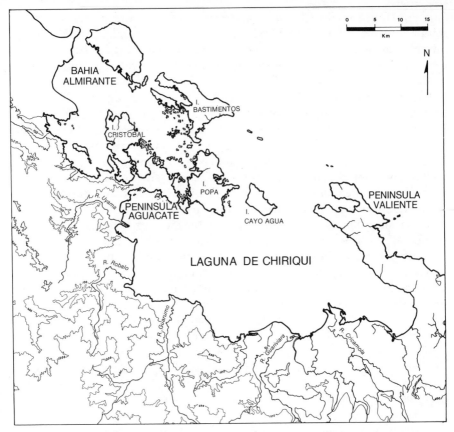

Figure 5.0-2: Map of the Chiriqui Lagoon, Atlantic Coast, Bocas del Toro province.

leafed plants, *Heliconia* and *Calathea* sp. ("bijao" and "chichica"), and small trees, *Cecropia* sp. ("guarumo") and *Anacardium* sp. ("marañon").

Most of the terrestrial mammals hunted by the Cerro Brujo inhabitants in the past (section 12.0) invaded disturbed habitats and thrived on cultivated or fallowed fields (Linares 1976). Hence, these slopes, planted with tangled gardens, must have been preferred hunting grounds for the caviomorph rodents *(Dasyprocta* and *Cuniculus)* and the peccary *(Tayassu tajacu)*, which the inhabitants took in substantial numbers.

The nearest sizable river, the Uyama, is 10 kilometers away on the mainland. On the Aguacate Peninsula itself, the largest stream is Quebrada Juliana, which flows from the foothills of Cerro Brujo south into the Chiriqui Lagoon. Due to the constant rains, it has some water the year round, as have the smallest streams that flow at the base of every ridge on the peninsula. Besides providing the ancient inhabitants with the only fresh water available, they must have also served as a habitat for the mammalian species that were hunted.

Below the 40-meter contour line are found extensive swamps, known locally as "swampos," which were and are largely uninhabited except for

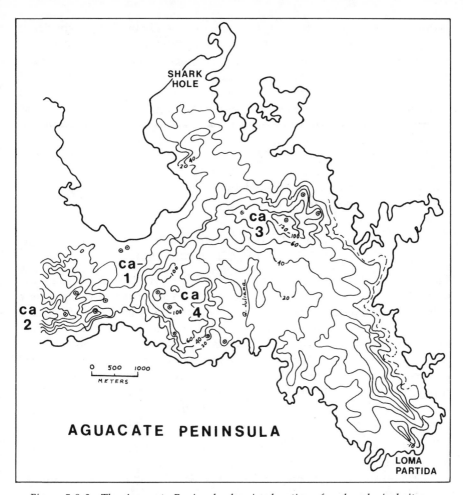

Figure 5.0-3: The Aguacate Peninsula showing location of archaeological sites.

marine birds, crabs, turtles, and raccoons, none of which were extensively utilized in the past. The "matumba" or *Raphia* palm grows luxuriantly in this habitat and may have been used for thatching; its fruits, leaves, and sprouts are consumed by peccaries.

Fringing the shore are stands of mangrove of the genera *Rhizophora* and *Avicennia* that extend quite far inland in the Chiriqui Lagoon. Their stilt roots are used now for firewood and, occasionally, for house construction. Another shore-dwelling plant species is the seaside grape (*Coccoloba uvifera*), useful for its tannic acid and edible fruit.

The immediate marine inshore substrate environment is made up of large flats of turtle grass (*Thalassia testudinum*) growing on silt and sand and coral rubble. These marine grasses provide feeding grounds for the green turtle and the manatee which the CA-3 inhabitants hunted in substantial numbers (Wing, section 13.2). Where mangrove stands occur, the mangrove oyster (*Crassostrea rhizophorae*) is found in great quantities attached to the roots. Mangrove channels also provide good habitats for a species of snapper and a species of snook that were important in the prehistoric diet.

Live coral heads of *Acropora cervicornis* (staghorn coral), *Porites furcata* (finger coral), *Acropora millepora* (stinging coral), and sponges start right off from the shallows, continuing into deeper waters (Rodaniche, personal observations). Where mangrove stands are missing, the immediate inshore substrate is mostly sand and dead coral. This is also the environment preferred by the molluskan species gathered prehistorically *(Arca zebra, Arca imbricata,* and *Chama macerophylla),* which live attached to rocks in shallow water and must have been collected by wading (section 14.0). Coral and rocky reefs are also inhabited by a number of fish species such as snapper, grunt, jack, and grouper.

5.3   SETTLEMENT AND COMMUNITY PATTERNS IN THE AGUACATE PENINSULA

Two surveys of the Aguacate Peninsula (the first in 1969, the second and more thorough one in 1974) were undertaken in order to investigate a number of problems concerning the overall distribution of archaeological sites (i.e., their settlement patterns) and their internal arragements (i.e., their community patterns). To facilitate interpretations about ancient population distributions vis-à-vis available resources, we focused on a limited number of questions formulated as testable propositions. Because of its small size, it was possible to survey the entire Aguacate Peninsula, thus eliminating problems of sampling. The results of these surveys are discussed below under each of the propositions investigated.

1.   All inhabitable parts of the peninsula were (were not) settled at one point or another in the archaeological past.

We found that roughly one-half of the peninsula had never been inhabited, at least not by people leaving behind detectable refuse. (Even though shell middens are easiest to discover in the lush vegetation, they are by no means the only sites regularly found by peasant cultivators as they clear the vegetation with their machetes. The only sites we could have consistently missed are midden deposits, without shell, located in areas not cleared in the last decades; there are few such areas on the peninsula.) The scarcity of sites is most apparent in the areas between Cerro Brujo (CA-3) and Shark Hole, and between CA-3 and Loma Partida (fig. 5.0-3).

2.   Within the inhabited area, archaeological deposits are (are not) found in all sorts of habitats.

As previously mentioned, refuse deposits were found consistently in the higher ridges and hilltops, often on the backbone of the peninsula and never on or next to the shoreline.

Within the ridged area, the largest ancient deposits are usually on the crests, above the 80-meter contour, while smaller middens tend to be located on the peripheral slopes in the 40- to 80-meter contour.

3. Refuse deposits are (are not) distributed continuously over the ridged area.

Midden deposits occur discontinuously, either singly or in clusters, one to several hundred meters apart. Each isolated midden, or cluster of middens, has been considered as a dwelling locality. Several such localities are to be found dispersed within a one-kilometer radius. Between an area where middens are found and another such area, there may be one or two kilometers of uninhabited territory.

The area within which midden localities are found was designated an "archaeological site" and was assumed to have corresponded to a dispersed, or loosely localized, hamlet or residential unit. Four such hamlets, composed each of several midden localities, were found in the Aguacate Peninsula and labeled CA-1, CA-2, CA-3, and CA-4, with the affix CA standing for the district of Cauchero, and the numbers standing for the sites in the order found. (One of these hamlets, Cerro Brujo [CA-3] was the scene of intensive excavations (report no. 6).

The occupation of Cerro Brujo involves two phases. The earlier or pre-shellfish occupation (the Aguacate phase; ca. A.D. 600) occurs in strata C and D; the more recent or shellfish-collecting phase (Bocas phase; ca. A.D. 900) is confined to strata B-1 and B-2. Using phase and stratigraphic distinctions, we can summarize the overall community history of the Cerro Brujo site as follows:

Locality 3a, or the main midden spot (fig. 5.0-4), comprises nine areas, each of which was initially designated as an "activity area" despite the fact that only two classes of "above-surface features" were represented: living or habitation spots and trash heaps. The only subsurface constructional units (i.e., "features") encountered during excavation were "natural floors," burial pits, and caches. Neither specialized above-surface structures, such as platform mounds or defensive walls, nor specialized subsurface constructions, such as hearths, ovens, or storage pits, were encountered in the excavations.

During the Aguacate phase, the first Cerro Brujo inhabitants settled on the flatter central portion of the 3a locality, discarding most of their damaged artifacts at this (area 9) and at another (area 4) spot. In the first part of the Bocas phase, while the trash middens were still low, people trod upon them to discard their rubbish, contributing to the formation of "natural floors" recognizable by compacted, crushed, and lensed shell-layers. In the latter part of this same phase (ca. A.D. 930), the trash middens were too high to be walked upon and therefore shell was dumped from the side, in activity areas 1-3, 5-8. During this time, the rest of the localities (3b, 3c, 3d) were established. These localities seem to have been even less internally differentiated than the 3a locality and certainly much smaller. The principal Cerro Brujo locality (CA-3a) was occupied for the first time around A.D. 600-700. No radiocarbon determinations exist for the older or Aguacate phase occupation at the site, but cross-ties with other sites indicate a short period, some time after A.D. 600 and before A.D. 900 (section 7.8). These

Figure 5.0-4: Aerial photograph of the excavations at the main Cerro Brujo midden (Locality 3a).

older inhabitants did not practice a shell-fishing economy and were not yet fully adapted to coastal habitats. The ceramic traditions that they brought to the site share basic similarities with those of the Chiriqui highlands, specifically with those of Cerro Punta and El Hato. If not the direct descendants of these highland groups, the Cerro Brujo people were undoubtedly related in some manner to groups that had formerly occupied the interior valleys and coastal plains of western Panama (section 7.9).

A short time after settling in Aguacate, the Cerro Brujo people adapted a lifeway oriented toward the sea, discarding veritable middens of shell on top of ridges and slopes right next to where they had their dwellings. These middens built up very fast, probably within a few decades. Together with this change in lifeways came a change in ceramic repertoire. Local materials, such as shell and reeds, and motifs portraying the local fauna came to be used to decorate the pottery. During this time, regular contact was maintained with peoples of the Pacific coast. Then, shortly after A.D. 930, the hamlet was abandoned, probably to be rebuilt elsewhere.

While it lasted, Cerro Brujo was a modest hamlet marked by refuse deposits covering a total area of at most .5 hectare and no more than six dwellings (two at locality 3a and one at each of the other localities). These dwelling localities were at some distance from each other, atop ridges and hill slopes. The hamlet was internally differentiated only insofar as the main locality was larger and had more "activity areas" than the other secondary localities.

Differences between hamlets in the Aguacate Peninsula, probably dating within the same century, seem to have been minimal. In layout, stratigraphic sequence, and artifactual inventory, Sitio Machuca (CA-2) duplicates very closely the Cerro Brujo site.

5.4 CONCLUSIONS: THE AGUACATE SETTLEMENT SYSTEM, A RECONSTRUCTION

The immediate environment of the Aguacate Peninsula was characterized by habitat diversity and by much variety in the kinds of resources available to the prehistoric inhabitants. Besides ridges, slopes, and fringing bogs, there were two lagoons to exploit, each with a slightly different ecology. In such a setting it was possible to raise different crops, to gather all sorts of fruits, wild and semitended, to hunt on land and sea, to fish, and to collect several species of mollusks.

Despite the variety, however, two important habitats were missing altogether from the Aguacate area: broad alluvial plains and fringing beaches or mudflats. These two are among the most highly productive areas in the tropics. To the absence of these important habitats, we may add the uniformly high rainfall and limited seasonality and the tides of low amplitude, factors which tend to decrease the efficiency of agriculture and fishing.

In fact, the multiple resources available to the Aguacate people were either in small supply or patchily distributed or easily depleted, or all these things. Land suitable for cultivation — the slopes, that is — was steep and subject to constant erosion as well as to rapid weed invasion under the rainfall regime. Similarly, although many species of fish and mollusks are found in coral reefs, they are patchily distributed and difficult of access. The same is true of terrestrial mammals, except for those found in house gardens and cultivated fields. All these factors seem to have contributed to a settlement strategy emphasizing small and scattered hamlets of short duration.

Four such dispersed hamlets, each designated as an archaeological site, existed on the Aguacate Peninsula around A.D. 900. Each site is thus defined as the area in which dispersed dwelling localities are found. Within each site, the typical community pattern involved a larger and more centrally located midden cluster placed on the crest of a ridge above the 80-meter contour. Anywhere from three to five smaller "secondary" midden clusters or satellite dwelling localities were scattered in the contours immediately below. The areas within which we found dwelling localities measured anywhere from 0.8 to 1.5 kilometers. Each of these areas is thought of as a hamlet unit, probably with paths, dooryard gardens, and houses once encompassed within. The separate houses or dwelling localities were probably occupied by families related by kinship, as among the present-day Guaymí of this area (Young, section 15.0).

Between one such hamlet and the next were uninhabited tracts of low-lying land two or more kilometers wide. We have interpreted these as overlapping site-catchment areas where gatherable resources and hunting tracts were once located.

A dispersed settlement pattern on ridge tops was probably adapted to a very extensive type of "nomadic" agriculture, not unlike that practiced by the modern Guaymí of this area. The present system can be described as a long forest-fallow, slash-and-mulch cultivation system whereby fields, preferably located on flat ridges, are cleared but not burned, planted with tubers such as *otoe* for one or two years, and left fallow for up to fifteen or twenty years. These tangled gardens and abandoned fields also offer ideal conditions for the survival of the small mammals that the Cerro Brujo peoples took in such numbers (section 12.0). Nowadays, the Bocas Guaymí constantly abandon old structures and build new ones. In the three years during which we visited the Cerro Brujo site, the group of consanguineally related males living nearby had cleared several new fields, abandoned several others, and built two new structures, all within a radius of a few kilometers. Not only was the increasing distance to new clearings a cause for moving, but also being able to defend crops against animal predators. Additional households must also be set up in response to the normal developmental cycle of the domestic group. The relative ease with which new structures can be built from readily available construction materials, weighed against the effort needed to repair old houses, facilitates this mobility among the Bocas Guaymí.

Although fishing and shellfish-collecting were important pursuits among the ancient Aguacate inhabitants, they did not seem to have influenced their choice of dwelling localities. Hamlets were placed on ridge tops and not at the water's edge. Enormous quantities of shellfish were then hauled up to their living areas. Besides being near their cultivated fields, an important consideration for living on the highest spots seems to have been a view of both bays, probably as an insurance against incursion and possible attack. If we recall, disarticulated and mutilated human skeletons were found at the CA-3 site, a sure indication of hostile relations in the area.

It is possible to suggest a maximum population density for the Aguacate Peninsula at around A.D. 900. We must start with the assertion that all four Aguacate hamlets were the size of Cerro Brujo — though only one in fact was, the rest being somewhat smaller — and that all were contemporaneous. Since CA-3 had an adult population probably not exceeding 30 adults (six houses with five people in each), the total population in the Aguacate Peninsula could not have exceeded 120 persons. Now, since the total area of Aguacate is 31.5 square kilometers, this would give a rounded population density figure of no more than three or four persons per square kilometer.

This figure may well represent the upper limits of the long-term carrying capacity of a backwater area such as Aguacate. Low population densities represent a successful pantropical mammalian adaptive strategy. In an interfluvial area with a steep relief and scattered resources, it may well have represented a very viable adjustment.

6.0

Ecology and Prehistory of the Chiriqui Gulf Sites

O. F. LINARES

6.1 INTRODUCTION

In a recent volume discussing coastal adaptations in Middle America, we find the following introductory remark:

> The two coastal plains that border the Middle American land mass provide similar physical and biotic conditions to which humans have adjusted their lives. Because of the environmental similarities, the two coasts can be treated as a single broad analytic unit (Stark and Voorhies 1978, p. 1).

The data presented in this volume, as well as information contained in previous publications (Linares 1976, 1977), cast serious doubts on Stark and Voorhies's assumption made above. Not only do the two Panamanian coasts differ markedly in physical and biotic parameters (section 2.1) but the Bocas settlement system on the Atlantic coast was characterized by low population aggregates with a great deal of mobility, exploiting a variety of resources that were fairly abundant but patchily distributed (section 5.0). In contrast the bulk of the pre-Hispanic population on the Pacific coast seems to have been congregated into large villages on the floodplains, where fairly intensive cultivation practices were possible. The site of La Pitahaya (IS-3) described in the section that follows seemed to have functioned as a socio-ceremonial and economic center of some importance, despite its location, away from major rivers. No such "centers," or paramount chief villages, have ever been reported — nor do I believe they ever will be reported — from the equivalent interfluvial area on the Atlantic side.

6.2 TERRESTRIAL AND MARINE HABITATS IN THE GULF OF CHIRIQUI

The Gulf of Chiriqui stretches all along the southern or Pacific coast of western Panama, from Punta Burica on the west to approximately Bahia Honda on the east. A number of complex embayments are found on this stretch of coast. The one that concerns us here is Bahia de Muertos (fig. 6.0-1), extending 40 to 50 kilometers southeast of the city of David, at 8°11' N latitude and 82°15' W longitude (Linares 1968b). At least seven rivers, whose headwaters are in the continental divide, flow into Muertos Bay:

> Streams which flow into the estuary drain a large area of volcanic terrain, providing large quantities of clay and sand-sized materials to the estuary. Clay and fine silt are deposited in the back-water mangrove swamp areas of the estuary, whereas the sand tends to concentrate in the stream and tidal channels and is eventually transported to the outer fringes of the estuary where it is concentrated in sand bars, spits, and beaches. During low tide great expanses of mud and sand are exposed as tidal flats (Bishop ms. 1961, p. 6).

The bay is roughly 8 by 9 kilometers, or about half the size of Almirante Bay, and in depth it is quite variable (2 to 7 fathoms). Large islands protect Muertos from tidal action. Some of these islands, such as Sevilla and Isla Mono, are hardly more than extensive mangrove flats barely projecting above water. Others, like Muertos (or Villalba), Cedro Island, and Isla Boca Brava are rocky islands varying in elevation between 50 and 100 meters above sea level.

> Rocks composing the islands southeast of the estuary and the mainland east of the estuary are highly deformed, and they appear to be older than the strata of the estuary and the marine plain. They consist of shale, siltstone, sandstone, and graywacke. Deformation has resulted in severe fracturing, faulting, and recementation of the rocks. Minor recrystallization has occurred in some instances (Bishop ms. 1961, p. 7).

Boca Brava itself is a long island, measuring 11 kilometers east to west and 4.5 kilometers north to south at its widest point. It is placed across the mouth of the Estero de Horconcitos forming the southern end of Muertos Bay. At a point opposite the mainland town of Boca Chica, the channel that divides the island from terra firma is barely 250 meters across. As recently perhaps as just a few thousand years ago, Boca Brava was probably part of the mainland. Both its flora and fauna are indistinguishable from that of corresponding habitats in the rest of Chiriqui province.

The southern end of Boca Brava projects eastward to form a point referred to somewhat misleadingly as Isla Palenque despite the fact that it is permanently attached to Boca Brava by a beach and mangrove strip 200 meters across. By all accounts Palenque should be thought of as a peninsula and not an island. In fact, it and Boca Brava together form one peninsula (roughly the size of Aguacate), which is almost attached to the mainland south of the town of Horconcitos.

Palenque itself is a small peninsula, measuring 1.6 kilometers across and 2.4 kilometers in length, divided into roughly two topographic areas. The higher sector, averaging 60 meters in elevation, is found on the eastern or broader end, while the flatter, sandier, and more swampy terrain is found on the western or narrower part of the peninsula. The pre-Hispanic population of the island was nucleated into one continuous village on the eastern half. The total land area available in this sector is close to .5 square kilometers (or 50 hectares) of which 8.5 hectares (or 21 acres) are covered by a

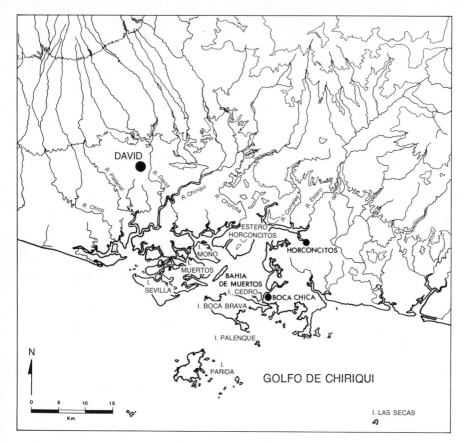

Figure 6.0-1: Map of the Gulf of Chiriqui on the Pacific coast, Chiriqui province.

continuous cap of archaeological materials. The principal biotopes in Palenque utilized in times past were forests, mangrove swamps, palm groves, beach communities, inshore substrates, and offshore waters.

A semideciduous forest approaching a fairly mature stage is now found on the formerly occupied eastern sector of Palenque. (The Palenque forest is one of the few surviving forests on the Pacific side of Panama that is this close to the mainland.) Among the most useful wood-bearing trees found here are *Bombacopsis quinatum* ("cedro espino"), which grows to 2 meters width and is used in boat and house construction; *Tabebuia penta-phylla* ("roble") which is good for house building, but not for boats; *Calophyllum brasiliense* (or "Maria") and *Chlorophora tinctoria* (or "mora") whose woods are used to make house beams; and *Anacardium excelsum* ("espave") which is useful in all sorts of construction. Besides these species, there are a number of other trees whose fruits are edible for animals and sometimes man. Some of these species, however, may be overrepresented at Palenque now, since they are protected and in some cases even planted in order to feed the prosperous population of pigs being raised here. Many of the same species, however, must have once grown in Palenque and Boca Brava, contributing to the maintenance of a wild animal population that could be hunted. Terrestrial mammals that currently eat fallen fruit are the white-tailed deer *(Odocoileus virginianus)*, the two peccaries, and the caviomorph rodents (mainly agouti and paca), while all sorts of birds, monkeys, and squirrels feed on fruit in the canopy. In fact, a lively population of howler monkeys *(Alouatta villosa* or *A. palliata* of some authors) lives in the Palenque canopy now, feeding mostly on the fruit of the *Ficus* sp. tree. Besides the latter, other species with edible fruit are *Luehea seemanii* ("guásimo colorado"), *Bursera simaruba* ("almacigo" or turpentine tree), *Spondias* sp. ("jobo de puerco"), *Gustavia* sp. ("membrillo"), and *Swaertzia* sp. ("naranjillo"). Finally, there are a number of tree species growing in Palenque which seem to be useful only for shade: the *Sterculia apetala* (the Panama tree), and the false silk-cotton tree *Pseudobomba barrigon* (or "barrigón").

All of the species mentioned above are typical of mature semideciduous forests in areas with a pronounced dry season. Totally absent from the present-day Palenque vegetation are the small tree species characteristic of degraded soils and grasslands maintained by constant burning: species like *Curatella* ("chumico"), *Xylopia* sp. ("malagueto"), *Byrsonima* sp. ("nance") and *Cassia* sp. ("cañafístula"). These species now dominate the landscape of Boca Brava and the mainland area opposite Muertos Bay, as well as most of the Pacific slopes all the way across the Isthmus where cattle are raised. Also missing from Palenque is the regrowth vegetation typical of cleared fields: species like *Cecropia* sp. ("guarumo") and the *Heliconia* sp. ("chichica" or "bijao"). In fact, the current vegetation of Palenque probably represents the original flora of the area *before* it became densely populated in pre-Hispanic times. At the time of maximum occupation, much of the natural vegetation had been cleared to make room for dwellings, house orchards, palm plantations, and small milpa fields (section 10.5).

Besides being covered with archaeological materials, the eastern half of Palenque is also strewn with unworked, angular rocks of all sizes, representing the natural or bedrock substrate. At the time of occupation, these rocks had been cleared off to make room for living structures and house buildings and had been piled up onto natural ridges, forming large artificial mounds. Hence, these mounds are made up of fill of a special sort (report no. 7).

The western or narrower end of Palenque averages 10 meters above sea level and is covered by mangrove swamps. Immediately inshore, surrounding the shallow estuary, one finds a mangrove community of the genus *Rhizophora* sp. ("mangle colorado") whose stilt roots are used now for firewood and wharf construction, while its bark and leaves are used for tanning. Slightly farther inshore is a plant association consisting of *Avicennia* sp., the black mangrove (for some reason called "mangle blanco" in Panama), which produces honey and edible seeds, if cooked, and *Conocarpus*, the button mangrove which makes good firewood. These species grow "on slightly higher mud flats that are only seasonally flooded" (report no. 17).

Extensive stands or groves of the common coconut palm *(Coccus nucifera)* border the beaches on the southwestern edge of Palenque and Isla Brava, while large plantations of other native species occur farther inland. Among these are *Scheelia zonensis* ("corozo gunzo") and *Acrocomia vinifera* (the "corozo pacora"), which C. E. Smith (section 10.5) believes were actually cultivated by the Isla Palenque inhabitants in pre-Spanish days. On Isla Brava, palms of the genus *Scheelia* (the "palma real") are protected from constant burning, as the leaves serve for thatching.

Several kinds of beaches are found in Palenque. Since the prevailing dry-season trade winds are from the northeast, the windward side of the island is also the best protected. On the north side of Palenque is found a narrow boulder-and-gravel beach (fig 6.0-2) which probably was (it still is) used for landing, as it was the safest and nearest to the ancient settlements. To the northwest, on the same side, is another somewhat more exposed beach, made up of gray sand. This beach borders on Boca Brava as well, providing an excellent habitat for the common clam nowadays gathered here in great quantities.

On the leeward side, facing the open ocean, is a long, sandy, light-gray beach, continuing into Boca Brava, which is buffeted by strong wind and water action. This is the perfect habitat for small crustaceans, including the mantid shrimp and crabs, both of which are eaten in great quantities now.

Despite the fact that sand-beach communities are extensive on Palenque and Boca Brava, and that these communities are known to be rich in species of considerable biomass, the ancient inhabitants did not seem to have

Figure 6.0-2: Protected narrow gravel beach on the north side of Isla Palenque.

collected shellfish or crustaceans to any appreciable degree. Even if we were to assume that the position of the beaches and their microecology has changed dramatically at Palenque and Boca Brava during the last thousand years, it seems unlikely that beaches were ever totally absent from Muertos Bay. Certainly shellfish was being harvested in greater quantities than at Palenque by people living at the same time in nearby places like Villalba (Linares 1968b). A possible explanation for the indifference shown toward these marine resources by the Palenque inhabitants may be found in their engagement in intensive agricultural pursuits (more on this point later).

Inshore substrates in the Chiriqui Gulf have been described by Glynn (1972). In the Gulf, coral formations and sea grass beds, with their associated faunas, are less developed than in the Caribbean. The same is true for epibenthic mangrove communities like the mangrove oyster which on this ocean do not survive prolonged low-tide exposures. On the other hand, the Gulf of Chiriqui's rocky intertidal communities and mid- and high-tide levels are more densely populated with sessile organisms such as oysters and barnacles.

Offshore waters contain a rich fish fauna. The fish fauna of both Panamanian coasts have been described by Robins (1972), who points out the lower species diversity but greater biomass in the Pacific as compared with that of the Atlantic Ocean. Nonetheless, the Pacific waters are known to be rich in many kinds of lobsters and shrimp, not to say many kinds of pelagic fish such as tuna. However, as Wing (section 13.5) notes, pelagic species together account for only 5 percent of the minimum number of fish at IS-3, while 50 percent alone is accounted for by the marine catfish or Ariidae family which thrives in shallow, turbid, brackish waters like those in existence in the estuaries along Muertos Bay.

6.3   THE CHIRIQUI GULF SITE SURVEY

The Gulf of Chiriqui was first surveyed in 1961 as part of a project (Interrelationship of New World Culture: Project G) covering the Pacific coast of western Panama from Punta Burica to Punta Mariato. A total number of 37 sites were recorded from the Chiriqui Gulf islands and adjacent mainland points. The results of preliminary and limited excavations in the Chiriqui Gulf were reported by Linares (1968b), while Ranere (ibid., appendix 2, pp. 107–119) discussed the surface collections from the neighboring districts of Punta Burica, San Felix, and Remedios in Chiriqui. Here we will only mention in passing the sites that were found in the area around Muertos Bay, not all of which appear in the previously mentioned publications.

It is important to note that archaeological sites are found on practically all of the inhabitable areas around the Bay: on the mainland districts of Alanje and San Felix, to the east and west, respectively, of Muertos Bay; on the mainland part of Horconcitos district where the Cangrejal site was found; and on practically all the inshore islands such as Villalba. Farther offshore, there are archaeological sites on the San Jose Islands, 2.25 kilometers southeast from Palenque, and on Isla Parida, 7.5 kilometers to the southwest. The archaeological sites found on the latter two islands are contemporaneous with the Palenque occupations though considerably smaller in overall size.

It is not possible at present to make definitive statements about patterns of settlement on Boca Brava itself in pre-Hispanic times. However, two preliminary surveys, one in 1961, the other in 1975, failed to reveal other than two small sites located on one of the northern ridges. Although the possibility exists that a "spectacular" site will one day be found here, all evidence to date suggests that Boca Brava was largely uninhabited, or sparsely inhabited, during pre-Hispanic times. Apparently the bulk of the population was concentrated in the Palenque Peninsula, at one large nucleated "center" we have called La Pitahaya (IS-3) from the common name for a wild cactus that grows abundantly here. Even though Boca Brava may have been relatively empty of people, it may nonetheless have been used as farming and hunting territory by the people of Palenque.

6.4 THE SITE OF LA PITAHAYA (IS-3) AND ITS ACTIVITY AREAS

La Pitahaya (IS-3) is a single archaeological locality whose boundaries were determined, after clearing and mapping, by the presence of a continuous cap of surface artifacts, discernable on the clean forest floor, despite the absence of shell debris. Potsherds and groundstone tool fragments were found over an area 260 meters north to south by 330 meters east to west, giving a total site area of 85,800 square meters, or 8.5 hectares (21 acres), of which only 44,800 meters (4.5 hectares) were mapped in detail. The detailed contour mapping extends between the 53.0-meter and 62.5-meter contours. Between these contours, five very different activity areas were recognized and subsequently tested.

The five activity areas (report no. 7) can be put into several distinct categories. Most conspicuous among these are the artificial mounds (areas 1 and 3), which had been built by piling up angular rocks occurring naturally on the forest floor, onto the higher ridges and contours (fig. 6.0-3). Mixed with this special sort of "fill" were cultural materials in the form of broken artifacts, pottery, and organic remains. The main mound, with carved basalt columns on top and intrusive burials at the bottom, could have fulfilled special socioceremonial functions.

A second kind of activity area found at IS-3 (area 2) is simply a strongly sloping natural surface (not a ridge), on which cultural trash, with some angular rock again as fill, has been deposited. This area has neither the intrusive burials nor the carved basalt columns of area 1. A third kind of area is simply a special-purpose structure. Although not enough was excavated of activity area 4, there are strong indications that this was a hard-packed, trod-on, "plaza floor" associated with the numerous carved basalt columns lying about, which must have served as pillars for a structure of some sort. Finally, the dwellings were placed on the flatter and wider contours (area 5); these spots were swept clean of angular rocks, leaving a layer, 20 centimeters deep on the average, of cultural materials spread

Figure 6.0-3: Artificial rock-filled mound at IS-3. (For scale, left to right, I. Borgogno, J. Alden, E.J. Rosenthal.)

evenly on the surface. Rather than forming trash middens, this kind of surface trash accumulates normally on house floors and around the periphery of houses.

6.5   THE DEPOSITIONAL HISTORY OF IS-3

To reiterate, within the Pitahaya site area we find artificial refuse mounds up to 1.5 meters in height and 55 meters in length, refuse deposits up to half a meter deep on the natural slopes, and broken artifacts all over the surface, including the flat areas otherwise clean of angular rocks. Very few spots at IS-3 were found to be devoid of cultural material.

The general site stratigraphy consists of six strata. The bottom level (F) was usually devoid of cultural materials, except for the southern edge of the main mound (area 1, trenches 3 and 4), where the bottom strata have been dug into to form shallow basins on which to deposit the dead. These burials (features 1-8) are intrusive from above.

The next to the bottom stratum (E) shows some variation between trenches. In the main mound (area 1), it consists of a somewhat thin (average 20 cm) layer of weathered tuff, largely sterile except for intrusive burials. In area 2 (Trench I), however, it is a thicker layer, devoid of rocks, made up of a reddish-brown silty soil containing much cultural material. The intermediate strata (B, C, and D) also show marked variation between the different IS-3 activity areas. Although their soil matrix is generally the same — a light to dark brown sand silt — these levels do not always contain large amounts of angular rocks.

The apparent variation in amount of rock found in the IS-3 middens reflects the localized nature of this "rock-piling." This activity simply did not take place all over the site at the same time nor, apparently, for the same reason. At the main mound, where at least two-thirds of the deposit contains enormous amounts of rock, the purpose seems to have been twofold: to build up a high area on which to erect some type of structures associated with the carved basalt columns on top, and to cover up the burials deposited at the bottom. In contrast, in mounded areas (2 and 3) where rocky strata are less thick and basalt columns or burials are absent, these periodic rock-piling events may have been aimed at "clearing" the neighboring surrounding surfaces of rock in order to place on them the dwellings and/or house orchards. Whether this hypothesis is proved or disproved depends, however, on much more extensive excavations than have been conducted to date.

6.6   CONCLUSION:
THE PITAHAYA SETTLEMENT SYSTEM, A RECONSTRUCTION

By the first few centuries of the Christian era, during the Burica phases (equivalent to late Bugaba in the Volcan Baru region), most segments of the Chiriqui plains and midelevation highlands seem to have been inhabited. The survey conducted in 1961 by McGimsey, Bishop, and Linares revealed a densely settled coastal belt stretching from Punta Burica in the west to Punta Mariato in the east. Thus, it seems safe to propose that the push into the islands of the Chiriqui Gulf (as well as the push into the highlands above 1,500 meters) may have resulted from population pressures along the large floodplains and coastal valleys of Chiriqui province. These are the habitats preferred by agricultural peoples, now, as they provide the best irrigated bottomlands. However, none of the coastal sites surveyed in 1961, and certainly none existing today, is to my knowledge as large or as complex as La Pitahaya (IS-3). The same applies to other "island" sites in the Gulf of Chiriqui, all of which are smaller and lack the sizable mounds and/or carved basalt columns characteristic of IS-3. The fact that most, if not all, of the population at Isla Boca Brava was concentrated in La Pitahaya argues for this site having played a special role in the coastal economy.

One of the specialized activities performed at IS-3 may have been trading. Although by no means "overwhelming," the number of trade sherds from the central region (Cooke, report no. 11) argues for prolonged contact between these sites, especially in the centuries between A.D. 500 and A.D. 900. More important evidence of outside contacts is provided by the stone tool assemblage. As Shelton Einhaus (report no. 15) has argued, points and blades requiring skilled workmanship were probably imported ready-made by the IS-3 inhabitants, while the raw materials out of which most of the other implements, including celts, manos, and metates, and pounding-mashing stones, were made were either imported or procured at mainland quarries or in major mainland river beds. The category of "imported" materials even included the large basalt columns and the numerous stones used in the sculptures.

What the IS-3 inhabitants may have been trading in exchange is not, however, clear from the archaeological evidence. It may have been perishables such as salt and dried fish, or perhaps the products extracted from the *Acrocomia* palm, such as palm wine and palm oil. As C.E. Smith (section 10.5) remarks of the palm fruit kernels found archaeologically on the site: "the range of variation suggests that the palm fruit was being harvested from trees that were purposely planted and that they were not gathered from natural populations of palm trees." These palm plantations, as well as many subsistence crops, may have been grown not at IS-3 itself but on the much larger Boca Brava. Hence, La Pitahaya could have served as a "port of anchor," or a trading post of some sort.

We seem to be on surer ground when we suggest that IS-3 was also a socioceremonial center of some importance. The above-surface features found at the site point in that direction: large mounds containing intrusive burials, marked by rows of basalt columns on top, seem to have been used for special rituals. Hundreds of maize-processing tools, some of them fairly elaborate, were probably used for preparation of fermented chicha, associated with enormous lidded jars (belonging to the Isla Palenque Maroon Ware, thick variety) found at the site.

Be that as it may, what interests us most about the site is its size and the apparent density of its occupation. Whereas a few hundred sherds and a few tools per excavation unit came out of the Volcan deposits, and perhaps twice as much from the Cerro Brujo excavations, the Pitahaya deposits yielded several thousands of sherds and several hundred stone tools per excavation unit. Without many more seasons of excavation, it will be impossible to given an accurate estimate of the total population living at the site during the San Lorenzo phase (A.D. 700-A.D. 1000), when it was most intensively occupied. However, a rough guess of several hundred persons does not seem excessive. In contrast to the Volcan villages, which contained a shallow refuse layer lightly spread over the entire area, at La Pitahaya refuse was concentrated into artificial mounds 1.5 meters in height and over 50 meters in length, made up almost entirely of closely packed cultural materials. Even the unmounded areas contained a solid half-meter of cultural deposits. And not a single spot of the site surface was devoid of cultural materials. In order to pack these many people into a site covering 8.5 hectares, very little of the vegetation must have been allowed to survive, and hunting of the white-tailed deer, the only mammal found in any numbers at IS-3, must have taken place some distance away.

To conclude, La Pitahaya was a large and nucleated "center," probably the seat of a paramount chief, with a considerable population living from terrestrial resources, possibly practicing a short-fallow swidden system based on maize and manioc on the adjacent area of Isla Boca Brava. Protein resources came from the bay of Muertos, where sea catfishes prospered, and from hunting the white-tailed deer. Extensive stands of the corozo palm grew in between the houses, and possibly on the nearby Boca Brava island also. Extensive trade relations were probably kept up with peoples to the east, as well as intensive ritual relations with peoples of the adjacent coast and islands.

PART THREE

CULTURAL INFERENCES FROM ARTIFACTUAL REMAINS

Any artifact can be regarded from two contrasting but fully complementary points of view. First, we regard it in terms of its role and meaning in the immediate cultural setting in which we find it. Here then our interest concerns "what was going on," that is, the artifact itself as it was manufactured and in turn used among a given group of people. Second, we can view the artifact not for its own sake but rather as an indicator of the historic or "genetic" framework of its cultural setting, in other words the network of relations which allied our given group of people with other such groups and over which the culturally conditioned ideas and practices it shared with them were transmitted (Sackett 1973, pp. 319–320).

The generalization above may simplify somewhat the complex ways in which artifacts are usually regarded. Nonetheless, it describes the difference between Linares's section 7.0 on ceramics and Ranere's section 8.0 on stone tools. Both are concerned with inferring patterned behavior, but Linares's use of ceramics is almost purely for the sake of their historic or "genetic" framework, while Ranere's analysis is broader. He focuses on how stone tools were manufactured and used, that is, on their function, as well as on what they can tell us about the organization of economic relations within and between social groups. The ninth section, a short description of special objects, is mentioned below only in passing. Most of the discussion will center on Linares's and Ranere's contributions.

The first purpose of the ceramic analysis was to establish chronologies against which to evaluate major shifts in settlement patterns and subsistence techniques, as these are discussed in subsequent chapters. To this end, the ceramic collections from the excavated sites were hand-sorted into types and wares, and then quantified to allow comparisons, using chi-square statistics, between excavation units at one locality, between different localities at one site, between different sites in a region, and, finally, between different regions.

A second aim of the ceramic section was to detect past movements and contacts between ancient populations on the basis of pottery similarities and differences. By the only useful method we could devise, namely, by making minute comparisons in stylistic attributes that were distinctive enough for easy identification, we set out to test the hypothesis that the populations from the highlands were ancestral to those of either coast of western Panama. The results were summarized in a number of propositions having to do with the chronological priority of the Bugaba style (A.D. 200 – A.D. 600) in the Volcan highlands and the probability that the Bocas groups (A.D. 600) migrated from this region. The evidence for deliberate migration from the highlands is much weaker for the earlier occupations (ca. A.D. 600) of the Chiriqui Gulf than for those of Bocas. Linares has concluded that the coastal plains on the Pacific side may have been settled earlier than either Volcan or the Chiriqui Gulf.

Ranere's analysis begins by describing the tool kits of preceramic peoples in the Rio Chiriqui, the people of the Volcan sites, and the groups that occupied both coasts. His inferences about tool function and site activities incorporate recent advances in the study of lithic assemblages. By combining replication experiments with the observation of wear patterns under magnification, he not only sets up a sound typology but also proposes that their tools were used for three activities: stone working, woodworking, and plant processing. Elsewhere (section 3.7) he has suggested that the simplicity of the preceramic stone assemblage may be related to the fact that many of these tools were used to make other and more sophisticated tools of wood, such as spears and arrows. In this section (8.0) he is more concerned with the sociology of stone tool production. It may not surprise anyone that tree felling and woodworking were very important activities in these forested environments, from the Boquete phase (2300 B.C.) onward.

However, the idea that interactions among these tropical forest groups may have been structured around the manufacture, exchange, and maintenance of celts is an interesting one. From its very beginnings, successful agriculture in the tropics must have depended on the efficiency with which the forest could be cleared. That the first prosperous agriculturalists in western Panama seem to have settled in the Volcan highlands and inland plains, near the sources of dense volcanic rock preferred for celt manufacturing, cannot be a coincidence.

Be that as it may, Ranere's analysis of stone tools does indicate that an important organizational shift took place between the preceramic communities and those of later ceramic periods. During the Talamancan and, to a large extent, the Boquete preceramic phases, tool-making skills seemed to have been widely distributed in the population; tools were made in situ, and were neither exported nor imported. By A.D. 200, however, a radical shift in the direction of specialization had taken place among the Volcan Baru communities. While some tools like scrapers, knives, and milling stones were produced by all households, other tools like celts, manos, and metates were manufactured by specialists, in major production centers, probably in or near quarries. A few specialists in repairing damaged or blunted celts also resided in the larger villages such as Sitio Pitti-Gonzalez (BU-17).

By A.D. 900 the dependency on outside specialists for most stone tools was almost complete among the coastal communities of La Pitahaya and Cerro Brujo. Remarkably little stone manufacturing was done at either place. Most chipped stone and all ground and polished artifacts were imported. Some celt resharpening activities did take place locally, but the absence of all suitable hard and dense rock in these coastal contexts precluded most stone tool manufacture. Large nucleated paramount chief villages like La Pitahaya and small dispersed probably egalitarian villages like Bocas were equally dependent on regional exchange systems for tools to survive.

It may be instructive to contrast the kind of exchange represented at IS-3 and CA-3 with the systems operating more than 2,000 years earlier in the Formative periods of Mesoamerica. The closest parallel seems to be with the model of Pires-Ferreira and Flannery (1976): "Exchange of unworked nonutilitarian commodities for conversion by part-time specialists, with most villagers having access to the finished product" (p. 288). The important difference, however, is that the commodities exchanged from A.D. 200 onward in the Panamanian regions under consideration, namely stone tools, were utilitarian items of direct survival value. The items being exchanged in return by the CA-3 and IS-3 inhabitants may have included things like salt, dried fish, and cultivars.

As Lathrap (1973) has pointed out using ethnographic parallels, most exchanges in the tropics involve perishable items, which leave few traces in the archaeological record. Hence, a vigorous trade in feathers, skins, foodstuffs, and a multitude of other degradable materials could have existed in western Panama even as early as pre-ceramic times. Later on, however, most special objects that were preserved (section 9.0) were made locally and not exchanged, except for two clay disks on polychrome sherds at IS-3 and a jade bead at BU-17. Hence, it is difficult to avoid the impression that exchange systems were more rudimentary and nonexclusive in western Panama than in Mesoamerica and that they did not involve complex sociopolitical organizations such as Rathje (1972) suggests.

7.0

The Ceramic Record: Time and Place

O. F. LINARES

7.1 INTRODUCTION

The purpose in section 7.0 is to establish regional ceramic chronologies that will be useful later on in discussions of settlement and subsistence changes within and between our study areas. A second aim of this study, one that will be emphasized here, is to attempt a reconstruction of past movements and contacts between ancient Panamanian communities on the basis of differences and similarities in ceramic assemblages.

Initially, our comparisons between ceramic collections had a deceptively simple aim in mind. We wanted to determine whether pottery from different sites was or was not stylistically similar, and why. Following Sackett (1977, p. 377), we assumed "that since the choices underlying style are socially transmitted, the degree of stylistic similarity found among historically related loci directly expresses the degree of social interaction participated in by their occupants." In making this assumption, however, we were not unaware of the immense difficulties involved in defining with precision the kinds of social interactions that may be expressed by ceramic differences and similarities (see Flannery 1976, pp. 251-282).

The regions whose pottery we will discuss are: (a) the upper drainage of the Rio Chiriqui, (b) the highlands near Volcan Baru between Cerro Punta and El Hato, (c) the Aguacate Peninsula in Almirante Bay, Bocas del Toro province, and (d) the Palenque Peninsula in the Gulf of Chiriqui, in the province of Chiriqui. A diagram of the distances between the most important sites we studied in each area is shown in figure 7.0-1. The maximum distance (80 kilometers as the crow flies) is between Cerro Punta (BU-17) and La Pitahaya (IS-3) to the southwest, while in the opposite direction, to the northeast, a slightly shorter distance (55 kilometers) separates BU-17 from Cerro Brujo (CA-3) on the Atlantic coast. Between BU-17 and the Rio Chiriqui shelters on the same side of the continental divide, there are 35 kilometers of highland terrain. These distances are on the average about twice as great as those between the Oaxacan prehistoric communities

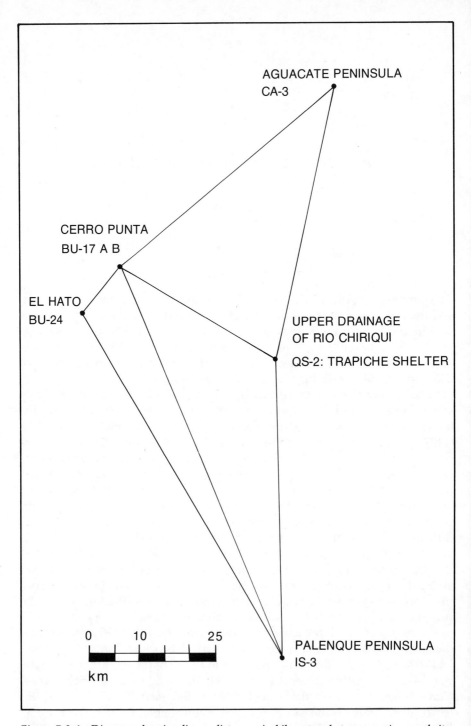

Figure 7.0-1: Diagram showing linear distances in kilometers between regions and sites discussed in monograph.

whose interaction intensity and ceramic similarities were studied by Plog (1976). Nonetheless, the Panamanian communities we studied are within easy commuting distance. A person walking at a fast clip along the well-traveled Third of November Trail takes about twelve hours to cross the mountains, from Chiriquicito on the Atlantic side to Paja del Sombrero on the Pacific side. Actual travel time from the Atlantic coastal edge near the Aguacate Peninsula to the Pacific coastal edge near the Gulf of Chiriqui would be about two long days. This is considered a normal commuting distance by present-day Guaymí Indians of Bocas and Chiriqui.

7.2   THE CERAMIC COLLECTIONS

These are very different in quantity as well as quality. The oldest ceramics encountered in our study areas came from the Rio Chiriqui shelters excavated by Ranere (section 3.0). These shelters were preceramic during most of their occupation, yielding a total sample of only 876 sherds from the top levels of two shelters. This sample was too small to detect ceramic changes through time, but it was large enough to allow comparisons with the other collections from nearby areas.

Pottery from Volcan, particularly the collections from the Pitti-Gonzalez (BU-17) site and from Barriles (BU-24), was more abundant and profusely decorated than the ceramics from the shelters. Also, the Volcan collections came from more diverse archaeological contexts: different stratigraphic units, different features and activity areas, and several sites besides the ones we excavated. Despite their diverse proveniences, however, the Volcan ceramics seemed at first remarkably uniform in paste, surface finish, decorative techniques, and shapes; they seemed to belong to the same general "tradition" or "style." Only after much reanalysis and reclassification were we able to establish clear differences in the time and place distribution of different wares within the Volcan tradition. These distinctions became crucial to our understanding of the relations between the Volcan sites and the oldest components of the coastal sites.

Reexcavation of La Pitahaya (IS-3) in 1971 yielded an immense and unwieldy quantity of ceramics which, besides confirming our previous sequence (Linares 1968b), were useful in intersite comparisons. However, the new collections only suggested, without adequate testing, the extent to which intrasite variation in time and function between utility areas was present at IS-3. Without much more extensive excavation, the underlying complexity of this immense and probably specialized center will remain undocumented.

Excavations in Bocas del Toro during 1970 uncovered abundant and previously undescribed ceramics in the top layers. However, we were only beginning to define the oldest ceramic component at the Cerro Brujo site when a 70-hour deluge wiped out our excavations before we had secured a larger sample of the oldest ceramics and enough carbon to date the oldest phase.

The first step in the classification was to decide on the ceramic classes that would best reflect intrasite variation and those that would be used best in intersite analysis. A dual typology thus had to be developed, one that would permit detecting ceramic differences through time at a single site, while at the same time allowing for the possibility of comparisons between sites on the basis of widespread but chronologically restricted ceramic attributes. Our hypothesis, that at the beginning of the sequence we were dealing with a style (Bugaba) which first developed in the highlands and then spread to either coast during the initial stages of coastal settlement, remained to be tested by our ceramic analysis.

A dual classification of western Panamanian ceramics was first attempted some years ago (Linares 1968b), with a type analysis used in determining chronological differences at any one site and a modal analysis used mainly in intersite comparison. Although we employed the seriation method, intercalating levels and sites on the basis of percentage frequencies of types (a procedure that has been shown since to be misleading), it is important to stress that the types determined in that analysis, and even the rough time-ordering of these types, were essentially correct and have withstood reexamination. Nonetheless, the seriation method per se, with its "smoothed-out" battleship curves, actually obscured the relations between sites and impeded the correct interpretation of La Pitahaya deposits as middens built up from "fill" of a special kind.

Following our first field season on Bocas del Toro, we began a computer cluster analysis program of the Bocas ceramics in order to define ceramic types. A great amount of time and effort was spent coding, and then running, a cluster analysis of Bocas ceramics before deciding that crude ceramics, showing only moderate variations in decorative technique or in shape, for our purposes could be more economically sorted out by inspection rather than by machine. When Borgogno's study (report no. 13) of the time spent hand sorting versus computer sorting of the La Pitahaya (IS-3) ceramics was concluded, we decided definitely to do the initial classification by hand, leaving the testing on intra- and intersite ceramic variation to machine manipulations. This is what Drennan (1976) has essentially done.

All ceramics from a site or a region were thus hand sorted first into several mutually exclusive classes of different degrees of inclusion. At the most inclusive level is the class we call "style," an easily recognized group sharing the same paste and decorative treatment and belonging to the same time period. The notion of style was useful in making interregional comparisons. As the analysis proceeded, we were able to define regional stylistic variants. These stylistic variants shared some, though by no means all, of the specific decorative attributes that characterized a style in its "homeland" area.

With a site, or cluster of sites, we used attributes of rim shape or mode shape (i.e., handle or supports) or, as in Bocas, more inclusive categories such as wares and types to do the initial tabulation of the ceramics according to stratigraphic layer, site features, or activity loci.

The second step in the analysis came later, after the initial sorting and counting, when the task in hand was to establish a local ceramic chronology for the areas studied and the particular sites excavated. We started with a simple hypothesis, namely that adjacent strata, separated during excavation on the basis of "natural" aspects in the deposit, were also different with respect to their ceramic content. For this purpose we used a computer program which employed chi-square statistics according to Siegel (1956). The cross-tabulations involved excavation layers along one axis and number of items in mutually exclusive ceramic classes along the other axis. Later we compared ceramic frequencies from different areas or localities within a site. As Cowgill (1977) has amply warned us, however, significance tests do not in any way constitute explanations. If, for example, two excavation layers, say A and B, show statistically "meaningful" differences in the frequency of ceramic items in the same classes, we are still called upon to explain if and why this difference may be "culturally" significant. In the sections that follow, we will discuss the results of our chi-square tests and of interpretations of their "meaning" for each of the areas studied.

Once local ceramic chronologies had been established, and once intrasite variation in time and function had been explored, the third and final procedure of the analysis was to compare chronologically equivalent ceramic assemblages from our four different regions. Here the analysis necessarily turned to interpretation and explanation. Our aim was to show that ceramic differences and similarities between regions could be attributed to population movement and/or cultural contacts. The limited extent to which our cultural interpretations are convincing at this level will become obvious in the pages that follow.

7.4 A CERAMIC SEQUENCE FOR THE VOLCAN BARU SITES

Ceramics from the region of Volcan Baru are discussed first because they precede in time and may have been ancestral to the ceramics found in the bottom levels of the coastal sites. Numerous surface collections and several stratified samples from excavated sites make up the total assemblage. Despite its fairly wide distribution, the Volcan pottery belongs to a coherent and easily recognized style, which, following Sackett (1977, p. 370), we will define in conveniently general terms as "a highly specific and characteristic manner of doing something . . . peculiar to a specific time and place." Because it is found in its most elaborate form in the district of Bugaba, we will refer to this style as the Bugaba style. It is characterized by a fine-grained, compact paste in which fine river sand and feldspar were used for temper; by the total absence of polychromes; by the presence of an orange to dark red slip or wash applied in zones that alternate with unslipped areas that may be plain, incised, brushed, or decorated with punctations; by a wealth of varied appliqué motifs made up from clay pellets and strips; and, finally, by a number of distinctive support and handle shapes.

7.4.a. The Pottery Analysis: Sitio Pitti-Gonzalez (BU-17)

The collections from the one extensively excavated site in the Cerro Punta valley (BU-17) were used to establish the first chronology known for a site in the Volcan area. The BU-17 pottery came from two separate localities at opposite ends of the same site: the Gonzalez locality (BU-17a) and the Pitti locality (BU-17b) — report no. 4. We will begin the discussion with the ceramics from the second of these places because the stratigraphy is clearer.

The Pitti pottery was first classified by Spang (ms. 1976) into a number of wares: Cerro Punta Orange, Valbuena, Bugaba Engraved, Zoned Bichrome, and Cotito Scarified. Following Drennan (1976, p. 21), a ware is here defined as a ceramic class sharing attributes of paste and surface finish. (For a detailed description of the Bugaba pottery, see report no. 9.)

Despite Spang's assertion that percentage frequencies of the BU-17b ceramics "indicate a single phase occupation" (Spang ms. 1976, p. 63), she herself noticed differences in the percentage frequencies of certain wares. At activity area no. 1 (the oval dwelling) and at its periphery (the area of block 14), as well as in activity area no. 4, the Cerro Punta Orange Ware, and to some extent the Combed Ware, decreased through time, while Valbuena and Bugaba Engraved increased through time (Spang ms. 1976, pp. 67–71). In order to see if these differences were statistically significant, I ran chi-square tests on contingency tables involving, along one dimension, the same ware frequencies as Spang used to calculate percentages and, along the other dimension, excavation levels in three localities: the oval dwelling (blocks 3, 5, 15), its periphery (block 14), and feature 4 (block 1). (It was necessary to combine some wares so as to fit the parameters set by our Contingency Table Analysis, namely, no empty cells and no more than 20 percent of the cells with five or fewer items.) Only the units above-floor and the floor itself in the oval dwelling showed significant differences (table 1).

Now, in order to see if less inclusive, more finely drawn, classes would show some differences in frequency between the floor and the below-floor units, even though wares did not, I reclassified the BU-17b collection (fig. 7.0-2) into three vessel-shape classes (restricted bowls, open bowls, and jars), five mode classes (ringstands/pedestals, tripod feet, tabs, strap handles, and appliquéd lobes and nubbins), and five classes of surface treatment (incising/grooving, engraving, zoned bichroming, combing or brushing, and representational appliqué). The results of the chi-square tests comparing the floor (units 3 and 4) and below-floor areas (units 5–9) in terms of these new classes (table 2) indicated a difference between these two units in vessel shape and mode frequencies, and not in surface treatment. With respect to appendages, tabs, and lobes/nubbins, these were more abundant below the floor than above the floor itself; the reverse was true of ring-stands/pedestals and tripod feet, which were more abundant on the floor unit. Because the comparisons using the frequencies of vessel-shape classes (restricted bowls, open bowls, and jars) between the floor and the below-floor units gave a significant but low chi-square value, I broke down the shape comparisons further.

TABLE 1   A 2 × 3 CONTINGENCY TABLE OF COMPARISONS BETWEEN THE FREQUENCIES OF THREE CERAMIC WARES

(In units below the floor, floor, and above the floor in cuts 3, 5, and 15 of the oval dwelling at BU-17 in the Volcan region)

	Cerro Punta Orange Ware	Valbuena and Bugaba Engraved	Others: Plain Zone Bichrome Cotito Combed White Painted	Chi-square scores; d.f. 2, L .05, critical value = 5.99
Above floor (Units 1, 2)	479	238	87	
				$\chi^2 = 29.96$
Floor (Units 3, 4)	110	12	9	
				$\chi^2 = 5.89$
Below floor (Units 5–9)	120	3	8	

TABLE 2   THREE CONTINGENCY TABLE COMPARISONS OF THE FREQUENCIES OF CERAMIC CLASSES BY SHAPE (TABLE A), BY MODES (TABLE B), AND BY SURFACE TREATMENT (TABLE C)

(Between the floor [units 3, 4], and below floor [units 5–9] in the oval dwelling at BU-17 in the Volcan region)

	Restricted bowls	Open bowls	Jars	Chi-square scores; d.f. 2, L .05, critical value = 5.99	Ringstands and pedestals	Strap handles	Tripod feet	Tabs	Lobes and nubbins	Chi-square score; d.f. 4, L .05, critical value = 9.49	Incised or Grooved	Engraved	Zone Biochrome and Combed or Multiple-Incised	Representat. Appliqué	Chi-square scores; d.f. 3, L .05, critical value = 7.82
Floor (Units 3, 4)	198	48	214	$\chi^2 =$ 9.72	59	60	34	13	25	$\chi^2 =$ 64.36	59	29	17	13	$\chi^2 =$ 1.68
Below floor (Units 5–9)	82	24	149		11	44	12	39	50		28	11	12	5	

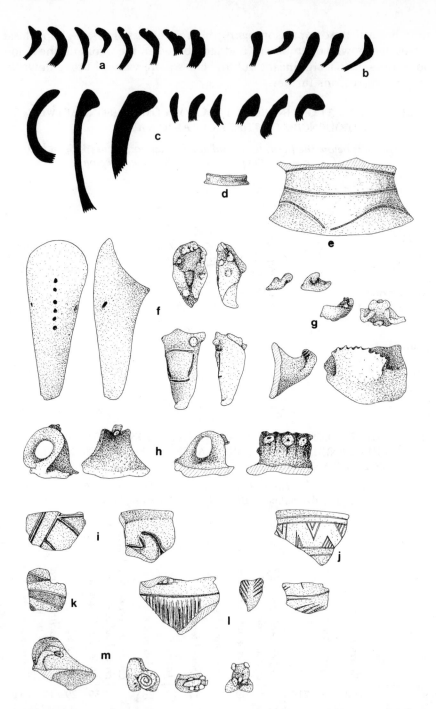

Figure 7.0-2: Ceramic classes from the Volcan sites (BU-17b collections): a. restricted bowls; b. open bowls; c. jars; d. ringstands; e. pedestals; f. tripod feet; g. tabs; h. strap handles with appliquéd lobes and nubbins; i. incising/grooving; j. engraving; k. zoned bichroming; l. combing or brushing; m. representational appliqué.

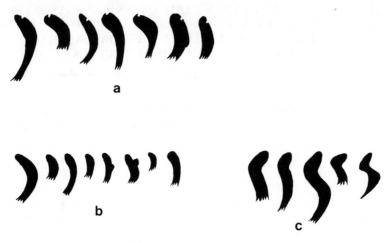

a

b

c

Figure 7.0-3: Classes of restricted rims from the Volcan sites: a. carinated; b. simple; c. s-shaped.

If the frequencies of the restricted shallow bowls (fig. 7.0-3) with a bright red slip and "notched," carinated rims (class *a*, technical report no. 9) are compared with the frequencies of simple and S-shaped restricted bowls (ibid., classes *b* and *c*) at the dwelling locality, important differences emerge. In terms of absolute presence and absence, carinated or notched rims belonging to the Cerro Punta Orange Ware class of pottery occur alone in the bottom units (6–8) of the oval dwelling deposits; neither class *b* nor class *c* rims belonging to the Valbuena and Bugaba Engraved wares occur in these same units. Moreover, if one runs chi-square tests comparing the frequencies of rims *a* versus *b,c* between the floor (units 3 and 4) and the below-floor (unit 5) in the oval dwelling (units in which both rim groups occur), significant differences also show up (table 3). The hypothesis that these two rim groups are differentially distributed in time thus receives support.

Unfortunately, however, I did not get as conclusive results as I had hoped for from contingency tables involving other areas in the Pitti-Gonzalez site. Whereas in BU-17b, block 1, the top units (4 and 5) and the bottom units (6–15) did show significant differences (x^2=5.83, L.05, d.f. 1, crit.val. =3.84) in rim frequencies between class *a* versus classes *b* and *c* in blocks 7 and 14 of the same locality, the chi-square results were in the borderline of the arbitrary 0.05 point needed for acceptance or rejection of the null hypothesis. In short, although there is a lack of positive (i.e., nonrandom) association between depth of deposit and rim class frequencies in some excavation units of the Pitti-Gonzalez site, even in these units a general trend shows up in the percentage frequencies of rim class *a* versus rim classes *b-c*: to wit, a decrease in class *a* bowls, and an increase in classes *b-c* bowls, toward the top or more recent levels of the deposit (table 4). Thus, I have tentatively concluded that two phases were represented at the BU-17b, or Pitti, locality, but that these were not so far apart in time for entirely new

TABLE 3 A 2 × 2 CONTINGENCY TABLE OF COMPARISONS BETWEEN TWO RIM CLASSES (CLASS A AND CLASS B) IN THE FLOOR (UNITS 3 and 4) AND BELOW THE FLOOR (UNIT 5) OF THE OVAL DWELLING AT BU-17B IN THE VOLCAN REGION

(Note that Class B rims do not occur in the bottom three units)

Units	Class A rims (carinated)	Class B rims (simple and S-shaped)	Chi-square scores: d.f. 1, L .05, critical value = 3.84
3, 4	55	131	} $\chi^2 = 20.83$
5	33	17	
6	8	0	
7	7	0	} cannot be done
8	8	0	

TABLE 4 PERCENTAGE FREQUENCIES OF CLASS A RIMS (CARINATED) AND CLASS B RIMS (SIMPLE AND S-SHAPED) IN THE EXCAVATION UNITS (TOP TO BOTTOM) OF THREE BLOCKS

(BU-17b locality of Sitio Pitti — Gonzalez in Cerro Punta, Volcan region)

	Class A rims		Class B rims	
	No.	(%)	No.	(%)
Block 1				
Units 4, 5	12	(.50)	12	(.50)
Units 6–15	35	(.81)	8	(.19)
Block 7				
Units 1, 2	10	(.32)	21	(.68)
Units 3–5	19	(.56)	15	(.44)
Units 6–9	12	(.52)	11	(.48)
Block 14				
Units 3–5	6	(.09)	60	(.91)
Units 6, 7	9	(.21)	34	(.79)

wares to have appeared or old ones to have dropped off. In most site areas, the same pottery classes occur throughout the BU-17a-b deposits; only their frequencies change in time and, even then, not always very markedly. The dwelling locality itself is an exception; it may have been occupied long enough for marked differences between ware frequencies to show up between the floor and the above-floor units.

To summarize, the only ceramic trends noted for the Sitio Pitti locality are (a) the slight increase through time of two wares, Valbuena and Bugaba Engraved and their associated rim classes, plus ringstand/pedestal and tripod feet modes in the second or more recent of the occupations, and (b) the slight decrease through time of the Cerro Punta Orange Ware with its characteristic notched rim, shallow bowl class. As I will discuss later on, this evidence bears on our interpretations of the initial settlement of the coastal sites (La Pitahaya and Cerro Brujo) where Valbuena and/or Bugaba wares, and not Cerro Punta Orange, are most popular in the lowest levels. Hence, I have tentatively defined two subphases for the BU-17b locality: the oldest subphase, which we have called Early Bugaba (A.D. 200 to A.D. 400) is represented by the floor and the below-floor units in the dwelling, and by the middle and the bottom levels elsewhere. At this time, Cerro Punta Orange and Cotito were abundant. A second, more recent subphase which we call Late Bugaba (A.D. 400 to A.D. 600) was represented by the top units everywhere, when Valbuena and Engraved wares, plus ringstands/pedestals, and tripod feet were increasing in popularity.

At the Gonzalez locality (BU-17a), on the southern end of the same site, only the later of the two subphases is present. The 2x2 contingency tables that I ran, using pairs of contrasting rim classes from the two stratigraphic units we had segregated in excavation in blocks 1-9, failed to show significant chi-square values. This suggests that this part of the site was occupied only during the Late Bugaba phase (A.D. 400–A.D. 600).

7.4.b. The Pottery Analysis: Barriles (BU-24)

Pottery was generally abundant at Barriles though nowhere did the counts equal those at Cerro Punta. The Barriles pottery came from seventeen (17) posthole "sondages" and from two test excavations (blocks 1 and 2) — report no. 5, fig. 5/1. The statistical analysis was based on the pottery from these two blocks, which was classified using the same ceramic code as in BU-17a-b. Frequencies of ceramic wares were quantified following the natural stratigraphy established during excavation, and compared using chi-square tests. The ceramics from block 2, the most productive of the two cuts, were also sorted into classes based on vessel shape, appendages, and surface decoration

Block 2 at BU-24 showed *no* significant difference between the three main stratigraphic units with respect to the frequencies of four ceramic wares and the three vessel shapes occurring in large enough numbers to quantify. (Shallow restricted bowls belonging to the Valbuena Ware could not be included in the comparisons because they were numerically insignificant. However, the large jars with flaring necks and thickened lips belonging to the Valbuena Ware, and possibly used as burial urns, are present in Barriles, a fact discussed later on.) Similarly, block 1 showed no significant difference between the two main occupations with respect to the four most popular wares. However, when we compared all of block 1 with all of block

2, on the basis of the most popular wares, these two areas turned out to be very different (table 5). This difference is increased by a consideration of the small, nonquantifiable, but very revealing decorative techniques associated elsewhere with the so-called Concepción phase of Chiriqui dated to 300 B.C. or before (Haberland 1962). Three of them (namely, Shell Impressed, Reed Incised, and Deep Incised), plus one very diagnostic mode (a "webbed foot"), occur only in block 2 and *not* in block 1. This agrees well with the radiocarbon dates which are earlier for block 2 (starting at A.D. 200) than for block 1 (ranging from A.D. 600 to A.D. 800). We also have a date of 60 B.C. ± 275 from the unit at the very bottom of block 2. Thus, the ceramic chronology and the dates suggest that the "ceremonial" area near block 1, where Stirling (1950) excavated some time ago and found a rectangular floor of massive slabs, large urns belonging to the Valbuena Ware, elaborate giant metates, and fragments of stone statues, is more recent in time than the more peripheral, older area of block 2.

TABLE 5   A 2 × 5 CONTINGENCY TABLE OF COMPARISONS BETWEEN THE FREQUENCIES OF THE FIVE MOST COMMON WARES IN BLOCK 1 AND BLOCK 2

(Barriles, BU-24, site in El Hato Basin, Volcan region)

	Cerro Punta Orange	Zone Bichrome	Bugaba Engraved	Grooved Ware	Combed Ware	Chi-square scores; d.f. 4, L .05, critical value = 9.49
BU-24, Block 1	273	22	57	5	24	
BU-24, Block 2	283	20	40	43	11	$\chi^2 = 37.85$

7.4.c.   A Comparison of Sitio Pitti-Gonzalez (BU-17) with Barriles (BU-24)

A short chi-square test (table 6) comparing BU-24 (block 2) and BU-17b (blocks 3, 5, 15) in terms of frequencies of four ceramic techniques (namely Incising or Grooving, Engraving, Zoned Bichroming, and Combing), suggests there was a significant difference in these techniques between the top units (3–5) of BU-24, and the floor unit of the oval dwelling at BU-17b, but *not* between the bottom units of BU-24 and the units below the floor at BU-17b. Unfortunately, the sample from the above-floor units was not large enough to use in chi-square testing. Nonetheless, the evidence points to some chronological overlap between the older occupation at Barriles and the initial occupation of the Pitti (BU-17b) locality.

Turning to the radiocarbon dates, and to the presence or absence of ceramic wares, we can tentatively suggest that Barriles (BU-24) near El Hato was occupied prior to the Early Bugaba phase, possibly before the Christian era. Both Cerro Punta and the Barriles areas were also occupied during the Early Bugaba (A.D. 200–400) and Late Bugaba (A.D. 400–600) phases. However, while the Cerro Punta villages were abandoned about A.D. 600, Barriles apparently grew in importance as a ceremonial center, lasting well into A.D. 800. This was probably due to its greater distance from Volcan Baru, which erupted around A.D. 600–700. An explanation for the absence of Valbuena shallow bowls and the presence of only the big Valbuena jars at Barriles may lie in the former being a village-based utilitarian ware, while the big jars were used as urn burials or storage jars, or for special activities that were conducted at the bigger center. Finally, a very late radiocarbon date (A.D. 1210 ± 150) from the top unit of block 2, above the pumic layer, indicates that Barriles was reoccupied for a short time during the Chiriqui phase discussed later on.

TABLE 6　TWO CONTINGENCY TABLE COMPARISONS OF THE FREQUENCIES OF FOUR CERAMIC WARES: TABLE A BETWEEN THE TOP UNITS OF BLOCK 2 AT BARRILES (BU-24) AND THE FLOOR UNIT OF THE OVAL DWELLING AT SITIO PITTÍ-GONZALEZ (BU-17B) AND TABLE B BETWEEN THE BOTTOM UNITS OF BU-24 AND THE UNIT BELOW THE FLOOR AT BU-17B

	Incised or Grooved	*Bugaba Engraved*	*Zone Bichrome*	*Combed Ware*	*Chi-square scores; Table A: d.f. 3, L .05, critical value = 7.82 Table B: d.f. 1, L .05, critical value = 3.84*
Table A					
BU-24, Block 2, Units 3–5	16	17	12	6	$\chi^2 = 11.64$
BU-17b, Floor	59	29	14	3	
Table B					
BU-24, Block 2 Units 6–8	16	12	10		$\chi^2 = 1.63$
BU-17b, Below floor	28	11	12		

7.4.d.　Surface Collections from the Volcan Baru Survey

In our article on settlement and subsistence patterns (Linares, Sheets, and Rosenthal 1975) and in report number 2, the region of Volcan Baru was divided into five "natural zones" (Cerro Punta, Bambito, Intermediate, Los Llanos, and Southwest) on which Sheets plotted sites, using five size classes.

Here I will discuss surface collections, made and classified by Bruce Dahlin, from the 45 Volcan sites he surveyed. Many of these sites yielded a woefully inadequate ceramic sample and, as could be expected, much of the surface materials was badly weathered. To offset the effects of small samples, whose randomness had not been statistically assured, we clustered the collections from each of the natural zones and compared the results of chi-square tests with those obtained from clusters drawn on the basis of site-size classes. The ceramic wares we used in these comparisons had shown significant time and/or place differences in the sites excavated, namely Sitio Pitti-Gonzalez (BU-17a-b) and Barriles (BU-24).

TABLE 7   A 2 × 5 TABLE OF ALL POSSIBLE COMPARISONS BETWEEN THE FREQUENCIES OF FIVE CERAMIC WARES IN THE SURFACE COLLECTIONS FROM THE CERRO PUNTA, BAMBITO, AND SOUTHWEST REGIONS IN VOLCAN BARU

	Cerro Punta Orange	Valbuena Ware	Bugaba Engraved	Zone Biochrome	Combed Ware	Chi-square scores; d.f. 4, L .05, critical value = 9.49
Cerro Punta region	311	80	50	14	12	
Bambito region	434	83	83	11	14	$\chi^2 = 9.49$
Southwest region	535	27	27	9	14	$\chi^2 = 80.82$

$\chi^2 = 43.96$

Chi-square tests (table 7) comparing the frequencies of five wares (Cerro Punta Orange, Valbuena, Bugaba Engraved, Zoned Bichrome, and Combed) in three natural zones (excluding the Intermediate area, where only one ware — Cerro Punta Orange — was abundantly represented, and Los Llanos, which had no sites) showed that sites in Cerro Punta and Bambito had almost the same pottery class frequencies. However, by the same criterion, these two zones were very different from the Southwest area where Barriles (BU-24) is found. In terms of percentage frequencies of ceramic wares, it is interesting to note that the Southwest zone had a slightly higher percentage of Cerro Punta Orange Ware, but lower percentages of all the other wares, in contrast with the other two regions considered (Bambito and Cerro Punta). This evidence reinforces our hypothesis that the Southwest or Barriles zone may have been settled earlier than the zones at higher altitudes.

A second series of chi-square tests (table 8), comparing site-size classes with reference to the frequencies of three ceramic classes (Cerro Punta, Valbuena, and Bugaba Engraved), showed that only sites of sizes 2 and 3 were "homogeneous"; that is, they were the only ones that did not differ significantly ($x^2 = 5.2$) in ceramic content. The rest of the size-classes had very different frequencies of the same pottery classes. In this connection, it may be interesting to note that, except for the higher percentage frequencies of Valbuena and Bugaba Engraved wares in sites with refuse covering an area between 400 and 700 meters long (size 4 sites), there was no apparent correlation between the sizes of sites and the abundance of certain wares.

TABLE 8   TABLE OF CHI-SQUARE SCORES OF ALL POSSIBLE COMPARI-
SONS BETWEEN THE FREQUENCIES OF THREE CERAMIC
WARES (CERRO PUNTA ORANGE, VALBUENA, AND BUGABA
ENGRAVED) IN SITES OF SIZES 1-4, AS DETERMINED BY THE
VOLCAN SURVEY

(Report No. 2 and Section 4.4); d.f. 2, L .05, critical value = 5.99)

	Site size 1	Site size 2	Site size 3	Site size 4
Site size 1	*	21.50	40.02	8.02
Site size 2	*	*	5.20	30.19
Site size 3	*	*	*	43.23
Site size 4	*	*	*	*

7.5   CERAMICS FROM THE RIO CHIRIQUI SHELTERS (QS-2 AND QS-3)

Despite the small size of the samples (58 sherds in the Trapiche Shelter — QS-2, 126 sherds in the Horacio Gonzales Shelter — QS-3), the predominant, if not exclusive, ceramic class represented in the top levels of the shelters is Valbuena Ware with its two diagnostic bowl rim shapes (*c* and *d*). No sherds belonging to the Cerro Punta Orange Ware, with its characteristic bright red polished slip and notched bowl rim (class *a*), occur in the Rio Chiriqui shelters. Moreover, it is curious to note that Bugaba Engraved Ware, a class of pottery which occurs with some abundance in the Volcan sites 35 kilometers to the west, is extremely rare in the shelters, being represented by a single sherd. Inconclusive as the evidence may be, chi-square tests comparing ceramics in the Rio Chiriqui shelter deposits with excavation units in the dwelling of the Pitti (BU-17b) locality showed less of a difference (though still a significant one) between the shelters and the above-floor unit than between the shelters and the other two dwelling units (table 9). Another comparison of the frequencies of all restricted bowls and all short-necked jars between the Rio Chiriqui shelters and the Late Bugaba deposits in the Gonzalez (BU-17a) locality showed no significant difference ($X^2 = 0.02$, 1 d.f.). Thus, we tentatively conclude that the Rio Chiriqui shelters were occupied by ceramic-using peoples during the second or Late Bugaba occupation (A.D. 400-600), and not during the first. In the interim, between the end of the preceramic Boquete phase (ca. 300 B.C.) and the beginning of the Late Bugaba phase, the shelters were probably abandoned.

TABLE 9   A CONTINGENCY TABLE OF ALL POSSIBLE COMPARISONS
BETWEEN THE FREQUENCIES OF SIX CERAMIC CLASSES IN THE
RIO CHIRIQUI SHELTERS AND IN THE ABOVE FLOOR, FLOOR,
AND BELOW FLOOR UNITS OF THE PITTI LOCALITY (BU-17B)
IN THE VOLCAN REGION

Chi-square scores:
A = d.f. 2, L .05, critical
    value = 5.99
B = d.f. 5, L .05, critical
    value = 11.07
C = d.f. 5, L .05, critical
    value = 11.07

	Bowls	Jars	Incising	Engraving	Supports	Other decorative motifs			
Rio Chiriqui shelters	29	29	49	1	6	4	A	B	C
				*60					
BU-17b: Above floor	7	19		*14			$\chi^2 =$ 7.43		
								$\chi^2 =$ 161.52	
									$\chi^2 =$ 104.14
BU-16b: Floor	397	320	59	39	146	55			
BU-17b: Below floor	110	150	28	11	96	34			

*Grouped for comparison.

7.6   A CERAMIC SEQUENCE FOR THE
BOCAS DEL TORO (AGUACATE) SITES

The total number of sherds analyzed from the principal localities excavated at Cerro Brujo (CA-3a to CA-3d) came to about 17,000. They were divided into the following six wares: Bocas Brush-Pinched, Bocas Smooth-Polished, Bisquit, Bugaba, Chocolate Incised, and Plain. Seven modes are characteristic: double handles, round handles, strap handles, solid tripods, hollow tripods, "bisquit" tripods, and bisquit appliqué and pellets (fig. 7.0-4). For a description and illustration of these classes, see report number 12.

After sorting the sherds into the above classes, the next step was to test for significant differences in the frequency distributions of these ceramic classes through time (i.e., between stratified layers) and through space (i.e., between site features). Ceramic counts used in the chi-square contingency tables represented subtotals from adjacent excavation layers that were clearly and unambiguously related by stratigraphy. At CA-3a, the four stratigraphic layers defined in report number 6 served as the basis for comparing sherd classes from several proveniences.

In the first test, using the Cerro Brujo pottery, I ran a 2 x 2 contingency table of all possible comparisons, using subtotals and frequencies, between pairs of the four most common ceramic wares in the features having the two

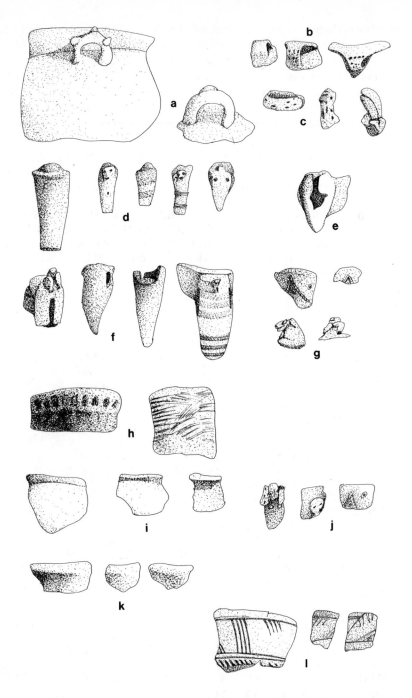

Figure 7.0-4: Pottery classes at Cerro Brujo (CA-3): a. double handles; b. strap handles; c. round handles; d. solid tripods; e. Bisquit tripod; f. hollow tripods; g. Bisquit appliqué and pellets; h. Bocas Brushed-Pinched Ware; i. Bocas Smooth-Polished; j. Bisquit; k. Bugaba; l. Chocolate Incised.

main stratigraphic units represented; the most recent occupation comprised layers A and B and the oldest (levels C and D) in features 1–4 and 9 at locality CA-3a. The chi-square results indicate marked differences in the frequencies of the four ceramic classes in either occupation. Incidentally, the highest chi-square values were obtained between the Bugaba Ware and all others. It is clear even by inspection that Bugaba Ware is much more abundant (90 percent) in the older occupation than in the most recent (13 percent).

A second significance test was run on the CA-3a ceramics in order to determine whether natural strata (levels A, B^1, B^2, C, and D) were or were not different from each other with respect to the frequencies of three

TABLE 10   FOUR 2 × 3 CONTINGENCY TABLES SHOWING ALL POSSIBLE COMPARISONS BETWEEN THE FREQUENCIES OF THREE CERAMIC WARES IN THE LEVELS OF FEATURES 1–4 AT THE CA-3A LOCALITY OF THE CERRO BRUJO SITE IN BOCAS DEL TORO

| | Bocas Brushed-Pinched | Bocas Smooth-Polished | Bisquit Ware | | Chi-square scores; d.f. 2, L .05, critical value = 5.99 | | | |
					A	B^1	B^2	C
FEATURE 1								
Levels: A	259	13	161	A	*			
B^1	177	23	123	B^1	7.43	*		
B^2	607	147	188	B^2	76.17	48.62	*	
C	136	50	53	C	63.85	31.34	5.41	*
FEATURE 2					A	B^1	B^2	C–D
Levels: A	201	29	201	A	*			
B^1	756	107	256	B^1	84.48	*		
B^2	414	68	109	B^2	94.01	5.34	*	
C–D	205	59	65	C–D	67.32	17.71	8.39	*
FEATURE 3					A	B^1	B^2	C–D
Levels: A	41	29	60	A	*			
B^1	80	25	25	B^1	27.28	*		
B^2	27	5	55	B^2	11.99	44.04	*	
C	10	4	17	C	1.48	16.56	?	*
FEATURE 4					A	B	C^1–C^2	C^3–D
Levels: A	30	17	38	A	*			
B	64	35	58	B	1.40	*		
C^1–C^2	243	124	138	C^1 & C^2	10.58	5.39	*	
C^3–D	16	32	22	C^3 & D	11.78	13.82	19.23	*

ceramic wares (Bocas Brushed-Pinched, Bocas Smooth-Polished, and Bisquit Ware) in features 1–4. The results of this test (table 10) were far from satisfactory. In all four features, most levels seemed to differ significantly from each other, which seems as meaningless as if all had turned out to be "homogeneous." The only consistency in the results appeared to concern adjacent levels. With the exception of feature 3, whose levels A and C turned out to be "homogeneous," most of the levels which showed no significant differences were adjacent to each other: levels B^2 and C in feature 1, levels B^1 and B^2 in feature 2, and levels A and B, and B and C^1–C^2, in feature 4.

In order to see if I could obtain more consistent results, I ran another chi-square contingency-table analysis, comparing frequencies of three ceramic wares in A, B^1, B^2, and C levels of three adjacent features in the main mounded locality (CA-3a). The scores, unfortunately, were like those before: all ware frequencies turned out to be statistically different between equivalent stratigraphic levels in two separate features.

The only explanation I can offer for this apparent fluctuation in ware frequencies between adjacent stratigraphic levels, and between adjacent features, lies in the nature of most shell midden deposits. Shell middens, as opposed to living floors, tend to accumulate haphazardly; shells, from a particular collecting trip (or trips), get dumped (and presumably so do broken pots) first in one spot, then in another, resulting in a patchy distribution.

Despite this problem, we can still observe some regularities (table 11). The bottom shell-less layer (C and/or D) in features 2 and 4, and all layers in feature 9 have the Bugaba Ware securely represented in them. On the other hand, the types Chocolate Incised and Negative, plus double handles and round handles, seem to characterize only the top levels. Although Bisquit Ware drops off markedly toward the bottom levels, it does occur right along with Bugaba Ware in feature 4, a phenomenon that can be attributed only to mixing.

To summarize, features 2, 4, and 9 of the main locality (CA-3a) have Bugaba Ware represented in the bottom levels. This occupation has been called the Aguacate phase and, by association with the Volcan sites, has been dated to A.D. 600. The second occupation, which we have called the Bocas phase, has been estimated on the basis of radiocarbon determinations to date from ca. A.D. 900.

At the second Cerro Brujo locality (Co-Idewe or CA-3b), Bugaba Ware also shows up in the bottom levels of three test excavations in appreciable quantities: 24 percent, 18 percent, and 13 percent of all the ceramics in these levels are in the Bugaba style. Although most of the other pottery is plain ware, there are still some typical Bocas wares (Brushed-Pinched and Smooth-Polished) found together with the Bugaba Ware, as in the main locality (CA-3a). Nonetheless, a chi-square test based on the frequencies of the most popular wares in the stratigraphic units of two CA-3b blocks reveals significant differences between the middle or shell-containing,

		Bugaba Ware	Bocas Brushed-Pinched	Bocas Smooth-polished	Bisquit Ware	Plain	Chocolate Incised	Negative or Fugitive	San Lorenzo Banded	Double Handles	Round Handles	Strap Handles	Solid Tubular Tripods	Hollow Tubular Tripods	Bisquit Tripods	Bisquit Appliqué and Pellets
F.1	A	0	259	13	161	96	0	1	2	3	1	0	5	7	1	0
	B1	0	177	23	123	90	4	0	0	5	2	14	7	9	1	5
	B2	0	607	147	188	135										
	C	?	136	50	53	103	0	0	0	0	0	0	0	0	0	0
F.2	A	0	201	29	201	109	4	0	0	0	2	1	2	15	0	4
	B1	0	756	107	256	207	2	0	9	1	8	22	21	25	1	5
	B2	0	414	68	109	200										
	C	?	205	53	65	143	0	0	1	0	0	3	1	3	0	0
	D	16	0	6	0	0	0	0	0	0	0	0	0	0	0	0
F.3	A	0	41	29	60	4	0	0	0	0	0	2	0	3	0	0
	B1	0	80	25	25	7	0	0	0	0	1	9	3	16	0	0
	B2	0	27	5	55	5										
	C	?	10	4	17	7	0	0	0	0	0	3	0	0	0	0
F.4	A	0	30	17	38	8	0	0	2	1	1	0	0	1	1	0
	B	3	64	35	58	13	0	0	0	4	0	2	2	13	4	1
	C1, C2	22	243	124	138	248	0	0	0	0	0	3	0	7	0	0
	C3, D	70	16	32	22	143	0	0	0	0	0	7	1	1	0	0
F.7	0–10	0	50	13	4	17	1	0	0	0	0	0	0	0	0	0
	10–20	0	84	30	33	36	0	0	0	0	2	0	1	7	0	1
	20–30	0	46	31	6	46	0	0	0	0	1	0	1	2	0	0
F.8	0–10	0	33	51	33	22	0	0	0	0	0	0	1	0	0	0
	10–20	0	51	16	3	38	0	0	0	0	0	1	0	0	0	0
	20–30	0	40	14	5	10	0	0	0	0	1	2	1	1	0	0
	30–40	0	15	11	5	6	0	0	0	0	0	0	0	4	0	0
	40–50	0	10	3	0	2	0	0	0	0	0	0	0	0	0	0
F.9	0–10	32	6	3	1	33	0	0	0	0	0	0	0	0	0	0
	10–20	110	6	0	4	101	0	0	0	0	0	0	0	0	0	0
	20–30	84	0	0	0	26	0	0	0	0	0	2	0	0	0	0

TABLE 12 TWO 2 × 5 CONTINGENCY TABLE COMPARISONS BETWEEN THE FREQUENCIES OF FIVE CERAMIC WARES IN THE B AND C LEVELS OF BLOCKS 2 AND 4

(Co-Idewe [CA-3b] locality of the Cerro Brujo hamlet in Bocas del Toro)

	Bocas Brushed-Pinched	Bocas Smooth-Polished	Bisquit Ware	Plain Ware	Bugaba Ware	Chi-square scores; d.f. 4, L .05, critical value = 9.49
BLOCK 2						
Surface	24	15	16	36	0	
All B levels	319	141	67	244	7	$\chi^2 = 172.45$
All C levels	14	14	1	83	25	
BLOCK 4						
Surface	55	13	9	30(.28)	0	
All B levels	85	41	13	23(.13)	9	$\chi^2 = 39.13$
All C levels	6	2	8?	13(.34)	9	

( ) = percentage frequencies.

typically Bocas phase, B units, and the bottom or shell-less Bugaba phase, or C units (table 12).

Although the main (CA-3a) and the "secondary" (CA-3b) dwelling localities were occupied at the same time during the Aguacate phase, the other localities in the Cerro Brujo cluster were not. Neither CA-3c, nor CA-3d, yielded a trace of Bugaba Ware in the bottom levels. These two dwellings, then, formed part of the hamlet only during the most recent of the two Bocas phases.

The only other hamlet we excavated in the Cerro Brujo peninsula (Sitio Machuca, CA-2) was a purely Bocas phase site. Not one of the 7,929 sherds analyzed from the excavations at this site belong to the Bugaba Ware. Furthermore, a chi-square test comparing the frequencies of the Bocas Brushed and Bisquit wares showed either a borderline chi-square value or no significant differences between the occupational layers at Sitio Machuca.

7.7 A CERAMIC SEQUENCE FOR THE GULF OF CHIRIQUI AT LA PITAHAYA (IS-3)

The number of sherds excavated from La Pitahaya (IS-3) was over a million. Because a rough chronology already existed for this site (Linares 1968b), only the ceramics from the blocks with the clearest stratigraphy were analyzed in the different activity areas. These comprised: (a) blocks 1 and 2 of trench II in area 1, (b) block 2 of trench I in area 2, and (c) trench VII in area

3. Even then, the quantity of sherds was so great (about 40,000 for a 2 x 2-meter block) that a further reduction was necessary. Hence, we classified only rim sherds, or only rim sherds plus appendage modes (i.e., handles and supports). For rim sherds we used the intuitive and computer types which in Borgogno's exercise (report no. 13) turned out to be comparable (fig. 7.0-5). With the appendage modes we used nine easily distinguished handle and support classes previously established (Linares 1968b) and known to be good chronological markers (fig. 7.0-6). For a brief description of the rim and appendage classes used here in the chi-square tests, see technical report number 10.

1. Trench I, block 2, was the central unit of a three-block trench in activity area 1. It was dug by natural stratigraphy. Careful control was exercised by having first removed the two end blocks so that the center could be excavated by cultural layers that were exposed on two sides. The percentage distribution of each of the three wares that the 1968 analysis had shown to be diagnostic of one of the Chiriqui Gulf occupational phases is given for this block in table 13. Despite some degree of overlap, layers A and B clearly belong in the Chiriqui phase, layer C in the San Lorenzo phase, and the bottom layers D and E in the Burica phase, according to Linares's (1968b) old chronology.

In order to test further ceramic distributions, I ran a series of chi-square contingency tables comparing rim class frequencies in different excavation layers. As mentioned above, the seven rim classes used had been established by computer and hand sorting (report no. 13). Again, in terms of the old typology, rims 1, 2, and 3 belong to the Isla Palenque Maroon Slipped type, a class of pottery which defined the Burica phase in the Gulf; it is identical to the Valbuena Ware of the Bugaba phase in the Volcan sites; rims 6, 7, and 8 belong to the San Lorenzo phase pottery types, and rims 11 and 12 belong to the Chiriqui phase pottery types. The results of our chi-square tests (table 14) are contradictory. They indicate that adjacent layers A and B are very different from each other while layers B and C, which are also adjacent, are not. Layers C and D are, again, very different while D and E are not. However, the chi-square tests of the distribution of ceramic classes in the other trenches (see below) are more consistent. For that reason I infer that the two principal ceramic "breaks" in the deposit lie between A-B and C layers, on the one hand, and between C and D-E layers on the other hand.

Figure 7.0-5: Rim shape types (showing correspondence between computer and intuitive typing; see report no. 13 from La Pitahaya (IS-3), used in chi-square tests: 1. jar with exteriorly thickened rim; 2. straight-sided bowl; 3. convex-sided shallow bowl; 4. jar with outstanding rim; 5. deep convex-sided bowl; 6. outwardly slanting straight-sided bowl; 7. outwardly slanted concave vessel; 8. thin-walled straight jars; 9. short-necked everted jar; 10. long-necked everted jar. In the classification by O.F. Linares, 1968b: Types 1-3 belong to Isla Palenque Maroon Slipped; Type 4 crosscuts several types; Type 5 belongs to Cangrejal Red Line; Types 6 and 7 to Zapote Red Banded and Castrellon Red Slipped; Type 8 to Tarrago Bisquit Ware; Types 9 and 10 to Villalba Red-Streaked.

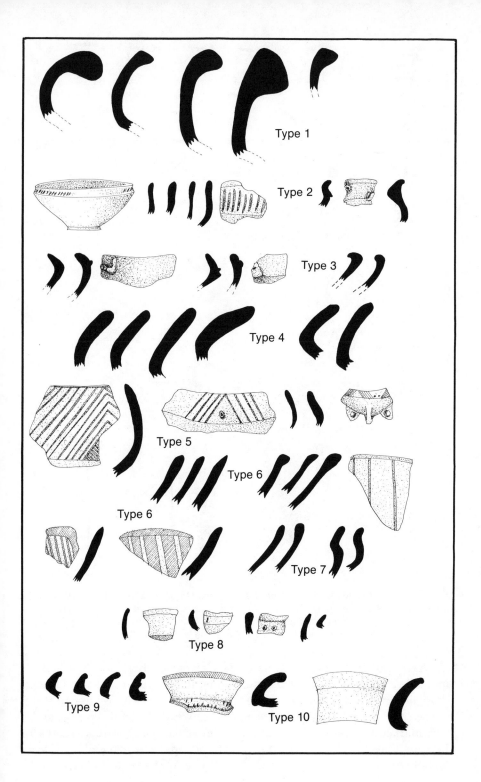

Type 1

Type 2

Type 3

Type 4

Type 5

Type 6

Type 6

Type 7

Type 8

Type 9

Type 10

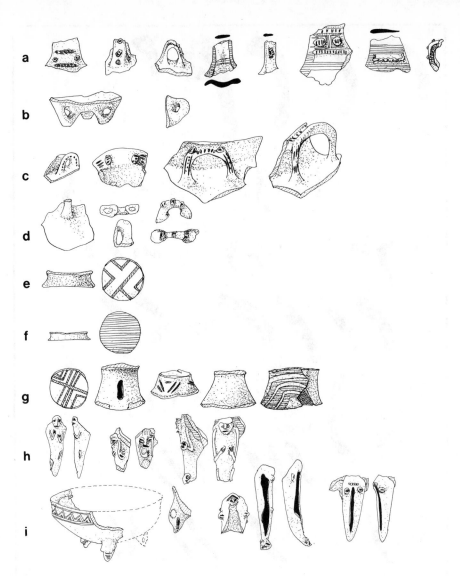

Figure 7.0-6: *Appendage classes from La Pitahaya (IS-3), established by O.F. Linares, 1968, and used in chi-square tests in this section: a. strap handles; b. strapped feet; c. double handles; d. round handles; e,f. ringstands; g. pedestal bases; h. solid tripods; i. hollow tripods. After Linares 1968b, figs. 30, 32-36.*

2. A contingency table chi-square analysis for trench II, block 1, in activity area 2 (table 15) gave the following results: the Chiriqui and San Lorenzo phase layers A and B showed no significant differences in frequency of rim classes (provided rim types 9, 11, and 12 are excluded), while layers B and C were markedly different. Unfortunately, however, the chi-square scores for the appendages are somewhat equivocal; the top two layers and the C layer are not similar but very different, while the sample size for the layer at the

TABLE 13   PERCENTAGE FREQUENCIES OF THREE COMMON WARES IN THE EXCAVATION LEVELS OF LA PITAHAYA (IS-3), TRENCH I, BLOCK 2

Layers	Bugaba Ware (Isla Palenque Maroon)	San Lorenzo Wares (Red Banded)	Bisquit Ware
A and B	.13	.08	.79
C	.30	.47	.22
D and E	.91	.09	.00

TABLE 14   CONTINGENCY TABLE COMPARISONS (2 X 2 AND 2 X 3) BETWEEN THE FREQUENCIES OF THREE RIM TYPE GROUPS IN ADJACENT LEVELS AT TRENCH I, BLOCK 2 OF LA PITAHAYA (IS-3) IN THE GULF OF CHIRIQUI

(Comparisons A, B, C: d.f. 1, L .05, critical value 3.84; comparisons D & E: d.f. 2, L .05, critical value = 5.99)

		Burica Phase rim types 1, 2, 3	San Lorenzo Phase rim types 6, 7, 8	Chiriqui Phase rim types 11, 12	
Surface		27	124	161	D $\chi^2 = 12.27$
	Chiriqui phase	12	25	17	E $\chi^2 = 160.68$
Layer A					
Layer B		92	132	6	A $\chi^2 = 5.83$
	San Lorenzo phase				
Layer C		68	97	0	B $\chi^2 = 31.89$
Layer D		155	65	0	C $\chi^2 = 4.30$
	Burica phase				
Layer E		65	13	0	

very bottom is too small to use in this particular chi-square test. If simple percentage frequencies of appendage modes are compared, however, it is clear that the biggest popularity differences between the A and B versus C layers are in the classes of double and/or round handles and thick ringstands. The former make up 40 percent of all appendages in the A and B layers, but only 8 percent in the C layer; thick ringstands are only 2 percent of the total in the top layers, increasing to 14 percent in the middle or C layer. Going back to a previous publication (Linares 1968b), we note that double handles are characteristic of the Chiriqui phase, and thick ring-

TABLE 15 A 2 × 3 CONTINGENCY TABLE OF COMPARISONS BETWEEN GROUPS OF RIM TYPES IN THE THREE MAIN STRATIGRAPHIC LAYERS (A, B, C) OF LA PITAHAYA (IS-3), TRENCH II, BLOCK 1

	Burica Phase rim types 1, 2, 3	San Lorenzo Phase rim types 6, 7, 8	Plain rim types 5, 10	Chi-square scores; d.f. 2, L .05, critical value = 5.99.
Layer A	45	275	609	
Layer B	82	561	1172	$\chi^2 = .58$
Layer C	193	52	135	$\chi^2 = 614.88$

Note: Rim rypes 9, 11, 12 were excluded because they only occur in the top A level only.

stands of the San Lorenzo phase. Finally, if we reconsider rim classes 11 and 12, which characterize the Chiriqui phase, then simple presence and absence shows a difference between the top A and B stratigraphic layers, where these rim types comprise 4 percent of the total, and the C and below layers where they do not occur at all.

3. The rim class evidence for trench VII, block 1, is, again, consistent with that from the block analyzed above: excluding rim classes 9, 10, and 11, and including 1–3 and 6–8, gives us a "homogeneity" between A and B versus C layers and a marked difference between the C versus the D and E layers (table 16). If we take into account the excluded rim classes, however, then clearly the top level, where rims 10 and 11 occur, is different from the middle and bottom levels where they do not. A comparison of appendage frequencies also leads us to the same conclusion: there is a difference between the top and the middle layers, but only in the frequencies of two appendage modes, namely double handles and thick ringstands.

4. A cursory inspection of the sherds from the nonmounded area of trench VI, in the vicinity of a basalt column concentration, suggests a slightly different depositional sequence from that of the mounded areas where trenches I, II, and VII, discussed above, were located. In this locality (no. 4; the area of trench VI), Bisquit Ware and the late modes (i.e., double handles) are entirely missing. The shallow deposit consists preponderantly of the Bugaba Ware, with about 20 percent of red-banded San Lorenzo Ware. Slight as this evidence may be, it does suggest that the Burica (or Bugaba) phase can be isolated as a single-phase component in parts of the IS-3 site.

To summarize, the ceramic analysis from the three mounded areas of La Pitahaya (areas 1, 2, and 3) shows a continuity throughout all strata of most ceramic classes. The exceptions are Bisquit Ware, and its associated rim type (12), and Villalba Red Streaked Ware (see Linares 1968b), with its associated rim class (11) and double handle mode; these classes occur only

TABLE 16 A 2 × 3 CONTINGENCY TABLE COMPARISON OF THE FREQUENCIES OF THREE RIM TYPE GROUPS BETWEEN STRATIGRAPHIC LAYERS (A AND B, C, D AND E) OF TRENCH VII, BLOCK 1 OF LA PITAHAYA (IS-3) IN THE GULF OF CHIRIQUI

	Burica Phase rim types 1, 2, 3	San Lorenzo Phase rim types 6, 7, 8	Plain rim types 5, 10	Chi-square scores; d.f. 2, L .05, critical value = 5.99
Layers A and B	12	98	229	
				$\chi^2 = .109$
Layer C	27	220	491	
				$\chi^2 = 56.69$
Layers D and E	14	9	27	

Note: Rim types 9, 11, 12 are excluded; there are 17 in the A & B layer & none in other layers.

in the top A and B stratigraphic units and not in the bottom ones (D and E) of the mounded areas. All other ceramic classes occur throughout the entire depositional sequence, even though, as for example in trench I, area 1, Bugaba Ware rims 1, 2, and 3 constitute 80 percent of all rims at the bottom, but only 10 percent at the top; another example of frequency differences in rim classes within the same stratified deposit is that of rim classes 6, 7, and 8, which make up 17 percent of all rims at the bottom, over 50 percent in the middle or San Lorenzo phase strata, and 40 percent at the top in the Chiriqui phase.

An explanation of these overlaps in ceramic frequencies may be found in the nature of the La Pitahaya deposits (see report no. 7). Most of the site areas were apparently occupied, perhaps as early as A.D. 400, but certainly by A.D. 600, by peoples of the Burica (or Late Bugaba) phase (see below). A short period of abandonment may have preceded the subsequent San Lorenzo phase (A.D. 700–900), dominated by local wares that show strong stylistic influences from neighboring areas to the east, probably as a result of increased interaction with the "central region" of Panama (report no. 11). At this time, during the San Lorenzo phase, the inhabitants of the island gathered and piled up fist-sized angular rocks and larger boulders, which they swept up periodically from the surrounding terrain onto natural low ridges, resulting in artificial mounds that were built up even further by having broken pottery and stone artifacts discarded on them. Subsequently, probably during the latter part of the San Lorenzo phase, the main mound (area 1) was used for burial. The dozen or so burials found in area 1 in the bottom or Bugaba phase layers (D and E) of trenches II to V are associated with San Lorenzo phase pottery, as defined by Linares (1968b), and are therefore intrusive from above. In trenches without proper burials in the bottom, such as trench I, human bones were nonetheless found throughout the deposit as an indication that some disturbance had taken place. Of the areas tested, only number 3, where we placed trench VII, had no sign of burial activities; and it is this trench which gave the clearest evidence of a marked break in ceramics between the Bugaba Ware and those of the subsequent San Lorenzo phase. This suggests that there was a cultural discontinuity between these two phases, and probably a short period of abandonment as well. Between the San Lorenzo (A.D. 700–900) and the Chiriqui (A.D. 1000–1100) phases, minor ceramic differences exist, but there is little evidence for any sort of cultural break.

7.8 A SUMMARY OF THE CERAMIC CHRONOLOGY FOR WESTERN PANAMA

In figure 7.0-7 we have diagrammed, with a one-sigma range, the 28 radiocarbon determinations obtained from samples collected in the Volcan, Bocas, and Chiriqui Gulf sites (the ones for the preceramic shelters are listed in section 3.4). We have chosen to disregard the following samples: I-5871 because it is way out of line with the other dates for that site, and SI-1833, 1835 because they came from a possibly disturbed area where an earth oven was found. (In a previous publication, Linares, Sheets, and Rosenthal 1975, we tended to accept these dates, which after the ceramic analysis I now reject.) Sample SI-1846 dates the *end* of the preceramic phase in the Trapiche Shelter and not necessarily the beginning of the ceramic phase. Although sample I-7262 from the bottom level of block 2 at Barriles "could only be pretreated for the removal of carbonates and not for humic acids because of (its) small size and soluble nature of basic solutions" (J. Buckley, personal communication), it will be accepted here; with a one-sigma deviation, it overlaps the other dates for Volcan. Moreover, a few sherds of "Scarified ware" (fig. 7.0-8), which Haberland (1962) and others have placed in an earlier phase called La Concepción, came out of this level. The bulk of the Bugaba deposits, however, fall in the time span between A.D. 200 and A.D. 600. Using a one-sigma deviation, all these dates overlap around A.D. 400. Unfortunately, we could not obtain sufficient charcoal to date the oldest occupations in the coastal sites, namely the Aguacate phase of Cerro Brujo and the Burica phase of La Pitahaya. However, comparisons with the pottery from the Cerro Punta deposits suggest a date between A.D. 400 and A.D. 600. The San Lorenzo phase in Chiriqui (A.D. 700–A.D. 900) and the Bocas phase in Bocas del Toro (A.D. 900) seem to be securely dated by a number of fairly consistent radiocarbon determinations. A summary of the chronology is provided in table 17.

Figure 7.0-7: Radiocarbon determinations, diagrammed with one-sigma range, for ceramic occupations from: BU-17a Gonzalez locality, BU-17b Pitti locality, QS-2/BO-2 Trapiche Shelter, BU-24 Barriles, IS-3 La Pitahaya, CA-3b Cerro Brujo (Co-Idewe locality), CA-3a Cerro Brujo (main midden locality). Phase designations are given above the dates; laboratory numbers under the dates.

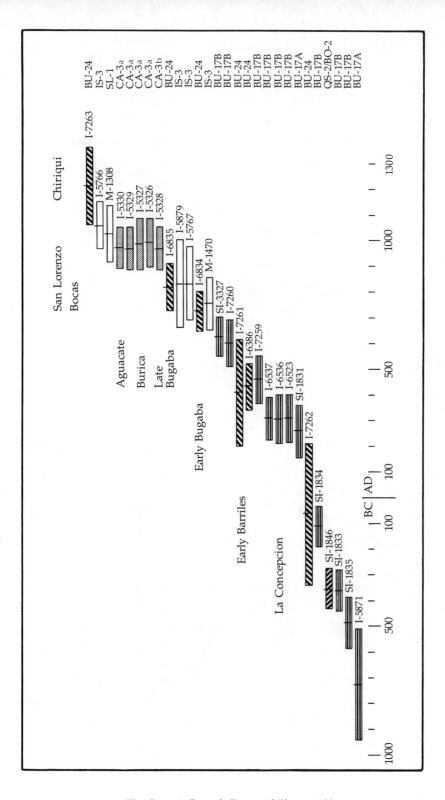

Figure 7.0-8: Whole vessels of the "Scarified" ware from the site of Finca Solano near La Concepción: a. corrugated bowl; b. "vulture" shape; c. "florero" shape; d. round bowl.

TABLE 17 SUMMARY OF THE CERAMIC CHRONOLOGY FOR CHIRIQUI AND BOCAS

Dates	Chiriqui highlands	Chiriqui plains	Chiriqui coast and islands	Bocas coast and islands
1200	Chiriqui phase	Chiriqui phase	Chiriqui phase	
			San Lorenzo phase	Bocas phase
800				
	Late Bugaba phase	Late Bugaba phase	Burica phase	Aguacate phase
400				
	Early Bugaba phase	Early Bugaba phase		
B.C./A.D.				
	Barriles phase	La Concepción phase		
400				
800				

7.9 CONCLUSIONS AND INTERPRETATIONS

In previous sections we have discussed intrasite ceramic variation within each of our four study areas. Here we will take up a number of linked propositions bearing on the nature of, and probable explanation for, ceramic similarities between our various sites. These "propositions" may be stated as follows: (1) A number of ceramic attributes of shape and surface finish, including whole classes of pottery, are shared by the Volcan Baru collections on one hand, and those from the Early Bocas phase at Cerro Brujo and the Burica phase at La Pitahaya, on the other hand. These collections can be considered as belonging to a single style we have called Bugaba. The shared ceramic attributes are of such nature that their independent invention at each site seems unlikely (fig. 7.0-9). (2) The Bugaba-style pottery of the coastal sites belongs to only one of the two subphases represented in the Volcan chronology. (3) Ceramic similarities between occupational components in the Bugaba period can be explained in terms of population movements or contacts. (4) During the following Early Bocas and San Lorenzo phases the ceramics on both coasts differed greatly. These differences reflected a period of minimal or no contact between the populations on either coast.

I will discuss each of the above prepositions in the order mentioned above.

1. The principal diagnostic attributes of the Bugaba style in the Volcan sites have been listed across the side of table 18, with an indication whether they are more common in the Valbuena Ware or in the Cerro Punta Ware, or

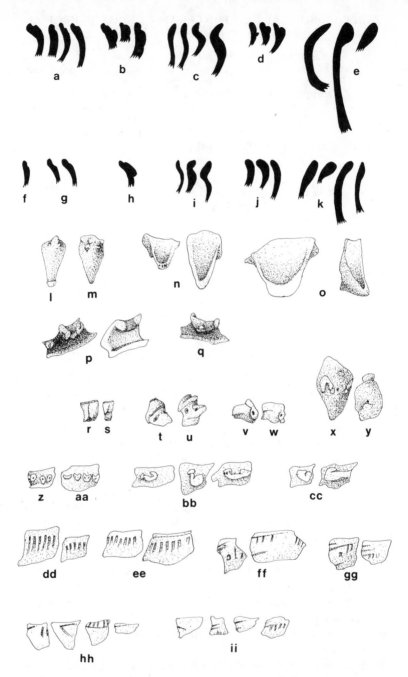

Figure 7.0-9: A comparison of ceramic attributes from the three oldest ceramic periods: the Bugaba phases from Volcan, the Aguacate phase at Cerro Brujo, and the Burica phase at La Pitahaya: a-e. rim shapes Bugaba, compared with f. Burica and g-k. Aguacate; solid tripods: l. Bugaba, m. Aguacate; concave tabs: n. Bugaba, o. Aguacate; tab handles: p. Bugaba, q. Aguacate; split tripods: r. Bugaba, s. Burica; man with conical hat motif: t. Burica, u. Bugaba; Toucan motif: v. Burica, w. Bugaba; applied arm on solid tripod: x. Burica, y. Bugaba; appliquéd pellets: z. Burica, aa. Bugaba; appliquéd arm motif: bb. Burica, cc. Bugaba; fluting on exterior of shallow bowls: dd. Burica, ee. Bugaba; engraving: ff. Burica, gg. Bugaba; incising: hh. Burica, ii. Bugaba.

whether they occur in both wares (if nothing is indicated, they are difficult to assign to any one ceramic group). Along the vertical axis of this same table, I have recorded the presence (+), absence (−), or low representation (√) of less than five items of the Bugaba style attributes in the oldest occupations of the coastal sites. As we can see, the Aguacate phase at Cerro Brujo (CA-3) includes 15, and the Burica phase at La Pitahaya (IS-3) includes 25 of the 33 Bugaba period Volcan attributes listed in this table. The absence of many of these attributes from the Aguacate phase must be related to the smallness of the sherd sample: about 375 sherds in total, including body sherds. In contrast, the Burica phase sherds inspected from IS-3 amounted to several thousand. (Body sherds and the supports from some excavations were not coded, however; the classification was done on rims, among which shapes 1, 2, and 3 were indistinguishable from those of the Volcan Bugaba periods.) As expected, more Bugaba style attributes are present at IS-3 than in Cerro Brujo. What we did *not* expect, however, was discovering that most of the attributes *missing* from the early coastal phases were those associated with the Cerro Punta Orange Ware. Except for a few carinated rim sherds found at each coastal site, these collections lacked the elaborate bowls with appliquéd pellet figurines and the high-relief animal *adornos* so characteristic of the Cerro Punta Orange Ware.

Now, it seems obvious that some attributes, like a sandy paste or a red slip, are general enough to be duplicated in pottery collections anywhere. Others are much more specific: for example, arm motifs, S-shaped bowls with parallel exterior ridges, double-leg and "Venus tripods," or "toucan" appliqués and human faces with conical hats. More important than the "specificity" of particular motifs, however, is the fact that the Bugaba style attributes of the coastal sites are not randomly associated with this or that extraneous pottery type. Instead, they are associated with each other, forming clusters of shapes, surface finish, decoration, and appendages that are identical to, and virtually indistinguishable from, the pottery classes we call Valbuena and Bugaba Engraved in Volcan. Hence, we are not talking here of "vague" similarities, but of the very same classes of pottery appearing in the Volcan sites as well as in the bottom levels of the coastal sites. This is the phenomenon we must try to explain.

2. For the Volcan Baru highland sites we tentatively divided the Bugaba period into two subphases: Early Bugaba (A.D. 200–400) and Late Bugaba (A.D. 400–600). The evidence for these subdivisions is not absolutely conclusive, however. Although a contingency table analysis for the pottery from the oval dwelling at Sitio Pitti-Gonzalez (BU-17) revealed significant chi-square differences between the frequencies of three wares and several modalities in the above-floor, floor, and below-floor units, the same was not true of other areas in the same locality; at cuts 1 and 14, for example. For this reason we first lumped all the Volcan wares into a single phase. Later on, when we looked at collections from neighboring areas in Panama, including the other sites excavated in Bocas and Chiriqui, and compared these with nearby collections from sites in the Costa Rican highlands, 25

(As they appear in the oldest phases of the coastal sites)

Volcan attributes	IS-3 Burica Phase	CA-3 Aguacate Phase
A sandy, homogeneous paste (V)	X	X
A fugitive maroon slip or wash on the interior and exterior of thin-walled bowls (V)	X	X
A polished, thick, bright red slip in the interior and exterior of thick-walled bowls (CPO)	−	−
Zone bichroming on urns	−	−
Combing or multiple incising	√	√
Scalloped-necked jars (CPO)	−	−
Deep, widely separated single incisions (V and CPO)	X	X
Engraved lines in parallel, concentric, geometric or representational motifs	X	−
Raised ridges placed vertical to the lip of bowls (CPO)	−	−
Punctuations below the lip (CPO)	−	−
Appliqué; high-relief animal motifs (CPO)	−	−
Simple appliqué lobes (CPO and V)	X	X
Serpentine applied motifs (CPO)	−	−
Arm motif (V)	X	−
Restricted bowls with simple rims (CPO and V)	X	X
Restricted bowls with carinated rims (CPO)	√	√
Restricted bowls with exteriorly thickened lip	X	√
Restricted S-shaped bowls with low ridging on exterior (V)	X	X
Restricted composite silhouette bowls with raised ridges or incisions	X	√
Deep bowls with exterior thickening	X	X
Tecomate shape (CPO)	−	−
Very shallow open bowls with interiorly thickened lip	X	√
Open bowls with composite silhouettes	X	−
Small jars with exteriorly thickened lips	X	X
Low, thin ringstands with a red slip (V)	X	−
Special strap handles (CPO AND V)	√	−
Labial flanges in the interior of shallow bowls (for holding a lid? (V)	X	−
Tripods in the shape of human legs (V)	√	−
Female figure ("venus") tripod (V)	√	√
Stilt and nubbin supports (V)	√	−
Tabs used as handles or as feet	√	√
Adorno: "toucan" motif	√	−
Adorno: human head with conical hat	√	−

Note: V = Valbuena Ware; CPO = Cerro Punta Orange Ware

kilometers to the west, a separation between the two areas emerged. Some collections had only the Valbuena and Bugaba Engraved wares, plus very large burial urns, represented; other collections, including those from Costa Rica, had only the Cerro Punta Orange Ware represented. On both the plains and the Chiriqui highlands, sites containing one and not the other wares occurred in close proximity.

Now, as we discussed previously, a resorting of the Volcan collections permitted separation of the shallow, restricted bowls into two classes (fig. 7.0-3): carinated rims (class *a*; report no. 9) of the Cerro Punta Orange Ware and simple or S-shaped rims (classes *b* and *c*; report no. 9) of the Valbuena and Bugaba Engraved wares. These two rim groups were then submitted to a contingency table analysis, with the chi-square results being as inconclusive as those obtained using whole ceramic wares. To reiterate, some, but not all, of the BU-17 utility areas, and definitely not the BU-17b locality, showed a significant association between one rim group and a stratigraphic unit. Thus, the evidence for the existence of two phases within the Bugaba period in the highlands in only suggestive but not conclusive. By the same token, we cannot be certain of the precise time when the coastal sites were first occupied.

3.   Because the eruption of Volcan Baru deposited a fairly deep layer of sterile pumice on the Cerro Punta area, the Pitti-Gonzalez site was abandoned, apparently around A.D. 600. Now, if we ignore the uncertainty surrounding the problem of exactly when the coastal sites were first settled, an obvious question suggests itself. Could the first coastal inhabitants of Cerro Brujo and La Pitahaya have been refugees from the highlands? Let us see how this suggestion would fit in with the ceramic evidence. Taking the Cerro Brujo site as a whole, differences between the Aguacate phase ceramics and those from the following Bocas phase seem at first to be quantitative rather than qualitative. Not only does Bugaba pottery occur from bottom to top of the deposit, but non-Bugaba wares are also found in the bottom (C and D levels) of some of the features. However, at features 2, 4, and 9, the Bugaba Ware is found either alone or as the dominant ware in the bottom levels. Additional evidence, such as the absence of shell, the predominance of hunting over fishing pursuits, reinforces the view that the Aguacate phase represented an earlier inland-derived occupation at the Cerro Brujo site. For the IS-3 occupations, the evidence for the Burica phase being isolated in the bottom levels of any feature is less clear. Rim types 1, 2, and 3, which belong to the Bugaba style, occur right along with types 6, 7, and 8, which belong to the San Lorenzo wares, even though the latter are less common in the bottom levels.

In short, there is some ceramic evidence to support the hypothesis that during the Aguacate phase peoples, probably from the nearby highlands, moved right on to the Bocas coastal edge, carrying with them a "pure" Bugaba-style pottery tradition. There is no evidence, on the other hand, for assuming the same deliberate migration of peoples from the Volcan area to

La Pitahaya. In fact, the Bugaba phase pottery seems to have more antecedents in the coastal plains than in the highlands. Sites belonging to the Concepción phase (ca. 300 B.C.), such as Sitio Solano in Chiriqui and Sitio Guacamayo in Veraguas, are located at elevations below 300 meters. Although the Cerro Punta Orange pottery seems to be predominately highland in distribution (at Sitios Guanico and Guayabal near Caldera and also at the Costa Rican sites), it occurs at least at one site (Finca Toreto, in Estero Majaguales) which is on the Chiriqui coast. Besides the sites discussed in this report, we know six others which contain Valbuena and/or Bugaba Engraved pottery; half of them are on or near the coast. Scanty as the evidence will remain until a systematic sampling survey of the Atlantic and Pacific plains is conducted, it does suggest that the Pacific coast was heavily populated before and during the Bugaba phases. At the moment there is as much evidence for the Cerro Punta and El Hato populations having come directly from the Chiriqui coastal plains as there is for the Pacific coastal populations having come from the highlands. In fact, plant remains suggest a coastal to highland movement rather than the reverse (section 6.2.f.). All we can, or should, suggest is an expansion of peoples or techniques all over the highlands and the coastal plains on the Pacific side during the Bugaba phase (A.D. 200–A.D. 600) and probably before.

4. Marked stylistic differences separate the Early Bocas ceramics of the Atlantic coast from the San Lorenzo wares of the Pacific coast in the period between roughly A.D. 700 and A.D. 900. While large, crude, double-vessel jars with brushed or pinched monochrome surfaces and appliquéd marine faunal motifs are typical of the Bocas wares, bowls and jars painted with red bands and resting on strapped feet and pedestal bases characterize the San Lorenzo wares. Except for a handful of red-banded sherds found in the main Cerro Brujo midden locality (CA-3a), and a few more at each of the other localities, the ceramic assemblages from both coasts resemble each other very little at this point in time.

If we assume that stylistic similarities in the pottery of two sites results from some measure of social interaction between its makers (Plog 1976), should we also assume that lack of such similarities imply lack of interaction? Clearly, two interacting groups may make very different pottery. However, it seems reasonable to suggest that if two groups do not overlap in range, their ceramics are bound to be different unless one is deliberately copying from the other. If we recall, the highlands seem to have been avoided — or at least to have been lightly settled — following the eruption of Volcan Baru. To the existence of this barren land may perhaps be attributed the lack of apparent interaction between the coastal populations on the Bocas and Chiriqui sides in the period between A.D. 700 and A.D. 900.

The period following A.D. 900 sees the resumption of contact between the inhabitants of the Bocas coast and those of the Chiriqui coast. About one-third of the Late Bocas pottery, and about half of the diagnostic Chiriqui phase pottery, is constituted of an easily recognized and very distinctive ware known, under one guise or another, as Bisquit Ware. The fact that Bisquit Ware is more common in Chiriqui than in Bocas, appearing in the latter area virtually unchanged in the midst of other local wares, argues for its having been carried by actual people across the mountains. Without succumbing to the doubtful practice of some archaeologists always to link ceramic groups with ethnic groups, it seems reasonable to suggest that the makers of the Chiriqui and Bocas ceramics were the ancestors of the Guaymí Indians, who, a few centuries later, were found by the Spaniards living in the same areas.

8.0

Stone Tools and Their Interpretation

A. J. RANERE

8.1 INTRODUCTION

Careful analysis of lithic assemblages from tropical forest contexts has been infrequent for two very different reasons. On the one hand, the preceramic chipped stone assemblages have often been described as amorphous or as consisting of generalized cutting and scraping tools; not the sort of material that elaborate typologies and cumulative indexes are made of. On the other hand, the well-made but rather unvarying tools associated with ceramic periods are looked upon as rather insensitive indicators of archaeological cultures and chronological phases; if you've seen one celt you've seen them all.

Recent advances in technological and functional analyses of stone tool assemblages, particularly replicative experiments and wear pattern analysis, have altered this situation rather dramatically. These advances, coupled with a sharpened interest in systematics, have greatly improved our potential for recovering information about extinct cultural systems from the analysis of stone tools. This potential has yet to be fully realized. The frontiers are being pushed further and further out by lithic specialists, more rapidly than their approaches can be incorporated into the repertoire of many archaeologists. Most studies are still experimental, meant to illustrate the value of different experimental/microwear/systematic approaches (here I include the use of computer-aided statistical treatments) rather than to explain a particular body of data (e.g., Swanson 1975; Rosenthal ms. 1976; Sheets 1975).

However, in the present volume we have attempted to apply at least some of the newer approaches to the entire sample of stone artifacts recovered in the various subprojects of the western Panama project. In doing so we have tried not to neglect the obligation of any researcher to provide as complete and accurate a description of the collections as possible so that these materials can be compared with those from other archaeological sites in other regions. To do this, more less traditional artifact descriptions have been provided, as well as photographs, drawings, and tables of distributions.

In presenting the typologies for each collection, the tools were first placed into classes based on the final method of manufacture (e.g., ground and polished stone, chipped stone). They were then divided into major functional categories (e.g., celts, adzes) which in turn were subdivided into types based on formal attributes (e.g., Type A pear-shaped celts, Type B straight-sided celts). In the process of analysis, many of the tools were replicated and then used. Stereoscopic microscopes (6x-50x) were employed to examine wear patterns on both archaelogical and replicated tools. In addition, tools and flakes from archaeological and experimental collections were examined under the microscope in order to identify those attributes resulting from the manufacturing process. The reader is referred to report numbers 8, 14, 15, and 16 in this volume for detailed descriptions and analysis of collections from each of the four subareas examined in western Panama. I will, however, summarize the major features of these collections before turning to questions of tool function and the organization of tool production.

8.2   THE LITHIC COLLECTIONS

8.2.a. The Rio Chiriqui Canyon

Four rock shelters and one open campsite were tested in the canyon of the Rio Chiriqui. The bulk of the 45,000 stone specimens recovered came from preceramic occupation layers in the four shelters. A series of ten radiocarbon dates, six from Casita de Piedra and four from the Trapiche Shelter, place the preceramic occupation between 5000 and 300 B.C. (see section 3.4). Two phases were defined based on changes in the lithic assemblages. The division between the earlier Talamanca phase and the later Boquete phase falls at about 2300 B.C.

The rock shelters are all quite small, none containing more than 30 square meters of protected floor space (see report no. 1). Occupational debris did, however, extend beyond the protected space (i.e., beyond the dripline) in all cases. Ten and twelve square meters were excavated in Casita de Piedra and the Trapiche Shelter, respectively, the shelters with the deeper and more clearly stratified deposits. Five square meters were excavated at the Horacio Gonzales Site and two square meters at the Zarsiadero Shelter.

Within each phase, the tool types and chipping debris from shelter to shelter were quite similar, suggesting that all had been put to similar uses. Therefore, I will discuss the assemblages by phase, drawing primarily on data from Casita de Piedra and the Trapiche Shelter, where stratigraphic separation of the phases was quite clear.

Most of the tools of the Talamanca phase were made of chipped stone, or were used in the making of chipped stone tools (hammers and anvils). The chipped stone technology represented was quite simple: direct percussion using a hammerstone, and occasionally an anvil stone, was probably the only knapping method employed. Platform preparation was minimal to nonexistent. Large blocks of andesite, the most common raw material found during the Talamanca phase (over 90 percent of all flakes and tools), were normally reduced by detaching flakes from any convenient platform. Thus most andesite cores are irregular. There are, nonetheless, a few conical cores and bifacial cores in the collections. Smaller chunks of material, most often chalcedony and quartz, were reduced using the bipolar flaking technique. In this method, the core is placed on an anvil stone and a hammer is swung directly onto the top of the core. Although a rather crude technique, it does facilitate the fracturing of small pebbles.

Used flakes of various shapes and sizes were the most commonly encountered tools. These flakes, modified only through use, were employed in cutting, engraving, scraping, planing, and chopping. Unifacial retouch was used to manufacture scraper-planes, some steep scrapers and some gravers. Bifacial retouch was used primarily for the manufacture of large celtlike wedges. A few choppers exhibit bifacial retouch as well. The only other technique employed was the detachment of a burin spall to make rather delicate burins.

In addition to these chipped stone tools, hammers, and anvils, the Talamanca phase deposits contained tools made on unmodified cobbles and boulders. The most distinctive tools are edge-ground cobbles, generally flat and somewhat oval in outline with a facet worn along the narrow edge. These cobbles were presumably used against milling stone bases, also recovered from Talamanca deposits, for mashing and grinding. The flat to slightly convex facet on the edge-ground cobbles and the flat to slightly concave face of the milling stones were produced by the action of one upon the other. A less common artifact is the nutting stone, so called because it appears to have been used for cracking the hard nut or kernel of the corozo palm. Similar stones are still used in Panama for this purpose. They are simply cobbles in which a small depression has been made.

The chipped stone assemblage of the Boquete phase (2300–300 B.C.), also preceramic, is in most respects similar to that of the Talamanca phase. Both phases share most of the same tool types. However, bipolar flaking does become more common in the Boquete phase because of the increased use of chalcedony, quartz, and obsidian, materials normally available only as small pebbles or nodules. During this phase bifacial wedges cease being made; instead, small tabular wedges or chisels (pièces ècaillées) are found in quantities reaching 50 percent of the tools recovered in some layers. Quartz crystals are also used as wedges or chisels during the Boquete phase.

Edge-ground cobbles and milling stone bases continue to be found in Boquete phase deposits. Nutting stones occur as well. In addition, a few handstones are found whose working facets are on the flat face of the cobble or offset toward one edge. Small pestles also occur for the first time during the Boquete phase.

Both the cobble tools and the chipped stone tools from the two preceramic phases are quite simple to make. In fact, in the majority of cases the "making" consists of selecting a flake or cobble with the proper shape and size. However, a few ground and polished stone tools — celts, chisels, and axes — were also found in Boquete phase contexts. These are, of course, quite sophisticated tools, demanding skills in bifacial flaking for preforming the tools as well as skills in pecking, grinding, and polishing. The amount of time necessary to complete one of these ground and polished stone tools far exceeds the time needed to make the other tools found in the preceramic phases. More will be said about ground and polished tools in the context of later ceramic phases where they become increasingly important. It is, nonetheless, important to remember that the tools first appear in preceramic contexts.

The Rio Chiriqui shelters ceased being intensively used after the introduction of ceramics into western Panama at about 300 B.C. Better evidence for the use of stone during the post-300 B.C. ceramic period is provided by stone assemblages from the highland region of Volcan, from the Aguacate Peninsula along the Caribbean coast, and from Isla Palenque along the Pacific coast (see report nos. 14, 15, and 16). The sites examined in the Volcan region are dated earlier than those along either coast, and in some sense seem ancestral to them (see section 7.9). For this reason I will discuss the Volcan site first, then the site of La Pitahaya on the Pacific coast, and finally the sites on the Aguacate Peninsula.

8.2.b. The Volcan Highlands

In the Volcan region, one site, Pitti-Gonzalez (BU-17), was extensively excavated and two others, Barriles (BU-24) and Fistonich (BU-22), were tested. An additional 42 sites were located in an intensive survey of the region (see report nos. 2–5). Stone tools were collected from the surface of these sites as well as from the excavations. A large series of radiocarbon dates from Sitio Pitti-Gonzalez and Barriles fix the main occupation of these sites between A.D. 200 and A.D. 600 (see section 7.4.c.). Cross-dating of the surface pottery collections with those from the excavated sites suggests that with a few possible exceptions, all sites located in the survey fall within this same time span. Slight differences in the ceramic collections enable two main ceramic phases (Early Bugaba and Late Bugaba) to be distinguished, each lasting approximately 200 years. No such distinctions could be made based on the much smaller lithic collections (see report no. 14, tables 1–3). This is not to say that distinctions between lithic assemblages from these two phases do not exist, only that much more extensive collections are needed in order to determine whether or not such distinctions exist. In any event, the collections for all of the Volcan sites will be grouped together for consideration. There are nearly 300 tools and 3,000 flakes in the combined collection.

The chipped stone industry of the Volcan sites has been aptly characterized by Sheets (1975) as a cottage industry. Flakes were struck from unprepared cores with hammerstones and used with little or no modification. Some scraper-planes, scrapers, and perforators were formed by simple unifacial retouch. Other scraper-planes and scrapers were not retouched before use, as was the case with knives and choppers. These flake tools and the cores from which they were struck were widely distributed, being found in the smallest as well as the largest habitation sites.

A variety of tools recovered from the Volcan sites were used in grinding, mashing, and pounding activities. Most common among these were metates, both legged and slab varieties, and cylindrical manos. These tools were almost certainly used to grind maize. Also numerous were milling stones, made of suitably shaped but unmodified boulders, and the oval and spherical handstones that were presumably used with them. Large stone mortars, some formed in bedrock and others in boulders, were also present. Several small slabs ("palettes") with smoothed surfaces were apparently used for grinding or pulverizing small amounts of materials, perhaps pigments.

Ground and polished stone tools were recovered from a number of sites in the Volcan region. With few exceptions, all such tools were celts that can be placed in two categories. Type A or pear-shaped celts have a bit which extends in an unbroken curve back along both sides of the implement. Type B celts have straight sides which taper slightly from the bit to the butt end. A single small celt (Type C) had incurvate sides. One chisel was also recovered from Sitio Pitti-Gonzalez. The skills required to manufacture these ground and polished stone tools and the time invested in their production suggest that this activity was in the hands of specialists.

8.2.c. La Pitahaya in the Gulf of Chiriqui

Test excavations were carried out in several parts of the large site La Pitahaya (IS-3), located on Palenque Peninsula just off the mainland of Chiriqui. The excavations produced approximately 1,000 stone tools and an additional 1,000 flakes. Shared ceramic similarities between the bottom of La Pitahaya deposits and the upper layers of Sitio Pitti-Gonzalez place the beginnings of the IS-3 occupation at A.D. 600, if not earlier (see section 7.7). The earliest phase at La Pitahaya, the Burica phase (Linares 1968b), was contemporary with the Late Bugaba phase in the highlands. The middle layers of the site are dated to A.D. 700–900 and attributed to the San Lorenzo phase. The Chiriqui phase is represented by materials in the top layers of the site which date to A.D. 1000–1100 (section 7.8). Although there are some differences in the frequencies of stone tool types for these three phases, the types themselves continue to be found throughout the deposits. Here I will summarize the assemblages of the site as a whole, and save discussion of the changing frequencies of tool types until later.

The ground and polished stone tool industry at La Pitahaya is very much like that described for the Volcan sites even though the collection is considerably larger (199 vs. 40 specimens). Pear-shaped Type A celts and straight-sided Type B celts were the most common tools encountered. A smaller celt type ("C") is thinner in cross section than other celts. A small number of adzes and chisels was also recovered. These ground and polished stone tools had invariably been broken and/or reused as hammerstones.

Like the Volcan sites, metates and cylindrical or bar manos were the principal grinding tools at La Pitahaya. A number of ovoid manos occurred at the site as well. Milling stones, while present, were rare. Nutting stones were very common tools (38 specimens) as were large and battered pounding-mashing stones (pestles). Three tool types were unique to La Pitahaya and seem to reflect its coastal location. Notched and grooved pebbles, thought to have been used as net weights and line weights, were found in considerable numbers. Several rasps or sandstone saws were also present. These thin flat pieces of sandstone have sharp beveled edges and are thought to have been used for working shell.

The chipped stone industry has two very different aspects. There was at La Pitahaya a household industry where flakes were detached from unprepared cores and used without further modification for cutting, scraping, and perforating. Small nodules were reduced by the bipolar flaking technique; both bipolar cores and anvils were recovered from the site. Shelton Einhaus (report no. 15) has suggested that some of the small quartz chips produced by bipolar flaking may have been grater chips, or teeth set in wooden graterboards. Used flakes and possibly these grater teeth were the only products of this household industry. Purposeful retouch was very rare if not completely absent.

In contrast, there are two artifact types, blades (and tools made on blades) and trifacial points, that are clearly the product of a sophisticated technology. The long straight blades were detached from prepared cores with considerable skill. The trifacial points are triangular in cross section, flaked across all three surfaces and tanged. Both tool types were most certainly the products of specialists.

8.2.d. The Aguacate Peninsula, Bocas del Toro

Major excavations were conducted at the dispersed hamlet of Cerro Brujo (CA-3) on the Aguacate Peninsula. Test excavations were also undertaken at the neighboring Sitio Machuca (CA-2). Two components were recognized at the CA-3 locality. The major occupation occurred in what is called the Bocas phase and is dated by several radiocarbon determinations to A.D. 900. An earlier occupation is dated by ceramic cross-dating with highland Volcan sites to A.D. 600–700 (section 7.6). Little of the initial or Aguacate phase occupation was excavated at Cerro Brujo, and an Aguacate phase at CA-2 was absent altogether. Only six tools (two Type A celts, three Type B celts, and one chisel) and nine flakes were recovered from Aguacate phase contexts. Therefore, my discussion will be restricted to the 145 tools and 112 flakes recovered from Bocas phase contexts.

Ground and polished stone tools were the most common artifacts recovered in the Aguacate Peninsula sites. The straight-sided Type B celts and pear-shaped Type A celts were the dominant forms (50 and 18 specimens, respectively). Small celts with incurvate sides (Type C) were also present. In addition to these celts, one axe and a number of chisels and adzes were found. Like La Pitahaya, most of the ground and polished tools were broken and/or recycled as hammerstones.

Unlike all previous areas discussed, tools for grinding and mashing are either rare or absent. Only two possible handstones and two pestles were recovered in the excavations. Similarly, only four tools can be considered as products of a household chipping industry (along with five cores and twelve flakes). Most of the chipped stone tools at Cerro Brujo and Sitio Machuca are made on blades. Tangs were flaked on a number of these blades to faciliate hafting. Some blades were used as struck, others were modified by unifacial or bifacial retouch. Still others had narrow, chisellike bits produced by grinding and polishing. Blades were used for slicing, scraping, sawing, perforating, drilling, whittling, and chiseling (see report no. 16).

8.3 TOOL FUNCTION AND SITE ACTIVITIES

In the discussions above I purposely concentrated on describing the technology of tool production because it is the least speculative aspect of lithic analysis. It is somewhat more difficult to determine the nature of the material on which the tool was employed. One can, for example, be more confident in identifying a tool as a scraper than identifying it as a *hide* scraper. Nonetheless, experiments to replicate tool functions and microwear analysis, particularly under high magnification, have proved to be surprisingly accurate in a controlled test situation (see Keeley and Newcomer 1977).

In our analysis of the western Panama tool assemblages, we conducted a number of experiments with replicated tools in order to study tool function. A stereoscopic microscopic (6x-50x) was used to examine tools and flakes for evidence of wear. The functional interpretations based on the tool use experiments and on the microwear analysis are discussed in report numbers 8, 14, 15, and 16 (see also Ranere 1975) in some detail. Certain implications of these studies are presented below.

While interpretation of function is a more hazardous undertaking than the interpretation of technology, it often provides information on site activities available from no other source. This is particularly true in the humid tropics where preservation of archaeological materials is generally poor. For example, we are almost entirely dependent on functional interpretations of stone tools for information on activities carried out during the preceramic occupation of the Rio Chiriqui shelters.

Three general kinds of activities are indicated by the stone tools for both the Talamanca and Boquete phases in the Rio Chiriqui canyon: stone working, woodworking, and plant processing. Hammerstones and anvils were the only tools recovered that were used for making stone tools, and most likely they were the only ones used at the shelters. They were, at any rate, the only tools I needed in order to replicate the range of stone tools found at the sites (ground and polished tools excepted). The 45,000 flakes and cores recovered from the shelter deposits clearly document the importance of stone tool manufacturing at the sites.

Most of the chipped stone tools from the Rio Chiriqui shelters appear to have been used in working wood. Included here are bifacial wedges, tabular wedges, broad-based wedges, scraper-planes, choppers, burins, gravers, spokeshaves, used quartz crystals, and at least some steep scrapers, flake scrapers, and flake knives. Not all tools in these categories had identifiable use wear. Some were either not used, or not used enough for wear to be discernable under the magnification we employed in our analysis. Moreover, the surfaces and edges of a number of andesite tools were so altered by weathering that only the largest use flakes could be recognized. Nonetheless, a number of tools in each category had seen heavy use, and the resultant wear was visible under the microscope. In addition, the wear patterns were duplicated on replicated tools in laboratory experiments where wood was chopped, split, planed, chiseled, scraped, engraved, and whittled (report no. 8 and Ranere 1975). The emphasis on woodworking at the sites seems reasonable, both in the light of the emphasis placed on it by later tropical forest peoples and in light of the similarly interpreted contemporary assemblages in other parts of the tropics (section 3.8.c.).

More difficult to interpret are the edge-ground cobbles and milling stone bases, the principal plant processing tools in both Talamanca and Boquete phases. The use facets along the narrow edges of the edge-ground cobbles are very pronounced, but in all of the Rio Chiriqui specimens, the cobble surfaces were too heavily weathered for the preservation of any microwear attributes. However, well-preserved edge-ground cobbles have been recovered from the Aguadulce Shelter and Monagrillo site in central Panama (Ranere and Hansell 1978). These cobbles often have use flakes driven off the edges of the working facet. Many have one longitudinal edge of the facet more rounded than the other as if the tool was slightly rolled while in contact with the milling stone base. In addition, striations perpendicular to the long axis of the facet can be seen on some specimens. These wear patterns suggest that the tools were used against milling stones in a motion combining pounding and grinding, wherein the cobble was struck against the milling stone and then drawn toward the user. In laboratory experiments, unmodified cobbles and flat boulders were used in this manner to mash a variety of tubers, including manioc. The tools seemed quite efficient, particularly if the tubers were first cut into sections. Wear patterns identical to those on the archaeological specimens from central Panama were produced experimentally (Moser ms.1977).

It is one thing to show that manioc and other tubers *could* have been mashed by edge-ground cobbles and quite another to show that manioc and other tubers *were* mashed by edge-ground cobbles in the Rio Chiriqui shelters. Still, our experiments indicated that these narrow-faceted tools were much less efficient at grinding maize than were broad-faceted manos (just as one might expect); yet they were more efficient than manos for mashing starchy tubers. Edge-ground cobbles and milling stone bases are common tools in the Rio Chiriqui sites and were presumably used in the every day activity of food preparation. The most obvious choice of food in a tropical forest environment is starchy tubers, among which manioc was the most important historically; the question whether these tubers were wild or domesticated also remains to be answered.

Interpreting tool function during the later ceramic phases is less problematic because of the continuity with the historic period and because plant and animal remains from the excavations provide corroborative evidence. The identification of the archaeologically recovered manos and metates as maize-grinding implements is supported by the historic and modern use of nearly identical objects in Panama and elsewhere in tropical America. Moreover, carbonized maize remains and maize pollen were recovered from both Sitio Pitti-Gonzalez and La Pitahaya. Wear pattern analysis and experimental use of manos and metates to grind maize, though consistent with this identification, seem somehow superfluous. The association of manos and metates with maize is so well documented, in fact, that their absence from the Aguacate Peninsula sites assumes considerable significance. One is almost forced to conclude that maize was not used as a staple at these sites, in marked contrast to those sites on the Pacific side of the continental divide.

The use of ground and polished stone celts and axes for woodworking and particularly for felling trees is well documented historically. Given the botanical evidence for agriculture at the Volcan sites and at La Pitahaya, little doubt remains that these tools were used in felling the vegetation prior to planting. The celts at Cerro Brujo were almost certainly also used in clearing the forest to make agricultural fields as well, although maize was probably not a major crop. Even though carbonized remains of domesticated plants were not recovered at Cerro Brujo, the presence of large numbers of celts provides good indirect evidence for cultivation at the site.

Woodworking other than tree felling continued to be an important activity during the ceramic period, just as it had been previously. Ground and polished stone chisels and adzes replaced a number of chipped stone tool types, but some chipped stone woodworking tools were still used (whittling knives, scrapers, and spokeshaves).

Hammerstones are found in all the assemblages dating from the ceramic period, but are particularly numerous at La Pitahaya and Cerro Brujo. In both sites, damaged and broken celts (and most of the recovered celts fit this category) almost invariably were reused as hammers. Pounding facets are generally quite broad, and we are probably safe in calling these implements pecking hammers. There was not enough chipping debris at either site to support the contention that they were knapping hammers (the ratio of flakes to hammers at Cerro Brujo is about 2 to 1!). These pecking hammers appear to have been used primarily to reshape damaged and dulled celts and other ground and polished stone tools. Whetstones and pebble polishers, found in Volcan, Aguacate, and La Pitahaya sites, were also used for reshaping and sharpening ground and polished stone tools (see discussion below).

Other implements whose function seems reasonably clear include the notched and grooved stones found in large numbers at La Pitahaya. One notched stone was found at Sitio Machuca on the Atlantic as well. These stones have been identified as net weights and line weights used in fishing. Both net fishing and line fishing are implied by the species of fish recovered from La Pitahaya deposits (see section 13.0). No such weights were found at Cerro Brujo, however, possibly because nets are difficult to use over coral reefs (section 13.3).

"Nutting stones" appear to be accurately named. Similar stones are still used in Panama to crack the hard shell of the corozo palm nut while leaving the nut meat in one retrievable piece (without the depression in the nutting stone the nut meat is sometimes smashed into bits). These tools were found in the Rio Chiriqui shelters, Sitio Pitti-Gonzalez, and La Pitahaya, as were carbonized remains of the corozo palm nut (see section 10.6).

A number of other tools made of cobbles and boulders present at the Volcan sites and in La Pitahaya can be loosely described as plant-processing tools. These include milling stones, mortars, pestles or pounding-mashing stones, and handstones of various kinds. These implements were probably used to process foods other than maize since manos and metates were available for that purpose. It is interesting to note that at La Pitahaya, these "non-maize" food-processing tools (including nutting stones) are much more common in the latest Chiriqui phase than they are earlier, while the number of metates increases only slightly. Shelton Einhaus (report no. 15) speculates that this may reflect increased reliance on foods other than maize, particularly tree crops and root crops that allow the land to stay in production longer. Such a shift in food production may have represented an attempt to feed a growing population, or an attempt to adjust to tropical soils impoverished from too many years in maize production.

Shelton Einhaus has further suggested that a number of small quartz flakes from La Pitahaya might well have been insets for graterboards. Such graterboards were widespread historically in South America east of the Andes and in the Caribbean. They were (and still are) used for shredding bitter manioc so that the poisonous juices could be squeezed out. Grater-board teeth were not necessarily made of stone, but this was often the case (cf. Lathrap 1973). The specimens from La Pitahaya are only slightly larger than some ethnographic samples reported by DeBoer (1975). Of course, the La Pitahaya specimens may not be grater teeth at all, or they may be grater teeth and the grater may have been used for grating something other than manioc. Notwithstanding, manioc pollen was recovered in sediments near La Pitahaya which were contemporary with the occupation (report no. 17). If edge-ground cobbles and milling stone bases are an earlier (and perhaps less efficient) alternative to graterboards for reducing manioc to a pulpy mass, as I suspect, then the presence of grater chips at La Pitahaya but not edge-ground cobbles and the presence in the Rio Chiriqui shelters of edge-ground cobbles but not grater chips makes a good deal of sense.

8.4   THE ORGANIZATION OF STONE TOOL PRODUCTION: EVIDENCE AND IMPLICATIONS

The one aspect of lithic analysis that inspires most confidence is the technology involved in the production of stone tools. The tools themselves are available for analysis, waste flakes and workshop rejects or mistakes representing different stages in the manufacturing process can often be examined, and many of the tools used to make stone tools are recoverable. Moreover, experimental replication of stone tools has a long history, and has witnessed an impressive resurgence of interest during the past decade (see Johnson 1978 for a recent assessment). Hence, it is not by accident that my summaries of the lithic assemblages from western Panama focused on the technology. Because the stone technology from this area is reasonably well understood, it seems worthwhile to examine it more closely for the information it can provide on craft specialization and intersite contact.

In this section I would like to examine the proposition that within a 3,000 year period populations living in self-sufficient communities in western Panama were transformed into populations whose communities were integrated at the regional level. I will limit my discussion for the most part to evidence provided by the changing technology of stone tool production. The Talamanca phase (5000–2300 B.C.) and the Bocas phase (A.D. 900) represent the beginning and end points of this organizational transformation. During the Talamanca phase social groups appear to be completely autonomous and independent with respect to stone tool production; on the other hand, the Cerro Brujo residents appear almost completely dependent on outside specialists for tool production. Although there is little common ground for making a technological comparison between Talamanca and Bocas phase assemblages, the assemblages from the Boquete, Bugaba, Burica, and San Lorenzo phases bridge the gap nicely.

8.4.a. Stone Tool Production During the Preceramic Period

A number of lines of evidence indicate that during the Talamanca phase occupation of the Rio Chiriqui canyon, all of the tools made in the shelters were also used in the shelters, and all the tools used in the shelters were made in the shelters. That is to say, the shelter inhabitants were neither producing tools for use elsewhere, nor were they importing tools for use at the shelters. It is important, I think, to establish the facts that (1) these Talamanca groups were self-sufficient at least insofar as the production of stone tools is concerned, and (2) the skills to produce *all* of the Talamanca tools were widely distributed in the population (i.e., none was the product of specialists).

That tool production was an important activity in the Rio Chiriqui sites should be evident from the quantities of waste flakes recovered (nearly 45,000 in 31 cubic meters excavated). The materials used for making stone tools were readily available to the canyon occupants, and they appear to have brought blocks, cobbles, and pebbles of these materials back to the shelters to make their tools. Flakes with cortex on their dorsal surfaces were quite common in the collections and several cobbles and pebbles of andesite, chalcedony, quartz, and obsidian were recovered that had been carried into the shelters but never used.

A rough index of the amount of chipped stone tool manufacturing carried out at an archaeological site can be arrived at by looking at the ratio of flakes to finished tools. In a lithic workshop site where most of the finished tools are exported, the ratio should be quite high. At the other extreme, at sites where tools are imported in finished form, the ratio should be quite low. Table 1 lists the ratios of flakes to chipped stone tools for the most extensively excavated sites in western Panama by phase. The ratios listed in the table indicate very clearly that a lot of stone tool manufacturing was going on during the Talamanca and Boquete phases in the two Rio Chiriqui shelters and during the Bugaba phase at Sitio Pitti-Gonzalez. The ratios also indicate that very little manufacturing was going on at La Pitahaya and Cerro Brujo.

I have already noted that the technology for the Talamanca phase was relatively simple. Not only was there very little skill involved in making many of these tools, but they could be made in a matter of seconds. The only exceptions were bifacially flaked celtlike wedges which demand a moderate amount of skill to make. Still, judging from my replicative efforts, it probably took less than ten minutes to make a bifacial wedge.

Despite the greater skill needed to produce them than to produce any of the other tools, bifacial wedges appear to have been manufactured at all the Rio Chiriqui sites containing Talamanca phase deposits. There are simply too many flakes in the collections that were clearly struck from bifaces (i.e., flakes which retain part of the biface edge and opposite face on their platform) to assume they all came instead from the few bifacial cores and choppers present. In a sample of 1,070 flakes from an excavation unit in

TABLE 1   THE RATIO OF WASTE FLAKES TO CHIPPED STONE TOOLS
FOR THE PRINCIPAL SITES EXCAVATED IN WESTERN PANAMA*

Phase	Site	Flakes	Tools	Ratio
Talamanca (4600–2300 B.C.)	Casita de Piedra	15,488	368	42.1:1
Talamanca	Trapiche Shelter	13,340	282	47.3:1
Boquete (2300–300 B.C.)	Casita de Piedra	8,685	561	15.5:1
Boquete	Trapiche Shelter	3,095	108	28.7:1
Bugaba (A.D. 200–600)	Sitio Pitti-Gonzalez	2,051	104	19.7:1
Burica (A.D. 600–700)	La Pitahaya	311	65	4.8:1
San Lorenzo (A.D. 700–900)	La Pitahaya	273	72	3.8:1
Chiriqui (A.D. 1000–1100)	La Pitahaya	201	73	2.8:1
Bocas	Cerro Brujo	22	28	0.8:1

*Celt flakes are excluded from the flake count; cores are included in the tool count.

Casita de Piedra, 24 or 2.2 percent were struck from bifaces. I should point out that most flakes removed in the manufacture of bifacial wedges cannot be identified as such. In analyzing the chipping waste from one experimentally manufactured bifacial wedge, I was able to classify only 10 of 205 flakes (larger than 1/4 inch) or about 5 percent as unmistakable products of bifacial reduction. If this result is at all applicable to chipping waste from prehistorically produced bifacial wedges, then about 44 percent, not 2.2 percent of the waste flakes from Talamanca deposits were the product of bifacial flaking. This amounts to some 6,000 flakes or 125 flakes for every bifacial tool and tool fragment recovered in Casita de Piedra (the ratio is about 100 to 1 at the Trapiche Shelter). This ratio is not terribly different from the 187 to 1 ratio of flakes to bifacial wedges for tools I have made experimentally (n=5). If bifacial fragments from Casita de Piedra are counted as half of a finished tool, then the Talamanca flake to tool ratio is 167:1, very close to the experimental value. But this is dangerously close to playing with numbers (if fragments are counted as one-third of a finished tool, the experimental and archaeological ratios are closer still!), and I need not belabor the point further. Bifacial wedges were almost certainly manufactured at all the Talamanca phase sites, and therefore the skills necessary to make *all* the tools from Talamanca assemblages are judged to have been widely distributed in the population.

The idea that the Rio Chiriqui sites were not *just* workshops, however, is supported by two lines of evidence. First, few of the unused, unfinished (blanks and preforms) or rejected tools normally encountered in a lithic workshop are present in the shelters. Second, a large number of tools show evidence of use (see discussion above). Bifacial wedges, for example, exhibit use polish and striations on their bits and on high spots back along both faces. The butt ends have also been heavily battered. Moreover, a number of resharpening flakes retaining the worn bit edge of the wedges were also recovered. This suggests that the wedges were resharpened perhaps several times before being discarded. The existence in the collections of wedges that were abandoned after unsuccessful attempts at resharpening, and short wedges that were reused as hammers, provides further evidence that these tools were heavily used.

Tools made on unmodified flakes and cobbles can only be identified as tools because they show use wear. Hammerstones, anvils, edge-ground cobbles, milling stones, cobble spall choppers, flake choppers, flake scrapers, and flake knives all fit into this category. Wear polish, striations and/or use flakes were also observed on scraper-planes, steep scrapers, concave scrapers, gravers, and burins (Ranere 1975).

As a final check on the production versus the use of tools during the Talamanca phase, I determined the ratio of waste flakes (over 1/4 inch) to cores and core tools for the Trapiche Shelter and Casita de Piedra. I included bifacial wedges, irregular bifacial wedges, bifacial fragments, bifacial choppers, scraper-planes, conical cores, bifacial cores, and irregular cores but not small bipolar cores in the count of cores and core tools. The ratios for Casita de Piedra and the Trapiche Shelter were 171:1 and 145:1, respectively. These ratios are very close to the 187:1 ratio produced in the experimental manufacture of bifacial wedges. Thus, all lines of evidence support the proposition that the tools made at the sites were used at the sites and vice versa.

I would be remiss if I did not note that a single large fragment of a stone bowl was recovered from Talamanca phase deposits in Casita de Piedra (see report no. 8). The fragment represents the only artifact that may well have been imported into the site, and the only artifact that was probably the product of a specialist.

A very similar picture of tool production and tool use can be seen for Boquete phase deposits. If anything, the chipped stone technology was even simpler since bifacial wedges were no longer made (there is a corresponding drop in flakes produced in bifacial reduction). A few scraper-planes, bifacial choppers, and scrapers were made by secondary retouch, but most tools were simply appropriately shaped flakes or cobbles modified through use. The dominant tools — small tabular wedges or chisels — are easily made by bipolar flaking. The ratio of flakes to tools (about 15 to 1; see table 1) in the Boquete deposits lends support to the proposition that the tools used at the sites were also made there.

A half dozen of the 800 artifacts from Boquete phase contexts do not conform to the pattern described above. These include five ground and polished stone tools, among them a grooved axe, a celt, and a chisel, as well as an incised rim sherd from a stone vessel and a cup-shaped stone mortar (figs. 3.0-4 and 8/9). In spite of their small numbers, the ground and polished tools are important in that they signify the introduction of a new technology for stone tool manufacturing, requiring skills in bifacial flaking for preforming the tools, as well as skills in the pecking, grinding, and polishing needed to complete them. Each tool, in addition, represents a considerable investment in time, one measured in hours, not minutes or seconds as is the case with other Boquete tools.

These ground and polished stone tools may have been made at the shelters. Tools that I have described as "pestles" are limited in the Rio Chiriqui sequence to the Boquete phase and may, in fact, have been pecking hammers. However, no other implements associated with the production of ground and polished stone tools, e.g., whetstones and pebble polishers, were recovered. Therefore, it seems more likely that the tools were made elsewhere and imported into the Rio Chiriqui sites. This is probably true of the stone bowl and cup-shaped mortar as well. (More will be said about the production of ground and polished stone tools in the context of later ceramic phases where they become more common.)

8.4.b. Craft Specialization and Regional Interaction During the Ceramic Period

The character of the lithic assemblages from western Panama changes rather dramatically after 300 B.C., or at the time when pottery is added to the cultural inventory. Stone celts become common tools in the assemblages from highland Volcan sites. These same assemblages also contain large numbers of manos and metates, the latter often quite elaborate. Both the ground and polished stone tool industry and the mano and metate industry point to the existence of well-established craft specialization. This specialization is documented in a spectacular fashion by the large stone sculptures known chiefly from Barriles, which include life-sized human figures, the enigmatic stone "barrels" which gave the site its name, and enormous (over six feet in length) legged tables or metates (Stirling 1950; Linares et al. 1975).

Existing alongside these specialized crafts was a chipped stone tool industry consisting of little more than the production of flakes from unprepared cores. These flakes were then simply used as detached, or on rare occasion modified by light unifacial retouch. At Sitio Pitti-Gonzalez, the ratio of flakes to tools is high, indicating that these chipped stone tools were made on the spot. The household nature of this industry is also confirmed by the widespread occurrence of cores and flakes in surface collections from both large and small sites in the survey area.

One chipped stone artifact type, dacite laterally flaked slabs, deviates from this pattern by being restricted in distribution to a few larger sites and by requiring more skill and time in its manufacture.

Thus, during the Bugaba phase (A.D. 200–600), the production of a number of tools, like knives, scrapers, and milling stones, was still in the hands of the household, or at least of the local community. The production of other tools, like celts and metates, was clearly in the hands of specialists, however. Celts and metates are essential components of any household inventory of subsistence farmers, just as essential certainly as chipped stone knives, scrapers, and milling stones. It is of some importance, I think, to know where these tools were produced and how they were distributed. An examination of the evidence (or lack of evidence) for celt and metate production leads me to suggest that (1) only a few of the largest sites in the region were involved in the production, maintenance, and distribution of the tools, and (2) the major production center(s) for ground and polished stone tools, and perhaps for metates and manos as well, lay outside the surveyed zone.

Because the materials used to manufacture celts and other ground and polished stone tools differed with few exceptions from those used to make other stone tools, waste flakes from celt preforming and celt resharpening can be distinguished from other chipping debris (report no. 14). In the case of celt resharpening or reshaping by percussion flaking, a portion of the polished or ground surface is often retained on the detached flakes. Celts that have been reused as cores also produce flakes with ground or polished facets (a few were also undoubtedly produced in accidental damage to the celts). These "celt flakes" are clearly not the result of initial celt production, but rather indicate celt reshaping or celt recycling. Of course, not all flakes removed in celt reshaping or recycling will retain remnants of the tool surface. In one resharpening experiment which I conducted, 14 out of the 48 flakes detached (over 1/4 inch) or 29 percent showed no evidence of having been removed from a celt, and, if found in archaeological contexts, could not be classified as celt flakes.

Celt flakes were recovered from only nine of the 45 sites recorded in the Volcan region, including the three sites where excavations were conducted. Only six sites yielded flakes of celtlike materials (possible celt manufacturing flakes) and two contained only a single flake each. All of these sites are large in absolute terms, or large in comparison with the sites that surround them. Even though the sample size is small (see table 2), the data suggest that both celt repairing and particularly celt manufacturing were carried out at only a few important sites.

At the large Sitio Pitti-Gonzalez site, the only one where extensive excavations were undertaken, 363 flakes of celtlike materials were recovered. One hundred of these are classified as celt flakes since they have retained part of the celts' ground and/or polished surfaces. The remaining 263 flakes are possible celt manufacturing flakes. Some of these undoubtedly came from resharpening activities as did the one hundred celt flakes. However, if the ratio of flakes with ground and polished surfaces to flakes without such surfaces produced in experimental celt resharpening is representative (1.0:0.4), only about forty of the Sitio Pitti-Gonzalez possible celt manufacturing flakes can be accounted for by celt resharpening. At least *some* initial celt manufacturing was carried out at the site.

Granting this, it seems unlikely that very much manufacturing was going on at the site. Few of the tools associated with the manufacturing of celts were recovered at the site. Nor were there preforms or celts in any other stage of being manufactured with the single exception of a pecked celt.

TABLE 2   CELT (RESHAPING) FLAKES AND POSSIBLE CELT
MANUFACTURING FLAKES FROM WESTERN
PANAMA SITES

Site	Celt flakes	Possible celt manufacturing flakes
Sitio Pitti-Gonzalez (BU-17)	100	263
Barriles (BU-24)	3	6
Fistonich (BU-22)	9	0
BU-15	2	1
BU-16	1	0
BU-33	1	0
BU-39	2	3
BU-49	5	3
BU-55	3	0
BU-65	0	1?
La Pitahaya (IS-3)	191	19
Cerro Brujo (CA-3)	80	31

Moreover, even if *all* of the 263 flakes that were clearly not resharpening flakes are considered to be celt-manufacturing flakes, the number is still quite small. In replicative experiments, an average of 160 flakes (over 1/4 inch) per celt blank (n=5) was produced. Even if tools were being produced for use at this one site only, the number of flakes recovered is off by more than an order of magnitude. Nineteen celts and one chisel were recovered from Sitio Pitti-Gonzalez. To judge from the replicative experiments, somewhere on the order of 3,200 flakes were removed to produce just the tools found at this site. We might recall that the ratio of flakes to core and core tools in the Talamanca deposits was 150 to 1, again suggesting that about 3,000 flakes would have been removed in making the twenty ground and polished stone tools from Sitio Pitti-Gonzalez. Most of the tools involved in establishing the Talamanca phase ratio of flakes to core and core tools were bifacial wedges, which are very similar to celt blanks. Thus the application of this ratio to Sitio Pitti-Gonzalez seem justified. Of course, if specialists at the site were making celts for other settlements, more chipping than 3,000–3,200 flakes would be expected.

Sitio Pitti-Gonzalez is a large site, and only small parts of it were excavated. Thus the possibility exists that within its boundaries a large celt making station will one day be discovered. Nonetheless, I think it more likely that most of the celts used by the Volcan area residents, including those from Sitio Pitti-Gonzalez, were made at large quarry workshop sites outside of the surveyed area. I have visited one such site at India Vieja, midway between the Volcan basin and the Rio Chiriqui canyon, where celt-manufacturing flakes occur thousands upon thousands. There is the possibility that only the preforms were made in quarry workshop sites and that the time-consuming tasks of pecking, grinding, and polishing were carried out at sites like Sitio Pitti-Gonzalez. This possibility however, is not supported by the scarcity of pecking hammers, whetstones, and pebble polishers found at the site.

The interpretation that I feel best accommodates the evidence is that Sitio Pitti-Gonzalez and perhaps another five or six sites in the region served as celt maintenance centers, not manufacturing centers. Celts would originally have been made at quarry workshop sites and imported into the region as finished tools. One or more resident individuals at sites like Pitti-Gonzalez were specialized in repairing damaged and dulled celts, and even occasionally made new ones. The grave of just such a repairman who lived a few centuries earlier than the Bugaba occupation in central Panama has been excavated by Cooke (1978). The tool kit buried with "El Hachero" at Sitio Sierra consisted of 41 basalt polishing pebbles, 1 jasper polishing pebble, 3 heavy basalt hammerstone, 1 basalt pecking hammer, 1 dacite whetstone, 2 small basalt flakes, 2 jasper flakes, a jasper side scraper made on a blade, 8 celts in various stages of reshaping and a basalt cobble fragment flaked along one side (Cooke 1977b).

The manufacture of metates from vesicular basalts and andesites was also a specialized craft. Like celts, they too were probably produced in special quarry workshops and imported by the Volcan settlers. Unlike celts, however, metates and manos are self-sharpening and do not need repair, only replacement. Since we have no specific information on where the source of the stone for metates and manos might be located, and since we have no information from the Volcan sites pertaining to metate manufacturing, it seems prudent not to speculate further. It is interesting, perhaps, to note that the large stone sculptures at Barriles, including the large "ceremonial metates" were made of the same stone as many of the utilitarian metates and manos, and were undoubtedly made "on site." Therefore, craftsmen skilled in working vesicular igneous rocks were available at least at one site in the region.

The move toward specialization in stone tool production and away from any household production continues on both Pacific and Atlantic coasts during the phases that follow the highland Bugaba phase. At the site of La Pitahaya, the ratio of flakes to chipped stone tools is quite low, even during the earliest Burica phase, and gets progressively lower in the succeeding San Lorenzo and Chiriqui phases (table 1). Still, over 800 waste flakes and a number of cores were recovered at the site, as well as 63 tools which were simply used flakes. Thus household production of the very simplest tools appears to continue, albeit on a smaller scale. The small quartz flakes that may have served as insets for graterboards also were made at the site. Bipolar cores of quartz and quartz debitage occur along with the possible grater chips.

Nevertheless, an important part of the chipped stone industry, i.e., the production of blades and trifacial points, was in the hands of specialists. The absence of blade cores and any workshop debris that could be associated with the production of blades or trifaces indicates that these specialists resided elsewhere and that the tools were imported as finished objects.

Similarly, there is no evidence for the manufacture of ground and polished stone tools at La Pitahaya. Fully 191 of 210 flakes of celtlike materials retained the ground and/or polished remnant of the celt. Only 19 are possible celt manufacturing flakes, and they are best interpreted as celt-reshaping flakes as well, in light of the experimental resharpening data discussed earlier. A number of celts showed evidence of reshaping by flaking, pecking, grinding, and polishing. Pecking hammers are also numerous, most being made on broken or exhausted celts. Two whetstones were found at the site, as were a number of pebble polishers (which, of course, could have been used for polishing pots as well as celts). One can easily picture celt repairmen similar to "El Hachero" at Sitio Sierra described by Cooke (1977b) working to return these valuable tools to serviceable condition. The dense igneous rocks employed in making celts do not occur on the island where La Pitahaya is located; thus the need for continual reshaping of old celts is understandable. The recycling of exhausted celts as pecking hammers is also understandable, given the lack of tough dense stone on the island.

Metates and cylindrical (or bar) manos are also made of stone not found on the island and appear to have been imported as finished products. On the other hand, pestles (pounding-mashing stones), nutting stones, notched stones, and grooved stones were made locally of local rock. All these artifacts are easily made and therefore were probably not the handiwork of specialists.

Remarkably little stone manufacturing took place during the Bocas phase occupation of the Aguacate Peninsula (ca. A.D. 900). As mentioned earlier, only four flake tools, twelve waste flakes and five cores can be positively attributed to a household chipping industry. Chipped stone tools are almost entirely made on blades. The absence of blade cores and debitage associated with blade removal clearly indicates that the blades were imported. The ground and polished stone tools from the Aguacate sites were likewise imported as finished implements. Only 21 of 111 flakes of celtlike materials (29 percent) could not be classified as celt flakes. However, since 29 percent of the flakes produced in experimental celt resharpening cannot be classified as celt flakes either, all of the Bocas phase flakes can probably be considered by-products of celt reshaping.

Many of the celts, adzes, and chisels from the Aguacate Peninsula sites show evidence of resharpening by flaking, pecking, grinding, and polishing. Additional indication of celt repair activities is provided by the enormous numbers of pecking hammers found at the sites. As at La Pitahaya, these are made on exhausted or broken celts. Dense, tough stone is no more common on the Aguacate Peninsula than it is at La Pitahaya, and celts have been recycled here in exactly the same manner.

With very few exceptions, all of the stone tools used during the Bocas phase occupations were imported as finished tools. Not only was stone tool production almost entirely a specialized activity, but in addition none of it was carried on at the sites investigated. Cerro Brujo and Sitio Machuca are not large internally differentiated sites like La Pitahaya, Barriles, and Sitio Pitti-Gonzalez. Instead, they are small dispersed hamlets of perhaps a half dozen to a dozen households each. Yet they participated in a regional exchange system as fully as these large centers, since they depended on others for many of the tools needed in obtaining their livelihood.

8.5 SUMMARY AND CONCLUDING REMARKS

From 5000 to 2300 B.C., the production and maintenance of stone tools in western Panama seemed to have been household activities. In fact, until about 300 B.C., they remained household activities with minor exceptions; minor in terms of the number of tools involved. Nonetheless, beginning at around 2300 B.C., ground and polished stone tools requiring both skill and time for their making began to be substituted for chipped stone tools. After 300 B.C., households can no longer be considered self-sufficient since a significant number of the tools they used were produced by craft specialists. Moreover, these specialists were located in only a few places, which meant that celts, axes, metates, and manos had to be imported by most communities. Still, a number of simple chipped stone tools and cobble tools were produced by the households that used them. By A.D. 900, even these simple tools were rarely made or used. They were in the main replaced by tools made on blades by skilled craftsmen. Thus, in some communities like Cerro Brujo, nearly every stone tool used by the residents was imported.

Looking only at the evidence provided by the lithic assemblages, interaction between settlements during the preceramic period can only be characterized as sporadic. Beginning early in the ceramic period, this interaction intensifies to the point where it becomes an essential factor in the functioning of all communities, large and small.

To conclude, I have been concerned with documenting the existence of interaction between communities, pointing out the increasing importance of this interaction through time. I have not attempted to discuss the nature of this interaction, important though it may be, because such a discussion would quickly lead to a consideration of more than lithic assemblages. What, for example, were the commodities given in exchange for celts and metates? What did celt repairmen receive in exchange for their services? Was the exchange reciprocal like the salt for axes system described by Rappaport (1968) for the New Guinea Maring? Or were commodities accumulated and redistributed by a central authority in much the same manner as Flannery (1968b) described for parts of Mesoamerica during the Formative Period? Arriving at answers to these questions is an important goal of archaeological research (cf. Pires-Ferreira and Flannery 1976). Even though this examination of stone tool technology does not provide all the answers, it does provide some (for example, which tools are received in exchange and which are not), which is a step in the right direction.

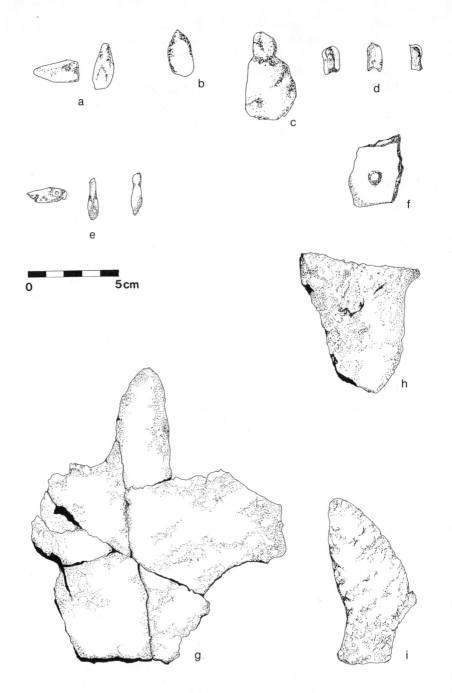

Figure 9.0-1: *Special objects from the Volcan Baru sites (see table 1 for proveniences): a-c.*
pumice objects; d,e. jade beads; f. perforated sherd; g- i. dacite laterally flaked slabs.

9.0

Miscellaneous Artifacts of Special Use

O. F. LINARES

9.1 INTRODUCTION

Practically all of the excavations reported in this volume were of domestic refuse, discarded in shell middens (at CA-3), in mounds filled-in with rocks (at IS-3), or in house floors and living areas (at BU-17). The only burials we found were placed intrusively into middens and mounds and were accompanied only by pots, celts, and other utilitarian everyday objects. Special-purpose cemeteries have been described at Barriles containing burials with lidded urns and giant metates (Stirling 1950). In addition, numerous scattered graves of both Early and Late Bugaba phases have been dug haphazardly by "huaqueros" here and there in the Volcan area. However, the objects they contained did not seem very different from those found in trash deposits. The same appears to have been true of the grave objects found in cemeteries of the San Lorenzo and Chiriqui phases (Linares 1968b) on the mainland adjacent to the Gulf and of the burials at the bottom of the trenches at IS-3. Graves have not been reported from the Bocas side, which raises the possibility that the "local" dead were thrown directly into the sea; the mutilated remains of persons (captives?) whom they cannibalized and of infants and diseased individuals were carelessly buried in the trash heaps. In short, very few if any of the objects described in this section can be assigned precise "ideotechnic" or "sociotechnic" functions (Binford 1962) even though they were obviously used on special occasions.

The category of special objects include such few items that we will describe them below, rather than in a separate report.

9.2 DESCRIPTION OF THE ARTIFACTS

I. Objects from the Volcan Baru Sites (fig. 9.0-1; table 1):

TABLE 1   SPECIAL OBJECTS FROM BU-17B, BU-45, BU-60

Figure	Object	Provenience	Context	Phase
9.0-1a	pumice object	BU-17b, cut 16 unit 3	house floor	Early Bugaba
9.0-1b	pumice object	Bu-17b, cut 7, unit 4	house floor	Early Bugaba
9.0-1c	pumice pendant (?)	BU-17b, cut 14, unit 5	below house floor	Early Bugaba
9.0-1d	stone bead (jade?)	BU-17b, cut 8, unit 3	house floor	Early Bugaba
9.0-1e	stone bead (jade)	BU-17b, cut 1, unit 6	below house floor	Early Bugaba
9.0-1f	perforated sherd	BU-17b, cut 11, unit 3	house floor	Early Bugaba
	dacite slabs	BU-17b, cut 6, unit 3	house floor	Early Bugaba
	dacite slabs	BU-17b, cut 16, unit 3	house floor	Early Bugaba
	dacite slabs	BU-17b, cut 15, unit 5	below house floor	Early Bugaba
9.0-1g	dacite slabs	BU-17b, cut 5, unit 8		Early Bugaba
	dacite slabs	BU-17b, cut 12, unit 9		Early Bugaba
9.0-1h	dacite slabs	BU-45	surface	no date
9.0-1i	dacite slabs	BU-60	surface	no date

A.   Pumic objects (fig. 9.0-1a-c): These are small oval-shaped objects (biggest is 4.5 cm long; smallest is 2.4 cm long) made from naturally occurring pumice. Their use is problematic. The largest of these objects is grooved around the top, possibly for use as a pendant.

B.   Beads of stone (jade) (fig. 9.0-1d, e): A fragment of a plain hollow, tubular bead, 1 cm in diameter, with one end ground and the other broken; the length cannot be estimated; the material looks like jadeite. The other is a nicely carved, polished, and perforated specimen made of blue-green jade; incised lines have been made on one of the narrower faces for decoration.

C.   Perforated sherd (fig. 9.0-1f): A small (.5 cm) hole has been drilled on a red-slipped sherd. Because such perforations are very rare, the likelihood is that the sherd was used as a pendant.

D.   Dacite laterally flaked slabs (fig. 9.0-1g-i): Twenty-five specimens, all fragmentary, have been described by Sheets, Rosenthal, and Ranere, as follows: Naturally flat laminar dacite has been bifacially worked into some sort of stemmed object. The most complete specimen (actually seven fragments glued together) measures 184 mm along the axis parallel to the stem and 174 mm perpendicular to this axis. The specimen is incomplete. The edges of the objects are crushed, sometimes quite heavily so. The stems, where measureable, vary from 60 to 90 mm in length, from 30 to 54 mm in width, and 8 to 16 mm in thickness. Nonstem fragments vary from 4 to 22 mm in thickness. These stemmed, apparently multipointed objects do not appear to have been used for any utilitarian purpose. The nature of the bifacially flaked and sometimes battered or crushed edges suggests that the overall shape of the objects, not the edge morphology, was of paramount importance. Hafted on the end of a long shaft, these objects may have served as some sort of emblem or staff.

Dacite slabs are found only in the large habitation and burial sites. A number of dacite waste flakes were recovered from BU-17, indicating that this was one of the sites where these implements were manufactured.

II.   Objects from La Pitahaya (IS-3) (fig. 9.0-2; table 2):

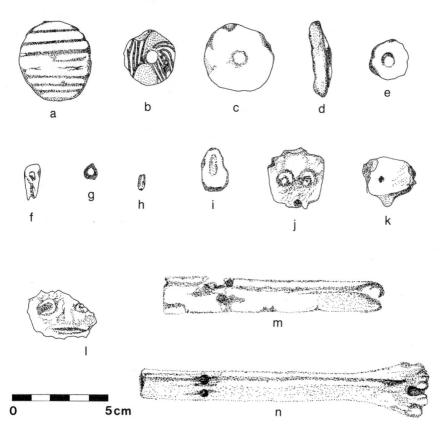

Figure 9.0-2: Special objects from La Pitahaya (see table 2 for proveniences): a-e. perforated clay disks; f-h. stone beads; i-l. miscellaneous clay objects; m. deer metatarsal (original); n. deer metatarsal (replica).

TABLE 2 SPECIAL OBJECTS FROM IS-3

Figure	Object	Provenience trench (tr.)	Context	Phase(s)
9.0–2a	nonperforated clay polychrome disk	tr. 1, cut 2, layer B	fill and trash from activity area 1	San Lorenzo Macaracas*
9.0–2b	perforated clay polychrome disk	tr. 2, cut 1, 20–30 cm	fill and trash from activity area 1	San Lorenzo and/or Chiriqui
9.0–2c	plain, perforated, large clay disk	tr. 2, cut 1, 90–100 cm	fill and trash from activity area 1	Burica (?) Macaracas
9.0–2e	plain, perforated, small clay disk	tr. 3, 50–100 cm	experimental trench; no secure context	not known
9.0–2f	tubular stone bead	tr. 1, cut 1, 100–110 cm	fill and trash from activity area 1	Burica
9.0–2g	ring bead	tr. 1, cut 2, 70–80 cm	fill and trash from activity area 1	San Lorenzo
9.0–2h	jade (?) bead	tr. 2, cut 2, 0–10 cm	fill and trash from activity area 1	Chiriqui
9.0–2i	clay adorno	tr. 1, cut 3, 90–100 cm	fill and trash from activity area 1	Burica
9.0–2j, k	clay whistle	tr. 2, cut 1, 0–10 cm	fill and trash from activity area 1	Chiriqui
9.0–2l	clay face	tr. 2, cut 1, 20–30 cm	fill and trash from activity area 1	Chiriqui
9.0–2m, n	worked bone object	tr. 2, cut 1, 100–100 cm	fill and trash from activity area 1	Burica

*Macaracas phase, Pica-Pica variety, A.D. 700–900, central region, report no. 11

A. Perforated clay disks (fig. 9.0-2a-e): These are round pottery disks of various sizes; smallest has a diameter of 2 cm; largest of 4 cm. All specimens, with the exception of one, are drilled in the middle with a small hole. The function of these flat objects is not clear, as they are not of the rounded shape associated with spindle whorls. The possibility that these disks were used ornamentally, as pendants, is suggested by the fact that two have been made out of polychrome sherds from the central provinces, (Cooke report no. 11). These sherds have been rounded off by grinding around the edges.

B. Stone beads (fig. 9.0-2f-h): Small tubular or ring-shaped beads made of stone, one of them being jade. These beads are all drilled through the middle. The jade specimen is the smallest (1 cm x ½ cm), an indication perhaps of the rarity of this material. Because it was found on the top stratum, we have surmised that it is very recent, from the end of the Chiriqui phase.

C. Miscellaneous clay objects (fig. 9.0-2i-l): These are fragments of adornos and a whistle. The most diagnostic of these objects is a small "nut-shaped" little adorno in the Bugaba style, similar to the ones occurring on pots of the Valbuena Ware in the Volcan highlands.

D. Worked bone object (fig. 9.0-2m, n): This is a metatarsal of a white-tailed deer *(Odocoileus)* with the proximal end sawed off deliberately and the distal end missing. This object was perforated with small circular holes, two on the sides and one on the top, a few centimeters from the proximal end, probably for suspension from a cord. R. Cooke (personal communication) has found roughly similar deer metapodials split longitudinally through the hinge which were and are still being used in the central provinces of Panama as huskers for removing maize grains.

III. Objects from Cerro Brujo (CA-3) (fig. 9.0-3; table 3):

TABLE 3   SPECIAL OBJECTS FROM CA-3A

Figure	Object	Provenience stratum (str.)	Context	Phase(s)
	clay pellet	cut 6H, str. A	trash, area 1	Bocas
	clay pellet	cut 6H, str. B	trash, area 1	Bocas
	clay pellet	cut 6I, str. C	trash, area 1	Aguacate
9.0-3a	clay pellet	cut 6L, str. A	trash, area 2	Bocas
	clay pellet	cut 7L, str. B	trash, area 2	Bocas
9.0-3b	clay pellet	cut 8L, str. C	trash, area 2	Aguacate
9.0-3c	clay bead	cut 6I, str. C	trash, area 1	Aguacate
9.0-3d	clay whistle	cut 8L, str. B	trash, area 2	Bocas
9.0-3e	clay whistle	cut 4H, shallow pit	trash, area 3	not certain
9.0-3f	shell trumpet	cut 7H, str. B	trash, area 1	Bocas
9.0-3g	fragment, shell trumpet	cut 8L, str. B	trash, area 2	Bocas
9.0-3h	bone pendant	cut 9L, str. B	trash, area 2	Bocas

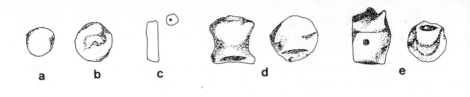

a   b   c   d   e

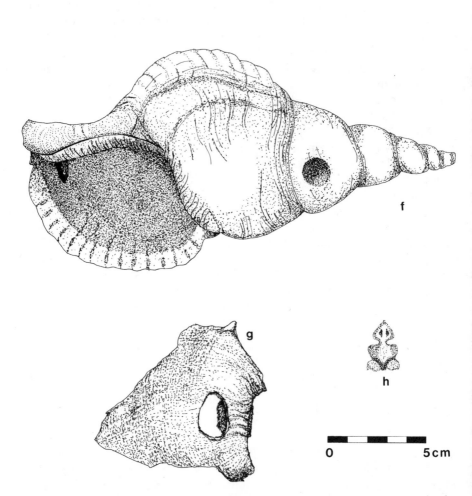

Figure 9.0-3: Special objects from Cerro Brujo (see table 3 for proveniences): a,b. clay pellet; c. clay bead; d,e. clay whistles; f. shell trumpet; g. shell trumpet fragment; h. bone pendant.

A. Clay pellets (fig. 9.0-3a, b): These are small (1.2 – 2.0 cm) round clay pellets, probably used as rattles inside the hollow legs of tripods. These kinds of vessels are very common in the Chiriqui phase pottery of that province (Linares 1968b), a small amount of which also occurs in the Bocas

phase at Cerro Brujo (ca. A.D. 900). The only explanation for the two specimens from the Aguacate phase levels (ca. A.D. 600) at Bocas is that they are
intrusive from above.

B. Clay bead (fig. 9.0-3c): This small (2 cm long x .75 cm wide) tubular
bead is perforated through the middle and covered with a red slip. It was
probably strung in some sort of necklace.

C. Clay whistles (fig. 9.0-3d, e): Both specimens are fragments of the
mouthpiece section of a whistle. They are perforated at the end with a slit,
through which the air was blown, and on the sides with either one or two
slits/holes for letting air out.

D. Shell trumpets (fig. 9.0-3f, g): The complete specimen of the "Trumpet
Triton" (*Charonia variegata*) measures 9 inches in length and is perforated
with holes 1½ cm in diameter, one in the under surface of the spire, the
other on the outer lip. It still emits a hollow sound when blown. Shell
trumpets are still important among the Guaymí Indians of the region who
use them during the *balsería* (or stick game) to summon the participants.
The other trumpet is a fragment from a different gastropod, possibly a
Strombus sp.,which has been perforated with a hole of the same size (1½
cm), but differently located, from the first specimen.

E. Bone pendant (fig. 9.0-3h): A small (2.4 cm x 1.5 cm) pendant made of
bone, carved in the shape of a small frog. It is perforated through the "neck"
portion with two small holes for suspension. A very similar frog pendant
was reported from the Chiriqui Gulf site of Las Secas (IS-11) by Linares
(1968b, p. 63).

9.3 CONCLUSIONS

Most of the special objects found in our excavations were made from local
raw materials, abundant at each of the sites. Thus, pumice objects and
laminar dacite slabs are common at BU-17, where pumice and dacite
abound, while artifacts of clay, like perforated disks and whistles, are
dominant at IS-3, which yielded large amounts of pottery. Not surprisingly,
the most distinctive artifacts found at CA-3 were shell trumpets and a bone
pendant.

On the other hand, many of the common everyday objects used by the
coastal peoples were made of foreign raw materials. For example, most of
the stone tools found at Cerro Brujo and La Pitahaya were imported
ready-made or partly finished (Ranere, section 8.4.b.). None of the hard
dense volcanic rocks employed in making these tools occur naturally on the
islands; they obviously occur in the highlands around Volcan Baru, where
large quarry sites seem to have been exploited from early (pre 200 B.C.)
times on.

PART FOUR

CULTURAL INFERENCES FROM ORGANIC REMAINS

The archaeological record of organic remains from our sites is uneven and incomplete. Whereas plant remains in the form of carbonized seeds were found in the highlands, in the deposits of the Rio Chiriqui shelters and the Volcan Baru villages, these sites did not yield any faunal remains. The reverse is true for the coastal sites, which did not yield plant remains, but did contribute substantial faunal assemblages. Poor preservation outside shell-midden contexts may explain the lack of animal bones in the highland deposits; the fact that hearths were not excavated in the coastal sites probably explains why no charred seeds were found.

While these lacunae in our records are lamentable, they are by no means crippling. Inferential evidence about the use of plants can be provided by wear-analysis of stone tools, and extrapolations about hunting and fishing can be made from modern species distributions of animals in the Panamanian mid- to high-elevation environments. In short, it is not our purpose here to discuss the numerous problems of sampling and analysis that can affect the interpretation of organic remains from archaeological sites. These problems have been treated at length in many publications by other authors. Keeping in mind that our samples may be far from perfect, we will proceed to summarize, and elaborate upon, some of the ideas presented in the sections concerned with organic remains.

The carbonized plant remains from the Rio Chiriqui shelters (section 10.2) are among the oldest (4800 B.C. – 500 B.C.) such evidence from the humid tropics of the New World. Only four species were represented in these deposits: two palms and two seasonally flowering trees. All indications are that the fruits of these trees were collected from wild, and not cultivated, populations. Even now, little human effort is exercised in selecting for large seed size in these species, although trees of *corozo* palm, *nance,* and *algarrobo* are regularly tended and occasionally propagated. As Harris (1977) points out, harvesting of tree crops may be one of the systems of food procurement that did *not* lead to agriculture. The extraordinary persistence of the same unmodified tree species from preceramic to modern times may be due to their unsuitability for domestication, as most trees are cross-pollinated and take a long time to bear fruit. However, under special circumstances, palms may have been under cultivation at the site of La Pitahaya (see below).

There is little evidence in the actual plant record for, or against, Ranere's idea, formulated on the basis of the stone tools (section 3.8), that manioc agriculture was present in the shelters by 2300 B.C. The presence of manioc cultivation elsewhere in lower Central America is somewhat ambiguous (Linares 1979). Pickersgill and Heiser (1977) have also pointed out that the evidence for manioc pollen in Panama in cores dated to the beginning of the Christian era (Bartlett and Barghoorn 1973) is not conclusive. Apparently, the pollen of wild Euphorbiaceae may not have been rigorously eliminated from the identifications. Be that as it may, Ranere's suggestion that agriculture was present in the shelters by 2300 B.C., and that it probably involved manioc, should be seriously entertained. Because the soft parts of this tuber do not preserve well (nor do they caramelize like those of sweet potatoes), it would have been surprising if manioc had been found in the Rio Chiriqui shelters, even if it were of overwhelming importance.

The next plant remains discussed by Smith (section 10.3) were from the house floor (layers 3 and 4) of the Cerro Punta oval dwelling, dated at A.D. 400–600. According to Smith, the numerous cobs of *Zea mays* found in these deposits were fairly uniform in size. He also found only one species of bean, *Phaseolus vulgaris*, represented in the collections. We have tentatively proposed (section 16.0) a rapid radiation of maize- and bean-growing peoples all over western Panama several centuries before and after the Christian era.

Galinat's observation (section 11.0) that the Cerro Punta maize was a relic descendant of a much earlier southward spread of a Zea cultivar corroborates the statement by Pickersgill and Heiser (1977, p. 807), that the "archaeological data are thus compatible with the idea that maize agriculture spread gradually from Mesoamerica to South America by an overland route." While both Galinat and Smith classify the Cerro Punta maize as intermediate in type between Nal-tel and Pollo, they disagree slightly on their areas of origin. Smith mentions a center for development of Pollo in northwest South America, while Galinat regards Pollo, not as a separate species, but as an offshoot of the Mesoamerican Nal-tel/Chapalote races. In any case, the important point Galinat makes is that the low condensation (i.e., compaction of the rachis) giving the Volcan maize the same quality of hardness found in Pollo, may have been separately evolved in response to cold and wet conditions. Thus, there is no reason to believe that the Central American maize, including that of Panama, shows introgression from the South American Pollo race, as previously suggested by several investigators (a review of this issue is found in Linares 1979).

Other plants identified by Smith from the Cerro Punta deposits include the ubiquitous palms, the *algarrobo* (*Hymenaea* sp.), and, possibly, the sweet potato (*Ipomoea batatas*). Some doubts have been expressed (Pickersgill and Heiser 1977) as to the correctness of the identification of Ipomoea pollen in the sections of the cores from Gutun Lake in Panama analyzed by Bartlett and Barghoorn (1974) and dated to A.D. 200. The Cerro Punta sweet potato, however, fits in well in time with this evidence.

Finally, a word about the few plants recovered from La Pitahaya (none were found at Cerro Brujo). Smith (10.5) suggests that the palm trees growing here in pre-Hispanic times were being cultivated. This fact corroborates the general impression, given by the faunal evidence, that intensification and specialization of resources had taken place to some degree on this island by the first millennium A.D., if not before. Certainly this was the most densely populated of the sites investigated, and the one with the most intensive form of cultivation. This is important in view of Boserup's (1965) theories about population pressures discussed later on (section 16.0).

Sections 12.0 and 13.0 are concerned with the analysis of faunal remains from the coastal sites. The summary and interpretations offered below extend the comparisons to include fish populations under natural conditions, as well as archaeological faunal assemblages from other areas.

1. A Comparison of the Fish Fauna from Both Coasts

Some knowledge of natural conditions is required before we can make valid comparisons between archaeological marine faunal assemblages on both sides of the Isthmus. Leaving aside the important question whether the samples at CA-3 and IS-3 are large enough to allow making confident statements about cultural preferences for certain species, we will mention other, perhaps more interesting, factors concerning differences in the natural distribution of species on both sides of the Isthmus.

With respect to aquatic animals, it is interesting to note that the same species do not always occur on both oceans, or they occur with different abundance. The most obvious example is the manatee *(Trichechus)* which, as everyone knows, occurs only on the Atlantic side. Therefore, its presence in the sample from CA-3, but not in the sample from IS-3, should not surprise anyone. The tarpon *(Elopidae)*, however, presents a different problem. It occurs in the Pacific, and thus might be expected to occur at IS-3, even in as low numbers as at CA-3 (4.6 percent of the aquatic fauna biomass). However, experts tell us that it is one of the few species that came across when the Panama Canal was built in 1914; before then, there were no tarpons on the Pacific side (R. Rubinoff, personal communication). Hence, there were none in the IS-3 deposits.

Why other fish species occur at one but not the other coastal site is more difficult to explain. For example, the Serranidae (groupers) comprises 57.5 percent of the fish biomass at CA-3, but 0 percent at IS-3; similarly, the Lutjanidae (snapper) is 7.9 percent of the CA-3 biomass but only a negligible 0.8 percent of the IS-3 biomass. It would be tempting to conclude that groupers and snappers are simply more abundant in the Atlantic than in Pacific waters; yet we know this is not necessarily true. On the other hand, it is true of the snook family (Centropomidae) and of the barracuda family (Sphyraenidae); these fish are more abundant in the Atlantic, both in number of species and probably in number of individuals within each species (R. Rubinoff, personal communication). Because snooks and barracudas occur more frequently in the CA-3 deposits than in those from IS-3, their "natural" and "cultural" abundances are in agreement, unlike the groupers and snappers.

In fact, most of the frequencies of fish in our samples are also in agreement with their natural biomass. For example, the following species are represented in much higher numbers at the Pacific site of IS-3 than at CA-3: the drums or *corvina* (Sciaenidae), the sea catfish (Ariidae), the tuna and mackerel (Scombridae), and the puffers (Tetradontidae). These species are naturally much more common in the Pacific waters of the Isthmus than in those of the Atlantic (R. Rubinoff, personal communication). This is also true of sharks (A. Rodaniche, personal communication) which, like the other species just mentioned, are also more common in the IS-3 than in the CA-3 deposits. Hence, the general tendency was for the people on either coast to utilize the most common species available, rather than to search for rare forms.

It may be interesting to ask why some species should be naturally more abundant in the waters, and hence in the archaeological deposits, of one or the other coast. The answer seems to reside in the different inshore and littoral environments. While coral reefs are well developed all along the Atlantic coast of Panama, they are less well developed — except perhaps around the offshore islands of Secas and Contreras (Glynn 1972) — in the Gulf of Chiriqui. In particular, "the reefs around Paridas (in the Gulf of Chiriqui) are small and patchy in contrast to those in the Atlantic" (P. Glynn, personal communication). On the other hand, the Gulf has more developed brackish-water estuaries, with extensive mangrove formations, than Almirante Bay. Hence, reef fishes, including the grouper and snapper, are rare or missing at IS-3, while shallow, turbid-water species, such as marine catfishes, and to a lesser extent *corvina* and puffers, abound.

2. Comparison with Other Marine Faunal
Assemblages in Other Areas

So far, our comparisons have involved marine faunal assemblages from sites on both coasts of the Isthmus. It may be instructive to compare assemblages from the same coast of lower Central America to see if they are more similar. On the Atlantic side, the nearest site yielding a quantifiable faunal collection comparable to that of CA-3 is the Selin Farm site in the department of Colon, in northeastern Honduras (Healey 1978), which is more than 1,000 kilometers northwest of CA-3. While at both sites the pecomorph fishes (the grouper/bass, snappers, snook, grunts, and jacks) were very important, the jack *(Caranx hippos)* alone constituted over half (53 percent) of the total number of bony fish in the Selin sample. At CA-3, jacks made up less than 1/10th (about 8 percent of the minimum number of individuals — MNI) of the sample from both periods. On the other hand, snappers, snook, and groupers are more common at CA-3 (16 percent, 27 percent, and 10 percent of the MNI) than at Selin (6 percent and 8 percent and 5 percent of the MNI). Thus, fishing at Selin appears to have been a specialized endeavor, centered on the jack, a highly gregarious, schooling fish often found in offshore waters. The fishing system of Cerro Brujo was more generalized, with at least four important bony fish represented, all of them reef species.

On the Pacific, the nearest site with a well-analyzed faunal sample comparable to that of La Pitahaya is Sitio Sierra (Ag-3), 12 kilometers from the Parita Bay coast, on the shores of the Santa Maria river in the central region of Panama, about 400 kilometers by sea from IS-3. This site was excavated by R. Cooke, and its faunal assemblage was studied by E. Wing. While two marine catfish species constituted an important component of the IS-3 aquatic faunal assemblage (40 percent of the MNI), at Sitio Sierra five catfishes (four marine and one riverine) dominate the assemblage (70 percent of the MNI). On the other hand, sharks and rays are more common, both in species and in numbers, at IS-3 (13.5 percent of the MNI) than at Sitio Sierra (3.5 percent). These differences indicate a greater degree of specialization on a single species at Ag-3, and more reliance on terrestrial forms.

3. The Use of Marine Versus Terrestrial Resources in the Coastal Sites

It may also be interesting to explore the degree to which the inhabitants of CA-3 and IS-3 were oriented to the faunal resources from the ocean vis-à-vis those from the land. These differences are summarized in table 1.

In the sample from CA-3, fish constituted about two-thirds of the total faunal assemblage (67 percent of the MNI), while at IS-3 they constituted 90 percent of the assemblage. Conversely, at CA-3 land mammals constituted 22 percent of the assemblage, while at IS-3 they constituted only 4 percent. From these data alone one would conclude that the inhabitants of La Pitahaya were relatively more ocean-oriented in their search for proteins than the CA-3 inhabitants. When usable meat, rather than minimum numbers, becomes our unit of comparison, however, and when all the ocean and all the terrestrial animals are taken into account, a different picture emerges: the ratio of meat from the ocean versus meat from the land is higher at CA-3 than IS-3 (namely 3:1 or 76 percent: 24 percent at CA-3, but only about 2:1 or 65 percent: 35 percent at IS-3). This is highly significant. A contingency table X^2 comparison of the usable meat derived from the ocean versus the usable meat derived from terrestrial and fresh water resources at CA-3 and IS-3 is given in table 2.

The change in relationship between the relative importance of numbers of animals and meat they may have provided, first noted by E. Wing, is related to the fact that at CA-3 marine organisms (manatee and sea turtles) are common, while at IS-3 a larger terrestrial animal (deer), is more abundant. Even the bony fish from La Pitahaya were on the average smaller than the bony fish in the Cerro Brujo sample (E. Wing, section 13.0). This in itself is interesting in view of the popular, though untested, impression that fish are on the whole larger in the Pacific than in the Atlantic waters of the Isthmus. At IS-3, the smaller size of the fish, vis-à-vis those from CA-3, may be related to their probably having been caught in nets placed across the mouth of estuaries.

A final word should be said about the molluskan fauna from our archaeological sites on both Panamanian coasts (section 14.0). It is obvious that shellfish gathering was a more important activity at CA-3 than at IS-3. Furthermore, at CA-3 five different species of bivalves, forming extensive beds in nature, were harvested, while at IS-3 no one species was consistently utilized. Since the natural biomass of mollusks may well be higher in the Pacific than in the Atlantic, their scarcity at IS-3 can be explained only in terms of cultural preference for other foods and/or scheduling conflicts, especially

149

with other subsistence activities such as farming. We should also keep in mind the argument "that marine food resources are inferior to terrestrial resources, especially mammals, both in terms of human labor investment and in terms of protein yield" (Osborn 1977, pp. 160–161). If by hunting the white-tailed deer on the nearby mainland, by cultivating the oil and protein-rich palms, and by fishing catfish in large numbers the inhabitants of La Pitahaya were meeting their protein requirements, it is understandable why they did not waste time in less productive endeavors.

TABLE 1   A COMPARISON OF MARINE AND TERRESTRIAL FAUNA
FROM CA-3 AND IS-3

	CA-3 (both periods)				IS-3 (all periods)			
	MNI	%	Usable meat (kg)	%	MNI	%	Usable meat (kg)	%
OCEAN AND BRACKISH								
Fish (bony and cartilaginous)	299	.67	1,076.86	.41	297	.90	377.06	.52
Sea turtles	25	.056	641.40	.24	4	.01	95.85	.13
Sea cow	3	.007	287.0	.11	0	0	0	0
TERRESTRIAL AND FRESHWATER[1]								
Mammals[2]	99	.22	543.16	.21	12	.04	212.132	.29
Reptiles (turtles, iguana, crocodiles)	7	.02	87.34	.03	16	.05	40.9	.06
Amphibians (frogs)	10	.02	0.5	.0002	0	0	0	0

1. excluding a few birds

2. excluding rats

TABLE 2   A 2 X 2 CONTINGENCY TABLE
COMPARISON OF THE USABLE
MEAT DERIVED FROM THE
OCEAN VS. USABLE MEAT
DERIVED FROM THE LAND
AT CA-3 AND IS-3

	CA-3	IS-3	Chi-square scores; d.f. 1, L .05, critical value = 3.84
From ocean	2005	473	$\chi^2 = 35.72$
Terrestrial and freshwater	631	253	

10.0

Plant Remains from the Chiriqui Sites and Ancient Vegetational Patterns

C. E. SMITH

10.1 INTRODUCTION

Plant remains from wet tropical habitats are thought to be rare in the archaeological record for several reasons, the most important being the axiomatic belief that biological materials disintegrate rapidly in this sort of climate. While this is partly true, the information included in this section contradicts this widely held belief. Once plant tissue has become carbonized, it is virtually impossible to destroy it by chemical means. It is nearly insoluble in all common solvents including water. Careful recovery techniques can yield a very fine sample of plants used at archaeological sites which have always had a warm, wet climate since the time of deposition.

The most ancient plant material recovered from preceramic shelters in Panama has persisted under difficult climatic conditions for at least 6,000 years. We will begin our discussion with that material. The other sections cover more recent plant remains from the Volcan Baru villages (A.D. 200 to 700) and from La Pitahaya (A.D. 700 to 1100).

10.2 PLANT REMAINS FROM THE RIO CHIRIQUI SHELTERS

The Rio Chiriqui drainage has its tributaries in the mountains dividing the northern Bocas province from the southern province of Chiriqui (Ranere, section 3.2). Because the trade winds in Panama blow from the northeast, these mountains are a continental divide and something of a vegetational divide. On the northern or Bocas side, the trade winds bring in much moisture so that the vegetation at high elevations is montane rain forest, grading into lowland rain forest downslope. On the southern side, montane forest and rain forest are restricted to the top; downslope in the rain shadow, the forest becomes progressively more seasonal with higher proportions of deciduous trees.

It is on the southern slopes at fairly high elevations that the sites of Casita de Piedra (QS-1) and Trapiche (QS-2) are located (section 3.3) At the present time, they are within easy access of a trail which crosses the divide. Casita de Piedra is near the junction of the Casita de Piedra and Chiriqui rivers, at an elevation of about 700 meters. Trapiche is only about a kilometer downstream along the Rio Chiriqui. At the present time, much of the original forest of the area has been removed, but enough remains to judge that the forest around the rock shelters was once a mixture of montane forest and seasonal forest with a much higher proportion of deciduous trees.

The occupational sequence of the shelters has been presented by Ranere in section 3.4. To summarize, the Talamancan phase (4600 B.C. to 2300 B.C.) is preceramic and, probably, preagricultural as well. The Boquete phase (2300 B.C. to 300 B.C.) is preceramic but, according to Ranere (section 3.8.a.), may be agricultural, probably based on tree and root-crop cultivation.

Fortunately, all throughout the preceramic sequence the occupants of the shelters lost fully as much plant material in their fires as did their more settled brethren of later periods. Thus we have something of a record of their plant food preferences during four thousand years. This record is summarized in table 1.

10.2.a. Seed Fragments and Problems of Species Identification

Because of differences in the nature and thickness of the excavation strata, more specimens were recovered from some strata than from others. Furthermore, only those remains of seeds that were sufficiently large to be measured were counted. Smaller fragments are less securely identified than larger ones and, in some instances, may have broken off from the same fruits as the latter. Inasmuch as it is highly fortuitous that fragments fell into the campfire in just the right position to become carbonized without turning to ash, it is highly improbable that these counts bear any relationship to the actual number of fruits consumed. If we add to this the number of fragments that were probably discarded when the firepits were cleaned, it quickly becomes apparent that the number of fragments has no significance beyond indicating the plants locally available and desirable for food.

The species of plants represented in the Chiriqui rock shelters show a remarkable continuity during a long period of time. From the earliest levels to the latest levels, the plant remains are dominated by fragments of palm seeds. In many levels in both the QS-1 and QS-2 deposits, the next most conspicuous element is seed of *Byrsonima* sp. ("nance") (fig. 10.0-1). *Hymenaea courbaril* ("algarrobo") (fig. 10.0-2) occurs in only two places: the uppermost stratum B of Casita de Piedra and the lowermost stratum E of the Trapiche Shelter. Other, unidentifiable fragments are present in very small proportions.

The palm fragments are obviously important, but it is necessary to eliminate any misconceptions that may arise concerning the species of palms in use. The remains from which the identifications have been made

Species	Shelter	Excavation level	No. Fragments measurable	Length mm	Width mm	Diam. or Range Diams. mm	Mean Diam. mm	Comment
Boquete Phase (2300–300 B.C.)								
Acrocomia sp.	Casita	B	2 kernel			9.0	9.0	small
Scheelia sp.	Casita	B	1 kernel	13	4.5			
	Casita	C	11 kernal	11.5–19.0	5.5–10.5			
	Casita	D	1 kernel	16.5	9.0			
Acrocomia sp. or *Scheelia* sp.	Casita	B	11 shell			9.8–19.2	13.0	
	Casita	C	46 shell			7.4–25.0	15.64	
	Casita	D	43 shell			7.4–35.6	17.1	
	Trapiche	B	10 shell			8.2–22.0	16.1	
	Trapiche	C	26 shell			6.8–26.6	17.7	
Byrsonima sp.	Casita	B	2 seed			5.5–6.5	6.0	unusually large
	Casita	D	1 seed			6.0		
Hymenaea courbaril	Casita	B	2 seed	11.0–12.0	5.0–6.0			thickness 3.5–4.0
Talamancan Phase (4600–2300 B.C.)								
Acrocomia sp.	Casita	E	3 kernel	11.0–19.0	3.0–11.0	12.0–17.0	15.0	
Scheelia sp.	Trapiche	D	4 kernels	15.0	7.0			
	Trapiche	E	1 kernel					
Acrocomia sp. or *Scheelia* sp.	Casita	E	118 shell			6.4–34.0	14.0	
	Casita	F	60 shell			7.6–15.0	13.9	
	Casita	G	8 shell			10.0–16.2	11.9	
	Trapiche	D	106 shell			6.0–27.6	15.4	
	Trapiche	E	3 shell			13.0–20.6	17.6	
Byrsonima sp.	Casita	E	3 seeds			5.0–6.5	5.5	
	Casita	F	13 seeds			5.0–6.0	5.4	
	Casita	G	5 seeds			4.5–5.5	5.1	
	Trapiche	D	4 seeds			4.5–6.0	5.2	
	Trapiche	E	20 seeds			4.0–6.0	5.1	
Hymenaee courbaril	Trapiche	E	1 cotyledon	9.0	7.0			length incomplete

Figure 10.0-1: Leaves and fruits of Byrsonima crassifolia *(nance).*

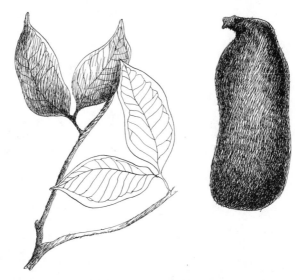

Figure 10.0-2: Leaves and fruit of Hymenaea courbaril *(algarrobo).*

consist either of fragments of the hard and durable seed coat, or fragments of kernels. In no instance in the carbonized material was a whole palm fruit recovered. Thus, the identification is made in part by eliminating those species of palms which the fragments cannot represent. Fortunately, this eliminates many species of palms that are not native to Panama. However, it leaves us with several possibilities (Bailey 1943 a and b). From among these, many species may again be eliminated because they are not known to

Figure 10.0-3: Drawing of palm fruit Acrocomia vinifera *(corozo pacora).*

Figure 10.0-4: Drawing of palm fruit Scheelia zonensis *(corozo gunzo).*

grow in the area of Chiriqui province near the rock shelters. Among the remaining possibilities, the best candidates from an ethnographic standpoint are the two species known as *Corozo pacora* (fig. 10.0-3) and *Corozo gunzo* (fig. 10.0-4), used traditionally by the mestizo and by the Guaymí Indians of the area. The former, which bears spherical fruit, is *Acrocomia* cf. *vinifera* Oerst, while the latter, which bears ellipsoidal fruit, is *Scheelia zonensis* Bailey (fig. 10.0-5a,b).

All larger fragments of palm fruit coat were measured, and the diameters calculated. An inspection of the figures obtained showed that the diameters did not clearly cluster at any point other than around 13 mm with a secondary peak at 16 mm (the number of fragments was plotted against the diameters, disregarding mm fractions). From a series of measurements on kernels of present-day fruit of *Acrocomia* from Chiriqui, we obtained an average diameter of 23.2 mm. Similarly, for modern *Scheelia* kernels we obtained an average length of 42.7 mm and an average diameter of 21.2 mm. Because changes in the dimensions of palm fruit fragments due to changes in the curvature of the fragments because of shrinkage are unknown, errors in measurements may have been inevitable. However, a certain consistency in the results tends to establish the general validity of the measurements.

Several partial palm kernels were recovered in sufficiently large pieces to provide measurements of length, width, and thickness for *Scheelia* kernels and of diameters for *Acrocomia* kernels. The *Acrocomia* kernels range from 9 mm to 17 mm in diameter, for an average diameter of 12.6 mm. This is approximately one half the average diameter of modern dried fruit of this palm for Chiriqui. The *Scheelia* kernel fragments vary in diameter from 3 mm to 11 mm (average is 7.6 mm) and in length from 11 to 19 mm (average is 14.3 mm). The average diameter of the fresh fruit is 21.1 mm, as we have seen, making the archaeological diameters only somewhat more than a

Figure 10.0-5: Photograph of palm fruit racimes: a. Acrocomia; *b.* Scheelia.

third of the modern fruit; the average length of the modern *Scheelia* fruit is 42.7 mm, making the length of the archaeological fragments almost exactly one third of the modern sample. The archaeological sample fits so well proportionally that I feel the identification is correct.

The problem of size difference between ancient and modern fruits cannot be met by assuming that the seeds came from other species of palms native to the area. Species of several genera, largely *Bactris, Chamaedora,* and *Geonoma,* are known from Chiriqui, but they invariably have smaller seeds than the diameters obtained from the archaeological specimens. Hence the size difference must be due primarily to shrinkage during carbonization.

Nowadays, both the *Acrocomia* and the *Scheelia* palms are saved when encountered during clearing operations. Their fruits are not only eaten extensively, but the long fronds of *Acrocomia* are also used in thatching. The abundance of *Scheelia* kernel fragments recovered from the shelters, as compared with *Acrocomia* fragments, may reflect something about their relative hardness and the manner in which their fruit was eaten. Fruits of the *Scheelia* palm nowadays are peeled first, then sucked for their watery and sweet flesh; the kernels, which have such hard seed coats that only agoutis and squirrels can eat them, are usually discarded. The *Acrocomia* fruit, on the other hand, is seldom consumed for its flesh. The whole fruit is usually boiled, peeled, and then the soft-coated seed or kernel is cracked; the white flesh inside of it is eaten as it is, or mashed down further to make *chicha* or to extract the oil.

While it would be tempting to speculate on the beginnings of cultivation for these two species, the evidence from the diameters derived from the palm fruit remains is not conclusive. In Casita de Piedra (QS-1) the mean diameters for the reconstructed fruits is given in table 2.

The gradation from small to large upward in the QS-1 deposit may

TABLE 2   MEAN DIAMETERS OF PALM FRUITS FROM THE SHELTERS

	Casita				Trapiche		
Stratum	Mean Diameter mm	Range Diameters mm	C^{14} Dates B.C.	Stratum	Mean Diameter mm	Range Diameter mm	C^{14} Dates B.C.
B	13.05	9.8–19.2	940	B	16.06	8.2–22.0	350
C	15.64	7.4–25.0	2125	C	17.7	8.8–26.6	1920
D	17.1	7.4–35.6	2135	D	15.42	6.0–27.6	
E	14.04	6.4–34.0	3845	E	17.6	13.0–20.6	{ 2735 3900
F	13.92	7.6–25.0	3730				
G	11.92	10.0–16.2	4610				

actually indicate a selection for fruit size in planted trees. However, the comparison figures for Trapiche Shelter (QS-2) (table 2) do not support this at all. Stratum E at Trapiche has fruit fragments with a mean diameter within 0.1 mm of the largest mean for any stratum. Hence there is no clear evidence that selection for cultivation has resulted in fruit enlargement in the latter periods.

The next most important plant material found in the shelters is the carbonized seed of *Byrsonima* ("nance" in Panama, "nanche" in some parts of Mexico). This member of the Malpighiaceae family is a common weedy shrub or small tree on the dry Pacific slope of North America, from southern Mexico to Panama, and must have grown in the vicinity of the shelters. In Panama, *Byrsonima* trees flower at the end of the rainy season and fruit between January and April at the height of the dry season. Although, like the palms, *Byrsonima* could theoretically have been under cultivation in this climatic zone, at present it is very little cultivated and does not appear to be highly selected for. Furthermore, the fragments that were clearly identifiable and measurable all fall within a close range in size so that means of diameters range from about 5.1 mm to 5.4 mm. The seed size of currently available specimens collected from wild plants does not vary significantly from this. It appears that nance fruits, which are slightly acid and can be eaten raw or cooked, were locally collected from native plants. In general, the identification has been left as *Byrsonima* sp. It is almost certainly *Byrsonima crassifolia,* although other species have been recognized in the genus and might have been present in the original vegetation rather than the more weedy *B. crassifolia.* I have no information on the seed size of the other species and, therefore, I shall leave the seeds without specific identification.

The only other identifiable material from the two shelters is leguminous cotyledons of *Hymenaea courbaril.* Toward the end of the dry season, numerous large pods are produced on the "algarrobo" and locally collected for the sweet, mealy pulp around the seeds. Currently, this may be eaten directly or made into refrescos or fermented beverages. Presumably, the seeds of algarrobo were discards from fruits used for similar purposes during the occupations of the rock shelters. *Hymenaea* still grows in the deciduous forest of the Pacific slope of Panama near the shelters. The few archaeological seeds recovered probably bear little relationship to the amount actually used but, even so, it is doubtful that this was ever a major item of food.

10.2.b. Significance of the Plant Remains from the Rio Chiriqui Shelters

Altogether the carbonized plant material was sparse at both Casita de Piedra (QS-1) and Trapiche Shelter (QS-2), but it is important. For the first time we have an indisputable record of the food supply of preceramic peoples living in a deciduous forest of tropical America covering a period of 4,000 years. During the Talamancan phase (4600 B.C. to 2300 B.C.), these people may have been only moving through the area, relying on local resources for food. By the Boquete phase (2300 B.C.), sedentary groups were certainly living in the area and clearing the forest, most probably for cultivation (section 3.8). However, the shelters may have continued to be used by transients. Even now, the QS-1 shelter is used as an overnight stopping place for people walking across the mountains along the Third of November Trail.

The plant remains are remarkably uniform from bottom to top of the deposits. The major plant food utilized was seeds of palms belonging to two species, *Corozo gunzo* (*Scheelia zonensis* Bailey) and *Corozo pacora* (*Acrocomia* cf. *vinifera* Oerst). Palms supplied carbohydrates, vitamins, and possibly oil. The next most plentiful plant remains were seeds of *Byrsonima* cf. *crassifolia*, "nance," which is rich in vitamins, especially vitamin C, and in minerals. The only other identifiable plant parts were cotyledons from seeds of *Hymenaea courbaril*, the "algarrobo." In addition to providing carbohydrates, *Hymenaea* is also one of the richest sources of calcium and phosphorous of the fruits native to the upper Rio Chiriqui region. If the fruits of palms, nance, and algarrobo were consumed together, they would have provided a well-balanced diet, except for proteins which we presume came from animal sources.

The fact that no other remains of wild food plants were recovered is no indication that other plant foods were not utilized, however. Foliage of some plants almost certainly was used as greens and it is highly probable that some starchy roots were also utilized, without being preserved. Furthermore, a number of forest fruits were probably eaten on the spot.

Inasmuch as the trees represented in the plant remains are normally present in the dry forest of the Pacific slope of Chiriqui at the present time, they indicate that there has been no major change in climate over the period of time represented by the shelter deposits.

10.3 PLANT REMAINS FROM CERRO PUNTA (BU-17)

Excavations in the Cerro Punta area have yielded a sample of plant material from a habitation floor of an oval dwelling (locality b; activity area 1; blocks 3, 5, 15; layers 3 and 4) which has been bracketed by radiocarbon (C[14]) dates between A.D. 200 and 400 (sections 4.3 and 7.8). Additional plant remains were found where floors were not encountered, but most of the material represents household debris from the oval dwelling which was thrown out during housecleaning.

The plant remains include several species that are obviously cultivated. Neither maize nor beans are known to be naturally distributed under the climatic conditions prevalent at the Cerro Punta site. The fragments of palm fruit may have been gathered from wild trees, or they may represent trees which were purposely planted and cultivated. The charred fragment of cane and the seed of a leguminous tree were almost certainly gathered from wild plants.

10.3.a.   Cultivated Plant Remains (fig. 10.0-6)

Fifty-four out of a total of 64 *Zea mays* cobs were found within the Cerro Punta house-floor layers. The rest came from two widely separated localities (blocks 7 and 14). The maize specimens have been examined by Dr. Walton C. Galinat (section 11.0), who reports them as belonging to a type intermediate between the races Nal-tel and Pollo. Altogether 62 cobs were sufficiently intact to count the row number, which Galinat describes as 8- to 10-rowed ears. Rachis diameters ranged from 6 to 11 mm. Mean row number is 8.4 and mean rachis diameter is 7.1 mm. In terms of variation in maize, the Panamanian maize is relatively uniform. In Peru or in Mexico, maize is frequently much more variable in row number and in rachis diameter. It is unlikely that this uniformity was a result of the Cerro Punta peoples being isolated from regular communication with other areas. If anything, it suggests the opposite: a rapid radiation of maize-carrying people or of a maize-growing pattern into western Panama a few centuries before and after the Christian era (section 16.0). The identification of the races of maize in the Volcan area this late in time as Nal-tel or Pollo may indicate a conservatism in accepting additional varieties from outside areas, especially if these are the best adapted races for the cool but wet Cerro Punta climate. Whatever the case, this is the first recovery of prehistoric maize from the important Isthmian area and it is significant that it is the Pollo/Nal-tel derivative of the Chapalote/Nal-tel complex. Inasmuch as the center of development for Pollo is in the northern Andes, the implication is that the Panamanian maize was derived from South America rather than Mesoamerica.

From the amount of carbonized cob fragments recovered, it is obvious that maize was an important part of the carbohydrate portion of the diet of these people. The amount of carbonized cob material furthermore indicates that dry cobs may have been used as fuel for cooking fires.

Another important cultivated plant of the Cerro Punta site is the common bean. A number of charred fragments of beans from the floor of the dwelling (activity area 1) and from a deep hearth (area 3, block 7) were examined by Dr. Lawrence Kaplan, who comments, "The material is clearly *P. vulgaris* but in view of the similarity of the Guitarrero Cave and Pichasca collection to Mesoamerican varieties, I could not say whether the Panama beans are

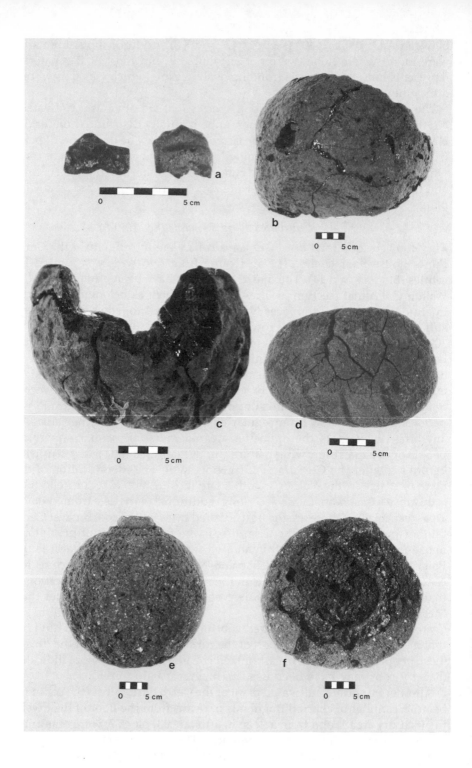

Mesoamerican or highland Andean" (Kaplan, personal communication). A column sample from the floor of the dwelling yielded 15 additional bean fragments of which two were too small to measure. The measurements of the others are given in table 3.

TABLE 3   MEASUREMENTS OF BEAN COTYLEDONS FROM BU-17, CERRO PUNTA

(In millimeters)

Provenience (dwelling-floor units)	Length	Width	Thickness
3	8.0	4.5	2.0
3	7.0	4.5	2.0
3	7.5	4.0	2.0
3	8.0	4.5	2.0
3	7.0	4.0	2.0
3 (whole bean)	9.0	5.0	3.5
2*	10.0	4.0	2.0
?**	10.0	7.0	4.0 + (probably whole bean)
?**	9.7	4.5	—

*Edges of cotyledon inrolled and width extrapolated.

**Measurements furnished by L. Kaplan.

The uniformity of the measurements indicates that only a single variety of common bean is involved in these remains. This is somewhat unusual (often several varieties of common bean are utilized in an area or they may even be intercropped in the same field) and may perhaps be due to the same factors as those involved in maintaining uniformity in the maize remains. The number of fragments suggests that the common bean was an important dietary item for the household.

Figure 10.0-6: Plant remains from the Volcan sites: a. When maize cobs burn, the softer, less consolidated tissue becomes ash more quickly than the dense tissue of the cupules shown here. b. A reconstructed palm kernel measuring 30 mm in diameter has probably expanded during the carbonization process. c. At 24 mm in diameter, this reconstructed fragment of palm kernel is more nearly the average size for the outer diameter of modern corozo pacora fruits, but it is probably the expanded remains of a smaller than average fruit. Note that both of these kernels came from spherical fruit like that borne by Acrocomia. *d. The outer surface of a carbonized cotyledon of* Hymenaea courbaril *from BU-17; e. cast of an entire corozo pacora fruit from BU-24 showing plastic material forming the cast and the point of attachment of the spherical fruit; f. palm fruit cast from BU-24 split in half to show preservation of fleshy layer of fruit, dense shell of seed, and representation of kernel at the center.*

10.3.b.   Other Plant Remains

The most common carbonized fragments other than the obvious fragments of maize and beans were the remains of carbonized palm fragments. In some cases, a sufficiently large fragment of the dense outer seed coat is preserved so that an estimate of the diameter of the fruit can be derived. In two cases, the specimens consisted of fragments of the carbonized inner meat of the palm fruit. One from the floor (cut 5, unit 3) measured 2.4 cm in diameter after reconstruction. The other from fill above the floor (cut 5, unit 2) measured 3 cm in diameter after reconstruction. Error during reconstruction may have resulted in an erroneous diameter, because diameters derived from shell fragments are only 1.14 cm and 1.5 cm for two samples. Another explanation lies in the probable differential shrinkage between dense outer shell tissue and softer, oily palm fruit meat during the carbonization process. It is also possible that different species of palms are indicated by the difference in diameters, but I find the same difficulty with this argument as I did before. As I mentioned previously (section 10.2.a.), in Chiriqui province two *Corozo* palms are currently saved during clearing operations: *Acrocomia vinifera* Oerst, known locally as *Corozo pacora*, and *Scheelia zonensis* Bailey known locally as *Corozo gunzo*. The spherical seeds of *Corozo pacora* average 2.32 cm in diameter. The diameter of the elliptical seeds of *Corozo gunzo* averages 2.12 cm, but the length of these seeds averages 4.27 cm.

The diameter of the first archaeological specimen mentioned above could place this as *Corozo pacora*. The second is much larger than the average size for the *Corozo pacora* seeds from the modern individual measured.

A single leguminous seed, 1.8 cm long and 1.1 cm wide, was found in cut 5, unit 4. It is clearly a seed of *Hymenaea courbaril* L., or algarrobo. As the sweet, mealy pulp around the seeds is still eaten, we can assume that the archaeological seed represents a pod that was gathered for the pulp.

Perhaps the most intriguing specimen found comes from below the floor of the oval dwelling. It is the completely charred end of a rhizome or tuber which tapers from one end to the other. The open spaces in the carbon were probably formed during the carbonization. The carbon between is dense and the broken surface has a glassy luster. Similar bubbling and formation of dense glassy char results from burning sugar. Usually maize kernels have sufficient sugar so that carbonized maize kernels have a characteristic bubbly texture which is like a miniature of the structure of this specimen. The only rhizome or tuber with which I am acquainted which has sufficient sugar to char in this way is sweet potato *(Ipomoea batatas)*. Thus, while it cannot be proven, I suspect that the fragment is a small burned portion of sweet potato and that sweet potato formed a regular part of the cultivated food supply.

10.4   PLANT REMAINS FROM BARRILES (BU-24)

The few remains from this site date to about A.D. 600. They were recovered from a column taken out for flotation from an old latrine hole, about 20 meters north of block 1, in the general area where platforms and anthropo-morphic stone statues were once standing (Stirling 1950). (For a description of the site and its chronology, see sections 4.3, 4.4, and report no. 5.)

The evidence for plant material from the Barriles site is very unusual. While some small fragments of carbonized plant material were recovered (largely flecks of wood charcoal), all of the large, recognizable plant parts are casts of the original organic material. The material which forms the casts is not a uniform plastic, which is the normal cast-forming substance when a plant part rots away and the mold is filled, nor is it a crystalline material, which is often the result of replacement of plant material by water-borne minerals. The material which forms the casts at Barriles is a plastic material probably little different from the surrounding fill. It includes crystals, rounded bits of rock, and soil particles. The mechanism by which the cast is formed and subsequently holds its shape is unknown.

The column was removed by the natural observable stratigraphy. Only layers 6 to 10 contained cultural materials, all dating to about A.D. 600. Although the relative ages of the strata are not important, the units will be discussed in numerical order. The casts from unit 6 include only casts of fragments of seed coat (5 fragments) as do those from unit 7 (13 fragments). These were measured to establish the length of the chord from one side of the fragment to the other and the distance from the chord to the outside arc of the fragment. From these figures was derived the radius of the circle (sphere) from which they were broken (fig. 10.0-7).

Referring back to our previous palm fruit measurements, the figures for radii from measurement of the casts were consistently too small. For in-stance, fragments from unit 7 belong to fruit having radii ranging from 3.3. mm to 13 mm. The explanation for this may lie in the misidentification of the species of palm used, but the more probable explanation is error in measuring. This is confirmed by a cast of a complete fruit from unit 8 which measures 25 mm in diameter (12.5 mm in radius). Altogether, 14 casts of palm fruit fragments (shell) from Barriles were large enough to be mea-sured. From these, eight radii ranging from 9 mm to 14.5 mm (diameters of 18 mm to 29 mm) are within a possible range of variation for spherical fruit from *Acrocomia vinifera (Corozo pacora)*.

10.5   PLANT REMAINS FROM LA PITAHAYA (IS-3)

Although the archaeological site of La Pitahaya is extensive, the tests from which the following plant remains were recovered were fairly limited (sections 6.4, 6.5, and 7.7). The material recovered here dates from A.D. 800 to 1100 and is thus chronologically later than plant material recovered in Barriles and Cerro Punta (section 7.8).

The bulk of the plant remains consisted of fragments of the dense shells of palm fruit. Most of these fragments are from activity area 2, which was a living area lacking the intrusive burials or the basalt columns found on the artificial mounds. The fragments come from all three blocks of trench I, mostly from the San Lorenzo and Chiriqui phase layers, though a few were

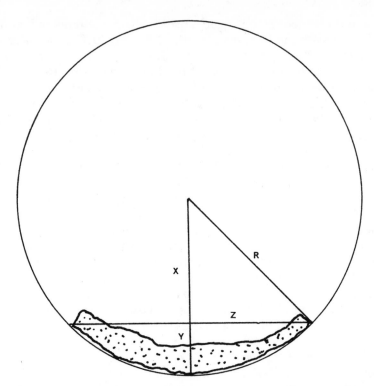

Figure 10.0-7: The radius of palm fruit represented only by shattered fragments of shell can be reconstructed by measuring the length of the chord (Z) and the distance from the chord to the arc (Y). Then, $Y^2 + (1/2Z)^2 = R$, where R is the radius of the circle or sphere from which the fragment was broken. Obviously, fragments of ellipsoidal or obvoidal fruit will provide a different radius depending upon whether the long curvature or the short curvature is measured. Some of the variation encountered in the radii derived from palm shell fragments from Chiriqui may have resulted from this factor.

also found in the Burica phase bottom level of block 3. At the bottom of trench 2, block 2, occurred a fragment of carbonized material probably originally elliptical in shape with parallel lines on the surface. It has a diameter of 1.25 cm and it appears to be a fragment of palm kernel, perhaps of *Scheelia zonensis*. One palm fruit shell fragment in the Bugaba bottom layer of trench I, block 3, is thicker than usual and markedly ridged on the outer surface; I have not yet identified the species to which this belongs. All of the larger fragments were measured in order to calculate diameters in an effort to establish the identity of the species to which they belong.

Altogether, 29 palm fruit fragments were measured and from these the radii were calculated. The derived diameters are as small as 6 mm and range upward to 20 mm. Even the largest calculated diameter is small for mature palm fruit of *Acrocomia*, or *Corozo pacora* (average 23.2 mm), or even *Scheelia*, or *Corozo gunzo* (21.2 mm). (This same problem was encountered with the two fragments reported for BU-17.) However, some of the casts from BU-24 were calculated to have dimensions that placed them within a range of variation which might be expected for fruit of *Corozo pacora*. I have previously indicated that I do not think the fragments come from a different species of palm, but it is possible. The probability that error in measurement will consistently give such a reduction in fruit size is unlikely, particularly when the even more difficult to measure casts from BU-24 provide a series of calculations which plausibly fit into a size range for *Corozo*. The answer to the problem almost certainly lies in distortion introduced in the fragments during the burning process, as well as a reduction in size due to loss of part of the structure during carbonization.

When the sizes of the numerous fragments of palm fruit are arranged in rank order, I find no good indication that more than one size class is involved. Were both *Corozo gunzo* and *Corozo pacora* represented, in spite of the nearness of the average sizes for diameters of modern seeds, a differential shrinkage or distortion would be expected in the burned fragments, which should show up as a marked break in the rank order of diameters. The nearest approximation of a marked change in size occurred between 10.6 mm and 12.8 mm, although a larger change occurred near the upper end of the series between 16.6 mm and 19.2 mm. This, I suspect, is a function of the few pieces from which large diameters were calculated, rather than a significant gap between fruit with different diameters. The evidence furnished by the fragments of seed coat seems to indicate that a single, continuously varying palm fruit was being harvested from trees which were purposely planted and that they were not gathered from natural populations of palm trees. While the sizes of fruits and seeds vary in a natural population, the variation is within predictable limits. When man interferes with the natural restraints placed on variation by environmental factors, he usually looks for or selects for increased size. For a long period of time, cultivated populations included both trees producing fruits and seeds in the size range of the natural populations and trees selected for an enlarged fruit and seed size. Only in relatively sophisticated modern agriculture are the smaller fruit variants rigorously routed out of cultivated populations, leading to monocultures of the large-fruited varieties. Therefore, extensive size variation, like that seen in the current sample of palm fruit fragments, suggests palm trees in cultivation.

All of the maize at IS-3 came from trench I, block 2, from the same area as the palm fruit fragments. Some kernels recovered from layer A (Chiriqui phase) apparently were very sweet. In the process of burning, the sugar caramelized, forming gas bubbles that were captured in the carbon during the final phases of carbonization. Maize materials from the same block, only in the middle or San Lorenzo phase layers, included a cob as well as a mass of charred kernels which have what appears to be the imprint of a maize leaf captured by the carbonization.

The only other notable plant fragment from IS-3 is a carbonized fragment of grass stem found with burial no. 5 in activity area 1, the main mound. While it is possible that this is a carbonized maize stem, it may equally well be a fragment of the New World cane commonly called "caña brava" (perhaps *Guadua* sp.).

From a series of rock shelters along an ancient trail which passes to the east of Volcan Baru, carbonized plant remains have been recovered which represent several thousand years of use, from 4600 B.C. to 300 B.C. The species represented do not include obviously cultivated species such as maize and beans, despite a sample of several hundred identifiable plant fragments. Although Ranere has postulated root-crop agriculture here by 2300 B.C., carbonized remains of tubers are hard to come by, and phytolith or pollen analyses of the rock-shelter sediments are yet to be made.

The majority of the fragments from the shelters are portions of the cracked outer seed coats of *Corozo* palm fruits. Of these, 433 were measurable and the radii were calculated for all of them. The mean diameter for the seeds was 16.52 mm, and the diameters of the individual seeds ranged from 6 mm to 35 mm. Obviously, the extremes represent errors in measurement or seed coats from different species of palm. For these early seeds, the latter may be the case, because travelers along the trail would undoubtedly have gathered any palm fruit which they encountered in suitable condition (I know of no poisonous palm fruit, although some are vastly more preferable than others in flavor, texture, ease of use, and so forth).

For much later sites, the mean seed diameters for palm fruits are 13.2 mm for Cerro Punta, 17.23 mm for Barriles, and 11.78 mm for La Pitahaya. If anything, the greater mean diameter from the early sites can be considered a function of the much larger sample of fragments measured in which errors in measurement became ameliorated by the larger numbers of more nearly correct measurements. Another possible interpretation for the larger mean is that many of the fruits were being gathered from a cultivated population exhibiting some of the great variability accompanying hybridization of two different stocks. As yet, archaeology has supplied no positive information on the origin of cultivation of palm species in the Old World or the New World. Even the earliest dates for material from the early Panamanian sites is well within the time scale for the beginnings of plant cultivation in the New World and none of the evidence is negative. On the other hand, we have no evidence that artificial selection for larger fruit size, improved flavor, or other attributes took place among cultivated palms.

The one fact which is prominent from the plant remains recovered from BU-17, BU-24, and IS-3 is that the diet of all three sites was not entirely dissimilar. The archaeologists indicate that the Cerro Punta plant remains represent the debris from a household floor. Not all of the other remains from the other sites were associated with clearly identified living floors, but they certainly represent the debris from living areas (as opposed to "ceremonial" mounds) from human food preparation. Had the La Pitahaya palm fruit fragments been opened by animals, the tooth marks would have persisted on the fragments. Only humans shatter such hard seeds by hammering so that they break in angular pieces.

The diet at all three sites contained cultivated plants. Cerro Punta and La Pitahaya are not native areas for maize, which appears at both sites. I have noted above that the range of variation of fragments of palm seeds suggests that the palm trees were cultivated. The social organization indicated by the architecture of Barriles alone would suggest cultivation there. Unfortunately, the Barriles samples did not include maize or beans, which were certainly in cultivation, but the test from which the plant remains were recovered was apparently small. Also, the palm remains were casts of fragments, rather than carbonized remains, and maize and beans may not have survived in this medium of preservation.

While the diet at all three Chiriqui sites, Cerro Punta (BU-17), Barriles (BU-24), and La Pitahaya (IS-3), was similar, the habitats are not, nor were they any more similar in the past. At the present time, the natural vegetation in these areas is badly disturbed. Surprisingly enough, the forest on La Pitahaya, although second growth, was the best developed as recently as 1975. The Barriles area has been cleared except for an occasional palm or guava tree, and the pastures are being invaded by a variety of weedy shrubs, some of which are foreign to Chiriqui. Cerro Punta is an area of intense truck-gardening of recent development.

As is generally well known, one of the strongest controls on the vegetation of an area is exerted by both the quantity and the pattern of the rainfall. Hence, the vegetation provides a clue to the rainfall, both by its composition and by its habit. Temperature is limiting for vegetation in combination with rainfall when it nears the extremes which the species will tolerate. Thus, the Cerro Punta region is a montane evergreen forest (fig. 2.0-2), clearly indicating that the rainfall at the 1,800-meter to 2,375-meter elevation is nearly evenly distributed throughout the year. Mean annual precipitation is 2,260 mm (section 2.1).

The position of the Cerro Punta basin on the north side of Volcan Baru insures an ample precipitation from the trade winds crossing the Isthmus from the Caribbean. However, at this elevation, frost occurs, undoubtedly eliminating some frost-sensitive species from the flora. At the time BU-17 was occupied, the entire area was certainly covered with a continuous montane evergreen forest that would have had to be felled to provide an opening for cultivation. The volcanic increment in the soil makes the fertile Cerro Punta soil available for long-term cultivation rather than for the usual pattern of shifting agriculture, which must be practiced in most tropical areas with a rainfall pattern of this kind and volume. Unless weedy shrubs and trees became too much of a problem, it is doubtful that the occupants of BU-17 had to move their fields, and clearing may only have been done to accommodate production to an expanding population.

It is also apparent that the pattern for cultivation was well set when the pioneer occupants entered the Cerro Punta basin because the gatherable wild fruits and seeds of the region fail to appear, except for *Hymenaea courbaril*, which is not a species of the montane evergreen forest anyway; it belongs with the vegetation of the region of seasonal rainfall to the south.

Similarly, while the native range of the *Corozo* palms has been so disturbed by human intervention that we can no longer define it accurately, the adaptation of both *Scheelia* and *Acrocomia* to a seasonal rainfall regime is obvious (fig. 10.0-8). The fruit of *Corozo* used at BU-17 was either brought into the area from the south or the occupants of the site planted *Corozo* palm as part of the cropping system. In fact, all of the identifiable food-plant remains recovered from Cerro Punta indicate a dependence on cultivation or importation from a seasonal rainfall area. How this fits in with inferences, arrived at independently, on population movements and contacts between the highlands and the Pacific coastal plains in the period between 300 B.C. and A.D. 300 is discussed in section 7.9.

Barriles may have been the immediate area from which the occupants at BU-17 migrated. The rainfall at Barriles averages 3,100 mm annually, but the separation into a wet and a dry season strongly influences the vegetation. To the south, behind the continential divide, even at the 1,200-meter to 1,340-meter elevation of Barriles, Panama has seasonal rainfall patterned by the seasonal shift in the trade winds in the Caribbean. The Pacific slopes of the Isthmus receive very little rainfall from the beginning of December until about the end of April, and the vegetation is composed principally of species which are seasonally deciduous. Palms of the genera *Scheelia* (fig. 10.0-9) and *Acrocomia* (fig. 10.0-10) are left standing so that they are prominent in the second growth invading pastures. It is probable that all of these were native species in the primary deciduous forest, although the palms could also have been brought into the area in cultivation at an earlier time. They are so well adapted to this habitat and other related species are so often found in areas of seasonal rainfall that we will probably never know the original range of the *Corozo* species on the Pacific slope of Panama.

At the time of the occupation represented by the plant remains from Barriles, the area was probably already largely cleared of primary deciduous forest. The Barriles palm fruit fragments include a cast of a whole fruit of *Acrocomia* and a number of casts of the angular, shattered seed coat fragments normally resulting from human activity. The former proves the presence of this palm in the area and the latter the human use, but neither indicates whether or not the palms were cultivated or native around Barriles.

La Pitahaya is adjacent to the coast of Chiriqui near the mouth of the Rio Chiriqui. At the present time (1975), the peninsula is nearly completely covered with a second-growth deciduous forest which is approaching mature dimensions. The climate of the southern coastal region is strongly divided into dry and wet seasons (section 2.1). At the end of the dry season, the coastal vegetation is living in a virtual desert. The crop system must have been adjusted to the climate inasmuch as the dry season has too little rainfall in an unpredictable pattern for growing corn and beans.

Despite the more recent time period represented by the Pitahaya plant remains than by those of Barriles and Cerro Punta, there is an interesting continuity in subsistence pattern. In both areas, the subsistence crops

Figure 10.0-8: View of the Chiriqui plains.

appear to have been maize and palm fruit *(Corozo)*. As before, the plant products that may have been gathered from native plants do not appear in the carbonized remains. Their absence may indicate a number of things, but the most probable is that the native vegetation at La Pitahaya had been nearly completely destroyed in favor of making space for cultivation. Rarely are wet debris, like peelings from tubers, thrown into a fire, yet we know that root crops were being grown in both areas: frost-resistant sweet potatoes in the Cerro Punta highland valley, and drought-resistant manioc in the dry seasonal lowlands of La Pitahaya. Whether or not the continuity in dietary preferences is an indication of continuity of political organization, social organization, or even cultural pattern, I leave to the archaeologist.

10.7   THE PLACE OF THE PANAMANIAN PLANT REMAINS IN THE NEW WORLD

The Panamanian plant remains represent unique material in several ways. Although the samples were recovered from small excavations, they clearly demonstrate the value of even a limited volume of evidence. Furthermore, the Panamanian remains represent the first collection of archaeological plant remains from wet, tropical areas of the New World. The deposits of the Mexican highlands are from areas of reduced, seasonal rainfall in which the native vegetation is much different, as are the conditions for preservation of plant remains. The Peruvian plant remains from the Callejon de Huaylas are from the dry slope of an area of sparse and markedly seasonal rainfall. Other Peruvian plant remains have largely come from the very dry coastal desert where preservation is particularly good, but where agriculture presents some special problems.

It is generally conceded that the beginnings of agriculture in the New World were either in Mesoamerica or in highland Peru, although some

Figure 10.0-9: Palm of the species Scheelia zonensis *(corozo gunzo).*

Figure 10.0-10: *Palm of the species* Acrocomia vinifera *(corozo pacora).*

evidence is found for the origin of some cultivated plants in eastern South America (Pickersgill 1969). For a few crops, the evidences for the origins of their cultivation seem to be reasonably secure. Perhaps the most positive evidence so far has been found for maize. In the caves of the Tehuacan Valley cobs and other material were recovered which Paul Mangelsdorf has interpreted as wild maize (Mangelsdorf et al. 1967). Upward in the time scale exemplified by the stratigraphy of the deposits, the results of artificial selection are clearly demonstrated by the trends in variation. The influence of different germ plasm introducing tripsacoid characteristics is clearly seen with the resulting proliferation of variation which finally becomes selected to the early forms of ancient Mexican maize races, Chapalote and Nal-tel.

From the highlands of Peru in the Callejon de Huaylas, maize which is not securely dated has been recovered from Guitarrero Cave. It may be as early as 4000 B.C. at the earliest level, or it may be only around 100 B.C. The upper level may represent accretion as late as A.D. 1000. Morphologically, cobs are similar to the early maize found in the Tehuacan Valley of Mexico and Bat Cave in New Mexico, but they are clearly varying toward the ancient race Pollo from the highlands of Colombia in at least one of the lines of selection. None of the lines of variation is clearly equatable with modern Peruvian races of maize which may indicate that the Guitarrero Cave maize is very old.

Both the Tehuacan maize and the Guitarrero Cave maize are from areas of highly seasonal rainfall. The Panamanian maize from Cerro Punta is from an area of more evenly distributed rainfall as well as higher rainfall. In spite of the differences in the habitats, the Panamanian maize can be clearly placed with respect to the Mesoamerican maize and the Andean maize. Galinat (section 11.0) identifies 36 cobs as intermediate between Nal-tel (Mexico) and Pollo (Colombia), 12 definitely have the characteristics of Nal-tel, and 16 have the characteristics of Pollo. Panama, on this evidence, can be assumed to be receiving maize races radiating from more ancient centers of distribution in Mexico and in Colombia. The Panamanian material is datable to at least A.D. 200 and may be earlier still (section 7.8). Although the ease with which it can be assigned to the races Nal-tel and Pollo may be interpreted to indicate that this is near the date for the introduction of maize into Panama, it is unlikely. Palynological evidence shows that maize was introduced into the lowlands of Panama at a much earlier date (Bartlett, Barghoorn, and Berger 1969). I suspect that lack of repeated later introductions into the highlands preserved the characteristics of the original races. In other words, the archaeological maize from the Volcan sites illustrates a relict population of some antiquity.

The common beans from the Cerro Punta site are clearly of no special morphological type which can be readily referred to another geographical area. Because of the continuity of Chiriqui with Mesoamerica through Costa Rica, where wild beans have been collected, I hypothesize that *Phaseolus vulgaris* probably came into Panama from the west and north. It is impossible to tell from the current evidence whether its introduction into Panama coincided with the introduction of maize or not. Additional evidence from other sites is going to be needed before a more exact provenience for the common bean can be determined. Ecologically, the common bean is a plant of arroyo slopes in dense second-growth shrubs (Gentry 1969) in Mexico and Central America and it is always possible that wild *Phaseolus vulgaris* was once, or still is, a native of a drier habitat in Panama.

The area of origin of the cultivated palms is unknown at the present time. In Mexico, *Acrocomia mexicana* (coyol) seeds were recovered from the caves of the Tehuacan Valley (Smith 1967). Coyol remains came into the deposits at about 4800 B.C. Coyol is adapted to a more mesic area than the Tehuacan Valley and it is grown today on the sides of the irrigation ditches. It appears to have been introduced into the Tehuacan Valley as a cultivar after hydraulic or irrigation farming was developed. No palm material has yet been recovered from South America, so far as I know. Thus, the Panamanian recovery of palm material tells us of its importance in the agriculture on the Pacific slope of Panama, but it gives no additional information on the development of palms as crops or on the changes which may have occurred with selection for superior fruit qualities.

Actually, the kind of cultivation under which palms are grown in the New World tropics is not a European or Asiatic version of intense cultivation. Seeds may be selected and planted purposely, but many palm fruits are eaten out of hand and the seeds indiscriminately discarded. If a new palm tree grows from such a discarded seed in a place where it can be tolerated, it will not be removed. When shrubs and trees are cleared for pastures, palm trees in the area will be preserved. When a *chacra* is cleared in a previously cultivated area, palm trees will be left standing. In fact, I have encountered severe resistance to the cutting of palm trees for botanical specimens in spite of an offer of money. This tolerance for palm trees which bear useful fruit and which appear from discarded seeds, no matter the quality of their source, may mean that very little change in fruit size occurs between wild and cultivated populations of palms of the same species. This may account for the continuity in seed size from preceramic to pre-Conquest times.

The lack of remains of wild plants other than trees in the Chiriqui sites is not surprising. The amount of fill processed for carbonized remains was limited, and the chances for a specimen of any gathered material undergoing just the correct amount of carbonization are very remote. Had some plant material from the native flora been the principal starch source on which the human population depended, the chances for preservation would still have been remote. The possible native species which furnish tubers or rhizomes would rarely have found their way into the fire. No grass of the area promises much of a return in grain. Such species as were probably gathered on a casual basis when the fruits were mature, or when they were encountered during an outing, would have had very little chance of appearing as carbonized specimens. Thus, the inhabitants of Cerro Punta, Barriles, and La Pitahaya were probably using a much more varied assortment of species of native plants than will ever appear among the carbonized plant remains.

With its strategic position between Mesoamerica and the Andean high-lands, Panama may have served as an intermediate transfer point for both goods and ideas, just as it did during the colonial Spanish period between western South America and Spain. As more plant evidence becomes available, I expect to find that maize and other cultivated plants reached Panama relatively soon after they came into common use in their areas of origin. It would be surprising if the variety of crops represented did not improve dramatically with additional sampling. The development of local preferences and accommodation to ecological conditions will also be illustrated more successfully with a larger sample.

11.0

The Archaeological Maize Remains from
Volcan Panama – A Comparative Perspective

W. C. GALINAT

A collection of archaeological maize *(Zea mays)* from the highlands of western Panama is identified here as being intermediate in type between the races Nal-tel and Pollo. Its date (A.D. 200–400) makes it very recent in comparison with other maize finds. *Zea* pollen from the Gatun Basin of Panama was previously dated from associated organic matter at 1200 ± 60 B.C., or in nearby cores at the same level at 5350 ± 130 B.C. and 4280 ± 80 B.C. (Bartlett et al. 1969). Much earlier *Zea* pollen, associated with human occupation, came from Guila Naguitz cave in northern Oaxaca, Mexico (Schoenwetter 1974), where radiocarbon dates for units B, C, and D range from 6910 B.C. to 8750 ± 350 B.C. Somewhat younger maize cobs at about 5200 B.C. came from Tehuacan in Puebla, Mexico (Mangelsdorf et al. 1967). In the highlands of Peru at Ayacucho, a Nal-tel–Pollo type of maize is known to have occurred by 3000 B.C. (Galinat and MacNeish, in preparation). Cultivated *Zea* may have had a long and almost undocumented history of evolutionary changes in the wet coastal areas of Central and South America, where there is little or no preservation of organic remains. This is suggested by the large, highly evolved kernels of maize dated at 2000 B.C. that were preserved as ceramic imprints at coastal Ecuador (Zevallos et al. 1977) and by the phytolith evidence (Pearsall 1978). In any case, if maize spread southward through Panama, early archaeological contexts of around 4000 B.C. for this cultivar in the area would seem to be in accord with the present evidence, including the pollen data of Bartlett et al. (1969).

The sample of Panamanian maize to be described here probably then represents only a relict descendant from a much earlier (ca. 4000 B.C.) spread southward of *Zea* cultivars. A study of these cobs is important, however, because they represent the largest sample we have so far from the lower Central American area. The record may never be complete because we can know only the material which has happened by circumstance to find its way into dry caves that ideal for its preservation over the millennia. But such limited data are not irrelevant pieces of a complex jigsaw puzzle. As additional pieces of data accumulate, the parts should fit together so that an overall conception of the spread and evolution of maize becomes possible.

After his study of some archaeological maize from Venezuela (Mangelsdorf and Sanoja 1965), Mangelsdorf (1974) revised his earlier suggestion with other authors (Roberts et al. 1957) that Pollo of Colombia was of independent origin. He now (1974) considers Pollo to be an offshoot from the Nal-tel/Chapalote complex that has its ancient roots in Mexico and Guatemala. The reduction in rachis diameter and condensation appears to be an adaptation to insure the drying and curing of mature ears in humid parts of the Andean highlands (Galinat 1978). This rapid ear drying to about 13 percent moisture is important to the popping qualities of various popcorn races such as Pollo, Pira, Confite Puntiagudo, and Confite Morocho.

The botanical characteristics of the Cerro Punto (BU-17) maize cobs are listed in table 1 according to several contexts, including house floors and hearths. There was a total of 64 cobs divided into seven collections from separate layers, not counting a sample of isolated cupules. The definitive characters of the cobs that allowed their identification are kernel row number, rachis diameter, and internode (rachis-segment) length. An index of the degree of condensation or compaction in the rachis has been calculated by dividing the kernel row number by the rachis-segment length in millimeters. On this basis, the cob specimens may be identified as either Pollo or Nal-tel according to the formula that an index of 2.0 or less is Pollo and 2.5 or more is Nal-tel. If the rachis diameter is 10 mm or more in these cobs, it is Nal-tel even though condensation may drop to 2.25. Thereby, the identifications are 36 cobs that are intermediate between Nal-tel and Pollo, 12 cobs that are Nal-tel, 16 cobs that are Pollo. Representative specimens of these three types are shown in figure 11.0-1. One specimen (table 1, last sample) that fits the criteria for Pollo may actually be an elongated tip of a Nal-tel ear. Condensation is usually lower toward the tip of an ear and it may have given a phenocopy of Pollo in Nal-tel. There were seven carbonized kernels, all of which, except for length, fall within the range of variation for that of Nal-tel and Pollo (table 5). A slight reduction in length was caused by a loss of the "tip cap" in the carbonization process of the archaeological kernels.

The justification for a classification of Pollo as having a lower level of condensation represented by an index of 2.0 in comparison to Nal-tel, which is more condensed at a 2.5 level, is apparent in tables 2 and 3, respectively. In table 2, it is seen that, on a basis of condensation, the archaeological cobs from El Tiestral, Venezuela (date 200 B.C.) and from Severo Ledesma, Costa Rica (date A.D. 345) are actually closer to the highland subraces of Nal-tel than they are to Pollo. Thus, Pollo and Nal-tel appear to diverge from a single stock. This is consistent with the hypothesis of a southward spread of maize from Mexico to South America. It is also consistent with the contention that the farther back into maize's history that we go, the fewer

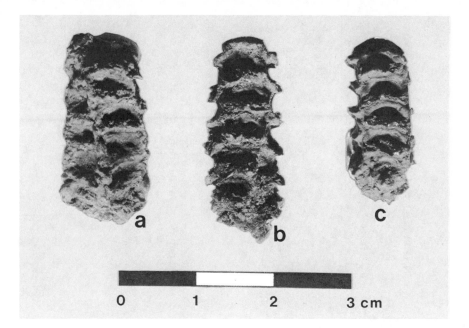

Figure 11.0-1: Three types of Zea mays *cobs from the Pitti-Gonzalez (BU-17) site: a. Nal-tel; b. Pollo-Nal-tel; c. Pollo.*

the number of races. An exception to this principle is the recent genetic erosion resulting from inbreeding and selection by a limited number of seed producers.

In table 4 the condensation of present-day Confite Morocho from Peru is seen to be not only lower than that of the Cerro Punta, Panama, maize in the present study, but also lower than that of Pollo or any other maize. The archaeological Confite Morocho at Ayacucho, Peru, is not in the oldest strata, but it also has comparatively large kernels for a supposed "primitive wild race" (Galinat and MacNeish, in preparation). The low condensation of this and other highland maize may be a specialized condition rather than a primitive one. The extreme form of low condensation that occurs in Confite Morocho, known as the "string-cob" trait, is controlled by only two incompletely dominant genes (Galinat 1969) and these genes are adaptive for rapid ear drying and seed curing under humid conditions (Galinat 1978). The presence of low condensation in certain Nal-tel maize types from the Panamanian highlands, as described by Linares, Sheets, and Rosenthal (1975), need not necessarily be considered as evidence of introgression from the South American Pollo, but rather just a similar result from an independent adaptation to a similar environment.

Walton C. Galinat is professor of genetics, University of Massachusetts — Amherst, 240 Beaver Street, Waltham, Massachusetts 02154. This section is Mass. Agricultural Experiment Station Paper No. 2321.

TABLE 1 CARBONIZED MAIZE COBS FROM SITIO PITTI (BU-17) IN THE CERRO PUNTO BASIN OF CHIRIQUI, PANAMA

(Approximate date A.D. 200)

Blocks	Layers	Phase	Number of cobs	Average kernel row no.*	Average diam., rachis, mm	Average length* rachis segment, mm	Index conden.	Identity
Hearth								
7	6,8	Early Bugaba?	5	8.85	8.85	4.0	2.21	Nal-tel Pollo
House floor								
3, 5	3, 4		9	8.93	8.83	3.53	2.53	Nal tel
3, 5	3, 4	Early Bugaba	15**	8.0	8.4	4.03	1.99	Pollo
3, 5	3, 4		30	8.28	7.48	3.64	2.28	Nal-tel Pollo
Periphery of dwelling								
14	6	Early Bugaba?	3	9.0	10.0	4.0	2.25	Nal-tel
14	6	Early Bugaba?	1	8.0	6.0	3.5	2.29	Nal-tel Pollo
14	6	Early Bugaba	1	8.0	5.0	6.0	1.33***	Pollo

*The kernel row number is used here on the assumption that the kernels are paired (rather than single as in teosinte) and that there is no significant degree of interlocking (as occurs in Piricinco-Coroico types of maize). There were no intact cobs in terms of length. Some were also fragmentary in diameter.

**Two of these were fragments in which data were estimated.

***This may be an elongate tip of a Nal-tel ear.

Index of condensation = row number/length, mm.

I.C. = 2.0 or less = Pollo; I.C. 2.5 or more and/or rachis diameter of 10.0 mm or more = Nal-tel.

TABLE 2   THE CHARACTERISTICS OF MODERN AND ARCHAEOLOGICAL
POLLO TYPES

(In comparison to the archaeological maize from BU-17)

Source	Average kernel row no.	Average diam., rachis, mm	Average length internode	Index conden.
Venezuela (mod.)[1]	9.8	13.0	5.2	1.88
Colombia (mod.)[2]	10.0	8.1	5.0	2.00
El Tiestral (Ven.)[3]	8.6	4.6	3.2	2.32
Severo Ledesma (C.R.)[4]	8.0	7.0	3.3	2.42
Present Study	8.4	7.1	3.7	2.27

[1]Grant et al. (1963).

[2]Roberts et al. (1957).

[3]Mangelsdorf and Sanoja (1965):200 B.C.

[4]W.C. Galinat, in M. J. Snarskis (1976): A.D. 345.

TABLE 3   THE CHARACTERISTICS OF MODERN NAL-TEL FROM MEXICO
AND GUATEMALA

(In comparison to the archaeological maize from BU-17)

Source	Average kernel row no.	Average diam., rachis, mm	Average length rachis segment	Index conden.
Mexico[1]	11.4	9.2	3.9	2.92
Guatemala[2] (five subraces below)				
Amarillo Tierra Baja	11.7	*	4.1	2.85
Blanco Tierra Baja	12.0	*	3.9	2.93
Amarillo Tierra Alta	12.0	*	5.5	2.18
Blanco Tierra Alta	12.0	*	4.7	2.55
Nal-tel Ocho*	11.0	*	4.8	2.29
Present Study	8.4	7.1	3.7	2.27

[1]Wellhausen et al.(1952).

[2]Wellhausen et al.(1957).

*Unfortunately only cob diameters are given. The rachis diameters are necessary because the chaff is eroded or burned away to some degree in archaeological cobs. While Nal-tel Ocho averages 11 rows, eight rows are thought to be the basic type.

TABLE 4   THE CHARACTERISTICS OF MODERN CONFITE MOROCHO
FROM PERU

(Compared to the archaeological maize from BU-17)

Source	Average kernel row no.	Average diam., rachis, mm	Average length rachis segment	Index conden.
Ayacucho, Peru[1]	8.0	5.2	4.55	1.76
Present Study	8.4	7.1	3.7	2.27

[1]Grobman et al. (1961), in Table 5.

TABLE 5   COMPARISON OF KERNEL CHARACTERS OF POLLO AND NAL-TEL TO THOSE OF BU-17 MAIZE*

Source	Length mm	Width mm	Thickness	No. kernels
Pollo, Venezuela[1]	10.1	9.9	5.2	
Pollo, Colombia[2]	8.54	7.94	4.96	
Nal-tel, Mexico[3]	7.4	6.7	3.9	
BU-17, TP7, Unit 8, 649	6.0	7.0	4.5	6
BU-17, TP7, Unit 5, 647	6.0	8.0	5.0	1

*All BU-17 kernels carbonized, smooth crown.
[1]Grant et al. (1963).
[2]Roberts et al. (1957).
[3]Wellhausen et al. (1952).

12.0

TERRESTRIAL FAUNA FROM CERRO BRUJO (CA-3) IN BOCAS DEL TORO AND LA PITAHAYA (IS-3) IN CHIRIQUI

O. F. LINARES AND R. S. WHITE

12.1 INTRODUCTION

In his analysis of the Cerro Brujo mammalian fauna, Grayson (1973, 1978) discusses a number of problems affecting the calculation of minimum number of individual taxa for a given collection. The minimum numbers method (MNI for short) determines the necessary numbers of individuals of a species accounting for all identical bone elements found in a given collection (Grayson 1973). As Grayson points out, not only does the MNI vary significantly with the analytic units used for the calculations, but also with the size of a sample from which the MNI was derived. To illustrate this point, he compares MNI based on individual excavation strata (the maximum distinction or Mx method) with MNI based on the whole site taken as one unit (the minimum distinction or Mi method). Grayson (1973, table 2, p. 436) provides us with the calculations given in the first two columns of table 1.

Now, as useful as Grayson's calculations may be for illustrating a methodological point, they are less helpful to the archaeologists who must interpret these data. As we have previously discussed (sections 5.3 and 5.4), the site of Cerro Brujo was made up of four hamlet localities, the largest of which, CA-3a, provided the bulk of the collections Grayson analyzed. Within this locality we distinguished two different occupations: the Aguacate phase (ca. A.D. 600) and the Bocas phase (A.D. 900). Furthermore, we also distinguished a number of features representing separate activity areas. It is in terms of these features, and of the two periods represented in them, that the MNI should, from the beginning, have been calculated. These features, and not the separate strata or the whole site, are most likely

181

TABLE 1   TERRESTRIAL MAMMALS FOUND IN THE CERRO BRUJO (CA-3) DEPOSITS

(Grayson's 1973 figures, A, are compared with revised figures, B)

		A					B		
Taxon	Colloquial name	Number of specimens (Grayson 1973)	MNI* Mx	% of total	MNI Mi	% of total	Revised Number of specimens (R. White)	MNI by feature	% of total
Dasyprocta	Agouti	822	204	43.8	29	38.7	411	41	38.0
Cuniculus	Paca	224	104	22.3	9	12.0	172	21	19.4
Dasypus	Nine-banded armadillo	186	69	14.8	10	13.3	191	17	15.7
Tayassu tayacu	Collared peccary	94	27	05.8	3	04.0	66	11	10.2
Odocoileus	White-tailed deer	20	14	03.0	2	02.7	16	6	05.6
Hoplomys	Armored rat	8	3	00.6	2	02.7	8	3	02.8
Sigmodon	Cotton rat	28	16	03.4	8	10.7	18	2	01.9
Mazama	Brocket deer	3	2	00.4	1	01.3	3	1	00.9
Caluromys	Wooly opossum	2	1	00.2	1	01.3	1	1	00.9
Didelphis	Opossum	5	1	00.2	1	01.3	5	1	00.9
Oryzomys	Rice rat	16	11	02.4	3	04.0	16	1	00.9
Trichechus	Manatee	13	9	01.9	3	04.0	13	3	02.8
Tayassu pecari	White-lipped peccary	15	4	00.9	2	02.7	0		

*Minimum number of individuals

TABLE 2   THE MOST COMMON SPECIES OF TERRESTRIAL MAMMALS
FROM THE CERRO BRUJO (CA-3) SITE ON THE AGUACATE
PENINSULA IN BOCAS DEL TORO

*(A comparison of minimum number of individuals, MNI,
their total biomass, and usable meat)*

Terrestrial CA-3: mammals	MNI	Live wt. (kg)	Biomass	%	Butchered wt. (% of live wt.)	Usable Meat (kg)
Dasyprocta	41	2.26	92.66	.11	.66	61.16
Cuniculus	21	6.33	132.99	.16	.66	87.77
Tayassu tajacu	11	24.0	264.0	.31	.70	184.8
Odocoileus	6	39.32	235.92	.28	.62	146.27
Dasypus	17	5.30	90.1	.11	.54	48.65
Didelphis	1	3.0	3.0	.04	.50	1.5
Caluromys	1	.9	.9	.01	.50	.45
Mazama	1	20.25	20.25	.02	.62	12.56

to represent discrete time-behavior units, thus reducing the chances that the bones of an individual animal be spread over more than one unit.

In 1975, R. White reanalyzed the Cerro Brujo data at Linares's request. The total number of bone specimens he reports (920) is considerably less than the 1,436 reported by Grayson (1973, table 2) for the following reasons: (a) only elements that were completely identifiable were used (excluding, ribs, vertebrae, other than atlas and axis, and so forth); (b) considerable time was spent fitting bones of adjacent strata and repairing broken bones, thereby reducing the number of fragments; (c) loose teeth (± 150) were not recorded under *Dasyprocta;* and (d) only the CA-3a bone was analyzed. As a result of using features and the two periods as the analytic units, the total MNI (107) calculated by White was considerably less than that obtained by Grayson using the Mx method, but more than that obtained by him using the Mi method (table 1). Furthermore, White found that some bones from one stratum fit those of another stratum (thus casting doubt on the Mx method); in no case did a bone fragment from Period 1 fit into a fragment from Period 2 (thus casting doubt on the Mi method).

In the discussions that follow we will be using the revised calculations provided by White. The best way to represent these figures is as percentage frequencies. It should go without saying that the MNI number derived for a species is bound to be an underrepresentation. Certainly an MNI of 21 pacas at Cerro Brujo means that at least 21 pacas were killed; it is a near certainty that many more were in fact killed, but there is at present no way of estimating the relationship between the MNI recorded from a site and the actual number of animals killed there, nor can we imagine any such method being developed in the future.

12.2   THE MOST COMMON TERRESTRIAL MAMMALS
IN THE CA-3 COLLECTIONS

The ecology and behavior of the most common Cerro Brujo mammals have been summarized in Linares (1976). Here we will discuss some of the characteristics of the archaeological fauna itself (table 2).

1.   Caviomorph rodents: The agouti, *Dasyprocta punctata* (fig. 12.0-1a) (see Smythe 1978), accounted for a minimum of 41 individuals represented by 411 identified elements from feature contexts. The sample of agouti bones is large enough to allow investigation of the age structure of the population. Nearly all the animals represented are of adult size; only five elements came from animals that were clearly subadult in size. The remaining animals are of varying age as demonstrated by epiphyseal union of the long bones. If we make the assumption that each set of elements in the collection came from the same set of animals (that is, we assume that the humeri are from the same animals as the femora), then a count of the sealed and unsealed bones should yield a schedule of the order of epiphyseal sealing, with those elements showing the highest frequency of closure being those that seal first. Table 3 presents such data from the collection for those elements present in significant numbers.

When examples of known age become available, it will be possible to estimate the actual age structure of the archaeological population with fair accuracy.

We will here follow Smythe (1978) in considering *Cuniculus paca* (fig. 12.0-1b) as the valid generic name for the dasyproctid rodent often referred to as *Agouti* Lacepede 1799 (see, for example, Hall and Kelson 1959). This animal, vernacularly called the paca, is sometimes confused with *Dasyprocta punctata*, the agouti. The latter was less important as a food source at CA-3 than was the paca, represented by 21 individuals, due to a difference in meat weight of the two animals. Smythe (personal communication) obtained an average weight per individual agouti of 2.26 kilograms, and an average weight per individual paca of nearly three times that, or 6.33 kilograms. If the ratio of number of individuals, 41 agouti to 21 paca, is converted to potentially available biomass (i.e., live weight) then a ratio of 1:1.5 is obtained. Paca therefore provided 1.42 times the amount of meat to the diet provided by the agouti.

2.   Remains of the nine-banded armadillo, *Dasypus novemcinctus* (fig. 12.0-2a), were very common at Cerro Brujo, with 191 fragments recovered, representing some 17 animals. The armadillo can attain a weight of 7.71 kg (Hall and Kelson 1959), but animals of 4.54 to 5.44 kg weight are commonest for animals taken in Texas. Assuming that an adult animal might weigh from 4 to 6 kilos on the average (as determined by Nietschman 1973), an estimate of the relative percent of meat from the armadillo can be made. Using an average of 5.3 kg per individual, then the ratio of armadillo meat to agouti meat is 0.95:1. Armadillo and agouti contributed roughly equally to the meat protein consumed.

Figure 12.0-1: Most common Cerro Brujo mammals hunted in the past: a. agouti (Dasyprocta punctata); b. paca (Cuniculus paca); c. collared peccary (Tayassu tajacu); d. white-lipped peccary (Tayassu pecari). Reprinted from O.F. Linares, Human Ecology, 1976, vol. 4, no. 4, fig. 5, p. 346.

TABLE 3   EPIPHYSEAL UNION SCHEDULE FOR DASYPROCTA

Element	N	% unsealed	% partly sealed	% completely sealed
Distal humerus	16	0	0	100
Distal tibia	12	41.60	0	58.30
Proximal femur	17	64.71	5.88	29.41
Distal femur	17	70.59	0	29.41
Proximal humerus	16	56.25	31.25	12.50
Proximal tibia	12	83.33	16.66	0

3.   Grayson's original analysis of this fauna indicated that both species were present, but that the collared peccary (*Tayassu tajacu;* fig. 12.0-1c) outnumbered the white-lipped peccary (*Tayassu pecari;* fig. 12.0-1d) by a ratio of six to one (Grayson 1973). Closer inspection of the material from Cerro Brujo leads White to conclude that only the collared peccary is certainly identifiable. Only three specimens are identifiable to the species level, and all are *T. tajacu.* The characters used to make this identification are summarized in Hall and Kelson (1959, p. 995) and in Olsen (1964, p. 58); present in each of the three specimens was a distinct ridge connecting the canine and second premolar.

Information regarding the age structure of the Cerro Brujo peccary population is slight. Of the 79 specimens identified, 13 are skeletally mature (that is, with epiphyses sealed), 10 are skeletally immature (with unsealed epiphyses), and 56 specimens are indeterminate. If these numbers reflect the actual ratio of young to old animals, then it would seem that there are unnaturally high numbers of young animals in the population. Given the common practice among the contemporary Guaymí of Bocas of penning young peccaries captured wild (personal observations), the possibility that such a practice was being carried out at Cerro Brujo suggests itself. However, as Wing (personal communication) remarks: "If epiphysial fusion is comparable to pigs then many epiphyses are only fused at 3½ years, and vertebral epiphyses at 4-7 years, so the young need not be so very young."

The alteration in the number of Tayasuid species present in the Cerro Brujo fauna does not effect the previous argument that the collared peccary is more likely to be taken when garden-hunting is practiced (Linares 1976); it does, in fact, strengthen the thesis.

4.   The cervid material from Cerro Brujo was carefully compared with skeletons from both the white-tailed deer, *Odocoileus virginianus* (fig. 12.0-2b), and the red brocket deer, *Mazama americana* (fig. 12.0-2c). Both comparative skeletons are from animals taken in the Chiriqui highlands.

Nineteen specimens of *Odocoileus* and three of *Mazama* were identified. It seems likely that at least some of the scrap bone, and much of the bone identified only as "large mammal," came from one of these two cervids.

All of the *Mazama* bones and most of the *Odocoileus* bones came from animals of adult size.

a

b

c

Figure 12.0-2: Most common Cerro Brujo mammals hunted in the past: a. nine-banded armadillo (Dasypus novemcinctus); *b. brocket deer* (Mazama americana); *c. white-tailed deer* (Odocoileus virginianus). *Reprinted from O.F. Linares,* Human Ecology, *1976, vol. 4, no. 4, fig. 5, p. 346.*

Although a fair amount of antler material was recovered from Cerro Brujo, little can be deduced concerning the seasonality of occupation. Six fragments of antler from the white-tailed deer were recovered. Three came from antlers that had been shed from live individuals, two came from antlers that had been forcibly removed from the animals' skulls, and one fragment came from a nondiagnostic part of the antler. The two fragments which represent antlers broken from the skull both came from completely developed antlers, indicating that the animals in question were killed some time after the velvet had been dropped, but some time before the antlers themselves were dropped.

White-tailed deer are normally found in ecotone situations between woodland and savanna; brocket deer are normally found in woodland environments. Brocket deer, however, are common today in areas of considerable disturbance, and white-tailed deer can be found in fairly dense forest situations. If *Odocoileus* was indeed hunted near Cerro Brujo, some reduction of the rain forest must have taken place at the time of occupation of Cerro Brujo. It is possible, however, that deer were being sought some distance away (more on this point later).

12.3 DIFFERENCES THROUGH TIME IN THE CA-3 FAUNA

In table 4 we have listed the occurrence of the most important terrestrial mammals in the Cerro Brujo collections in each of the two phases. (The total MNI of 34 for the older or Aguacate phase may be slightly exaggerated by the inclusion in the faunal analysis of all the C and D layers in the CA-3a locality, even though not all of them contained the Bugaba Ware.) A contingency table chi-square analysis comparing the total live weight (or biomass) of the five most common species shows a significant difference between the Aguacate and Bocas phases (table 5). Obviously, the same is also true of the usable meat. The greatest difference between the two phases is accounted for by the larger animals. Peccary accounts for 39 percent and deer for 16 percent of the biomass in the Aguacate phase, while the same two species account for 30 percent and 35 percent, respectively, of the biomass in the Bocas phase. Limited as the evidence may be, it does suggest that more forest was around in the earlier period, when peccary was hunted more, than in the latter, when *Odocoileus,* an open-brush species, was more common. The agouti *(Dasyprocta)* remains a more or less constant component of the diet of both periods; it is 10 percent of the usable meat in the Aguacate phase and 12 percent in the Bocas phase. We are reminded of the agouti's importance by Smythe (1978, p. 1), who remarks, "For many of the chronically protein-deficient poor people within the range of the agouti, it is one of the most important meats."

12.4 LA PITAHAYA FAUNA

La Pitahaya (IS-3) mounds were not "true" shell-middens, even though they did contain some shell. Conditions leading to the preservation of bone

TABLE 4   OCCURRENCE OF THE MOST IMPORTANT TERRESTRIAL
MAMMALS IN EACH OF THE TWO PERIODS (PERIOD I,
AGUACATE PHASE; PERIOD II, BOCAS PHASE) AT CERRO BRUJO

(In features 1-8 of the main midden locality CA-3a)

	MNI[1]	%[2]	Live wt. (kg)	MNI × l.w. (kg)	%	b.w.[2] % usable	Usable meat	%
Period I Aguacate phase								
Dasyprocta	11	.32	2.26	24.86	.10	.66	16.41	.10
Cuniculus	8	.24	6.33	50.64	.20	.66	33.42	.21
Dasypus	7	.21	5.30	37.10	.15	.54	20.03	.12
Tayassu	4	.12	24.00	96.00	.39	.70	67.20	.42
Odocoileus	1	.03	39.32	39.32	.16	.62	24.38	.15
Others	3	.09						
Period II: Bocas phase								
Dasyprocta	30	.41	2.26	67.80	.12		44.75	.12
Cuniculus	13	.18	6.33	82.29	.15	ibid	54.31	.15
Dasypus	10	.14	5.30	53.00	.09		28.62	.08
Tayassu	7	.10	24.00	168.0	.30		117.60	.32
Odocoileus	5	.07	39.32	196.60	.35		121.89	.33
Others	9	.12	—	—	—		—	—

[1]Minimum number of individuals.

[2]Butchered weights.

TABLE 5   CONTINGENCY TABLE COMPARISONS OF LIVE WEIGHT
FREQUENCIES (BIOMASS) AND USABLE MEAT FREQUENCIES
(BUTCHERED WEIGHTS) OF THE FIVE MOST IMPORTANT
TERRESTRIAL MAMMAL SPECIES IN THE AGUACATE VS.
THE BOCAS PHASES AT THE CERRO BRUJO (CA-3) SITE IN THE
AGUACATE PENINSULA, BOCAS DEL TORO

	Live wt. (biomass)					Usable meat (butchered wt.)				
	Dasyprocta	Cuniculus	Dasypus	Tayassu	Odocoileus	Dasyprocta	Cuniculus	Dasypus	Tayassu	Odocoileus
Aguacate phase	24.86	50.64	37.10	96.00	39.32 ⌉A	16.41	33.42	20.03	67.20	24.38 ⌉B
Bocas phase	67.80	82.29	53.00	168.00	196.60 ⌋	44.75	54.31	28.62	117.60	121.89 ⌋

A = chi-square 34.69; d.f. 4, L .05,   B = chi-square 21.57, d.f. 4, L .05,
critical value = 9.49   critical value = 9.49

were therefore less optimal here than in Bocas. Nonetheless, as Wing's analysis indicates (section 13.0), over 1,529 fish specimens were well enough preserved at IS-3 to be identified at least to the familial level. Hence the paucity of bones of terrestrial mammals here (263 elements, excluding rats; 12 MNI) contrasts markedly with their abundance at Cerro Brujo (1,437 specimens; 104 MNI) (table 6). This contrast will be discussed later on.

The most abundant animal at IS-3, by any reckoning, is the white-tailed deer, which alone contributes 80 percent of all usable meat from terrestrial mammals. It is a well-known fact that this species of deer prefers open habitats. Both the deer and the cottontail or *Sylvilagus* specimen confirm the accessibility to the IS-3 inhabitants of grasslands and low-brush habitats, possibly located nearby. Open habitats accord well with inferences about the history of land use all along the Pacific coast (Bennett 1968; Linares 1977b). However, all the other mammals eaten by the inhabitants of IS-3 are forest-dwelling animals. Even though the caviomorph rodents, as well as the collared peccary and the puma *(Felis concolor)*, are represented by only one individual each at IS-3, the inhabitants of this site must have had some access to forested habitats for hunting. Because most felids require fairly extensive territories, it is likely that the puma specimen reported here was hunted on the mainland.

Very few bones (less than ten, including all the unidentified scrap) showed evidence of burning or charring. The preferred method of cooking must have been pot boiling. None of the bones showed butchering or skinning marks either. This may be due to the small sample size and the generally poor preservation of the bone surfaces.

12.5 A COMPARISON OF THE TERRESTRIAL FAUNA FROM BOTH SIDES OF THE ISTHMUS

The total biomass of terrestrial mammals at Cerro Brujo, excluding the rats, is 840 kg; the total at La Pitahaya is 343 kg (table 7). At both places, however, marine, rather than land, vertebrates supplied the bulk of the proteins consumed (section 13.0).

With the exception of white-tailed deer, the animals hunted by the Cerro Brujo people are predominantly forest-dwelling species. They are also predominantly frugivorous, even though the paca, agouti, and collared peccary also eat cultivated crops and live near human settlement. Just as in the past, these are the preferred animals hunted by the Guaymí and non-Guaymí populations now living on the Aguacate Peninsula.

At La Pitahaya, paca, agouti, and collared peccary are represented by only one specimen per species. If we apply the argument that the biomass of these animals at Cerro Brujo may have been artificially increased by letting them feed on domestic crops (Linares 1976), we may wonder why this was not being done at La Pitahaya. Obviously, food alone is not the only limiting factor for these species. If very little forest was left on or near IS-3, these animals would not survive. Much of the area may, in fact, have been in grasslands and open brush.

TABLE 6 INFORMATION CONCERNING THE TERRESTRIAL MAMMALS FOUND IN THE ARCHAEOLOGICAL COLLECTIONS FROM LA PITAHAYA (IS-3), TRENCHES 1-5, 7

Taxon	Number of elements	MNI[1]	%	Live wt.	MNI × l.w.	% usable	Usable meat	%
Dasyprocta	2	1	.08	2.26	2.26	.66	1.49	.007
Cuniculus	4	1	.08	6.33	6.33	.66	4.18	.02
Sylvilagus	1	1	.08	.79	.79	.63	.498	.002
Tayassu	1	1	.08	24.00	24.00	.70	16.8	.08
Odocoileus	254	7	.58	39.32	275.24	.62	170.65	.80
Felis concolor	1	1	.08	34.00	34.00	.55	18.7	.09

[1]Minimum number of individuals.

Almost as many deer turned up in the Cerro Brujo faunal collection as in the IS-3 collection. If we assume a sparse human population during Cerro Brujo times, with densities roughly comparable to those existing ten years ago in the Aguacate Peninsula (about 3.4 persons per square kilometer), then very little land may have been cleared in the immediate vicinity of the site, and deer were being hunted some distance away. Incidentally, white-tailed deer is *not* found in Aguacate today (the nearest it occurs is in Changuinola), and *Sylvilagus* has not been reported from the Bocas side.

To summarize, the inhabitants of Cerro Brujo hunted more land mammals than did the people of La Pitahaya. Their favorite species were forest-dwelling, largely frugivorous, medium-sized animals which also eat cultivated crops and may become commensals of man. Garden-hunting (Linares 1976) may have been facilitated by leaving cut vegetation to decay, without burning it. Possibly the Cerro Brujo people were also occasionally "penning" collared peccaries for food, as the Aguacate people commonly do today. Snares and traps, and probably bows and arrows, were used in hunting. It is very likely that much of the area surrounding the site was forested at the time of occupation, as it is now.

The people of La Pitahaya hunted the white-tailed deer almost exclusively. This species thrives in open, disturbed habitats, like those created by slash-and-burn cultivation techniques. In fact, the white-tailed deer may have been the staple game throughout 7,000 years of prehistory on the Pacific Panamanian coast, becoming the preferred and protected food of high-ranking individuals in the periods immediately preceding the Conquest (Cooke ms. 1978).

TABLE 7 A COMPARISON OF THE TOTAL BIOMASS OF TERRESTRIAL
MAMMAL SPECIES AT CERRO BRUJO (CA-3) AND AT
LA PITAHAYA (IS-3)

(During approximately the same time span, A.D. 600–1000)

CA-3: Aguacate Phase and
Bocas Phase

IS–3: San Lorenzo and
Chiriqui Phases

	MNI	Live wt. (kg) of individual specimens	Biomass	%	MNI	Live wt. (kg)	Biomass (kg)	%
Dasyprocta	41	2.26	92.66	11.03	1	2.26	2.26	0.66
Cuniculus	21	6.33	132.99	15.83	1	6.33	6.33	1.85
Tayassu tajacu	11	24.0	264.0	31.43	1	24.0	24.0	7.00
Odocoileus	6	39.32	235.92	28.09	7	39.32	275.24	80.33
Dasypus	17	5.30	90.1	10.73	0	0	0	0
Didelphis	1	3.0	3.0	.36	0	0	0	0
Caluromys	1	.9	.9	.12	0	0	0	0
Mazama	1	20.25	20.25	2.41	0	0	0	0
Felis concolor	0	0	0	0	1	34.0	34.0	9.9
Sylvilagus	0	0	0	0	1	.79	.79	0.23

13.0

Aquatic Fauna and Reptiles from the Atlantic and Pacific Sites

E. S. WING

13.1 THE BOCAS MARINE ENVIRONMENT

The marine environment of the Bocas coast has been described in detail in section 5.2. To summarize, shallow-water lagoons and reefs are very well developed in this portion of the Caribbean coast, while beaches and mud-flats are not. Species diversity of fish is high, possibly connected with the presence of extensive coral formations. Turtle grass beds and mangrove stands are very common.

Information about the use of aquatic resources by the people who lived at Cerro Brujo is based on the identification of a large sample of faunal material excavated from the four archaeological localities at the site. A total of 2,013 bone and tooth specimens were identified to at least the familial level. In addition, 4,526 specimens lacking diagnostic characteristics were identified to class only. Because of the great differences between the number of identifiable bones in different fish species, a bias is introduced if analysis is based on numbers of identified specimens. Therefore, this analysis is based on minimum numbers of individuals (MNI) determined for each cultural period in the same manner described in section 12.1. (For a discussion of the minimum numbers method see Chaplin 1971, pp. 69–75 and Grayson 1973.) These data are summarized in tables 1 and 2, which list the species according to their importance in the CA-3 collections and not in phylogenetic order.

13.2 THE CERRO BRUJO AQUATIC FAUNA

The following identifications were made at the Florida State Museum by Elizabeth Wing, Kathleen Byrd, and Kathleen Johnson. (Descriptions of the habits and habitats of the different fish species were abstracted from Böhlke and Chaplin 1968, and Randall 1968, by O.F. Linares.)

1.   Bony fish: Sixteen different families of bony fish are represented in the CA-3 collections, but only six are very common: (a) Centropomidae: snook or robalo of the genus *Centropomus* is the most abundant fish. Four species were identified: *C. parallelus, C. pectinatus, C. poey,* and *C. undecimalis;* of these *C. undecimalis* (fig. 13.0-1) is the most common. Snooks are elongate fish which live in estuarine waters near mangrove sloughs and river deltas. *C. undecimalis* can live in fresh or salt water, but prefers brackish conditions. It is carnivorous, feeding on crustaceans and fish. (b) Serranidae, the sea basses or groupers follow the snook in abundance in the faunal collections. Of the two occurring genera, *Epinephelus* and *Mycteroperca* (fig. 13.0-2a), the former is more common. Five species of *Epinephelus* were identified, among which *E. itajara* and *E. striatus* are dominant. All Serranidae are bottom-dwelling, robust-bodied fish with fairly large mouths; they vary greatly in size, those from Cerro Brujo weighing from 1 kilogram to 42 kilograms, with a mean at 10.83 kilograms. The fact that they have no intramuscular bone makes them excellent eating (Randall 1968, p. 57). *E. itajara* (fig. 13.0-2b) is a giant sea bass, living in caves and large coral growths and feeding almost exclusively on crustaceans; *E. striatus* is about half the size, lives in reefs and over turtle grass beds, and is one of the least shy of reef fishes. (c) Lutjanidae or snappers are the third most abundantly represented family of fish in the faunal collections. Seven species of the genus *Lutjanus* were identified (*L. apodus* [fig. 13.0-3], *L. analis, L. campechanus, L. griseus, L. purpureus, L. mahogoni, L. synagris*). They are all approximately equally represented. Snappers are mostly inshore living species, entering mangroves, which some species use as nursery grounds, and feeding on crustaceans and fish. All of the species represented at Cerro Brujo occur naturally in shallow bays and reefs. (d) The

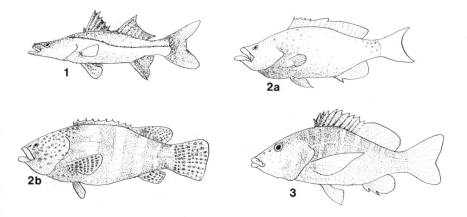

Figures 13.0-1–13.0-3:13.0-1, snook or "robalo" (Centropomus undecimalis); *13.0-2, sea basses (groupers) or "meros": a.* Mycteroperca *sp.; b.* Epinephelus itajara; *13.0-3, snapper or "pargo" of the species* Lutjanus apodus. *(Figures 13.0-1 to 13.0-10 are drawn from photographs in J.E. Randall 1968, figs. 9-12, 15, 58, 66, 73, 103, 126, 140, 156.)*

Carangidae or jack family of fish is represented in our collections by three identified species: *Caranx crysos, C. hippos,* and *C. ruber. C. hippos* (fig. 13.0-4) is slightly more abundant than the other two. Jacks are fast-swimming, silvery fish which usually spawn offshore but eventually drift inshore, living near reefs and feeding on other fish. *C. hippos* can occur on highly saline flats, as well as up in coastal rivers. (e) The tarpon family, *Elopidae,* is represented by the species *Megalops atlantica* (fig. 13.0-5), which spawns offshore, but its larva feeds in shallow waters, in mangroves and marshes. The young of *M. atlantica* can live in stagnant waters, and adults of the species are equally at home in fresh as in salt water. (f) Pomadasyidae, the grunt family, is represented by a few individuals of the *Haemulon* genus (fig. 13.0-6). Species in this genus range in size from 20 cm to 46 cm. Some occur in large schools on reefs during the day, dispersing to feed at night, mostly on small invertebrates of the plankton community near the bottom.

Among the less common bony fish we find the following edible families represented: (g) Sphyraenidae or barracudas of the genus *Sphyraena* (fig. 13.0-7) are represented by six individuals, ranging in weight from 1.39 to 5.04 kilograms. Smaller individuals (up to 30 cm) prefer inshore shallows and sandy or weedy bottoms, while larger ones (60 cm or more) are found offshore or on the reefs. As is well-known, barracudas are almost completely carnivorous. (h) Scaridae (parrotfishes) of the *Scarus* and *Sparisoma* genera, are colorful reef fishes that graze heavily on sea grass and reef algae. While the genus *Scarus* is pantropical, *Sparisoma* occurs only in the Atlantic. Grown parrotfishes of the genus *Scarus* range from 27 cm to 118 cm in length, while those of the *Sparisoma* genus are slightly smaller on the average (27 cm to 52 cm). (i) Sparidae, or porgies, of the *Archosargus* and *Calamus* genera, were identified but are rare in the sample. Porgies are accustomed to dwelling on flat bottoms even though they are found in reefs. (j) Albulidae, or bonefish, is represented by only one individual of *Albula vulpes,* which lives on sand and feeds primarily on clams and crabs. (k) the well-known Sciaenidae, the drum or corvina family, is represented at CA-3 by only one individual. Drums are inshore, bottom-dwelling shallow water fishes, highly valued nowadays for their flesh. (l) Eleotridae, sleepers, are represented by four individuals two of which are identified to *Gobiomorus dormitor* the bigmouth sleeper. These are common in brackish freshwater swamps and streams. (m) Only one specimen of the rudderfish or sea club (Kyphosidae family, *Kyphosus* genus) was found at CA-3. Rudderfishes live as adults in reef areas, and are mostly herbivarous. (n) Diodontidae or porcupine fishes of two genera, *Chilomycterus* and *Diodon,* are fairly abundant, with *Chilomycterus* being slightly more common. Porcupine fishes (also called puffers) have inflatable spine-covered bodies. They inhabit bays and harbors. (o) The Batrachoididae or toadfish family is represented by a few individuals. Toadfishes are fairly small (though some may reach 44 cm in length), bottom-dwelling voracious, hardy fishes. Some species of toadfish are commonly eaten today despite their unpalatable appearance. (p) Belonidae or needlefishes are easily distinguished because of their

Figures 13.0-4–13.0-10: 13.0-4, jack or "pampano" of the species Caranx hippos; *13.0-5, tarpon of the species* Megalops atlanticus; *13.0-6, grunt or "pez loro" of the species* Haemulon plumeieri; *13.0-7, barracuda of the genus* Sphyraena; *13.0-8, eagle ray of the species* Aetobatus narinari; *13.0-9, stingray of the species* Dasyatis americana; *13.0-10, hammerhead shark of the species* Sphyrna lewini.

pointed beaks. Some species live inshore, in bays and protected harbors, feeding on great quantities of small fish. Nowadays they are only occasionally eaten.

2. Cartilaginous fish: Two families of rays and one family of sharks are represented in the collections. (a) Myliobatidae or eagle rays of the *Aetobatus* genus (fig. 13.0-8) can grow to over two meters in length and weigh over two hundred kilograms. The archaeological specimens are from very young animals which have not even attained a weight of one kilogram. Eagle rays are active, free-swimming species, living near land and feeding on clams and oysters. (b) Dasyatidae (genus *Dasyatis;* fig. 13.0-9) or stingrays lie on the bottom, in lagoons and bays, buried in sand, where they feed on worms, mollusks, and crustaceans. The stab from their tail can be very poisonous. Both types of rays may be eaten. (c) Sphyrnidae or ham-

merhead sharks of the genus *Sphyrna* (fig. 13.0-10) are found inshore and offshore, feeding on other sharks, rays, and fish. Adults can attain sizes of over three meters; the archaeological specimens at Cerro Brujo were very young individuals ranging from approximately one to five kilograms in weight. Hammerhead sharks are extensively eaten where they occur; very young sharks appear regularly in the Panama City market.

3.   Reptiles; marine turtles: The family Cheloniidae is represented in our collection by four out of the five existing genera. (a) *Chelonia:* green turtles (fig. 13.0-11) being primarily herbivorous are found in shallow lagoons where marine grasses do well. Their migrations, occurring over hundreds of kilometers with their mass arrivals for nesting, render them particularly vulnerable to predation by man. The Thalassia beds in Almirante Bay and the Chiriqui Lagoon are important fishing grounds for individuals that nest on Tortuguero Beach, as evidenced by the many returns on marked animals from a tagging program in Costa Rica conducted by Dr. Archie F. Carr, a foremost authority on sea turtles. Some green turtles are caught throughout the year, but most are caught in early fall on their return from the beaches in Costa Rica to their feeding grounds in Colombia. The weight of the green turtles that Dr. Carr tagged in Costa Rica ranges from 45 to 182 kilograms; he believes the proportion of exceedingly large individuals was greater in the days before they became so relentlessly hunted. Nietschmann (1973, table 20, p. 165) gives the weight range for *Chelonia* specimens caught by the Miskito Indians of Nicaragua as 86 to 95 kilograms. Here we will use a 90-kilogram average weight. This is only a rough estimate, as turtles vary considerably with age, water temperature, and food availability (Rebel 1974, pp. 35-45; Nietschmann 1973, p. 164). Following Rebel, we have estimated that about 40 percent of the weight of the green turtle is flesh. (b) *Eretmochelys* or hawksbill turtles (fig. 13.0-12) are largely confined to tropical warm waters; they are generally more sedentary, and prefer more ocean front, than green turtles, even though both species occur together. "Typical [hawksbills] habitats are coral reefs, shoals, lagoons, and lagoon channels and bays, where a growth of marine vegetation provides both vegetable and small animal food" (Rebel 1974, p. 47). In feeding habits, hawksbills are omnivorous, eating such unlikely foods as mangrove leaves, fish, sponges, Portuguese man-of-war, sea urchins, and sea grasses. Like the *Chelonia,* they were probably valued for their eggs as well as their meat. Hawksbills seldom reach a weight of 68 kilograms; at maturity they weigh about 36 kilograms. At present, these turtles nest in small numbers on beaches near Bocas. (c) Loggerhead turtles belonging to the genus *Caretta* are represented by only one individual in the Bocas collection. Although loggerheads may reach a maximum weight of 110 kilograms, a six-year-old mature individual averages 45 kilograms. Adult turtles eat shellfish, barnacles, conchs, and, to a lesser extent than the other genera, sea grasses. In former days, a tortoise shell industry, using the epidermal scutes of *Caretta,* was centered at Bocas (personal communication, A. Carr). (d) *Dermochelys* (leatherback turtles) are also represented by only one specimen in the Bocas collection. Leatherbacks are among the

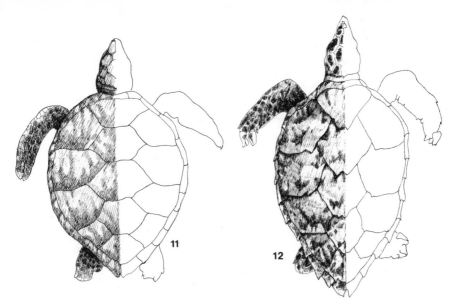

Figures 13.0-11–13.0-12: 13.0-11, the green turtle Chelonia mydas, *after B. Nietsch-mann 1976, fig. 11, p. 24; 13.0-12, the hawksbill turtle* Eretmochelys imbricata, *after B. Nietschmann 1976, fig. 9, p. 21.*

largest of the marine turtles, their average weight having been given by Rebel as 318 kilograms or, for the smallest nesting specimens, as 295 kilograms. They do not live in shallow lagoons, preferring pelagic waters of at least 45 meters depth, except when egg-laying (Rebel 1974, p. 48). (For information on all turtles see Archie Carr's numerous publications dating back to the 1940s. A convenient summary of sea turtles is presented in Rebel 1974, and a compilation of articles on all turtles, especially *Chelonia*, is found in Nietschmann 1977. Nietschmann [1973] describes how turtles are hunted, and the important role they play in the economy of the Miskito Indians of Nicaragua. Gordon [1969, pp. 47–48] gives a brief description of turtle hunting with nets and spears as a major industry among the Guaymí Indians of Bocas. The two most common species hunted by the Guaymí now, as in the past, are the green turtles and the hawksbill.)

4.   Freshwater turtles: One specimen of *Rhinoclemys* (old name, *Geomyda)*, a land turtle of the Emydidae family, is found in the Bocas collection. Two species of *Rhinoclemys* occur naturally in Panama — one species inhabits the forest floor, the other lives in ponds (S. Rand, personal communications to O.F. Linares). We do not know to which of the two species our archaeological specimen belongs.

5.   Other reptiles and amphibians: Remains of frogs and/or toads were found in the Cerro Brujo deposits, but they were not abundant, nor could they be identified as to genera or species. Crocodiles, on the other hand, formed a noticeable portion of the meat supply. The order Crocodylia is represented in Panama by caimans and crocodiles. Unfortunately, we do not know to which of the two groups our specimens belonged.

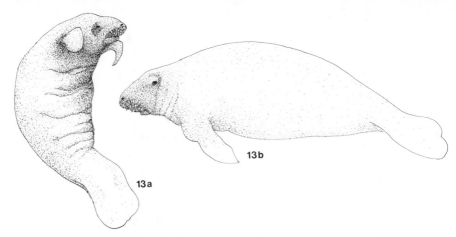

Figure 13.0-13: The manatee Trichechus manatus: *a. front view; b. side view. After photograph in E.P. Walker 1968, vol. 2, p. 1336.*

6.   Aquatic mammals: This class is represented by *Trichechus,* the sea cow or manatee (fig. 13.0-13a, b), whose dense bones are relatively easy to recognize. Manatees live in slow-moving rivers and in quiet marine bays where they feed nocturnally, strictly on vegetable matter consisting of either marine plants or overhanging terrestrial vegetation (Walker 1968, pp. 1336-1337). Although they are seasonally gregarious, these animals usually live singly or in small family groups. Walker gives the weight of the manatee as ranging from 140 to 360 kilograms, and their length as nearly 4.5 meters. Nietschmann (1973) gives their average weight as 500 lbs (227 kg). Here we have used the figure of 239 kilograms. Regardless of how one calculates their weight, however, a few manatee could have contributed a great deal of meat to the Cerro Brujo group. As a matter of fact, Bocas is an optimal habitat for and the center of abundance of the sea cow. Before the advent of the .22 rifle, sea cows were exceedingly abundant in these shallow coastal waters (Archie Carr, personal communication). As indicated earlier, this shallow bay with mangrove stands harbors a rich and varied fauna, including not only grazing sea cows and turtles but also shellfish of many kinds. Fishing for the manatee among the Miskito Indians of Nicaragua requires special harpoon heads, silent canoes, and even specially shaped paddles, as these shy animals have very acute hearing (Nietschmann 1973, p. 161). Despite great patience and skill, the Miskito have low returns per manatee hunting trip.

13.3   INTERPRETATION OF THE AQUATIC AND REPTILIAN REMAINS AT CERRO BRUJO

In order to gain a better understanding of the importance of various animals in the Cerro Brujo collections, we estimated their biomass (i.e., live weights) and usable meat (i.e., butchered weights). Weight estimates for mammals (see section 12.2) and for reptiles were simply extracted from the published evidence. Fish weights, on the other hand, were based directly on the faunal material. The method used is described by Casteel (1974) and is based on establishing a correlation between body weight and a linear measurement. I used a correlation established between the posterior width of the centrum of the first eight vertebrae, excluding the atlas, and the body weight of percomorph fishes. This relationship is described by the formula $\log y = 2.2602 (\log x) + .9807$ (where $\log y$ is the logarithm of the body weight in grams and $\log x$ is the logarithm of the centrum width in mm) $r = 0.9834$. I have also used this regression formula for estimating weights of shark. The resulting estimate will not be as accurate as for the percomorphs, but in testing the formula with our shark data I have found the error to be less than 15 percent which is I think the most accurate estimate that can be made until more comparative material is available. The formula used to estimate the weights of catfishes based on the cervical centrum width is $\log y = 3.0195 (\log x) + 0.1458$ (where $\log y$ is the logarithm of body weight in grams and $\log x$ is the logarithm of posterior centrum width in mm) $r = 0.9845$. The resulting estimates are presented in table 3. These average weights were used in determining biomass and usable meat represented in the faunal samples. Those species for which no measurement could be taken were compared with other species in the fauna and their size approximated. These estimates are preceeded by a ± designation in tables 1-3.

All the available forms of life are not harvested in a random way. As with even the most generalized subsistence system, selection in animals used for food is exercised. Linares (1976) has pointed out that a clear pattern can be seen in the hunting of terrestrial animals that are attracted to agriculturally disturbed land. Virtually no bird or mammalian arboreal forms are represented in the CA-3 faunal assemblage. Likewise, a relatively limited variety of the available aquatic fauna was intensively used, comprising members of only six fish families.

Many of the species used are generalized fish that can be found in various habitats. The most abundantly represented fish inhabit either mangrove sloughs and channels, or reefs (Randall 1968), habitats that are within easy access of the archaeological site. Fishes common in mangrove situations are the porcupine fish *(Diodon holocanthus)*, snook *(Centropomus undecimalis)*, and snapper *(Lutjanus griseus)*. In this assemblage only the parrotfish (Scaridae) are confined to coral reefs. The associated fishes which include a number of snappers *(Lutjanus analis* and *Lutjanus synagris)*, grunt *(Haemulon* sp.), jack *(Caranx* sp.), and grouper *(Epinephelus striatus)* are also around coral and rock reefs. Grouper *(E. striatus)* may also be found feeding over turtle grass.

The fishes represented in the site are predaceous, feeding on mollusks, crustaceans, and other fishes. They are also on the whole fairly uniform in size. Most of the fishes are estimated to range in size between one and five kilograms, with an occasional very large, up to 20 and 40 kilograms, tarpon and jew fish. These factors, their size and carnivorous feeding habits, would suggest that they were caught with hook and line. Some, for example, the snook, may also have been speared as they are so often today. Turtle

TABLE 1 SUMMARY OF THE AQUATIC FAUNA IN PERIOD I (AGUACATE PHASE) AT THE CERRO BRUJO (CA-3) SITE IN BOCAS DEL TORO PROVINCE ON THE ATLANTIC COAST

(The columns list from left to right: No. = number of elements, MNI = Minimum Number of Individuals, live weight = weight of live animal, MNI × l.w. = biomass, % usable = proportion of animal that is meat, usable meat = MNI × l.w. × % usable)

	No.	MNI	Live wt. (kg)	MNI × l.w.	% Usable	Usable meat
BONY FISH						
Centropomidae (snooks)						
Centropomus spp.	104	17	2.93	49.810	.90	44.829
Serranidae (sea basses/groupers)	16	1	10.826	10.826	.90	9.743
Epinephelus spp.	49	9	10.826	97.434	.90	87.691
Lutjanidae (snappers)						
Lutjanus spp.	22	9	2.00	18.00	.90	16.20
Carangidae (jacks)						
Caranx spp.	38	5	1.906	9.53	.90	8.577
Elopidae (tarpons)						
Megalops atlantica	13	1	9.122	9.122	.90	8.209
Pomadasyidae (grunts)						
Haemulon spp.	2	1	ca. 2.00	2.00	.90	1.8
Sphyraenidae (barracudas)						
Sphyraena spp.	1	1	3.188	3.188	.90	2.869
Scaridae (parrotfishes)	2	1	ca. 2.00	2.00	.90	1.8
Eleotridae (sleepers)	1	1	.133	.133	.90	.119
Sparidae (porgies)	0	—	—	—	—	—
Sciaenidae (drums/corvina)	0	—	—	—	—	—
Kyphosidae (rudderfishes)	0	—	—	—	—	—
Albulidae (bonefishes)	0	—	—	—	—	—

	No.	MNI	Live wt. (kg)	MNI × l.w.	% Usable	Usable meat
Diodontidae (porcupine fishes)						
Chilomycterus spp.	3	3	ca. .50	1.5	.90	1.35
Diodon spp.	11	3	ca. .50	1.5	.90	1.35
Belonidae (needlefishes)	1	1	ca. .10	.10	.90	.09
Batrachoididae (toadfishes)	2	1	ca. .10	.10	.90	.09
CARTILAGINOUS FISH						
Myliobatidae (eagle rays)						
Aetobatus narinari	2	2	1.339	2.678	.90	2.410
Dasyatidae (stingrays)						
Dasyatis sp.	1	1	1.339	1.339	.90	1.205
Sphyrnidae (hammerhead sharks)	0	0	—	—	—	—
REPTILES: TURTLES						
Cheloniidae (sea turtles)	53	5	57*	285.00	.35	99.75
Chelonia (green turtles)	—	—	—	—	—	—
Eretmochelys (hawksbills)	—	—	—	—	—	—
Caretta (loggerheads)	—	—	—	—	—	—
Dermochelys (leatherbacks)	1	1	318	318.00	.35	111.3
Emydidae (freshwater/marsh turtles)	0	0	—	—	—	—
REPTILES: CROCODILES						
Crocodylidae (crocodilians)	3	1	ca. 22.40	22.40	.60	13.44
AMPHIBIANS						
Anuran (frog)	20	3	.05	.15	.50	.075
AQUATIC MAMMALS						
Trichechus manatus (manatee)	1	1	239.00	239.00	.40	96.00
Total Period I:	346	68				

*Average weight for the three genera excluding leatherbacks.

TABLE 2 SUMMARY OF THE AQUATIC FAUNA IN PERIOD II (BOCAS PHASE) AT THE CERRO BRUJO (CA-3) SITE IN BOCAS DEL TORO

(Key to column abbreviations is found with Table 1)

	No.	MNI	Live wt. (kg)	MNI × l.w.	% Usable	Usable meat
BONY FISH						
Centropomidae (snooks)	403	53	2.93	155.29	.90	139.761
Serranidae (groupers/sea basses)	80	27	10.826	292.302	.90	263.072
Epinephelus spp.	177	25	10.826	270.650	.90	243.585
Mycteroperca sp.	1	1	10.826	10.826	.90	9.743
Lutjanidae (snappers)						
Lutjanus spp.	79	38	ca. 2.00	76.00	.90	68.4
Carangidae (jacks)	7	2	1.906	3.812	.90	3.431
Caranx spp.	152	19	1.906	36.214	.90	32.59
Elopidae (tarpons)						
Megalops atlantica	9	5	9.122	45.61	.90	41.049
Pomadasyidae (grunts)						
Haemulon spp.	17	10	ca. 2.00	20.00	.90	18.00
Sphyraenidae (barracudas)						
Sphyraena spp.	14	6	3.188	19.128	.90	17.215
Scaridae (parrotfishes)	4	4	ca. 2.00	8.00	.90	7.2
Albulidae (bonefishes)						
Albula vulpes	3	1	ca. .50	.50	.90	.45
Eleotridae (sleepers)	1	1	.133	.133	.90	.12
Gobiomorus dormitor	2	2	ca. .100	.20	.90	.18
Sparidae (porgies)						
Archosargus sp.	1	1	ca. 2.00	2.00	.90	1.8
Calamus spp.	2	2	ca. 2.00	4.00	.90	3.6
Scianidae (drums or corvina)	1	1	ca. 2.00	2.00	.90	1.8

	No.	MNI	Live wt. (kg)	MNI × l.w.	% Usable	Usable meat
Diodontidae (porcupine fishes)						
Chilomycterus spp.	277	8	.50	4.00	.90	3.6
Diodon spp.	57	8	.50	4.0	.90	3.6
Belonidae (needlefishes)	10	7	ca. .10	.70	.90	.63
Batrachoididae (toadfishes)						
Opsanus sp.	22	12	ca. .10	1.2	.90	1.08
	1	1	.10	.10	.90	.09
CARTILAGINOUS FISH						
Myliobatidae (eagle rays)						
Aetobatus narinari	1	1	1.339	1.339	.90	1.205
Dasyatidae (stingrays)						
Dasyatis spp.	5	4	1.339	5.356	.90	4.820
Sphyrnidae (hammerhead sharks)	7	2	1.338	2.676	.90	2.408
REPTILES: TURTLES						
Cheloniidae (sea turtles)	286	11	57.00	627.00	.40	250.8
Chelonia (green turtles)	6	4	90.00	360.00	.35	126.00
Eretmochelys (hawksbills)	5	3	36.00	108.00	.35	37.8
Caretta (loggerheads)	1	1	45.00	45.00	.35	15.75
Dermochelys (leatherbacks)	0	0	—	—	—	—
Emydidae (freshwater/marsh turtles)						
Rhinoclemys sp.	1	1	2.00	2.00	.35	.70
REPTILES: CROCODILES						
Crocodylidae (crocodilians)	5	5	22.40	112.00	.60	73.2
AMPHIBIANS						
Anuran (frogs/toads)	20	7	.050	.350	.50	.175
AQUATIC MAMMALS						
Trichechus manatus (manatee)	9	2	239	478	.40	191
Totals: Total Period II	1667	277				

and manatee are harpooned or netted today (Nietschmann 1973), as they may have been in the past.

In order to ascertain if at Cerro Brujo there were any differences in the bony fish employed during the older Aguacate phase versus the slightly more recent Bocas phase, we ran a contingency table chi-square analysis, using minimum number of individuals, biomass, and usable meat, between the same species in the two periods. The results (table 3) show the only significant difference to have been between the Serranidae or sea basses, which are slightly more abundant in the more recent Bocas phase (63 percent of all the bony fish in that period), than in the slightly older Aguacate phase (55 percent of all the bony fish in that period). Otherwise, the frequencies of the five most important bony fish families and/or genera were proportionally the same in both periods ($X^2 = 2.14$, 2 d.f.).

TABLE 3 A COMPARISON OF FREQUENCIES OF MOST COMMON BONY FISHES IN THE TWO PHASES AT CA-3

	Phases*	MNI	Biomass (kg)	Usable meat (kg)	Chi-square scores; d.f. 2, L .05, critical value = 5.99
Serranidae	B	10	108.26	97.43	$X^2 = 7.58$
	A	53	573.78	516.40	
Centropomidae	B	17	49.81	44.83	$X^2 = 1.516$
(*Centropomus*)	A	53	155.29	139.761	
Lutjanidae	B	9	18	16.2	$X^2 = 0$
(*Lutjanus*)	A	38	76	68.4	
Carangidae	B	5	9.53	8.56	$X^2 = 1.449$
	A	21	40.03	36.02	
Megalops	B	2	11.122	10.21	$X^2 = 0.169$
and *Haemulon*	A	15	75.61	59.049	

*B = Bocas phase; A = Aguacate phase.

13.4 AQUATIC RESOURCES AT LA PITAHAYA (IS-3)

The marine environment around the Gulf of Chiriqui has been described in Linares 1968b, with important clarifications and details added in section 6.2 of this volume. To summarize, the site of La Pitahaya is on a peninsula protected on the northern side by inshore islands and a quiet lagoon (Muertos Bay) but exposed to the more open Pacific waters on the leeward, southern side. Extensive mangrove stands and turbid, muddy waters characterize Muertos Bay, which forms the center of a complex embayment where numerous rivers discharge, while sandy beaches and intertidal rocky communities characterize the more open waters of the

Chiriqui Gulf. Coral formations and sea grass beds are little developed inshore in the Gulf (Glynn 1972).

The fish and reptilian sample from La Pitahaya is smaller than that excavated from Cerro Brujo, but it is large enough to provide us with a good idea of the resources that were used. The number of specimens identified is 1,688. The entire sample as a single cultural unit includes at least 317 individual aquatic animals (table 4). The analysis of this sample is the same as for the two Cerro Brujo samples. The following list summarizes our analysis:

Bony Fish:

Anguilliformes — a single bone of an eel of undetermined family is present.

Ariidae — sea catfish primarily of the genus *Arius* or *Ariopsis* (fig. 13.0-14) but also including a few *Bagre panamensis* are by far the most common type of fish present, constituting 50 percent of the fish fauna. The taxonomy of this family of fishes is presently being revised by Dr. R. W. Taylor, Smithsonian Institution. At this time it is not possible to assign precise taxonomic designations to specimens belonging to the *Arius-Ariopsis* group.

Belonidae — a single needlefish is represented.

Holocentridae — a single squirrel fish is represented.

Centropomidae — snooks are represented by three individuals.

Carangidae — jacks are represented by seven individuals.

Pomadasyidae — grunts are represented by two individuals.

Lutjanidae — snappers are also represented by two individuals.

Sparidae — porgy are represented by a single individual.

Sciaenidae — drums or corvinas (fig. 13.0-15) are fairly abundantly represented (10 percent of the fish fauna). Three genera are present and include *Bairdiella*, *Cynoscion*, and *Larimus*. Of these *Cynoscion* is the most common.

Sphyraenidae — barracuda of the genus *Sphyraena* are present.

Eleotridae — sleepers are present.

Scombridae — members of the mackerel (fig. 13.0-16) and tuna family are moderately abundant (7 percent of fish fauna).

Tetraodontidae — puffers of both genera *Lagocophalus* and *Spheroides*, with *Spheroides* (fig. 13.0-17) predominating are abundant in the sample. They constitute 13 percent of the fish fauna.

Diodontidae — porcupine fish are moderately abundant (fig. 13.0-18).

Cartilaginous Fish:

Orectolobidae — nurse shark *Ginglymostoma cirratum* (fig. 13.0-19a) is represented by one individual.

Carcharhinidae — both the tiger shark *Galeocerdo cuvieri* (fig. 13.0-19b) and the genus *Carcharhinus* are moderately abundant.

Sphyrnidae — hammerhead shark *Sphyrna* are also moderately abundant.

Dasyatidae — stingray *Dasyatis* are present.

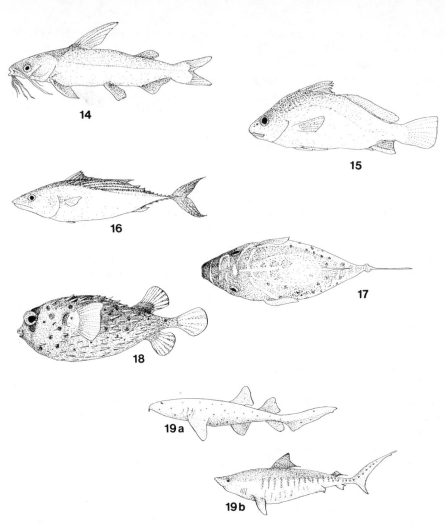

Figures 13.0-14–13.0-19:13.0-14, a generalized sea catfish to represent the Arius genus; 13.0-15, drums or "corvina" of the species Bairdiella armata, after S.E. Meek and S.F. Hildebrand 1925, vol. 15, part 2, plate 67; 13.0-16, mackerel or "sierra" of the species Sarda velox, after S.E. Meek and S.F. Hildebrand 1923, vol. 15, part 1, plate 24; 13.0-17, puffer of the genus Sphoeroides (top view), after S.E. Meek and S.F. Hildebrand 1928, vol. 15, part 3, plate 78; 13.0-18, porcupine fish of the genus Diodon, after photograph in J.E. Randall 1968, fig. 312, p. 282; 13.0-19, sharks of the species: a. Ginglymostoma cirratum; b. Galeocerdo cuvieri. After photographs in J.E. Randall 1968, fig. 1, p. 9, fig. 2, p. 10.

Reptile:

Iguanidae — iguana remains are moderately numerous. A few of these remains could be provisionally identified to genus and appeared to be *Iguana*.

Emydidae — two remains of pond turtle *Chrysemys scripta* are present in the collection.

Cheloniidae — remains of sea turtle are rare.

The most important elements of the aquatic fauna at La Pitahaya, which include the sea catfishes (Ariidae), shark (Orectolobidae, Carcharhinidae, and Sphyrnidae), corvina (Sciaenidae), and puffers (Tetraodontidae), may be characteristically found in shallow, turbid, brackish, coastal waters (Randall 1969). Sea catfishes are a resource that was most extensively used in prehistoric times from Mexico to Ecuador. Where they occur abundantly they are found as a prominent constituent of archaeological faunal samples. Sharks, where they are found, also may be represented by many and often large individuals. The La Pitahaya sample is one in which sharks with estimated weights up to 15 kilograms occur. The abundance of puffer fish is of interest from the standpoint of food preparation. The viscera of puffer fish are exceedingly toxic. In spite of this danger the meat is much esteemed. The Japanese today eat this fish and although the people who prepare it must be licensed, a number of fatalities from tetradon poisoning occur each year. If this fish was eaten at La Pitahaya, care must have been taken in its preparation.

A small portion of the fauna is composed of fishes that may be more typically found among reefs. These include barracuda (Sphyraenidae), squirrel fish (Holocentridae), and the consocies jack (Carangidae), snapper (Lutjanidae), and grunt (Pomadasyidae).

Another portion of the fauna is composed of tuna (Scombridae). Most members of this family occur in offshore pelagic waters, while some others may migrate inshore.

Estimates made of the sizes of the fishes in this sample indicate that with the exception of relatively large tiger and requiem sharks most of the fishes were small. They average 1.5 kilograms, ranging from 0.17 to 4.9 kilograms.

Evaluation of the data relating to the habits and sizes of the fishes used, the nature of the coastal waters fished, and archaeological remains of fishing equipment may provide some possible suggestions regarding the fishing techniques that were used. The magnitude of the Pacific tidal rise and fall is very great (5 to 7 meters), making the use of nets or weirs strung across tidal channels a likely capture method for fish that were uniformly small. Supporting this suggestion are abundant net sinkers excavated from the IS-3 site (report no. 15). All of the fish species represented are carnivores. Some are, in fact, voracious. This suggests the possibility that hook and line fishing would have been effective as well.

Sharks clearly would fall into this group described as voracious carnivores. They are most active during the night and could have been caught at that time by any of the means proposed. Many of the nurse (*Ginglymostoma*) and hammerhead (*Sphyrna*) sharks were small, but the remains of the tiger (*Galeocerdo*) and requiem (Carcharhinidae) sharks indicate that many of them were quite large (up to 16 kilograms). These would have provided a lot of meat. They also are a source of a valuable trade item, their teeth. Shark remains in the sample are almost entirely composed of vertebrae. Of the 261 shark specimens only two are teeth, one of which was drilled. If the entire animal was used at the site one would anticipate approximately equal

TABLE 4   SUMMARY OF THE AQUATIC FAUNA EXCAVATED FROM THE SITE OF LA PITAHAYA (IS-3) IN THE GULF OF CHIRIQUI ON THE PACIFIC SIDE

(Key to the column abbreviations are found with Table 1)

	No.	MNI	Live wt. (kg)	MNI × l.w.	% Usable	Usable meat (kg)
BONY FISH						
Ariidae (sea catfish)	830	54	1.245	67.23	.77	51.767
~ *Arius* spp. or *Ariopsis* spp.	150	60	1.245	74.7	.77	57.519
Bagre panamensis	16	13	1.245	16.185	.77	12.462
Sciaenidae (drums or corvinas)	51	17	1.11	18.87	.90	16.983
Cynoscion spp.	16	6	.826	4.956	.90	4.46
Larimus sp.	1	1	.173	.173	.90	.156
Bairdiella sp.	1	1	.173	.173	.90	.156
Scombridae (mackerels & tuna)	44	17	1.372	23.324	.90	20.992
Tetradontidae (puffers)						
Lagocephalus spp.	4	3	ca. .55	1.65	.90	1.485
Sphoeroides spp.	55	29	ca. .55	15.95	.90	14.355
Sphyraenidae (barracuda)						
Sphyraena spp.	15	8	.529	4.23	.90	3.80
Diodontidae (porcupine fish)	35	18	.549	9.882	.90	8.894
Eleotridae (sleepers or gobies)	13	9	.77	6.93	.90	6.237
Carangidae (jacks)	12	7	1.00	7.00	.90	6.3
Centropomus (snook)	8	3	2.16	6.48	.90	5.835
Lutjanidae (snappers)	2	2	1.00	2.00	.90	1.8
Pomadasyidae (grunts)	5	2	1.00	2.00	.90	1.8
Sparidae (porgies)	1	1	.738	.738	.90	.664
Holocentridae (squirrel fishes)	1	1	.50	.50	.90	.45
Belonidae (needlefishes)	2	1	ca. .100	.100	.90	.09

	No.	MNI	Live wt (kg)	MNI × l.w.	% Usable	Usable meat (kg)
CARTILAGINOUS FISH						
Orectolobidae (nurse sharks)						
Ginglymostoma cirratum	2	1	.469	.469	.90	0.422
Carcharhinidae (requiem sharks)	186	12	5.087	61.044	.90	54.94
Carcharhinus spp. (reef shark)	8	4	5.087	20.348	.90	18.313
Galeocerdo cuvieri (tiger shark)	18	6	11.008	66.048	.90	59.443
Sphyrnidae (hammerheads)						
Sphyrna spp.	47	16	1.116	17.86	.90	16.074
Dasyatidae (stingrays)	1	1	2.653	2.653	.90	2.388
Dasyatis spp.	5	4	2.653	10.61	.90	9.549
REPTILES						
Iguanidae (probably Iguana)	55	14	4.536	63.504	.60	38.102
Cheloniidae (sea turtles)	5	3	57.00	171.00	.35	59.85
Chelonia mydas	7	1	90.00	90.00	.40	36.00
Emydidae (freshwater turtle)						
Chrysemys scripta	92	2	4.00	8.00	.35	2.8
Totals	1,688	317				

quantities of teeth and vertebrae. The two types of shark (tiger and requiem) represented by the largest individuals are the kinds that have teeth that are most often used as tools or ornaments and traded inland. The risks involved in catching these large and dangerous animals were evidently considered worth taking for the meat and trade items they provided.

The reptilian faunal sample from IS-3 is very small, except for the genus Iguana that thrives on river-edges and man-made clearings. Considering the fact that a freshwater pond once existed in the vicinity of La Pitahaya (report no. 17), the paucity of remains of *Chrysemys scripta* (old name, *Pseudemys scripta*) can only be due to its having been depleted early on. This widely ranging pond turtle lives in swamps and lakes overgrown with plants and filled-up with mud (Stebbins 1954, pp. 177–179). Sea turtles occur in Pacific waters, as the few remains of Cheloniidae at IS-3 indicate, but they are far more common in Panamanian Atlantic waters, where turtle grass and other marine plants abound.

13.6   A COMPARISON OF THE AQUATIC FAUNA FROM BOTH SIDES OF THE ISTHMUS

Aquatic resource use on the two shores was quite different in spite of the fact that a number of the same types of fishes were used on both coasts (tables 5 and 6). The differences lie in the relative extent to which the various available marine resources were used. Sea cows and sea turtles were evidently of major importance to the diet of the people at Cerro Brujo, whereas fish were the predominant aquatic species of La Pitahaya. Not only do fish constitute different amounts of the aquatic fauna but also different species predominate in the two assemblages. At Cerro Brujo the most important species, from the standpoint of numbers of individuals represented and amount of usable meat they can contribute, are grouper (Serranidae), snook (*Centropomus* sp.), snapper (Lutjanidae), and jack (Carangidae). At La Pitahaya the important species are shark (Carcharhinidae, Orectolobidae, Sphyrnidae) and catfish (Ariidae). Furthermore, the fish from La Pitahaya were on the average only half the size of the fish in the Cerro Brujo sample (table 7).

The relative importance of different marine habitats to the fishing efforts of peoples on both coasts was also striking (table 8). The inhabitants of CA-3 were going out to coral reefs as often as to mangrove channels to fish, all the while staying close inshore. The inhabitants of La Pitahaya, however, were exploiting predominantly the mangrove fauna, venturing out to the rocky (and dangerous) offshore reefs to fish as infrequently as they set out to open seas in search of pelagic species. Related to the habitats used for fishing were the techniques employed. Fishing was probably done with hook and line and spears on the Bocas side, where tides are of low amplitude and seines or nets are difficult to use as they become entangled in the coral reefs. However, no fishing gear was recovered from the CA-3 shell-midden deposits, a fact that suggests the use of hardwoods for fishhooks and/or spears. On the Pacific side the technique that predominated at IS-3 seems to have been netting and/or seining. The small and relatively uniform size of the fish caught, especially in contrast with CA-3, suggests as much, as does the occurrence of net weights (i.e., notched stones) in the IS-3 deposits. Placing nets and traps across mangrove channels at high tide and trapping fish as the tide retreats is a common fishing strategy today all along the Pacific coast of Panama.

TABLE 5   A COMPARISON BETWEEN THE ARCHAEOLOGICAL AQUATIC FAUNA FROM CERRO BRUJO ON THE ATLANTIC AND LA PITAHAYA ON THE PACIFIC

BONY FISH	CERRO BRUJO Biomass (kg)	%	LA PITAHAYA Biomass (kg)	%
Serranidae (sea basses/groupers)	682.04	58.6	0	0
Centropomidae (snooks)	205.10	17.6	6.48	2.5
Lutjanidae (snappers)	94.00	8.1	2.00	0.8
Elopidae (tarpons)	54.73	4.7	0	0
Carangidae (jacks)	49.56	4.3	7.00	2.7
Sphyraenidae (barracudas)	22.32	1.9	4.23	1.6
Pomadasyidae (grunts)	22.00	1.0	2.00	0.8
Diodontidae (porcupine fishes)	11.00	1.0	9.88	3.8
Scaridae (parrotfishes)	10.00	0.9	0	0
Sparidae (porgies)	6.00	0.5	.74	0.3
Scianidae (drums or corvinas)	2.00	0.2	24.17	9.2
Kyphosidae (rudderfishes)	2.00	0.2	0	0
Batrachoididae (toadfishes)	1.40	0.1	0	0
Belonidae (needlefishes)	.80	0.1	.10	0.04
Albulidae (bonefishes)	0.50	0.04	0	0
Eleotridae (sleepers)	0.47	0.04	6.93	2.6
Ariidae (sea catfishes)	0	0	158.12	60.1
Scombridae (mackerels & tuna)	0	0	23.32	8.9
Tetradontidae (puffers)	0	0	17.60	6.7
Holocentridae (squirrel fishes)	0	0	.50	0.2
Totals	1,163.92	100%	263.07	100%

TABLE 6 A COMPARISON OF CARTILAGINOUS FISH, REPTILES, AND AQUATIC MAMMALS AT CA-3 and IS-3

	CERRO BRUJO (CA-3)			LA PITAHAYA (IS-3)		
	MNI	Biomass	Usable meat (kg)	MNI	Biomass	Usable meat (kg)
CARTILAGINOUS FISH						
Dasyatidae (stingrays)	5	6.695	6.026	5	13.263	11.937
Myliobatidae (eagle rays)	3	4.017	3.615	0	0	0
Sphyrnidae (hammerhead sharks)	2	2.676	2.408	16	17.86	16.074
Orectolobidae (nurse sharks)	0	0	0	1	0.469	0.422
Carcharhinidae (requiem sharks)	0	0	0	22	147.44	132.696
REPTILES						
Cheloniidae (sea turtles)	25	1743	641.4	4	261.0	95.85
Crocodylidae (crocodilians)	6	134.4	80.64	0	0	0
Iguanidae (iguana)	0	0	0	14	63.50	38.10
AMPHIBIANS						
Anuran (frogs/toads)	10	.50	.25	0	0	0
AQUATIC MAMMALS						
Trichechus manatus (manatee)	3	717	286.8	0	0	0

TABLE 7   ESTIMATES OF LIVE WEIGHTS (IN KG)
OF FISHES FROM CA-3 AND IS-3

*(Based on correlations with cervical
centrum widths)*

	N	Mean	Range
CERRO BRUJO			
Megalops	3	9.122	3.097–20.235
Centropomus	11	2.930	1.372– 5.625
Serranidae	6	10.826	1.112–42.756
Caranx	3	1.906	1.052– 2.679
Sphyraena	2	3.188	1.388– 5.037
Eleotridae	1	.133	
LA PITAHAYA			
Ginglymostoma	1	.469	
Carcharhinidae	4	5.087	1.112–12.595
Galeocerdo	4	11.008	9.118–15.896
Sphyrna	4	1.116	.681– 1.987
Dasyatis	2	2.653	.549– 4.757
Ariidae	3	1.245	.803– 1.626
Centropomus	2	2.161	2.072– 2.250
Sparidae	1	.738	
Sciaenidae	2	1.222	.942– 1.502
Cynoscion	2	.826	.508– 1.143
Bairdiella	1	.173	
Sphyraena	1	.529	
Eleotridae	2	.770	.301– 1.239
Scombridae	1	1.372	
Diodon	1	.549	

TABLE 8   A COMPARISON OF THE RELATIVE IMPORTANCE OF FISHES
ADAPTED TO THREE DIFFERENT HABITATS FOUND IN THE
ARCHAEOLOGICAL COLLECTIONS IN CERRO BRUJO (CA-3)
AND LA PITAHAYA (IS-3)

	CA-3 *(both periods)*			IS-3 *(all periods)*		
	No.	MNI	%	No.	MNI	%
Estuarine fish	941	140	46.8	1450	260	87.5
Reef fish	661	159	53.2	35	20	6.7
Pelagic fish	0	0	0	44	17	5.7
Totals		299			297	

14.0

Molluskan Fauna from Both Sides of the Isthmus

I. BORGOGNO AND O.F. LINARES

14.1 INTRODUCTION

When the Panamanian Isthmus came into existence some 3.5 million years ago, this "land bridge disrupted an extensive (mollusk) province to form the present Caribbean and Panamic provinces" (Woodring 1966, p. 430). A great number of species that once existed on both seas, became extinct, especially on the Atlantic side, leading to the "impoverishment of the present Caribbean fauna" (ibid.). Thus, the molluskan fauna on both sides of Panama are far from identical, with species such as *Strombus galeatus* occurring on the Pacific side only. The following section discusses the role of mollusks in the subsistence system of the Cerro Brujo inhabitants on the Atlantic coast and those of La Pitahaya on the Pacific. We will argue that cultural selectivity, rather than natural availability, seems to explain the differential use of mollusk resources between these two archaeological sites.

14.2 THE CERRO BRUJO MOLLUSKS

The following discussion is based on an analysis of the shells recovered from five column samples measuring 40 x 40 centimeters each from five different trenches at the CA-3 locality (report no. 6, fig. 3a, b). The shell was collected by stratigraphic units; unwashed, these units averaged almost 4,000 grams in size. To avoid contamination between units, shell was taken only from the center of each stratigraphic level; i.e., no material was saved from the centimeters that constitute the transition from one stratum to another, as mixing between strata is most likely to occur in this zone. The samples were screened on a 0.25-inch mesh, with everything remaining in the screen being recovered. According to a study by Greenwood (1961), shell screened to 0.25 inch provides a sample comparable to that obtained from smaller meshes, except where the shell being sampled tends to fracture into very small pieces. In the same article, Greenwood demonstrated that a shell sample of 500 grams is as accurate a measure of a level as the total amount of shell from that level. At Cerro Brujo, an attempt was made to collect samples that would measure 2,000 grams when clean and dry. After being washed in the laboratory and cleared of extraneous stone and pottery, the units ranged in size from less than 1,000 grams to more than 2,000 grams, most of them being between 1,000 and 2,000 grams. The identifiable sample size is reduced anywhere from 10 to 50 percent, however, as each unit contains numerous fragments. (It should be noted that many of these fragments seem to be of *Ostrea* sp.)

Some doubt arises as to the ability of any sampling technique to indicate all the species present at a site. The most notable omission for Cerro Brujo is *Lyropecten nodosus*, which does not occur in any of the samples, but which was noticed in small quantities in most of the cuts while we were excavating. The infrequency of occurrence at the site seems to indicate a negligible importance, but it would be of distinct interest to know the entire catalogue of species at a site. (There are probably other species of minor importance at Cerro Brujo which do not appear in the sample; *Lyropecten nodosus* is notable in absence because it is a spectacular shell.) It should be noted, however, that the column-sample method is entirely adequate for determining occurrence and proportions of the more important species, which is the information needed for an ecological analysis (Greenwood 1961).

A total of 25 different species, 17 pelecypods and 8 gastropods, was identified. Several very small species, of extremely doubtful use as food, were simply lumped into a "miscellaneous" category, which also includes the frequently occurring coral fragments. The vast majority of the species occur sporadically and/or in very small quantities. Two of the species only occur once. There are, however, five species which occur in *all* shell-bearing units, in comparatively large quantities. These five are: *Arca imbricata* Bruguière, *Arca zebra* Swainson, *Chama macerophylla* Gmelin, *Crassostrea rhizophorae* Guilding, and *Isognomon alatus* Gmelin (fig. 14.0-1). There do not seem to be any clear-cut trends in the frequencies of these species in the three shell-bearing layers (table 1).

These five species are all pelecypods with an intertidal/shallow water distribution. Furthermore, they all occur attached to some surface, usually rocks or mangrove roots; i.e., they form mollusk beds that can be easily harvested once they are located. Obviously, this description applies equally well to many of the other pelecypods present in the sample. However, these appear only infrequently and in such small quantities that it seems unlikely that there was any systematic utilization of them. While some of the gastropods, notably *Murex* sp., do appear frequently in the unit, hence arguing for consistent utilization, and also have an intertidal to shallow water distribution, they are mobile and do not form beds. Thus, they cannot be "harvested" in the way that sessile pelecypods can be. It seems likely, therefore, that the five species previously named were being harvested on a regular basis from well-known beds. Occasional interlopers – either other pelecypods adapted to those conditions and seeking to establish footholds, or predatory gastropods come to feast on their sedentary relatives – were gathered if and when they appeared among the regularly collected species.

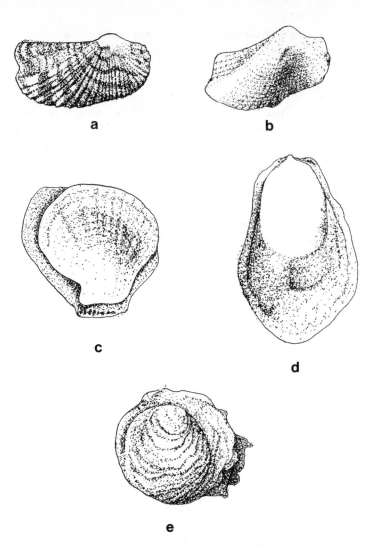

Figure 14.0-1: Five of the most common species of mollusks found in the Cerro Brujo deposits: a. Arca zebra; *b.* Arca imbricata; *c.* Isognomon alatus; *d.* Crassostrea rhizophorae; *e.* Chama macerophylla. *After photographs in G.K. Warmke and R.T. Abbott 1962, plates 30, 32, 35, 37.*

It has been assumed (Linares 1977a) that mollusks were an important supplement to the diet on the Atlantic coast. The degree of importance remains a matter of conjecture. The size of the midden suggests at first sight a rather heavy reliance on shellfish. However, the argument has been advanced (see conclusions) that a bucket of mollusks gives a lot of refuse and little food as compared to fish or game which leave a handful of bones but provide a considerable amount of meat (Osborn ms. 1977). Thus, it would be extremely useful to determine the amount of food represented by a given amount of shell: for Cerro Brujo, this could be done in terms of

TABLE 1 PERCENTAGE FREQUENCIES (BY WEIGHT) OF THE FIVE MOST IMPORTANT MOLLUSK SPECIES IN THE CA-3 SITE

Shell columns and layers	Arca imbricata gms (%)	Arca zebra gms (%)	Crassostrea rhizophorae gms (%)	Isognomon alatus gms (%)	Chama macerophylla gms (%)	Others gms (%)	Totals
A column							
A	653 (.22)	482 (.17)	467 (.16)	171 (.06)	1088 (.37)	63 (.02)	2924
B^1	934 (.31)	498 (.17)	295 (.10)	155 (.05)	996 (.33)	138 (.05)	3016
B^2	871 (.25)	529 (.15)	311 (.09)	155 (.05)	1555 (.45)	62 (.02)	3483
B column							
A	342 (.24)	380 (.27)	93 (.07)	62 (.04)	467 (.33)	78 (.06)	1422
B^1	1089 (.27)	685 (.17)	685 (.17)	310 (.08)	1181 (.29)	125 (.03)	4075
B^2	1120 (.27)	965 (.23)	233 (.06)	187 (.04)	1393 (.33)	311 (.07)	4209
C column							
A	280 (.27)	93 (.09)	62 (.06)	62 (.06)	342 (.32)	218 (.21)	1057
B^1	467 (.26)	404 (.22)	280 (.15)	140 (.08)	497 (.27)	31 (.02)	1819
B^2	482 (.19)	374 (.15)	265 (.11)	373 (.15)	933 (.37)	109 (.04)	2536
D column							
A	404 (.37)	249 (.23)	62 (.06)	47 (.04)	342 (.31)	0 (.00)	1104
B^1	280 (.42)	109 (.16)	78 (.12)	62 (.09)	124 (.19)	16 (.02)	669
B^2	249 (.19)	342 (.26)	140 (.11)	62 (.05)	373 (.29)	140 (.11)	1306
E column							
A	187 (.12)	218 (.14)	249 (.15)	171 (.11)	747 (.46)	47 (.03)	1619
B^1	233 (.19)	93 (.07)	249 (.20)	124 (.10)	529 (.42)	31 (.03)	1259
B^2	47 (.07)	31 (.05)	124 (.20)	124 (.20)	140 (.22)	171 (.27)	637

Note: A column was in feature 2, cut 9L; B column was in feature 2, cut 7L/8L; C column was in feature 1, cut 8H; D column was in feature 8; E column was in feature 4, cut 23 PQ.

grams of food per kilogram of dry shell for each of the five important species. This would eliminate any discrepancies between the species, as some species grow heavier shells than others. With these data, the amount of food represented by a shell sample could be determined.

Another matter for consideration is the distance that the mollusks were transported. The site CA-3 is located 140 meters above sea level, and here are found huge mounds of shell. Several factors may have contributed to this phenomenon. First, by leaving the animal alive and intact, the food could be preserved for several hours. This would be of extreme importance if shellfish gathering were an ancillary activity — that is, if the collecting was done while fishing or hunting — or some other activity that would prevent immediate transport and preparation. A second consideration may have been the actual mechanics of food preparation and distribution. While any of these contingencies is possible, when considered in conjunction with other problems of on-the-spot preparation, it would appear more convenient to carry the uncooked animal in its shell. This would especially be true if considerations of weight were unimportant.

Therefore, to summarize briefly: the inhabitants of CA-3 were consistently utilizing five species of mollusks throughout the shell-gathering phase. (To determine the exact usage patterns will require statistical analysis.) These five species occur intertidally in beds, lending themselves to easy harvesting. Mollusks were carried alive and whole up to the living area because (1) the food did not spoil as quickly, (2) the mechanics of preparation and serving were more convenient, and (3) transportation of large weights was not a major consideration.

As a final point, it is interesting to note that modern inhabitants of the area still utilize shellfish, but not as consistently and possibly not the same species (at least proportionately). Shell middens are not developed, however, because the refuse is discarded directly into the sea. This difference is due to a change in settlement pattern, which has shifted from the ridge-top to the coast as a result of modern influences, principally the introduction of the outboard motor (Linares 1970).

14.3   THE PITAHAYA MOLLUSKS

The midden deposits at IS-3 cannot under any definition be called shell mounds even though a few shell specimens occurred in every stratum. While the CA-3 middens were made of shell, at IS-3 they simply contained some shell. Because the quantity of shell was small, and because the IS-3 research of 1973 had other aims in mind, we did not attempt a quantitative analysis of shell species comparable to the one we did at CA-3. However, the pattern of consistent reliance on five species at CA-3 forms a striking contrast to the contemporaneous patterns established on the Pacific side during the San Lorenzo-Chiriqui phases (Linares 1968b, pp. 68-73), wherein there is no instance of constant utilization of even one species. The two species which occur most frequently in the Gulf of Chiriqui sites, *Melongena patula* and *Anadara grandis* (fig. 14.0-2), appear in less than one-third of

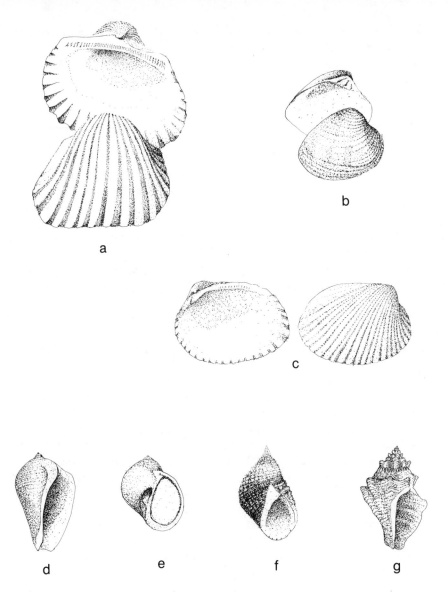

Figure 14.0-2: Species of mollusks found in La Pitahaya deposits: a. Anadara grandis; *b.* Anomalocardia subrugosa; *c.* Lunarca bucaruana; *d.* Melongena patula; *e.* Natica chemnitzii; *f.* Littorina varia; *g.* Strombus granulatus. *Only species a and b occur with any frequency, the rest being relatively rare. After photographs in A.M. Keene 1958, figs. 5b, 67, 178, 258, 338, 401.*

the units. They are not represented at Cerro Brujo because they do not occur on the Atlantic side. However, they are of minor importance as compared to the five major species of CA-3. It is of further interest that these two, *Melongena patula* and *Anadara grandis,* do not occur in beds. The other species in figure 14.0-2 are represented by only a few specimens.

To summarize, the quantity and variety of mollusks found in the IS-3 deposits is very much reduced even when compared to other estuarine sites in the Chiriqui Gulf, such as Villalba (IS-7), and San Lorenzo (SL-1); (see Linares 1968b). Hence, mollusks formed a negligible part of the diet of the IS-3 inhabitants.

14.4   CONCLUSIONS

The "natural" availability of mollusks on the Atlantic side of the Isthmus seems generally less than that of the Pacific, especially with reference to soft-bottom–dwelling species of pelecypods, whose biomasses are definitely higher on the Pacific, even in areas such as Chiriqui that do not get the direct effects of the upwelling (M. Bertness, personal communication). Yet the Cerro Brujo peoples were eating mollusks to a much greater extent than were the peoples of La Pitahaya. The obvious question to ask is why was this so?

As Osborn (ms.1977) has pointed out, the importance of shellfish as a staple food resource in the diet of prehistoric peoples has been exaggerated. "For example, one metric ton (1,000 kg) of mussels contains less calories than one white-tailed deer weighing 64 kg " (ibid., p. 13). Not only is the nutrient content of shellfish low, but as Osborn also demonstrates the exploitative costs of shellfish-collecting are higher than those of hunting and many times that of manioc and maize cultivation (ibid., table 5, p. 16). In fact, maize agriculture "generates more than 124 times as many calories per hectare per day than does the Peru Current which is one of the most productive ocean regions of the world" (ibid., p. 19).

Thus, the intensive maize-growing and probably palm-tending economy of La Pitahaya seems to have obviated the need to harvest "marginal" protein resources such as mollusks. In contrast, the subsistence system of the Cerro Brujo groups seemed well suited to the exploitation of a widely spaced resource; one that requires more labor and smaller returns per man-hours than almost any other subsistence strategy, except perhaps that of wild-plant gathering. Yet shellfish could be counted upon at CA-3 to contribute a steady and predictable dietary supplement, one that could be gathered by women and children, especially on days when other protein quests failed.

PART FIVE

CONTEMPORARY INDIAN SOCIETIES
IN WESTERN PANAMA

This part of the account switches from archaeological considerations to a brief description of the 50,000 Guaymí Indians living today in the province of Bocas del Toro and the Chiriqui highlands. All indications are that they, or their close relatives, once occupied a more extensive territory that probably included the coastal plains of Chiriqui, and possibly other areas as far east as the central provinces.

As Young (section 15.0) emphasizes, many of the Guaymí features of social, as well as economic and political, organization show strong continuities from the past. Their dispersed settlement pattern is obviously adapted to a traditional system of swidden cultivation. Some of their rituals, including the most important, the *balsería* and the *chichería*, still serve to encourage agricultural overproduction and to cushion against ecological disaster. In former days, these same rituals may have functioned as redistributive occasions for chiefs, such as the one that must have presided at IS-3, and as contexts where trade could take place among warring groups. It is interesting to note that one of the principal ritual items in the Guaymí *balsería*, the shell-trumpet, was also present in our Cerro Brujo excavations.

There are important differences in subsistence patterns between the Bocas and Chiriqui Guaymí populations. Generally speaking, crops such as maize and beans, which do better in areas with a prolonged dry season, are grown by the Guaymí on the Pacific slopes; crops that prosper under constantly humid conditions, such as tubers, including *Xanthosoma*, and peach palms are grown by the Bocas Guaymí. These different adaptations in cropping patterns are treated in more detail by Bort (report no. 20).

15.0

Notes on Guaymí Traditional Culture

P. D. YOUNG

15.1 INTRODUCTION

The Guaymí are the largest Indian population in the Republic of Panama. They occupy the isolated and largely inaccessible mountainous regions of the provinces of Chiriqui and Veraguas (fig. 15.0-1) and the mountains and some sectors of the coast in the province of Bocas del Toro (fig. 15.0-2). Formerly their territory was much more extensive, probably extending to the coast in eastern Chiriqui and almost certainly including most of the Bocas coast.

Little is known about the Guaymí of pre-Conquest times or about what happened to them during the first hundred years after contact. It is possible that the decimation and dislocation of native populations which occurred throughout much of Central America during this early period affected the Guaymí as well, though direct documentation is not available.

The earliest good account of the Guaymí is that of Fray Adrian de Ufeldre (also known as Fray Adrian de Santo Tomás) who lived among the Guaymí between 1622 and 1637 (Ufeldre 1682). A comparison of this and more recent accounts (Franco 1882; Pinart 1885; Johnson 1948; Alphonse 1956) with contemporary data (Young 1971, 1976; Bort 1976; Young and Bort 1976) attests to the presence by the early seventeenth century and the historical continuity of many of the features which today characterize Guaymí traditional culture. References to the Guaymí in Ferdinand Columbus's account of his father's fourth voyage to the New World in 1502-1503 suggest that much of Fray Adrian's descriptive material would hold true in general for Guaymí culture at the time of first European contact.

Fray Adrian notes that the Guaymí were subsistence farmers, but that hunting and fishing were also important subsistence activities. He points out that Guaymí settlements were very small and were located at some distance one from another. He makes it clear that polygyny, child betrothal, the levirate, the sororate, in-law avoidances and economic obligations to affinal as well as consanguineal relatives were all-important features of seventeenth-century Guaymí culture, and some of his remarks suggest the

Figure 15.0-1: A Guaymí dwelling in the highlands of San Felix in Chiriqui.

practice of postmarital virilocality. His descriptive accounts of *balsería*, the major Guaymí ritual, is strikingly similar to accounts I obtained in the 1960s and 1970s (Young 1976). While some of these features of early seventeenth-century Guaymí culture have declined considerably in importance, none has completely disappeared. Adjustments have been made to a changing cultural and natural environment, but in many respects the Guaymí have maintained a style of life similar to that of their ancestors, incorporating practices that in at least some instances may greatly antedate the appearance of Europeans on the scene. More ethnohistorical detail may be found in Young 1970.

15.2   SETTLEMENT PATTERNS

Today the Guaymí are virtually surrounded by rural-dwelling Panamanians, to whom they refer in Spanish as *latinos* or in their language as *suliá*. Their total population, according to the Panamanian census of 1970, was 42,857. Today there are some 52,000 Guaymí, and these figures do not take into account the heavy migration of Guaymí in recent years into the towns and cities of the Republic. Preliminary data from Chiriqui indicate that permanent migration out of the Indian area may range between 7,000 and 10,000 individuals. Sixty percent of the Guaymí live in Chiriqui, 30 percent in Bocas, and 10 percent in Veraguas (excluding migrants).

The Panamanian government estimates that the total land area presently occupied by the Guaymí is approximately 5,000 square kilometers. The boundaries of the *comarca* have never been surveyed. My own estimate of the territory they occupy is 6,000 to 6,500 square kilometers. By anyone's

Figure 15.0-2: A Guaymí dwelling in Almirante Bay, Bocas del Toro.

estimate, less than half of this land is now cultivable using the agricultural technology that the Guaymí possess.

Traditionally the Guaymí live in small hamlets called *caseríos,* with five to eight houses occupied by families related through kinship (report no. 20; fig. 20/1a, b). The distance separating one community from another is usually a kilometer or more. Due to the recent rapid increases in population, many hamlets are now much larger and are occupied by members of two or more distinct kin groups. The small communities scattered throughout the mountains represent an adaptation to their system of swidden or slash-and-burn agriculture, a pattern that has changed little since the time of Columbus. Slash-and-burn techniques in this area require several hectares of land to feed even a relatively small family of five or six, and Guaymí families are often much larger. The small size and dispersion of hamlets normally permit men to reside close to the plots of land they are cultivating.

15.3   SOCIAL ORGANIZATION

Among the cultural traditions of the Guaymí one finds the practice of extensive reciprocity among kinsmen with respect to food, the exchange of other products, and the exchange of labor; collective ownership and control of land by kin groups with use rights assigned to individuals; a form of marriage involving the symmetrical exchange of women between kin groups that established a series of rights and obligations, not just between spouses or between parents-in-law and children-in-law, but among all the members of the marriage-linked kin groups; polygyny, both sororal and nonsororal; mother-in-law/son-in-law avoidance; and residence after marriage in the hamlet of the husband. The levirate, the sororate, and child betrothal, all practices mentioned in historical documents, have become quite uncommon in recent years but have not completely disappeared.

A series of traditional rituals that served as focal points of cultural integration have disapppeared or greatly diminished in scale, frequency, and importance in the last two decades. The traditional means of achieving prestige and coming to be a man of importance — a leader — has been (until *very* recently) through the sponsorship of rituals such as *chichería* and *balsería* and others (Young and Bort 1976; Young 1976). In addition to serving as a means of publicly displaying one's prestige and accumulating more, these rituals serve to emphasize patterns of economic reciprocity among kinsmen and between kin groups and to express in symbolic form both the ideals and the realities of Guaymí society.

These same rituals also serve to encourage a level of agricultural production greater than that necessary to meet ordinary daily needs, for rituals can be sponsored only when surplus food is available. The rituals can thus be interpreted as serving an adaptive function, as providing a means by which adequate production may be assured even in years of poor harvests because the calculated overproduction intended for use in the sponsorship of rituals (which require large quantities of food and *chicha*) could always be used, in time of scarce resources, for the daily consumption of the family and other kinsmen in the event that the harvest was not sufficient to meet the demands of both daily needs and ritual needs.

While it cannot be conclusively proven that twentieth-century Guaymí rituals existed in pre-Hispanic times, there are grounds for suggesting that such an inference is reasonable. First, it is extremely unlikely that a ritual as elaborate as the *balsería*, described in great detail by Fray Adrian, not only came into existence but also became the major Guaymí ritual within a century of first European contact. It is thus reasonable to assume that the *balsería*, at least, was present at the time of first contact. Second, the ritual sibling relationship (Young and Bort 1976), of central importance to the *balsería*, appears to be the key relationship in many Guaymí rituals. Third, the fact that rituals structurally similar to those of the Guaymí are found or are known to have been present throughout much of native northern South America certainly strengthens the case for their antiquity among the Guaymí. It is highly unlikely that such widespread geographic distribution could have come about in post-Conquest times, especially when one considers that a primary task of the conquerors was to stamp out native rituals.

Since the *balserías*, of both the seventeenth and the twentieth centuries, were occasions for a good deal of trading, and since warfare is known to have been endemic throughout the area in late prehistoric and early historic times, it is possible that these rituals also served in the past as periods of truce during which freedom of movement between otherwise warring regions was possible.

15.4   ECONOMY

Guaymí traditional economy consists of subsistence agriculture utilizing slash-and-burn or slash-and-mulch (fig. 15.0-2) techniques, supplemented in some cases by the raising of a few cattle, chickens, or pigs and, to a considerably lesser extent today than in the past, hunting and fishing (fig. 15.0-3). Their most important crops, those which constitute the major part of the diet in one or another part of the Guaymí territory, are corn (fig. 15.0-4), beans, bananas, rice, various tubers such as otoe, sweet manioc, taro, and yams, and peach palm fruit. Fray Adrian mentions yuca, sweet potatoes, yams, squashes, and otoe as being cultivated by the Bocas Guaymí in the early seventeenth century and also points out that there was little corn and few bananas, but that peach palm fruit was of great importance and was found in great abundance. He makes no mention at all of beans. The relative importance of these foods in the diet depends to a large extent on environmental conditions, the greatest difference being between the Pacific and Atlantic slopes. Of major importance in Chiriqui, for example, are corn, beans, and bananas, while in Bocas the Guaymí diet depends heavily on root crops and bananas, and peach palm fruit during a part of the

Figure 15.0-3: Guaymí Indian of the San Felix highlands in Chiriqui using the long bow with blunted tip to catch birds.

year. (See John Bort's report no. 20 for more detail on the contrast in subsistence patterns between Bocas and Chiriqui.)

Of the above list, only taro (locally called *dasheen*), bananas, and rice are imported plants. None appears to have completely displaced any indigenous cultivar, though each has caused a shift in the relative importance of crops within the total inventory. Taro is raised only by the Guaymí living near the Caribbean coast and has partially displaced otoe and sweet manioc in the diet. I have no data on how early it was introduced but suspect it may have first come in with the black English-speaking Antillean population in the early twentieth century.

Bananas are mentioned by Fray Adrian as being of only minor importance in the early seventeenth century. Today they are a major staple on both sides of the cordillera, apparently having partially replaced root crops

Figure 15.0-4: Guaymí Indian women carrying maize from fields.

as a major source of carbohydrates in the diet. High productivity and a lesser susceptibility to predators are probably among the factors that account for the displacement of indigenous tubers by bananas.

Rice is of very recent introduction, not having been of any noticeable importance among the Guaymí of Chiriqui until some time after the 1930s and somewhat later in Bocas. The Guaymí appreciate its palatability as well as its easy marketability, but it is still a crop of very limited distribution.

The individual household is the basic economic unit in daily productive and consumptive activities (fig. 15.0-5), but larger groups regularly cooperate in clearing land, weeding fields, and occasionally in harvesting. Such labor is reciprocal and is a major aspect of the structure of production. Reciprocal labor groups, called *juntas,* are organized by and composed of males, though in harvesting, females often participate as well. Labor groups normally are made up of consanguineally related males. The coresidence of related males in a single hamlet is thus a factor in the organization of these labor groups since such coresident males often constitute the majority of a group's participants. Additional participants are recruited from among one's consanguines and affines in nearby communities.

Land is owned collectively by the kin group and its use is generally regulated to some extent by the senior resident male in consultation with

Figure 15.0-5: Interior of a Guaymí dwelling.

other resident kinsmen. Use rights are inherited bilaterally. This provides a man with at least two alternatives in seeking land to farm. If, for example, his father's kinsmen do not have sufficient land available, a man may seek to exercise his right to farm land belonging to his mother's kinsmen. Since women also inherit land-use rights, a man may also choose to exercise the rights of his wife. There are also other possibilities (Young 1971).

The distribution of surplus to kinsmen is a major aspect of the structure of consumption. Every visitor to a household (under traditional circum-stances, almost all visitors were kinsmen of one sort or another) is given at least a token quantity of food, either for immediate consumption or to take home (fig. 15.0-6). In times of localized scarcity, formalized patterns of food sharing, including the apportionment of part of one's standing harvest, serve to distribute food on a large scale among needy kinsmen. Other goods such as guns, axes, large kettles, large gourds for making *chicha,* and so forth, though owned by individuals or households, are freely borrowed by kinsmen residing in the same hamlet and sometimes by related individuals in other hamlets.

Figure 15.0-6: Guaymí woman husking maize to feed visitors.

15.5 CONCLUSIONS

The above brief remarks point to the fact that the Guaymí are traditionally adapted to a nonmonetary economy with a swidden agriculture base, and that their particular relationship to the land has been characterized by a relatively high degree of stability for several centuries. The early introduction of metal tools increased the efficiency with which swidden agriculture could be carried on, but it did not represent a major shift in means of production. In spite of increasing involvement in the cash economy, economic dependence on external institutions has remained subordinate to subsistence agriculture, but there are strong indications that this relationship is being altered rapidly.

PART SIX

16.0

Conclusions

O. F. LINARES

The object of this section is not only to summarize the prehistory of western Panama but to consider a more fundamental question. What have we learned about cultural systems in the tropics and the ways in which they changed? Here it may be necessary to insert some definitions we skirted in the Introduction. We assume that cultural systems are composed of sets of activities or practices (i.e., subsystems) that are adaptive in the long-run — i.e., that promote survival — and that may be tightly or loosely integrated at different times. Changes in one activity set or subsystem will probably not produce immediate, or even long-range, systemic change, unless they involve positive feedback relations with other such subsystems. While all cultural practices are multilevel, involving at least the individual, the cultural, and the ecological (Perlman 1977), we are forced here by the nature of the evidence to neglect the individual in favor of broadly defined social groupings and types of habitats. It should be understood, however, that if adaptation does occur, it does so first at the level of the individual, and then often in the form of new intangible ideas or perceptions that leave only indirect archaeological traces. It also should go without saying that not all cultural behavior is adaptive (Rappaport 1978).

For convenience I will begin by considering, like Durham (1978), the cultural traits or practices themselves, as these can be deduced from material evidence. I will then try to determine which practices had adaptive value, enhancing the ability to survive and reproduce in a given environment. The problem will be to reconstruct the environment as it presented itself to human groups at different points in their history. Only then can we hope to understand how the cultures evolved to cope with natural and social circumstances.

The data will be discussed in terms of three systems, or time-periods, that seem to represent important stages in human adaptations. These stages may be called the Tropical Forest Archaic, the Formative villages and Ceremonial centers, and the pre-Conquest Coastal Settlements. These three time-periods could be supposed to fit with a generalized model explaining organizational change: "a period of relative stability exhibiting dominantly negative feedback will — given a sufficiently long time span — be followed by a period of relative instability exhibiting dominantly positive feedback, which will finally (if the system survives) return to a state of relative stability and dominantly negative feedback" (Perlman 1977, p. 331). Of course this is only pertinent in a roughly constant environment, which we know the tropics are not (May 1973).

16.1 THE TROPICAL FOREST ARCHAIC (4800 B.C. to 500 B.C.)

The first inhabitants we have records of in western Panama — the preceramic peoples of the Talamancan phase — occupied rock shelters and open camps along the Rio Chiriqui, at elevations between 600 meters and 900 meters. They were by no means the first humans to penetrate the Isthmus, however, having been preceded by Paleoindian groups for at least 5,000 years. A few Paleoindian pressure flaked points have been found in the Panama Canal area, on the surface of what is now the artificial Lake Madden or Alajuela (Bird and Cooke 1978); but these finds are few and far between. It is tempting to attribute the meagerness of these data to a lack of interest or expertise on the part of local archaeologists. However, in Panama the search for Paleoindian occupations has been intensive (J. Bird, A.J. Ranere, and R. Cooke, personal communications). We should, therefore, conclude that Paleoindian hunter-gatherers were in the Isthmus in very small numbers. It is generally agreed that the complex and varied chipped stone tool assemblages found associated with Paleoindian occupations in temperate latitudes and in the dry highlands of Mesoamerica and the Andes were utilized to hunt mammalian herbivores adapted to relatively open savanna and brush habitats. Similar habitats may well have occurred in the Isthmus in small pockets, and the first Paleoindians may have moved between them. The remains of supposedly savanna type extinct animals have been recovered by Gazin (1957) from the drier sectors of the central provinces. In general, however, "The tropical American savannas supported relatively low herbivore populations, with few large species, at least by late- and post-Pleistocene times. Human occupation of these savannas seems to have been sparse and may not have occurred until late Pleistocene" (Harris 1979). Starting from what must have been a small population base, demographic growth between 10,000 B.C. and 5000 B.C. seems to have been extremely slow.

By 5000 B.C., however, we see a number of preceramic sites representing the remains of small mammal hunters, collectors of wild plants, and riverine and/or marine fishermen in several forested biotopes of the Isthmus (Ranere and Hansell 1978; Linares 1979). The obvious conclusion is that these groups had for the first time evolved an appropriate technology to cope with real forest. Among the Rio Chiriqui groups this technology comprised chipped stone tools with which to make more specialized implements of wood, e.g., projectile points. It seems important to know why the Tropical

Forest Archaic seemed to have occurred in the mid-elevation highlands of western Panama rather than on the coast. One reason may be that outcrops of hard igneous rock suitable for tools occur only in the highlands. People seem to have settled where the proximity of raw materials facilitated colonization of the forest. Another reason may be that the coastal edge was an inhospitable environment, almost pure mangrove. Scholars like Sauer (1969) have always assumed that seaside living offered the best options for preagricultural peoples. Recently, Osborn (1977a, pp. 160–161) has argued convincingly, using Peruvian evidence, "that marine food resources are inferior to terrestrial resources, especially mammals, both in terms of human labor investment and in terms of protein yield." Only when populations are experiencing density-dependent selection (i.e., some form of population pressure) does a shift to the exploitation of marine resources occur (ibid., p. 177). The few exceptions to the general poverty of coastal environments occur in areas of seasonal upwelling, with consequent enrichment of the local marine fauna. This certainly does not occur in Chiriqui. We have argued elsewhere (Linares and Cooke 1975; Ranere and Hansell 1978) that preceramic peoples were numerous in the Parita Bay coast of Panama, at sites such as Cerro Mangote (McGimsey 1956), simply because this area experiences the upwelling which is lacking in Chiriqui. A similar argument, with better documentation, has been advanced by Osborn (1977a) to explain why large shell middens were found on the north but not on the south coast of Peru. The important point to remember is that upwelling is a localized phenomenom. As Osborn emphasized, other marine environments may be low in productivity when compared with terrestrial habitats, especially so when vegetable as well as animal products are taken into consideration. (Very few marine plants are edible by man.)

What was the habitat of the Talamancan groups in the mid-elevation highlands of Chiriqui at 5000 B.C.? In the absence of evidence for major climatic shifts in the last five thousand years we assume that they occupied a seasonal, semideciduous forest (patches of which survive today). It is commonly believed that tropical forests are characterized by a high diversity of species but a low density of individuals of any given species. This has been taken to imply that the trees of any species should be sparsely and evenly distributed in space. "Any small unit of territory, specifically the unit of territory which can be conveniently exploited by a small human group, will only have a few individuals of each useful plant, a resource easily degraded" (Lathrap 1977). This generalization has recently been challenged. By mapping a large tract of dry forest in Guanacaste, Costa Rica, Hubbell (1979) found that most species of trees, including *Hymenaea courbaril* or algarrobo, whose fruits were collected by the Rio Chiriqui groups, exhibit significant adult clumping under natural conditions. He thus concluded that "adults of tropical dry-forest tree species are not uniformly dispersed in the forest " (ibid., p. 1,302). Furthermore, although some species seem to be governed by internal rhythms, most plants in the dry forest have their periods of flowering, and hence of fruiting, synchronized with the rains. They are clumped in time as well as in space. Thus, the

Talamancan peoples probably did not wander through the forest at random, but rather moved from one clump of fruiting tree to another according to a fairly regular schedule.

Did they live from the forest alone? Jackson (1975, p. 313) wonders whether societies can survive in the tropical rain forest solely by foraging, hunting, and gathering. It is true that recent foraging groups in the Neotropics lived in semiarid savannas or other open habitats, e.g., the Gran Chaco, the Patagonian pampas, the Chilean archipelago, and possibly parts of Matto Grosso. It is also true that the existing seminomadic tropical forest groups discussed by Martin (1969) practice limited horticulture in addition to foraging. Martin is of the opinion that groups like the Sirionó, Guayakí, Nambicuara, and Coroado, had "devolved" from sedentary agriculturalists because of warfare, displacement, and depopulation. Lathrap (1968) tends to agree. He suggests that the populations organized into small, widely dispersed and mobile social units of Amazonia were driven from villages near major rivers into interfluvial areas by more powerful neighbors.

Obviously, however, the Talamancan phase peoples at 4800 B.C. were too early to have devolved from advanced agriculturalists. There are still two questions to be considered. Did the Talamancans supplement foraging by some limited form of horticulture? Is horticulture, in fact, a prerequisite to invading forested habitats? The archaeological data we have are not conclusive on the point. All we know is that preceramic Panamanian peoples gathered wild, seasonal fruits, lived in small shelters and open campsites, in reduced (family?) units, and were able to stay at one spot for weeks, if not months at a time, preferably by a river's edge. We also know that other tropical groups like the Mbuti pygmies of Africa live at population densities well below the carrying capacity of their environment (Harris 1978b). In fact, many species of nonhuman primates, whose diet is generally similar to that of man, have evolved and flourished in large numbers in the New World tropical forest (Moynihan 1976). In places like the Congo (Bahuchet 1978), pygmies and chimpanzees compete for the same resources. Thus, we see no reason to postulate the practice of horticulture in Chiriqui during the earlier of the two preceramic phases.

It may be theoretically possible to survive in the forest on an almost purely vegetarian diet. As Beckerman (see comments to Ross 1978, pp. 17–19) points out, sources of vegetable protein, like palms, are widely available in the tropics; although less good as a source of amino acids than animal protein, vegetable protein can support large populations. Most South American tropical forest groups today make extensive use of wild plants (Lévi-Strauss 1950). This use may be important the year round, as among the Sirionó (Holmberg 1950), or seasonally important as among the Yanömamo (Chagnon 1968), the Trio (Rivière 1969), the Kalapalo (Basso 1973), the Sharanahua (Siskind 1973), the Warao (Wilbert 1976), and many other groups. Incidentally, palm products play a most conspicuous role among these groups. Similarly, the Guaymí of Chiriqui, and especially those of Bocas, collect and even propagate the peach palm (*Gulielma gasipaes*), storing their fruit for several months (Bort, report no. 20). If any one family of plants made possible the colonization of tropical habitats it was the palms, whose products have a multitude of uses for food and shelter. Among the preceramic groups of Chiriqui, palms were probably much more important than the fruits of tree legumes.

As it happens, however, the Talamancan peoples probably also got an appreciable amount of animal protein. They could hardly have done much fishing, as the highland streams are too swift and shallow. But they must have been able to hunt terrestrial animals, which are thought to be as dispersed as plants in the tropics. Disagreements have risen in the last few years concerning the effects of this presumed dispersal on cultural patterns among hunter-gatherers. Some scholars have argued that Amazonian cultural features, such as small group size, seminomadism, warfare, food taboos, and so forth are the result of the low biomass and spatial dispersal of tropical animals, especially terrestrial mammals, on which peoples who did not fish were dependent for their protein supply (Ross 1978). Other students, myself included, would attribute the same cultural features to a complex set of factors in the natural and social adjustments of these groups (see comments to Ross's 1978 article). Recently, Chagnon and Hames (1979) have put the protein-limitation hypothesis to rest by demonstrating quite conclusively that the Yanömamo, whom Ross (ibid.) used as an example of a protein-limited group, have an ample protein supply. Among them levels of protein consumption are not neatly correlated with any of the above-mentioned practices, least of all warfare.

I may add that riverine environments seem to be optimal, not only for agriculturalists, but also for hunting-gathering populations. Most species of plants, including many palms, thrive on riverine environments. Other species of animals besides aquatic ones, e.g., mammals, birds, reptiles, and even insects, concentrate at the water's edge, especially during the dry season.

Doubtless some cutting of the trees for shelter if not for food began almost immediately. It seems unlikely, however, that Talamancan peoples had the capacity to clear the forest in any massive way. None of the tools they used — not even the large bifacial wedges — would appear to be very suitable for felling trees rapidly and easily. More important, there must have been few incentives to clear sizable tracts of land before agriculture became important. It is probably true that preagricultural peoples did set fires, as Harris (1977) has suggested. This may have extended the orginally small patches of grasslands and the ranges of species, such as *Byrsonima*, which are typical of them. It is still true that forests would be difficult to burn continuously, over immense distances, if the vegetation had not been previously felled and dried. In short, changes in the forest must have been slow at the beginning, when population densities were low.

The introductior of axes and celts about 2300 B.C., during the Boquete phase, presumably indicating the real beginning of horticulture, should have greatly increased man's extrasomatic abilities to modify the environment. Nevertheless, this new technology does not seem to have produced immediate or drastic changes in the pattern of adaptation. Despite the probable addition of root crop cultivation, people continued to live in small (family?) groups, to use natural rock shelters and open campsites, and to collect the same wild plants and animals as before. It seems important, therefore, to try to identify the negative feedbacks that maintained this cultural system in relative stability for about 4,000 years.

Panama is not the only New World region where previllage adaptations lasted for a long time. In Mesoamerica, groups remained semimobile as late as 1500 B.C., even though they had cultivated several species of plants since at least 5000 B.C. (MacNeish 1972). Flannery (1972) attributes the delay in the appearance of permanent villages in Mesoamerica to the comparatively low productivity of early maize and other local plants (much less productive than the wild barley and wheat of the Near East). Conditions for the development of settled agriculture would seem to have been even less favorable in Panama than in Mesoamerica, perhaps very much less favorable.

Doubtless some of the species of plants that were domesticated in the agricultural hearths of Mesoamerica, the Andes, and Amazonia (Pickersgill and Heiser 1977) also grew in Panama. A quick perusal of the plants mentioned in Simmonds (1976) is revealing. Sweet potatoes, yams, small seeded beans, peppers, *Xanthosoma,* and a host of what later became minor cultivars such as cashew, soursop, guava, sapodilla, and so forth, may at one time or another have grown in Chiriqui and have been collected by preceramic peoples. However, the wild ancestors of two of the most important cultivars, namely maize and manioc, probably never occurred naturally in the Isthmus. Teosinte, the most likely ancestor of *Zea mays,* apparently never spread beyond the semiarid uplands of Guatemala (Flannery 1973), while all the species that could have given rise to *Manioc esculenta* seem to be adapted to much drier conditions (Jennings 1976) than those which existed in the Isthmus. Harris (1979, p. 396) touches on an important point when he remarks: "Most tropical crops originated in savanna environments." By tropical savanna, Harris means the lands intermediate between the equatorial rain forest and the perennially dry desert, or the semiarid tropics of other authors.

There may be several reasons why agriculture should have been earlier in semiarid environments than in the humid tropics. Problems of clearing land and controlling weeds are obviously easier in semiarid habitats than in the humid tropics (Pickersgill and Heiser 1977). For example it takes an Amahuaca Indian of Amazonia 828 man-hours to clear a 1 ha. plot with a stone axe (Carneiro 1968, p. 247). Moreover, the highly seasonal semiarid environments, including tropical savannas, usually experience a marked flush in vegetation at the beginning of the rains (Harris 1979). In Mesoamerica, groups of food collectors made intensive use of the annual flushes by collecting a number of seasonal, localized stands of wild plants including grasses, many of which are still being gathered today (Messer

1979). Annual grasses are much less abundant in the forest floor than in open areas, and they certainly do not occur in dense stands there. When Hubbell (1979) talks about the clumping phenomenon in forest trees, he is referring to a dozen or so adult *algarrobos* occurring within 100 meters of an adult of the species. When Flannery (1968a, p. 72) is talking about plants occurring in dense stands in the Tehuacan valley, he is talking about such things as mesquite (*Prosopis* sp.), and guajes (*Lucaena, Mimosa,* and *Acacia*) which at the peak of the pod-bearing season can supply "truly impressive" amounts of food within a tiny area. In the tropics, it is doubtful if any single wild resource was abundant enough to permit concentrating upon it.

It is significant that the genetic changes, or "deviation amplifying" processes that made possible the expansion of one system — wild grass procurement centered on maize, or rather on teosinte (Flannery 1973) — involved a self-pollinated annual that occurs in thick stands. Conditions in the humid tropics, on the other hand, must have been very different. If ancient Panamanians had wanted to increase tree fruit production by selecting for large seed size or other favorable characteristics, they would soon have been discouraged by the fact that trees are cross-pollinated and take a long time to yield (Harris 1977, pp. 206–208).

Perhaps the key element of the negative feedback system is that mobility, with or without agriculture, has certain well-known demographic consequences. This is especially true of "logistic mobility," when only certain members of the group move about in the food quest (Harris 1978b, p. 407). Recent studies of surviving hunter-gatherers have shown that "they live at population densities well below the capacity of the physical environment to support them" (ibid., p. 403), as a result of slow population increase. From the research of Lee and De Vore (1976), we know that the !Kung San have a very slow demographic growth. Howell (1976, p. 138) concludes that "in general, hunters and gatherers are characterized by fertility and mortality levels that are relatively low by the standards of agricultural peoples." In fact, there are some reasons to believe that the !Kung's growth rate of less than 0.5 percent per year (Howell ibid., p. 150) may be higher than that of ancient hunter-gatherers or mobile horticulturalists in the tropics. At least disease among mammals and birds tends to be relatively higher in the humid tropics than elsewhere (Moynihan 1971). Hence, there may be an adaptive advantage in these latter environments to being widely spaced and dispersed rather than concentrated.

Scholars have emphasized that a common pattern among hunter-gatherers in semiarid regions — e.g., the !Kung Bushmen mentioned above, or the Southern Paiute, the Australian tribes, the prehistoric inhabitants of Tehuacan, Oaxaca, and so forth — is seasonal aggregation into multifamily bands at times of marked resource abundance, followed by periodic dispersal and occasionally severe food shortages. The preceramic Rio Chiriqui inhabitants probably did not congregate in such large groups. There is no evidence for aggregation in the archaeological record, nor is there any reason to believe that food was often extremely scarce. I would suggest that the absence of extremes — marked periods of abundance when people could congregate and marked periods when the threat of famine was present — must have reduced the stresses on the systems of tropical forest peoples. This itself must have reduced the incentives for change of any kind, including the intensification of agriculture. What Harris (1978a, p. 132) has said of the tropical rain forest hunting-gathering aborigines of Queensland could just as well be said of the ancient Panamanians: "Negative feedbacks . . . [by which Harris means demographic regulators] . . . maintained the subsistence system at a level that can be characterized as selective foraging within a broad spectrum resource use."

16.2 LATE FORMATIVE VILLAGES AND CENTERS AFTER 500 B.C.

Settled village life based on maize agriculture did not have an autochthonous or gradual development in western Panama. This cultural system seems to have appeared full-blown, and to have expanded all over the lower montane and highland plains, sometime between 500 B.C. and A.D. 1. Whereas the Tropical Forest Archaic is represented by only a few sites, there are dozens of sites with Scarified Ware of La Concepción complex, and at least a hundred Early Bugaba phase sites, along the courses of major rivers of Chiriqui province. Not only do ceramics appear for the first time at these sites, but also a sophisticated ground and polished stone tool industry that included numerous celts, and grinding implements (e.g., manos and metates) associated with maize agriculture.

It is not our purpose to try to trace in detail the origins of seed-crop cultivation in western Panama. Maize itself may have been cultivated in the central part of the Isthmus by 1680 ± 95 B.C., during the Monagrillo phase at the Aguadulce shelter (Piperno ms. 1979; Linares 1979, pp. 34–35). But at this time, maize does not seem to have been very productive or been grown very intensively. It would be tempting to accept Myers (1978) date of 2200 B.C. for the Scarified tradition of Chiriqui, which he sees as sharing decorative principles with Valdivia C pottery of coastal Ecuador, and argue for a South American introduction of maize into the Isthmus. It will be recalled that maize was grown intensively during Valdivia times (Lathrap et al. 1977; Pearsall 1978). It was also an important plant during Scarified times. The Scarified tradition burials at the type-site of Finca Solano, near the town of Concepcion, contain numerous metates piled-up, as if in ritual fashion, around the edges of the graves. Unfortunately, however, there is very little solid evidence for Myers's dating, or for his stylistic ties between Scarified and Valdivia. Indeed the very status of the Scarified "complex" is problematic. All indications are that Scarified and Bugaba ceramics are part of a single, evolving tradition with ties to such complexes as the so-called Zoned Bichrome period of the nearby Nicoya Peninsula in Costa Rica. I would suggest that the probable dates of the Zoned Bichrome period are 500 B.C. to A.D. 1, even though Lange (1971) thinks that it was earlier. Judging from the radiocarbon dates we have for the earliest levels of the Barriles site (fig. 7.0-6), which yielded a few Scarified sherds, the ceramics of La Concepcion complex are not much older than 500 B.C. and may in fact be considerably more recent.

In short, while Monagrillo phase maize may have been introduced from Mesoamerica or from South America, it looks as if the much later maize found in the Scarified-Bugaba phases (section 11.0) was part of a rapid but localized expansion of seed-crop agriculture (and/or agriculturalists) from the adjacent area of eastern Costa Rica, starting about 500 B.C. The introduction of the maize-bean crop system during the second half of the first millennium B.C. triggered a rapid transition from a small-group (extended family?) way of life based on root-crop cultivation supplemented by hunting and gathering in the Boquete phase (2300 B.C. to 300 B.C.), to a fully sedentary existence in sizable farming (multifamily?) villages with some degree of craft specialization, and by A.D. 400 the germ of a site hierarchy.

What were some of the positive feedbacks involved in the rapid expansion of maize cultivation in the Chiriqui plains and highlands? In several classic papers, Harris (1969, 1972b) has compared two crop complexes — vegeculture and seed culture — in terms of their ecological requirements and consequences for human settlements. He suggests that protein-rich seed crops such as maize and beans make more demands on the supply of nutrients in the soil than starch-rich vegecultural root crops such as manioc. Hence seed crops tend to be unstable, to exhaust the soil more rapidly, and to demand longer fallow periods than root-crops. In those parts of the seasonal tropics where traditions of seed-crop swidden have evolved, "as among the maize cultivators of the American tropics, . . . swidden settlements will tend to be less stable and more liable to progressive migration than those of the tropical vegeculturalists" (Harris 1972b, p. 254). Because maize-dominated systems, especially when combined with beans, provided a protein-rich and complete diet, they permitted sedentary settlement, unlike the systems in which the hunting of animals or gathering of nuts for protein was essential. With the adoption of seed-crops, there began a process of positive, amplifying interactions among sedentary life, demographic growth, and the ever-increasing need for cultivating and fallowing larger amounts of land.

The adoption and explosive spread of maize agriculture in Panama should be understood in terms of a model, such as the one Harris proposes, that places emphasis on the imbalances inherent within the system itself. However, certain external characteristics of the environment may have also contributed significantly to the success of maize farming in Chiriqui. First, the coastal plains and highlands of the province up to the altitude of El Hato have a marked dry season that not only makes slash-and-burn cultivation possible but also is essential for the proper growth and maturation of the maize plant. Secondly, Chiriqui is crisscrossed by a large number of important rivers that flow across the plains and provide, especially in the belts of lands between the coast and the highlands, wide expanses of fertile alluvial soils on which to farm. Most of the sites in the Concepción and Bugaba occupational phases are found along these major rivers. Finally, the lands surrounding Volcan Baru are both the most fertile in the country and close to the sources of hard igneous rocks, including vesicular basalts and andesites, from which celts and maize processing tools were made.

Stone tool production and distribution may have provided a mechanism for the economic and possible ritual integration of the Volcan villages. Whereas such tools as knives, scrapers, and milling stones were produced by every Volcan household, other implements such as celts and metates were almost certainly produced by specialists (section 8.0). As a result of his replicative experiments, Ranere concludes that the major manufacturing centers for these tools were outside the surveyed zone, at quarries such as India Vieja, thirty kilometers to the east of the Volcan villages in the same highland chain. He also suggests that a few specialists in larger Volcan villages were charged with the repair and distribution of these tools. The actual manufacture of celts and metates may have been done by the same specialists during visits to the quarry sites, or by local experts of the quarry region. In either case, the proper circulation of essential tools must have involved some form of structured interpersonal relations such as trade or payment to specialists. Interesting examples of trade in stone axes can be found in the ethnographic literature (Sharp 1968; Townsend 1969). It does not seem necessary, however, to postulate that the pattern of resource distribution in the tropical forest is such that political, economic, and social power would inevitably be concentrated in the hands of those who control long-distance trade in such things as metates (Rathje 1972). Certainly, one of the most elaborate tropical forest long-distance trade networks occurs in Amazonia (Lathrap 1973), without complex sociopolitical organization.

When in use, celts have to be constantly maintained. For example, among the Heve of New Guinea, stone axes have to be sharpened roughly every 4 hours, a task that takes approximately 1 hour (Townsend 1969, p. 201). An Amahuacan Indian of the Amazon told Carneiro (1979, p. 41) "that aboriginally when the forest was being cleared for garden plots, men had to sharpen their stone axes every morning." The resharpening of a normally blunted celt may have thus been done by the owner himself, in his garden or at his home, even though the repair of a really damaged celt was in the hands of specialists.

So far we have discussed the production and maintenance of tools used by the Volcan inhabitants directly for subsistence. In addition to this utilitarian activity, there existed another, more spectacular, industry for the production of monumental lapidary objects of probable socioceremonial function. These include the well-known giant "alter-ego" statues and the large stone drums and metates found by previous expeditions at the site of Barriles (see Linares et al. 1975, cover and figs. 5–7). Undoubtedly, these statues were also produced by specialists for special use at regional centers, but we know very little about their manufacture, except that they must have been made in situ (Ranere, section 8.0). No systematic analysis has been made of Barriles art and iconography. However, certain themes are striking and all-pervasive in this art. They must reflect important principles of the social organization and ideology of these people. The first theme is status and rank and includes statues of persons wearing conical hats, holding staffs, and being carried on the shoulders by others. A second theme emphasizes warlike aspects and includes such items as ceremonial weapons (dacite laterally flaked slabs?) and trophy heads. A third is concerned with maize: enormous metates, which Lange (1971) interprets as ceremonial stools and chairs, lidded burial urns probably used as *chicha* jars, pregnant "Venus" figurines possibily connected with agricultural rites, and men wielding what look very much like stone axes. It is interesting to note that some of the same elements (e.g., men with conical hats, men carrying staffs, Venus figurines, warriors, and so forth) are duplicated in the ceramics from sites such as Pitti-Gonzalez (see report, 9, figs. 9/4, 9/5, 9/8). Although further speculation on the subject of Barriles iconography is not justified, it is important to note that the association between rank, war, and maize does not seem to have been fortuitous. The art of Barriles conveys the overwhelming impression of a group of expansionistic maize agriculturalists, organized under warring chiefs who lived in socioceremonial centers such as Barriles, and who wielded some (coercive?) influence over the inhabitants of nearby villages.

The precise nature of supravillage territorial organization in the Volcan region must, for the moment, remain inferential and somewhat vague. More is known about the types of settlement-subsistence adaptations existing at the local village level than at the regional level. The Volcan villages were based on a seed-crop intensive farming economy complemented by cold-adapted root crops such as sweet potatoes and by the gathering of fruits such as palm nuts. Fishing probably was less important than hunting. Settlement was a variant of a linear stream and river system, with villages located on the flat lands of the high stream terraces in the best agricultural lands. Villages varied in size; the smallest were less than two hundred meters long and probably were inhabitated by fewer than thirty persons; the largest were more than seven hundred meters long and may have been inhabited by more than a hundred persons. Households within the village were placed about fifty meters apart and were probably separated by gardens. The life-span of a single dwelling at any one spot seems to have been relatively short. Moves of dwelling locality, and village fission and relocation farther upstream, cannot be attributed to simple factors such as soil depletion. The deep volcanic soils of the Cerro Punta basin, only half of which was occupied at the time of abandonment (A.D. 600–700), could have probably supported much larger and more permanent villages under a sustained-yield agricultural system. Thus, some of the movements must have been due to social rather than ecological factors.

A few of the largest villages, such as BU-17, had craft specialists living in them who specialized in the repair, if not the manufacture, of stone tools. Specific ties between farming villages and centers such as Barriles may have been political, ceremonial, based on kinship, or all these things. At some level, however, they were also economic, structured around a subsystem that included both the ground stone and polished tool technology and the growing and processing of the crops for which the tools were used. The technology and the subsistence system, in turn, were related to the organization of village life and to its articulation with socioceremonial centers. The whole successful pattern seemed to be flourishing at the time when it was cut off by the last eruption of Volcan Baru.

16.3 THE PRE-CONQUEST COASTAL SETTLEMENTS

In an article on adaptive strategies in western Panama (Linares 1977a) I reviewed the archaeological evidence for and against the hypothesis of a common highland origin for populations on the Atlantic and Pacific coastal edge of western Panama after A.D. 600. Because these problems remain more or less where I left them, it may be worthwhile to quote some of the previous conclusions:

> The idea of a common origin for the coastal Chiriqui and Bocas populations rests on evidence that is suggestive, but also inconclusive and difficult to evaluate. In favor of the "common heritage" hypothesis are similar ceramics, similar stratigraphic contexts for these ceramics, good chronological overlap, clear-cut antecedents in the highlands, mid-way between both areas and a few days walking from each. In addition, the oldest Chiriqui and Bocas occupations appear to represent the remains of swidden agriculturalists who had not yet begun to exploit littoral resources. The limitations of our data, however, are equally inescapable. There is almost exclusive reliance on ceramics during the earlier periods which are usually characterized by poor preservation and/or absence of accompanying cultural materials. Also, the presence of other pottery types in the oldest Chiriqui occupations suggests that other groups, besides our supposed migrants from the highlands, may have been present from the beginning. This is important in view of competition theory. Moreover, the Volcan ceramics, as well as those from Bocas and Chiriqui coastal sites, have widespread counterparts elsewhere, so their area of origin cannot be really pin pointed with exactitude. Finally, intermediate settlements have been located in the areas between highlands and coast on the Chiriqui, but not on Bocas side (Linares 1977a, p. 312).

I did suggest that there were more indications of purposeful movement in the Bocas situation than in Chiriqui:

> To take up our Panamanian example once again, the evidence for purposeful group-migration looks very doubtful indeed, especially on the Chiriqui side where a number of other sites containing early Volcan-like materials have been found on the plains half-way between mountains and coastal edge. These cover a long period (300 B.C. to A.D. 600), and suggested that people spent a long time moving down, assuming that the prevailing movement was from highland to coast. On the Bocas side, a very wet cloud-forest separates the highlands from the coastal ridges. No archaeological sites have been reported from this mid-way area. Here it looks as if small groups did, indeed, move down purposefully to colonize the area around the central embayment. This area offered splendid opportunities for the utilization of marine resources, but obvious drawbacks to some types of agriculture (discussed later). Their movement appears late (after A.D. 500) and deliberate. They seem to have encountered at least a partially vacant area (Linares 1977a, p. 313).

Several factors could have been responsible for whatever displacements may have occurred:

As to the causes of the movements outlined above we must rely on the fact that warring chiefdoms and crowded villages characterized the Basin of El Hato by A.D. 300 (Linares, Sheets, and Rosenthal 1975). Population densities, however, had by no means reached the maximum carrying capacity of Cerro Punta, the closest highland valley to the Atlantic or Bocas side, before depopulations had occurred. Unpalatable as I have always found most "catastrophic" explanations for migration, the possibility that Bocas was settled by refugees from volcanic activities cannot be discarded. On the other hand, population pressures on scarce resources, or all of these factors are equally satisfactory (or equally unsatisfactory) as explanations for the Chiriqui migrations (Linares 1977a, p. 313).

There is no question but that the inhabitants found in the islands and peninsulas in the Chiriqui Gulf and Almirante Bay after A.D. 600 had moved there from farther inland, from the adjacent coastal plains if not directly from the highlands. What Sanders (1978, p. 270) remarks of other Middle American areas is equally pertinent to western Panama: The "contrast in cultural evolution between the immediate coastal zone and the riverine plains of the adjacent lowlands is striking." In Chiriqui, maize agriculture probably made its first appearance (during Scarified times) in the numerous riverine plains of the lowlands. From here, the system probably spread out to the highlands in one direction, and to the adjacent coastal edge in the other direction. In Bocas, extensive lowland plains are confined to the Changuinola and Cricamola rivers, which are as far, or even farther, from the Aguacate Peninsula itself as are the highlands. Because Bugaba-phase occupations have, to my knowledge, not been found in the Changuinola or Cricamola plains, the most likely place of origin for the first inhabitants of Bocas is still the adjacent highlands. Even now, the Guaymí Indians of Bocas and the Chiriqui mountains speak the same dialect variant, intermarry regularly, and participate in some of the same ceremonies, including the *balsería*.

From the cold but fertile highland valleys, where fishing was unproductive, the Aguacate migrants to Bocas at A.D. 600 entered a highly diverse environment, rich in species of marine and terrestrial organisms but with less optimal conditions for agriculture. The limitations of farming in the Bocas environment are both topographic and climatic. In Almirante Bay there is no coastal plain, and virtually no dry season. The typical vegetation of the area is a dense rain forest which regenerates very rapidly after cutting. While a sturdy race of flint corn can be, and is, grown today in Bocas, seed crops seem to do much less well in this environment than wet-adapted root crops (e.g., *otoe*) and many species of trees (e.g., palms and cacao). Furthermore, in some years, and in some areas, the rains effectively prevent the burning of the felled vegetation. In these circumstances, slash-and-mulch, that is cutting the vegetation and leaving it to rot, is the only alternative. Although effective, this system usually restricts the amount of land that can be cleared.

The marine environment surrounding the Aguacate Peninsula is highly variegated (section 5.2). Large beds of turtle grass, and many species of corals, grow from the shallows into deeper waters. On the immediate shore, two kinds of mangrove are found in profusion. Although the low amplitude of the Caribbean tides (rarely more than 60 cm) has prevented the formation of extensive sand beaches, so that mollusks, crustaceans, and echnoids are less diverse here than on the Pacific (Vermeij 1978), there is still an abundance of mollusks in Almirante Bay.

What are the settlement-subsistence adaptations of the inhabitants of Bocas after A.D. 600? To begin with, they apparently cultivated root and tree crops without maize. (Not a single maize-processing tool came out of the excavations.) This type of agriculture was probably extensively nomadic. The Bocas peoples lived in scattered and discontinuous hamlets of short duration. These were on ridge tops, possibly for defense. Only half of the Aguacate Peninsula was occupied at any one time. Dwellings were so scattered that it is difficult, if not impossible, to draw exact boundary lines around each hamlet. Within a settlement such as Cerro Brujo, only two types of "activity areas" could be distinguished: the flat, central part of the ridges, where the houses were located, and the edges and slopes, where the trash was discarded. Apparently, very few, if any, "special" structures existed at the site.

Animal protein was, and is still, abundant in the Bocas environment, especially in the ocean (Vermeij 1978, p. 259, notes that there are at least 900 species of fish in the western Atlantic as compared with 650 species in the eastern Pacific). The Cerro Brujo peoples derived three times as much meat from marine animals as from terrestrial ones. Marine turtles and manatees provided especially huge, if intermittent, feasts. The regular day-to-day animal protein came from mollusks, smaller fishes, and terrestrial mammals that were probably hunted in and around house gardens and abandoned fields (Linares 1976).

There is no way that the peoples of Bocas could be characterized as "protein limited." Yet their small and shifting settlements were more similar to those of interfluvial groups along the Amazon, who are supposed to suffer from scarcity of animal protein (Ross 1978), than to those of riverine groups in the same region (Carneiro 1968; Lathrap 1968) who obviously get plenty of fish. The scattering of populations in Bocas cannot be attributed to a single factor. It was an aspect of the entire system: "The larger problem remains one of the total human use of the environment" (comment by A. Johnson, in Ross 1978, p. 21). In an area of extreme diversity, the best subsistence strategy was to remain or become a generalist and to exploit as many different terrestrial and marine biotopes as possible. This generalized pattern of resource use may, in turn, have delayed such processes as demographic growth, the intensification of agriculture (Boserup 1965), and the evolution of centralized polities, for at least one thousand years. It may be wrong to state that "In Panama the Caribbean coast proper has not been a focus of settlement at any time" (Helms 1978, p. 145). However, "if the environment is stable, not subject to great seasonal changes or major instabilities as to source and quantity of foods, we may expect greater behavioral redundancy and a greater role for unreasoned acceptance of traditional strategies for living" (Binford 1978, p. 455). The Aguacate people would seem to have been a good example of this conservatism.

Turning now to the Pacific side of western Panama, that is, to the province of Chiriqui, we note that it is markedly different from the Atlantic or Bocas side (section 2.1). Chiriqui is characterized by relatively large plains, and alluvial-rich rivers, and a very seasonal climate. The pronounced dry season, lasting four or five months, has contributed to the progressive disappearance of the natural semideciduous forest. The first agricultural populations in this part of the Isthmus lived on the plains along the rivers. For these peoples, moving to the coastal edge, and beyond into the Chiriqui Gulf islands, must have involved the abandonment of fertile riverine land, a reduction in territory, and even a decrease in fishing (at least freshwater fishing) possibilities. Thus, it is difficult to believe that they would have moved to a place such as La Pitahaya for reasons other than necessity, perhaps related to a buildup of population pressures on the plains.

The several hundred inhabitants of La Pitahaya occupied one large nucleated, continuous village covering 8.5 hectares. Several distinct special-purpose utility areas can be distinguished at IS-3, including artificial, rock-filled mounds which served as burial grounds and shrines and a "plaza" floor with stone columns. These features suggest a special function for the site. Its location in a protected embayment as well as the appearance of pottery from the central provinces and numerous imported stone tools, ready-made or as raw material, imply some sort of trading center. Unlike the earlier socioceremonial site of Barriles, which probably exerted some coercive influence over nearby villages, IS-3 seems to have been a peaceful place, dedicated to the production of such things as salt, dried fish, and possibly palm products for trade with mainland groups in the interior.

Life in a nucleated village like IS-3 was made possible by maize agriculture, supplemented by root crops and palm products. Not only agriculture, but also some of the other subsystems had advanced considerably in the direction of intensification and specialization. Hunting was centered almost exclusively on the white-tailed deer, and fishing on marine catfish. These latter species must have been abundant in the brackish estuaries that surround the site. Less productive subsistence alternatives — such as collecting of shellfish — seem to have been almost ignored. Scheduling conflicts, as well as the abundance of other subsistence alternatives, are the most likely explanations for this selectivity.

To conclude, the results of this research may appear to be overly ecological and deterministic, but this is probably the way it worked. Up to the present, the Guaymí of the Bocas region live in scattered hamlets, practice tree and root crop cultivation, and are politically atomistic. On the Pacific side, in Chiriqui, there has of course been a huge turnover of population, but the local peoples are still clustered in large towns, practice relatively intensive agriculture, and are continuously changing. Ecology may not have been the only factor involved in these differential adaptations, but it certainly provides some of the most obvious correlations.

REPORTS

Report Number 1

The Rio Chiriqui Shelters:
Excavation and Interpretation of the Deposits

A. J. RANERE

INTRODUCTION

The nature of a site's stratigraphy and the way it is handled determine in large measure the precision with which archaeologists can talk about past cultural patterns. The associations that can be made among excavated materials, whether they be artifacts, faunal remains, botanical remains, or the sediments themselves, all depend on (1) the way these materials were first deposited, (2) on any later displacement of these materials, and (3) on the control exercised by the excavator in recording their positions vis-à-vis each other. Water, wind, man, animals, and plants are all agents of deposition and, for that matter, of postdepositional relocation of site materials as well. Ideally, we would like to recover artifacts, bone, shell, carbonized plant fragments, and features such as hearths just as they were left by prehistoric peoples. Similarly, we would like pollen grains to remain where they fell, covered up by sediments that also remain as they were initially deposited. Unfortunately, patterns of deposition are seldom left undisturbed, if not by the occupants themselves — sweeping the floor clean, reusing hearth stones and scattering the ashes and charcoal, digging storage pits, burial pits, roasting pits — then by burrowing animals, insects, plant roots, or erosion.

It is important, I think, to assess the processes behind the distribution of materials at a site. Reconstructing cultural patterns and building chronological sequences on the basis of spurious associations is worse than useless; it is misleading. The third factor controlling the reliability of the archaeologist's inferences, then, is his ability to recognize the influence of the first two factors in accounting for the distribution of materials encountered in his excavations, that is, he must be able to distinguish between materials in the place of their initial deposition and those that have been disturbed and be able to evaluate the extent of the disturbance. It is a question of recognizing proper associations and providing the correct interpretation. Are the tools and hearth found side by side the result of a single evening's meal, of a temporary camp, of sporadic use of a site for several years —

several hundred years? The levels on which associations are made vary widely, and the temptation is great to propose a finer level of association than is warranted by one's material. Thus, for example, tools found close together may be identified as parts of a "tool kit" when other evidence, such as the lack of identifiable living surfaces or the absence of a cache pit for the tools, suggests that they might well have been deposited at different times. They might still be considered "associated" as part of a culture's stone-tool inventory; a perfectly good and useful association, even if not as specific as the proposed "tool-kit" association.

In the following section, I would like to discuss in some detail my interpretation of the processes involved in the deposition of materials in the Rio Chiriqui sites, the postdepositional rearrangement of these materials, and, finally, my control of the excavations. This discussion will, I hope, make clear the limits placed on any interpretation of the sites' cultural and natural histories by these three factors.

CASITA DE PIEDRA

Casita de Piedra is a boulder overhang located near the confluence of the Rio Chiriqui and the Rio Casita de Piedra (see section 3.2 for a description of the site and surrounding area). The site was first visited in 1970, when it was tested to a depth of 70 centimeters in a .5-square meter pit. This was done simply to verify the suspected preceramic nature of the deposits. The following year a 5 x 2-meter cut was made at the site, excavated in blocks measuring 1 x 2 meters and 1 x 1 meter.

The initial test pit at the site was a 1 x 2-meter block oriented with its long axis perpendicular to the back of the shelter. The digging was done in 10-centimeter levels, maintaining the surface slope unless natural stratigraphic breaks were recognized. In such cases, they formed the boundaries of the excavation units rather than the arbitrary boundary at 10-centimeter intervals. After the original test pit was excavated into sterile sediments, the sequence of natural and/or cultural layers was worked out and became the basis for the excavation of the remaining five blocks. Since the strata were almost always thicker than 10 centimeters, they were subdivided and excavated in arbitrary 10-centimeter levels. Thus, in block 2, layer C was approximately 30 centimeters thick and was excavated in three separate units, C_1, C_2, and C_3, each 10 centimeters thick. Depending on the slope and thickness of the layer, the arbitrary levels within, while generally being 10-centimeter units, often were smaller. Furthermore, they might be 10 centimeters thick at one end and 3 centimeters thick (or 15 centimeters thick) at the other, depending on the slope of the natural layer. That is to say, natural and cultural stratigraphic divisions were followed whenever this was possible, even if excavation units of slightly different sizes resulted.

The size and composition of the excavation crew varied from two (one workman and myself) during the initial testing of the site, to eleven (seven workers, three student assistants, and myself) near the end of the excavations, when we were using the waters of the Rio Casita de Piedra as an aid in sifting dirt through fine screens to separate out microfossil remains. A crew of three or four workmen plus myself was the more normal situation. Hand troweling was the method of excavation used most frequently; shovels were used occasionally for excavating surface levels and portions of the lowest deposits, particularly those below evidence of human occupation. All the sediments were sifted, using quarter-inch mesh screen, except for selected units which were sifted in water, using fine-mesh window screen. This technique produces similar results to flotation and water-separation techniques often employed in the recovery of botanical specimens (Struever 1968). Actually, very little of the material could be "floated"; so the separation was done by picking through the residue left on top of the screen after it had been dried. The results of this fine screening technique were at the same time disappointing and gratifying: disappointing in that more was not recovered, gratifying in that it showed that little was being missed in the troweling and screening methods used in most of the site. We did increase the size of our carbon samples and recovered a few more carbonized seeds in the lowest layers in the site, where both were relatively scarce. Also, we recovered the small flake category which otherwise passed through our quarter-inch mesh screens (although later analysis was to show that these very small flakes provide little information not more easily acquired from the larger flakes). The technique also confirmed the fact that no bone was preserved in the deposits.

Methods of excavation were chosen with an eye to recording meaningful distributional data for the artifacts, the charcoal, and the sediments, and to minimizing the recording of irrelevant distributional data. For example, since there were no living floors intact and, as we have suggested, archaeological materials were almost all horizontally moved from their initial placement, it makes little sense to measure tools and flakes in situ and to plot their horizontal distributions. Thus, vertical locations of materials were carefully noted, while horizontal locations were for the most part limited to designating which 1 x 1- or 1 x 2-meter block held the artifact, charcoal sample, fire-cracked rock, and so forth. However, features such as hearths and pits were mapped in both vertical and horizontal dimensions.

The rock-shelter sediments were primarily silts and clayey silts, all testing slightly acidic (pH ca. 6.0) except for the uppermost layer which was neutral (pH 7.1). Subtle changes in sediment color, composition, texture, and compactness served to separate one layer from the other (fig. 1/1). Boundaries between layers were most often gradual rather than sharp and sometimes became indistinguishable (noted as dashed lines on the profiles). The strata all had two facies, one inside and one outside the dripline, clearly a result of the more protected depositional environment inside the dripline (or underneath the overhang). Sediments inside were finer and less weathered, whereas rock-fall blocks from the face of the overhang and other rubble from on top were added to the sediments outside the shelter, as well as some water-deposited material from the two small fans on either side of the shelter. Also, the increased moisture content beyond the protec-

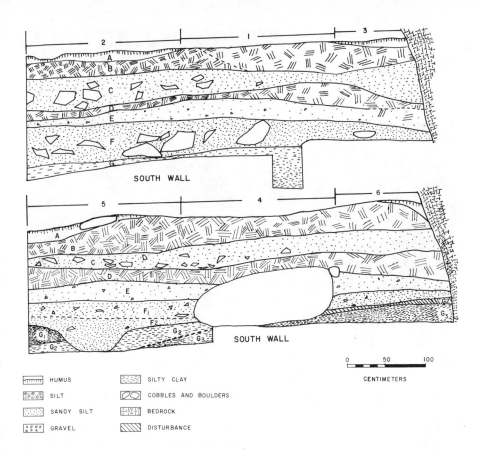

SOUTH WALL

SOUTH WALL

HUMUS	SILTY CLAY	
SILT	COBBLES AND BOULDERS	CENTIMETERS
SANDY SILT	BEDROCK	
GRAVEL	DISTURBANCE	

Figure 1/1: Profiles of the stratigraphy at Casita de Piedra; the south wall of blocks 2, 1, 3, and the south wall of blocks 5, 4, and 6. Adapted from figure 5, Proceedings of the First Puerto Rican Symposium on Archaeology, *Fundación Arqueológica, Antropológica e Histórica de Puerto Rico.*

tion of the overhang caused faster weathering of the sediments. After a rainy period, the penetration of moisture into the deposits, visible in the block walls, almost exactly coincided with the facies shift observed in the layers. The change in amounts of pebbles, cobbles, and boulders in the shelter fill (from very infrequent inside to abundant outside the dripline) was more gradual than the change in weathering, but nonetheless quite well developed (see figure 1/2). Interestingly enough, there was an increase in rock fall in all layers at the very back of the shelter, where exfoliated flakes from the rear wall were added to the shelter fill.

The deepest unit excavated in the site, layer G, can be contrasted to all those above it on several counts. First, it is separated from layer F above by an unconformity, the only sharp break between layers in the site. Second, its sediments are primarily silty clays, dark red beyond the dripline and orange within. Layer G also contains a subunit of large subrounded boulders and cobbles, present in all but the back meter of deposits, in quantities

Figure 1/2: The profile of the south wall of blocks 5, 4, and 6 in Casita de Piedra as it appeared after completion of the excavations.

far surpassing anything encountered higher up in the site. Finally, the only evidence of human occupation attributable to the deposit are fifteen flakes and some small charcoal flecks at the extreme eastern end of the excavations (in blocks 2 and 4) beyond the dripline. These occur in G_1, a lens of dark red silty clay which overlies G_2 or the major unit of the layer. There is some reason to believe that the flakes and charcoal are intrusive, since one of the flakes glues to another found in layer F immediately above it (they are flakes from a bifacial or irregular core). Intrusive flakes and charcoal had been noted for other parts of layer G, where they were encountered in fossil insect burrows, and, although no such disturbances were noted for these flakes (and careful attention was paid to this), there is still the possibility that the disturbances existed and went unrecognized.

The contact between layers G and F looks like an erosional surface, or at least a stable surface on which weathering had taken place. If such is the case, layer G has a fossil soil developed on it whose surface formed the floor of the shelter at the time of its initial occupation. The profile of this proposed fossil soil closely resembles the modern lateritic soil profile on the flat just 20 meters above Casita de Piedra (this is the location of the Schoolyard Site). The fossil soil lacks the thin, dark, surface humus zone of the modern soil and has perhaps a higher concentration of clay; both understandable results of having been buried for several thousand years. The contact between layers F and G is marked by a concentration of angular rock, much of it almost certainly roof fall. This thin layer appears to be either a lag deposit on an erosion surface left after finer sediments had been eroded away, or simply exfoliated flakes from the roof and other rock accumulating on a stable surface. In addition, some huge boulders also rest on or are slightly "indented" into the surface of layer G, while others which extend deeply into the layer exhibit different weathering characteristics above and below the F/G boundary. This would seem to lend further support to the proposal that the top of layer G represents a stable surface present for a lengthy period of time.

The predominantly subrounded pebbles, cobbles, and boulders found in all but the back two meters of the layer seemed to have been a slope wash or fan deposit spilling into the shelter from off the slope on its north side. The back part of the layer is a fine silty clay with some sand and a few disintegrating granite rocks which probably fell from the roof of the overhang. The layer went deeper than 185 centimeters below ground level, the bottom of the excavations, and ended on the contact with layer F at 120–130 centimeters below ground level.

Layer F is a compact, brown to reddish brown, clayey silt with some sand. Beyond the dripline it contained granules and small pebbles of decomposed granite, but few larger cobbles and boulders. The bottom of the layer rested unconformably on the top of layer G and was easily recognizable. The separation of strata F and E rested on F being lighter in color, more compact and having a higher clay content than E. At the outer edge of the deposits, beyond the overhang, the distinctions became blurred, and the two layers could not be positively separated. This layer varied in thickness from 15 centimeters near the rear of the shelter to more than 40 centimeters in the extreme front part of the site and was divided into two to five excavation units. It extended from 95–110 centimeters to 120–130 centimeters below the ground surface. Substantial amounts of charcoal, flakes, and artifacts were recovered from this stratum, which probably holds the earliest cultural remains in the shelter (those in G are suspected of having originated in F also). Charcoal collected in insect burrows from the top five centimeters of layer G and almost certainly associated with layer F yielded a radiocarbon date of 6560 ± 120 years (4610 B.C., sample number I-6278).

Layer E is a dark brown clayey silt with sand, granules, and pebbles of decomposed granite increasing in density toward the front of the excavations. The boundary between layers E and D was quite sharp, E being considerably darker and having more sand granules and pebbles than D. The stratum varied from 20 to almost 40 centimeters in thickness, extending from 65–90 centimeters to 95–110 centimeters below the ground surface. It was subdivided into two to four units for the purposes of excavation. Artifact and flake concentrations were far higher here than in any other layer in the site. Charcoal concentrations were also high. Charcoal collected from subunit E3 in block 6, where this was the bottom of the layer, yielded a radiocarbon date of 5795 ± 105 years (3845 B.C., sample number I-5765). A second determination of 5680 ± 105 years (3730 B.C., sample number I-5764) from charcoal collected from a pit extending down through layer F and into layer G probably dates this layer also, although when the sample was taken the pit walls could be traced no higher than into layer F.

Layer D is composed almost entirely of clayey silt, which is light orange to tan inside the dripline, changing to brown beyond the dripline. The upper boundary of the layer is not nearly as distinct as the lower one. Inside the dripline the sediments can be contrasted to those of C because of their lighter color and almost total absence of large rock inclusions. Beyond the dripline the color blurs and, in the east or outside wall of the excavations, layers C and D cannot be separated. Layer D was 10–15 centimeters in thickness. It was excavated as a single unit in all but the rear blocks (3 and 6), where it was subdivided into three parts. The stratum extended from 40–70 centimeters to 65–90 centimeters below the surface. Flakes and artifacts were plentiful, although much less so than for layer E. Charcoal was also abundant, though less occurred here than in the strata above and below it. A radiocarbon date of 4085 ± 75 B.P. (2135 B.C., SI-1845) on charcoal from unit D_3 in block 6 should date to a time shortly after the layer began to form.

Layer C is a dark brown clayey silt with some fine sand, pebbles, and cobbles intermixed beyond the dripline, but diminishing in quantity toward the rear of the shelter, finally disappearing altogether. Though not easily separated from D beyond the dripline, the layer is quite distinct from B, the layer overlying it, which is lighter in color and finer textured. Layer C extended from about 30 centimeters below ground surface to between 40–70 centimeters below it, varying in thickness from 10 to almost 40 centimeters. It was divided into three excavation units. Charcoal concentrations were higher than for any other layer in the site. Artifacts and flakes were abundant in the upper two subunits, C_1 and C_2, but near the bottom of the layer the concentration dropped off sharply. A charcoal sample from sublayer C_3 in block 1 produced the radiocarbon date of 4075 ± 105 years (2125 B.C., sample number I-5614) which should apply to the beginning of the layer deposition.

Layer B is a fine silt, tan-orange inside the dripline changing to light brown beyond. The sediments contained very few rock particles larger than fine sand. The contact with both layer C below and layer A (surface humus) above was quite clear. Layer B is beneath A at not more than 10 centimeters below the surface in the front and rear sections of the excavations and formed the surface of the site in the central area. It extended down to 30 centimeters below the surface and was divided into three units for the purposes of excavation. Charcoal was less plentiful here than in layer C but was still abundant. Artifacts and flakes were numerous, although a decline in numbers was noticeable in the lowest part of the layer. A charcoal sample from near the top of the layer (10–20 cm below the surface level) produced a radiocarbon date of 2890 ± 70 B.P. (940 B.C., SI-1844). The intensive use of the shelter must have ended shortly thereafter.

The upper layer in the site was not a depositional unit but rather a disturbed weathering zone or surface humus. It was a brown silt with a blocky structure and high organic content. Where present (at the rear of the shelter and out beyond the dripline), it was always less than 10 centimeters thick and highly disturbed. Glass, porcelain, nails, clay pipe fragments, and plastic, as well as stone flakes and tools, came from the stratum.

It is assumed that minor changes in depositional environments were responsible for the changing nature of the sediments identified and discussed above. These minor changes may have had a climatic basis, for changes in mean annual temperature and precipitation during the past 7,000 years have been suggested on the basis of pollen data for other parts of Panama (Bartlett and Barghoorn 1973). On the other hand, the changing intensities of human occupation might have been at least as important as climatic change in forming distinguishable layers. The laterization highly in evidence for layer G, deposited before the site was intensively occupied, is only weakly developed in any higher section of the profile. It seems likely, therefore, that the amount of organic material contributed to the deposits as a result of human occupation has arrested the laterization process; more completely in zones of heaviest occupation (layers E and C) than in others. It is tempting to suggest that layers E and F were deposited under the same natural depositional environment and are separable on the basis of more organic material in the former, and that A, B, C, and D were deposited under the same natural depositional environment (but one different from that of E and F) and are separable on the basis of higher organic content in C. At this time the suggestion cannot be verified and so must be classified as speculation. It seems best to consider each layer (A excepted) as a separate depositional unit without concern as to what combination of natural and cultural factors account for its formation.

With a few exceptions to be noted later, features of any sort were conspicuously lacking in the site. Instead of hearths, we recovered charcoal and fire-cracked rocks widely scattered in the deposits. The few features encountered were near the back wall of the shelter, beyond what we might consider the central living area. Moreover, artifact and flake densities were considerably higher near the back wall and out in front of the shelter, an area also beyond the central living area (fig. 1/3). The concentrations of fire-cracked rock and charcoal had similar back-wall and out-front distributions. This suggests to me that the central area of the site was generally swept clean. The pattern persisted into the historic period, for not only are historic artifacts concentrated beyond the overhang and in the rear of the shelter, but the entire surface humus layer has been removed, or kept from developing, in the central area. The shelter was even used as a camping spot by several Guaymí after I had initiated excavation of the site. They were there on a weekend after having crossed from the Atlantic side along the Third of November Trail. The only evidence of their camp was charcoal and ashes from a small fire near the back of the shelter (where block 3 was later to be dug) and a half dozen kernels of corn and a like number of beans thrown off to one side (although a couple of corn kernels did fall into the excavations). Thus, the pattern of site use has persisted to the present day.

The occupants themselves, then, had altered the fragile pattern of associations which might have allowed us to reconstruct the ways in which they used the shelter, instead of the ways in which they cleaned it up. In most cases, we cannot identify cooking areas, food processing areas, tool manufacturing areas, or various tool kits. On the other hand, with one excep-

Figure 1/3: A view of one of the two hearths uncovered in Casita de Piedra, in block 6, layer C, 45 cm below ground level. The arrow indicates north and points to a stone mortar found at the same level.

tion, our rock-shelter inhabitants did not dig into the floor of their dwelling, and so tools and charcoal from a single occupation remained in the same stratigraphic layer or even sublayer in which they were initially deposited. Horizontal displacement of materials by the occupants themselves was pronounced; vertical displacement was minimal.

In addition to one large pit dug by the early inhabitants, there is some evidence for vertical displacement of materials by tunneling insects, primarily termites. Charcoal and small flakes in layer G_2 were entirely confined to fossil termite (or other insect) tunnels which penetrated the layer to a depth of 4 to 6 centimeters. The bright orange, compact, silty clay sediments of the undisturbed layer were easily distinguished from the looser black-brown-orange mottle of sediments inside the tunnels. Farther up in the deposits where adjacent layers were distinguished by more subtle color and texture differences, these small burrows could not be identified, although we can be fairly certain that they existed. These observations can be interpreted to mean that small flakes, small artifacts, and particularly charcoal were liable to have been displaced vertically a few centimeters by insect disturbances, whereas large tools and flakes would be unaffected.

In contrast to the insect tunnels, two large animal burrows (ca. 15 cm in diameter) were easily recognizable by the looseness of their sediments and could be cleaned out without disturbing the natural deposits. Root disturbance, although present in the site, was confined primarily to the upper 60 centimeters of the fill and could not have caused more than minimal displacement of materials.

In sum, horizontal displacement of materials after initial deposition was primarily a function of human activity (clearing off the central living area). Any further horizontal movement by the activities of tunneling insects is inconsequential. This tunneling activity was, however, the primary cause of vertical displacements. Root growth and human activities are very minor factors. Although these disturbances rule out the possibility of reconstructing the fragile patterns of site use, they in no way restrict us from identifying more general associations. On the positive side, we should remember that the deposits are stratified (a condition in itself not usually reported in sites in the tropics); layer distinctions can be drawn, artifact distributions are patterned and show breaks at layer boundaries, and, finally, the radiocarbon determinations are internally consistent and of the right order of magnitude. Thus, although we are, for the most part, limited to talking about associations in terms of thousand- or several hundred-year periods, we can be reasonably confident that the associations are valid ones.

THE TRAPICHE SHELTER

This site is a boulder overhang similar in size to Casita de Piedra, which is located about one kilometer upstream (section 3.2). It was first visited in 1970 when a small surface collection was made. The initial test pit, dug in 1971, led to the excavation of 12 square kilometers in the site later in the year.

Sediments in the Trapiche Shelter and the cultural remains enclosed were very similar to those from Casita de Piedra and were handled in a like manner. With the exception of two pits apparently dug by the shelter occupants into the culturally sterile layer F, no other features were recognized in the deposits. Considerable amounts of charcoal and fire-cracked rock were found scattered throughout the shelter fill. The concentration of tools at the rear of the shelter underneath a low ceiling was quite pronounced, again as at Casita de Piedra. Horizontal displacement of materials at the hands of the inhabitants seemed as obvious here as in Casita de Piedra Shelter.

Vertical displacement in the Trapiche Shelter appeared to be slight, caused primarily by root disturbances which were encountered in places to a depth of 70 centimeters. These disturbances were easily recognizable, however, and every attempt was made to segregate the material in the disturbance zones from those in undisturbed contexts. One large animal burrow along a rock face was noted, and the material contained within was similarly segregated. Finally, there were two pits, both ca. 70 centimeters in diameter and 15 centimeters deep, dug into layer F from the layer above by the site inhabitants. Disturbance by tunneling insects was either absent or very slight (and not recognized), for in layer F, a bright yellow-orange clayey silt below the occupation, no trace of their tunnels could be seen.

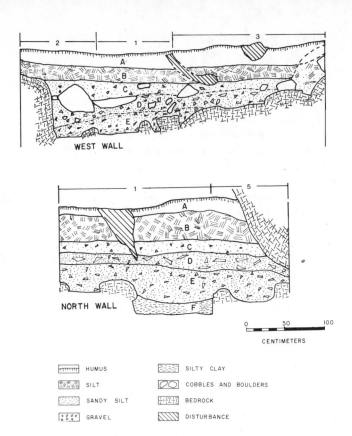

WEST WALL

NORTH WALL

0   50   100
CENTIMETERS

	HUMUS		SILTY CLAY
	SILT		COBBLES AND BOULDERS
	SANDY SILT		BEDROCK
	GRAVEL		DISTURBANCE

Figure 1/4: Profiles of the stratigraphy at the Trapiche Shelter; the west wall of blocks 2, 1, and 3, and the north wall of blocks 1 and 5. Adapted from fiigure 7, Proceedings of the First Puerto Rican Symposium on Archaeology, *Fundación Arqueológica, Antropológica e Histórica de Puerto Rico.*

Furthermore, not a single flake was recovered here. Vertical displacements, then, seem to have been less frequent than in Casita de Piedra.

Excavation techniques were in every respect parallel to those described for Casita de Piedra. After an initial 1 x 2-meter test pit, the natural strata, subdivided into 10-centimeter levels where appropriate, formed the basic excavation unit. The digging was done primarily with trowels, and all sediments were sifted through a quarter-inch mesh screen, except those units sifted with water through fine-mesh window screen. As was true for all sites examined along the Rio Chiriqui, the acidity of the sediments prevented the preservation of bone.

The original test pit was dug by myself and one workman. The remainder of the excavation was quite ably carried out either by E. Jane Rosenthal or John Alden, with a crew of three or four workmen. Both had worked with me at Casita de Piedra before assuming responsibility for the excavation of the Trapiche site. Also, since the two shelters were only one kilometer

Figure 1/5: The profile of the north wall of block 1 in the Trapiche Shelter.

apart, I was able to visit the site daily and discuss the progress of the work with them.

All the layers in the Trapiche Shelter are predominately silts, with noticeably less clay than found in Casita de Piedra (figs. 1/4, 1/5). The sediments under the overhang are more protected and therefore drier than those at Casita de Piedra; consequently, the facies shift inside and outside the dripline is pronounced, with pebbles and cobbles in the outside deposits even in layers that are almost totally fine silt back underneath the protection of the overhang. There are, on the other hand, numerous boulders under the roof of the shelter, some exposed on the surface but many more buried at various depths in the deposits.

The lowest layer encountered in the excavations was designated layer F, a compact clayey silt with a considerable amount of coarse sand, presumably from completely disintegrated blocks of granite. Also occurring here were disintegrating cobbles and boulders of granite (many of which could be troweled through with little difficulty and thus show up in cross section in photographs of the profiles). The layer changes in color from a red-orange at the rear of the shelter to yellow toward the front. It extends deeper than 155 centimeters below the surface, the bottom of the excavations, and ends between 100 and 120 centimeters below the ground surface. With the exception of two intrusive pits, the stratum is culturally sterile.

Layer E is a compact brown (reddish brown in the rear of the site) silt with coarse sand, granules, and pebbles of decomposed granite. The larger particles occur with greater frequency beyond the dripline than within it. The contact between E and F was clear in all parts of the site. Layer E varied from 20 to 30 centimeters in thickness and was divided into three excavation units. It began between 70 and 85 centimenters and ended between 100 and 120 centimeters below the ground surface. The considerable numbers of tools and flakes, as well as a modest amount of scattered charcoal, found here mark the initial occupation of the rock shelter. Charcoal collected in block 1 from units E_2 and E_3 (90–110 centimeters below the surface) and from the pit dug into layer F presumably from the same level were combined to obtain a sample sufficiently large to run a carbon-14 determination. The sample dated 5850 ± 110 B.P. (3900 B.C., I-5613). A second charcoal sample from slightly higher in the layer (E_2, 90–100 cm below surface level) in the adjacent block 2 produced a date of 4685 ± 85 B.P. (2735 B.C., SI-1848).

Layer D is composed of angular and subangular boulder- and cobble-sized particles, many of which seem to be roof fall, in a matrix of compact brown silt. The quantity of rocks in the layer serves to set it off from those both above and below. The layer varies in thickness from 15 to 35 centimeters and was divided into three excavation units. It extended from 40–60 centimeters below the floor of the site to 70–85 centimeters. The amounts of flakes, tools, and charcoal recovered from this stratum far surpassed those from any other stratum in the shelter.

Layer C is a compact, fine, brown silt with some pebbles and cobbles. It is lighter in color and contains very little rock near the rear of the shelter. It is very much like the matrix for layer D but lacks the latter's quantity of larger rock particles. However, where larger rocks are present in that part of C beyond the dripline, the two layers cannot be distinguished with certainty. In most parts of the site, layer C was less than 15 centimeters thick and was excavated either as a single unit or divided into two sections. It extended from between 25–50 centimeters to 40–60 centimeters below the surface. Flakes, artifacts, and charcoal were all plentiful in the deposit, even though representing a considerable drop from the densities found in layer D. Charcoal from the top of the layer in block 3 (C_1, 40–50 centimeters below surface level) dated 3870 ± 75 B.P. (1920 B.C., SI-1848).

Layer B is composed almost entirely of fine, loose, brown silt and is easily distinguished from layer C below, which is compact and contains some large rock particles. This layer contained rock only at the extreme outer edges of the shelter beyond the dripline. The top of the layer was not so easily distinguished, for in places the disturbances of the shelter's floor reached 15 centimeters into the shelter fill and into the top of layer B. In such cases, the disturbed part of the layer was removed with the upper layer, A. Where intact, layer B had an upper boundary 15–20 centimeters below the ground surface and extended down 25–50 centimeters into the shelter fill. The undisturbed part of the layer was excavated in two units. Occupation continued to be heavy, judging from the amounts of flakes, tools, and charcoal contained in the stratum. Charcoal collected from the top of the undisturbed deposits (20–30 cm below surface level) in block 3 provided a date of 2300 ± 75 B.P. (350 B.C., SI-1846).

Layer A is not a depositional unit, but a highly disturbed surface humus zone. Where preserved unaltered, it is a brown silt with a blocky and friable structure. For the purposes of excavation, this humus plus any surface disturbance was labeled layer A. It extended no deeper than 20 centimeters below the surface. Potsherds, as well as stone tools and flakes, were recovered here. No material evidence of a historic or modern occupation of the shelter was recovered. Surface disturbances were probably related to the fact that the shelter sits in a coffee grove.

The major break in the shelter deposits is between layers B and C. The loose brown silt of both layers A and B (which belong to the same depositional unit) stands in marked contrast to layers C, D, and E below, which are more compact and which contain considerably more sand, pebbles, cobbles, and boulders than A and B. Furthermore, beyond the dripline where all layers have large rocks, and at the extreme rear of the shelter where none do, C, D, and E appear almost as a single layer with gradually increasing proportions of clay and sand at the expense of the silt fraction.

THE HORACIO GONZALES SITE

This small rock shelter is 50 meters downstream from the Trapiche Shelter. The site was visited for the first time in 1970 but was not tested until the following season. Although the shelter has considerably less area underneath its overhang than either of the other two shelters upriver, it has a comfortably high ceiling and perhaps more usable floor space than is available at the Trapiche site today. A 1 x 2-meter test pit was dug in the center of the floor with its long axis oriented north-south or perpendicular to the rear wall of the shelter and one meter from it. Large boulders were uncovered almost immediately and at 40 centimeters below the surface took up over three-quarters of the pit. A 1 x 1-meter extension (block 2) was added to the front or south end of the test pit in order to obtain a clearer picture of the depositional sequence. At a later date we returned to the site and excavated block 3, a 1 x 2-meter unit east of block 2 and the front meter of block 1 and contiguous with them. In total, five square meters were excavated with all but the very front of blocks 2 and 3 being within the dripline.

The excavation procedures were similar to those already described for the Casita de Piedra and Trapiche shelters, with the exception that no fine sifting of sediments was carried out. The digging was done by myself and two workmen. No features were recorded in the site deposits and, for this reason, there is assumed to be considerable horizontal dislocation of cultural remains as in Casita de Piedra and the Trapiche Shelter. Since the shelter had been recently used as a pigsty, and on occasion as a horse stable (for one horse), the surface was heavily disturbed by these animals. Furthermore, the animals were secured by tying them to stakes driven deep into the deposits, disturbing them still more. The site was originally tested in hopes that major occupation levels occurred beneath the effects of these disturbances. This did not prove to be the case. Thus, although the site is stratified and the nature of the strata are reasonably clear (fig. 1/6), there was enough mixing of the deposits to obscure the cultural record slightly; the general pattern shown in the artifact distributions is clear enough, but the associations for the charcoal samples are not (and for this reason have not been dated).

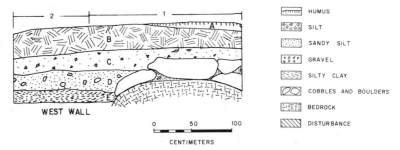

Figure 1/6: Profile of the stratigraphy at the Horacio Gonzales site; the west wall of blocks 1 and 2.

The lowest stratum exposed was an orange silty clay without any large rock particles included and was designated layer E. It extended from 60–70 centimeters below the ground surface down to at least 85 centimeters, the lowest part of our excavations. Because of the large boulders in block 1 and block 2, it was present in only the front meter of the excavations. No evidence of human occupation was recovered from the layer.

Layer D is a brown clayey silt with some pebbles and cobbles. It is between 10 and 20 centimeters thick and was excavated in two units. Only four flakes were contained in the bottom 10 centimeters of the layer, and these were added to the bulk of the cultural material which came from the upper part of the stratum. Still and all, there were only a handful of flakes and artifacts to document the occupation of the layer.

Layer C, a brown silt, is the bottom deposit in most of blocks 1 and 2 where it sits on large boulders (bedrock?). Elsewhere it can be separated from layer D only on the basis of having smaller particles included. It varies from a few centimeters in thickness above some of the boulders to about 20 centimeters in thickness at the front of the shelter. It extended from 25–30 centimeter below ground level to a maximum depth of 50 centimeters. Although cultural remains are predominantly stone flakes and tools, some potsherds were recovered near the top of the layer. A modest amount of charcoal was present as small flecks scattered throughout the sediments.

Layer B is a tan compact silt with no large rock particles. At the front of the shelter where some leveling had been done previous to excavation, layer B was exposed at the surface. Toward the rear of the shelter it was capped by a surface humus horizon designated layer A. The stratum varies from 15 to 30 centimeters in thickness and was divided into two or three excavation units. The contact with layer C, 25–30 centimeters below the shelter floor, is a reasonably clear one. Considerable amounts of flakes, stone tools, and potsherds came from the layer, although only a trace of charcoal was observed. Also, quantities of modern trash occurred in the top of the layer where it was exposed at ground level.

THE ZARSIADERO SHELTER

This small shelter is located alongside the Rio Zarsiadero, one kilometer above its confluence with the Rio Chiriqui. It is only about two kilometers from Casita de Piedra (see section 3.3, for further description of the site). The Zarsiadero Shelter was first visited in 1970 and was tested later that same year. The small .5-square meter test pit, dug to a depth of 70 centimeters, documented the presence of a preceramic component. During the 1971 field season, this was the first site to be tested. A 1 x 2-meter block with its long axis perpendicular to the back of the shelter was excavated by two workmen and myself. The digging was done with both shovels and trowels, and all dirt was sifted through a quarter-inch mesh screen. Besides the surface disturbances caused by the recent occupation of the site by farm workers, several pits had been dug into it by rooting pigs and had to be avoided in the placement of the test pit. We were also to find that from about 10 to 30 centimeters below the ground surface, the deposits were full of burrowing grubs, which must have made some contribution to the vertical displacement of small tools, flakes, and sherds.

Since the deposits appeared to be homogeneous, the excavation units were arbitrary 10-centimeter levels which held the gentle slope of the shelter floor. Unfortunately, the culturally sterile yellow-tan silt that underlay the occupation layers sloped more steeply than the surface, indicating that our arbitrary levels, at least the ones near the bottom of the block, cut across depositional lines instead of being parallel to them. This would have been corrected in further excavation of the site. However, in the press of time we never had the opportunity to continue. Thus we must rely on the results of the single 1 x 2-meter test pit for information on the nature of the occupation at the Zarsiadero Shelter.

The lowest layer in the site, a compact yellow-tan silt, began between 55 and 65 centimeters below ground surface, and extended below 70 centimeters at the bottom of the excavations. This layer D contained no cultural remains.

Layer C is composed of angular and subangular cobbles and pebbles in a matrix of dark brown silt. The stratum extends from 35–40 centimeters to 55–65 centimeters below the shelter floor, sloping down toward the front of the shelter. A number of flakes and tools came from this layer, but no potsherds. A concentration of charcoal in the southeast corner of the block between 48 and 50 centimeters below the surface is well within the layer and should provide an accurate date for it. Only small charcoal flecks occurred elsewhere in the sediments. All cultural material in excavation units 40–50 centimeters, 50–60 centimeters, and 60–70 centimeters below ground surface came from this layer, as did some of the material in excavation unit 30–40 centimeters below the surface.

Layer B is a dark brown silt similar to layer C except that it lacks the high concentration of rock particles. It extends from 10 centimeters below ground surface to 35–40 centimeters. Flakes and stone tools were recovered in great numbers throughout the deposit. Potsherds were common at the top of the level but quickly dropped off in numbers toward the middle and were probably absent in the lowest 10 centimeters of the layer. Small flecks of charcoal were scattered throughout the deposit. Excavation units 10–20 centimeters and 20–30 centimeters below the surface fall entirely within this layer, as does part of the unit 30–40 centimeters below the surface.

Layer A was a highly disturbed surface humus zone which did not seem to extend deeper than 10 centimeters into the shelter fill. In addition to great quantities of flakes, tools, and sherds, it also contained some bone, plastic, glass, nails, a spoon, and other assorted historic and modern trash.

THE SCHOOLYARD SITE

At the very end of the 1971 field season, a 1 x 2-meter pit was dug into a terrace of the Rio Chiriqui behind Casita de Piedra in order to expose the soil profile. Cultural remains were encountered to a depth of 70 centimeters, the bottom of our excavation. Lack of time prevented us from excavating further, even though we were not altogether sure that we had reached the bottom of the occupation. The results of this limited test are included here simply to document the fact that open campsites as well as rock shelters hold preceramic occupations in the Rio Chiriqui area, and that such occupations are likely to be buried at some depth. In such open campsites one might be able to find evidence of special activity areas, tool kits, and perhaps even dwellings.

The lowest sediments were red-orange silty clay with some highly weathered pebbles and cobbles included. A few flakes and a charcoal sample came from the lowest 10 centimeter level excavated (60–70 centimeters below surface level). The sediments become redder and more silty higher up in the profile and contain fewer pebbles and cobbles. The flakes of andesite and the potsherds found at the 40–60 centimeter level were much more heavily weathered than those recovered from the protected deposits in the four rock shelters examined. Slightly higher in the deposits (the 20–40 centimeter level) two additional flakes and a modern copper rivet represented the first cultural remains unearthed. The dark red clayey silt was capped by a thin (less then 10 centimeters thick) surface humus horizon.

The Volcan Baru Region: A Site Survey

P. D. SHEETS

INTRODUCTION

The region surveyed measured 62 square kilometers along both banks in the headwaters of the Rio Chiriqui Viejo. It comprises all of the habitable area, and all of the archaeological sites, in and between the two highland basins of Cerro Punta and El Hato. The land extends from a minimum of 1,180 meters along the river near Barriles to a height of 2,375 meters at Cerro Punta. Sites were found at elevations from 1,200 to 2,000 meters. A preliminary summary of the results appears in Linares, Sheets, and Rosenthal 1975.

GEOLOGIC HISTORY

The geology of the Volcan region has been described recently by Stewart (ms. 1978), whose preliminary report gives the most authoritative account to date of the Early Tertiary to Recent history of this area. We are concerned here with Stewart's interpretations of the events following the beginnings of Pliocene times, when the province of Chiriqui as we know it today began to take form. From this time on, vulcanism in this region seems to have been constant. During one of the phases of volcanic activity, what Stewart calls "the Primary Baru Phase," a very large composite volcanic cone built up and, in the process, numerous andesitic lava flows went in various directions. Three of these flows went west, forming lava dams across the Rio Chiriqui Viejo at the spot where we now find the town of Bambito. The backed-up waters from the river created a substantial lake in the area where the town of Cerro Punta is located. For hundreds and thousands of years, the lake became filled with sediments washing down from the nearby volcano. Finally, the dam eroded away and the Cerro Punta lake was drained, "leaving behind the extremely rich lake and volcanic soil mixture we find here today"; afterwards, "man moved into the area and began his agricultural existence there" (Stewart ms. 1978, p. 36).

During the time when the Cerro Punta volcanic lake was filling up with sediments, a volcanic field had developed, covering about 400 square kilometers and forming more than 80 small craters. It was located to the south, extending from the towns of Nueva California and El Hato halfway to the town of La Concepción. The archaeological site of Barriles "is in and along the edge of one of the old craters of the Barriles Phase . . . . This old crater contained a deep lake which had deposited in it a considerable thickness of diatomaceous earth deposits derived from the silica-bearing diatom plants that lived in the water. Later, the Rio Chiriqui Viejo reached the northwestern part of the crater and drained the lake. The lake terrace left behind became an ideal place for the development of a large Indian settlement, especially as there was an abundant supply of fresh water from an artesian spring that runs year round" (ibid., p. 32).

After a period of inactivity, another phase of renewed vulcanism (the "Secondary El Baru Phase") began, with eruptions occurring for thousands of years. "The last eruption of El Baru contained . . . an enormous amount of fine pumice which was widely distributed by the winds. This layer, actually two layers of pumice, each 10 to 15 cm thick and about 30 cm apart, have been found covering an area from Cerro Punta southward beyond Nueva California and El Hato and eastward as far as Boquete and the Rio Caldera" (ibid., p. 35). In our archaeological work, we have dated the end phase of volcanic activity, which drove people out of the area at ca. A.D. 600.

METHODS

The survey of the Volcan Baru region was designed to locate and determine the size of all the sites occurring in the strip alongside the Rio Chiriqui Viejo between the basins of El Hato and Cerro Punta. We wanted to see if there was any patterning in the distribution of sites and with what factors it could be correlated. Thus, the entire survey area was walked meter by meter, and constantly checked for evidence of occupation (sherds, chipped stone, ground stone, or petroglyphs). Where the ground surface was well exposed and had been disk-plowed, as was generally the case in the Cerro Punta and Bambito regions, noting the decrease and disappearance of surface materials was considered sufficient to define site boundaries.

However, in undisturbed areas occupation debris was often buried by some 20 centimeters of volcanic pumice and contemporary humus. In these areas we had to check in arroyos which had eroded through the overburden, watch for areas of treefall where the roots would bring up materials, and check in such man-made features as road cuts and drainage ditches. In areas where even these methods of "seeing" below the pumice failed, we used the posthole digger to get a soil profile and check for occupation debris (see report no. 3).

When an occupation was discovered, all chipped stone and ground stone were collected, and, during the first stages of site collection, all ceramics. If the site was at all sizable, then it was impractical to pick up *all* ceramics, and we focused on collecting diagnostics (rim sherds, decorated sherds, and so forth).

Occasionally, while surveying an otherwise vacant area, we came across small concentrations of a few sherds — often looking like an area where a pot or two had broken. These locations were noted as sherd concentrations and plotted as such on the map. It is possible that some of the sherd concentrations were small sites, but it is unlikely that many were. We found a total of twenty sherd concentrations.

At all but two locations, the petroglyphs recorded were associated (by proximity) with occupation sites and therefore are included with those sites. However, in two cases petroglyphs were found with no nearby occupation debris and so were given separate site numbers.

The location of any feature or collection, whether a site, sherd concentration, petroglyph, or posthole sondage, was noted within a grid covering the entire surveyed area. Each grid square was one kilometer (1,000 meters) on a side, and was subdivided into ten units vertically and ten horizontally. These finer lines were spaced 100 meters apart. This system provides mapping accuracy to within 100 meters, certainly quite sufficient for sites in a 62 square kilometer area.

NATURAL ZONES

The surveyed area was divided into five zones which are, respectively, from northeast to southwest: Cerro Punta, Bambito, Intermediate, Los Llanos, and the Southwest (or "Lower Barriles"). The regions are distinguished from each other on the basis of environmental and topographic differences. Description of these regions follows.

1. Cerro Punta is a highland basin filled in with alluvial sediments deposited on an essentially flat or gently sloping land. The flat, cultivable, and habitable land of the Cerro Punta region is estimated to be between 7 and 8 square kilometers (700 to 800 hectares), roughly two-thirds of this basin. Only half of the habitable area was occupied; the sites encountered clustered toward the lower portion of the region, from 1,810 to a maximum elevation of 2,000 meters.

The mean annual precipitation for Cerro Punta, which is in the rain shadow of Volcan Baru, is 2,300 mm (actually 2,260, based on eight years of records). The range is from 1,704 mm to 3,464 mm, the maximum being twice the minimum. Local people tell us that frost used to be a much more common occurrence as recently as ten years ago, before the extensive forest clearance denuded so much of the present landscape. The degree of forest clearance on the hillsides at the time of occupation could have been somewhere between the mature evergreen forest of fifty years ago and the present treeless landscape, perhaps not unlike conditions ten to twenty years ago. Nowadays the basin is planted with potatoes, onions, and other vegetables or given over to the raising of cattle for milk.

2. Topographically, Bambito is much more dissected than Cerro Punta, since, due to its close proximity to the lava dams, Bambito has suffered much more erosion in the form of deeply entrenched *quebradas*. The Rio Chiriqui Viejo ranges from 100 meters below the main terrace edge to deeper than 300 meters below it. Less than one-third of the terraces are flat, habitable lands, in contrast with the less-eroded Cerro Punta, with two-thirds habitable.

In terms of climate, Bambito and Cerro Punta are virtually identical. We could not detect differences in the pre-eruption soils either. The lowest elevation of the region is 1,570 meters, and the highest of the surveyed area is about 2,050 meters. Sites range from 1,610 to 1,910 meters. A total of eight sherd concentrations were located and recorded.

3. Los Llanos is the only region surveyed that did not contain a single site, not even a sherd concentration. Its rainfall must be close to that of the Southwest region described below. Los Llanos itself is geologically very recent. As a rapid volcanic outwash composed of fine pumice and ash boulders, it is a difficult surface for humic buildup. Hence the vegetation is composed of low scattered scrub trees, a few bushes, and a sparse growth of grasses and lichens. It is almost a desert, not due to the lack of rainfall, but due to the rough and recent nature of the deposit. The elevation range within the surveyed area is from 1,380 to 1,720 meters.

4. Topographically very little of the Intermediate region is river terrace. Most of the terrain is steep and hilly, with elevations ranging from 1,400 to 1,800 meters. Flat, cultivable land is available nowadays only where the Rio Chiriqui Viejo makes a southward loop, near the towns of Tisingal and Paso Ancho. Rainfall is probably close to the Nueva California figure mentioned below, and temperatures would be higher than at Bambito or Cerro Punta. In some places, for example around Tisingal, conditions may have been too swampy for settlement. However, some of the flat area beyond the Tisingal town itself is habitable, along with most of Paso Ancho. Even the two large hills dividing these towns are fairly low for Volcan, below 1,700 meters, in contrast to El Alton ridge, which we have also included in the Intermediate region, but which is above 2,000 meters. The habitable segments of Paso Ancho and Tisingal are covered with a fine-grained humus, rich in organic content. However, as we shall see, very few archaeological sites were found here.

5. The climate of the Southwest region is more seasonal than that of Cerro Punta even though the annual overall rainfall is greater. Nueva California averages 2,800 mm of rain a year, or about 500 mm more than Cerro Punta. Also, temperatures in the Southwestern region are higher because of the slightly lower elevations. In short, the region around Barriles has a wet and dry climatic regime, more similar to that of the Pacific coastal lowlands of Chiriqui than to the Cerro Punta climate, which is colder and more continuously wet. Elevations in the inhabited area of the Southwestern region are 1,200 to 1,340 meters, or about 500 meters lower than in the settled parts of the Cerro Punta basin. Almost two-thirds of the land is flat and cultivable.

There are four river terraces in this area, the largest of which is the oldest, and the only one that supported massive zones of occupation. The humic horizon (pre-eruption) that has built up on this terrace is relatively thick and fine-grained. This high terrace abuts on the eroded remnants of geologically much earlier lava flows (again predominantly dacitic in composition).

SITE SIZES AND DISTRIBUTIONS

By recording the surface distribution of cultural materials and, where exposure was insufficient, by surveying below the surface with the posthole digger, we were able to determine site boundaries with some confidence. Size categories, based on a rough index of the site areas, were then devised. Sites in class 1 had occupational debris spread over an area less than 200 meters long; sites in class 2 covered areas between 200 and 300 meters long; sites in class 3, between 301 and 400 meters long; sites in class 4 between 401 and 700 meters long; and sites in class 5 had debris covering areas more than 701 meters long. Obviously, these categories are rather crude and do not correspond to any ethnographic reality, but they help to discuss site distributions in the five natural zones outlined above.

The location, including the site number and size-class of the sites discussed below, is given in figure 2/1, while table 1 compares the number of sites found in each of the natural zones.

1. A total of 14 habitation sites (and one lithic site) was discovered in Cerro Punta, along with 9 sherd concentrations. The sizes of the Cerro Punta sites range from 1 to 4 on the 5-point scale, and average 2.5. A subdivision of the Cerro Punta region was made, creating three clusters of sites.

A. The first cluster consists of seven sites, ranging in size from 1 to 3, and averaging 2.1. The impression is that of a cluster of very small to moderate-sized hamlets.

B. The second cluster in the center of the basin contains five sites, all of size 3 or 4, with a mean site size of 3.6. This is considerably larger than the hamlets in the first cluster, and indeed larger than any settlements until we get to the Southwest region. Of the five central Cerro Punta sites, Sitio Pitti (BU-17) was clearly the largest and most internally differentiated. Here we found ritual and utilitarian celts and the debitage from their manufacture, slab and legged metates (one *very* large), dacite sculptures, and a high percentage of incised and appliqué-decorated pottery.

C. The third cluster is a tiny one, composed of only three sites. The sites are small, of sizes 1 and 2, averaging only 1.3.

2. The survey encountered a total of 23 sites in Bambito, with an average size of 2.0. Bambito sites are generally smaller and lack anything like the central Cerro Punta cluster of large sites. Bambito sites are usually on the ends of the plateaus (dissected remnants of the major terrace), overlooking the Rio Chiriqui Viejo at the bottom of the canyon, or on lower river terraces. Those along the river are quite small; the larger sites are on higher terraces. Several site clusters can be recognized within the Bambito area:

A. The first cluster is composed of six sites, all on the major, high terrace. Mean site size is 2.0, with a range of 1 to 4. Elevations of sites are between 1,800 and 1,900 meters. Both BU-18 and BU-11 are relatively large sites, but the rest are quite small. BU-18, in fact, is the largest site in areal extent in Bambito, but is smaller than Sitio Pitti (BU-17), the largest in Cerro Punta.

B. The second cluster of Bambito sites is composed of ten sites on lower stream terraces, closer to the Rio Chiriqui Viejo than either of the other clusters. Mean size is 1.9, ranging from 1 to 3, indicating the consistently small size of the Bambito hamlets located near the river. The sites range in altitude from 1,610 meters up to 1,820 meters. It is possible that because the

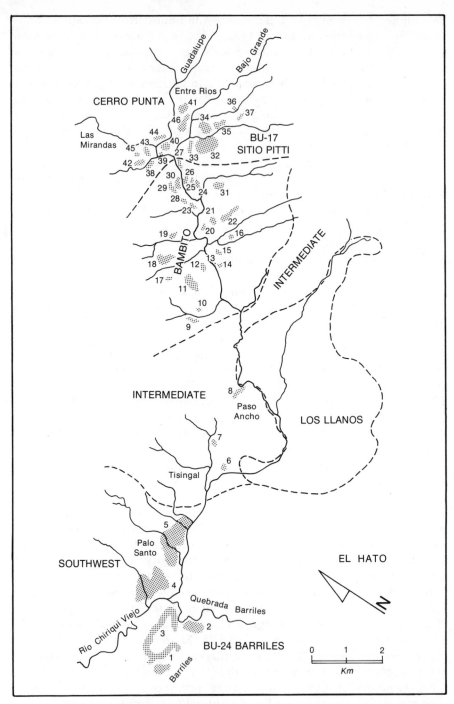

Figure 2/1: Distribution of archaeological sites in Volcan Baru by area. The numbers indicate the sites and the stippling their sizes. After O.F. Linares, P.D. Sheets, and E.J. Rosenthal, in Science, *1975, vol. 187, no. 4172, fig. 3, p. 140 (© 1975 by the American Association for the Advancement of Science).*

TABLE 1 NUMBER OF SITES IN EACH OF THE FIVE SITE-SIZE CLASSES BY SURVEYED ZONE IN THE VOLCAN BARU REGION, CHIRIQUI HIGHLANDS

	Class 1 <200m	Class 2 200-300m	Class 3 301-400m	Class 4 401-700m	Class 5 701->1,000m	Totals
Cerro Punta (sites 32-45) (1,800-2,375m)	3	5	4	2	0	14
Bambito (sites 9-31) (1,570-2,050m)	8	8	6	1	0	23
Intermediate (sites 6-8)	0	3	0	0	0	3
Los Llanos (none) (1,380-1,720m)	0	0	0	0	0	0
Southwest (sites 1-5)	0	0	0	0	5	5

lower terraces are geologically more recent, the humus buildup is not quite as rich as on the high terrace, partially explaining the smaller site size here.

C. The third Bambito cluster has seven sites, with a mean size of 2.1 and a range of 1 to 3, not unlike the first cluster. Three moderately large sites (size 3) are located toward the center of the cluster, specifically sites 31, 22, and 21. Altitudes range from 1,820 to 1,880 meters.

3. As mentioned, not a single site was discovered in the region of Los Llanos.

4. The Intermediate region covers a rather large area between Bambito, Los Llanos, and the Southwest regions. Much to our surprise in surveying this region, particularly around Paso Ancho and Tisingal, where fairly deep, rich soils occur, we found sites to have been small and far apart. There were only three occupation sites (all size 2), two sherd concentrations, and one petroglyph site in the entire area.

The three sites encountered range in elevation from 1,380 to 1,540 meters. There is a high sherd concentration in this region, to the east of the river, at 1,870 meters. This hilly ridge leading up to El Alton was almost completely covered either by pasture grasses or coffee fields, so we had problems with exposure in this area. It is possible that we could have missed a small site, or even two, but it is very unlikely we could have missed a major site in this area.

5. Even though the Southwest region is the smallest area covered by the survey, it was by far the most densely inhabited in prehistoric times. Here the sites are not small, discrete areas of refuse, but long, continuous zones of dense habitation debris.

As with Bambito and Cerro Punta, there was a marked preference for settling on the high major stream terrace of the Rio Chiriqui Viejo. We surveyed three sites (BU-3, 4, 5) completely by finding all site boundaries, and all are clearly size 5. The two other sites which were incompletely surveyed will probably turn out on future work to be size 5 as well. All of the sites in the Southwest region were found within 20 meters (above and below) the 1,300-meter contour line; in other words, 1,300 meters is the mean elevation for occupation in the Southwest region.

The BU-3 site is curiously shaped as a sinuous band of cultural material, 100 meters or more in width and almost three kilometers long, surrounding what was probably a lake, formed in one of the numerous old craters in this area.

SITE CHRONOLOGY

The analysis of surface collections from the Volcan Baru survey (section 7.4.d.) indicates that Cerro Punta and Bambito were similar to each other but different from the Southwest region in the frequency of major ceramic wares. Similarly, sites in classes 2 and 3 were ceramically homogeneous but different from those in the other size classes. Although no great time differences are involved, it is important to note that the Southwest region, or more precisely the area around Barriles, was settled earlier, and the occupation lasted longer, than in the regions farther north.

A SUMMARY OF SETTLEMENT PATTERNS IN THE VOLCAN REGION

"A settlement pattern, as the name implies, is the pattern of sites on the regional landscape; it is empirically derived by sampling or total survey, and is usually studied by counting sites, measuring their sizes and the distances between them, and so on" (Flannery 1976, p. 162).

In total 45 sites were found in and between the basins of El Hato and Cerro Punta in a complete survey of a 62 square kilometer strip extending along both banks of the Rio Chiriqui Viejo. The river flows from an elevation of 2,000 meters at Cerro Punta to an elevation of 1,200 meters at El Hato, over a distance of about 16 kilometers; thus the average gradient is 50 meters per kilometer. The salient characteristics of the Volcan settlement pattern can be summarized as follows:

1. The predominant pattern is a variant of a linear stream and river system as discussed by Flannery (1976, pp. 173–180). However, though settlement followed the course of the Rio Chiriqui Viejo, most sites were located at some distance back from the river channel on high terraces varying in elevation from a few to several hundred meters above the river itself. The sites most distant from the river are found in the Bambito region where the Chiriqui Viejo cuts a deep channel; those nearest the river are on the flatter basin floors of Cerro Punta and El Hato. Hence the Volcan settlement was not a typical lowland floodplain pattern, like the one that predominated all along the Pacific coast of the Isthmus, especially in the central provinces (Cooke 1972; Linares 1977b), but a piedmont pattern characteristic of tropical mountains with incident rivers.

2. The upper limit of human occupation seems to have been 2,000 meters. Settlement farther north was probably arrested by a cloud forest uninhabited even nowadays.

3. Sites were located on the only flat land available on top of river terraces, flanked by deeply entrenched streams. The area covered by a particular river terrace determined the number of sites placed on it.

4. Within the Cerro Punta and Bambito regions there was usually one or at most two sites that were conspicuously larger (class 4) than the rest. Hence, larger sites tended to be farther apart from each other than smaller sites.

5. In these same regions sites in classes 1–3 tended to be at a minimum distance of 150 meters and at a maximum distance of approximately 300 meters. Hence, they were fairly evenly spaced.

6. Despite the availability of flat cultivable land near Tisingal and Paso Ancho, the Intermediate region was very sparsely inhabited. The three sites found here were located at distances over 500 meters, and were all of one small site size. We have suggested elsewhere (Linares, Sheets, and Rosenthal 1975) that social, and not simply natural factors, must have accounted for the lack of settlement near the two modern towns mentioned above. More precisely, the Intermediate region may have served as a buffer zone between the large and powerful villages of the Southwest area and the smaller villages of Bambito and Cerro Punta (see section 4.4).

7. The emptiness of Los Llanos is probably more apparent than real. According to Stewart (ms. 1978) the most recent eruption of Volcan Baru (which according to our radiocarbon determinations occurred around A.D. 600) deposited a layer of lava and ash flow, 20 meters deep in some places, over the entire area. If so, numerous sites in Los Llanos could have been buried underneath the ash flow.

8. Unlike Cerro Punta, the Southwest or "Lower Barriles" region was dominated by five large villages, three of them measuring over one kilometer in length. Natural factors, such as the availability of cultivable flat land, a seasonal rainfall which is optimal for maize and manioc farming, and absence of frost, must have accounted in part for the "prosperity" of these large villages. In addition, the Southwest area was settled earlier than the rest, probably by groups moving upland from the Chiriqui coastal plains. Nonetheless, the Southwest villages may have been large as a response to political and social pressures — in order to dominate, and possibly even to extract tribute from, the smaller villages in the area. How this hypothesis fits in with the material evidence from ours and other people's excavations in the Volcan Baru region is discussed in section 4.3.

Surveying the Volcan Region with the Posthole Digger

B. H. DAHLIN

THE TESTING (OR SONDAGE) TECHNIQUE

At a number of locations, both occupied and unoccupied, within the 62 square kilometer survey area stretching on both sides of the Rio Chiriqui Viejo (report no. 2), a series of soundings were made by means of an ordinary posthole digger with a blade diameter of about 20 centimeters (see Fry 1972). Such soundings were deemed necessary (1) to locate sites where there was little or no ground surface exposure, (2) to determine subsurface stratigraphy, (3) to determine depth of occupation debris, (4) to locate subsurface features, and (5) to define site limits where there was reason to believe that the distribution of surface debris was misleading.

A "sondage" survey requires at least two persons for maximum efficiency: one to manipulate the posthole digger and another to examine the soils and the cultural materials extracted at each thrust and to record by means of profiles the results of each sondage. The value of this technique exceeded our expectations. The vertical position of anything worthy of note could be accurately measured and distinct stratigraphic changes in color, texture, or compactness could be recorded within about two or three centimeters. Soundings were made where optimum results could be achieved. In larger surveys employing sampling methods, a grid-plan and randomizing procedures should also be imposed on the posthole soundings.

For obvious reasons the sondage survey was not attempted at sites where adequate information could be gained by other means, such as examining road clearings, river cuts, arroyos, drainage ditches, and wells. Throughout the survey area the culture-bearing strata are capped by a more or less thick layer of pumice with a contemporary humic zone on top. Unless a site has been plowed, or otherwise disturbed, there is little likelihood that cultural debris will be uncovered in quantities adequate to define a site. Much of the arable land, particularly in the Southwestern sector, is also under pasturage. The low mat of grasses which almost entirely blankets the ground surface provides very little opportunity for surface collection. In all these instances the posthole digger is the only recourse.

SUBSURFACE STRATIGRAPHY

As I just mentioned, a layer of pumice capped the culture-bearing strata. Using the sondage technique enabled us to tentatively assess the variable effects of the pumice fall. In recording the amount, size, and angularity of the pumice particles and the nature of their deposition at any and all locations within the survey area, we were able to identify the source of the pumice as Volcan Baru and conclude that it affected the entire survey area. How helpful this information will be in future efforts to establish relevant contemporary climatic conditions is difficult to say without more detailed work, for certainly the volcanic eruptions must have temporarily had an enormous effect on the local wind, rain, and transpiration patterns.

The Intermediate region in particular posed a serious problem to understanding subsurface stratigraphy. Despite favorable ecological conditions for settlement, evident on the surface of some subareas, few sites were found here, and those that were recorded were generally small. In addition to putting in soundings at BU-8 near Paso Ancho, several others were made at what appeared to be totally unoccupied areas. This was done in an effort to ascertain natural factors that may have accounted in part for the sparseness of settlement in parts of this large area. We also wanted to make sure that the paucity of occupation was not due to having the cultural evidence otherwise buried under the pumice layer. The BU-8 site is a particularly good case in point. There is little or no slope; drainage is good even in the rainy season; a few small clear streams lace the area; soils appear to be fine, composed of rich black humus; and foot transportation along the nearby Rio Chiriqui Viejo seemed relatively easy. Widely spaced sondage units also showed that the rich soils were uniformly deep, often exceeding 100 centimeters. We proposed that some cultural factor may have retarded movement into this otherwise advantageous settlement area (see section 4.4).

Additional soundings were made along part of the apparently unoccupied north bank of the Rio Chiriqui Viejo in the Intermediate region. This area was thought beforehand to have been either an extension of BU-5 or perhaps an as yet undefined site extending to the northeast. The reason for the lack of cultural materials became evident from our sondage units: the humic horizon was very thin, in all likelihood discouraging settlement by intensive maize farmers.

TESTING THE DEPTH OF OCCUPATION DEBRIS

The settlement survey benefited from this test at at least three sites. At BU-12 we discovered the greatest concentration of cultural materials found anywhere on the surface. The location of such a concentration was unexpected because our assessment of the arable land available did not seem sufficient to support a large population. Moreover, no other site in the survey area suggested such a long depositional history. Eight strategically placed sondages indicated that the upper soil zone was relatively thin, and that the plowed zone was extraordinarily deep, extending down to about 80 centimeters. Therefore, we concluded that almost all surface materials were due to recent disturbance. The same was true of BU-11 which also looked promising on the surface. The sondage survey therefore saved us time by obviating extensive test-pitting. The sondage technique tests for depth of occupation at a site in a tenth or even twentieth of the time required by a 2 x 2-meter test.

Most of the field season was spent excavating the productive Pitti-Gon-zalez site in Cerro Punta. However, we also wanted to understand the relationship of this site to Barriles, the type-site for the Southwest region. Therefore, an extensive series of soundings (17 in all) was initiated at Barriles in an effort to locate areas of deep, undisturbed midden. Two relatively good areas were located and subsequently tested by excavation. Even better results were achieved at Sitio Pitti-Gonzalez (BU-17).

LOCATING SUBSURFACE FEATURES

Our main concern at site BU-17 was to locate subsurface features such as living floors, hearths, burials, and midden deposits, not only for purposes of excavation, but also to define activity areas at the site. Forty-seven posthole soundings were made at BU-17 in order to approximate site limits, to locate subsurface features upon which to define activity loci, and to clarify the site stratigraphy. As a result we were able to suggest at least four tentative activity areas (section 4.3; fig. 3/1). Area 1 contained a dense layer of refuse which upon excavation turned out to overlie an oval dwelling (report no. 4). Immediately surrounding the dwelling, we encountered a zone with sediments that were uniformly dark and fine owing to their high organic content. The suggestion has been made that this organic matrix resulted from periodic sweepings of vegetable debris from the living floor of the dwelling (Spang ms. 1976).

Roughly 50 meters to the northwest of area 1, the posthole soundings revealed another dense area of refuse (area 2) which probably marked the presence of another dwelling. Farther north, about 80 meters from area 1, an open hearth was unearthed (area 3) by opening up block 7 at a spot where a single posthole sounding had revealed a fairly deep refuse deposit. Finally, to the southwest of the dwelling, we discovered an area of redeposition (area 4) on a small hillock.

One of the aims of the 1972 season was to retest Barriles (BU-24) with the purpose of linking its stratigraphy and ceramic sequence with the rest of the

TABLE 1   NUMBER OF SHERDS IN THE POSTHOLES AT
BU-17B *(see report no. 3, fig. 3/1)*

Number of Sherds	Postholes
None	1, 4, 6, 22, 34
1–10	5, 7, 11, 12, 13, 16, 17, 23, 29, 35
11–20	2, 8, 10, 14, 19, 21
21–30	15, 31, 32, 33
31–40	20, 24, 28
41–50	3, 18, 26, 27
> 50	9, 25, 30, 36

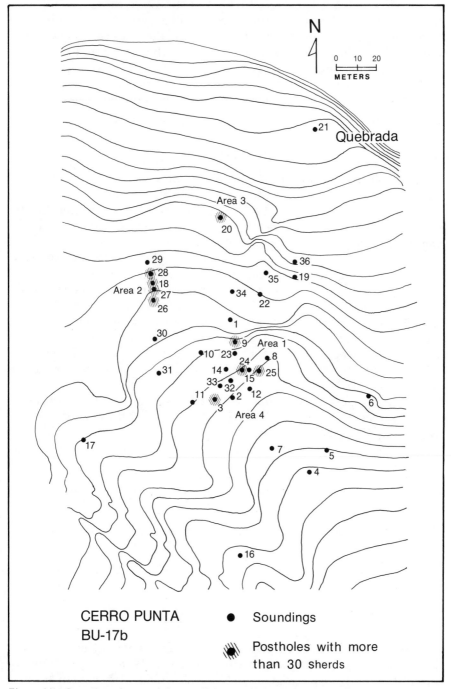

Figure 3/1: Location of most of the posthole soundings made at the Pitti locality (BU-17b) in Cerro Punta. Postholes with more than thirty sherds are indicated by shading; these served to define four activity areas. (This figure and figure 41/3 are after site maps by B. Dahlin and P. Sheets.)

Volcan sites, most especially with that of BU-17. Because the site was covered with a thick matting of grass, the use of the posthole digger became essential. Of the seventeen postholes dug at the site, two showed the following characteristics: they were in undisturbed areas (indicated by a thick consolidated pumice layer), they yielded abundant cultural material going through at least two stratigraphic layers, and they contained charcoal. These spots became the location of test excavations (blocks 1 and 2; report no. 4).

CONCLUSIONS

The posthole digger sondage survey of the Volcan region was essential to the success of the 1972 season in several important respects:

1. It served to determine the total extent of the area affected by the deposition of wind-transported pumice during the last Volcan Baru eruption, which occurred about A.D. 600.

2. It served to locate many of the sites that otherwise would have lain undetected under the layer of pumice or in unplowed pastures.

3. It suggested that other than natural processes may have been involved in the sparseness of the occupation in the Intermediate region.

4. It corrected wrong impressions, gained from the abundance at some sites of cultural materials on the surface, by showing that the deposits were not especially deep, but the sites had been plowed especially thoroughly.

5. It allowed the definition of activity loci at sites Pitti-Gonzalez (BU-17) and Barriles (BU-24).

6. Finally, it permitted the discovery of the most important feature excavated that season — the oval-dwelling at BU-17a — and the placement of the two productive tests at Barriles.

Report Number 4

The Pitti-Gonzalez (BU-17) Site: Excavations and Stratigraphy

S. SPANG AND E. J. ROSENTHAL

INTRODUCTION

The site straddles the road entering the Cerro Punta valley from the direction of Bambito. It is located on rich alluvial lands that slope up gently toward the south, away from an eastward-flowing stream known as Quebrada Callejon, between the 1,860- and 1,900-meter contours. Potsherds and other artifacts were found intermittently over an area 600 meters in length and about half that much in width. On the western end of the site, near the existing road, we excavated the BU-17a or Gonzalez locality in 1971; in 1972 we excavated the BU-17b or Pitti locality, some 300 to 390 meters to the east. Both localities constitute the BU-17 site.

THE EXCAVATIONS

1. The Gonzalez Locality (BU-17a; fig. 4/1)

The first 2 x 2-meter cut at BU-17a was opened April 1971 and was ex-cavated by arbitrary ten-centimeter units. Screening began when the first sherds were encountered and continued to a depth of 100 centimeters below the surface. After cut 1 was profiled to determine the natural stratigraphy, we decided to continue the testing. A trench was established running north-south of, and adjacent to, cut 1. A total of seven 2 x 2-meter cuts were placed here, of which six were completed; the seventh was partially exca-vated by representatives of the Museo Nacional (this was only 1 x 2 meters).

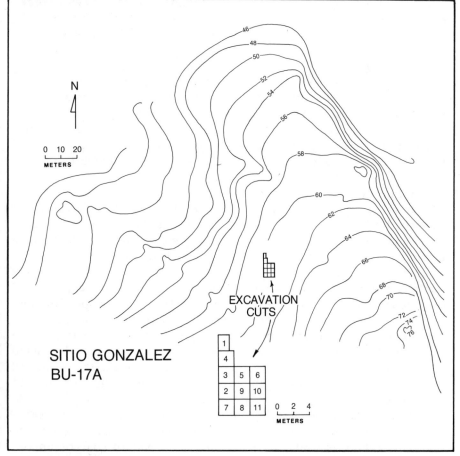

Figure 4/1: Map showing location of excavations at the Gonzalez locality (BU-17a) of Sitio Pitti-Gonzalez.

The final appearance of the site was a 9-meter long trench running north to south, and an adjacent 4-meter trench running east from cut 3.

The testing program suggested that although the deposit was secondary, the pottery and tools were well enough preserved to encourage further excavation in the general area.

The excavation of BU-17a was continued during the 1972 season (fig. 4/2). One month was spent slowly removing with trowels four 2 x 2-meter cuts in the eastern sector abutting cuts 1 and 2, and in the southern sector abutting cuts 5 and 6. The purpose for continuing excavations at this site was the single radiocarbon determination of 735 ± 110 B.C. (I-5871); the necessity of confirming this date (which we do not now accept) was obvious then.

The method of excavation was as follows: Cuts were numbered in counterclockwise order, with cut 8 adjacent to cut 1 being the first. It was decided to trowel down 8 and 10, then remove 9. The topsoil was removed with a shovel, and trowel excavations were begun before noticing that cut 10 was badly disturbed. So the initial plan of attack was abandoned in favor of removing cuts 8 and 9 by natural stratigraphy. As we excavated we recorded all stone tools, debitage, and sherd clusters, both spatially and vertically, below the pumice. Carbon samples were taken from the levels in general and also from specific quadrants or concentrations as they appeared. As a final control before the removal of cut 11, a large column sample measuring 50 square centimeters was removed from the southwest corner of cut 11. This was done after the profiling of the north wall of cut 8 had established a standard stratigraphy. This column was floated and analyzed for pollen, without much success. After the column sample was taken out, the crew removed by troweling the cultural zone of cut 11 and recorded again all material of interest. Finally, all long walls were profiled and photographed. The site was backfilled.

2. The Pitti Locality (BU-17b; fig. 4/3)

During the dry season of 1972 a second, more extensive survey of the valley had led to the discovery of particularly abundant surface remains on land owned by Dr. D. Pitti. We placed a single 2 x 2-meter test (cut 1) on a gentle slope where a large metate fragment had been found. This cut yielded a significant quantity of artifacts which first appeared just below the topsoil and continued throughout the soil deposits to a depth of 160 centimeters. However, the stratigraphy suggested that the slope of the land had been sharper in prehistoric times than at present. Therefore, this deposit of cultural remains probably represented not a primary, but a secondary deposit washed down from farther upslope. We then decided to situate our next excavation following the slope upward to the south and west with hopes of discovering the living site from which the debris in cut 1 had come.

Pitti's field was in fallow at the time. In the general southwestern area we noticed two different types of cover growth, a short and a long grass. The short grasses grew in scattered circular areas. This pattern led us to suppose that if, indeed, we were dealing with a prehistoric village site, then these circular patches might indicate the outlines of individual dwellings. Our

Figure 4/2: Excavations at BU-17a in progress.

next test pit intersected one of these circles. Fortunately, that one circle did represent a house site. Unfortunately, we lost the unique opportunity to map these circular patches by concentrating all our efforts on the recovery of organic remains; this was probably the gravest of all mistakes, but it was too late in the season and the site owner could not postpone any longer the plowing in his field to plant potatoes.

The BU-17b excavation consisted of 18 cuts (fig. 4/3). Cut 1 mentioned above was approximately 150 meters upslope and to the south of the Quebrada Callejon which crossed Pitti's land. Cut 2 was 50 meters to the west of cut 1. This one meter-square cut was intended to uncover a possible burial, but it served only to expose a pothunter's backdirt. Cut 7 was located 40 meters north of cut 2 and was closer to the Quebrada than either cuts 1 or 2. This was a two-meter square cut placed in an area where surface material indicated occupation.

The central area of excavation (where we later on encountered the dwelling) consisted of cuts 3-6, 8-18. These cuts were located some 20 meters upslope to the southwest of cut 1. All were two-meter squares, except cut 4 which measured 1 x 2 meters and cut 15 which measured 2 x 3 meters. Only cuts 1, 3, 5, 7, 14, and 15 were excavated to sterile, because of heavy rains and lack of time at the end of the season; the rest were excavated to a depth of 40 centimeters below the topsoil.

All excavation units and artifacts were vertically controlled by their mutual relationship to a single datum stake assigned an arbitrary elevation. We excavated according to natural stratigraphy when we could interpret it. Otherwise, we worked with arbitrary levels of five or ten centimeters when

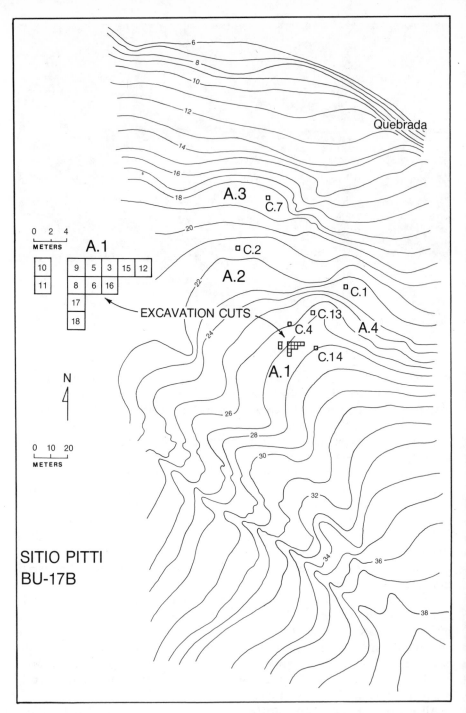

Figure 4/3: Map showing location of excavations at the Pitti locality (BU-17b) of Sitio Pitti-Gonzalez. A.1, A.2, and so forth, mark the activity areas. Inset on left is an enlargement of area 1.

Figure 4/4: Pattern of post molds (i.e., house post impressions) defining an oval dwelling in area 1 of BU-17b.

the stratigraphy was obscure, or when a single stratum was broken up for purposes of control over artifact provenience. We shoveled and screened the fill of levels containing few cultural remains. We troweled and screened where occupation was dense, or when cultural features (artifact clusters, rock clusters, post molds, or pits) appeared.

Near the end of the season, we encountered post molds in cuts 3, 5, 8, 9, 11, 16, and 17 (fig. 4/4). They first appeared at 40 centimeters beneath the surface of the topsoil. The processes of discovery and excavation were delicate. No change in soil color or texture distinguished their outline. However, the soil in the post molds themselves was slightly less compact than the surrounding soil. We could often anticipate post molds by tapping the handle of a trowel on the soil surface and listening for a hollow sound resulting from a change in soil density. We excavated most post molds by hollowing them out with a dental pick. Due to lack of time at the end of the dry season, we cross-sectioned only two: one in the south wall of cut 3 and another in the center of cut 6.

We were able to distinguish post molds from burrows, root cavities, or other uninterpretable holes by their size and shape. Their diameters at the widest point varied between 10 and 15 centimeters, and their depths between 10 and 25 centimeters. One post mold in cut 6, however, was 50 centimeters deep. They all narrowed at the bottom to a blunt point. Only one (in cut 8) was buttressed by rocks. We could safely count 22 certain post molds arranged in an apparently oval outline. We could not establish closure on the southeast simply because we did not have time for further excavation. The outline we did expose measured seven meters in diameter

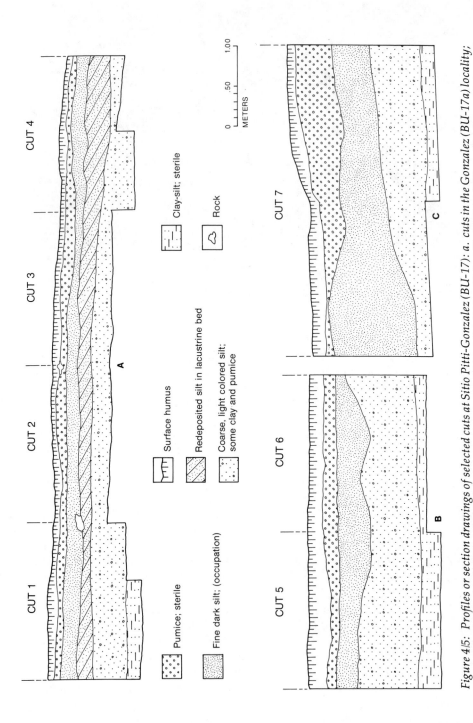

Figure 4/5: Profiles or section drawings of selected cuts at Sitio Pitti-Gonzalez (BU-17): a. cuts in the Gonzalez (BU-17a) locality; b cuts in area 1 of the Pitti (BU-17b) locality; c. cut in area 3 of the Pitti (BU-17b) locality. After field profiles by crew.

Pumice; sterile

Fine dark silt; (occupation)

Surface humus

Redeposited silt in lacustrine bed

Coarse, light colored silt; some clay and pumice

Clay-silt; sterile

Rock

CUT 1   CUT 2   CUT 3   CUT 4

CUT 5   CUT 6   CUT 7

A   B   C

METERS

0   .50   1.00

along the east-west axis and six meters along the north-south axis. (For more detailed discussions of the BU-17b excavations see Spang ms. 1976.)

SUMMARY OF THE STRATIGRAPHY AND DEPOSITIONAL SEQUENCE

Despite its secondary nature, the depositional sequence at the Gonzalez or BU-17a locality clearly demonstrates an association between the period of human occupation and a sedimentary alluvial soil built upon Pleistocene lacustrine beds (fig. 4/5a). This occupation was capped, in turn, by a fairly thick pumice deposit which was responsible for the rapid depopulation of this area.

At the Pitti locality (BU-17b), a three-strata depositional sequence became clearly defined. The bottom stratum represents lacustrine sediments mixed with weathered pumice; they vary in color from brown to yellow, and in texture from sandy to clayey, but they are devoid of any cultural material. The occupational layer above is defined by a light brown, fine-grained alluvial silt in which was embedded a layer of closely packed cultural remains. This cultural layer averaged 10–30 centimeters in thickness in area 1 (fig. 4/5b), but was thicker in area 3 (fig. 4/5c). The occupation is also overlain by a dense layer of unweathered pumice in a light brown

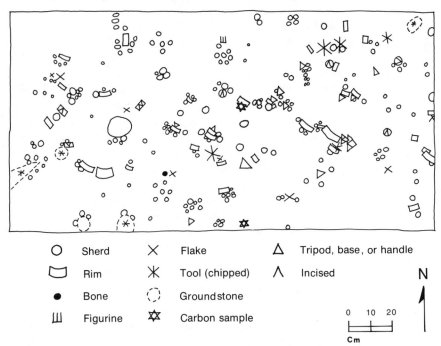

O	Sherd	✕	Flake	△	Tripod, base, or handle
⊔	Rim	✳	Tool (chipped)	∧	Incised
●	Bone	(˙)	Groundstone		
⊞	Figurine	✪	Carbon sample		

0   10   20
Cm

N

Figure 4/6: Diagram showing location of cultural items on the floor of the oval dwelling at BU-17b.

matrix representing the last eruption of Baru, dated to ca. A.D. 600. During the millennium or so following the abandonment of Cerro Punta, a humic layer varying in thickness between 10 and 20 centimeters gradually built up upon the pumice. The modern recolonization of this area was placed upon this base. Hence in Sitio Pitti-Gonzalez we have a clearly defined natural stratigraphy involving an occupational unit (unit 3; fig. 4/6), sandwiched between a lacustrine layer below and a sterile pumice deposit above. Where dwellings occurred, stratigraphic breaks are defined on the basis of cultural breaks, such as those below, on, and above the house floor of the oval dwelling.

Report Number 5

Excavations at Barriles (BU-24): A Small Testing Program

E. J. ROSENTHAL

INTRODUCTION

The site of Barriles (BU-24) is in the Southwest area of the Volcan Baru region, near the town of Nueva California, at 8°7' N latitude and 82°41' W longitude. A *quebrada* named Barriles (from the drum-shaped carved stone cylinders found at the site) flows to the south of the occupation area. The site elevation is 1,200 to 1,300 meters. Barriles was first described by Stirling (1950) as a "ceremonial center" consisting of a raised area approximately 50 x 30 yards, lined with stone slabs and boulders. According to him, off to the east of the "center" stood a row of retainer statues that already had been removed to the Museo Nacional de Panama. Rocks covered with petroglyphs and elaborate shaft tombs containing large carved metates or lidded urns were also mentioned, but despite a two-month stay at the site, Stirling does not provide us even with a sketch map indicating the approximate location of these features. It was not until Ichon (1968) briefly visited the site that we had both a sketch map of the site (fig. 5/1) and an idea of its ceramic stratigraphy.

PURPOSE OF EXCAVATION

Our small testing program was undertaken with several specific purposes in mind. A high point of our third field season was the discovery of an undisturbed occupation at the Pitti locality (BU-17b) in the Cerro Punta valley. Its subsequent excavation suggested strong links with Barriles. For chronological comparisons, a series of radiocarbon samples from BU-24 was obviously desirable. Furthermore, a type collection from Barriles was necessary. Unfortunately, the ceramics of previous excavations of the site

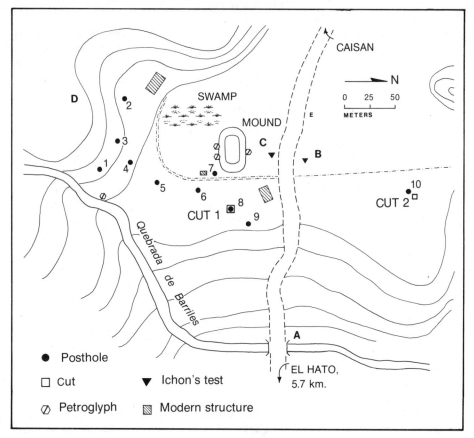

Figure 5/1: Sketch map of Barriles (BU-24) showing location of posthole sounding, the two test cuts, and other features. Letters indicate: a. place where the stone drums which give the site its name were found; b. general area from where came the big "metate" at the Museo del Hombre Panameño (fig.4.0-3a); c. general location of the giant stone statues at the Museo del Hombre Panameño; d. burials. Adapted and expanded from Ichon 1968b, fig. 1, p. 20 by E.J. Rosenthal.

(Stirling 1950; Ichon 1968) had failed to remain in Panama; nor had Ichon recovered any charcoal for dating.

In addition to these two primary reasons for excavating we had several other limited hypotheses to test at Barriles: (a) that the site had been settled prior to the Cerro Punta occupations, (b) that the occupation of Barriles lasted longer because the area was less affected by the Volcan Baru eruption than Cerro Punta, which was nearer to the cone, and (c) that population movements had been from the plains to the interior highlands via the natural conduits of the Rio Chiriqui Viejo.

The formal hypothesis for testing Barriles was, therefore, that in areas of natural (nonceremonial mound) deposition the stratigraphy should reveal an occupation intermediary in time between coastal and highland materials.

METHODOLOGY

Following the suggested hypothesis, it is obvious that a major problem for the investigator was determining the proper placement of test cuts. The need to find well-stratified deposits eliminated the immediate environs of the disturbed mound and ceremonial plaza from consideration. The thick cover of *cuzcuzo* grass interfered with surface survey techniques for determining an area of domestic accumulations. Likewise, a random method of square selection seemed dangerous in a site extensively disturbed by *huaqueros*, for there would be a possibility of excavating, unwittingly, another man's backdirt. Nor was it possible to obtain back-hoeing equipment to strip away the topsoil. It was decided, instead, to place a series of posthole soundings (report no. 3) into apparently undisturbed areas to determine excavation prospects. The seventeen soundings not only gave information as to where to dig but also greatly clarified the general depositional sequence of the area.

First, both Stirling's and Ichon's reports mentioned that the cultural material was overlaid by pumice. Undisturbed areas should therefore display a thick consolidated pumice layer below the topsoil. Secondly, the desire to date the occupation stressed the selection of an area with carbon. Thirdly, the most revealing soundings should show an occupation comprising at least two different strata. From the sample of seventeen soundings, two, numbers 8 and 17, suggested the appropriate configuration of attributes to warrant further investigation: an intact pumice layer, dark organic soils containing charcoal, two or more of Ichon's pottery types, and at least one apparent stratigraphic change within the sherd matrix.

Cut 1 was therefore placed near sounding 8, while cut 2 was placed one meter north of sounding 17. Each cut was a two-by-two-meter square established due north-south with a Brunton compass.

THE EXCAVATIONS AND STRATIGRAPHY

Excavation techniques used a combination of natural and metric stratigraphy. Within each natural unit established by the criteria of soil color, grain size, or inclusions, ten centimeter units were removed as a control.

Because it most closely duplicates the soundings, I shall first describe from bottom to top the stratigraphy of cut 2, as pictured in the accompanying profile (fig. 5/2a). In profiled section, layer E designates the *talpetate*, a yellow brown, hard-packed volcanic ash which is compactly packed and sterile except for an intrusive rodent burrow. Overlaying the *talpetate* is a medium grain compact brown sediment which has pockets of black clay and yellow weathered pumice pieces suggestive of fluvial deposits; few sherds were encountered in this stratum (layer D).

Layer C which overlies the brown zone comprises occupation units 6, 7, and 8. This layer contrasts with the one below not so much in color as in texture, grain size, and moisture content. Layer B was a very damp, dark black silt with many rodent disturbances. Units 3, 4, and 5 are contained in

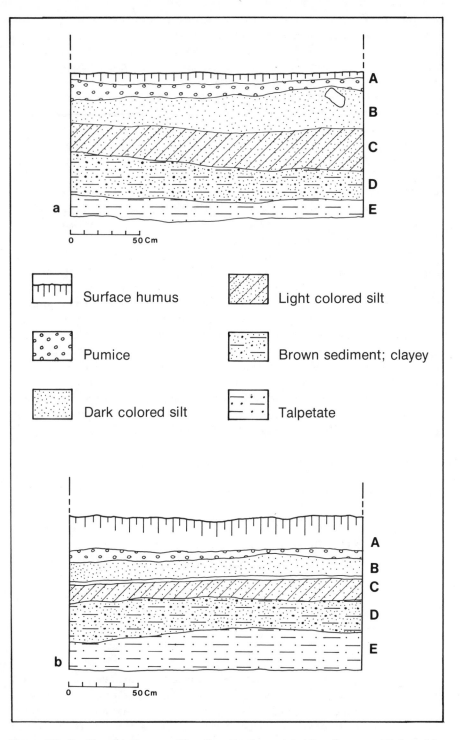

Figure 5/2: Profiles of test excavations (i.e., 2 x 2 m cuts) at Barriles: a. cut 2; b. cut 1.

Excavations at Barriles   291

this stratum. The A layer and the top were the air-deposited pumice and the topsoil (surface humus), respectively.

Cut 1 (fig. 5/2b) revealed a similar stratigraphy with one important exception. Layer E is again the hard-packed sterile *talpetate* that forms the irregular undulating floor of the cut. Above it is layer D, a brown sedimentary unit of considerable compaction, with yellow weathered pumice and heavy deposit of sherds in units 8 and 9. Layer C is a fine, dry, sediment similar to that in cut 2, only darker. However, in cut 1 this stratum is separated from the black silt of layer B by an intervening stratum of black sediment which is mottled with white. Interestingly, this depositional stratum is also culturally sterile. Units 6 and 7, dated to A.D. 820 ± 85 (I-1130), are in the dark sediment below it, and units 3, 4, and 5 are in the black silt above it. Layer B terminates the occupation at 56 centimeters below datum and is overlain by a pumice and topsoil layer approximately 20 centimeters in thickness (layer A).

To summarize, the BU-24 site rests on a compact, yellow, weathered ash (known as *talpetate* in Mesoamerica) which is sterile of cultural material (layer E). Above it are lacustrine sediments with black clay pockets, usually at depths exceeding 50 centimeters; they contain some cultural material, probably intrusive from above (layer D). The occupation layer (C) is embedded in heavily organic fluvial sediments of a dark brown color representing at least three organic inputs and a considerable span of time. Throughout the site, the occupation was capped by a layer of air-deposited pumice, low in silica content, of fairly uniform thickness (8 to 10 centimeters). This pumice came from the last eruption of Volcan Baru. Finally, atop the pumice is layer A (8 to 10 centimeters thick), representing modern humus or soil buildup occurring after the previously mentioned volcanic event.

Report Number 6

The Aguacate Sites in Bocas del Toro: Excavations and Stratigraphy

O. F. LINARES

SITE DESCRIPTIONS

The settlement pattern of the Aguacate communities has been summarized in section 5.3. There I have included a short description of each of the four sites encountered on the peninsula (fig. 5.0-3), including a brief summary of excavation procedures at each locality. Because the Cerro Brujo site (CA-3) was the most thoroughly investigated, it will be treated separately.

This report is intended to serve as background for the more general discussions in sections 5.3 and 7.6.

1. CA-1 is a small site consisting of several midden clusters within a half kilometer radius near a spot known as Hope Well. The middens averaged 35 centimeters in depth and in diameter were seldom bigger than five meters. Surface collections revealed cultural materials indistinguishable from those found on the rest of the Aguacate middens.

2. CA-2, Sitio Machuca: This site was first surveyed and tested by myself (Linares 1970), followed by more intensive work the year after (Linares 1971; Linares and Ranere 1971). The area where middens are intermittently found extends for about 1,000 meters on the fairly flat crest of a ridge and on secondary slopes that drop off sharply to the northwest. A small stream runs east-west at a distance of about 50 meters. The site comprised four midden localities, but only one (CA-2a) was tested by three cuts measuring 2 x 2 meters. Smaller middens— (CA-2b and CA-2c) — were located to the northeast and northwest, respectively. The largest of the middens (CA-2d) was unusual in not being placed on the crest of the Machuca ridge but on a secondary ridge running east-west that had extensive middens stretching downslope; this midden covered a 10 x 30-meter area and was as large as or slightly larger than the main midden at Cerro Brujo (CA-3a, features 1-3) discussed below.

3. CA-4, the Rojas site: The distribution of shell middens at this site followed the general rule for the Aguacate area, namely that they tended to be on the higher ridges, either on the crest or downslope. The largest CA-4 midden was 10 meters across and was surrounded by smaller shell accumulations. Other midden clusters were encountered at distances varying between 400 meters and 800 meters from each other; these were recorded but not tested.

THE CERRO BRUJO (CA-3) LOCALITIES

Four separate midden clusters comprised the CA-3 site (fig. 6/1).

1. Locality 3a, the main midden cluster, was found on the crest of a ridge measuring 30 meters across and sloping abruptly in three directions, except to the southeast where the ridge continued more or less flat. A conspicuous midden averaging one meter in depth and having three mounded areas was found on this level area, while shallower deposits were strewn over the edge of the steeper slopes and displaced downhill for considerable distances. The central part of the hilltop was devoid of shell, but pottery and stone tools were found here embedded in a shallow brown soil, probably marking the spot where the principal dwelling(s) had been located (see below). A total of 118 square meters of deposits varying in depth from 50 to 100 centimeters was excavated at this locality.

2. Locality CA-3b: This spot was about 800 meters to the southwest of 3a on a lower contour. Refuse middens of respectable size were found on the southwest slope, while at the crest of the ridge little or no shell was

Figure 6/1: Aerial photograph showing the location of the separate midden clusters which constitute the Cerro Brujo hamlet.

discarded, suggesting again that these flat spots were reserved for houses. The excavations here covered 18 square meters.

3. Locality CA-3c consisted of a single shell midden measuring eight meters in diameter, located 400 meters to the southwest of 3a on a very narrow ridge where at most a single small dwelling could have fit. The midden was tested by a single 2 x 2-meter block or cut.

4. Locality CA-3d was to the northeast of 3a, at a distance of about 400 meters, on the opposite side of the same ridge. One 2 x 2-meter cut and another 1 x 2-meter cut were placed in what must have been refuse from a single dwelling.

THE CERRO BRUJO EXCAVATIONS

1. Working conditions: The excavations at Cerro Brujo presented particular logistic difficulties associated with the constant rains. (The longest period without rain was one week and the "dig" had to be closed about a week ahead of schedule because the site was washed out by a 70-hour downpour that caused severe floods in Bocas province and elsewhere.) Trenches had to be covered at all times and excavation was under tarpaulins; the deposit was often moist and therefore difficult to sift, and mapping or photography was restricted to short periods of sunshine during the day.

2. Participants in the excavation, besides myself as principal investigator and Anthony J. Ranere as field supervisor, were Irene Borgogno and E. Jane Rosenthal (both from the University of Pennsylvania) and Máximo Miranda (University of Panama), plus a crew of six to eight men who came by boat and on foot, often wading through swamps and streams, from the town of Aguacate one to two hours away. Field headquarters were in a rented house in the town of Bocas, Isla Colon, about one and a half hours by outboard from Cerro Brujo. Hence, excavated materials had to be taken by outboard to the field laboratory once a week. While the excavations were going on, we camped in tents at the base of the Cerro Brujo site.

3. Clearing locality CA-3a: This phase lasted one week and was done by a team of six to eight local men using axes and machetes. Large trees were felled, regrowth vegetation was cut down, and the whole locality was raked down, with the cut vegetation thrown over the edges of the site, away from the cultural deposits.

4. The map: A contour map of the 3a locality was drawn up, using 25-centimeter contour intervals for the mounded area and 50 centimeters for the steeper slopes (fig. 6/2). All excavation was done with reference to this map.

5. The grid system: Once the clearing of the CA-3a locality was terminated, while the site was being mapped, the reference grid was put up by staking the entire area into 2 x 2-meter squares oriented to "grid north" (slightly to the east of true north). The quadrats were then numbered 1, 2, and so on, north-south, and given letters east-west. All excavations were horizontally located with reference to this grid.

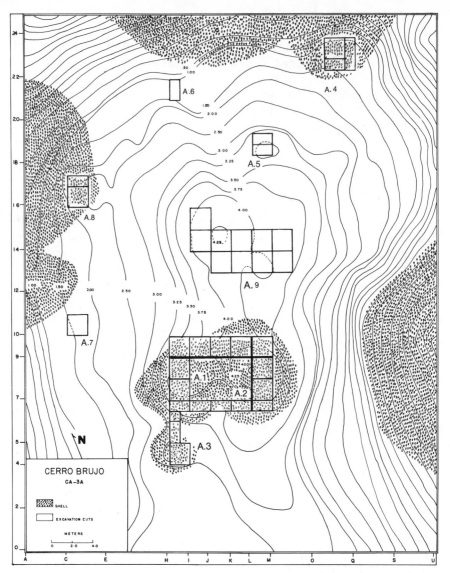

Figure 6/2: Site map of the main midden area (3a) at Cerro Brujo. Excavation cuts were located on the grid coordinates; for example cut 9 H is the top left 2 x 2-meter cut of area 1 (A1).

6. The pilot trench: This initial trench (6H-6L) was dug first, opening up blocks 6H, 6J, and 6L by arbitrary 10-centimeter levels and profiling the walls prior to doing the two intermediate blocks 6I and 6K. Agreement about the natural stratigraphic divisions to be used in the rest of the excavations was reached at this point and adhered to throughout excavation.

7. The block excavations: After opening up trench 6, we proceeded to open up, by natural and/or cultural stratigraphy, blocks 7L and 7H, 8L and

8H, and 9L and 9H, all of which cut through the center of areas 1 and 2, respectively. Area 3 was explored next, by putting in the 4H to 6H trench. Following this, we tested the peripheral shell middens on the slopes by opening up blocks 16-17C (area 8) and 22-23PQ (area 4). Finally, we opened up a number of 2 x 2-meter blocks in the center of the 3a ridge, looking for postholes (areas 13 j-m, 14 i-m, 15 i).

In actuality, the excavations were conducted by straightforward cultural levels (A, B-1, B-2, C, and D), with minor subdivisions therein (B-la or B-2b, and so forth) in most of the blocks, and by artificial levels within cultural ones (e.g., B-1, 0–10 centimeters; B-2, 10–20 centimeters, and so forth) when minor subdivisions within major strata were not immediately obvious during excavation. These techniques were standardized.

8. The other three Cerro Brujo localities, namely 3b, 3c, and 3d, were tested with one to several 2 x 2-meter blocks.

9. Column samples of both soil and shell were collected mainly from the main locality 3a. This was done after the whole site was profiled and the stratigraphy clarified. The soil columns were used for pollen analysis and for clarifying soil horizons; the shell samples served for a quantitative analysis of the mollusks gathered at the site (section 14.0).

10. Recovery techniques: These were complicated by the incessant drizzle which compacted the earth in the strata and prevented easy screening, except through one-quarter inch mesh. Despite these difficulties, recovery was good, resulting in a respectably large faunal sample.

STRATIGRAPHY OF THE CA-3A LOCALITY

Stratigraphic distinctions were drawn on the basis of shell and soil deposition.

1. The soil horizons were determined by observations during excavation, as well as from a laboratory analysis of sediments from column B done by geologist James Clary. Except for the top and bottom strata, most of the soil deposited in between the shell layers is a fine- to medium-grained silty sand, varying in color from tan to brown.

2. The shell profile was drawn during excavation by noting the abundance, compactness, or the state of the shells involved. The deeper layers were more compact, and the shell more lensed and/or crushed than in the top layers.

3. Depositional units: Five cultural-natural strata, drawn on the combined basis of soil and shell characteristics, were determined right at the beginning of excavation and recognized throughout the site (fig. 6/3a).

A. The A stratum: This was the surface humus, largely disturbed by roots and animal burrows. Although it contains some shell, mostly worked in from below, this stratum is made up largely of an organically rich, silty soil, dark brown mottled with white, mostly deposited by wind and rain action after the site was abandoned and built up through vegetation decay.

B. The B-1 stratum: Abundant and loosely packed shell in a very fine-grained silty sand matrix containing shell fragments, carbonized wood,

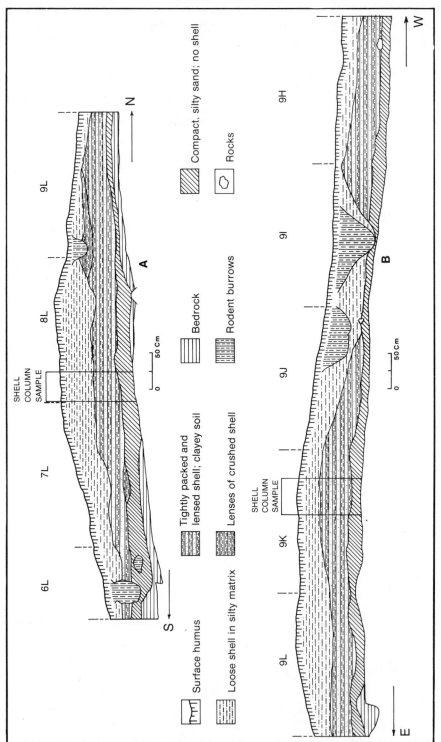

Figure 6/3: Profile or section drawings of the excavations at CA-3a: a. the L trench; b. the 9 trench.

Legend:
- Surface humus
- Loose shell in silty matrix
- Tightly packed and lensed shell; clayey soil
- Lenses of crushed shell
- Compact, silty sand; no shell
- Bedrock
- Rocks
- Rodent burrows

bone, and metamorphic minerals. The color of the soil varies from tan to brown, with the latter color usually found right under the A stratum and probably produced by the soil percolating from above. The soil divisions within the B-1 stratum seem to reflect natural phenomena and are without much cultural import. However, the looseness of the shell deposits is probably due to the fact that shell in these layers was dumped all at once, from the side of the mound once it had grown to a certain height.

C. The B-2 stratum: These are more tightly packed shell layers with comparatively less shell and more soil than the ones above; otherwise not too different, except the soil in these strata is more clayey and lighter in color. In the profiles, these strata have been differentiated on the basis of their compactness and lensing, both probably caused by constant treading on the surface of the mound while it was still low, before it had built up to any height.

D. The C stratum: This is a compact, brown, silty sand with a high pumice content. In excavation it felt clayey and sticky when wet, forming fist-sized lumps. The cultural material in this stratum belongs to the earlier of the two Cerro Brujo occupations.

E. The D stratum: This is a yellow-tan weathered and "decayed" bed-rock, forming a loose silty sand. Chunks of "decomposed" pumice are found to crumble easily. The level was sterile, except for a few sherds on each block thought to have floated down from above.

DEPOSITIONAL SEQUENCE AT THE CA-3A ACTIVITY AREAS

The nine activity areas of the principal Cerro Brujo locality (CA-3a) had somewhat different stratigraphic sequences.

1. The main mound activity (areas 1–3): A somewhat thin C stratum underlies the whole midden and is followed by lensed and/or compacted shell layers (the B-2 stratum), capped by looser shell layers above (the B-1 stratum). This sequence is characteristic of the entire locality. There is some reason to believe that the eastern half of the mound (activity area 2) was built up before the western half (activity area 1). This shows up on the south wall profile of trench 9 (fig. 6/3b), where area 2 has more B-2 stratum and also underlies area 1, in section 9J. Unfortunately, however, the juncture be-tween activity areas is somewhat obscured by disturbance in the form of burrows.

A burial pit and a skeleton appeared in the bottom of blocks 6H and 7H in activity area 1 (fig. 6/4). It soon became apparent in excavation that only the head and shoulders of the skeleton were present, and that it was intrusive, being associated with typical pottery of the Bocas or more recent of the two Cerro Brujo phases. Associated with the burial were two, almost complete, plain crude vessels and two large *Strombus* sp. shell trumpets. This burial constitutes one of the few specific features found in the entire site.

2. Activity area 4 is constituted of a shell-and-soil lens on the northeast edge of CA-3a , where the ridge dips down steeply toward the north, and more gradually toward the west. The top strata (A and B) in the three blocks

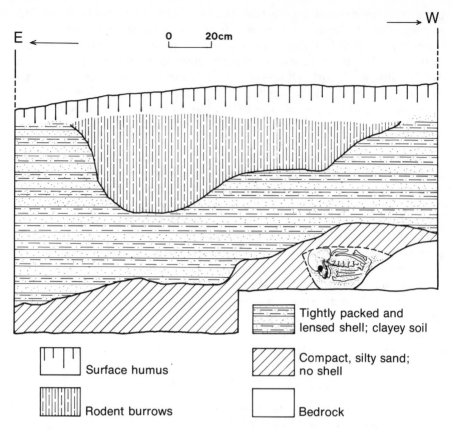

E ⟵   0   20cm   ⟶ W

	Tightly packed and lensed shell; clayey soil
	Surface humus
	Rodent burrows
	Compact, silty sand; no shell
	Bedrock

Figure 6/4: Section drawing of cut 6 H, activity area 1, showing burial pit.

conform to the strata in the rest of the 3a locality, but the C stratum differs markedly. At least two-thirds of the deposit on this spot belong to the C stratum, with scarcely any shell. This spot also contained less charcoal and fewer stone tools than the other localities. More important, the pottery belongs to the Bugaba Ware, diagnostic of the older or Aguacate phase at Cerro Brujo. In the C-1 and C-2 layers, Bugaba Ware appears slightly mixed with some sherds of the more recent phase, but in layer C-3 it was unmixed. In short, area 4, like area 9 on the center of the site, represents the first settlement at this Cerro Brujo locality.

3. Activity area 5 was an inconsequential small hillock which we tested, but which turned out to have been natural.

4. Activity area 6 was a depression on the true north end of the locality which we thought might represent some sort of palisade. Excavations were carried down to the yellow bedrock, but no cultural material or postholes were discovered.

5. Activity area 7 was on the western edge of this locality. (It was dug to satisfy Young's idea that it may have been the location of a house.) Instead of postholes, we encountered a shallow midden only 30 centimeters deep with few, if any, distinctive characteristics.

6. Activity area 8 was a thin, shell lens on a slope falling off to the west. It was begun as a 2 x 2-meter square which turned sterile at 20 centimeters and was thus extended toward the north. The stratigraphy at this spot seemed the reverse of the usual, with the more packed and compact shell layer at the top, and the looser B-1 unit below it. This disposition shows the distinction between the B-1 and B-2 units to have been functional rather than chronological as a result of treading on the surface of a refuse midden. Besides having an intrusive burrow, the two bottom strata here were the same as elsewhere in this locality.

7. Activity area 9 was the result of having a large section of the central flat area of the CA-3a locality scraped down in search of postholes, the general concensus of the crew and ethnographer being that this was the appropriate area where dwelling(s) would be placed. The top 4–5 centimeters, as elsewhere, was a black humus A stratum. Directly below was a brown, clayey silt (stratum C) deposited over a yellow-brown sterile soil. The spot contained absolutely no shell debris; but sherds belonging solely to the Bugaba Ware indicated that the first settlers, who did not collect any shell, settled on the central part of the midden. Although no postholes were found at this stage, they probably would have been located had it not been for the 70-hour rainstorm which terminated our excavations by wiping out the site. A total of 118 square meters was opened at CA-3a.

THE DEPOSITIONAL SEQUENCE OF THE
OTHER CERRO BRUJO LOCALITIES

1. Locality CA-3b (Co-Idewe) was in the midst of a cacao grove, on the side of a ridge with a strong slope to the southwest (fig. 6/5). Test excavations were conducted here in order to determine the cultural and chronological sequence of this dwelling locality vis-à-vis that of the main 3a locality.

The same strata as previously described for CA-3a also occur at CA-3b, but with important differences (fig. 6/6). At 3b the deposit is less deep, undoubtedly the result of being located on a very steep slope. Secondly, and more important, the C stratum marking the older of the two occupational phases is thinner at 3b. As might be expected, cultural remains in this C stratum are also scarcer; few artifacts besides pottery were recovered from this unit at this locality.

Despite the not-so-negligible excavations covering 18 square meters, few, if any, "activity areas" were detected at this spot. We must therefore assume that dwellings were placed on top of the ridge, where we found no soil, and that all of the trash was thrown downslope.

2. The CA-3c locality consisted of only one small, shallow midden, eight meters in diameter, probably belonging to a single dwelling, perched up on a narrow ridge with a sharp dropoff to the north and west and a sharp rise to the east. Like 3b, this locality lacked most of the C component. Only four square meters of deposit were excavated here.

3. Finally, there was the CA-3d midden, which was also very small, despite its being in the same ridge system as 3a. The deposit here (we

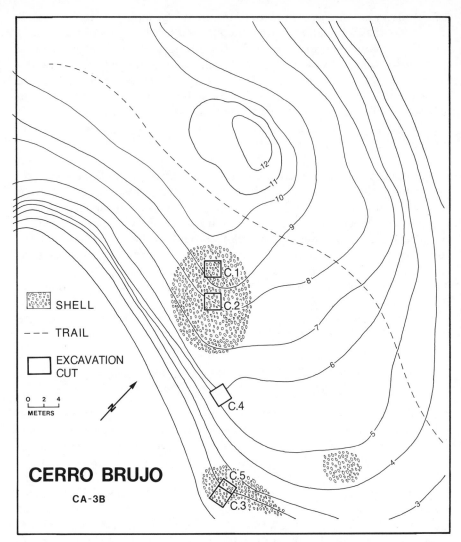

Figure 6/5: Site of the Co-Idewe (CA-3b) locality showing location of excavations. Contour intervals are 0.50 cm.

excavated six square meters of it) was mostly shell with very little in the way of a soil matrix, suggesting that this deposit was built up very fast and lasted for a shorter time than the deposits in the other localities. This general impression was confirmed by the fact that, although a thin C stratum was present, it seemed to contain the same pottery types as the previous levels.

SUMMARY

Cerro Brujo (CA-3) is one of the four dispersed hamlets in the Aguacate Peninsula and the one which received most intensive excavation (fig. 6/7).

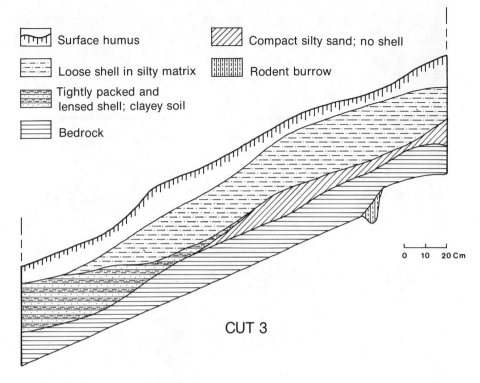

Figure 6/6: Profile or section of cut 3 at the CA-3b locality.

The four dwelling localities making up its internal or "community" pattern are found within a 1.5-kilometer radius. These localities were distinguished by the occurrence of single or clustered trash middens whose deposition was the result of several direct, or indirect, human processes.

Most important among these depositional processes, accounting for the bulk of the Cerro Brujo deposits, is the great amount of refuse, mainly shell plus faunal remains and broken artifacts, discarded on the crest of ridges, or on slopes, right next to spots where dwellings were placed. The resulting strata are therefore distinguished as "occupational layers" (see Swanson 1972). A second and more indirect process resulted in natural sediments being deposited or displaced as a result of human occupation of these ridges. For example, the silty sand accompanying the shell "occupation" layers has resulted from deforestation and/or a loosening up of the surface soils by treading, sweeping, and digging into, with consequent redeposition by wind and water action. A third, and last, process represented in the Cerro Brujo strata is the embedding of artifacts into natural deposits, as occurred in stratum C (see below).

It is important to stress here the "incidental" character of the Cerro Brujo deposits. Not the slightest evidence suggests that middens were built up purposefully in order to serve as house platforms, shrines, or burial places. Although human bones were found in the deposits, they were disarticu-

Figure 6/7: Excavating the southern extension of the H trench at CA-3a.

lated and/or mutilated, facts that suggest they were considered "trash" and treated as such.

The CA-3 trash middens were only partly visible on the surface. In fact, one of the principal difficulties in working in the humid tropics is one of gaining adequate "horizontal exposure." Vegetation is often so tangled that archaeologists, once they find a deposit, tend to restrict excavation to

Figure 6/8: Photograph of the corner of the 9 and L trenches at CA-3a showing natural stratigraphy.

that one spot, losing all perspective of sites as functional "wholes." In order to avoid this danger, considerable effort was spent prior to excavation in clearing off the vegetation of the CA-3 localities. As a result of the increased exposure, midden clusters that had been assumed to represent different sites turned out to be different localities in the same site.

A second difficulty involved in doing archaeological work in the tropics is that of recognizing depositional strata clearly enough, and also early enough, to permit excavation by cultural strata (fig. 6/8), thus avoiding the ubiquitous metric stratigraphy that has caused so much confusion. Hence, initially to facilitate making cultural-natural stratigraphic distinctions at Cerro Brujo, a "pilot trench" was first opened up and five cultural strata were then determined. These constituted the basic stratigraphy of the Cerro Brujo site.

The five strata can be summarized from top to bottom as follows: stratum A, the surface humus, was a layer formed by decomposing vegetation and natural weathering, mostly after the site was abandoned, to which was added some cultural material mixed in from below and many root and animal disturbances; stratum B-1 was made up of loose shell in a silty matrix dumped, probably from the side, when the midden was high enough to discourage normal walking upon it; stratum B-2 was composed of tightly packed shell layers, in some places compacted and lensed, indicating "natural floors"; stratum C was a brown silty sand with some pumice inclusions and fairly abundant artifacts but not shell; stratum D was a highly weathered, light-colored bedrock, usually sterile except for sherds floated down from above.

Following the previous discussion about depositional processes, we can add that the A and D strata are most entirely "natural," while the B-1 and B-2 are almost purely cultural, being designated as "occupational layers," stratum C, on the other hand, represents a "natural layer" in which cultural remains have been embedded.

Report Number 7

La Pitahaya (IS-3) in the Gulf of Chiriqui: Mapping and Excavation

O. F. LINARES

INTRODUCTION

La Pitahaya (site IS-3) was explored in 1961 (Linares 1968b), but the very limited nature of the test excavations, plus the lack of any adequate mapping, made it imperative to return to the site. Ten years later, we initiated a second testing program to obtain settlement-subsistence data comparable to that of Cerro Brujo on the Atlantic side. Contour mapping of the site, recovery of organic remains, and analysis of stone tools took precedence over the recovery of ceramics since a ceramic chronology had been established before (Linares 1968b). Nonetheless, an effort was made to check the old sequence against the larger sample recovered in 1971 (section 7.7).

Palenque's isolation (it can be reached only by water) and the lack of proper facilities for camping on the island, which included a large population of howler monkeys and pigs, made working conditions less than optimal. Transporting all of the heavy stone artifacts out of the island to the laboratory in David was nearly impossible by canoe; hence, many of the heavier groundstone artifacts (such as manos, metates, and composite nutting stones) had to be photographed on the spot and left behind. Although hundreds of gunnysacks containing hundreds of kilos of ceramics were removed to the laboratory, an almost equal amount had to be inspected on the spot and then discarded. In the two months spent at La Pitahaya, we recovered useful comparative data on ecology and subsistence, but the site is so large and complex that it would have required many seasons to study it adequately. However, the limited comparative material we were after was more or less satisfactorily obtained.

CLEARING AND MAPPING THE IS-3 ACTIVITY AREAS

The entire crew spent three weeks clearing the vegetation from the central area by cutting the underbrush and some medium-sized trees and raking

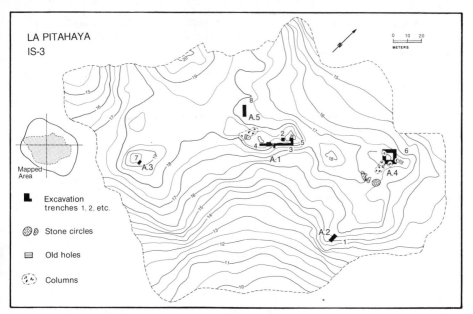

Figure 7/1: Map of La Pitahaya (IS-3) showing location of trenches (1, 2, and so forth) and of activity areas (A.1, A.2, and so forth). Inset on left shows stippled area as the proportion of the site that was mapped. Contour intervals are 0.50 cm. Original site map by J. Alden.

the site. The clearing operations revealed a number of mounds stretching in an arc from east to west.

Contour mapping of the cleared area by J. Alden took approximately a whole month and was done with alidade and plane table along sighting points (fig. 7/1). Contour intervals were first assigned values ranging from 10 to 19.5 meters. Then a bench mark, assumed to be 43 meters above sea level, was overlapped with the lower contour, giving the higher contour an absolute elevation value of 62.5 meters above sea level, thus bringing it in line with the 63-meter elevation given for this part of Palenque in the 1:50,000 map of the Instituto Cartográfico Nacional.

As a result of the clearing and mapping program, we were able to distinguish a number of above-surface features which we provisionally identified as "activity areas," worthy of excavation.

1. Area 1 was the main mounded area, which measured close to 50 x 10 meters and was located on the 61-meter contour. Stratified deposits, made up largely of angular rocks swept up from the surrounding area and deliberately piled up on top of the natural ridge to form oblong mounds, were excavated by trenches (II, III, IV, and V), covering 30 square meters. Most of these trenches were found to contain intrusive burials in the lowest levels.

2. Area 2 was located on a fairly steep north-south gradient near the eastern edge of the mapped area and tested by one trench (I), consisting of three blocks measuring 2 x 2 meters.

3. Area 3, located on the highest mound feature near the southern edge of the site, was tested by a small excavation, trench VII.

4. Area 4 had large basalt columns on top, some of them carved, and a hard-packed floor that we tentatively identified as a plaza floor(?). A trench, 1 meter wide and 10 meters long, dug all around this spot to a depth of 40 centimeters, revealed ceramics belonging mostly to the older of the Pitahaya phases.

5. Area 5 was the flat, nonmounded area to the northwest of the main mound. The surface was devoid of the angular rocks that cover most of the peninsula, which were probably swept up to form the mounds in area 1. A trench (VIII) measuring 2 x 8 meters was dug to a depth of 48 centimeters, but we were unable to locate postholes. However, the swept-up surfaces and the presence of some cultural materials suggest that this as well as the other more or less level areas without angular rocks between the 60-meter and 61-meter contours were the preferred spots for dwellings.

THE EXCAVATIONS

An initial 2 x 2-meter cut (trench I) was placed in area 2 in order to determine the stratigraphy and concentration of material. Arbitrary 10-centimeter units were removed from this block by careful troweling and screened through one-quarter inch mesh. We were overwhelmed by the amount of cultural materials that came out from this small unit: 31 gunnysacks (made to hold 100 pounds of grain) filled with ceramics and at least 20 kilograms of stone artifacts. We thus decided to make another similar test in the central area. Again we encountered not only equal amounts of artifacts, but also greater stratigraphic depth and burials. A decision was then made to direct

Figure 7/2: Beginnings of excavation of trench I, area 2 at IS-3.

excavations to two objectives. First, to recheck the previously established chronology and, second, to clarify the nature of the deposits and establish whether the mounds were a product of natural deposition or were artificial (fig. 7/2).

With the above objectives in mind, two trenches were placed along the southern portion of the central or main midden area (area 1, trenches III and IV). The sole purpose of these trenches was to open up an area large enough to permit inferences about how the material had accumulated. These trenches revealed thick, chronologically uniform strata, suggestive of deliberate dumping. Further, near bedrock, several large pots associated with burials were found in both trenches. In all, at least ten individuals were found in these narrow trenches. In each case, burial was intrusive into the lowest stratum (level E). Another trench to the southeast (trench I) was less disturbed, thus providing a clearer stratigraphy.

The rest of the field season was spent testing the peripheral areas where trenches VI, VII, and VIII were placed. These excavations revealed that deposition in the flatter sectors was shallow and belonged to the San Lorenzo phase. Trench VII suggested the presence of a hard-packed plaza floor, and trench VIII the possible presence of dwellings.

STRATIGRAPHY

The IS-3 strata appear to be both natural and cultural in origin. Stratigraphic separations were established by evaluating silt and clay components, the presence or absence of angular rock fragments, root disturbances, and compaction, and the intermingling of cultural materials. Five depositional strata have been identified for all of IS-3, with minor local variations between activity areas (marked in the original individual profiles). The five general strata are, from top to bottom, as follows:

1. Stratum A: Surface to maximum depth of 40 centimeters; average depth, 18–20 centimeters. A gray to brown, usually loosely compacted, humus with decaying vegetal material and many roots. Large angular rocks and much disturbance are characteristic.

2. Stratum B: Minimum depth 13 centimeters, maximum depth 50 centimeters, average depth 45 centimeters. A beige to brown silt, varying in compaction, with large root-disturbances and numerous angular basalt fragments. Distinct lensing of the pottery occurs at many of the B strata at the site. Abundant cultural materials are found in this stratum.

3. Stratum C: Minimum depth 22 centimeters, maximum depth 104 centimeters, average depth variable. A compact, friable, granular, sandy silt, varying in color from light to very dark brown. Although fist-sized, angular rocks are present, they are not abundant in this stratum and are sometimes entirely absent. Heavy concentrations of sherds and other artifacts are found in this level.

4. Stratum D: Minimum depth 55 centimeters, maximum depth 128 centimeters, average depth 110 centimeters. A light-colored silty sand,

composed of well-rounded to subangular grains of quartz and other materials, including small pumice fragments. Angular rocks are usually absent.

5. Stratum E: Minimum depth 96 centimeters, maximum depth 171 centimeters, average depth 130 centimeters. The final stratum before bedrock consists of a red to yellow silty, clayey sand with abundant fragments of weathered tuff, chalcedony, and obsidian flakes and churned-up shell and bone fragments.

6. Stratum F and bedrock: The bedrock at IS-3 is a yellow compact tuff(?), which sometimes weathered at the top, forming a weathered yellow band that we distinguished as stratum F since it sometimes contains a few sherds, probably worked in from above.

In summary, IS-3 presents an accumulation of mounded cultural material capped by recent humus. This artificial construction has been deposited over a stratum of clay and decomposing stone, superimposed on a weathered tuff surface. Further division of the silt unit is possible. Recognition of inclusions of large, angular rock fragments like the ones that cover the surface of IS-3 everywhere, except where they had been purposely cleared off, and the leaching of the soil, provide a separation of strata B and C. Increasing amounts of clay and decreasing amounts of pottery and other artifacts also permit the establishing of stratum D. Basically, the IS-3 deposits are largely the result of deliberate dumping of rocks and cultural refuse on slightly raised areas. These mounds were used for burial and, to judge from the basalt columns that are found on top, to carry on special activities, possibly associated with shrines.

DEPOSITIONAL HISTORY OF THE IS-3 ACTIVITY AREAS

The depositional sequence at each of the IS-3 areas was characterized by the alternation of levels composed mostly of sandy silt and levels composed mostly of angular rocks of different sizes, some of them large enough to be called boulders, embedded in a silty matrix. These silt and rock levels were sandwiched in between a top level (the surface humus) and a bottom level (the natural bedrock). Distinct lensing of the pottery occurred in the top levels. The levels made up of great amounts of rock represented periodic "sweeping-up," or "piling-up," of the angular rocks composing the natural surfaces of the peninsula. The soil matrix in these rock-filled levels, as well as in the less rocky levels, was composed of "silt and sand aggregates, well-rounded to subangular grains of quartz, angite, dacite(?) and some olivene, actinoline, apatite, and iron nodules. To this sandy silt component was added highly weathered shell fragments, opalized bone and carbonized wood" (J. Clary, personal communication).

Because each of the IS-3 activity areas represented a somewhat unique depositional sequence, they will be discussed separately.

1. Activity area 1: The stratigraphy of trench II deserves detailed discussion, as the stratigraphy in the other trenches was highly disturbed by the presence of intrusive burials deposited on a red clay zone, mixed with decomposed tuff (level E), right above the bedrock. (These burials will be discussed below.)

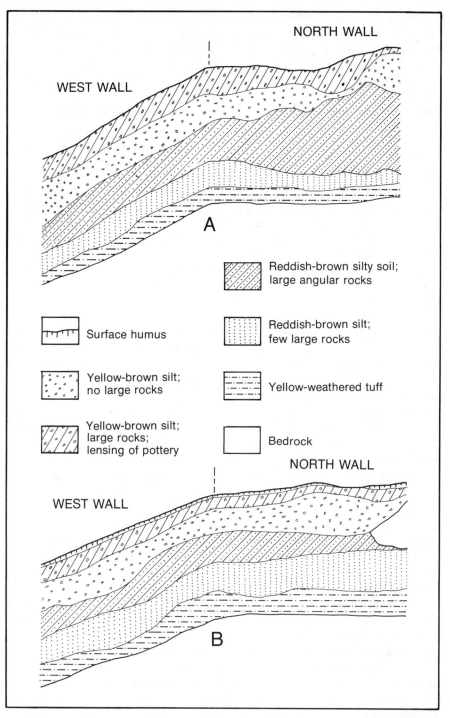

Figure 7/3: Profiles or section drawings of IS-3 deposits: a. trench II, block 1, west and north walls; b. trench II, block 2, west and north walls. From field profiles by excavation crew.

Trench II consisted of two 2 x 2-meter blocks (block 1, fig. 7/3a and block 2, fig. 7/3b) separated by an unexcavated center area. The depositional sequence, from top to bottom, was as follows: A very thin gray-brown disturbed soil (surface), deposited after the site was abandoned, was followed by a level varying in thickness between 10 and 20 centimeters, containing a loosely packed gray-brown silt and many roots (level A). On this level were found many fist-sized angular rocks and signs of disturbances, such as large roots, burrows, and so forth. Cultural material was abundant throughout the level. Directly below (level B) the soil became more compacted and lighter in color, and the deposit was twice as thick. Otherwise it was very similar to the one above, with large rocks present. Stratum C varied in the amount of rock that was found in each of the two cuts. The texture was loosely compacted and the amount of cultural material was still abundant. With stratum D there was an abrupt change to a dark-colored, very moist and fine-grained silty sand, variable in thickness, containing few large rocks. The amount of pottery and other artifacts declined in this level; these ceramics belong mostly to the Burica or older of the three phases at the site. Finally, the bottom stratum (E) was a weathered tuff, with little cultural material, deposited over sterile bedrock.

To summarize, the bulk of the deposit at activity area 1, trench II, was composed of large rocks which were most abundant in strata A and B, but also occurred in stratum C, suggesting that this mound is largely artificial. This idea receives corroboration from the pottery type sequence at cuts 1 and 2, which shows a certain amount of mixing, despite the overall gradual change in ceramic modalities.

Trenches III and IV were placed along the long axis of the main mounded area and were opened up expediently once it became obvious that the stratigraphy was greatly disturbed by burial activities. In trench IV, at depths between 130 and 160 centimeters (in strata E and F), we encountered several burials intrusive from levels C and D above. These burials represented a number of different practices and can be listed as follows. Features 1 and 2 consisted of two infant bundles from the south wall, and feature 3 was a large vessel containing a child burial. Features 4 and 5 were two whole skulls and 1 crushed skull, surrounded by disarticulated human bones. The most interesting was feature 6 (fig. 7/4), an extended "ritual" burial, flanked by two fairly large, lidded pots also containing burials, and another bundle burial on the wall of the pit itself. Although these burials are not reported here in any detail, as they did not represent a sample large enough to provide reliable information, they do indicate that these artificial mounds were used as burial grounds for infants as well as adults. However, very few "fancy objects" were buried with the dead at this particular spot.

The same general situation held for the bottom levels of trench III, which lay along the same axis as trench IV. Two extended burials were recovered from a semisterile red clay zone, lying right on top of the bedrock, or cut into the bedrock and filled with red clay.

Trench V was a 2 x 1-meter block connecting trench II, block 2, with the northern end of trench III, yielding nothing of note.

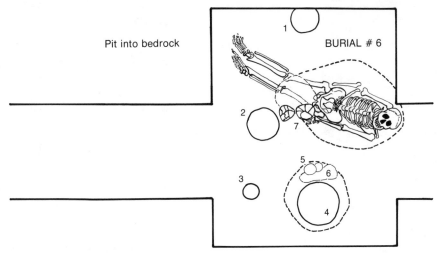

Figure 7/4: Feature 6 at bottom of trench IV at IS-3 was an extended burial surrounded by the following items: 1. lidded vessel; 2. vessel containing bones of infant; 3. small pot; 4. lidded vessel; 5. skulls of two children; 6. bundle burial of child; 7. crushed skulls.

2. Activity area 2: Three 2 x 2-meter cuts (trench I) were placed in this area and oriented north to south, following the natural dip in the strata. Refuse deposit at this spot was accumulated on a natural ridge sloping southward, rather than on what may be called a mound.

The depositional sequence in area 2, trench I (fig. 7/5a) showed some important differences from that of area 1. To begin with, the surface humus in area 2 was a fairly thick layer averaging 10 centimeters, resulting from less erosion and more chance for a humic buildup than in area 1. Furthermore, only layers A and C included great quantities of fractured rocks, and these were intercalated with two strata of silty soil, suggesting that the "sweeping-up" and "piling-up" of rocks was more sporadic in area 2 than in area 1. Also, a more gradual buildup of cultural and natural deposits occurred in area 2, in contrast to area 1, where nearly two-thirds of the deposit was the result of rapid and deliberate dumping.

Although the deposits in area 2, especially in block 1, contained enormous boulders, there was no indication whatsoever that these had been carried to this spot. Instead, the deposit seems to have grown around these boulders, as if a naturally unusable spot had been chosen to become a trash heap.

3. Activity area 3: This area lay on a second large mound near the southern border of the mapped section of the site. The stratigraphy at this spot (trench VII) duplicated that of the mounded area (activity area 3), only it was clearer and less disturbed by burrows, burials, or boulders (fig. 7/5b). Nonetheless, large roots penetrated far into the deposit, adding to the difficulty of excavation. A thin layer of surface humus (stratum A) was followed by a thick and compact, somewhat clayish brown soil level (stratum B) containing fist-sized rocks and abundant ceramics, some of it lensed, suggesting "natural flowers." The next layer (stratum C) was a more

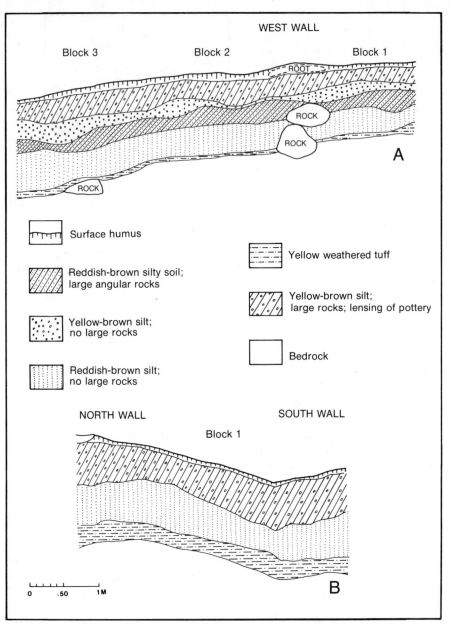

Figure 7/5: Profiles or section drawings at IS-3 of: a. trench I, activity area 2; b. trench VII, activity area 3. From field profiles by crew.

loose deposit with darker silty soil, containing few rocks. The bottom level represented the decomposed bedrock and weathered tuff, mixed with a sandy, clayey, silty soil (D and E). As elsewhere, the bottom level was a sterile bedrock (F). In general, the deposits in area 3 were somewhat deeper

Figure 7/6: Field shot of the basalt columns at IS-3.

than at the other areas, with the bedrock being encountered at a depth between 140 and 160 centimeters, rather than at a depth of 120 or 130 centimeters.

4. Activity area 4: Where carved basalt columns had been exposed in clearing operations (fig. 7/6), a one-meter band was roped off around a 10-meter square, and surface collections were made down to a depth of 10 centimeters. Our intention was to clarify the association between surface artifacts and stone columns. Then, two 1 x 1-meter blocks were dug down to bedrock in the corner of the square. The depth of the deposit was 50 to 60 centimeters. It, as well as the surface collections, contained abundant ceramic and lithic artifacts from the Burica and San Lorenzo phases.

5. Activity are 5: This was the flat area to the northwest of the main mound (area 1) between the 60.5-meter and 61.0-meter contours. It was tested by an 8 x 2-meter trench (trench VIII) which went down to 48 centimeters in places. Although no postholes were found — due probably to the limited nature of this test — the flat, swept-up area devoid of rocks to the north, east, and west of the main mound, including the area of trench VIII, seems the "logical" place for the ancient dwellings and house orchards.

Stone Tools from the Rio Chiriqui Shelters

A. J. RANERE

INTRODUCTION

The four rock shelters I excavated in 1971 in the upper Rio Chiriqui drainage in the province of Chiriqui, Panama (Ranere 1972b), are all located near the bottom of the Rio Chiriqui canyon at elevations between 645 meters and 900 meters. Eight kilometers to the north, the continental divide rises to an average elevation of 2,000 meters (see section 3.2 for a description of the region). All four rock shelters are small, none containing more than 30 square meters of protected living space.

Casita de Piedra contained preceramic deposits to a depth of 1.4 meters. Six radiocarbon dates, ranging from 4610 B.C. to 940 B.C., fix the time of its occupation. The Trapiche Shelter contained 1.2 meters of predominantly preceramic deposits. Four radiocarbon dates place its preceramic occupation between 3900 B.C. and 350 B.C. The Horacio Gonzales site (undated) contains both preceramic and ceramic components in its shallow deposits. From the fourth site, the Zarsiadero Shelter, we recovered both preceramic and ceramic materials in 70 centimeters of somewhat disturbed cultural deposits. Ten square meters of the first site, twelve square meters of the second, five square meters of the third, and a 1 x 2-meter pit in the fourth site were excavated. This report concerns the more than 45,000 stone flakes and tools recovered from these four shelters.

THE APPROACH TO THE ANALYSIS

The analysis of the lithic assemblages from the Rio Chiriqui shelters presented a number of problems, in part due to the large numbers of specimens that had to be processed but in the main due to the nature of the tool assemblages themselves. The preceramic chipped stone assemblages from the Rio Chiriqui sites differ considerably from those found in North America, the Andean area, and even in the ceramic horizons of Central America. Moreover, while it is quite probable that other sites within the tropical forested regions of South America have similar assemblages, none are adequately described (the problem of comparing the Rio Chiriqui assemblages with others in South America is dealt with elsewhere).

Tool categories such as projectile points, bifacially flaked knives, drills, and blades are either nonexistent in the Rio Chiriqui stone tool inventory or are applied only at the risk of distorting the true nature of the inventory. Forcing chipped stone tools into familiar predefined categories is not only tempting but almost unavoidable in a first encounter with a strange assemblage. Consequently, during the excavation of Casita de Piedra and the other shelters, my impression, as the tools were being found, was that a number of parallels to North American and Andean tool types could be drawn even though some important differences certainly existed. It was on this basis that I first discussed the Rio Chiriqui tools in a preliminary fashion (Linares and Ranere 1971). Unfortunately, first impressions are not always reliable, for, in this case, I overestimated the importance of the few pieces which resembled burins and blades, while underestimating the importance of small wedges which occurred by the dozens, but which were tools unfamiliar to me.

Rather than use categories of tools designed to describe the more familiar kinds of New World assemblages, it was decided to define new tool types based on a study of the Rio Chiriqui materials themselves. Therefore, the first step in the analysis was to examine every flake in the collections, separating out for individual cataloguing those pieces which were tools or tool fragments or which showed any sign of human modification other than the single blow which detached the flake from its parent block. During this initial sorting operation, no attempt was made to separate pieces into categories beyond the distinction between "unmodified, unused flakes" and "all others." Throughout this rather lengthy process, a stereoscopic microscope was used regularly to look for signs of wear, which could indicate how the tool was used, and for evidences of the manufacturing or flintknapping techniques employed in making the tools. When the patterns of tool form, function, and manufacturing techniques began to emerge, I initiated a series of experiments in an attempt to replicate the forms and technological characteristics of tools in the collections. The tools made in these experiments were then used to perform a variety of tasks in an attempt to replicate the wear patterns observed under the microscope. Additional experiments in lithic technology were carried out in order to reproduce the range of flakes found in the sites and thus to identify stone-working techniques known to the prehistoric inhabitants of the Rio Chiriqui valley (see Ranere 1975 for a lengthier discussion of the replicative experiments).

By the end of the initial sorting, and after a number of experiments, I was considerably more aware of the kinds of tools and stoneworking techniques represented in the collections. From this relatively knowledgeable position, the entire collection was reexamined. All chipped stone from a single occupation layer was laid out on the laboratory tables, and tools (including tool fragments) were separated once again from "unmodified unused flakes," correcting the identifications made during the initial examination where necessary. Also, at this time attempts were made to match artifact fragments, flakes with their cores, and flakes with flakes, with modest success.

Finally, all tools and tool fragments from each individual site were grouped together, then classified without regard to layer provenience. It was at this stage of the analysis that artifact categories were first formally defined. Tools from all sites were laid out on tables at the same time, and every precaution was taken to insure that artifact categories were consistent from site to site as well as from layer to layer.

A similar procedure was followed in the classification of nonchipped stone tools, but one made simpler because of the fewer numbers of tools to consider. All artifacts from one site made on pebbles, cobbles, and boulders, whether purposely manufactured or shaped through use, were put out together on the laboratory tables and sorted into categories. Again, replicative experiments were carried out in order to better understand the function of the tools and the techniques of manufacture. As with the chipped stone tools, the cobblestone tools were classified without regard to layer provenience, and the categories are considered to be consistent from site to site.

The artifacts were divided into major groups based on the final method of manufacture (e.g., chipped stone, ground and polished stone). Within these groups, artifact types are defined primarily in functional terms and only secondarily in terms of form. In large measure, the emphasis on function in defining artifact types reflects the nature of the stone assemblages themselves. Form seems to be important only in those characteristics that directly affect function (for example, large bifacial wedges have straight bits and taper gradually to a thick body; choppers are large enough and heavy enough to use for chopping). The technological repertoire represented in the assemblages was simple but effective; it appears that as little work as possible went into making a functional tool. Almost all the non-chipped stone tools were not purposefully shaped at all but were suitably sized cobbles or boulders which could be used as found. The modification of these cobbles into recognizable (and classifiable) forms came about only through use.

DESCRIPTION OF ARTIFACTS

A word of caution must be introduced here before going on with the tool descriptions. A great many tools from these shelters consist of flakes, spalls, cobbles, and so forth, used without modification. Identification of these specimens as tools depends on the analyst's ability to detect evidence of their use. In order to do this, the wear patterns on the working surfaces of the tool must be preserved reasonably intact after the tool has been discarded. Unfortunately, some of the rocks used for tools in the Rio Chiriqui sites weather rapidly when a fresh surface is exposed. Most of the andesite used for chipped stone tools and the granite cobbles used for grinding and mashing are included in this category. The weathering of some andesite pieces is so great that evidence for use retouch would not be preserved. Other andesite specimens are not so heavily weathered and use retouch can be detected, although wear polish and striations cannot. As figures 8/1 and 8/2 indicate, andesite accounts for between 48 percent and 96 percent of the chipped stone found in major stratigraphic units. Therefore, a considerable number of tools, particularly those modified only through use, have necessarily gone unrecognized. Flake knives, flake scrapers, and

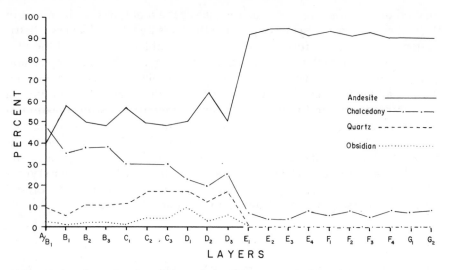

Figure 8/1: *Percent of andesite, chalcedony, quartz, and obsidian chipped stone by layer in Casita de Piedra*

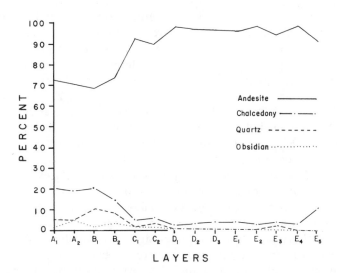

Figure 8/2: *Percent of andesite, chalcedony, quartz, and obsidian chipped stone by layer in the Trapiche Shelter.*

gravers, in particular, are certainly more common than is indicated in the discussion to follow.

I. Chipped Stone

In this section, the major classes of chipped stone artifacts (e.g., scrapers, choppers, wedges) are subdivided into different varieties (e.g., steep scrapers, concave scrapers), and these form the basic descriptive unit. The method of manufacture and probable use of the tool types are included in the description, as is the description of the tools by site and layers. Distributions of artifacts are further broken down to sublayers in each of the sites and recorded in tables 1–4. Dimensions are given for the largest and smallest artifact in each category and for the artifact in the median position (having a like number of objects larger and smaller than itself). Providing measurements for individual specimens rather than listing maximum-minimum values for each dimension may convey a better picture of tool proportion (that is, the relationship between its length, width, and thickness). Distinctions made in the raw materials used in tool manufacturing were limited to five: andesite, chalcedony (which includes other cryptocrystalines such as jasper and agate), quartz, obsidian, and "other" (primarily coarse-grained volcanic and metamorphic rocks).

A. Cores

1. Conical cores (fig. 8/3 j-l). These have a single striking platform from which flakes have been detached. Negative flake scars extend completely around the perimeter on most specimens and more than halfway on the remainder. The cores are not supported on an anvil; therefore, the flakes curve underneath the core on detachment, giving the distinctive conical shape. Most of these small cores were simply discarded as exhausted. However, some of the specimens considered as scraper-planes may have been made on conical cores. One unusually large specimen made on a small boulder produced flakes large enough to be used as choppers.

Dimensions: largest, 21.0 x 13.5 x 7.4 cm; smallest, 2.6 x 1.6 x 1.4 cm; median, 4.2 x 4.1 x 2.9 cm. Material: At Casita de Piedra, 5 andesite, 1 other (total 6); at Trapiche Shelter, 3 andesite. Distribution: At Casita de Piedra, 1 in layer E, 3 in F, 2 in G (disturbed); at Trapiche Shelter, 1 in B, 2 in E.

2. Bifacial cores (fig. 8/3 p,q). Several bifacially flaked objects in the collections appeared to serve no purpose other than as cores for removal of flakes. Instead of having a flat striking platform, these cores have an edge functioning as the striking platform with flakes removed in two directions. One of these bifacial cores is made on a small boulder and has flakes removed on alternate sides along one edge. The smaller cores tend to be disk-shaped or round, and biconvex in cross section; the perimeter of the disk is the striking platform and the flakes terminate at the center of the two opposing faces. None of the specimens show evidence of having been used as a chopper or wedge. Furthermore, they are not the proper shape to be considered blanks or preforms for bifacially flaked wedges.

Dimensions: largest, 15.4 x 14.4 x 8.2 cm; smallest, 5.0 x 4.9 x 2.3 cm; median, 6.7 x 5.5 x 3.0 cm. Material: Casita de Piedra, 2 andesite, 1 other (total 3); Trapiche Shelter, 2 andesite, 3 chalcedony (total 5); Zarsiadero Shelter, 1 chalcedony. Distribution: Casita de Piedra, 2 in layer C, 1 in E; Trapiche Shelter, 1 in A, 1 in B, 3 in D; Zarsiadero Shelter, 1 in B.

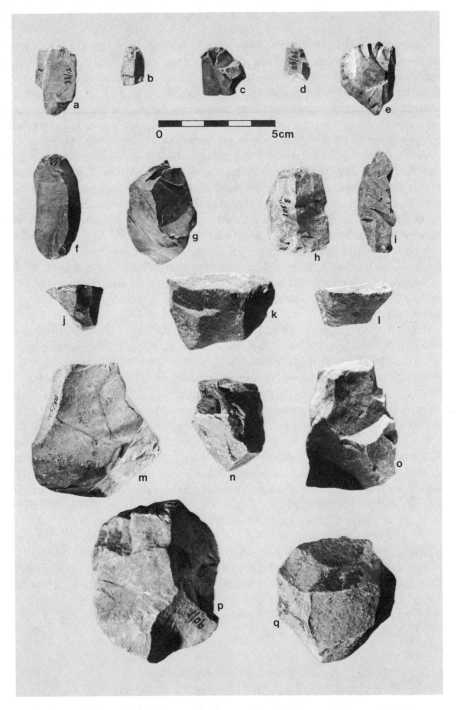

Figure 8/3: a-i. Bipolar cores; j-l. conical cores; m-o. irregular cores; p,q. bifacial cores.

3. Bipolar cores (fig. 8/3 a-i). Included here are cores, core remnants, or fragments which have negative flake scars originating at opposite ends of the specimen. This indicates that an anvil was used in the flake removal process. Such a method of flake detachment is called the bipolar flaking technique, since a single blow from a hammer results in force being applied simultaneously to both distal and proximal ends; that is, at the point of contact between the core and the hammer and at the point of contact between the core and the anvil. In the Rio Chiriqui sites, small rounded pebbles were supported on a stone anvil and struck by a hard stone hammer. Although the bipolar flaking technique lacks precision (cf. Sollberger and Patterson 1976), it is an efficient way to reduce small pebbles into usable flakes. With force being applied simultaneously at both ends of the core, flakes cannot "curve under" the distal end of the core and are therefore quite straight. Core remnants themselves are often straight, parallel-sided tabular pieces. Both flakes and core remnants produced by the bipolar flaking technique are ideal for use as small wedges. Numerous specimens classified as tabular and broadbased wedges are bipolar cores which show subsequent flake removal and polish, having been used as wedges or chisels. Specimens listed below do not show any additional evidence of use other than as cores.

Dimensions: largest, 3.8 x 3.5 x 1.4 cm; smallest, 0.9 x 0.7 x 0.6 cm; median, 2.5 x 1.2 x 0.8 cm. Material: Casita de Piedra, 97 chalcedony, 3 quartz, 1 obsidian, 2 andesite (total 103); Trapiche Shelter, 25 chalcedony, 2 quartz (total 27); Zarsiadero Shelter, 5 chalcedony. Distribution: Casita de Piedra, 9 in layer A/B, 8 in B, 26 in C, 19 in D, 31 in E, 4 in F, 1 in G (disturbed), 5 in ABC; Trapiche Shelter, 6 in A, 8 in B, 4 in C, 7 in D, 2 in E; Horacio Gonzales Site, 3 in C; Zarsiadero Shelter, 1 in B, 1 in B/C, 3 in C.

4. Irregular cores (fig. 8/3 m-o). Blocks of material which have had flakes removed in a random manner are grouped together as irregular cores. Some are exhausted cores from which further flake removal is impossible. Others have very few flakes removed and seem to have been abandoned because the material was not suitable for flaking. None of the pieces included in this category appears to have been used after functioning as a core.

Dimensions: largest, 16.4 x 9.7 x 8.9 cm; smallest, 2.2 x 1.6 x 1.2 cm; median, 3.8 x 2.8 x 2.6 cm. Material: Casita de Piedra, 14 chalcedony, 10 andesite, 2 quartz (total 26); Trapiche Shelter, 1 chalcedony, 8 andesite, 1 obsidian (total 10); Zarsiadero Shelter, 1 chalcedony, 1 andesite, 1 quartz (total 3). Distribution: Casita de Piedra, 2 in layer A/B, 5 in B, 7 in C, 3 in D, 6 in E, 1 in F, 2 in G (disturbed); Trapiche Shelter, 2 in A, 1 in B, 5 in C, 1 in D, 1 in E; Zarsiadero Shelter, 1 in A, 1 in B, 1 in C.

B. *Large Wedges*

1. Bifacial wedges (fig. 8/4 a-f, k). These are large, bifacially flaked implements which have celtlike forms; that is, they are long and thick bodied. They were not hafted either as axes or adzes, but were used as wedges or chisels. The bit end on complete specimens was carefully flaked to a sharp,

Figure 8/4: a-f, k. Bifacial wedges; g-j. irregular bifacial wedges.

relatively straight edge. It tapers gradually back to the thick, center section of the tool at about a 45° angle. Wedges which have been resharpened depart from these ideal characteristics, more or less depending on the success of the resharpening. Often the resharpened bit may be straight and sharp, but hinging of the resharpened flakes increases the angle and the smoothness of the taper. The butt end of these wedges almost always has an area of heavy battering slightly offset from the long axis of the tool. Frequently the battering occurs on a small portion of cortex which seems to have been purposely left intact in shaping the wedge. This would be reasonable since the cortex of the andesite blocks is stronger than the freshly exposed rock and can withstand more hammering. The bit is more heavily worn on the corner directly opposite the battered portion of the butt than in any other place. Wear polish, which also extends for three-fourths of the length of the tool on the high spots, is more heavily developed on the most convex side of the tool (the cross sections of the wedges tend to be plano-convex). Striations visible in the polished areas run at an angle of ca. 30° from the long axis of the tool. The lateral edges of the tools are usually blunted. These various wear patterns and manufacturing characteristics strongly suggest that these tools were handheld at a 30° angle (more or less) to the wood being split or chiseled, and driven in with a mallet of hard wood or perhaps stone.

In experiments, I replicated several of these wedges using only a hammerstone to remove flakes. One of these I used repeatedly in splitting wood blocks, holding the tool at an angle and driving it with a hard wooden mallet. As a result, wear patterns virtually identical to those on the archaeological specimens were produced.

Many of the specimens had been resharpened, and others had been broken in the resharpening attempt. A series of flakes that carried off the worn bit end of these wedges were recovered. These flakes show that the tool length was reduced at least 7 to 10 mm during each resharpening. This suggests that some of the wedges in the collection were resharpened several times before being discarded. One of these wedges (from layer E in Casita de Piedra) was reused as a hammerstone after several resharpenings (it is short relative to its width and thickness). It has blunted lateral edges and heavy wear polish on its faces, but it has a battered, rounded end where the bit should be.

Dimensions: largest, 12.0 x 4.1 x 3.4 cm; smallest, 7.0 x 3.3 x 1.6 cm; median, 9.3 x 3.9 x 2.3 cm. Average weight: 150 gm. Material: Casita de Piedra, 14 andesite; Trapiche Shelter, 28 andesite, 1 chalcedony (total 29); Zarsiadero Shelter, 11 andesite. Distribution: Casita de Piedra, 11 in layer E, 3 in F; Trapiche Shelter, 2 in B, 2 in C, 20 in D, 5 in E; Zarsiadero Shelter, 5 in B, 3 in B/C, 3 in C.

2. Irregular bifacial wedges (fig. 8/4 g-j). These tools appeared to function as wedges or chisels in the same way as the celtlike wedges. They differ in that they are made on cobbles and large flakes with a minimum of shaping by bifacial flaking. Most have wear polish on the bit edge and on the faces of the tools, most noticeably on the more convex side. Most also have a battered area at the butt end.

Dimensions: largest, 11.5 x 4.6 x 3.6 cm; smallest, 4.9 x 2.9 x 2.4 cm; median, 7.0 x 5.6 x 2.1 cm. Materials: Casita de Piedra, 6 andesite; Trapiche Shelter, 6 andesite. Distribution: Casita de Piedra, 5 in layer E, 1 in F; Trapiche Shelter, 5 in D, 1 in E.

3. Biface fragments. Most specimens are probably bifacial wedge fragments, since this is the most common bifacially worked artifact type found at the shelters. However, a few pieces may be from bifacial cores or bifacial choppers.

Material: Casita de Piedra, 31 andesite, 2 chalcedony (total 33); Trapiche Shelter, 29 andesite; Horacio Gonzales, 1 andesite; Zarsiadero Shelter, 5 andesite. Distribution: Casita de Piedra, 1 in layer A/B, 4 in B, 4 in C, 18 in E, 5 in F, 1 in ABC; Trapiche Shelter, 1 in A, 2 in B, 6 in C, 19 in D, 1 in E.

C. Small Wedges

1. Tabular wedges (fig. 8/5 a-y). These are small tools generally made on a flake, but are also made on core remnants. They average about 2.0 centimeters in length and weigh approximately 20 grams. Flakes are removed from opposite ends of the artifact and from both faces, creating a wedge- or chisel-shaped edge at one or both ends of the artifact. These edges have a series of small, generally hinged, use flakes evident. Some of these tabular wedges exhibit wear polish on the bit edge and on the high spots of both faces. Striations visible in the polished areas indicate that the tool was

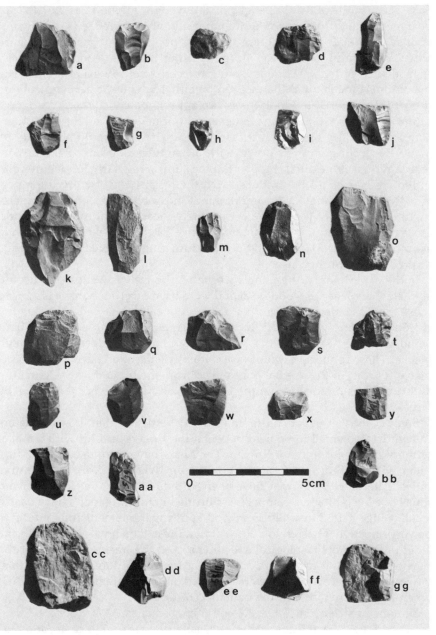

Figure 8/5: a-y. Tabular wedges; z-gg. broad-based wedges.

driven directly into the material being worked (probably wood) since they parallel the working axis of the tool. In some cases, sets of striations perpendicular to each other can be observed, indicating that the tool had two different and adjacent bits. More often, if a wedge had more than one edge used as a bit, the two edges were opposite each other. Occasionally, flake scars will extend the length of the wedge, giving it a "fluted" appearance. The fluting occurs quite naturally when a wedge is deeply embedded in wood, and therefore rigidly supported, and meets resistance when an attempt is made to drive it further into the wood. I produced several such fluted specimens during the course of my experiments. The maximum dimension of the tool can be either parallel or perpendicular to the working axis of the tool; many are approximately square.

Some wedges seemed to have been intentionally shaped for use, others simply shaped by use. In most cases, this distinction could not easily be made. By hitting straight down with a hammerstone on a flake or core remnant on a stone anvil (bipolar flaking), quite regularly formed double-bitted wedges could be produced. On the other hand, by driving a previously unmodified flake or core remnant into a block of wood and reversing the direction of the wedge occasionally, nearly identical forms result. Once the purposefully manufactured wedge has been used long enough to acquire wear characteristics, it becomes indistinguishable from the wedge formed solely through use.

In the experiments, these tools worked quite well as wedges, and could split sizable pieces of wood if several were used at a time. I have also used these tools as chisels; in fact, the decision to call them wedges instead of chisels was purely arbitrary. In my experiments, a limb section of hard wood was used as a mallet to drive the unhafted wedges into wooden blocks. These replicated wedges were identical to the archaeological specimens in form, in the use flakes removed from the bit end, in the crushing and use flakes removed from the butt end, and in the wear polish on the faces.

Some of the wedges are quite small (many being less than 1.5 centimeters in length); too small to be held between the fingers and hit with a mallet without endangering your fingers. They may have been used by holding them with something like a doubled green twig — a kind of primitive pliers. Alternately, they may have been hafted in wood, bone, or antler and thus have been bits in a composite splitting or chiseling tool. I have used a small wedge hafted in antler as a wood-splitting implement and found it to be very effective. I hasten to point out that the extension of wear polish, the length of some archaeological specimens, and the heavy battering of the butt ends seem to argue against the hafting of the tools. It is possible, however, that these wedges were reversed or turned sideways in their haft when the original bit became damaged or dulled.

Dimensions: largest, 5.6 x 3.0 x 1.5 cm; smallest, 1.1 x 0.9 x 0.5 cm; median, 2.1 x 1.5 x 0.5 cm. Material: Casita de Piedra, 110 chalcedony, 57 quartz, 17 obsidian, 2 andesite (total 186); Trapiche Shelter, 32 chalcedony, 17 quartz, 11 obsidian, 2 andesite (total 62); Horacio Gonzales Site, 14 chalcedony, 1 quartz (total 15); Zarsiadero Shelter, 14 chalcedony, 1 obsidian, 1 andesite (total 16). Distribution: Casita de Piedra, 15 in layer A/B, 37 in B, 73 in C, 40 in D, 9 in E, 1 in G, 11 in ABC; Trapiche Shelter, 23 in A, 32 in B, 3 in C, 3 in D, 1 in E; Horacio Gonzales Site, 1 in A/B, 13 in C, 1 in D; Zarsiadero Shelter, 5 in A, 7 in B, 4 in B/C.

2. Broad-based wedges (fig. 8/5 z-gg). The description of this artifact type closely follows that given for the tabular wedges except that the bit is opposed by a broad flat platform instead of a narrow one. Thus, whereas the tabular wedges could be and often were reversed when being used, the broad-based wedges could be oriented only one way, having a bit end distinct from the butt end. The bases of these wedges generally show crushing and small, hinged, use flakes around the periphery as a result of being pounded by a mallet. Broad-based and tabular wedges seem to be functional equivalents although the more blocky shape of the broad-based variety makes it a somewhat stronger tool; it can be driven with more force without fracturing.

Dimensions: largest, 3.7 x 2.4 x 1.9 cm; smallest, 1.0 x 0.9 x 1.4 cm; median, 1.8 x 1.5 x 1.4 cm. Material: Casita de Piedra, 18 chalcedony, 4 quartz (total 22); Trapiche Shelter, 4 chalcedony, 3 quartz (total 7); Horacio Gonales Site, 1 chalcedony; Zarsiadero Shelter, 4 chalcedony. Distribution: Casita de Piedra, 2 in layer A/B, 10 in B, 6 in C, 2 in D, 1 in E, 1 in F; Trapiche Shelter, 2 in A, 5 in B; Horacio Gonzales Site, 1 in C; Zarsiadero Shelter, 2 in A, 1 in B/C, 1 in C.

3. Probable small wedges. This is not a third distinct wedge variety, but simply a category including all those specimens which appear to have been used as wedges or chisels but which either lack some diagnostic characteristic or else are too fragmentary to be positively identified as wedges. It was often the case in my experiments that flakes used as wedges did not develop the pattern of use flakes described for tabular and broad-based wedges. This was particularly true for wedges made from "brittle" material which tended to snap at the point where the wedge entered the wood rather than having use flakes removed along the edge of the bit. Thus, it is my feeling that all specimens in this category can be considered wedges even though this cannot be demonstrated as convincingly as for the tabular and broad-based wedges.

Dimensions: largest, 3.2 x 2.6 x 0.9 cm; smallest, 1.0 x 1.0 x 0.3 cm; median, 2.2 x 1.5 x 0.6 cm. Material: Casita de Piedra, 89 chalcedony, 32 quartz, 3 obsidian (total 124); Trapiche Shelter, 27 chalcedony, 11 quartz, 5 obsidian (total 43); Horacio Gonzales Site, 6 chalcedony; Zarsiadero Shelter, 4 chalcedony, 3 quartz (total 7). Distribution: Casita de Piedra, 6 in layer A/B, 42 in B, 42 in C, 24 in D, 6 in E, 4 in ABC; Trapiche Shelter, 14 in A, 23 in B, 3 in C, 3 in D; Horacio Gonzales Site, 5 in C, 1 in D; Zarsiadero Shelter, 6 in B, 1 in C.

D. *Choppers*

1. Bifacial choppers (fig. 8/6 i-k). A few chopping tools in the collections had bifacially flaked edges. These were large heavy cobbles flaked completely around the periphery with one edge battered. Most of the specimens are fragmentary.

Dimensions: largest, ? x 6.5 x 3.5 cm; single complete specimen, 7.0 x 6.3 x 3.1 cm. Material: Casita de Piedra, 4 andesite; Trapiche Shelter, 1 andesite; Zarsiadero Shelter, 2 andesite. Distribution: Casita de Piedra, 1 in layer B, 3

Figure 8/6: a-h. Scraper-planes; i-k. bifacial choppers; l-n. flake choppers; o-q. cobble spall choppers.

in E; Trapiche Shelter, 1 in C; Zarsiadero Shelter, 1 in B, 1 in B/C.

2. Cobble spall choppers (fig. 8/6 o-q). These large flakes or spalls have been detached from rounded cobbles. The flakes are generally round and flat with one edge showing battering or removal of use flakes or both.

Dimensions: largest, 10.5 x 8.9 x 2.8 cm; smallest, 6.5 x 6.0 x 1.2 cm; median, 8.8 x 7.5 x 2.1 cm. Material: Casita de Piedra, 4 andesite, 1 other (total 5); Trapiche Shelter, 4 andesite; Zarsiadero Shelter, 2 andesite. Distribution: Casita de Piedra, 3 in layer C, 1 in D, 1 in G (disturbed); Trapiche Shelter, 1 in A, 1 in C, 2 in D; Zarsiadero Shelter, 1 in B, 1 in C.

3. Flake choppers (fig. 8/6 l-n). The specimens in this category are very much like cobble spall choppers but are made on large flakes struck from

andesite cores. Some show intentional bifacial flaking, but most of the flake removal can be attributed to use of the tools in chopping. A few of these tools may have been used as large splitting wedges.

Dimensions: largest, 8.8 x 7.5 x 3.1 cm; smallest, 3.8 x 3.5 x 0.7 cm; median, 6.2 x 4.6 x 1.6 cm. Material: Casita de Piedra, 11 andesite; Trapiche Shelter, 8 andesite; Horacio Gonzales Site, 1 andesite. Distribution: Casita de Piedra, 4 in layer C, 2 in D, 3 in E, 1 in F, 1 in ABC; Trapiche Shelter, 1 in A, 1 in C, 5 in D, 1 in E; Horacio Gonzales Site, 1 in C.

E. *Scraper-planes (fig. 8/6 a-h)*

Scraper-planes are heavy tools which have been unifacially flaked around their entire perimeter (with a few exceptions). A number of them are made on thick flakes and are domed or keeled. Working edges can be straight, "toothed," or (rarely) concave. Edge angles are most commonly between 60° and 70°, but range between 45° and 95°. Wear polish occurs on the edges and occasionally along the high spots on the adjacent ventral surface. On some specimens, use flakes are found on the ventral surface as well. Replicated scraper-planes, when used against wood with the ventral surface down, develop the same wear patterns as those observed on the archaeological specimens. These tools are all large enough to be used without hafting. On the other hand, replicas of the smaller specimens were much more effective when hafted. Such hafted tools bear a strong resemblance to the hafted "adze flakes" used by Australian aborigines (Gould et al. 1971). I could not determine from an examination of the archaeological specimens whether or not any had been hafted. (See Hester and Heizer 1972 for a discussion of other uses for scraper-planes.)

Dimensions: largest, 10.7 x 7.5 x 5.2 cm; smallest, 4.1 x 3.1 x 2.1 cm; median, 6.4 x 3.2 x 1.1 cm. Material: Casita de Piedra, 13 andesite; Trapiche Shelter, 22 andesite; Horacio Gonzales Site, 1 andesite; Zarsiadero Shelter, 1 andesite. Distribution: Casita de Piedra, 3 in layer B, 2 in C, 1 in D, 3 in E, 4 in F; Trapiche Shelter, 3 in B, 1 in C, 11 in D, 7 in E; Horacio Gonzales Site, 1 in A/B; Zarsiadero Shelter, 1 in B.

F. *Scrapers*

1. Steep scrapers (fig. 8/7 f-m). One edge of these flakes has been purposely chipped to form a steep-angled scraping edge. The angle of the working edge varies from 70° to 90°. Five of the scrapers had the working edge on the distal end of a short wide flake. Several were quite small (maximum length 3 cm) and had carefully flaked and rounded scraping edges.

Most of the wear polish on steep scrapers extends from the working edge back along the ventral surface, indicating that these tools were used as planes. Some of the heaviest wear occurred on the smallest specimens. I could not exert enough force to replicate the heavy wear polish or use flakes on experimental specimens without hafting them. A simple socket haft greatly increased the amount of force which could be applied when planing wood with these small tools.

A few specimens had light polish extending from the working edge onto the protruding ridges left by flake scars on the dorsal surface. Rather than being used as planes, these tools were drawn across the surface of the material being worked (probably wood) with the dorsal face downward.

Dimensions: largest, 7.9 x 6.1 x 1.2 cm; smallest, 1.4 x 1.0 x 0.9 cm; median, 2.8 x 2.5 x 0.8 cm. Material: Casita de Piedra, 31 andesite, 4 chalcedony (total 35); Trapiche Shelter, 12 andesite, 3 chalcedony; Zarsiadero Shelter, 6 andesite, 1 chalcedony. Distribution: Casita de Piedra, 2 in layer B, 1 in C, 3 in D, 22 in E, 7 in F; Trapiche Shelter, 4 in A, 2 in C, 7 in D, 2 in E; Zarsiadero Shelter, 4 in B, 2 in B/C, 1 in C.

2. Concave scrapers (spokeshaves) (fig. 8/7 a-e). All scrapers with one or more concave scraping edges were placed in this category. The scrapers were made on a variety of flakes. The diameter of the concavity or notch varies from 1.8 cm to 0.4 cm with no noticeable clustering. A number of these specimens have convex or straight scraping edges as well as a concave scraping edge.

Wear polish occurs most commonly on the concave working edge, occasionally extending a short distance back along the flake scar ridges on the dorsal surface (where edge angles are steep). Use flakes most often occur on the dorsal face as well. This wear pattern can be duplicated by drawing a spokeshave along a wooden shaft with the ventral surface facing the direction of motion. Use flakes occur less frequently on the ventral surface of spokeshaves (sometimes occurring together with use flakes on the dorsal surface). This suggests that sometimes the tools were used with the dorsal surface facing the direction of motion.

Dimensions: largest, 8.0 x 5.7 x 3.1 cm; smallest, 1.4 x 1.1 x 0.3 cm; median, 3.6 x 2.5 x 1.1 cm. Material: Casita de Piedra, 40 andesite, 26 chalcedony, 1 quartz (total 67); Trapiche Shelter, 40 andesite, 24 chalcedony, 1 quartz (total 65); Horacio Gonzales Site, 5 andesite; Zarsiadero Shelter, 8 andesite, 4 chalcedony. Distribution: Casita de Piedra, 2 in layer A/B, 5 in B, 9 in C, 9 in D, 31 in E, 10 in F, 1 in G (disturbed); Trapiche Shelter, 2 in A, 8 in B, 9 in C, 35 in D, 10 in E, 1 on surface; Horacio Gonzales Site, 5 in A/B; Zarsiadero Shelter, 1 in A, 6 in B, 5 in B/C.

3. Flake scrapers (fig. 8/7 n-t). This is a category of flakes and spalls which shows unifacial use retouch on at least one edge. The scraping edges are generally convex but can be straight. The angle of the working edge varies enormously, as does the size and the shape of the flake or spall which has been used for scraping. A few of the specimens show heavy wear polish on the flat, unretouched side, showing that they were used as scraping planes or push planes. Sixteen flake scrapers have a rounded scraping edge formed at one corner of a generally large flake. Otherwise, there is no particular pattern shown by the tools in this category. These tools were not intentionally manufactured, and it would appear that any flake which had a serviceable working edge was a candidate for scraping.

Dimensions: largest, 10.0 x 7.6 x 1.7 cm; smallest, 1.4 x 0.8 x 0.4 cm;

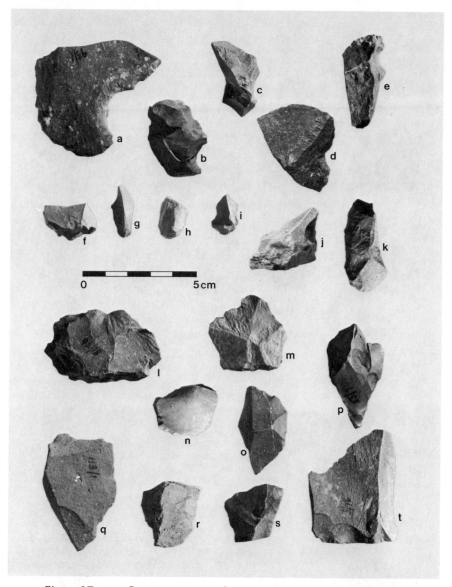

Figure 8/7: a-e. Concave scrapers; f-m. steep scrapers; n-t. flake scrapers.

median, 4.1 x 2.9 x 0.7 cm. Material: Casita de Piedra, 96 chalcedony, 73 andesite, 1 quartz (total 170); Trapiche Shelter, 27 chalcedony, 30 andesite (total 57); Horacio Gonzales Site, 2 chalcedony, 4 andesite (total 6); Zarsiadero Shelter, 9 chalcedony, 8 andesite (total 17). Distribution: Casita de Piedra, 7 in layer A/B, 14 in B, 24 in C, 17 in D, 70 in E, 31 in F, 2 in G (disturbed), 5 in ABC; Trapiche Shelter, 8 in A, 8 in B, 8 in C, 24 in D, 9 in E; Horacio Gonzales Site, 3 in A/B, 3 in C; Zarsiadero Shelter, 6 in A, 2 in B, 6 in B/C, 3 in C.

Figure 8/8: a-f. Used quartz crystals; g-l. burins; m-q. gravers; r-x. flake knives.

G. Flake Knives

Flake knives (fig. 8/8 r-x) are not intentionally manufactured tools, but they have use retouch or wear polish along one edge, indicating that they functioned as cutting tools. The working edge is generally straight and thin, an edge angle of less than 45° being most common. On most specimens, small flakes have been removed from both sides of the cutting edge. These use flakes are short and usually end in hinges or step fractures indicating that force was applied directly into the body of the tool. This pattern of use flakes contrasts with that found on flake scrapers where force is applied at an angle to the axis of the tool. Edge retouch on scrapers is unifacial, and the small flakes terminate smoothly rather than in step fractures. Flake knives with bifacial use retouch were probably used to cut hard materials, such as wood. In attempting to reproduce the pattern of use flake removal seen on archaeological specimens, I was most successful when using hafted flakes against hard wood. Knives with heavy use polish and no use flakes were probably used to cut meat and other soft materials.

Dimensions: largest, 6.9 x 4.0 x 1.9 cm; smallest, 2.4 x 1.5 x 0.3 cm; median, 4.6 x 3.1 x 0.8 cm. Material: Casita de Piedra, 49 andesite, 3 chalcedony (total 52); Trapiche Shelter, 24 andesite, 5 chalcedony (total 29); Horacio Gonzales Site, 5 andesite; Zarsiadero Shelter, 4 andesite. Distribution: Casita de Piedra, 1 in layer A/B, 1 in B, 8 in C, 8 in D, 25 in E, 7 in F, 1 in G (disturbed), 1 in ABC; Trapiche Shelter, 1 in A, 5 in B, 10 in C, 10 in D, 3 in E; Horacio Gonzales Site, 3 in A/B, 2 in C; Zarsiadero Shelter, 3 in B, 1 in B/C.

H. Engraving Tools

1. Burins (fig. 8/8 g-l). The strong, chisellike engraving end of a burin is formed by one or more blows directed perpendicular to the face of the stone being worked. Such a blow removes a burin spall or microblade from along one edge of the stone, leaving it with a squared-off or truncated edge. Two such truncations intersect to form the bit of the burin. Or, if a natural truncation was already present on the stone, the intersection of this truncation with one produced by a burin blow forms the bit of the tool. Numerous specimens in the Rio Chiriqui collections exhibit this specialized truncation or "burin facet." However, most are accidental by-products of the bipolar flaking technique or of breakage of small wedges while being used. The only specimens recorded as burins are those which are not obviously formed by accident. My feeling is that there is no strong burin industry represented in the Rio Chiriqui collections. Nonetheless, the specimens listed below do appear to be purposefully produced burins. Some have small flakes removed from their bits, showing that tools were used.

Dimensions: largest, 4.6 x 2.6 x 0.8 cm; smallest, 1.5 x 0.9 x 0.4 cm; median, 2.8 x 2.4 x 0.6 cm. Material: Casita de Piedra, 7 chalcedony, 3 andesite (total 10); Trapiche Shelter, 2 chalcedony, 2 andesite (total 4); Horacio Gonzales Site, 1 chalcedony; Zarsiadero Shelter, 1 chalcedony, 2 andesite (total 3). Distribution: Casita de Piedra, 1 in layer B, 5 in E, 3 in F, 1 in G; Trapiche Shelter, 2 in A, 2 in C; Horacio Gonzales Site, 1 in C; Zarsiadero Shelter, 1 in B, 2 in B/C.

2. Gravers (fig. 8/8 m-q). These tools have short projections or spurs which exhibit heavy use. On some, the spurs are isolated by fine unifacial retouch. The concavities which result from this retouch look like concave scraping edges (spokeshaves). However, microscopic examination indicates that wear occurs only on the spurs, not on the concavities. Some specimens are simply fortuitously pointed flakes which have been used without modification. All of these gravers have heavy use polish on the tip, and most have small use flakes removed from the tip's ventral surface.

Dimensions: largest, 4.9 x 2.5 x 0.9 cm; smallest, 2.2 x 1.3 x 0.6 cm; median, 3.4 x 1.9 x 1.0 cm. Material: Casita de Piedra, 4 chalcedony, 3 andesite (total 7); Trapiche Shelter, 1 andesite; Horacio Gonzales Site, 1 chalcedony; Zarsiadero Shelter, 1 chalcedony. Distribution: Casita de Piedra, 2 in layer B, 3 in E, 2 in F; Trapiche Shelter, 1 in B; Horacio Gonzales Site, 1 in C; Zarsiadero Shelter, 1 in B.

I. *Used Quartz Crystals (fig. 8/8 a-f)*

Evidence of wear is shown on the chisel-shaped point at the end of the crystal. Often the opposite end shows the effects of battering. These tools probably functioned as chisels or wedges.

Dimensions: largest, 2.8 x 1.2 x 1.1 cm; smallest, 1.4 x 0.5 x 0.4 cm; median, 2.1 x 1.2 x 1.0 cm. Distribution: Casita de Piedra, 3 in layer B, 1 in C, 3 in D, 1 in ABC; Trapiche Shelter, 5 in B.

J. *Blades*

Blades can be defined as parallel-sided flakes which are twice as long as they are wide. The striking platform is perpendicular, and the direction of applied force parallel, to the long axis of the blade. True blades are detached from prepared cores. Nonetheless, flakes having all the proper characteristics of blades can be produced accidentally in the process of manufacturing tools such as bifacial wedges, scraper-planes, and choppers. I doubt that blades were purposely produced tools in the Rio Chiriqui sites, since no blade cores were recovered. Instead, all cores were designed to produce short, wide, thin flakes, although bladelike flakes might have been detached in preparation of the core. In an experimental replication of a flake core, where short, wide flakes were the desired end-product, 5 out of 162 flakes could be considered blades. In a similar experiment to reproduce a celtlike wedge, 8 out of 205 flakes could be considered blades. Therefore, it is not at all unreasonable to suggest that the 79 blades recorded in the Rio Chiriqui collection of more than 45,000 stone flakes were accidentally produced. The fact that none of the blades exhibited use flakes or wear polish supports this position.

Dimensions: largest, 15.3 x 3.5 x 1.7 cm; smallest, 2.0 x 0.9 x 0.2 cm; median, 3.8 x 1.7 x 0.5 cm. Material: Casita de Piedra, 23 andesite, 8 chalcedony, 2 quartz (total 33); Trapiche Shelter, 31 andesite, 1 chalcedony

TABLE 1 DISTRIBUTION OF CHIPPED STONE IN CASITA DE PIEDRA

	Flakes	Totals (tools)	Blades	Used quartz crystals	Gravers	Burins	Flake knives	Flake scrapers	Concave scrapers	Steep scrapers	Scraper-planes	Flake choppers	Cobble spall choppers	Bifacial choppers	Probable small wedges	Broad-based wedges	Tabular wedges	Biface fragments	Irregular bifacial wedges	Bifacial wedges	Irregular cores	Bipolar cores	Bifacial cores	Conical cores
A, B_1	485	47	2				1	7	2						6	2	15	1			2	9		
B_1	220	16		1	1				2						7	1	3	1				1		
B_2	945	60		2	1	1		6	3	1	2			1	19	5	14				4	2		
B_3	889	62	4				1	6		1	1		2		16	4	20	1			1	5	1	
C_1	1,085	71	1				3	10	3		1	2	1		13	2	23	2	3	3	3	8	1	
C_2	1,251	69		1			3	5	3	1					12	1	32		2	6	2	6		
C_3	990	74	1				2	9	3		1	2	1		17	3	18			2	2	12		
D_1	404	27		1			2	3	8					2	3	1	12				2	5		
D_2	1,587	66		1			2	7	1			2			11	1	16				1	12		
D_3	401	40	1	1	1	1	4	7	2	3				1	10		12					2		1
E_1	1,156	36	2		1	2	4	9	16	6	1	1			1	1	5	7	1	3	4	9		
E_2	5,194	114	2		1	1	7	30	9	8	2	2			1		1	9			2	18	1	
E_3	3,918	91	11		1	1	11	25	2	6					1			2				3		
E_4	696	21	1			1	3	5	1	2					1							1		
F_1	279	5						2	2		1											2		2
F_2	443	6	2		1	2	1	3	5		1	1					1	4			1	2		1
F_3	2,016	51	5			1	5	16	1	4	3					1		1				1		
F_4	966	26				1	1	9		3														
G_1	16	2	1				1	2	1															
$G_{dis.}$	316	11											1		2						2	2		2
$E_{dis.}$	488	5		1			1	5				1					3	1						
A, B, C	428	29													4		11							
Totals	24,173	929	33	8	7	10	52	166	64	35	13	11	5	4	124	22	186	31	6	14	26	103	3	6

TABLE 2 DISTRIBUTION OF CHIPPED STONE IN THE TRAPICHE SHELTER

	Flakes	Totals (tools)	Blades	Used quartz crystals	Gravers	Burins	Flake knives	Flake scrapers	Concave scrapers	Steep scrapers	Scraper-planes	Flake choppers	Cobble spall choppers	Bifacial choppers	Probable small wedges	Broad-based wedges	Tabular wedges	Biface fragments	Irregular bifacial wedges	Bifacial wedges	Irregular cores	Bipolar cores	Bifacial cores	Conical cores
A₁	838	38	4			1	1	5		1					7	2	12				1	4		
A₂	1,033	34				1		3	2	3		1	1		7		11	1			1	2	1	
B₁	1,044	41	2	2			2	3	3		1				9	3	9			2	1	6	1	1
B₂	2,051	67	2	3	1		3	4	5		2				14	2	23	2	2		5	2		
C₁	1,898	47	4				8	7	6	2	1			1	1		3	5	2	2		4		
C₂	505	16	1			2	2	1	3			1	1		2			1	1	10	1	1	1	
D₁	3,251	62	4				3	9	10	4	4	2	1		1		1	9	1	8		4	2	
D₂	3,256	78	6				6	7	16	2	7	2	1		2		2	10		3	1	2		
D₃	1,941	31	6					8	9	1		1								2		2		
E₁	1,263	26	2				2	5	6	2	2							1		2		2		2
E₂	928	14						3	2		3	1					1			1				
E₃	298	8	1				1	1	2		2													
Totals	18,306	462	32	5	1	4	29	56	64	15	22	8	4	1	43	7	62	29	6	29	10	27	5	3

TABLE 3   DISTRIBUTION OF CHIPPED STONE IN THE HORACIO GONZALES SITE

Tool	A, B	C₁	C₂	D	Totals
Bipolar cores			3		3
Irregular bifacial wedges	1				1
Tabular wedges	1	4	9	1	15
Broad-based wedges			1		1
Probable small wedges		4	1	1	6
Flake choppers			1		1
Scraper-planes	1				1
Concave scrapers	5				5
Flake scrapers	5	3	1		9
Flake knives	3	1	1		5
Burins			1		1
Gravers		1			1
Blades		2	2		4
Totals (tools)	16	15	20	2	53
Flakes	729	1,587	446	55	2,817

TABLE 4   DISTRIBUTION OF CHIPPED STONE IN THE ZARSIADERO SHELTER

Tool	A	B	B/C	C	Totals
Bifacial cores		1			1
Bipolar cores		1	1	3	5
Irregular cores		1	1	1	3
Bifacial wedges		5	3	3	11
Biface fragments		1	2	3	6
Tabular wedges		5	7	4	16
Broad-based wedges		2	1	1	4
Probable small wedges		6	1		7
Bifacial choppers		1	1		2
Cobble spall choppers		1	1		2
Scraper-planes	1				1
Steep scrapers	4	2	1		7
Concave scrapers	1	6	5		12
Flake scrapers	6	2	6	3	17
Flake knives	3	1			4
Burins		1	2		3
Gravers	1				1
Blades		4	2	6	12
Totals (tools)	16	47	31	20	114
Flakes	306	1,765	787	631	3,489

(total 32); Horacio Gonzales Site, 2 andesite; Zarsiadero Shelter, 12 andesite. Distribution: Casita de Pedra, 2 in layer A/B, 4 in B, 2 in C, 1 in D, 16 in E, 7 in F, 1 in G (disturbed); Trapiche Shelter, 4 in A, 4 in B, 5 in C, 1 6 in D, 3 in E; Horacio Gonzales Site, 2 in C; Zarsiadero Shelter, 4 in B, 2 in B/C, 6 in C.

K. *Waste Flakes*

Nearly 45,000 apparently unmodified and unused flakes were recovered from the Rio Chiriqui excavations. Most were by-products of tool manufacture. However, an indeterminant number of these flakes must have seen some use. The extreme weathering of some of the andesite used so extensively in the shelters would have destroyed any wear patterns that might once have existed on flakes of this material. Other indications of wear undoubtedly went undetected. Still, the great majority of these flakes can be considered manufacturing debris. They clearly document the fact that these shelters did function as lithic workshops.

II. *Ground and Polished Stone*

These are nonchipped tools made on pebbles, cobbles, and boulders, either purposefully manufactured or shaped through use.

A. *Grooved Stone Axe*

A single specimen (fig. 8/9 h) was recovered from layer C_1 near the rear wall of Casita de Piedra. The surface is badly eroded; therefore, no wear patterns were visible. The bit edge is convex and asymmetrical. The axe is completely encircled by a broad (ca. 2.0 cm), shallow (0.2–0.6 cm) groove to facilitate hafting. Dimensions: length 7.8 cm, width of bit 6.3 cm, width of butt 4.6 cm, width at groove 4.1 cm, maximum thickness 2.6 cm.

B. *Polished Celts*

A bit fragment of a polished celt (fig. 8/9 d) was recovered from the upper part (layers A, B, and C) of Casita de Piedra. The fragment came from the top 50 centimeters of a balk separating blocks 2 and 5. Striations from shaping the celt are clearly visible. They run parallel to the front edge of the beveled faces which form the bit. Dimensions: 3.5 x 1.0 x 1.4 cm.

A second bit fragment came from layer A in the Zarsiadero Shelter (fig. 8/9 e). This small fragment (3.0 x 1.6 x 0.8 cm), from a polished celt or chisel, tapers from a relatively wide, thick body to a narrow bit. The faces of the bit are polished; striations run parallel to the long axis of the tool. The beveled edges below the faces are ground but not polished.

A complete (?) polished stone celt was left in the wall of the excavation at the Zarsiadero Shelter. It remains 18 cm below the surface in layer B. The tool, approximately 4–5 cm wide and 2–5.3 cm thick, was plano-convex in cross section. About 7 cm of the tool projected from the wall, and the complete specimen probably measured about 12 cm in length.

Figure 8/9: a. Stone bowl fragment; b. stone bowl sherd; c. polished stone chisel bit; d. polished stone celt fragment; e. polished stone celt bit; f. beveled ground stone fragment; g. grooved stone axe; h. grooved ground stone fragment.

C.   Polished Stone Adze or Chisel

The specimen (fig. 8/9 c), which came from layer B₃ in Casita de Piedra, was snapped at the middle by pressure exerted perpendicular to the face of the bit. Only this bit end was found. Two sets of parallel striations resulting from the manufacturing process run diagonally across the faces of the stone and cross each other at right angles. Two incised lines encircle the tool almost at the point where it snapped. The lines were formed as the tool rubbed against its haft. The fragment measures 3.3 x 1.6 x 0.5 cm.

III.   Pecked, Ground, or Battered Stone (tables 5 and 6)

A.   Handstones

1. Edge-ground cobbles (fig. 8/10 a-f). These tools have their working facet on the side or edge of the cobble rather than on the face as is common

Figure 8/10: Edge-ground cobbles.

with most handstones or manos. The working surface may extend nearly the length of the tool. The working surfaces are quite smooth and regular. Facets are slightly convex along the short axis and vary from quite convex to almost straight along the long axis. The cross sections of the cobbles themselves range from rectangular to oval to triangular, with the first being the most common. These tools have been called "pebble grinders," "edge grinders," and "chopper-grinders" (Willey and McGimsey 1954; McGimsey 1956; Willey 1971). They presumably were used in the Rio Chiriqui region with boulder milling stone bases. The two tool types have similar distributions in the sites' deposits. I have suggested that these tools were used in grinding or mashing root crops (Ranere 1972, 1975). Experiments using intially unmodified cobbles to mash manioc on a flat boulder did produce edge-ground cobbles (and milling stones) similar to the archaeological specimens. Any number of other substances could have been substituted for manioc and produced the same result, since it is the action of the cobble handstone against the boulder base that causes the wear (see Sims 1971 for further discussion on "edged" cobbles).

Dimensions: largest, 13.8 x 11.5 x 8.0 cm; smallest, 7.3 x 5.8 x 3.6 cm; median, 10.8 x 6.8 x 5.0 cm. Distribution: Casita de Piedra, 3 in layer A/B, 6 in C, 1 in D, 10 in E, 2 in F, 1 in ABC (total 23); Trapiche Shelter, 1 in A, 6 in B, 4 in C, 14 in D, 1 in E (total 26); Horacio Gonzales Site, 1 in A/B, 6 in C (total 7); Zarsiadero Shelter, 1 in B.

2. Rectangular handstones or manos (fig. 8/11 a,b). At Casita de Piedra, two formed rectangular grinding stones were recovered together in layer C near the rear wall of the shelter. These tools may have functioned as hammers, as well as manos, for the ends are battered. Grinding surfaces occur on the other four facets of the cobbles. Dimensions: 11.4 x 5.8 x 4.2 cm and 10.8 x 5.8 x 4.6 cm.

3. Cobbles with offset grinding facets (fig. 8/11 c,d). A few grinding stones had facets which were neither on the face of the cobble nor on the side, but in some intermediate position. In three of four specimens, these facets occurred in combination with side facets (that is, on edge-ground cobbles). The offset surfaces appear to have been made by pecking and are rougher than those on either the edge-ground cobbles or manos.

Dimensions for the three whole specimens: 13.8 x 11.5 x 8.0 cm, 13.7 x 8.8 x 5.4 cm, and 10.1 x 9.6 x 4.2 cm. Distribution: Casita de Piedra, 2 in C, 1 in ABC; Zarsiadero Shelter, 1 in B.

B. Milling Stone Bases

These tools (fig. 8/12) consisted of large boulders with one flat surface, sometimes with a slight concavity. In the best specimen (and the only example packed out of the Rio Chiriqui valley), the shallow depression is circular, 13 cm in diameter and 0.3 cm deep. In specimens having no depression, the surface of the boulder is ground smooth.

Dimensions: largest, 46 x 30 x 17 cm; smallest, 23 x 21 x 8 cm; median, 34 x

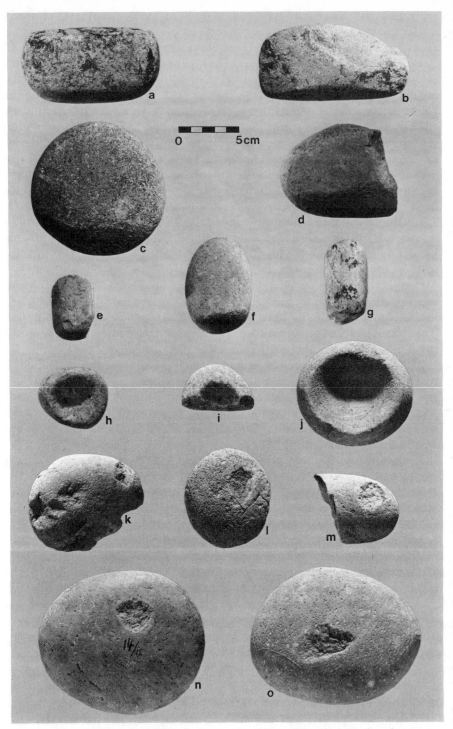

Figure 8/11: a,b. Rectangular handstones; c,d. cobbles with offset grinding facets; e-g. pestles; h-j. mortars; k-o. nutting stones.

0   5cm

Figure 8/12: Milling stone bases.

33 x 15 cm. Distribution: Casita de Piedra, 1 in layer B, 2 in C, 5 in E; Trapiche Shelter, 2 in layer D.

C. Pestles

These tools (fig. 8/11 e-g) were recovered only in the upper two layers in Casita de Piedra. The working surface is shaped like the gable on a house; the two facets join at an angle of ca. 120°. Either one or both ends of the pestle have this faceted surface. When in use, the tool was apparently held at an angle of approximately 60° to the mortar or milling stone base but not rotated in the hand (which would produce a rounded rather than a faceted working surface).

This type of tool was termed a "pestle" because specimens were made on elongated pebbles and cobbles. However, the working surfaces might as easily have been formed through use of the specimens as pecking hammers.

Dimensions: largest, 18.0 x 8.5 x 6.9 cm; smallest, 5.6 x 3.9 x 2.2 cm; median, 7.6 x 5.5 x 4.3 cm. Distribution: Casita de Piedra, 3 in layer A/B, 2 in C.

D. Nutting Stones

These tools (fig. 8/11 k-o) have one or more small (ca. 2–3 cm in diameter) pits pecked into their surface to a maximum depth of one centimeter. Such stones were presumably used in cracking nutshells; the nut being placed in the depression and hit with a stone hammer.

Dimensions: largest, 14.6 x 11.2 x 6.1 cm; smallest, 5.2 x 4.5 x 3.6 cm; median, 10.8 x 7.3 x 4.2 cm. Distribution: Casita de Piedra, 1 in layer B, 1 in F, 1 in ABC; Trapiche Shelter, 1 in A, 2 in B, 3 in C, 1 in D; Horacio Gonzales Site, 1 in C.

E. Hammers

1. Battered choppers/hammers (fig. 8/13e). Included in this category are bifacially flaked cobbles which have been heavily battered, so much so that broad facets characteristic of hammerstones occur along at least one section of the periphery and, on some specimens, around the entire periphery. The tools seem to have been originally manufactured and used as choppers, and later, after the edges had been so battered that they no longer served this function, they were used as hammerstones. In final appearance, these tools resemble the category "edge-battered cobbles."

Dimensions: largest, 10.5 x 10.0 x 4.7 cm; smallest, 3.9 x 3.1 x 2.4 cm; median, 7.0 x 5.6 x 2.1 cm. Material: Casita de Piedra, 8 andesite; Trapiche Shelter, 5 andesite, 2 chalcedony (total 7); Zarsiadero Shelter, 1 andesite. Distribution: Casita de Piedra, 1 in layer C, 1 in D, 4 in E, 1 in F, 1 in G (disturbed); Trapiche Shelter, 1 in A, 3 in B, 2 in D, 1 in E; Zarsiadero Shelter, 1 in B.

2. Edge-battered cobbles (fig. 8/13 g-i). Part or all of the cobble's circumference has been modified by hammering or battering. In the case of a few heavily used specimens, very broad, gently convex, hammering facets ring the cobble.

Figure 8/13: a-d, f. End-battered hammers; e. battered chopper/hammer; g-i. edge-battered hammers; j-m. anvils.

Dimensions: largest, 9.0 x 8.7 x 3.0 cm; smallest, 4.6 x 3.8 x 3.2 cm; median, 7.3 x 6.5 x 4.3 cm. Distribution: Casita de Piedra, 1 in layer A/B, 6 in B, 3 in C; Trapiche Shelter, 2 in A, 1 in B, 1 in D; Horacio Gonzales Site, 1 in C.

TABLE 5 DISTRIBUTION OF PECKED, GROUND, AND BATTERED
TOOLS IN CASITA DE PIEDRA

	Edge-ground cobbles	Rectangular handstones	Faceted handstones	Milling-stone bases	Pestles	Nutting stones	Battered choppers/hammers	Edge-battered cobbles	End-battered hammers	Anvils	Miscellaneous	Totals
ABC	1		1				1		2		1	6
AB₁	2				1			1		1	1	6
B₁						1		1				2
B₂								1	5			6
B₃	1			1	2			5	2	1	1	13
C₁	2	2	2	1			1	1	1	1	3	14
C₂	3			1	1			2	2		4	13
C₃	1				1				2	1	1	6
D₁												
D₂	1								1			2
D₃							1					1
E₁	2										1	3
E₂	4			4				2			1	11
E₃	4			1				2				7
E₄												
F₁												
F₂									1			1
F₃	2					1	1		1		1	6
F₄									1			1
G dist							1					1
Totals	23	2	3	8	5	3	8	10	19	4	14	99

3. End-battered hammers (fig. 8/13a-d, f). These elongated cobbles and pebbles are modified by hammering at one or both ends, but do not show evidence of heavy use. They were probably used in flintknapping, and so were discarded when the end of the tool became too blunted to accurately strike the implement being flaked.

Dimensions: largest, 13.9 x 8.0 x 4.3 cm; smallest, 3.6 x 2.4 x 1.2 cm; median, 9.9 x 7.0 x 4.6 cm. Distribution: Casita de Piedra, 8 in layer B, 5 in C, 1 in D, 3 in F, 2 in ABC; Trapiche Shelter, 2 in A, 4 in B, 2 in C, 6 in D; Horacio Gonzales Site, 2 in C.

F. Anvils (fig. 8/13j-m)

These cobbles and boulders have pitted surfaces on one or both faces where a chipped stone core has been supported during the process of flake

TABLE 6 DISTRIBUTION OF PECKED, GROUND, AND BATTERED TOOLS IN THE TRAPICHE SHELTER

	Edge-ground cobbles	Milling-stone bases	Nutting stones	Battered choppers/hammers	Edge-battered cobbles	Edge-battered hammers	Anvils	Miscellaneous	Totals
A₁				1		2		3	6
A₂	1			1		2	1	1	6
B₁				1	1	1			3
B₂	6		3	1	2	1			13
C₁	1		2						3
C₂	3		1			2	1		7
D₁	5	1			1	6	1		14
D₂	6	1		2			1		10
D₃	3		1						4
E₁	1			1			1		3
E₂								1	1
E₃	—	—	—	—	—	—	—	—	—
Totals	26	2	7	7	4	14	5	5	70

removal. Such anvils are necessary to produce the bipolar cores found so abundantly in the Rio Chiriqui collections.

Dimensions: largest, 22.0 x 10.4 x 9.3 cm; smallest, 5.4 x 4.9 x 3.3 cm; median, 12.3 x 6.5 x 4.5 cm. Distribution: Casita de Piedra, 1 in A/B, 1 in B, 2 in C; Trapiche Shelter, 1 in A, 1 in C, 2 in D, 1 in E.

G. *Miscellaneous Artifacts*

1. Stone mortars (fig. 8/11 h-j). One complete stone bowl or mortar, one fragment of a mortar, and one possible mortar came from Casita de Piedra (the first from layer C, the last two from layer E). The complete specimen, slightly oblong, had its surface entirely eroded away. Outside dimensions: length 8.7 cm, width 7.7 cm, depth 5.4 cm. Inside dimensions: length 6.5 cm, width 5.8 cm, depth 1.8 cm. The fragment was much like the complete specimen although smaller (outside ? x 5.4 x 3.1 cm, inside ? x 3.1 x 0.7 cm). The third specimen had a highly eroded surface and slightly irregular shape, making it doubly difficult to determine if it was made or used by man. The outside measurements: 5.4 x 4.6 x 3.0 cm; inside measurements: 4.1 x 3.6 x 0.5 cm.

2. Stone bowl (fig. 8/9 b). A single sherd, which appeared to be from the base and side of a stone bowl, was recovered from the Trapiche Shelter in layer E₂. Both inside and outside surfaces are smooth and regular. The

thickness varies from 2.0 cm near the base to a maximum of 2.2 cm, then tapers to 1.2 cm toward the rim of the bowl. Dimensions of the sherd are 9.5 x 5.7 cm.

3. Beveled, ground fragment (fig. 8/9 f). The entire surface of this fragment has been shaped, as striations are everywhere visible. Along one edge, where the specimen is intact, there is a polished concave section, suggesting that the specimen was once drilled. Opposite the concavity, the edge has been beveled to a thickness of 0.2 cm. Dimensions: 4.8 x 3.0 x 1.0 cm. Provenience: Casita de Piedra, layer C_2.

4. Pecked and ground stone tool fragment (fig. 8/9h). This small fragment, made on a flat rounded pebble, has been pecked and ground on both faces. A shallow notch has also been pecked into the edge. Dimensions: 7.4 x 3.6 x 1.4 cm. Provenience: Horacio Gonzales Site, layer C.

5. Pebble fragments with ground facets. Three specimens are very much alike, with ground opposing faces that taper to a rounded edge. Since much of the tool is missing in all cases, we can do no more than to suggest that they may have been fragments of manos. One fragment (dimensions 4.1 x 6.2 x 3.0 cm) came from layer A/B in Casita de Piedra, and two (dimensions 8.5 x 7.5 x 3.3 cm and 6.1 x 6.1 x 1.8 cm) from layer A in the Trapiche Shelter.

6. Grinding stone fragment (?). A small fragment of vesicular lava was recovered from the Trapiche Shelter, layer A. It shows no definite evidence of wear, but such evidence might easily go unrecognized on such a small fragment. Dimensions: 6.2 x 3.1 x 3.4 cm.

7. Small, flat, pointed pebbles. Two fragments of pebbles, both from layer C in Casita de Piedra, have ends ground to a rounded point. Although heavily eroded, worn facets are visible on the spatulalike ends. Dimensions: 3.1 x 3.1 x 0.6 cm; 3.1 x 2.5 x 1.2 cm.

8. Pebbles with striations. Several small specimens occur with striations visible on one or more surfaces. These may have served as abrading stones. Dimensions: 6.1 x 4.8 x 1.4 cm; 4.8 x 2.2 x 1.5 cm; 4.5 x 2.9 x 2.0 cm. Distribution: Casita de Piedra, 2 in layer C; Trapiche Shelter, 1 in layer A.

9. Whetstone (?). A flat, tabular piece of andesite that has both polishing and striations visible on one face. The piece came from layer F in Casita de Piedra. Dimensions: 4.8 x 3.6 x 1.2 cm.

10. Triangular polished stone. This small (2.5 x 1.6 x 0.3 cm) piece of stone is smoothed on all surfaces and quite even. It could be an unmodified piece, but the triangular or wedgelike appearance is unusual.

TECHNOLOGY

In spite of the enormous quantities of flakes and stone tools recovered from the Rio Chiriqui sites, the chipped stone industry is not a complicated one. The amount of chipping debris in the deposits reflects the fact that Casita de Piedra, the Trapiche Shelter, and the Zarsiadero Shelter were, in part, workshop sites. Lithic material, including obsidian, was plentiful within a kilometer or two of each site, and most kinds could be gathered from andesite outcrops or stream gravels less than 200 meters away from the overhangs. The range of tools produced throughout the sequence is quite limited, and the techniques used to produce them are simple. Moreover, very little change takes place in any aspect of the stone industry during the 4,500-year span of preceramic occupation of the valley. The conservative nature of the stone industry is a predictable consequence of the tropical forest adaptive pattern which emphasizes the use of other materials, principally tropical hardwoods, in manufacturing tools. Stone is simply not the important medium here, as it is in other preceramic patterns; thus, the stimulus to improve the technology was largely absent.

Stoneworking techniques represented in the Rio Chiriqui assemblages were simple but functional. All manufacturing was done by direct percussion, and hammerstones were probably the only flaking implements. Hardwood or bone billets may have been used also, but the flaking characteristics on the tools and discarded flakes can be accounted for by stone-hammer percussion only. Within the stone-hammer category itself, however, a wide range of sizes, hardness, and shapes is represented.

Two percussion-flaking techniques were used, depending largely on the characteristics of the material being flaked. Chalcedony (and other cryptocrystaline rocks like jasper, chert, and agate), obsidian, and quartz generally occurred as small nodules. These were broken up by using the "bipolar" flaking technique whereby a nodule or core is placed on a stone anvil for support and hit on the top surface with a hard hammerstone. For the chalcedony and quartz nodules, which are tough rocks to fracture, the use of an anvil greatly improves the ease with which flakes can be removed from a core. In addition, with the force being applied to the core simultaneously from the anvil as well as from the hammerstone, the detached flakes tend to be quite straight in profile. Often such flakes make suitable small wedges without further retouch. Use of the bipolar technique is documented for the entire preceramic sequence but is more common in the Boquete phase where 30 percent to 50 percent of the lithic material is chalcedony, quartz, and obsidian (figs. 8/1, 8/2). These materials account for less than 10 percent of the lithic specimens present in the preceding Talamanca phase.

Andesite can be found in large blocks in the immediate vicinity of all sites. The large andesite cores were not supported on an anvil, but were held free in the flaking procedure. Andesite flakes do not have the straight profile of the bipolarly flaked chalcedony ones; instead they curve underneath the core when being detached. This percussion technique, in which the core is not supported, was used more extensively in the Talamanca phase, where over 90 percent of the lithic material was andesite and from 30 percent to 55 percent of the tools were scrapers.

The lithic techniques represented in the Rio Chiriqui sites can be fairly characterized as being directed toward producing a serviceable tool with the least amount of work. This characterization holds true even for the celtlike wedge, the most sophisticated chipped stone tool in the preceramic period, ground and polished stone tools excepted. The category "irregular bifacial wedges" consists primarily of andesite flakes and spalls which were naturally wedgelike and needed little retouch to become functional tools. Celtlike wedges themselves take very little time to make. In experiments conducted to replicate the Rio Chiriqui tool types, I could produce a reasonable celtlike wedge in ten to fifteen minutes. All other tool types can be replicated in less than five minutes.

The ground and polished stone industry is represented by fewer than half a dozen specimens in the preceramic period, all found in Boquete phase contexts. The axe, celt fragments, and chisel bit found in Casita de Piedra represent the work of skilled craftsmen. With so few specimens present, it is not possible to say whether or not they were made at the site or imported. Still, the presence of a ground and polished stone industry in the Boquete phase represents a significant addition to the stoneworking repertoire of the Rio Chiriqui preceramic population.

Most of the other tools (i.e., those not made by chipping or by grinding and polishing) were not manufactured at all, but were simply suitably shaped cobbles and boulders formed through use. The only ones purposefully manufactured were two rectangular handstones (manos) from Boquete phase deposits in Casita de Piedra, plus three mortars and miscellaneous fragments from both Boquete and Talamanca phase deposits. In contrast to this small number of shaped tools, edge-ground cobbles, faceted grinding stones, milling stone bases, pestles, nutting stones, battered choppers/hammers, edge-battered cobbles, end-battered hammers, and anvils (over 150 tools) were shaped only through use. Moreover, these tool types occur throughout the preceramic sequence with even less change in frequencies than is the case for the chipped stone tools.

In summary, strong technological continuities exist between the Talamanca and Boquete phases in the Rio Chiriqui sequence. The only technological changes are the increase in the use of the bipolar flaking technique in the later phase, and the concurrent introduction of grinding and polishing stone as a method of forming axes, celts, and chisels.

TOOL USE

Throughout the preceramic sequence, stone tools were used in four activities: manufacturing stone tools, working wood, processing plant food, and processing animal products. In the first category are stone tools that were used for making other stone tools. These anvils and a variety of hammerstones (end-battered hammers, edge-battered cobbles, and battered chopper/hammers) are present in both the Talamanca and Boquete phases in roughly equal numbers. Also a part of the stoneworking complex are the various cores identified in the assemblages. Irregular cores and bifacial cores are equally represented in both preceramic phases while bipolar cores become more frequent in the later Boquete phase. Although few in number (seven), the clustering of conical cores at the base of the Talamanca phase deposits helps to distinguish it from the succeeding phases.

Woodworking tools are the most common tool types throughout the Rio

Chiriqui sequence. The large bifacial wedges have very distinctive technological and functional attributes which leave little doubt as to how the tools were manufactured and used (see description of bifacial wedges). This tool type is found only in Talamanca phase contexts and is its most diagnostic artifact. The small tabular and broad-based wedges are also quite clearly used as wedges or chisels in woodworking. These small wedges are best considered to be restricted to Boquete phase deposits. Of 277 small wedges recovered in Casita de Piedra and the Trapiche Shelter, all but 16 came from the upper depositional unit (Boquete occupations), and 10 of these 16 came from the upper sublayer in the lower depositional unit. The 10 found in this upper sublayer probably got there through mixing of deposits either before or during excavation. The remaining 6 are likely to have been misidentified, since the tools are simple ones, and in appearance very much like some of the bipolar core remnants. At any rate, the tools dominate the Boquete phase assemblages and are either absent or a very minor element in the Talamanca phase assemblages. Small wedges are not a part of the Burica-Aguas Buenas stone industry, either in the Rio Chiriqui valley (only 1 of the 22 small wedges found in the Horacio Gonzales Site came from the ceramic layer, and it is considered to be intrusive), or at other occupation sites in the province (Shelton Einhaus, report no. 15; Ranere and Rosenthal, report no. 16; Sheets, Rosenthal, and Ranere, report no. 14).

Other tools seem associated with woodworking tool kits, based on replicative experiments and microscopic analysis of wear patterns (Ranere 1975). A number of the scraper-planes show wear polish extending from the tool edge back along the ventral surface. A few of the large flake scrapers and steep scrapers exhibit the same wear. This pattern of wear has been duplicated experimentally by pushing these tools along the surface of the wood to remove shavings. Concave scrapers or spokeshaves also appear to be woodworking tools based on replicative experiments and wear pattern analysis. All of these tool types (scraper-planes, flake scrapers, steep scrapers, and spokeshaves) occur in larger numbers during the Talamanca phase than in the following Boquete phase.

The engraving tools found in the Rio Chiriqui shelters may well have been woodworking tools (they could have been used on bone as well or instead). Burins characteristically occur in Talamanca phase deposits, while gravers are found throughout the preceramic (and ceramic) sequence.

One final chipped-stone tool type appears to hold woodworking tools: flake knives. A number of these knives have bifacial use retouch, which I was able to replicate by using hafted specimens for whittling wood. Other unyielding materials, like bone, seem likely to produce the same wear.

An entirely new set of woodworking tools, the polished stone axes and celts, appear in the Boquete phase and continue into the ceramic phases. The single grooved stone axe was obviously hafted with the bit edge parallel to the handle and used in the same manner as modern axes. The polished stone celt left in the wall of the excavation at the Zarsiadero Shelter was plano-convex in cross section and tapered toward the butt end. It was probably hafted as an adze blade with the bit edge perpendicular to the handle. A much smaller bit from Casita de Piedra was similarly hafted and used as an adze or chisel. The two additional celt fragments were too small to indicate hafting methods, but both seemed to have adzelike or chisellike bits. Although only five polished stone tools were recovered, they document an important advance in the manufacturing of woodworking tools in the Rio Chiriqui sequence introduced during the Boquete phase.

Edge-ground cobbles and milling stone bases, with which they are almost certainly associated, dominate the tool kit used in the preparation of plant foods. The edge-ground cobbles and their bases might better be thought of as mashing implements used in processing starchy roots (both wild and cultivated), rather than as seed-grinding implements as has been suggested for similar tools found at Cerro Mangote and Monagrillo in central Panama (Willey and McGimsey 1954; McGimsey 1956; Willey 1971). There are several reasons for suggesting this. First, the narrow edge on these cobbles seems better suited for pounding or mashing than for grinding of seeds (or so our experiments indicated). Second, the use of roots as a food source is more characteristic of tropical forest cultural patterns than the use of seeds. Finally, edge-ground cobbles or "edge-grinders" never have been associated with the grinding of seeds, but they are associated with processing roots (*camus* bulbs) in the Pacific Northwest region of North America (Butler 1962; Sims 1971). Edge-ground cobbles and their bases occur in approximately equal numbers in the two preceramic phases in the Rio Chiriqui sequence, and are absent from the ceramic phases.

Nutting stones are presumed to have been used in cracking nutshells, perhaps from the Corozo palm. Similar stones are used today for this purpose by local residents of the province. These stones occur in small numbers throughout the Rio Chiriqui sequence.

Added to the food-processing tool inventory during the Boquete phase are rectangular grinding stones (manos) and offset faceted grinding stones, elsewhere commonly associated with seed grinding. Pestles are similarly restricted to the Boquete phase. However, of the three mortars recovered, two came from Talamanca phase contexts, indicating that the grinding or pulverizing function implied for mortars and pestles (presumably for foodstuffs, but possibly not) was a feature common to both preceramic phases.

The stone assemblages from the Rio Chiriqui shelters dimly reflect the hunting and processing of animals (butchering, hide preparation, and working of bone), which must have been an important aspect of the economy. Although not directly used as hunting implements, woodworking tools, particularly spokeshaves, were undoubtedly used to make spear shafts and wooden projectile points. Other stone tools may have been directly used in butchering, dressing hides, and working bone. Cobble spall and flake choppers are possibly butchering tools. (Although far removed from Panama, identical tools were used in the northern Rockies for fleshing hides by the Northern Shoshoni — see Swanson and Sneed 1966; Ranere 1971.) Flake knives may also have been used in butchering, since the pattern of edge polish on some specimens suggests that they were used on a soft, pliable substance like meat or hides.

SUMMARY

In summary, distinctions between the two preceramic phases can be made on the following bases: (1) over 90 percent of the chipped stone in the Talamanca phase was andesite, while in the Boquete phase, chalcedony, quartz, and obsidian accounted for at least 25 percent and up to 50 percent of the chipped stone; (2) bifacial wedges were restricted to the Talamanca phase deposits, whereas small tabular and broad-based wedges were restricted (in all probability) to the Boquete phase where they accounted for up to 50 percent of the tools recovered; (3) scrapers make up from 30 percent to 55 percent of the chipped stone tool inventory in the Talamanca phase, 11 percent to 22 percent in the Boquete phase; (4) choppers and flake knives were more common in the Talamanca phase than in the Boquete phase; (5) blades and burins were both more numerous in the earlier Talamanca phase; (6) conical cores, with one exception, were found only in Talamanca phase deposits; (7) restricted to the Boquete phase were used quartz crystals, manos, faceted grinding stones, pestles, polished stone celts, polished stone axes, and (with one exception) edge-battered cobbles. Recovered in approximately equal numbers in both preceramic phases were edge-ground cobbles, grinding stone bases, end-battered hammers, anvils, nutting stones, irregular cores, and bifacial cores.

The stone tool assemblages for the ceramic phase can only be described as impoverished in comparison to the preceramic assemblages. Even beyond the obvious fact that the Late Bugaba and Chiriqui Classic phases have pottery, and the Talamanca and Boquete phases do not, the contrast between ceramic and preceramic occupations is striking.

Report Number 9

Ceramic Classes from the Volcan Baru Sites

S. SPANG, E.J. ROSENTHAL, O.F. LINARES

INTRODUCTION

This report is little more than a description of the ceramic classes that make up what we have called the Bugaba style. This style (Sackett 1977) dominated the highlands in the centuries between A.D. 200 and 600 (section 7.4). In order to facilitate statistical comparisons, we classified the collections in terms of several different criteria. First we sorted the pottery according to seven easily distinguished wares "defined solely on the basis of paste and surface finish" (Drennen 1976, p. 21). Then we used vessel forms, which we classified into three large groups: jars, closed bowls, and open bowls. The vessel appendages were sorted by shape into two large functional classes: supports and handles. Finally, we distinguished a number of surface-treatment techniques.

Each of these ceramic classes (i.e., wares, vessel forms, appendages, and surface decoration techniques) were used in separate chi-square tests comparing ceramic frequencies within and between the Volcan Baru sites (see section 7.4.c.).

CERAMIC WARES

I. Cerro Punta Orange Ware (fig. 9/1 a-d)

Manufactured by coiling; faint coil junctions remain only on a few sherds with imperfectly finished surfaces. (All of the Volcan pottery was probably manufactured by the coil method, so this trait will not be mentioned again.)

A. *Paste*

1. Temper: numerous gray, angular particles, larger than a pinpoint, often with dead-white, irregularly shaped inclusions evenly distributed throughout the paste.
2. Texture: generally compact.
3. Color: buff to orange throughout cross section when completely oxidized; a dark gray core occurs when incompletely oxidized. Paste may be brown if incompletely oxidized, or uniformly very dark gray if unoxidized, reduced, or possibly smudged.

B. *Surface*

1. Color: buff to light brown to very dark gray. Fire-clouding is rare.
2. Treatment: slightly smoothed to produce an even surface but never polished.
3. Decorative technique: a fairly thick orange to red slip made from clay containing hematite is applied to the vessel surface. The slip is hard and shiny and therefore appears to be polished although striations are not obvious. Usually, the slip either covers the interior and exterior of the vessel completely, or it covers the interior and lip, stopping to leave an unslipped band on the exterior, and then resumes to cover the exterior of the base. These two motifs occur on all forms. A few body sherds show slip only on the interior or only on the exterior. On certain vessels which are incompletely oxidized, unoxidized, or smudged, the slip may be brown or black. Very occasionally, the slip color is a very light beige.
4. Additional decoration: ornamentation occurs on some but not all vessels. Only certain portions of the vessel are decorated, usually the areas near the rim.
    a. Lines: grooving (width greater than 2 mm), wide incising (width between 1 and 2 mm), or narrow incising (width less than 1 mm) appear in the following designs: single line, rectangular, triangular, parallel, curvilinear, or combinations of these. Fluting, or wide square grooves (approx-

Figure 9/1: Ceramic wares from the Volcan Baru sites: a-d. Cerro Punta Orange; e-h. Valbuena; i-l. Bugaba Engraved (with negative paint in interior); m-p. Cotito; q-s. Zoned Bichrome; t-x. Combed.

imately 1–1.5 cm in width), also occurs. Grooving and incision decorate all jar forms (with and without necks) and bowls, while fluting appears only on restricted bowls.

b. Appliqués: pellets (raised nubbins), fillets (raised vertical bands), raised horizontal bands, plain and incised lobes, zoomorphic or anthropomorphic representations. All appear on both necked jars and bowls, except zoomorphic or anthropomorphic figures which occur only on restricted bowls.

c. Punctation: round and oval punctations appear on a few body sherds and on open or restricted bowls. Punctation was more common on those vessels partially slipped on the exterior.

II. *Valbuena Ware (fig. 9/1 e–h)*

A. Paste

1. Temper: most often temper consists of small, fine, sandlike particles which are evenly distributed throughout the paste. The clay is generally finer than that of Cerro Punta Orange Ware.

2. Texture: compact; paste feels like fine sandpaper.

3. Color: buff to light beige when completely oxidized. Incomplete oxidation leaves a dark gray core.

B. Surface

1. Color: buff to light beige. Fire-clouding rarely appears.

2. Treatment: smoothed to an even surface.

3. Decorative technique: a dark red (maroon) fugitive slip is applied to the vessel. The slip is fairly thin and never polished. The slip may cover both the interior and exterior of the vessel completely; or the interior slip may continue over to the exterior of the lip and stop, leaving an unslipped, smoothed band, and then resume to cover the base. Some body sherds have slip only on the interior, or only on the exterior.

III. *Bugaba Engraved Ware (fig. 9/1 i–l)*

A. Paste

1. Temper: angular sand particles slightly larger than a pinpoint, evenly distributed throughout the paste.

2. Texture: compact.

3. Color: buff to reddish brown. Often completely oxidized. Occasional incomplete oxidation leaves a dark gray core.

B. Surface

1. Color: buff to reddish brown. Fire-clouding rare.

2. Treatment: smoothed to an even surface.

3. Decorative technique: a red, sometimes orange, and infrequently maroon slip is applied to the vessel. The slip is fairly thick and polished. The slip covers both the interior and exterior of the vessel. Occasionally

different color slips occur on the same vessel (red and maroon or red and orange-red) to produce a zoned bichrome effect.

4. Additional decoration:

a. All vessels are decorated with *post-fire* incising. These lines are very thin as if made with a sharp, pointed tool; hence the term Engraved. Designs: rectilinear, triangular, curvilinear, parallel lines, or combinations of these. Other design elements such as dots and commas may be added. These designs cover the exterior sides and bottoms of the bowls. A human face with conical cap may be engraved on the bottom of some bowls. These engraved lines are occasionally filled with white pigment.

b. Interior-resist painting in black occurs on some vessels. Designs: black bands, honeycomb, oval triangular, bands and dots combined.

IV.   Cotito Ware (fig. 9/1 m-p)

With a larger sample, this style may prove to be simply a variety of Cerro Punta Orange.

A.   Paste

1. Technique of manufacture: probably coiling.
2. Temper: fine- to medium-grained, sandlike.
3. Texture: compact.
4. Color: buff to reddish orange. Incomplete oxidation leaves a dark gray core. No oxidation or reduction causes paste to become dark gray throughout the cross section.

B.   Surface

1. Color: buff or dark gray. No fire-clouding.
2. Treatment: smoothed to produce an even surface.
3. Form: only body sherds found. Thickness: 5–10 mm.
4. Decorative technique: a thick, orange slip, which may turn black due to reduction, or lack of oxidation, or possibly smudging, is applied to the vessel and polished. Generally, slip and polish occur on both the interior and exterior of a vessel. On one body, the exterior was left plain.
5. Additional decoration:

a. All sherds have tight parallel grooving or incising on the exterior.

b. Appliquéd plain lobes arranged in a flower design or surrounded by round punctations may be superimposed on the parallel lines.

V.   Zoned Bichrome Ware (fig. 9/1 q-s)

A.   Paste

1. Temper: fine to medium, gray, angular, sandlike particles evenly distributed throughout the paste.
2. Texture: fine-tempered sherds are compact, fine-grained, and feel like fine sandpaper. Those sherds with larger grain, more angular temper are also compact, but rougher.
3. Color: fine-tempered sherds are light beige. Occasionally, incom-

plete oxidation leaves a thin dark gray core. Sherds with larger grain temper seem to be buff to reddish brown in color. Cores are occasionally found.

4. Decorative technique: slip and polish are applied to the interior. Color may be red or orange. On urns, the slip also covers the exterior of the lip. Occasionally, the interior is left unslipped and smooth. The exterior is smoothed. Thin pigments of two colors may be applied: red with buff, orange-yellow with maroon, orange with red, and orange with buff. Urns are characteristically decorated in the latter two color schemes. The restricted bowl combines orange and red. Highly polished slip occurs only on the interior. The differently colored pigments on the exterior are separated by grooves or wide incisions in geometric designs.

VI. Combed Ware (fig. 9/1 t-x)

A. *Paste*

1. Temper: either fine, round or larger, angular sandlike particles are evenly mixed into the paste.
2. Texture: compact.
3. Color: gray brown to dark gray throughout cross section.

B. *Surface*

1. Color: brown or dark gray on the surface. Fire-clouding was not observed.
2. Treatment: slightly smoothed. Surface remains rough in some places.
3. Decorative techniques: a thick slip (orange, red, or maroon) is applied on the interior and over the lip and then polished. The exterior remains smoothed but unslipped. In one case, the interior and exterior are both slipped; in another, both are unslipped.
4. Additional decoration:

a. All vessels are characterized by exterior combing or thin, incised lines running parallel to each other and slightly curved, or are crosshatched. This is the most important feature defining this style.

b. One vessel (represented by a body sherd), which is unslipped on both interior and exterior, has traces of white paint on the exterior.

c. Certain particularly thick body sherds show appliquéd bands in zoomorphic motifs.

VII. Plain Ware

This category may in part be truly a ware and in part represented by sherds in which the slip has worn off completely.

A. *Paste*

1. Temper: fine, round or larger, angular sandlike particles, well distributed throughout the clay.
2. Texture: compact to friable.
3. Color: buff, light brown, light gray, light beige. Incomplete oxidation leaves occasional dark gray cores.

B.   Surface

   1.   Color: buff, light brown or gray, light beige.
   2.   Treatment: smoothed or very rarely unsmoothed and rough.
   3.   Decoration technique: smoothing, no polishing, on exterior and interior. Surfaces are even. The interior and exterior of the vessel are both smoothed, although the exterior is more carefully finished.
   4.   Additional decoration:
      a.   Lines, grooves, wide and narrow incisions are found on bowls and jars. Interrupted linear design appears on one body.
      b.   Appliqué. Plain lobes and a zoomorphic representation were found on body sherds.

VESSEL FORMS

I.   Jars (fig. 9/2 a-c)

These are rims, everted at a 45° to 90° angle from the shoulder, belonging to rounded globular vessels with distinct necks. The curvature of the neck varies from a sharp C-curve to a gentle, almost straight, line. There are two well-represented classes of jars.

   A.   Jars with short necks between 1.5 and 3 cm long.
   B.   Jars with medium-long necks, varying in length from over 3 to 6 cm.
   C.   A third, less numerous, class of jars has necks up to 12 cm long and rim diameters of more than 40 cm.

Lip forms in all three classes can be variable, but the most common form is an *exteriorly* thickened lip which can be twice as thick as the vessel wall. Lips can be less than 1 cm thick to almost 3 cm. Less common jar lip forms are unmodified, exteriorly ledge-shaped or, rarely, flat or tapering. Rim diameters range from 8 to 20 cm in the short and medium-long necked jars, to more than 40 cm in the very long-necked jars.

Because our initial sortings showed little difference in the frequency of jar neck-length classes through time, all jars were put together for analysis. Jar shapes are found in most of the wares: Cerro Punta Orange, Valbuena, Zoned Bichrome, and Plain, but are nonexistent or at least not very common in the Bugaba Engraved and Cotito wares.

II.   Restricted Bowls (fig. 9/2 d-h)

These are "closed" bowls characterized by straight to incurved rims at angles of between 90° and 135°, either continuous with the vessel wall or meeting the shoulder at an angle. With the exception of the S-shaped bowls, restricted rims have no necks. They can belong to deep bowls, 6 to 12 cm in depth, or to very shallow bowls measuring less than 3 cm from the underside of the lip to the center point on the interior of the vessel. Both deep and shallow restricted bowls show variation in lip form and shape of vessel wall. Some of the variations are:

A.   Shallow bowls with incurved rims and either unmodified, tapered, or blunted lips. Their most characteristic features are a bright red polished slip and a wide incision or "carination" just below the lip, giving it a "notched" appearance in profile (fig. 9/2 e, f). These rims may be plain, decorated with punctations, or bear appliquéd or high-relief figurines serving as handles. They are characteristic of Cerro Punta Orange Ware.

B.   Simple, shallow bowls with sharply incurved rims, rounded or angular shoulders, and tapered lips that are *not* grooved or carinated like the ones above (fig. 9/2 d). These are covered with a fugitive, dark red (or maroon) slip or wash; roughly half of them also have a simple pellet or arm motif applied to the upper wall section. They are characteristic of Valbuena Ware.

C.   S-shaped bowls with gently curved body walls and either blunted or unmodified lips (fig. 9/2 g). These are covered with a maroon slip and usually decorated in the upper segment with parallel shallow ridges or incisions, vertically placed or at a slant to the lip. They are characteristic of Valbuena Ware.

D.   Composite silhouette bowls (fig. 9/2 h) that "have a curved upper wall segment which is convex inwards, separated from a lower wall segment which is either straight or convex outwards" (Drennan 1976, p. 25). They are characteristic of Bugaba Engraved Ware, which also has shallow unmodified simple incurved bowls.

E.   Deep restricted bowls (fig. 9/3 a-c) with narrow mouth apertures, averaging about 14 cm. (This is known as the "tecomate" shape in Mesoamerica.) They are characteristic of Cerro Punta Orange and Valbuena wares. Restricted bowls occur in almost all of the Volcan wares and are more distinctive but less common than jars.

III.   Open Bowls (fig. 9/3 d-f)

These are flaring, usually shallow bowls (though some deep ones do occur), with tapered, unmodified or very commonly, interiorly thickened, flat-topped lips. The interior may or may not be slipped, and the exterior may or may not be decorated with incisions, excisions (i.e., engraving), or wide-line "grooving." Very rarely, the interior may be decorated with low-relief appliqué. There are several variants:

A.   Open bowls with curved walls continuous with the vessel wall.

B.   Open bowls with insloping or everted walls that look slightly concave (viewed from the exterior) as they curve from lip to base.

C.   Bowls with rounded or flat bases, or with tripod feet, ringstands, or pedestal supports.

Open bowls are less numerous than restricted bowls; they are most common on the floor unit of the oval dwelling at the Pitti locality.

APPENDAGES

It is in this category of handles, supports, and appliquéd motifs that the Volcan pottery exhibits greatest variation and elaboration. Appendages are

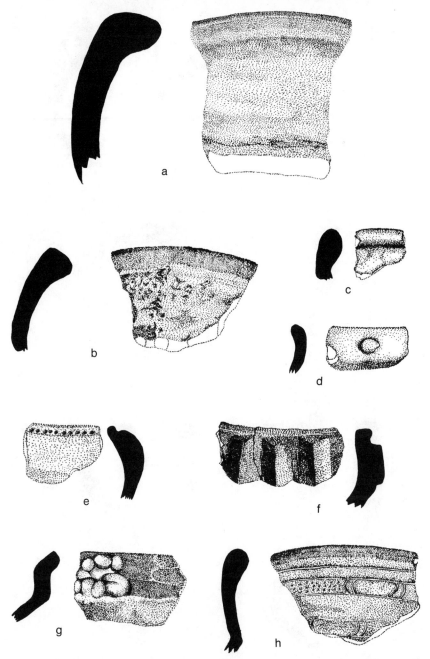

Figure 9/2: Vessel shapes from the Volcan Baru sites: a-c. jars; d-h. restricted bowls.

not always found attached to rims, nor do they always exhibit clearcut attributes of paste and surface finish characterizing the different wares. Thus we have chosen to describe appendages separately, linking them to wares and/or shapes only when we are certain of the connection. Within

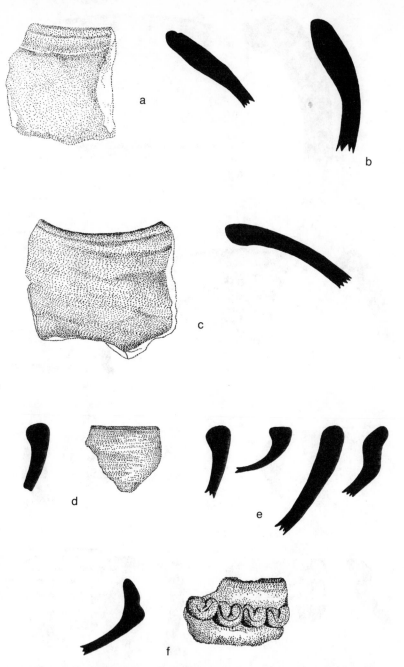

Figure 9/3: Vessel shapes from the Volcan Baru sites: a–c. deep restricted bowls; d–f. open bowls.

each category (i.e., handles, tripod feet, and so forth), attribute clusters, commonly known as modes (Rouse 1939; Linares 1968b, p. 48), can be recognized on the basis of shape, technique of manufacture, or decoration. Individual attributes (e.g., incising) are found in several wares (e.g., ring-

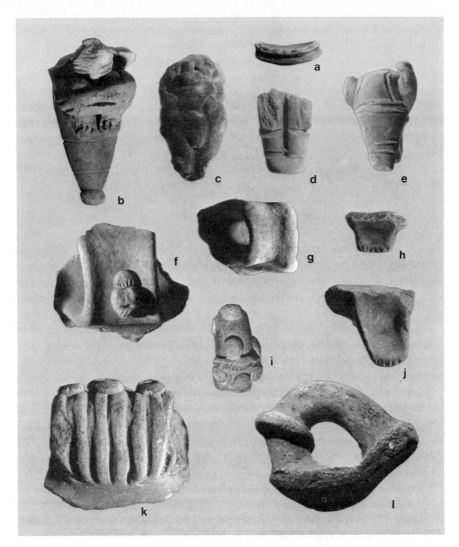

Figure 9/4: Appendages on vessels from the Volcan Baru sites: a. Ringstand; b. repre-sentational tripod; c. Venus tripod; d. double-legged tripod; e. grooved tripod; f. medium-sized strap; g. small strap; h. tab support; i. round handle; j. tab support; k. wide strap (corrugated) handle; l. round handle.

stands or tripod feet). The individual modes were not numerous enough to have tabulated separately, so they are purely descriptive classes.

I. Ringstands, Pedestals, and Basal Bands

A. Ringstands are circular base supports less than 2 cm high, with diameters ranging from 6 to 10 cm across the bottom (fig. 9/4 a). The exterior surface may be smoothed but unslipped, or it may be decorated with grooved lines where it joins the vessel bottom. Low ringstands, covered with a maroon slip on the inside and/or outside, belong with the Valbuena

Ware. A few ringstands are attached to parts of bowls that are engraved and thus belong with the Bugaba Engraved Ware.

B. Pedestal bases are tall, circular bases, between 2.5 cm and 6 cm high (fig. 9/5 b). The only complete specimen we have measures 15.5 cm in diameter on the underside at the widest point. The surfaces are smooth, never polished, and can be covered with a red, maroon, beige, or orange slip; in addition, surfaces can be decorated with widely spaced concentric or scalloped grooved and incised lines. A few have holes pierced through the center.

C. Basal bands are simply raised bands forming a circle on the vessel bottoms (fig. 9/5 a). Several specimens have a red slip.

II. Tripod Feet

This is a very varied category. Tripods may be hollow or solid, slipped or unslipped, tubular or bulging, plain or grooved, with unmodified or "nubbin" tips, with or without appliquéd motifs, with holes or with slits; they also may be "abstract" or representational. Some of the more common and/or more striking modes are:

A. Venus tripods (figs. 9/4 c, 9/5 c,d). These are solid, sometimes red slipped, in the shape of a bulging female figure with its sexual parts emphasized by pellet appliqués; in some the legs were not fused together, but split in the center as in mode B below. In the only specimen we have in which the legs are still attached, the vessel form is an open globular bowl.

B. Double-leg human (male?) tripods (figs. 9/4d, 9/5e). These are fairly straightsided, solid tripods, with a deep groove down the center, separating the legs; crossed grooves, plus pellets, were used to indicate knees and/or possibly details of body ornaments or armatures. No specimen is complete enough to show the top, but details of the buttocks and deemphasis of the pubic area suggest a male figure.

C. Grooved tripods (figs. 9/4 e, 9/5 f, g). These may be tapered and solid or, more commonly, bulging in shape and hollow, with "rattle" holes on the front and/or back. Wide, incised lines (i.e., grooves) occur and are placed horizontally across the bottom and midline, or vertically. The top of some tripods bears a pair of pellets. Some are slipped and at least one is zoned bichromed. The tips may be tapered, or end up in nubbins; a few are curled over in a scroll shape.

D. Representational tripods are all of humans in recognizable poses or with recognizable traits (figs. 9/4 b, 9/5 h). The most striking modes are a male figure carrying a staff and another figure squatting and holding its legs; both are common iconographic motifs in the well-known Barriles statues. Other human forms are recognizable, but less "realistic," with only a few body parts shown and not in proportion.

E. The only tall, plain tripods we have are hollow. One is an appliquéd (i.e., semidetached) specimen and the other is free-standing.

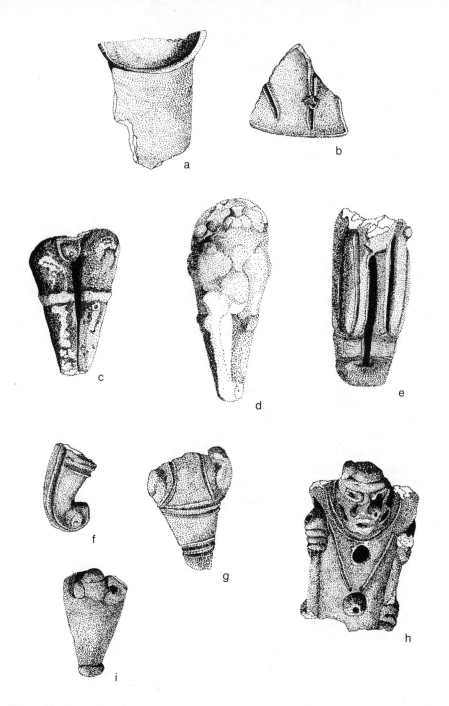

Figure 9/5: Drawing of appendages on vessels from Volcan Baru sites: a. basal band; b. pedestal base; c,d. Venus tripods; e. double-legged tripod; f,g. grooved tripod; h. representational tripod; i. semirepresentational (?) tripod.

III. Strap Handles

These are flat in cross section with rounded edges which are occasionally upturned, looking "swollen." Straps may be attached to the vessel just under the lip, on the shoulder, or just below the shoulder. They vary markedly in shape, size, and decoration.

A.   Small straps are less than 3 cm wide and are undecorated except for a red slip at the base and on the underside of the vessel to which they were once attached (fig. 9/4 g).

B.   Medium-sized straps are between 3 and 4.5 cm wide at the narrowest point; they may be gradually or very strongly tapered (figs. 9/4 f, 9/6 a-c). Unlike the small straps, they are often red-slipped on the top as well as on the base. One specimen is decorated with a pellet appliqué.

C.   Wide strap handles can measure up to 12 cm across (fig. 9/4 k). Two shapes are characteristic: gradually curved and sharply folded into a marked loop. Except for a red slip, they seem to have no other decoration on the surface.

D.   Corrugated strap handles are fairly wide (about 6 cm across), sharply curved, and are slipped on the "fluted" or corrugated surface as well as on the inside of the body to which they were once attached. One specimen has appliquéd "coffee-bean" motifs (fig. 9/6 d).

IV. Tabs (fig. 9/6 g,h)

These may have served as handles or as supports, and it isn't always possible to tell one group from the other. They are thin slabs, often indented in the middle, wider than they are long. They were attached at right angles to the vessel wall, just below the lip, if they served as handles, and to the underside of the vessel if they served as supports. The edges of the tabs may be scalloped in both the handles and the supports.

Some tabs are zoomorphic, extending out in a frog-head motif, and many of the relief appliquéd motifs described subsequently may have also served as handles.

V. Miscellaneous Appendages

These are not numerous enough to have been quantified and tested for intra- and intersite distinctions. However, some of these modes are so distinctive as to indicate unquestionable contemporaneity and contact between the Volcan sites and other Bugaba period sites or occupations in other regions. They are thus useful in regional comparisons.

A.   Webbed foot (figs. 9/4 m,n, 9/6 k). This is one of the most distinctive supports, occurring abundantly in the Concepción phase of the mid-elevation highlands and on the coast. Two such modes occurred in our collections, both on the lower stratigraphic units of sites BU-17b (below the floor) and BU-24 (cut 2, unit 6).

B.   Tab supports (figs. 9/4 h, j, 9/6 e,f). These are roughly tapered, thin, elongated slabs with upturned edges and occasionally scalloped tips.

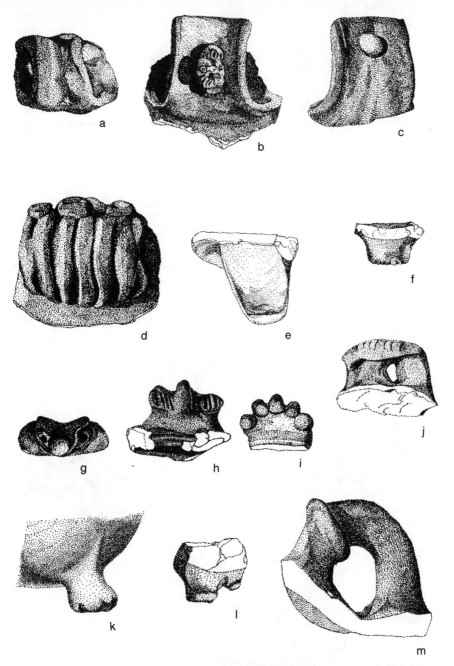

Figure 9/6: Drawing of appendages on vessels from Volcan Baru sites: a-c. medium-sized strap handles; d. carinated strap handle; e,f. tab supports; g-j. tabs (probably handles); k. webbed foot (La Concepción complex); l. square base; m. round handle.

C. Exterior flanges that may have facilitated lifting shallow bowls and/or other lightweight vessels.

D. Interior flanges that probably served to support lids.

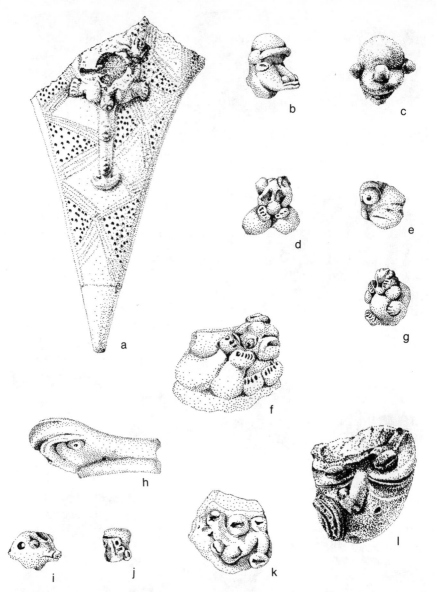

Figure 9/7: Drawing of appendages on vessels from Volcan Baru sites: a. stilt support; b–j. adornos; k,l. low relief appliquéd motifs.

E. Round handles that are twisted, decorated with raised bands and/or pellets, sometimes rendering zoomorphic motifs (figs. 9/4 i,l, 9/6 m).

F. Square bases that must have accompanied flaring bowls with or without supports (fig. 9/6 l).

G. Pierced "holes" that may have been put through pedestal bases.

H. Corrugated necks(?).

I. Stilt supports (fig. 9/7a). These are long, flat, triangular, outcurved flaps connecting with the vessel wall and tapering down to a point. They are uncommon, but very distinctive.

J.   Adornos (figs. 9/7b-j, 9/8 a-h, j). Numerous and varied appliquéd semidetached figurines, built up from rounded pellets and applied strips, are found in the Volcan ceramics. They seem to represent mammals with bulging coffee-bean eyes, protruding ears and snouts, and holding their heads. Some may have stood for humans. A "toucan" motif is also fairly common (figs. 9/7e, h, 9/8 j). Most appliquéd figurines were appended to bowls where they clearly served as handles.

K.   Low-relief appliquéd motifs. These are usually pellets, lobes, and bands, plain or incised. A few were made to represent faces, or a toucan, or a lizard. They are widely distributed within and between sites (figs. 9/7 k,l, 9/8 i).

SURFACE TREATMENT TECHNIQUES

I.   Incised or grooved body sherds have wide, shallow incisions, often arranged in pairs. Grooving occurs especially on the Cotito Ware (fig. 9/1 m-p), but is absent from the Bugaba Engraved and the Combed or Brushed wares. (Zoned Bichrome sherds are all grooved, but they are considered separately.) Any part of the vessel's exterior may be grooved, but grooving occurs most often at the base of the neck, at the shoulder, or on pedestal bases.

II.   Engraving is a special category of fine-line incising done after the vessel has been slipped in red and is very dry previous to firing. It is characteristic of Bugaba Engraved Ware (fig. 9/1 i, j). Engraved lines often have jagged "scratchy looking" edges; the incisions occasionally are filled in with white paint. Some of the most common engraved designs are combinations of parallel lines 20 mm to 35 mm apart, arranged at right angles or in concentric triangles and rectangles, or occasionally in a kind of animal "paw" motif. These designs cover the exterior walls and bottom of bowls. A human face with a conical cap and some other very complex and continuous design arrangements may be engraved all over the sides and/or bases of a bowl, usually extending right up to the lip area.

III.   Negative painting (fig. 9/1 k, l). Some engraved sherds also have negative-painted designs in the interior with black bands, honeycombs, ovals, triangles, bands, and dots, all combined.

IV.   Zoned Bichroming (fig. 9/1 q-s) is a technique whereby geometric designs, first grooved on the vessel exterior and the enclosed areas (or zones), are then painted with more than one thin layer or pigment of a red, yellowish and/or beige color. The *interior* of zoned bichromed sherds is usually slipped in red, and the body walls are usually thick (1 cm or more). This technique occurs on the body and rim of large jars, sometimes known as urns.

V.   Combed or Multiple Incised (fig. 9/1 t-x) is the technique that used to be called "Scarified" by Holmes (1888) and MacCurdy (1911). It consists of

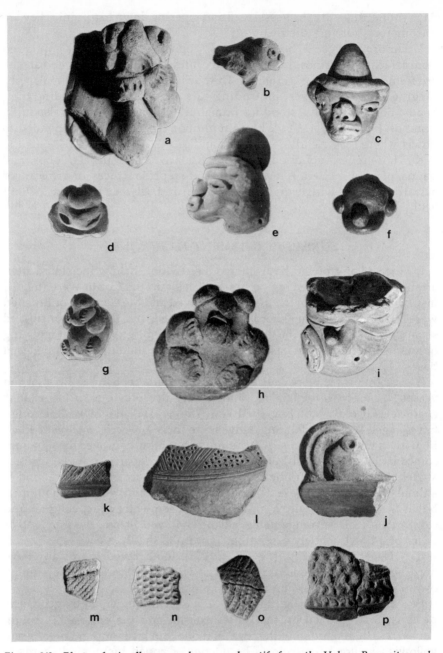

Figure 9/8: Photo of miscellaneous adornos and motifs from the Volcan Baru sites: a-h. adornos; i. low relief motif; j. adorno; k-p. surface treatment variations.

first smoothing the exterior of the vessel, then running over the surface with a multipronged instrument like a comb which leaves shallow, closely spaced but nonequidistant incisions.

VI. Miscellaneous surface treatments (fig. 9/8 k-p). Multiple small punctations, rows of raised "buttons," jab and drag, stamped circles, and shell impressions occur in combination with grooved lines and/or a red slip in certain portions of the vessel. A very few sherds (about three) have wide red bands on the exterior; these are not to be confused, however, with the San Lorenzo wares of site IS-3. For all intents and purposes, there are no painted wares in the Volcan collections.

Report Number 10

Ceramic Classes from La Pitahaya (IS-3)

O. F. LINARES

INTRODUCTION

Because the pottery from La Pitahaya has been thoroughly described (Linares 1968b), we will include here only a brief summary of the nine rim classes sorted by computer and by hand (see report no. 13) and of the seven appendage classes, all of them used in the quantitative analysis. The first three rim classes belong to the Bugaba phase, the next three to the San Lorenzo phase, and the last three to the Chiriqui phase.

RIM CLASSES

I.   Jars with long necks, flaring rims, and exteriorly thickened lips (fig. 10/1 a) that are always much thicker than the vessel wall (sect. 7.0, fig. 7.0-4, type 1; Linares 1968b, pp. 18–19, fig. 11).This group duplicates the medium- and long-necked jars of Valbuena Ware from Volcan (fig. 9/2 a,b).

II.   Straight-sided, gently S-shaped, and composite silhouette bowls with slightly thickened lips (fig. 10/1 b). Typically there are multiple parallel depressions or ridges on the exterior below and at an angle to the lip (sect. 7.0, fig. 7.0-4, type 2; Linares 1968b, group 3 rims, p. 19 and p. 20, fig. 12 i, j, n-t). This group duplicates the restricted S-shaped and composite silhouette bowls of the Volcan Valbuena Ware (fig. 9/2 g, h).

III.   A very shallow bowl with gently or sharply incurved rim (fig. 10/1 c, d) and lips that are slightly thickened, tapered, notched (sect. 7.0, fig. 7.0-4, type 3; Linares 1968b, p. 19, group 2 rims, fig. 12 k-m). This group duplicates the shallow bowls with incurving rims of the Volcan Valbuena Ware (fig. 9/2 d-f).

IV and V.   Plain convex rims from necked jars (fig. 10/1 f). There is a rounded but distinct shoulder, and the lip is unmodified in class 4 and flattened so that it slants inward in class 5. Decoration is usually absent, though the lip is frequently painted red. These rims belong to the Arayo Polished Line and Caco Red Slipped types of the San Lorenzo phase in the Gulf of Chiriqui (sect. 7.0, fig. 7.0-4, type 9; Linares 1968b, pp. 24–27, fig. 24 and fig. 17 a-c).

VI. Incurving rims belonging to shallow or to deep bowls typically decorated with painted line designs or red slip on the exterior upper wall sections (fig. 10/1 g, h). These bowls once rested on strapped feet. They belong to the Cangrejal Red Line and Caco Red Slipped types of the San Lorenzo phase in the Chiriqui Gulf (sect. 7.0, fig. 7.0-4, type 5; Linares 1968b, pp. 26–29, figs. 17 and 18).

VII and VIII. Outflaring open bowl rims (fig. 10/1e, i-k) belonging to a platterlike vessel with outwardly slanting rims which are gently S-curved and straight (sect. 7.0, fig. 7.0-4, types 6, 7). Both classes often have a red painted lip and a red painted design, on the interior, composed of red slipped areas or parallel bands and lines. They rested on ringstands and pedestal bases. These bowls belong to the Castrellon Red Slipped and Zapote Red Banded types of the San Lorenzo phase in the Gulf of Chiriqui (Linares 1968b, pp. 30–31, 35–36, figs. 19 and 24).

IX. A globular vessel, with a slightly concave, outward slanting rim, which rises from a gently rounded and barely perceptible shoulder. The lip is either unmodified or tapered. This seems to be a new class which has merged with classes 10 and 11 for quantification. It belongs to the Chiriqui phase of the Gulf of Chiriqui (Linares 1968b, pp. 37–43).

X. Outflaring jar rims with short to fairly long necks and folded-over lips that give it a bulging, rough exterior (fig. 10/1 l, m). These rims are characterstic of the type Villalba Red Streaked (sect. 7.0, fig. 7.0-4, types 9, 10; Linares 1968b, pp. 41–43, fig. 27), which in turn is diagnostic of the Chiriqui phase.

XI. Thin-walled, salmon-colored jars with small, straight to outflared rims that are often exteriorly thickened (fig. 10/1 n-p). They are usually decorated on the neck with appliquéd leaf and/or circle motifs. These rims are easily recognized, as they belong to the Tarrago Bisquit Ware, characteristic of the Chiriqui phase in the Gulf (sect. 7.0, fig. 7.0-4, type 8; Linares 1968b, pp. 38–41, fig. 26a-d and t-v).

APPENDAGES

These are supports and handles, usually found alone; when they occur attached to rims, they are still classified as appendages.

I. Wide, strap handles are flat in cross section and may be fairly straight-sided or strongly tapered (fig. 10/2 a-c). They range in width between 6 cm and 12 cm, and are often decorated with a red band on the sides and/or appliquéd motifs. They belong to the San Lorenzo phase (Linares 1968b, pp. 55–56, fig. 35).

II. Strapped feet and/or narrow handles are flat, ribbonlike straps (2–4 cm wide) which may have occurred in sets of three and served as supports; when they are found isolated, it is impossible to tell if they were supports or

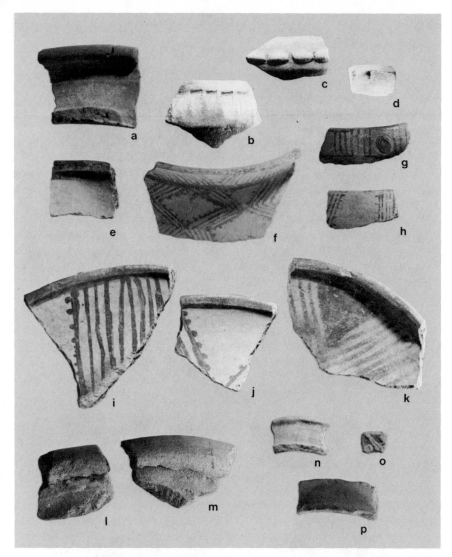

Figure 10/1: Rim classes from La Pitahaya (IS-3): a. rim with exteriorly thickened lip belonging to long-necked jars; b. straight or gently curved rim from shallow bowls; c,d. incurved rim from very shallow bowls; e. outflaring rim from open bowl with red lip; f. convex rims from plain necked jars; g, h. incurved rims from medium-deep bowls with painted exteriors; i-k. outflaring rims from open bowls with red painted lines; l-m. outflaring jar rims with folded lip; n-p. thin-walled Bisquit small jar rims.

strapped handles (fig. 10/2 d,e). They are usually plain, belonging to the San Lorenzo phase in the Gulf of Chiriqui (Linares 1968b, pp. 53–54, fig. 33).

III.   Double handles are large, looped handles, horizontally placed on each side of the vessel, curving upward and fusing with the lip (fig. 10/2 g). They may be as small as 6 cm or as large as 15 cm between points of attachment. Although some occur in the San Lorenzo phase, they are characteristic of the Chiriqui phase (Linares 1968b, pp. 54–56, fig. 34).

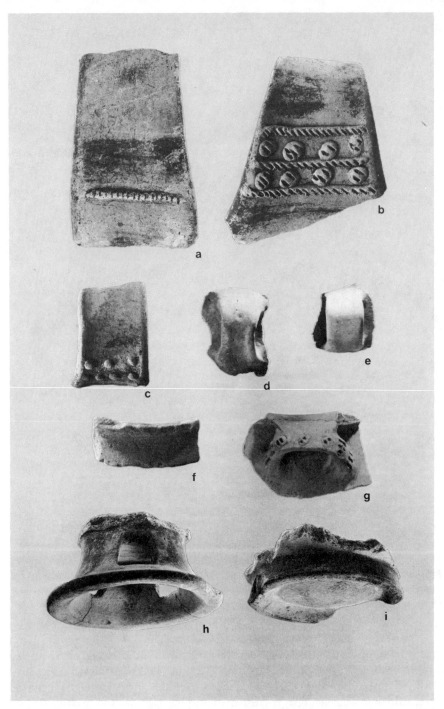

Figure 10/2: Appendages from La Pitahaya (IS-3) ceramics: a-c. wide and medium-width strap handles; d,e. strapped feet and/or narrow handles; f. low, thick ringstand; g. double handle; h. pedestal base; i. thin ringstand.

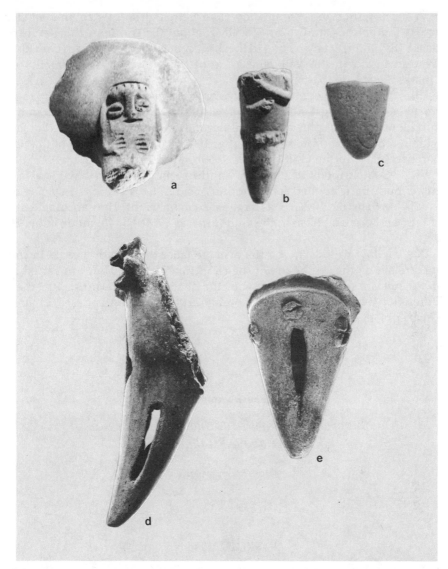

Figure 10/3: Appendages (tripods) from La Pitahaya (IS-3) ceramics: a,b. solid anthropo-morphic; c. small, nonrepresentational; d,e. hollow with rattles.

IV. Round or double handles may actually be fragments from the mid-section of double handles and are, therefore, grouped with that class.

V. Low, thick ringstands range from 2 to 4 cm in height and from 7 to 14 cm in diameter across the bottom (fig. 10/2 f). They have fairly thick walls (1.0 cm) and are usually decorated on the inside (on what would be the vessel's bottom) with a red slip or red bands; in some, the exterior is also slipped. Thick ringstands go with the Zapote Red Banded type and are diagnostic of the San Lorenzo phase in the Gulf of Chiriqui (Linares 1968b, p. 51, modes b, c, d, fig. 31d).

VI.   Thin ringstands are smaller (1.0–1.5 cm high and 4–8 cm in diameter across the bottom) and thinner walled (about 0.5 cm) than ringstands of class 5 (fig. 10/2 i). They belong to the Burica phase of the Chiriqui Gulf (and are also found in the Valbuena Ware of Volcan). (For more details see Linares 1968b, pp. 50–51, fig. 31.)

VII.   Pedestal bases are taller (6 cm or more) and usually larger (up to 12 cm across) than ringstands, and they also have slits or perforations in the middle of the base, plus additional decoration such as red slipped areas, wide red bands, and incised lines (fig. 10/2 h). They are typical of the San Lorenzo phase in the Gulf (Linares 1968b, pp. 51–53, fig. 32).

VIII.   Solid tripods are usually "anthropomorphic" in having a face and/or body parts applied at the top and/or sides (fig. 10/3 a,b). They may be as small as 6 cm (fig. 10/3 c) or as large as 25 cm in height. They are diagnostic of the San Lorenzo phase in the Gulf (Linares 1968b, p. 46, mode a, fig. 30 a-f).

IX.   Hollow tripods are on the average taller than solid ones (9–15 cm) and are slit on the center and/or the sides for "rattles." They are varied in shape but are usually abstract or in the shape of animals (fig. 10/3 d,e). Different types belong to the San Lorenzo and the Chiriqui phases (Linares 1968b, pp. 48–50, modes b-i).

Report Number 11

Polychrome Pottery from the Central Region of Panama at La Pitahaya (IS-3)

R. G. COOKE

INTRODUCTION

Thirty sherds recovered at IS-3 in 1961 (Linares 1968b, table 1) and 173 from the 1971 excavations (these representing at least 134 different vessels, table 1) bear painted designs that are anomalous in the total pottery sample from the site. By "painted" I mean employing a design that is painted in any color but red alone, either singly or in combination with other colors, upon a slip or the natural surface of the clay. With the exception of four sherds which are probably from Nicoya, Costa Rica, all of the others must have originated to the east of the present-day boundaries of Chiriqui, at one or more localities between the river Tabasara and the westernmost part of Panama province. Throughout this area — referred to elsewhere as the "central provinces" (Cooke 1972 and 1976a), or the "central region" of a tripartite, east-west division of the Isthmus (Cooke 1976) — an as yet unspecified number of manufacturing centers produced painted wares, using between one and five nonred pigments. These wares represent a gradually evolving technical and iconographic tradition that is markedly different from the one described in this volume for western Panama.

In addition to the painted wares, at least five red-slipped sherds have rim and appendage forms that are identical to those of the central region, and are likely to have been imported therefrom.

The possibility should also be entertained that some San Lorenzo phase pottery types characteristic of the locally made ceramics at IS-3 (Linares 1968b) were, in some way, imitative of central region pottery.

THE CENTRAL REGION AS A CULTURAL UNIT

Before discussing the relevance of the pottery from the central region to the archaeology of IS-3, it should be stressed that I do not accept the idea proposed by other authors, that the region be divided into two or three distinct "culture areas" called "Cocle," "Veraguas," and "Azuero" (Lothrop 1942, 1950, and 1966; Dade 1961; Ladd 1964; Willey 1971; Ichon 1974). Rather, I advocate (Cooke 1972, 1976a and b) the development of a distinct ceramic style west of Chame and east of Chiriqui, resulting from cultural contacts between antagonistic, but ethnically related social units occupying contiguous, environmentally circumscribed territories along the Pacific coastal plains and the larger montane valleys of both coasts (Linares 1977b). That differences in the painted ceramics found across the central region exist is indisputable (cf. Ichon 1974), but they are best regarded as local manifestations of a generalized cultural pattern. These differences were probably determined not by social or geographic isolation nor by foreign influences (cf. Ichon 1974, p. 317) but by more specific factors, such as the distribution and accessibility of raw materials, the location of manufacturing or trading centers, and the idiosyncracies of individual groups of potters.

THE CHRONOLOGY OF THE CENTRAL REGION

Those sherds that can be assigned with certainty to the central region (63.9 percent of the total, n=108) cover six periods, namely, periods IV to VIIB (Cooke 1976b, table 2). It seems that "trade" or some kind of direct or indirect contact between IS-3 and this area was most intense during periods V and VIA, from ca. A.D. 500 to ca. A.D. 900, with more sporadic contact just before and after this time-span. The relative dates that appear in table 1 are based on the 26 radiocarbon determinations now available for the periods relevant to our discussion.

A brief word about the nature and validity of the chronology proposed for the central region is in order. Temporal divisions have been based on "key" technological and decorative innovations within the painted pottery tradition. These "innovations" are displayed in one or two bichrome, trichrome, and polychrome "ceramic groups" per period; these groups are

TABLE 1   THE DISTRIBUTION OF NON–CHIRIQUIAN POTTERY AT IS-3, BY EXCAVATION UNIT

(Painted and red-slipped varieties)

Excavation Unit	EL HATILLO		PARITA		POST-MACARACAS		MACARACAS (Cuipo)		MACARACAS (Higo/P-Pica)		POST-CONTE		CONTE Polychrome		CONTE Red		MONTEVIDEO		TONOSÍ		NICOYA ?		Unclassifiable		TOTAL SHERDS	TOTAL VESSELS
	S	V	S	V	S	V	S	V	S	V	S	V	S	V	S	V	S	V	S	V	S	V	S	V		
TRENCH I, CUT I																										
A and B																									0	0
C							1	1	2	2	3	3	1	1			1	1					8	8	16	16
D and E																									0	0
TRENCH II, CUT 3																										
A and B			1	1																			3[b]	3	4	4
C									1	1			2	2					4	2			4	4	11	9
D and E									1[e]		3	3	1	1									9	9	14	13
TRENCH II, BLOCK I																										
Surface													1	1					1[d]	1					2	2
A and B													2	3					1	1			5	5	11	10
C	1?	2					2/1	3	7	2/19	2[c]	2	8	11	3	3	1	1			1	2	8	8	52	34
D and E	1	2[a]			1	1							4	5									2	2	8	7

TRENCH II, BLOCK II														
A and B					12 1	1 1[b]	4 3					5 5	22	10
C	1 1[a]			1 1	1 1	1 1	10 8				1 ? 1	3 3	18	16
D and E		1 1			1 1		3 3					1 1	6	6
TRENCH IV						1 1	3 1						4	2
TRENCH VI, CUT I											1 1		1	1
TRENCH VII, CUT I														
A (Surface)													0	0
B						2 2[b]	1 1						3	3
C	1 1[a]				2 2		2 2						5	5
D and E												1 1	1	1
Totals	5 5	2 2	1 1	5 3	38 15	13 13	48 37	3 3	2 2	6 4	4 3	49 49	178[f]	139
				45	20									
Approx. Date	1520	1300	1100	900	700			A.D.500		B.C.100?				
Period	VIIB	VIIA		VIB	VIA		V	V	IV	IV				

Key to symbols: a = Mendoza-style plates
b = Polychrome pedestals
c = Red pedestals + incisions
d = Has nubbin foot
e = Pottery disk
f = Of the 178 anomalous sherds, 173 are painted and 5 are red-slipped

sometimes further divided into varieties, following Ladd's (1964) original system.

The ceramic groups have been defined arbitrarily on the basis of a handful of pottery samples recovered and described from discrete contexts: the grave lots from Sitio Conte (Mason 1940; Lothrop 1942), various sites excavated by the National Geographic and Smithsonian expeditions (Ladd 1964), several localities in the vicinity of Tonosi (Ichon 1974), and domestic refuse from stratified sites in western Cocle (Ladd 1964; Cooke 1972) and Azuero (Ichon 1974; Ladd 1964). As each of the ceramic groups defined is part of a slowly and, apparently, intrinsically changing tradition that spans some 2,000 years, the temporal divisions that have been made are, by their very nature, artificial and must have between them an equivalent or greater number of "transitions." Two such "transitions" have already been suggested — the Montevideo "subgroup," between Tonosi and Conte (Ichon 1974, pp. 220–226; Cooke 1976b, pp. 128–129), and the so-called Late Cocle pottery from Sitio Conte that lies midway between Conte and Macaracas (Cooke 1972, chapter 4 and 1976b, p. 129).

In the interpretation of the small sample from IS-3, the temporary nature of these divisions must be borne in mind, and the assignment of comfortable round-figure dates to the periods must be viewed with caution. The flaws in the existing system typify the problem of maintaining a type-variety scheme, especially when one is working with highly complex designs recovered, for the most part, in sherd lots, rather than in properly excavated and dated funerary samples. The latter end of the sequence (A.D. 900–1520) is particularly blurred; this is unfortunate as far as IS-3 is concerned, as the final abandonment and/or change in function of the site seems to have occurred during this period.

THE "TRADE" SHERDS AND THEIR IDENTIFICATION

Table 1 summarizes the occurrence of the central region pottery — both painted and red-slipped — in the different excavation units at IS-3. The stratigraphic positions of the materials recovered in the 1962 digs are recorded elsewhere (Linares 1968b, table 1). Our comments pertain solely to the 1971 sample.

Table 2 presents, for the entire excavated area that contained traded pottery, the distribution of the various painted categories per period: both the "absolute number of sherds" (ANS) and the "minimum numbers of vessels" (to coin phrases from faunal analysis).

Before commenting on the vertical distribution of the sherds in the various cuts at IS-3, some information should be provided about those sherds which mark the beginning and end of the period under consideration, and whose classification is sometimes unclear.

I. Probable Period VII Mendoza-group Sherds

The characteristic bowl of Period VII in the central region has a lightly S-shaped profile and usually rests on a short, flaring pedestal (Ladd 1964,

TABLE 2 TOTALS OF CENTRAL REGION PAINTED WARES AT IS-3 ARRANGED BY PERIOD

(Those painted sherds which cannot be classified to period or group of periods have been excluded from this table)

Pottery group	ANS	%	MNV	%	Date
El Hatillo	5	4.2	5	6.2	A.D. 1520–1300
Parita	2	1.7	2	2.5	1300–1100
Either El Hatillo or Parita	1	0.8	1	1.2	
Period VII (total)	8	6.7	8	9.9	1520–1100
Macaracas (Cuipo)	5	4.2	3	3.7	1100– 900
Macaracas (Higo/Pica-Pica)	38	31.9	15	18.5	900– 700
Macaracas (all varieties)	2	1.7	2	2.5	
Period VI (total)	45	37.8	20	24.6	1100– 700
Sherds which are either Period VI or VII	11	9.2	11	13.6	1520– 700
Periods VI and VII (total)	64	54.6	39	49.3	1520– 700
Conte (Period V) (total)	48	40.3	37	45.6	700– 500
Montevideo	2	1.7	2	2.5	500– (400)
Tonosí	5	4.2	3	3.7	500– (100 B.C.)
Period IV (total)	7	5.8	5	6.2	A.D. 500– (100 B.C.)
Total all painted sherds	119		81		

Key to symbols ANS: Absolute number of sherds
MNV: Minimum number of vessels (see text)

fig. 7 r; Cooke 1972, vol.2, figs. 2,4,5 a, c and d; 1976 a, figs. 2–7; 1976b, table 2, top row). These vessels bear three principal designs: a stylized saurian, back-to-back triangles with tails, and linear arrangements of small dots (cf. Cook 1976b, table 2). There are also, in the western Cocle sample, a few sherds which have the decoration arranged not in concentric bands, but in isolated panels arranged radially on the interior, like the example from IS-3 in figure 11/1a.

Vessels with the three common designs were almost certainly being manufactured until the Spanish Conquest (Cooke 1976b, p. 132; Cooke and Camargo 1977, pp. 152–153). However, in spite of my seemingly confident assignment (Cooke 1976b, table 2) of these Mendoza-style bowls to El Hatillo group (A.D. 1300–1520), there is still some doubt as to exactly when they began to be manufactured, just how their designs might have varied through time on the same shape, and just what their relationship was to the possibly earlier Parita polychrome group, isolated first by Ladd (1964, pp. 66–95), and tentatively placed by me between A.D. 1100 and 1300.

One of the sherds from IS-3, is almost certainly off a Mendoza bowl with

Figure 11/1: Trade sherds from the "central region" of Panama found at La Pitahaya: a. Period VII Mendoza-group sherd; b. Period VII Parita polychrome-group sherd; c,d. Macaracas (Pica Pica and Higo varieties); e. Conte polychrome sherd.

the "back-to-back triangles" design, hence could date between A.D. 1300 and 1520. However, the other three, like that in figure 11/1a, have the rarer decoration of isolated panels. In the western Cocle sample, this mode is rare (1 percent, n=575). Moreover, the only precise analogue to the illustrated sherd's design is found on a vessel from Tomb 5 at Sitio Conte (Lothrop 1942, fig. 152). Tomb 5 is almost certainly one of the last in the sequence excavated by Lothrop and it should date, by virtue of the predominance of Macaracas (Pica-Pica/Higo) vessels, to between ca. A.D. 700 and 900. The vessel in question was "strange" to Lothrop (1942, p. 85); but it has a Macaracas shape and a good deal of purple paint, an item that is uncommonly found on Parita vessels and is absent from El Hatillo material.

These bowl sherds found at IS-3, though at first glance meeting my criteria for the El Hatillo (Mendoza) bowls, could be considered a "transitional form" dating from the beginning rather than the end of period VII. At some time between A.D. 900 and 1100, the central region potters apparently began to abandon polychromy and curvilinear naturalism in favor of trichromy and geometric abstraction; hence these sherds cannot date before those centuries.

II. Probable Period VII Parita-polychrome-group Sherds

Two sherds from IS-3 are assignable to Ladd's Parita polychrome varieties. The first (fig. 11/1b) is from a very large vessel — most likely a "frog" or

"Atlantean" effigy (Ladd 1964, figs. 17 e and 26 g). However, the same type of simple, geometric decoration is also seen on El Hatillo vessels (ibid., pp. 51–66), including Mendoza-shape bowls (Cooke 1972, vol. 2, fig. 18 g). As this sherd is significant stratigraphically, it should be stressed that it cannot be classified as Macaracas and ought to date after A.D. 1100.

The second Parita sherd at IS-3 is from the interior of a Yampí variety pedestal plate (Ladd 1964, fig. 24 d and h and plate 3 d). The precise chronological position of these vessels is unclear (Cooke 1976a, pp. 320–321). They probably represent the transition, in the central region bowl form, from Macaracas to Parita, and date from around A.D. 1000–1100.

There are, in addition, two eroded sherds of Period VII manufacture: an inverted rimless bowl (Cooke 1972, vol. 2, fig. 8b and c) and an El Hatillo or Parita exterior. The former was found on the surface of trench II, block 1, the latter in unit C of trench II, block 2.

III. Macaracas and Conte Polychromes

Of the classifiable polychrome sherds (n=120), 77.5 percent belong to these two groups. If I am correct (Cooke 1976b, table 2), in believing that Ladd's Cuipo variety outlasts or replaces the Pica-Pica and Higo varieties, the five representatives of Cuipo in the IS-3 sample may date between A.D. 900 and 1100.

The 38 Macaracas (Pica-Pica and Higo) sherds display the attributes ascribed to them by Ladd (1964): compare figure 11/1c of this report with Lothrop (1942, plate IIa) and Ladd (1964, plate 7a) and figure 11/1d with Ladd (1964, fig. 37a). Other design elements that occur at IS-3 are analogous to Lothrop's (1942, figs. 37 a and b and 40 k).

Of the 48 Conte polychrome sherds (A.D. 500–700), 21 have the characteristically "drooping" lip (cf. Lothrop 1942, fig. 29 and *passim*). There are five rims of the outflaring bowl type (ibid., fig. 159 and ff.), five shallow ring bases (cf. ibid., fig. 8 and *passim*), and one sherd exterior from a necked carafe (ibid., fig. 108).

Most of the designs on these IS-3 sherds are very fragmentary. The predominant element is illustrated in figure 11/1e which can be compared to Lothrop's (1942, figs. 137 b, 155 c, 158, et al.). Another direct comparison can be made between IS-3 sherds and the fill motif in Lothrop's (1942, fig. 52).

The Conte Red shapes include the "drooping lip" (Lothrop 1942, fig. 261 a) and flat-rimmed types (ibid., fig. 262 b).

IV. Period IV Materials

Period IV in the central region is characterized by the appearance of bichromy and the development of representational trichromy. There are three groups whose precise temporal and spatial relationship within this timespan are still unclear: the Aristide group (probably the ancestral form), the Tonosi group (a prestige ware?), and the Montevideo group (perhaps transitional between the Tonosi and Conte groups).

At IS-3 the Aristide group, which was certainly being made in Cocle by

240 B.C. ± 80 (Cooke and Camargo 1977, p. 143), does not occur. One Tonosi sherd and, possibly, three others from a single vessel (all found in IS-3, trench 1, cut 3, unit C) seem to be from typical double-vases (Ichon 1974, pp. 119–141), while a third, and a nubbin foot support, are from a three-color zoomorphic bowl type (ibid., fig. 45). There are now radiocarbon determinations for the double-vases stretching from 65 B.C. ± 80 at Sitio Sierra (Cooke and Camargo 1977, p. 144) to A.D. 450 ± 90 at La India in Los Santos province. However, when the zoomorphic bowls have black-and-white decoration on red, and four legs, as in these IS-3 examples, they appear toward the middle of period IV and remain popular until period V.

Thus, the evidence for exchange and/or contracts of some sort during period IV rests on eight sherds whose dates could run from as early as 100 B.C. to as late as A.D. 500. However, the facts that no Aristide sherds occur, that Tonosi and Montevideo material is rare in the whole sample vis-à-vis the subsequent Conte group, and that I have assigned Montevideo to a transitional position, make it likely that these activities did not get underway at the site until the end of the period (i.e., toward about A.D. 400).

CONCLUSIONS

Viewed as a unit, the sample of pottery from the central region of Panama at La Pitahaya (IS-3) in Chiriqui indicates that "contacts" between these areas were most prominent at the time when the Conte and Macaracas (Pica-Pica and Higo variety) polychromes were being manufactured; that is, between ca. A.D. 500 and 900. If we take the sample of sherds presented in table 2 (n=120), we find that 40 percent of the sherds and 45 percent of the vessels belong to the Conte ceramic group, while 31.7 percent of the sherds and 18 percent of the vessels are of the aforementioned Macaracas varieties. On the other hand, period IV types represent only 5.8 percent of the sherds and 6.1 percent of the vessels, while periods VI(B) and VII types make up 10.9 percent of the sherds and 13.5 percent of the vessels. Moreover, if our hunch about the transitional nature of most of the period VII sherds is right, and if the period IV material is, in fact, late, we can honestly limit nearly all the traded material to between A.D. 400 and 1300, a time-span which coincides well with the radiocarbon determinations for the site and Linares's estimates (section 7.7).

Ceramic Classes from the
Bocas del Toro Sites (CA-3 and CA-2)

M.O. KUDARAUSKAS, O.F. LINARES, AND I. BORGOGNO

CERAMIC WARES

Generally, the Bocas del Toro pottery was crudely made, neither very durable nor very varied. Five wares could be easily distinguished, two of which (Bocas Brushed-Pinched and Bocas Smooth-Polished) seem to be of local inspiration, and two of which (Bisquit Ware and Bugaba Ware) originated across the mountains in Chiriqui Province. In addition, there are two minor "types" (Chocolate Incised and Red Slipped) which may be of Costa Rican inspiration and/or origin; these two occur in too small frequencies to be treated quantitatively. Vessel shapes characteristic of each ware are described here, but the appendage modes are only mentioned and described separately.

All of the Bocas pottery was probably manufactured by the coil method, so this technique will not be mentioned again. Faint coil junctions remain on a few brushed sherds with imperfectly finished surfaces.

I.   Bocas Brushed-Pinched (fig. 12/1 a-g)

Except for plain sherds, this is the most abundant and localized of the Bocas del Toro wares.

A.   Paste

1.   Temper: Very coarse , angular particles.

2.   Texture: Most sherds are coarse and crumbly, breaking easily and unevenly. A few of the thinner-walled variety are more compact, however.

3.   Color: The paste is orange to medium-brown or gray, with a marked dark-gray core on some specimens caused by incompletely oxidized firing.

B.   Surface

1.   The color ranges from buff to light gray, with areas that are occasionally dark gray to black as a result of fire clouds. On a single vessel the color is relatively uniform. Surface hardness is 2.5 in the scale of Moh.

2.   Treatment: The exterior surfaces of vessels, including tripod feet bases and the necks, were conspicuously brushed with a tool, probably the edge of a large bivalve, possibly to facilitate carrying the vessel when wet. The interior is usually smoothed, and possibly in a few cases, covered with a thin wash. In addition, some sherds have wide "corrugations" which were probably made by "pinching" the wet clay gently between the thumb and middle fingers. Brushed and pinched areas do not usually overlap, but

pinching occurs only on thick brushed vessels and may be found on rims as well as on the body.

C. Form

1. Body walls belong in two distinct groups: (a) very thick (1–2 cm) and (b) thin (.3–.5 cm). There is a marked thickening of the vessel wall toward the bottom, possibly to add weight and balance to jars and bowls without visible supports.

2. Vessel shapes of the Bocas Brushed-Pinched are referred to as jars if the rims are discontinuous with the vessel wall (i.e., if the vessel has a visible neck and shoulder) and as bowls if the rims are continuous with the vessel wall. These categories may be further differentiated into:

a. Short-necked jars with gently everted short rims averaging 2 cm in length and unmodified, tapered, or blunt lips. There is a visible angle where the rim is attached to the vessel shoulder. Mouth diameters range between 18 and 24 cm.

b. Long-necked jars have everted rims which may be 5 to 7 cm long or, in the very long, 13 to 15 cm long and 1–2 cm thick. The thicker rims have blunt lips; the thinner ones may be tapered. Mouth diameter may be as much as 40 cm. Most of these jars probably served for carrying and storing liquids.

c. Hemispherical bowls have gently curved but vertically placed rims. These bowls may be fairly deep (25 cm from rim to midpoint on the inside). Mouth diameter may be as large as 36 cm. Some of the thinner and smaller rims may actually be from the top of a composite silhouette jar (see below).

d. Open bowls are outcurved bowls with open mouths. Some may be so flat and shallow as to approximate plates; others are definitely curved and may have been quite deep. The lip of open bowls is commonly painted in red and some of these open bowls have red bands in the interior (see Additional decoration). Rim diameters usually range in size from 20 to 30 cm.

e. Closed bowls have incurved rims that are continuous with the vessel wall. These bowls are often very small and may be pointed at the bottom and/or have long tripod legs attached to the underside.

f. Composite silhouette jars are curved in outline. Instead of being outflared or everted, the rim is gently concave inward, like the main body of the vessel. The rim is neither in- nor out-leaning, but vertically placed, so that the vessel looks like a jar or deep bowl with another flatter bowl on top, possibly serving as a funnel. These vessels are variable in size, from fairly small, with mouth diameters of 12 cm, to quite large, with mouths 24 cm across. The lip may be tapered or flat, and the rim may be plain, or, in the thin variety, bear rows of slashes and/or punctation, free or within incised lines.

3. The bases of the Brushed Ware are markedly thickened, probably to help balance the vessel. The open, shallow (platelike) bowls have flat bottoms, while most of the other jars and bowls have pointed bottoms.

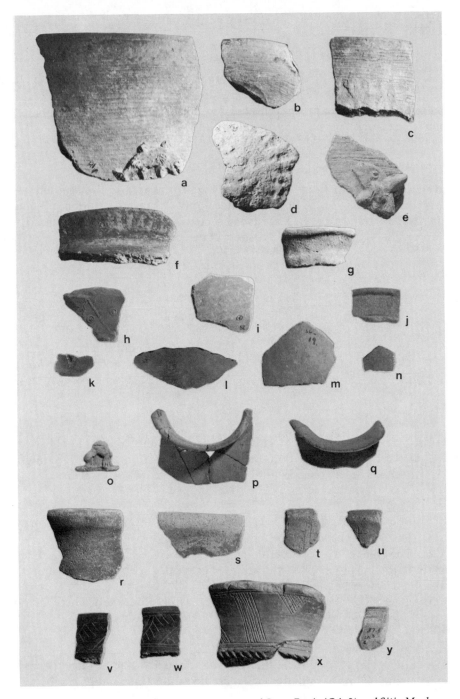

Figure 12/1: Ceramic classes from the Bocas sites of Cerro Brujo (CA-3) and Sitio Machuca (CA-2): a-g. Bocas Brushed-Pinched; h-n. Bocas Smooth-Polished; o-q. Bocas Bisquit Ware; r-u. Bugaba-style ware; v-y. Chocolate Incised.

(Tripod feet and handles are conspicuous in this ware, but they are described separately.)

D. *Additional Decoration*

1.   Red bands on lip or on interior of exteriorly brushed vessels seem to be an imitation of the Zapote Red banded type of La Pitahaya (IS-3).

2.   The most common appliquéd motif is a plain notched or incised band, but some "representational" appliqués also occur, depicting a fish, an "iguanid."

II.   *Bocas Plain Ware*

In almost all the attributes of paste, body wall thickness, and vessel shapes, this ware is identical to Bocas Brushed, only it has plain surfaces. Some sherds may, in fact, be the unbrushed sections of that ware. (For a description of this ware turn to the Brushed Ware section.)

III.   *Bocas Smooth-Polished (fig. 12/1 h-n)*

A. *Paste*

1.   Temper: Fine-grained light-colored, usually rounded in small particles.

2.   Texture is fairly compact, breaking along straight lines.

3.   Color of paste is usually light-colored (buff to reddish) and fairly uniform throughout, except for an occasional dark-colored core in cross section.

B. *Surface*

The exteriors may be light-gray to black to red and are highly polished, with polishing striations visible to the eye. The interiors may be left rough, or smoothed, or in some cases as highly polished as the exterior.

C. *Form*

1.   Body wall thickness ranges between .4 and .8 cm, with the majority consistently about half a centimeter in thickness.

2.   The characteristic vessel shape of this ware is a small jar with a short, straight to sharply everted thickened rim, and a globular body. Mouth diameters range between 10 and 16 cm.

3.   Bases appear to be rounded and not visibly thickened. There are no tripod feet, pedestals, and so forth, associated with this ware.

D. *Additional Decoration*

A band of slashes or punctations may be added to the area below the neck or to a small strap handle that often accompanies this ware.

IV.   *Bocas Bisquit Ware (fig. 12/1 o-q)*

This is exactly the same ware as the well-known Armadillo Terra Cotta Bisquit Ware of Chiriqui (see Linares 1968b,pp. 38–41). Although a careful analysis of the paste would be necessary before ascertaining its provenience, all indications are that the Bocas Bisquit Ware was brought into Cerro Brujo in substantial quantities, probably from the Chiriqui side. It does not seem to have been manufactured locally; the paste is "fine," unlike the other Bocas wares, and the vessel shapes, appendages, "adornos," and so forth, are identical with its Chiriqui counterpart. Short-necked jars with a "leaf" appliquéd motif, hollow "mammiform" tripods with rattles, rattle "armadillo"-shaped handles, little human figurines, and so forth, are all found in the Bocas Bisquit Ware. (For a detailed description of this ware see Holmes 1888, pp. 67–80; MacCurdy 1911, pp. 48–72; Linares 1968b, pp. 38–41.)

V. Bugaba-Style Ware (fig. 12/1 r-u)

This category overlaps the Volcan wares and is identical with them in all attributes of paste and surface finish (report no. 9, this volume). There are slightly over 400 Bugaba style sherds (the majority being body sherds) in the bottom levels of the Cerro Brujo localities CA-3a and CA-3b. In order to be as precise as possible in our comparisons between the Bugaba style sherds from Volcan (sites BU-17 and BU-24) and the less than 100 diagnostic (i.e., rims and appendages) Bugaba sherds that occur in Bocas, we will not use the Volcan ware categories, but use the vessel shape and mode classes that were defined for the Volcan pottery. We will include the Bugaba appendages in this section (and not under appendages), noting which attribute classes are present in Volcan but missing in Bocas. It is not possible for the moment to say with certainty where Bugaba style sherds of Bocas were manufactured. However, they certainly represent the first and oldest inhabitants of the Aguacate Peninsula and the Cerro Brujo Site.

A. Vessel Forms

1. Jars with short and medium-long necks occur at CA-3, but very long-necked jars like those of Volcan do not.
2. Although most of the Volcan restricted bowl variants occur in Bocas, the most common rims are those associated with the Valbuena Ware (report no. 9). The deep bowls are missing, however.
3. Open bowls are not found in the Cerro Brujo site.

B. Appendages

1. No ringstands, pedestals, or basal bands were found among the Bugaba Ware sherds at Cerro Brujo.
2. A hollow mammiform-shaped tripod slipped in red and a plain solid V-shaped small tripod occur at Cerro Brujo.
3. There are several specimens of tabs undoubtedly used as supports; these may be small (2.5 cm long by 3 cm wide) or longer (6 cm high). They have a depression in the center and are slipped in red.
4. A few very small strap handles (3 cm wide) in the bottom levels of CA-3 may belong to the Bugaba Ware.

C. High and Low Relief Motifs

While semidetached figurines (i.e., high relief) of Bugaba style are absent, the older CA-3 levels do contain a few lobes, nubbins, and pellet appliqués that are indistinguishable from those of Volcan.

D. Surface Treatment Techniques

A few incised or grooved sherds, one negative-painted sherd, and one multiple-incised sherd occur at CA-3, but neither engraving, zone bichroming, nor multiple incision is found among the Bugaba style sherds in the bottom levels of Cerro Brujo.

VI. Chocolate Incised (fig. 12/1 v-y)

A dark brown, black, or red slip is applied to both surfaces of fairly thin (.5 to .75 cm) outslanting rims of a fine-grained paste, and then polished, often to a high sheen. Motifs of slanting parallel lines, cross-hatching in V-shaped areas, and zig zag lines are incised on the exterior of the neck, extending in some cases over the lip into the interior of the rim, where they form a band up to 2 cm wide. The predominant vessel shape is an outflared bowl resting on "feline"-shaped hollow tripod feet (appendage below). (For a more complete description of the Chocolate Incised type see Linares 1968b, pp. 44–45.)

At Cerro Brujo this type, like the Bisquit Ware, is found in the A and B layers, but not in the C layers and is a time-marker for the more recent of the two occupations at the site.

LOOSE APPENDAGES

I. Supports

Most supports found in the Aguacate sites are tripod feet. A few other appendages accompany Bugaba Ware (fig. 12/2 a-e); for a description of Bugaba appendages see report number 9.

A. Tripod Feet

1. Solid tubular tripods are slightly incurved (concave inward) and tapered from top to bottom, ending in a thick, blunt tip (fig. 12/2 f,g,j). Complete specimens range in length from 3.5 cm to 8 cm and may be 2–4 cm at the top and 1.5 cm at the tip. They were first made hollow, and then "filled in" with a protruding clay core that served like a socket to insert the leg into the underside of the vessel. The surface was left plain, or it was brushed and/or painted with red horizontal bands varying in width from .75 cm to 2 cm. A few specimens were slipped in red. Tubular tripods are characteristic of Bocas Brushed-Pinched Ware.

2. Solid tubular tripods that are small (about 6 cm long) and decorated with a face motif, or with a small appliquéd figurine and transverse fillets (fig. 12/2 h). They are probably part of the Bocas Brushed Ware.

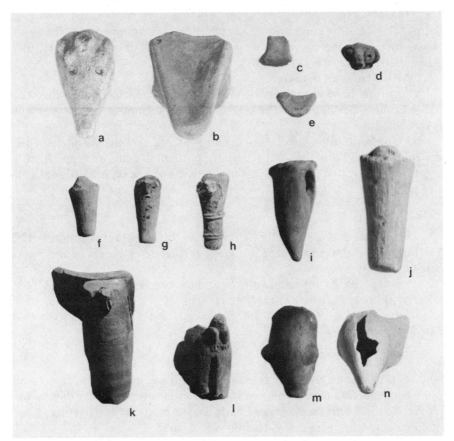

Figure 12/2: Appendages from the Bocas ceramics: a-e. Bugaba-style appendages; f,g. solid, tubular (often brushed) tripods, slightly tapered toward the bottom; h. solid tripod with face motif; i. bulging tripod with pointed tip; j. solid, tubular tapered tripod; k, l. hollow, tubular tall tripods; m. hollow tripod in the shape of an animal head (Chocolate Incised Ware); n. mammiform, rattle tripod (Bisquit Ware).

3. Tripods that are slightly outcurved (i.e., bulging) in the middle ending in a pointed tip (fig. 12/2 i). The same exact shape may be solid, or hollow with a slit. Complete specimens are 8 cm long, 3.5 cm at the top and 1.5 cm near the tip. Some bear traces of a red slip. They probably go with the red-slipped class.

4. Hollow tubular "rattle" tripods are tall, slightly out-bulging in the center and tapered toward the bottom (fig. 12/2 k, l). They are longer than their solid counterparts; no complete specimen remains, but some may have been as long as 25 cm or more. The width at the top may vary between 3 and 5 cm. They often have a small high-relief figurine sitting at the top, and either one or two slits on the body; the majority are also decorated with red horizontal bands the length of the foot. However, some are plain and/or have brushing, but no other decoration. They belong to the Bocas Brushed Ware.

5.   Mammiform "rattle" tripod feet belonging to the Bisquit Ware (fig. 12/2 n). They are bulging, and either plain or anthropomorphic. These are very common in the Chiriqui Bisquit Ware (see Holmes 1888; MacCurdy 1911).
6.   Miscellaneous tripods
a. Animal head characteristic of the Chocolate Incised Ware (fig. 12/2 m; see Linares 1968a, p. 50). These are late in the sequence, in Bocas as well as in Chiriqui.
b. Unidentifiable: Small (5–6 cm long) and either solid or hollow tripod feet that cannot be associated with any particular ware or type. Also, a larger, white-slipped curved tripod in the shape of a beak, possibly of Costa Rican(?) origin.

B. Other Supports

1.   Flat bases that are thinner (.75 cm) than the vessel wall (1 cm; fig. 12/3 q). They may belong to the open, shallow (platelike) bowls of the Bocas Brushed Ware.
2.   Pointed bases on small bowls and/or jars resting on tripod feet; belongs to Bocas Brushed Ware (fig. 12/3 r).
3.   (Bugaba Ware supports are described under the section for that ware.)

II.   Handles

A.   Strap handles are flat in cross section and extend from the vessel wall to the lip. They are one of the two most abundant types of handles in the Bocas collection, but they are not nearly as common nor as varied as in the Pitahaya ceramics. The Bocas handle classes are:
1.   Parallel-sided (i.e., nontapered) straps, 3–5 cm wide, that are gently curved between two points of attachment about 5 cm apart (fig. 12/3 a). They belong with Bocas Plain and (possibly) Brushed Ware.
2.   Straps that curve sharply between two closely spaced points of attachment (about 2.5 cm apart) (fig. 12/3 e). These straps are fairly wide across (4 to 5 cm) and are placed on the neck section of Bocas Brushed-Pinched short-necked jars.
3.   Small, narrow (1.5 to 2.5 cm wide) straps extending from lip to shoulders in small-necked jars of Bocas Smooth-Polished Ware (fig. 12/3 b). They are characteristically decorated with small punctations and/or slashes.
4.   Tapered handles are broader at one end (usually where they meet the lip) than at the other. This shape is very common in the San Lorenzo Ware of La Pitahaya and probably occurred in association with red-banded sherds in the Bocas collection.
B.   Double handles are the second most common category of grips at Cerro Brujo (fig. 12/3 f-h). They are nearly circular (as opposed to flat) in cross section and placed horizontally on the vessel's shoulder just below the neck, to which they are connected, near the rim, by a short transverse clay roll. A few of the specimens are actually fused to the rims. The top of the handle may be plain, or it may be decorated with pellet appliqués. Double

Figure 12/3: Appendages and decorative modes from the Bocas ceramics: a. nontapered medium-width strap handle; b. small narrow strap handle; c,d. round handle; e. sharply folded strap; f-h. double handles; i,l. slashed appliquéd bands; j, m-o. low relief animal motifs; k. twisted handle; p, s. adornos; q. flat base; r. pointed base

Ceramic Classes from the Bocas del Toro Sites   393

handles vary greatly in size, from 4 cm to 8 cm between points of attachment, and also in thickness, from 1 to 2.5 cm. They are characteristic of the Bocas Brushed-Pinched short-necked jars.

C. Most round handles may actually be fragments broken off the midsection of double handles, in the part often decorated with pellet appliqués (fig. 12/3 c, d). They probably belong to the Bocas Brushed Ware.

D. A few twisted handles were made by coiling one clay roll around another. They are probably associated with Bocas Brushed Ware (fig. 12/3 k).

E. Horizontal handles that are attached at two points on the vessel rim are almost as rare in the Bocas collections as twisted handles. Two complete specimens found are both decorated, one with slashes, the other with reed punctations. They are not clearly associated with any of the Bocas ceramic wares.

F. Effigy handles shaped into animal or human figures are also rare in Cerro Brujo.

III. Appliqué and Adornos

A. The most common appliqué on the Bocas pottery consists of straight or undulating raised bands that are slashed, often giving a ropelike effect (fig. 12/3 i,l). These are different from the simple rows of punctations, slashes, and jabs also found here. Both accompany the Bocas Brushed and Bocas Smooth-Polished wares.

B. In low relief, two animal motifs predominate: a curved "fish" (fig. 12/3 j, m-o) and a lizard or iguana. Both are found with the Bocas Brushed Ware.

C. In the adornos (i.e., high relief or appliquéd figurines) animals, as well as humans, occur (fig. 12/3 p,s). Several of these adornos belong to the Bocas Bisquit Ware, including the well-known "rattle" armadillo head that may have served not only as decoration but as a handle.

Report Number 13

Computer Typology – Pro and Con

I. BORGOGNO

INTRODUCTION

The purpose of this report is twofold: it is both an exploration into methodology and a preliminary attempt to redefine the ceramic typology of the Chiriqui area of Panama. The approach is primarily a computer-clustering of attributes. Computer use has attracted both defenders and opponents. Arguments pro and con have been offered, but no real test comparison of old and new approaches has been made. Therefore, this paper is concerned not only with the new computer approach toward typology, but also the older "intuitive" approach. The pottery sample used herein was typed both ways; the results will be compared for degree of similarity, and their relative merits weighed in terms of time, expense, reliability, and applicability. (This paper was written in 1971 as a master's thesis for the Department of Anthropology at the University of Pennsylvania.)

The material used in this exercise came from a 2 x 2-meter block in the center of trench 1, area 2 at the site of La Pitahaya (IS-3). The quantity of material removed from this single 2 x 2-meter cut was enormous; there was a total of thirty-one gunny sacks, each filled between one-half and three-quarters full. It was decided, primarily on the basis of expediency, to reduce this to a more manageable size by analyzing only the rim sherds. It was assumed that such a selection would provide a representative sample of all the kinds of pottery present, since by definition every pot must have a rim. It is naturally impossible to warrant the randomness of the sample, but two important factors other than expediency decided the matter. First, in quantitative analysis, it is preferable, if not essential, to hold constant as many nondistinctive variables as possible: i.e., it is better to compare two rim sherds than to compare a rim sherd with a body cum leg fragment sherd. Usually ceramic remains are not so abundant as to allow a selection of one sherd kind and still yield a large enough sample for quantitative analysis, unless the "sherd kind" be body sherds, which are the least informative on matters of pot shape. In this sample, however, most units yielded an average of two hundred and fifty rim sherds, which is adequate for quantitative analysis. Secondly, for the purpose of a methodological comparison, neither randomness nor representativeness is necessarily a prerequisite, since both methods are being applied to the same body of material and the comparisons are entirely internal. Of course, such an argument would have an adverse effect on the attempted establishment of a typology for the area, but in lieu of substantiating data either pro or con it is here assumed that rim sherds do provide a representative sample.

However, owing to many extraneous factors (such as the amount of time needed to code data for computer analysis), it was necessary to curtail the sample even further. To this extent, only the rim sherds from every other unit within each stratum was used. The end result was a sample drawn from nine levels and consisting of almost 1,500 potsherds.

TYPOLOGY

There are, basically, two different ways in which the construction of a typology may be approached: one focuses on the whole artifact, the other on individual attributes. If the whole artifact is the basis of grouping, the procedure is one of repeated trial-sortings until satisfactory groupings emerge; these groupings are then described by what appear to be the most characteristic attributes, although the basis of sorting may remain implicit. This is the "intuitive" approach to typology. If attributes form the initial basis of grouping, the procedure is different. Variations are described in a series of attribute classes, and clusters among these classes are sought by means of quantitative analysis. These clusters form the definitions of types, and the artifacts are then grouped into these clusters. This more explicit process is the basis of the typological development known as "attribute analysis," which was the necessary forerunner of typological analysis by computer, which is nothing more than a mechanized performance of the quantitive computations connected with attribute analysis.

A. By Eye

There are, basically, two different ways to approach nonquantitative sorting of artifacts into types. One can either successively subdivide a single set of material until all the same kinds are in a single class, or one can intuitively sort into homogeneous classes. In actual practice, some combination of the two is usually employed; such a combination was used in this analysis, with greater emphasis on the former.

A first division of the sherds was made on the basis of plain, slipped, and decorated (painted). These three were then subdivided by rim profiles, and it was seen that in large part certain profiles were associated with the slipped sherds, and different ones with the painted sherds. The plain sherds corresponded to the one group of profiles or the other, and probably represent sherds from which the slip or paint has disappeared. There were a few other relatively distinctive groups of sherds, and also a residue of pieces too small to present a recognizable rim profile. The basis of separation may be seen in the descriptions presented below, and it is soon obvious that shape was of primary importance, with decoration a useful secondary category. Some other bases were attempted and discarded, as they proved to be useless; notable among these was temper. The common temper used was grit, ranging from very fine particles to very coarse (0.4-4 mm) and in color being either black or gray. An attempt to separate on the basis of these differences led nowhere; all variations in size graded into one another and the colors cross-cut all size distinctions. Nor was there a noticeable correlation of temper with any other variable. In fact, shape, as determined by rim profile, appeared to be the only reasonable criterion for meaningful groupings, while presence of red slip seemed to have strong correlations with certain shapes.

The results of this analysis yielded twelve major types, three other small but distinctive groups, and a residue of two hundred and ten unassignable sherds. (For illustrations of the types see report no. 10.)

The first four "intuitive" types were distinguished, as a group, from the remaining types by the presence of a highly polished dark red slip, in previous work (Linares 1968b) called Isla Palenque maroon slip. The four types associated with this slip are differentiated by shape.

1. Vessels with globular bodies and flaring rims; the rims are concave and slanted away from the vessel interior. Necks are typically long, and rise from a rounded shoulder. The lip is usually much thicker than the body wall (186 specimens).

2. A relatively deep, somewhat angular, bowllike vessel, with a straight rim that is vertical or slanted away from the interior. The lip is slightly thickened and there is sometimes an exterior groove just below the lip. Typically, there are multiple parallel depressions or ridges on the exterior, below and at an angle to the lip, but never extending farther than an angular jointure, present on all examples about 4 cm below the lip, which is vaguely reminiscent of a shoulder (82 specimens).
3. A shallow, curved but flattened bowllike vessel, with a convex, vertical rim. It is almost invariably decorated with an appliquéd arm motif (50 specimens).
4. The fourth, an uncommon but distinctive shape, is a bowllike vessel with a convex, outward slanting rim. The lip is thicker than the body wall, and curves inwardly abruptly to form a hook-shape. The sides of the bowl are more linear than curved (16 specimens).

The next "group" consists of six types and comprises most of the bulk of the remaining sherds. They are distinguished as a group in not having the Isla Palenque maroon slips (nor the shapes associated with that characteristic) and by the frequent presence of red paint.

5. A simple jarlike vessel, with a slightly concave rim that slants away from the interior. There is a rounded but distinct shoulder, and the lip is unmodified. Decoration is usually absent, although the lip is sometimes painted red. Most rim necks are the same length, although some are rather short (35 sherds) and some are very long (64 sherds) (493 specimens in total).
6. A rounded bowllike vessel, with a convex and inward slanting rim. There are two variations: a shallower bowl whose body appears slightly flattened (58 sherds), and a deeper bowl with a more globular body (90 sherds). Typically, the sherds have red painted lips and exterior red painted designs consisting of thin lines or bands and dots (148 specimens).
7. A shallow, platterlike vessel, with outward slanting rims which are slightly convex or straight. Usually, there is a red painted lip and an interior red painted design composed of thick lines and blobs (146 specimens).
8. A globular and therefore deep bowl-shape, with a concave and outward slanting rim. These are frequently plain, but many (especially the smaller variety) have narrow painted lines of red and small appliquéd nubs (105 specimens).
9. A globular vessel, with a slightly concave, outward slanting rim, which rises from a gently rounded and barely perceptible shoulder. The lip is either unmodified or tapered. Decoration is usually absent (88 specimens).
10. In most respects, this one is just like 5 but with a modified lip. This lip is flattened interiorly, and angles inward toward the interior of the vessel. The lip is almost invariably painted red (43 specimens).

The remaining two "types" are actually wares that occur only late in the sequence, namely Bisquit Ware and Villalba Red Streaked (Linares 1968b).

11. Villalba Red Streaked is represented by a jarlike vessel with little or no neck. The rim is concave and slants outward; the interior of the rim bears a polished, bright orange-red paint that greatly resembles a slip. Where the paint does not occur, as on most of the exteriors, the surface is very rough, both unsmoothed and polished (72 specimens).

12. Tarrago Bisquit Ware is a very thin-walled ware, tan to salmon in color, with sand temper. The rim shapes are very distinctive and easily separated from the rest (21 specimens).

The three "small but distinctive" groups are:

1. Cocle Ware, trade pieces with a white slip background and polychrome paint in red, purple, and black; there were three examples.

2. A highly polished, red-slipped ware, very different from the Isla Palenque maroon slipped sherds in both slip color and vessel shapes, which included at least two compound vessels out of the five examples.

3. One sherd from an effigy vessel.

B. By Computer

The first step taken in the computer analysis of this sample of 1,500 potsherds was to describe each sherd on machine-readable OP-SCAN sheets. The code used for this purpose was a modified form of one developed earlier for analysis of material from Cerro Brujo. The variables in the code fall into two categories: those concerned with identification of the sherd (i.e., provenience), of which there are five, and those concerned with description, of which there are thirty-five. These descriptive variables (or attributes) fall into three groupings: nominal, ordinal, and ratio. All variables were reduced to nominal variables within the code by listing them in numbered classes; e.g., ratio variables were listed in comparable and convenient intervals, which were then numbered and used for coding. A list of the variables used may be found in Appendix 1.

The OP-SCAN sheets were machine-read and converted into eightycolumn IBM punched cards. A program for discovering errors (both human in mismarking the OP-SCAN sheets and machine in mispunching the IBM cards) was developed and the punched cards were submitted to this data "laundry" program. All detected errors were corrected.

The corrected data cards were next submitted to a standard University of Pennsylvania statistical program called Cross-Tabs. As described in the explanatory sheets:

> This program computes and prints out frequency tables among fifty or fewer variables in the manner specified on the "Design Cards." In addition, associated tables, such as cell percentages by row, and statistics, such as Chisquares, will be printed for each table, if requested (Cross-Tabs Program, p. 1).

The print-out from Cross-Tabs was used to reduce, where possible, the number of classes within each variable and also to eliminate any highly correlated variables, as the clustering program used assumes independent variables.

The reduced attributes were arranged in rough order of importance, quartered according to this ranking, and assigned coefficients of similarity. This information served to define a data transformation program, which punched out a new series of cards, with all the attributes recoded as two-state variables. (The previous thirty-five variables of one hundred and ninety-seven possible states were reduced to seventy-two two-state variables by elimination of infrequently and never used classes.) These new cards were the input for the clustering program.

The cluster analysis program used was essentially that developed by G.F. Bonham-Carter (1966) for use in geological analyses in which the data were primarily qualitative. This program was run in lots of two hundred sherds at a time, as that is the maximum sample size which it can handle efficiently. The sherds in each lot were drawn from all nine levels, in order to eliminate the possibility of time-related clusters. This step is the main part of the computer analysis, the preceding work being intended to prepare the data and the remaining steps being concerned with presenting the results in an easily read form.

The output of the clustering program was submitted to a modified form of DNPLOT (Demirmen 1967), which is a dendrogram plotting program. (A dendrogram is a treelike graph which allows a quick visual grasp of the level of association at which the objects — i.e., sherds — cluster.) The dendrogram runs were made in the same lots of two hundred as the cluster analyses. A rather low significance level (0.6500) was selected as the cut-off point for cluster; this was chosen because it yielded between ten and thirteen clusters of four or more objects in each of the runs. (Clusters of less than four objects were ignored as trivial; average cluster size was about fifteen objects.) This number of clusters was desired as it was comparable to the number from the analysis by inspection.

The clusters having been delimited, the data were submitted to the final computer run, a program which analyzed the clusters and printed out the shared characteristics. These cluster characteristics were compared among all the separate lots of two hundred, and reduced to a total of ten clusters:

1. An outward slanting, almost flaring, concave rim with an externally thickened lip, attached to a jar with an internal and an external red slip (167 specimens).
2. A bowl with a vertical, straight rim, and a lip that is slightly thickened externally; an external red slip is indicated (57 specimens).
3. A bowl with a vertical, convex rim and a tapered lip; a red slip is indicated in some of the runs (43 specimens).
4. A jar with an outslanting, straight rim; the lip is unmodified or tapered (401 specimens).
5. A bowl with an inward slanting, convex rim; the lip is unmodified or interiorly thickened (188 specimens).
6. An outward slanting bowl with a convex or straight rim; the lip is flattened or slightly thickened interiorly (68 specimens).

7. A vessel with an outward slanting, concave or straight rim; the lip is unmodified (34 specimens).
8. A vessel with an outslanting, straight rim, and an unmodified lip; there is an interior red slip (34 specimens).
9. A vessel with an outslanting, concave rim and a thickened lip (302 specimens).
10. A vessel with an outslanting, outcurving rim and a thickened lip (128 specimens).

There is a remainder of approximately one hundred sherds, consisting of sherds brought together above the 0.6500 significance level.

RESULTS

A comparison of the two sets of results immediately indicates both similarities and discrepancies. Seven of the computer types are very similar to seven of the intuitive types in description.

Intuitive		Computer	
1	(186)	1	(167)
2	(82)	2	(57)
3	(50)	3	(43)
5	(493)	4	(401)
6	(148)	5	(188)
9	(88)	6	(68)
11	(72)	8	(34)

However, the quantities are not the same, and discrepancies occur in both directions. Of the remaining three computer types, number 7 compares equally well with intuitive types 7 and 8, and computer types 9 and 10 are not directly comparable to any intuitive types.

There are several possible explanations for these discrepancies, all of them hinging on human error.

The first target for suspicion is the code by which the sherds were described for computer analysis. The code may have been inadequate for description of the material; this problem is particularly suspect in the case of computer type 6. The development of a satisfactory code is one of the most difficult steps in computer analysis; it is distinctly possible that considerable refinement is necessary before the code used herein will be fully acceptable.

A second area of error is in application of the code. An unconscious change in the mental decision-line of the analyst, due to increasing famil-iarity with the material, is not uncommon; where material is coded by predetermined lots, as here by excavation level, the difference may become very great. Choosing lots for analysis across excavation levels should miti-gate this effect, however.

Ranking and choice of similarity coefficient are vital to the clustering process; misapprehension or misunderstanding of the factors leading to visual clusters could cause discordant decisions of rank and coefficient.

This would lead to computer types derived from primary bases other than those used visually.

Another area of difficulty is the delimitation of clusters: what is a reliable cut-off for significance level? Perhaps the choice should not be affected by the expected number of clusters, but some criterion must be used.

It is, naturally, always possible to view the discrepancies as the results solely of the inaccuracies of by-eye sorting; the human mind cannot be relied upon to retain and combine, unaided, all pertinent variants in all possible combinations. This suggestion is extremely moot, however, where the main consideration is shape, and where the number of shapes is limited.

On the other hand, all responsibility may be shunted to the inherent problems of the program used and the need to work in lots of two hundred. Breaking a large sample into small units should be done randomly to insure that types are not dependent on some artificial basis created by the method of subdividing; however, this kind of breakdown would invariably mask infrequent types, no matter how distinctive, because they would show up as small clusters of one, two, or three members, a size here disregarded because of inability to determine the defining characteristics. (It is probably due to this that visual types 4 and 12 do not show up among the computer types.) Furthermore, once the clusters are determined and defined, it is necessary to correlate them across all the separate working-lots of two hundred; it is not always immediately obvious which clusters can be correlated and which cannot. This is in part due to an inadequate code, but it is even more dependent on the decision of the analyst of how many variations in description can be tolerated within the bonds of "identical."

On the positive side, it may be noted that there is a large amount of congruence between the majority of the types determined by each method. The curious fact that the intuitive types are almost all larger in quantity than the computer types may indicate an inherent tendency to lump on the part of the analyst, or possibly an inability on the part of the analyst to perceive distinctions readily apparent to the computer.

CONCLUSIONS

It is not possible, on the basis of the results obtained in this paper, to conclude with any fairness which of the two approaches produces the more reliable results. Due to the numerous possible sources of error, further investigations are necessary before a decision can be made, and it is suggested that three modifications be made to the approach used here. First, the code should be subjected to scrutiny and amended to be more accurate in terms of description of shape. Second, there should not be a concomitant attempt to establish a typology; the need for randomness that this secondary aim implies places unwieldy strictures on the choice of a sample (i.e., while numerically small types are lost, the need to cross-correlate clusters from different sample-lots of two hundred reduces the statistical accuracy which is the primary methodological objective). This is directly concerned with the third modification, that both the visual sorting and the computer sorting be done on the same subsamples of two hundred items. By removing ulterior typological considerations, the need for randomness — and the resultant methodological quandary of cross-correlations — is also removed. By applying the two methods to several individual groups rather than one enormous group, the results within each group are comparable to each other, and the relative reliability of the two methods in each of the separate groups may afterwards be compared to yield a conclusion on overall methodological reliability.

While no conclusion can be made on reliability, a conclusion on immediate relative expense can be made. In terms of both time and money, visual typing is much less expensive. At a conservative estimate, it required one hundred man-hours just to code the potsherds used for this computer analysis. Assuming that no problems were encountered in writing, running, and complying with the results of the computer programs, there is still a time requirement of *at least* fifteen additional man-hours, usually more. (And it should be noted that such uncomplicated encounters are rare in transactions with computers.) It is difficult to estimate the minimal monetary expenses for computer employment, but the amount is *not* negligible.

The final question to be considered is that of applicability. It was noted some time ago (Coult 1968) that one of the major problems in computer use is the tendency to employ the computer in the analysis of problems for which other techniques would give the same results with greater efficiency or economy, apparently the result of the lure of methodological sophistication. On the other hand, it may be argued that as the quantity of material increases, the unaided human mind produces results on the basis of a steadily decreasing *percentage* of the available material. While this paper has been concerned with a possible example of the first problem, it is still possible to conceive of situations where the material is patently too plentiful to be readily handled by observation alone. The work of True and Matson (1970) is a good example of this, where the concern is clustering objects from all categories of cultural remains to determine the nature and comparability of several sites. There is an unquestionable difficulty in trying mentally to manipulate and compare the entire inventories from several sites, looking for traceably repeated patterns of activities, and this difficulty is intrinsically greater, on the basis of sheer quantity, than the division of a large pile of potsherds into numerous small piles by virtue of shape. It seems probable that insofar as clustering is concerned, the computer may be of greatest use in archaeology where the data to be clustered are both plentiful and diverse, and not so easily comprehended at a glance as the shape of a pot. It seems improbable that the computer will totally supplant visual classification within a single class of material remains because of the ease of losing small but distinct variations in a large welter of statistical information. A solution may be found in a compromise combination, where a first visual sorting pulls out infrequent but distinct groupings, and the computer obligingly subdivides the remaining numerous but less distinctive categories.

Appendix 1
Attribute list

1. Sherd kind
2. Temper
3. Paste texture
4. Firing
5. Exterior paste color
6. Occurrence of polishing
7. Surface treatment other than polishing
8. Maximum body thickness
9. Angle of rim to body
10. Curvature of rim relative to vessel interior
11. Presence of a shoulder
12. Mouth diameter
13. Lip thickness
14. Lip form
15. Shape of vessel
16. Depth of bowls
17. Interior slip
18. Exterior slip
19. Interior painting in bands
20. Exterior painting in bands
21. Width of paint bands
22. Painting other than banding
23. Line incision
24. Circles
25. Zone incision
26. Coffee bean eyes
27. Lobes
28. Bas-relief bands
29. Appliquéd figurines
30. Bas-relief figurines
31. Incised figurines
32. Lip treatment
33. Presence of decoration on neck of a jar
34. Presence of decoration on shoulder
35. Presence of decoration on rim of a bowl

Stone Tools from Volcan Baru

P.D. SHEETS, E.J. ROSENTHAL, AND A.J. RANERE

INTRODUCTION

In 1971, we conducted preliminary excavations at the first locality (BU-17a) of Sitio Pitti-Gonzalez in the valley of Cerro Punta, Chiriqui province (report no. 4). The following year we did more extensive excavations in another section of the site (BU-17b). We also conducted test excavations at the nearby Fistonich site (BU-22) in 1972 and at the large archaeological site of Barriles (BU-24), downriver in El Hato basin (Stirling 1950; Ichon 1968b; Linares et al. 1975). In addition to the excavations in 1972, we completed an intensive survey of the Rio Chiriqui Viejo valley, from the Cerro Punta basin to the El Hato basin (report no. 2). The 3,100 pieces of worked stone collected in the excavations and survey operations from both years are the subject of this report.

The chipped stone assemblages and the ground and polished stone tools were initially analyzed by Sheets (1972). The cobble and boulder artifacts used in grinding and pounding were initially analyzed by Rosenthal (1972). The entire collection was reexamined in 1978 by Ranere. In this last examination, a stereoscopic microscope (6x to 50x) was used to detect wear patterns. The weathering of the igneous rocks used for manufacturing the overwhelming majority of the Volcan tools undoubtedly obscured most evidence of wear on tools used in the performance of light tasks and on tools used for short periods of time. However, wear patterns were detected on a number of tools that had received heavy use; these are discussed under the appropriate category in the section on artifact descriptions.

Tool categorization is based primarily on the final method of manufacture (see report no. 15). Tool form and inferred function were used to further subdivide tool categories.

CHIPPED STONE

Present in the Volcan Baru area in the early centuries of the first millennium A.D. was a chipped stone industry that can be called a cottage industry (Sheets 1975). A variety of cores are found at habitation sites, along with flakes modified and/or used as tools (table 1). The flaking was very simply done. Neither core preparation nor platform preparation was undertaken. Hard hammer percussion was the dominant and perhaps only flaking technique employed. The volcanic rocks used in the manufacture of stone tools are abundant throughout the region. It appears that blocks of raw material, often recovered from stream gravels, were kept at the sites and flakes were struck off as needed. Although we classified a few flakes as blades, their production is best considered fortuitous. There were no blade cores recovered from the survey or excavations. With two exceptions (discussed below), none of the tools produced necessitated any great skill at knapping. In fact, the modest skills required to produce these tools were probably possessed by most adults in the area.

There is in the collections a single example of a well-made keeled scraper-plane that seems out of place in the early first-millennium A.D. assemblages from Volcan Baru. It is, on the other hand, a diagnostic tool for the preceramic phases (5000–300 B.C.) documented for the Chiriqui highlands (Ranere 1975 and report no. 8). The artifact was recovered from the surface of site BU-28, which produced chipped stone from one section and ceramics from another, thus opening the intriguing possibility that the site has two components, one preceramic and one ceramic. A second site, BU-50, yielded only chipped stone tools and may have been preceramic (it was destroyed by road-building activities shortly after its discovery). However, none of the tools recovered was particularly diagnostic.

One further chipped stone artifact deserves special mention; a type we have called dacite laterally flaked slabs (see artifact description in section 9.0). It is difficult to imagine a utilitarian purpose for these flat, asymmetrical stemmed objects. The nature of the bifacially flaked and sometimes battered or crushed edges suggests that the overall shape of the objects, not the edge morphology, was of paramount importance. Hafted on the end of a long shaft, these objects may have served some sort of ceremonial or symbolic purpose. A number of dacite waste flakes were recovered from Sitio Pitti-Gonzalez, suggesting that these implements were manufactured there.

GROUND AND POLISHED STONE

In contrast to the chipped stone tools, the ground and polished stone tools (almost entirely celts) are quite well made (table 2). The finished tools are ground over most of their surface and often polished as well. The chipping out of the preforms (one complete example was recovered) was skillfully done as well. Celt manufacturing in the Volcan Baru sites was pretty clearly a specialized activity. The distribution of celt manufacturing and/or resharpening flakes supports this conclusion. Only 10 of the 45 sites recorded show any evidence for celt manufacturing or resharpening, and in three cases, only a single flake was recovered (see table 1). We hasten to point out that the sample size is small (9 or less specimens) in all cases except for the extensively excavated Sitio Pitti-Gonzalez (n=363).

It is instructive to compare Sitio Pitti-Gonzalez (BU-17) with La Pitahaya (IS-3) in the Gulf of Chiriqui (see report no. 15) in terms of celt recovery and evidence for celt resharpening and manufacturing. At IS-3, 67 ground and polished stone artifacts, primarily celts and celt fragments, were recovered. Of the 208 flakes of celtlike materials in the excavated collections, only 19 are possible celt manufacturing flakes. The remaining 189 flakes have polished,

TABLE 1   THE DISTRIBUTION OF CHIPPED STONE FROM VOLCAN BARU SITES

	Conical cores	Bifacial cores	Irregular cores	Miscellaneous cores	Blades	Scraper-planes	Flake scraper-planes	Flake choppers	Scrapers	Flake scrapers	Flake knives	Perforators	Dacite laterally flaked slabs	Chipped celts	Totals (tools)	Flakes
BU-17 surface	2	7	2			1	3		1		1	3			20	
BU-17a ex.	1	5				1	1	1		1	2	1			12	
BU-17b ex.	1	1	7	1	2	1	1		2	4	2	2	5		29	
BU-17b above floor	1	2									1				4	
BU-17b house floor						1	1		1	3			3		9	
BU-17b below floor	2		2			1			1	1			9		16	
BU-17b above floor level							1								1	
BU-17b floor level		1	1						1	2			1		6	
BU-17b below floor level	3		1					1					2		7	
BU-17 total	9	16	13	1	2	5	7	2	6	11	6	6	20		104	2,051
BU-14											1				1	
BU-15		2	3		1									1	7	45
BU-16									1						1	
BU-18			1								1				1	1
BU-20																5
BU-21			1												1	3
BU-22	2												1	1	4	74
BU-24	1					1						1			4	111

BU-28	1					1		1							[illegible]	[illegible]
BU-29								1							1	2
BU-31			1												1	5
BU-36	1														1	4
BU-38			1											1	2	2
BU-39	1		1										1		3	25
BU-40						1									1	6
BU-42		1			1										2	5
BU-43	3		1					1							5	12
BU-44		1	1												2	3
BU-45	1	4	1										1		7	23
BU-46		1			1							1			3	9
BU-49	2		2			1						1			6	65
BU-50	1	1	1						1						4	7
BU-51																1
BU-52																2
BU-53		1													1	1
BU-54																2
BU-55			1				3								4	39
BU-57	1			1		2							1		5	41
BU-60		1				1							1		3	11
BU-62			1												1	
BU-63																1
BU-64							1								1	
BU-65		2	1												3	11
No site		1													1	
Totals	23	31	32	2	5	13	11	8	8	12	7	9	25	3	189	2,591

TABLE 2   DISTRIBUTION OF GROUND AND POLISHED STONE FROM THE VOLCAN BARU SITES

	Type A celts	Type B celts	Type C celts	Celt fragments	Miscellaneous celts, pecked	Chisels	Polished pebbles	Totals (tools)	Celt flakes	Probable celt flakes
BU-17 surface	6			2				8		
BU-17b ex.	1				1	1		3		
BU-17b above floor	1							1		
BU-17b house floor	1			1				2		
BU-17b below floor		1	1					2		
BU-17b above floor level				1				1		
BU-17b floor level	2			1				3		
BU-17b below floor level	*									
BU-17 Total	11	1	1	5	1	1		20	100	263
BU-15	1			1			1	3	2	1
BU-16									1	
BU-20	1							1		
BU-22	1	1		2				4	9	
BU-24									3	6
BU-27		1						1		
BU-31	1							1		
BU-33									1	
BU-36				1				1		
BU-39				2				2	2	3
BU-44		1						1		
BU-45		1						1		
BU-46						1		1		
BU-49	1							1	5	3
BU-55				1				1	3	
BU-65										1?
No site		1						1		
Totals	16	6	1	12	2	1	1	39	126	277

*One specimen glued to piece from layer above

ground, or pecked dorsal surfaces and/or platforms, indicating that they were removed from already finished tools. In contrast, while only 20 ground and polished artifacts were recovered at BU-17, 263 possible celt manufacturing flakes were found. An additional 100 flakes with polished, ground, or pecked surfaces were recovered. Flakes which could have resulted from initial celt manufacturing are 40 times more common (per finished ground and polished artifact) at BU-17 than at IS-3. Thus while we can easily account for all celt flakes at IS-3 as products of reshaping, celt breakdown, or accidental removal, at least some initial manufacturing is indicated for BU-17.

Nonetheless, it would be erroneous to call BU-17 or any other site in the Volcan Baru area a celt manufacturing center on the basis of present evidence. In our limited excavation of a rather large site (BU-17), we did not encounter anything remotely resembling a lithic workshop, although one may well exist at the site. Only a few of the tools associated with celt-making (e.g., hammerstones, whetstones, pebble burnishers) were recovered. The largest concentration of flakes from celtlike materials occurred just to the east of the house. In all, 72 possible celt manufacturing flakes and 10 resharpening flakes were found together with a celt and two polished stone fragments (112 flakes of non-celtlike materials were also present). Experimental replication of chipped stone celt preforms produced between 95 and 201 flakes (minimum width 1/4 inch) per artifact (section 8.0), a result that suggests that the knapping activity represented by the flake concentration near the house was not extensive. Initial celt manufacturing must have taken place at quarry-workshop sites lying beyond the survey area. Such sites are known from an area twenty kilometers to the east, but closer sites probably exist as well.

It seems preferable to consider sites which contain celt flakes as celt maintenance or repair centers rather than as celt manufacturing centers; that is, places where damaged and dulled celts could be reshaped and resharpened by specialists. Six of the eight largest sites in the survey region yielded celt flakes, which we take to mean that they were celt repair centers. Four sites (Barriles and BU-3-4, and 5) occupy the Southwest or downriver end of the survey region (a fifth large site, BU-1, located in the same region was incompletely evaluated in the field and may be a repair center as well). The other two large sites (Sitio Pitti-Gonzalez and BU-34) occupy the center of the Cerro Punta basin at the upriver end of the survey region. Of the remaining 37 sites, only one, BU-18, yielded more than a single celt flake (BU-33-28 and 8 yielded single flakes). Interestingly, this site is located in Bambito, midway between the Southwest and Cerro Punta sites and had numerous small villages around it from which to draw clientele.

The probable sequence involved in the manufacture and subsequent reworking of a celt is summarized in figure 14/1.

PECKED, GROUND, OR BATTERED STONE

Tools for grinding, mashing, and battering are important components of the Volcan Baru lithic assemblages (table 3). The most easily recognized are metates and manos. Since charred maize kernels and cobs were recovered from Sitio Pitti-Gonzalez, the presumption that these tools were principally used to grind maize is warranted. The striations on the metates and manos indicate that a back and forth grinding motion was employed. A number of metates are legged, and thus are similar to the table metate, the standard maize-grinding implement throughout most of the Americas. These metates were manufactured from vesicular basalts and andesites, and were

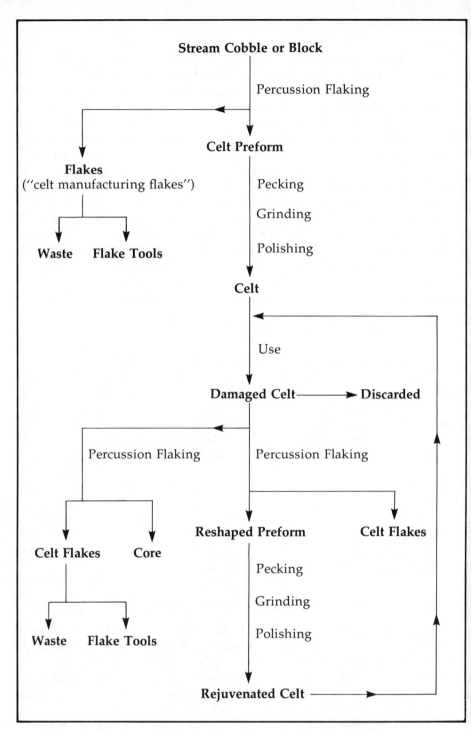

Figure 14/1: Celt manufacturing and use sequence.

pecked into final form. Some of the specimens have sculpted borders and legs (see Linares, Sheets, and Rosenthal 1975).

Other food processing tools occur as well. A significant number of boulder milling stones were encountered in the Volcan Baru region. These large boulders of dense volcanic rock have a circular shallow depression pecked and/or ground into one surface. Presumably the oval and subspherical handstones were used with these milling stones. These implements were apparently used with either a circular grinding motion or a pounding motion. At any rate, they were not used in the back and forth grinding motion documented for the manos and metates. The boulder milling stone bases and their handstones are best interpreted as being general mashing and grinding tools for use with a variety of substances.

A single boulder containing several small, deep depressions has been called a nutting stone. Similar stones are used today to aid in the cracking of palm nuts for meat extraction. Since palm nut fragments were recovered from BU-17 (section 10.3), the interpretation seems a reasonable one.

Two boulder mortars and one pestle were recovered from BU-17. In addition, a number of boulder or bedrock mortars were located along stream courses during the survey. These tools were presumably used for mashing vegetal foods and perhaps other materials as well.

ARTIFACT DESCRIPTIONS

In presenting measurements for incomplete specimens, the estimated original dimensions were placed within parentheses following the actual measurements. Edge angles were taken by measuring the angle made by tangents to the surface of both faces of an implement at a distance of 10 mm from the edge. The angle was measured at the center of the tool where possible, and rounded off to the nearest 5°. Proveniences for the artifacts are summarized in tables 1, 2, and 3.

I. Chipped Stone

A. Cores (fig. 14/2)

1. Conical, single platform: 23 specimens. Most are made on subrounded to subangular cobbles. Two large specimens are made on angular fine-grained andesite blocks. Occasionally, cores are reduced to the point where no cortex is left. Natural surfaces of the cobbles were commonly used as platforms, although exhausted or nearly exhausted cores had flaked platforms. The cores vary from having flakes removed from one side only to having flakes removed from the entire perimeter. Most of the larger cores are still capable of producing useful flakes. The smallest cores can be considered exhausted. Most of the cores are of andesite, although examples of dacite and granite are also present.

2. Bifacial: 31 specimens. An acute angled edge was used as the platform on these cores, and flakes were struck from both faces, that is,

TABLE 3 DISTRIBUTION OF PECKED, GROUND, AND BATTERED STONE IN THE VOLCAN BARU SITES

	Milling stones	Legged metates	Slab metates	Metate fragments	Mortars	Palettes	Nutting stones	Semicircular slab discs	Cylindrical manos	Oval manos	Spherical manos	Mano fragments	Smooth pebbles	Pestles	Hammers on cobbles	Hammers on cores and flakes	Whetstones	Miscellaneous	Totals
BU-17 surface	4	2	1	3	2				3	2			1					1	19
BU-17a ex.							1								1				2
BU-17b ex.	2			3						1		1	2				1		13
BU-17b above floor						1		1	1		2		1			1			5
BU-17b house floor	1										2		3		1	1			8
BU-17b below floor		2	1						2			1	2						8
BU-17b above floor level				1															1
BU-17b floor level	1									1			3		1	2			7
BU-17b below floor level		2	1										1						4
BU-17 total	8	6	3	7	2	1	1	1	6	4	4	2	13		3	4	1	1	67
BU-15																2			2
BU-21		1																	1
BU-22									3				1			1			5
BU-23				1															1
BU-24	4	1	1	1					1			1	1						10
BU-27		2		5					3			1		1					12
BU-29						1													1

	BU-30	BU-31	BU-32	BU-33	BU-36	BU-37	BU-39	BU-40	BU-42	BU-43	BU-44	BU-45	BU-46	BU-49	BU-57	BU-60	BU-61	BU-64	Totals
Totals	2	1	2	1	2	2	9	1	6	2	4	9	1	10	2	1	4	1	159
Miscellaneous						1													2
Whetstones												1		1					3
Hammers on cores and flakes							1			1		2							11
Hammers on cobbles																			3
Pestles																			1
Smooth pebbles							1					2							18
Mano fragments					1				1								1		7
Spherical manos	1	1				1			2			2							11
Oval manos		1		1									1	2					9
Cylindrical manos							2		1			2		1	1			1	21
Semicircular slab discs										1									2
Nutting stones																			1
Palettes			1				2		2										7
Mortars																			2
Metate fragments					1		1				2	1					1		20
Slab metates					1						2			1					8
Legged metates							1							1		1	2		15
Milling stones	1					1			1		1	1		1					18
Total																			159

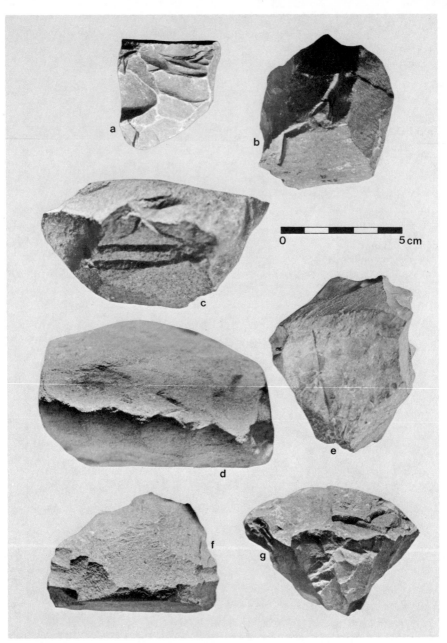

Figure 14/2: a-b. Unifacial cores; c-d. bifacial cores; e-g. multidirectional or irregular cores.

bifacially. A number of the smaller more completely flaked specimens are disk shaped and biconvex to biconical in cross section. Flakes were removed from only a single edge on many of the larger specimens. Cortex is visible on most large specimens and a few smaller ones. Most cores are made on subrounded to subangular cobbles. The larger cores could still be used for flake detachment with the exception of two specimens exhibiting multiple step fractures. The smallest cores appear to be exhausted. Andesite and to a much lesser extent basalt were the materials employed.

Some of these cores may have had light use as choppers or scrapers. The weathering of the andesite obscures use marks that are not moderately well developed.

3.   Irregular (multidirectional): 32 specimens. These cores are grouped together solely on the basis of having had flakes struck from more than two directions. Some of the larger cores have only three or four flakes removed, each one from a different platform and in a different direction. Some of the smaller cores are subspherical in shape and no longer useful for flake production. Cortex is visible primarily on larger specimens and indicates that these cores were made on rounded to subrounded cobbles. Andesite is the most common material employed, with a few specimens made of granite and dacite.

4.   Miscellaneous: two specimens. One core was made on a rounded boulder of what appears to be granite. Flakes were removed from a single platform from slightly over one-half of the perimeter of the core. If not for its enormous size, 170 x 170 x 70 mm, this core would have been considered a conical core.

A second large core, this one of dacite, is represented by nine large fragments, four of which can be fitted together. One piece has been modified after detachment by steep unifacial retouch and has been classified as a scraper-plane. The original core must have been a small boulder.

B.   Blades (fig. 14/3 a-d)

Very few specimens have attributes which conform with the definition of true blades, i.e., a flake whose length is at least twice its width, with the direction of force applied parallel to the long axis. All of the five specimens included here may well have been fortuitous. Only one specimen is complete (81 x 32 x 9 mm), although three others are missing only a small section of their distal ends. Two of these blades show evidence of use as knives and are described under the heading "flake knives."

There are a number of distal ends, proximal ends, and midsections of flakes that might have been blade fragments. None is twice as long as wide, however, and therefore they are not included in the specimen count.

C.   Scraper-planes (fig. 14/3 e-g)

Thirteen specimens. These tools have steep unifacial flaking on at least one edge, and in three cases completely around the perimeter. The largest specimen has wear polish clearly visible (using a stereoscopic microscope) on the flaked edge and extending back along the flat surface of the tool. Working edges of these heavy duty tools vary from convex (nine examples) to concave (two examples).

One tool (from BU-28) is a keeled scraper-plane unifacially retouched around the entire circumference. Made on a thick bladelike flake, the bulb of force has been removed by flaking of the ventral surface. All are made of andesite.

D. *Flake scraper-planes (unifacially retouched large flakes) (fig. 14/3 h-j)*

Eleven specimens. These tools have light unifacial retouch normally along one edge only. No wear patterns were identified, primarily because of the heavy weathering of most specimens. Their size and shape suggest that they would have served well as heavy duty planes. All were made of andesite.

E. *Flake choppers (bifacially retouched large flakes)*

Eight specimens. Light bifacial retouch occurs along one or more edges of these large flakes. Some crushing and small use flakes can be seen on a few of the specimens. All were made of andesite.

F. *Scrapers (fig. 14/4 a-f)*

Eight specimens. These tools are characterized by purposeful unifacial retouch along one or more edges. Working edges vary from convex (three examples) to straight (three examples) to concave (two examples). The contour of the working edge can be smooth (four examples) or jagged (four examples). One is made on a celt flake which still retains a polished surface and a portion of the bit as the striking platform. All are made of andesite.

G. *Flake scrapers (fig. 14/4 g-j)*

Twelve specimens. These flakes have edges appearing to be modified by use only. The use flakes are removed from one face of the working edge only. These presumed scraping edges occur on a variety of flake forms. Working edges vary from convex (four examples) to straight (four examples) to concave (four examples). They differ from purposefully made scrapers by having rather more acute working edge angles. Four tools have wear polish visible on the working edges. One is on the snapped edge of a large bladelike flake and appears to have been used as a small plane. Another tool of particular interest has two concave working surfaces exhibiting a high degree of polish on both surfaces, but no use flakes. The polished area extends 1–2 mm onto one face only of each working edge. There are striations visible in the polished facets perpendicular to the edge, suggesting that the tool was held at a 90° angle to the surface of the worked material (which was unyielding, perhaps wood) and moved in a scraping motion. All are made of andesite. Flake scrapers were undoubtedly much more common in the Volcan assemblages, but have gone unrecognized because of the obliteration of wear patterns by weathering.

H. *Flake knives (fig. 14/4 k-m)*

Seven specimens. These tools are distinguished either by having use flakes removed bifacially from the working edge or by having wear polish

Figure 14/3: a-d. Blades; e-g. scraper-planes; h-j. flake scraper-planes.

Figure 14/4: a-f. Scrapers; g-j. flake scrapers; k-m. flake knives (made on celt flakes).

extending onto both sides of the working edge. None appears to be deliberately manufactured. Three are on blade fragments, however. Six of the specimens have wear polish visible under the microscope as well as use flakes removed. One particularly well-used tool is a blade fragment (distal end) which has use polish extending away from the working edges 3–5 mm. Striations parallel to the working edges (both sides of the tool were used) suggest that the tool was used in a sawing motion. Another knife on a blade (distal fragment) has very shallow notches opposite each other near its proximal end. These notches along with polish on the high spots of both dorsal and ventral surfaces extending for 20 mm from the proximal end indicate that the tool was hafted (the polish is attributed to rubbing of the knife against the haft). The final knife on a blade fragment (distal end) has small bifacial use flakes and moderate polish along both edges and the tip of the tool.

Two of the remaining specimens are made on celt flakes; one, in fact, retains a full 23 mm of the bit end of what was probably a type A celt. It is the opposite end of the flake which has bifacial use flakes and polish. The tools are made of andesite and dacite.

I. Perforators

Nine specimens. There are several quite distinct tools that have a point or "nose" formed by unifacial retouch. One of the edges leading to the point is usually concave, the other straight. Five of the specimens have wear polish visible on the point and back some distance along both edges. One is particularly noteworthy as the polish is clearly visible without the aid of a microscope. This tool is made on a thick pointed flake, triangular in cross section. The rounded tip is nearly 5 mm across. Heavy rounding of edges and polish extends back along the total length of the acute-angled edge (74 mm) and back 35 mm on the straight edge and dorsal ridge. The polish follows the contours of the flake scars, suggesting that the tool was used on a soft yielding material. This tool is by far the largest of the perforators. The others are remarkably similar in size. All are made of andesite.

J. Bifaces

Three bifacially flaked specimens were recovered which appear to be preforms for either celts or chisels. The single complete specimen measured 68 x 35 x 25 mm, was planoconvex in cross section, and was heavily weathered (andesite). Two narrow bifacially flaked fragments were found that may have been preforms for chisels. Both were biconvex in cross section. One specimen measured 62 x 36 x 25 mm and was made of basalt. The other fragment, a midsection, measured 47 x 28 x 13 mm and was made of andesite.

K. Flakes

More than 2,500 flakes were recovered from sites in the Volcan Baru region (2,000 from BU-17), all but six made of igneous rocks, primarily andesite; the rest were, one of quartz and five of chalcedony. Cortex visible on a large number of flakes indicates that they were struck from rounded to subangular cobbles. Such cobbles are available in stream gravels throughout the region. Platforms tend to be wide, with "lipped" back edges. Bulbs of percussion are normally diffuse, and *éraillure* scars rare. The dominant mode of flake removal inferred is hammerstone percussion where the hammer is a soft rock and/or has a broad striking facet, and where the blow is struck well back from the core edge. All of these flakes might be considered as waste or debitage but for the fact that heavy weathering has undoubtedly destroyed the evidence of use on many of them.

II. Ground and Polished Stone

A. Celts (fig. 14/5)

1.   Type A (pear-shaped): 16 specimens. These celts have bits that extend in a smooth curve back along the sides of the tool, giving it a pear-shaped appearance. They are all biconvex in cross section although some are slightly asymmetrical. The entire surface of the bit end is ground and polished. The poll may be similarly treated, although sometimes it is left as a pecked or (rarely) a chipped surface. Some specimens have a center ridge (in one case double ridges) on either face near the poll end. More commonly, the surface contour of the faces is smooth. Some of the bits have clearly been reground. The new bit is made at a steeper angle than the original so that an obtuse angle is formed on the surface of the celt faces ca. 10 mm behind the bit. On one specimen the new bit angle measured 70° while the original bit angle was reconstructed to be closer to 55°. Most of the large celt fragments have been reused as cores.

Only two celts are complete enough to provide measurements; they are 86 x 46 x 20 mm and 145 (175) x 86 x 43 mm. Edge angles on the surviving bits varied between 40° and 70°. The celts are made from fine-grained andesite and basalt.

2.   Type B: six specimens. These celts have straight subparallel sides that taper gently from the bit to the butt end. All have a ridge along the midline and are diamond-shaped in cross section. Flake scars from the initial stage of manufacture are occasionally visible at the butt end. Evidence of pecking can be seen on most specimens from the midsection on back to the butt end. The bit end is completely ground and polished, and in a few cases the entire celt is similarly treated. The three bits left intact for measurement had edge angles of 55°, 55°, and 60°. The celts are made of fine-grained andesite and basalt.

3.   Type C: one specimen. This is a small, well-made celt with a flaring bit and incurvate sides. The butt end is missing. The well-controlled flaking is clearly visible on all but the bit section. Some pecking occurs on the middle of both faces, giving the celt a smooth biconvex cross section. Grinding and polishing are restricted to the bit itself. Bit angle is 40°. The celt measures 76 (100) x 68 x 16 mm, and is made of fine-grained basalt.

Figure 14/5: a-e. Type A celts; f-h. Type B celts; i. Type C celt.

4. Fragments: 12 specimens. A number of celt fragments were either too small or too altered to be categorized further. Seven are polls, four are midsections, and one is a bit section. The last mentioned fragment had been reworked (probably from a type A celt) and used as a chisel. The resharpened bit has an angle of 55°. All of the midsections and at least some of the polls were reused as cores. All were made of andesite and basalt.

5. Miscellaneous: One chipped and pecked celt preform was recovered. The bit on the tool had not yet been formed. It measured 78 x 51 x 24 mm and was made on rather coarse-grained andesite.

A flaked and pecked midsection recovered may have been a broken preform or perhaps a part of a chisel. The fragment measured 53 x 28 x 18 mm and was made of andesite.

B. *Chisel*

The bit fragment of a chisel (28 x 15 x 10 mm) was recovered from BU-17. The entire surface of the fragment was finely polished. The bit was only 7 mm wide, and had an edge angle of 40°. The tool was made of fine-grained andesite.

C. *Polished pebble*

A flat triangular-shaped fragment was recovered from BU-15 (33 x 29 x 14 mm). The fragment was polished on all surfaces, but a few flake scars remained incompletely obliterated on one edge. Its purpose is unknown.

D. *Celt flakes*

A total of 126 flakes retained pecked, ground, and/or polished surfaces on their striking platforms or dorsal sides. These flakes were either purposefully struck in order to reshape damaged cores or to produce flakes from damaged cores, or they were accidental by-products of heavy celt use. We suspect that most were deliberately struck from damaged celts; 23 of the total were clearly not from the bit end of celts and can be safely considered purposefully detached. Thirty-nine flakes retain a portion of the bit on their striking platforms (64 celt flakes could have come from either the bit or from somewhere else on the celt). The large number of celts showing evidence of resharpening and the large number of celt fragments that had been reused as cores support the inference that most celt flakes were deliberately struck. All celt flakes are of fine-grained igneous rocks.

E. *Possible celt manufacturing flakes*

A total of 277 flakes of fine-grained igneous rock *may* be by-products of celt manufacturing activities. Since flakes without pecked, ground, or polished surfaces can be removed in the celt reshaping process (ca. 30 percent in experimental reshaping — see Ranere, section 8.4) and in reusing celts as cores, not all of these flakes were manufacturing by-products. There are, in addition, a few nonground and polished stone artifacts made of fine-grained igneous rocks. Nonetheless, if these flakes of celtlike materials came only from reworking finished ground and polished tools, we would expect to find only 40 or so of them in the collections instead of 277. This estimate is based on celt reshaping experiments and on the ratio of celt flakes to flakes of celtlike materials from other sites in western Panama (section 8.4).

III.   Pecked, Ground, or Battered Stone

A. *Milling stones (fig. 14/6 h,i)*

Eighteen specimens. These implements are boulders of dense andesite or dacite having a pecked and/or ground shallow, circular depression on one

Figure 14/6: a-c. Slab metates; d. semicircular slab; e-g. palettes; h-i. milling stones.

side. The boulders used were generally rounded to subrounded (rarely angular). The two whole specimens recovered measure 211 x 178 x 93 mm and 226 x 156 x 97 mm. One large fragment had a diameter of 312 mm and a thickness of 115 mm. The handstones used with these milling stones were presumably used in a circular grinding motion and/or in pounding.

B. Metates

1. Legged (fig. 14/7): 15 specimens. These grinding tools were manufactured from vesicular igneous rocks by pecking. The working surface or table

is flat or slightly concave and is modified through use of a handstone against it in a back and forth motion. These metates have four legs which can be either tapered or straight, and either round or square in cross section. Some of the legs and table borders of these specimens are decorated with sculpted figures, trophy heads being most common. All specimens were fragmentary, so that their dimensions cannot be determined with accuracy. However, based on the size of the legs and the thickness of the tables, two size classes can be inferred. The most common (12 specimens) is a smaller size with a table thickness varying from 18 to 42 mm (averaging 26 mm). Legs are round in cross section and either tapered or straight. Maximum diameters of the legs vary from 41 to 87 mm (averaging 56 mm). In contrast, the larger metates (3 specimens) have a table thickness varying from 41 to 67 mm (averaging 58 mm), and legs that are square in cross section and average 120 mm across.

2. Slab (fig. 14/6 a-c): eight specimens. These metates are made of a volcanic rock somewhat denser than the rock used for legged metates. They are simply flat slabs having one surface dressed by pecking. The back and forth wear pattern on the working surface duplicates that found for the legged metates. The single complete specimen measured 364 x 231 x 38 mm. Fragments of other slab metates varied in thickness from 35 to 70 mm.

3. Fragments: 20 specimens. These metate fragments were too small to classify further.

C. Mortars

Two specimens. These boulders of andesite have deep, circular depressions pecked into one or more surfaces. Both are broken. One specimen has a main depression 85 mm deep and 150 mm in diameter plus two smaller depressions. The second mortar has a single depression 112 mm deep and 190 mm in diameter. Similar-sized depressions were noted in boulders and bedrock along stream courses in the survey region. These implements were presumably used with pestles in pounding or mashing activities.

D. Palettes (fig. 14/6 e-g)

Seven specimens. These artifacts are small slabs of dense andesite and dacite having one surface smoothly ground. Two specimens have slight circular depressions apparently formed through use. Perhaps these palettes were used in the grinding of pigments.

E. Nutting stone

One boulder of andesite (324 x 210 x 110 mm) contains five well-defined depressions and six incipient ones. The five definite depressions vary from 20 to 30 mm in diameter and from 6 to 12 mm in depth. Today such stones are used in the area for smashing palm nuts.

F. Semicircular slabs (fig. 14/6 d)

Two slabs of andesite were shaped by steep flaking and pecking into

Figure 14/7: Legged metate fragments.

semicircular forms. The smaller specimen, which is fragmentary, may have one surface altered by grinding. The larger one shows no signs of use. Their purpose is unknown.

G. Manos (fig. 14/8)

1. Cylindrical: 21 specimens. These implements are pecked into cylindrical form primarily from coarse-grained igneous rock (two specimens are of a finer-grained andesite). Through back and forth grinding against metate surfaces, flat work facets are developed on one to four faces. One well-used mano is rectangular in cross section. One specimen (224 x 87 x 87 mm) appears to be only partially complete. It has been pecked on all surfaces but is not uniform in appearance and is unused.

2. Oval: 9 specimens. These tools are rounded, flat river cobbles which have been used on one or both flat sides for grinding. They vary in outline from nearly circular to elongated ovals. The grinding surfaces are flat to slightly convex in contour. They are made of dacite and granite.

3. Spherical: 11 specimens. These tools are similar to oval manos in that they represent rounded stream cobbles modified only by use. They are all subspherical in shape, having two opposite faces that are somewhat flattened. These grinding facets are all somewhat convex. A circular grinding motion is inferred from the facet shape, although weathering of the surfaces obscured any striations which might originally have been present. All were made of dacite.

4. Fragments: 7 specimens. These handstone fragments could not be assigned to a more specific category.

Figure 14/8: a-g. Cylindrical manos; h-l. oval manos.

Figure 14/9: a-d. Smoothed pebbles; e. sculpted fragment.

H.   *Smoothed pebbles (fig. 14/9 a-d)*

Eighteen specimens. These are small oval (13) and round (15) pebbles of andesite and dacite which have definitely smoothed or possibly smoothed facets. Their function is unknown.

I.   *Pestle*

One elongated cobble of igneous rock was recovered which appeared to have been used as a pestle. It was almost square in cross section and tapered toward one end. A broad pounding facet occurs at the large end, and a small, off-centered facet at the opposite end. It measured 174 x 60 x 58 mm.

J.   *Hammerstones*

1.   Cobble: three specimens. All show heavy use as hammers. One (58 x 54 x 35 mm) is disk-shaped and has a hammering facet completely encircling its perimeter. The other two cobbles (76 x 57 x 54 mm and 50 x 32 x 28 mm) have broad hammering facets at opposite ends of the tool. All are made of fine-grained andesite.

2.   On cores and large flakes: 11 specimens. These hammers have been made (through use) on remnants of irregular and bifacial cores as well as on large flakes (2 examples). Facets range from broad and continuous around the tool perimeter to being light and localized along one edge. All are of andesite.

K.   *Whetstones*

Three specimens. One whetstone consists of an angular pumicelike stone which has one slightly concave, very smooth surface. Linear striations are visible, running parallel to the long axis of the tool. The opposite face and sides are unmodified. A second fragmentary specimen has one slightly concave, smooth surface, but no striations. The third specimen is a large flat dacite slab with a smooth, very slightly concave surface. Subparallel grooves 2–3 mm in width are visible on this surface as well as finer striations.

L.   *Incised cobble*

One elongated andesite cobble has a number of fine lines incised into its surface. No particular pattern can be discerned.

M.   *Sculpted fragment (fig. 14/9 e)*

A single piece of vesicular basalt has been sculpted in a fashion that resembles bas-relief. One side vaguely resembles a human face. It is probably a fragment from a metate table leg.

Stone Tools from La Pitahaya (IS-3)

C. SHELTON EINHAUS

INTRODUCTION

The 1971 excavations at La Pitahaya (IS-3) yielded approximately 2,000 lithic specimens produced and/or used by man. Of this total approximately one half, or 1,000, are tools; the others are by-products of tool manufacture.

Tools have been divided into categories on the basis of final method of manufacture, if manufacturing took place. We felt that such a descriptive typology would be more useful than others (e.g., a functional typology) for comparing the different sites we excavated in western Panama. Although functional interpretations of tools are of great interest to this study, in the current state of affairs they would be subject to almost constant revision. Furthermore, functional interpretations rely to a large extent on the study of wear patterns. Some tool uses leave no apparent wear; postdepositional weathering of tool surfaces often obliterates wear patterns; and replicative experiments on a very large scale are necessary to approach accuracy of explanation in functional analyses. Hence, the possible functions of IS-3 tools have simply been proposed as subcategories of the technological divisions.

The multiple wear displayed by these tools proved both informative and troublesome. It was informative because it emphasized the fact that at Palenque some kinds of stone were apparently more easily procured than others. Many of the materials used in the tools resemble the beach cobbles found on this peninsula today. Other materials must have come from the mainland, possibly from riverbeds, from the highlands, or from as far away as the Azuero Peninsula. Those materials that were not available locally appear to have been more highly valued, if extensive reuse can be taken as an indication of value. Multiple use also implies a certain lack of specialization in the assemblage. Finally, tools showing multiple usage present obvious problems in classification, in that there may be no way to distinguish which was the most important kind of wear, or if one kind of wear was equal to another.

Three avenues of investigation were pursued in identifying tool function: (1) microwear analysis, (2) ethnographic analogy, and (3) experimental replications. Microscopic analysis of wear patterns aids in identifying tool usage and in understanding variation in the macromorphology of tools (cf. Tringham et al. 1974, p. 195; Wilmsen 1968, 1970). Although archaeologists will not be able to discern every use to which every tool was ever put, wear patterns will teach them a great deal about specific sites and about the activities performed there.

Some tools from IS-3 so closely resemble ethnographic or historic ones that analogy seems justified, especially if corroborative evidence can be provided. Thus, manos and metates are considered by analogy to be maize-grinding implements, a fact corroborated by the recovery of maize kernels, cobs, and pollen from Isla Palenque.

A number of experiments were undertaken using raw materials from the site, from other areas of Panama, plus a few similar materials from the Philadelphia, Pa. area. These experiments reproduced and used tools similar to the excavated ones. As many archaeologists have pointed out (Coles 1973, pp. 15–18; Keeley 1974, p. 329; Odell 1975, p. 234), tool replication experiments do not tell us definitively what past use was made of excavated tools. They do, however, narrow the range of possible functional interpretations.

THE CLASSIFICATION

This typology divides artifacts into categories based on the final method of manufacture, where manufacture took place. It is an essentially descriptive typology that may be skipped over lightly by the nonspecialists. Subcategories within these groupings are based on inferred tool use and may be of more general interest.

Tables 1, 2, and 3 show the occurrence of each tool type by trench, block, and layer. These totals include some large artifacts that were not removed from the site. In table 4 tools showing clear evidence of more than one use have been listed, first according to the primary or heaviest kind of usage, then according to their secondary use. Artifacts photographed and discarded at the site have been included in the totals for table 3 and noted in the text, but omitted from table 4.

I. Chipped Stone

On the whole the IS-3 chipped stone industry does not appear to have been particularly well developed or complex. The most carefully made chipped stone artifacts, points and blades, are found in other Panamanian sites as well. These points are triangular in cross section and are known from other sites in the Chiriqui Gulf region (Linares 1968b) and from Sitio Conte and Nata in the other central provinces (Lothrop 1937; Cooke 1976a and personal communication). Stems from two large blades also resemble those from whole blades known from Cerro Brujo (see report no. 6) and from several sites in central Panama, including Sitio Sierra (Cooke 1976, personal communication).

Chipped stone tools were made of several varieties of chalcedony, as well as quartz and agate.

Chipping waste includes waste flakes, identified by such criteria as bulbs, striking platforms, éraillure scars and ripple marks, and shatter, resulting from the intentional breakdown of cores and flakes but not clearly exhibiting the above criteria. A flake with these identifying marks removed is thus classified as shatter. Waste flakes and shatter constitute the largest number (803 specimens) of chipped stone artifacts at La Pitahaya.

A. Core and Core Tools (table 1, fig. 15/1)

The principal materials for cores are a green or red chalcedony (jasper), a crystalline quartz sometimes combined with chert in the same specimen, white to gray cherts and white quartz. Of the 33 cores in the sample, eight are jasper and the remaining are gray cherts and quartzite.

1. Bipolar cores (fig. 15/1 a-c). At least 13 cores in the sample were flaked using a bipolar technique. This technique leaves crushing marks on the platform at two opposite ends of the core as a result of placing the core on a supporting anvil stone while it is being struck. The same technique also gives a flattened or straight-sided appearance to many flake scars, which is unusual in materials that break with concoidal fracture. Most of the bipolar cores are made of chert and quartz and exhibit nearly straight-sided breaks. Some of the quartz cores are under 2 centimeters in height, so small that support on an anvil might be necessary for flake detachment. The use of the bipolar technique can also aid in the flaking of larger cores of quartz, a material notable for its hardness. In the laboratory it was found that a supporting anvil was useful in anchoring the stone so that it could be smashed with a blow hard enough to break it.

2. Multidirectional, unidirectional, and other cores (fig. 15/1 d-f). None of the cores were flaked multidirectionally, that is, from more than one direction but not bipolarly. This group includes a few cores flaked in two directions. There are also 10 or possibly 11 unidirectionally flaked cores in this sample. Eighteen miscellaneous cores are listed under other cores in table 1.

Figure 15/1: a-c. Bipolar cores: d-f. multidirectional (irregular) cores.

TABLE 1 CHIPPED STONE FROM ISLA PALENQUE

Provenience and Types

Layer or cms below surface	Cores			Other	Used flakes	Perfo-rators	Possible grater chips	Unmodi-fied blades	Stemmed blades	Points on blades	Tri-facial points	Waste flakes	Shatter	Total
	Uni-directional	Bipolar	Multi-directional											
TRENCH I														
BLOCK 1														
Surface	—	—	—	—	—	—	—	—	1	—	—	3	—	4
A+B	1	1	—	—	5	—	11	1	—	—	3	46(6)[a]	4	78
C	—	2	2	—	3	—	2	1	—	—	—	56(8)	12	85
D+E	—	—	—	—	1	2	—	1	—	—	—	29(5)	4(3)	45
Block 1 Subtotal	1	3	2	—	9	2	13	2	1	—	3	134(19)	20(3)	212
BLOCK 2														
Surface	—	—	—	1	—	—	—	—	—	—	—	—	—	—
A+B	1	1	—	1	—	—	1	—	—	—	—	3	1(1)	8
C	1	1	1		2	2	3	1	—	—	—	24(13)	24(4)	76
D+E	1	2	—	1(BL)[b]	11	1	22	1	1	—	3	121(18)	50(3)	235
Block 2 Subtotal	3	3	1	2	13	3	26	1	1	—	3	149(31)	75(8)	319
BLOCK 3														
Surface	—	1	1	1	1	—	—	—	—	—	—	3	—	7
A+B	2	—	—	—	1	—	3	1	—	—	2	24(4)[a]	4(1)	42
C	1	2	1	5	8	1	6	—	—	2	—	67(10)	10(4)	117
D+E	—	1	—	2	4	—	3	1	—	—	2	45(6)	11(2)	77
Block 3 Subtotal	3	4	2	8	14	1	12	2	—	2	4	139(20)	25(7)	243

| | Cores | | | | | | | | | | | | | |
Layer or cms below surface	Uni-directional	Bipolar	Multi-directional	Other flakes	Used flakes	Perfo-rators	Possible grater chips	Unmodi-fied blades	Stemmed blades	Points on blades	Tri-facial points	Waste flakes	Shatter	Total
TRENCH II														
BLOCK 1														
Surface	—	—	—	1	—	—	—	—	—	—	—	1	—	2
A+B	1	—	—	—	—	—	4	1	—	1	1	30(5)	8	51
C	2	—	—	2	3	—	1	2	—	—	3	17(2)	3(1)	36
D+E	—	2	—	—	2	—	—	—	—	—	1	5(3)	1	14
Block 1 Subtotal	3	2	—	3	5	—	5	3	—	1	5	53(10)	12(1)	103
BLOCK 2														
Surface	—	—	—	—	1	—	—	1	—	—	—	4(1)	—	6
A+B	1	(1)	3	—	6	2	7	1	—	1	4	28(11)	14(4)	82
C	—	—	—	2	1	—	—	—	—	—	1	6(3)	(1)	15
D+E	—	—	—	—	—	—	—	—	—	—	—	2	—	2
Block 2 Subtotal	1	(1)	3	2	8	2	7	1	—	1	5	40(15)	14(5)	105
TRENCH III														
0–50	—	—	1	—	1	2	—	1	—	—	2	1(2)	—	8
50–100	—	—	—	—	—	—	—	—	—	—	—	2	—	4
100–sterile	—	—	—	—	—	—	—	—	—	—	—	—	—	—
Subtotal	—	—	1	—	1	2	—	1–	—	—	2	3(2)	—	12
TRENCH IV - none														

TABLE 1 continued

Layer or cms below surface	Cores			Other flakes	Used flakes	Perforators	Possible grater chips	Unmodified blades	Stemmed blades	Points on blades	Trifacial points	Waste flakes	Shatter	Total
	Unidirectional	Bipolar	Multidirectional											
TRENCH V														
Surface	—	—	—	—	—	—	—	—	—	—	—	—	—	—
A	—	—	—	2	—	—	—	—	—	—	1	4	1	8
B	—	—	—	—	1	—	—	—	—	1	1	3	—	6
C	—	—	—	—	—	—	—	—	—	—	—	—	—	—
D	—	—	—	—	—	—	—	—	—	—	—	—	—	—
Subtotal	—	—	—	2	1	—	—	—	—	1	2	7	1	14
TRENCH VI - None														
TRENCH VII														
A(Surface)	—	—	—	—	—	—	—	—	—	—	—	2	—	2
B	—	—	—	1(BL)	—	—	—	—	—	—	—	—	—	1
C	—	—	—	—	1	—	—	1	—	—	2	(1)	(1)	6
C?	—	—	—	—	1	—	—	—	—	—	—	1	2	4
D+E	—	—	—	—	—	—	—	—	—	—	—	2(1)	—	3
Subtotal	—	—	—	1(BL)	2	—	—	1	—	—	2	5(2)	2(1)	16
TRENCH VIII - none														
Artifact totals	11	13	9	18	53	10	63	11	2	5	26	530(99)	149(25)	1,024

[a] ( ) = possible specimen.
[b] BL = blade.

TABLE 2 GROUND AND POLISHED STONE FROM ISLA PALENQUE

Layer or cms below surface	Axe	Celt type			Adzes	Chisels	Flakes of celt material	Flakes with polish or pecking	Celt fragments	Totals
		A	B	C						
TRENCH I										
BLOCK 1										
Surface	—	—	3	—	—	—	—	—	1	4
A+B	—	—	4	—	1	—	1	11	11	28
C	—	1	1	1	—	—	—	17	3	23
D+E	—	—	—	—	—	—	1	6	—	7
Subtotal Block 1	—	1	8	1	1	—	2	34	15	62
BLOCK 2										
Surface	—	—	—	—	—	—	—	—	—	—
A+B	—	2	6	1	—	—	—	1	3	13
C	—	2	4	—	1	—	1	8	6	21
D+E	—	—	1	—	—	—	5	43(1)[a]	7	56(1)
Subtotal Block 2	—	4	11	1	1	—	6	52(1)	16	91(1)
BLOCK 3										
Surface	—	1	2	—	—	1 butt	—	4	1	9
A+B	—	—	2	—	—	1	—	10(1)	17	30(1)
C	—	—	—	—	—	—	6	18	9	33
D+E	—	—	—	—	—	—	3	18	5	26
Subtotal Block 3	—	1	4	—	—	2	9	50(1)	32	98(1)

TABLE 2 continued

Layer or cms below surface	Axe	Celt type			Adzes	Chisels	Flakes of celt material	Flakes with polish or pecking[a]	Celt fragments	Totals
		A	B	C						
TRENCH II										
BLOCK 1										
Surface	—	—	—	—	—	—	—	—	—	—
A+B	—	—	1	1	—	—	—	6	4	12
C	—	—	1	1	—	—	—	12	12	26
D+E	—	—	2	—	—	—	1	1	2	6
Subtotal Block 1	—	—	4	2	—	—	1	19	18	44
BLOCK 2										
Surface	—	—	—	—	—	—	—	1	4	5
A+B	—	1	1	—	—	—	—	10	5	16
C	—	1	1	1	—	—	—	5	3	11
D+E	—	—	—	—	—	—	—	1	—	1
Subtotal Block 2	—	1	2	1	—	—	—	17	12	33
TRENCH III										
0–50	—	5	3	1	—	—	—	2	19	30
50–100	—	—	—	—	—	—	—	1	—	1
100–sterile	—	—	—	—	—	—	—	—	—	—
Total	—	5	3	1	—	—	—	3	19	31
TRENCH IV										
0–100	1	1	6	1	1	1	—	—	3	14
100–sterile	—	—	—	—	—	—	—	—	1	1
Total	1	1	6	1	1	1	—	—	4	15

Layer or cms below surface	Axe	Celt type			Adzes	Chisels	Flakes of celt material	Flakes with polish or pecking[a]	Celt fragments	Totals
		A	B	C						
TRENCH V										
Surface	—	—	—	—	—	—	—	—	—	—
A	—	—	—	—	—	—	—	—	—	—
B	—	—	—	—	—	—	—	3	3	6
C	—	—	—	—	—	—	1	4	3	8
D	—	—	—	—	—	—	—	—	—	—
Total	—	—	—	—	—	—	1	7	6	14
TRENCH VI - none										
TRENCH VII										
A(Surface)	—	1	—	—	—	—	—	—	1	1
B	—	—	1	—	—	—	—	—	5	7
C	—	—	1	—	—	—	—	3	1	5
C?	—	—	—	—	—	—	—	3	2	5
D+E	—	1	—	—	—	—	—	1	—	1
Total	—	1	2	—	—	—	—	7	9	19
TRENCH VIII - none										
Totals	1	14	40	7	3	3	19	189(2)	131	407(2)

[a] ( ) = possible specimens.

TABLE 3   ARTIFACT TOTALS — GROUNDSTONE, COBBLE, AND MISCELLANEOUS ARTIFACTS FROM ISLA PALENQUE

Layer or cms below surface	Metates or milling stones	Manos and hand-stones	Hammers	Pounding-mashing stones	Anvils	Nutters	Notched stones	Grooved stones	Miscellaneous	Totals
TRENCH I										
BLOCK 1										
Surface	2	—	—	1	1	1	2	1	(1 sculpture)[a]	8(1)
A+B	7	5	5	5	4	2	3	—	(1 sculpture)	31(1)
C	3	3	6	—	1	3	6	1	—	23
D+E	—	—	2	—	—	—	—	—	—	2
Block 1 Subtotal	12	8	13	6	6	6	11	2	(2)	64+(2)
BLOCK 2										
Surface	—	—	—	—	—	—	—	—	—	—
A+B	17	20	9	2	1	5	6	1	1 grinding fragment	63
C	7	6	13	—	1	2	12	4	1 rasp / 1 sculpture	46
D+E	4	2	17	1	1	—	11	1	2 rasps / 4 grinding / 2 grinding fragments[b]	45
Block 2 Subtotal	28	28	39	3	2	7	29	7	11	154
BLOCK 3										
Surface	8	3	7	4	3	4	3	—	—	32
A+B	—	6	13	2	5	5	12	—	1 rasp	44
C	3	3	9	—	3	1	6	1	1 polisher	27
D+E	1	1	2	—	1	—	1	—	—	6
Block 3 Subtotal	12	13	31	6	12	10	22	1	2	109

Layer or cms below surface	Metates or milling stones	Manos and hand-stones	Hammers	Pounding-mashing stones	Anvils	Nutters	Notched stoned	Grooved stones	Miscellaneous	Totals
TRENCH II										
BLOCK 1										
Surface	—	—	—	—	—	—	—	—	—	—
A+B	—	—	14	—	1	1	10	1	3 rasps / 1 whetstone	31
C	3^c	8^d	8	—	—	2	25	1	1 sculpture / 1 whetstone	49
D+E	1	2^d	3	—	—	1	12	1	—	20
Block 1 Subtotal	4^c	10	25	—	1	4	47	3	6	100
BLOCK 2										
Surface	1	3	1	—	—	—	1	—	1 bead	7
A+B	—	—	7	2	1	3	5	—	1 geode / 1 sculpture	20
C	2	1	2	—	—	1	17	2	—	25
D+E	—	—	—	—	—	—	4	—	—	4
Block 2 Subtotal	3	4	10	2	1	4	27	2	3	56
TRENCH III										
0–50	2	5	18	—	5	5	26	2	—	63
50–100	—	—	—	—	—	—	—	—	—	—
100–sterile	—	—	—	—	—	—	—	—	—	—
Total	2	5	18	—	5	5	26	2	—	63
TRENCH IV										
0–100	—	—	—	—	—	—	2	1	—	3
100–sterile	—	—	3	1	—	—	2	1	—	7
Total	—	—	3	1	—	—	4	2	—	10

TABLE 3 continued

Layer or cms below surface	Metates or milling stones	Manos and hand-stones	Hammers	Pounding-mashing stones	Anvils	Nutters	Notched stoned	Grooved stones	Miscellaneous	Totals
TRENCH V										
Surface										
A	—	—	—	—	—	—	—	—	—	—
B	1	1	1	1	—	1	14	—	—	19
C	2	1	—	—	—	—	6	—	—	9
D	—	—	—	—	—	—	—	—	—	—
Total	3	2	1	1	—	1	20	—	—	28
TRENCH VI – none										
TRENCH VII										
A (Surface)	—	1	—	—	—	—	—	—	—	1
B	2	2	2	—	2	1	2	1	—	12
C	—	—	—	—	—	—	4	1	—	5
D+E	—	—	—	—	—	—	—	1	—	1
Total	2	3	2	—	2	1	6	3	—	19
TRENCH VIII – none										
Artifact totals	66	73	142	19	29	38	192	22	22(2)	603(2)
Percentage of total	10.9%	12.1%	23.5%	3.1%	4.8%	6.3%	31.7%	3.6%	4.0%	100%

a = possible specimens in parentheses.

b = 2 pieces of same stone in different levels, counted twice.

c = additional fragments discarded at the site.

d = two fragments of the same piece in separate layers, counted twice.

TABLE 4 USE ON GROUNDSTONE, COBBLES, AND MISCELLANEOUS TOOLS FROM ISLA PALENQUE

Layer or cms below surface	Metates and milling stones	Handstones and manos	Reused as handstones or manos	Hammers	Reused as hammers	Pounding-mashing stones	Reused as pounding-mashing	Edge-used	Anvils	Reused as anvils	Nutting stones	Reused as nutting stones	Notched stones	Other use with notches	Grooved stones	Other Use	Total
TRENCH I																	
BLOCK 1																	
Surface	2	—	1	—	—	1	—	—	1	—	1	1	2	—	1	(1 sculpture)[a]	
A+B	2	4	—	5	2	5	1	1	4	—	2	5	3	—	—	(1 sculpture)	
C	—	—	—	4	2	—	—	—	1	—	2	—	6	—	1	—	
D+E	—	—	—	2	—	—	—	—	—	—	—	—	—	—	—	—	
Block 1 Subtotal	4	4	1	11	4	6	1	1	6	—	5	6	11	—	2	(2)	62+ (2)
BLOCK 2																	
Surface	—	—	—	—	—	—	—	—	—	—	—	—	—	—	—	—	
A+B	—	2	—	2	1	—	—	—	1	1	1	1	2	—	2	—	
C	—	—	—	1	—	—	—	—	—	—	1	—	5	—	4	1 rasp, 1 sculpture	
D+E	—	—	—	1	—	—	—	—	1	—	1	—	—	—	1	2 rasps	
Block 2 Subtotal	—	2	—	4	1	—	—	—	2	1	2	1	7	—	7	4	31
BLOCK 3																	
Surface	7	3	1	7	3	4	—	3	3	1	2	4	3	—	—	—	
A+B	—	6	1	12	7	2	—	2	5	2	5	2	12	—	—	1 rasp	
C	1	1	—	8	3	—	—	1	3	3	1	—	6	—	1	1 polishing stone	
D+E	1	1	—	2	1	—	—	—	1	—	—	—	1	—	—	—	
Block 3 Subtotal	9	11	2	29	14	6	—	6	12	6	8	6	22	—	1	2	134

TABLE 4 continued

Layer or cms below surface	Metates and milling stones	Handstones and manos	Reused as handstones or manos	Hammers	Reused as hammers	Pounding-mashing stones	Reused as pounding-mashing	Edge-used	Anvils	Reused as anvils	Nutting stones	Reused as nutting stones	Notched stones	Other use with notches	Grooved stones	Other Use	Total
TRENCH II																	
BLOCK 1																	
Surface	—	—	—	1	—	—	—	—	—	—	—	—	—	—	—	—	
A+B	—	—	—	13	1	—	—	—	1	2	1	—	10	—	1	3 rasps, 1 whetstone	
C	3	3	—	8	—	—	—	—	—	1	2	1	24	—	—	2 sculptures,* 1 whetstone	
D+E	1	2^b	—	3	—	—	—	—	—	—	1	—	12	—	—	1	
Block 1 Subtotal	4	5	—	25	1	—	—	—	1	3	4	1	46	—	3	8	101
BLOCK 2																	
Surface	—	—	—	1	—	—	—	—	—	—	—	—	1	1	—	—	
A+B	—	1	—	5	1	1	—	—	1	—	3	—	5	1	—	1 sculpture	
C	2	—	—	2	—	—	—	—	—	—	1	—	17	—	2	—	
D+E	—	—	—	—	—	—	—	—	—	—	—	—	4	—	—	—	
Block 2 Subtotal	2	1	—	8	1	1	—	—	1	—	4	—	27	2	2	1	50
TRENCH III																	
0–50	2	5	—	18	5	—	—	—	5	2	5	2	26	2	2	—	
50–100	—	—	—	—	—	—	—	—	—	—	—	—	—	—	—	—	
100–sterile	—	—	—	—	—	—	—	—	—	—	—	—	—	—	—	—	
Total	2	5	—	18	5	—	—	—	5	2	5	2	26	2	2	—	74
TRENCH IV																	
0–100	—	—	—	—	—	—	—	—	—	—	—	—	2	—	1	—	
100–sterile	—	—	—	3	—	1	—	—	—	—	—	—	2	—	1	—	
Total				3		1							4		2		10

Layer or cms below surface	Metates and milling stones	Handstones and manos	Reused as handstones or manos	Hammers	Reused as hammers	Pounding-mashing stones	Reused as pounding-mashing	Edge-used	Anvils	Reused as anvils	Nutting stones	Reused as nutting stones	Notched stones	Other use with notches	Grooved stones	Other Use	Total
TRENCH V																	
Surface	—	—	—	—	—	—	—	—	—	—	—	—	—	—	—	—	
A	—	—	—	—	—	—	—	—	—	—	—	—	—	—	—	—	
B	—	—	—	1	—	—	—	—	—	—	1	—	14	—	—	—	
C	1	1	—	—	—	—	—	—	—	—	—	—	6	—	—	—	
D	—	—	—	—	—	—	—	—	—	—	—	—	—	—	—	—	
Total	1	1	—	1	—	—	—	—	—	—	1	—	20	—	—	—	24
TRENCH VI - none																	
TRENCH VII																	
A (Surface)	—	—	—	—	—	—	—	—	—	—	—	—	—	—	—	—	
B	2	1	—	2	2	—	—	—	2	—	1	—	3	—	—	—	
C	—	—	—	—	—	—	—	—	—	—	—	1	3	—	—	—	
C?	—	—	—	—	—	—	—	—	—	—	—	—	—	—	—	2	
D+E	—	—	—	—	—	—	—	—	—	—	—	—	—	1	—	1	
Total	2	1	—	2	2	—	—	—	2	—	1	1	6	1	—	3	21
TRENCH VIII - none																	
Total Use	24	30	3	101	28	14	1	7	29	12	30	17	169	19	18	13(2)	507+(2)

a = possible specimens in parentheses.

b = in two parts, with 2 numbers.

*One of these is on a metate.

B. Flake Tools

These are flakes with nibbling, crushing, unifacial retouch, or bifacial retouch on one or more edges. They may be divided into three categories, according to probable function (table 1).

1. Used flakes (fig. 15/2 oo-vv). Fifty-three flakes in our sample were probably used as scrapers, planes, and similar tools. Some cannot be assigned a special function but are included because of crushing, nibbling, retouch, or other indications of use. There was little or no polish visible on artifact edges under low magnifications. Forty-eight artifacts clearly show transverse or lateral retouch. One appears to be a spokeshave, three may have been used as knives. The majority are made of chalcedonies and quartz, the same materials as the cores from the site. Used flakes make up 5.2 percent of the chipped stone assemblages.

2. Perforators (fig. 15/2 hh-nn). Although usually associated with cores, waste flakes, and shatter, the ten quartz perforators in our sample differ from the latter in having sharply pointed ends showing crushing on the tips. They also tend to be larger than most quartz shatter and waste flakes. Perforators came from trenches I and II and make up 1 percent of the stone tools.

3. Possible grater chips (fig. 15/2 a-gg). These small flakes, mainly of quartz, were apparently detached from bipolar cores. There are 63 in the excavated sample.

Shapes are somewhat irregular, but tend to be thicker and blunter at one end and sharp at the other. The naturally rough cortex at one end gives an edge that holds up well, while the thickness provides added strength.

These flakes bear some resemblance to specimens classified elsewhere as insets for manioc grating boards, that is as grater chips. DeBoer (1975, pp. 419–433) notes a study by Barricklo giving modal dimensions for manioc grater chips in the collection of the American Museum of Natural History. These were: length 8 mm, width 6 mm, and thickness 2–3 mm. The grating edge was from 1–3 mm long. The modes for our sample of 63 chips were as follows: length 14 mm, width 5 mm, thickness 4 mm. Thus they were somewhat longer and only slightly thicker than the museum sample. The presence of thin cores and the regularity of our small chips suggest they were purposely manufactured to grate some product by setting them into wood. This product need not have been manioc, or other tubers, but possibly something completely different, like the kernel of the "corozo" fruit, from which oil is extracted today by boiling the pulp after it is grated. As Smith (section 10.5) has noted, this palm may have been under cultivation at IS-3. Fifty-one of the 63 chips were excavated from trench I, the remainder from trench II. They total 6.2 percent of the chipped stone.

C. Blades (fig. 15/3 a-f)

A blade is a flake twice as long as it is wide on which the direction of force is parallel to the long axis. There are 13 whole or partial specimens known from IS-3.

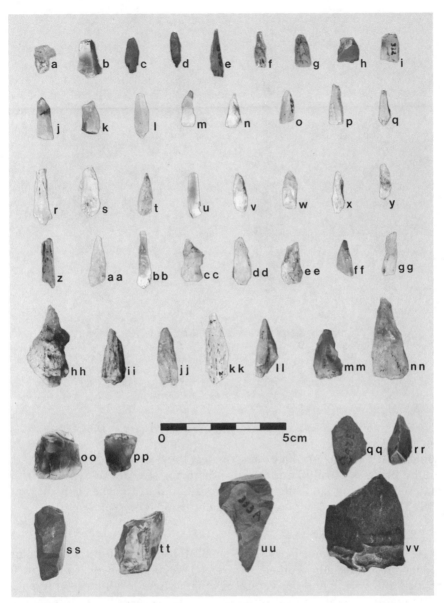

Figure 15/2: a-gg. Possible grater chips; hh-nn. perforators; oo-vv. used flakes.

Two large basal fragments of retouched blades were found at this site with their platform ends modified into stems for hafting (fig. 15/3 g,h).

On the smaller specimens evidence of use is found mostly along one or both edges or the tip and consists of use flakes or in one case polish. Six of these blades are ridged, four are backed, six show use on one edge, and three show use on both edges. In addition two blade specimens show wear on the tip, and one also has edge polish. One of the blades was unused,

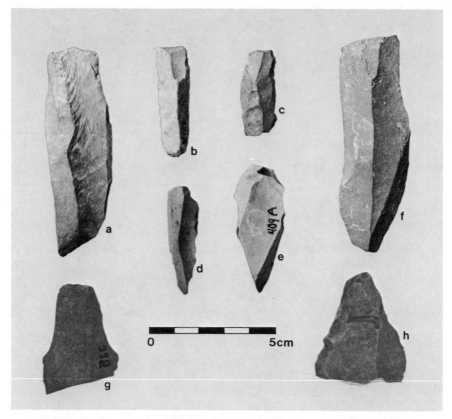

Figure 15/3: a-f. Blades; g,h. basal fragments of stemmed or tanged blades.

while wear patterns on the others suggest they were used for cutting.

One blade is of celtlike material, others are of chalcedony and a gray material, probably andesite. Blades were found in trenches I, II, III, and VIII. They make up 1.6 percent of the chipped stone sample.

D. Points (fig. 15/4 q-w)

1. Points made on blades. Five small, thin-stemmed points made on blades are unifacially worked with steep retouch. The platform end is shaped into a stem, and the ventral or inner surface is left more or less flat and unworked, while dorsal surfaces have ridges resulting from previous blade removal. They are made of a fine-grained gray material. All are broken, but length on complete specimens is estimated to vary from 3.5 to approximately 6 centimeters. These specimens must have been hafted, perhaps as projectile points. Other points like these were found by Linares in earlier survey work in the area and are illustrated in Linares (1968b, plate 20:a, c and description, p. 62). These points were excavated from trenches I, II, and V. They make up 0.2 percent of the chipped stone.

2. Trifaces (fig. 15/4 a-p). Twenty-six points with three faces and triangular cross sections are known from this site. On some specimens only two

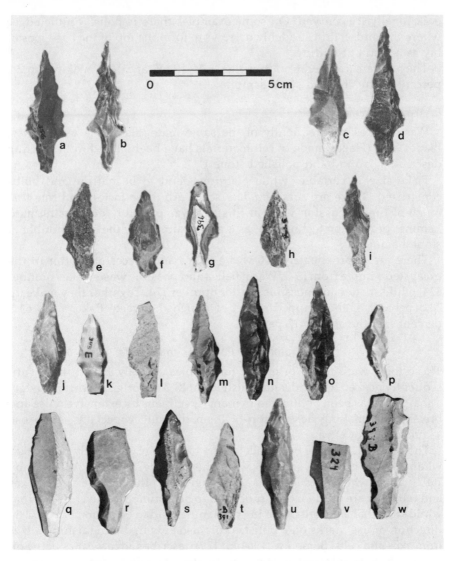

Figure 15/4: a-p. Trifaces; q-w. points made on blades.

faces are retouched or flaked while the third or ventral surface of the point is unmodified. The edges appear somewhat serrated.

At IS-3 the color range is wider for these chalcedony artifacts than for other cryptocrystalline artifacts. Many are in the tan-red-brown color range, which is not well represented in chipping debris at the site, raising the possibility that these points were imported, already made, from the mainland. They are known as far east as Veraguas and Cocle, where they are well documented (Lothrop 1937, 1950; Cooke 1972). Linares also found them in another nearby Chiriqui site (1968b, p. 62).

The inner or ventral surface of these points is usually nearly flat, although occasionally it is curved. On some examples there is polish on the edges where the midsection suddenly narrows to form the top of the base, possibly as a result of hafting.

They were excavated from trenches I, II, III, V, and VIII, making up 2.5 percent of the chipped stone sample.

E. Waste Flakes and Shatter

Waste flakes are frequently of the same materials as the used flakes, blades, etc. (Flakes made of celt materials have been placed in the section describing ground and polished stone.)

Flake size is variable, while platforms tend to be narrow and bulbs constricted. There are some *éraillure* scars. All these factors indicate that much of the percussion work at this site was probably done using hard hammer percussion techniques, as is also indicated by the large number of stone hammers.

There are approximately 800 waste flakes and pieces of shatter in the excavated sample from IS-3. Waste flakes and possible waste flakes number 629, while shatter and possible shatter number 174. Together they make up 78.5 percent of the chipped stone, of which the waste flakes form 61.5 percent and the shatter 17 percent.

II. Ground and Polished Stone Tools

These tools were made primarily on cobbles, usually flaked, then subsequently pecked, ground, and polished. At IS-3 the original working edge, a sharp bit, has been obliterated in many specimens by extensive reuse and breakdown, making description of them difficult, especially as the use sequence is not always clear.

Tools hafted with the bit parallel to the handle are commonly called axes when they are grooved, and celts when they are ungrooved (cf. Willoughby 1907). Tools whose bits form an acute angle with the haft are adzes. Axes and celts that are used for chopping tend to be symmetrical in cross section, while tools that are used in adzing or planing tend to be asymmetrical. The direction of use marks on a polished bit also aids in distinguishing adzes from axes and celts. Semenov (1964, p. 129) describes adze wear as being on the convex side of the bit as "grooves, thicker at the bottom and narrowing to fine lines. As a rule the striations lie along the axis of the tool more or less parallel to each other." In contrast axe wear shows up on both bit surfaces as diagonal striations.

Only 64 (27 percent) out of 236 ground and polished stone tool specimens preserved enough identifying characteristics to be included in the following typology. Most of these were complete or nearly complete specimens. However, the bits and edges were so battered that only three adzes were clearly recognizable from the excavations. Except for three chisels, the other polished tools having identifiable bits and more or less symmetrical cross sections have been designated as celts. Celts have been subdivided into three groups (A, B, and C), according to the shape of the celt and the length and curvature of the cutting edge.

Figure 15/5: Celt Type A.

Many of the bitted tools have lopsided bits, indicating heavier wear at one end than at the other. This can occur when tools are used either as choppers or as adzes; thus a lopsided bit is not diagnostic of any particular use (Semenov 1964, p. 130).

An additional tool included in the ground and polished category is the chisel, which though only half as wide as a celt, is biconvex in cross section, like a celt. Only one complete and two broken specimens occur in the collection.

A. Axe (fig. 15/7 i)

One fragment of an IS-3 specimen having the bit missing is constricted in the midsection like an axe. The remaining section has very smooth and polished surfaces. The butt is larger and flatter on the end than those of celts, adzes, or chisels. Edges and butt are somewhat battered, probably from reuse. This fragment comes from trench IV and measures 7.3 x 5.8 x 3.8 cm.

B. Celts (fig. 15/5)

1. Type A celts (13 in total) have an extended or "parabolic" bit, which is larger than that of the other celts described below, and a short butt. Their shape resembles a pear (see Lothrop 1937). Some pear-shaped celts were probably hafted, if roughening of the edge where the constriction occurs is an indication of hafting. These celts are biconvex in cross section.

In all but one specimen, celt bit angles are unreconstructable, being battered or having large flakes and chunks missing. Other celts were purposefully battered, probably by hammering or pecking, to produce a broad smooth facet replacing the sharp bit. The butts on all Type A celts are short and sometimes battered or partly broken off. In smaller specimens the butts

Figure 15/6: Celt Type B.

are proportionally larger than those of larger celts, suggesting that they may in fact be smaller because they have been extensively resharpened. Several breaks seem to have occurred at the point where the celts would enter the haft, if in fact these celts were hafted. On some celts the side edges remain smooth but on most they are heavily chipped.

Most Type A celts appear to have been polished from the bit edge to the constriction where the butt begins, though, on some celts polish may have stopped in the midsection. One small celt was clearly polished all over.

2.   Type B celts (38 in total) constitute by far the most numerous of the celt categories (fig. 15/6). Their bits make a sharp, angular junction with the sides, while the butts may be pointed or blunted. Some are almost rectangular in shape, while others are roughly triangular. In the latter, some of the taper from bit to butt may be the result of chipping and resharpening.

Most Type B celts are roughly chipped, lack polish, and appear to have been battered as a result of hafting or other wear. When viewed from the bit end, their cross sections vary from biconvex to diamond and hexagonal as a result of having surfaces beveled. However, some celts have two curved surfaces, others a curved surface and a ridged one, and still others a ridge or bevel near the center of both surfaces.

The edges along the sides vary from roughly chipped to smoothly polished. Beveled specimens have retained smoother edges than most others.

The Type B celts are on the average longer and thicker than other celts. The majority were probably hafted, as is indicated by having been polished from bit end to midsection only, with the rest roughly chipped or pecked. Several specimens also have scars in the midsection.

Figure 15/7: a,b. Celt Type C; c-e. chisels; f-h. adzes; i. axe.

3. Type C celts (seven in total) are generally smaller and less numerous than those in Types A and B (fig. 15/7 a-b). They may also have been formed from large flakes rather than from pebbles or cobbles. Type C celts also tend to be much thinner and have less curving surfaces, appearing to be almost flat rather than curved or beveled. Many are almost triangular in outline, with the bit forming the shortest side of the triangle. The butt is usually a thin oval in cross section. Proportionally more celts of this type have retained bits with sharp angles than those that are identifiably Type A or B.

C. Adzes (?) (fig. 15/7 f-h)

Three plano-convex tools, asymmetrical in cross section, may have served as adzes. However, they do not show wear-striations even though the bits have been chipped and worn. Hence, it is not clear how or if they were hafted. One specimen is broken in the midsection, another resembles a pear-shaped celt, and the third looks like Type B celts.

D. Chisels (fig. 15/7 c-e)

Three polished stone fragments are classified as chisels even though not confirmed experimentally. However, similar artifacts have been described elsewhere (McEwen 1946).

The single complete specimen in the collection measured 13.4 cm long, 2.9 cm wide, and 2.0 thick and was polished from the end of the bit to about 3 cm behind the bit. No wear striations were visible. Its bit angle measured 62°. Chisels are biconvex in cross section, resembling very narrow celts.

E. Celt Fragments

Celt fragments of various kinds, 131 in all, occur in the collection. Fourteen are nearly whole specimens, 37 are bits and bit ends, 38 are center sections, and 42 are celt butts. The large bit and butt sections may have broken off while the tool was being used. Most of the large fragments, excluding butts, appear battered and/or chipped.

F. Celt Flakes

In an attempt to determine whether or not celts were manufactured at the site, we isolated those flakes without polish or pecking that were made of the same materials as the celts. Only 19 flakes (9 percent) fit this description. Hence, it seems likely that celts were not manufactured at IS-3. In fact, the majority of the celt flakes (191; 91 percent) show polishing or pecking marks somewhere on the surface, as if they had broken off from finished or at least partially finished celts. This would have happened while the celt was being used as a tool or reused as a hammer, or while the celt was being resharpened by flaking.

III. Pecked and Ground Stone Tools

This group includes metates and milling stones as well as manos and other handstones. Metates were pecked into shape from large pieces of quarried stone, while barlike manos may also have been shaped by pecking. Nonetheless the ground-down surfaces of these tools resulted principally from use, even though some pecking or grinding may have occasionally been done to rejuvenate the surfaces. Other handstones are not visibly pecked as are the manos, but they are also ground down from usage.

A. Metates (fig. 15/8)

Four possible and 24 identifiable metate fragments were removed from the site. Approximately 37 other large fragments were left at the site.

All but a few metates removed from the site appear to be made of a stone having large phenocrysts, unlike the other types of artifacts that were made of more variable kinds of material. Semenov (1964, p. 69), describing the quality of sandstone grinding surface, notes that it is a "rock in which the grains are held together by a clay cement." On this surface the friction of an abrasive agent "destroys the links between its grains by the friction of the object against it, so that the blunted grains fall out, only to be replaced by new sharp grains from the agent." This appears to be the way metate surfaces were ground-down and rejuvenated during use at La Pitahaya, although the material is a large-grained igneous rock (probably porphyritic andesite) rather than sandstone. Such a metate surface becomes concave with wear.

The stone for the metates was first shaped by pecking it into a slab with tapered legs as supports. The slab was slightly concave to begin with and

Figure 15/8: Legged metate fragment.

becomes more so with use. On many metates there is a narrow, smooth band or raised rim around the top edge of the grinding table, probably to hold in whatever substance was being ground. The outer sides and legs of the metate are usually rough and weathered. Some unattached legs show secondary use as nutting stones.

All that remains of the larger metates are either the legs, or segments of slabs with legs attached. The height from the bottom of the leg to the rim varies from 11.8 cm to 19.4 cm for those specimens which could be measured. Some of the outer edges of the metate may have borne elaborate sculpture, but the only remaining sculpture is a plain lug. The largest remnant of a metate removed from this site measures 30 cm (the original width) and the legs are broken. The thinnest part of the basin is only 3 cm, while the thickest is 4 cm. (For similar metates, cf. MacCurdy 1911, figs. 18 and 30; Lothrop 1950, fig. 32, and 1937, fig. 50 a-f, fig. 62 a,b.)

B. Milling Stones

Milling stones are thick-walled basins without legs, deeper than metates. They are also made of a somewhat denser material.

Two fragments from the surface of trench I, block 3 at IS-3 have been tentatively classified as milling stones because they have thick-walled basins, even though it is unclear whether they were used with a circular grinding motion as were those in the highlands (report no. 14).

C. Bar Manos (fig. 15/9 a-e)

Eleven of the 30 grinding stones removed from IS-3 are or were originally barlike in shape. Two of these fragments are part of the same mano, although one section comes from a depth of 80–90 cm and the other from 140 cm, in trench II, cut 1 (see note b, table 4). Many of these faceted handstones were made of the same material with the large phenocrysts and self-sharpening qualities as the metates. They have grinding surfaces and broken or roughly pecked ends. Presumably they were used, together with metates, for grinding maize, but they could also have been used for grinding other substances such as pigments, spices, or other foodstuffs.

Only one of the manos in this group has just one grinding surface, while seven have two used surfaces and three have three grinding facets. The ends of most are broken off so that the original size is not clear.

D. Handstones

Handstones, like manos, frequently have smoother surfaces near the edges and roughened areas in the center of the grinding surface. Also the surface frequently curves outward so that it is thinner at the sides than in the center, which is the opposite of a metate basin.

1. Ovoid handstones (fig. 15/9 f-i) constitute a highly variable category, for some are true ovals, almost loaflike in appearance, while others are more irregular. Six specimens out of a total of 15 were ground on only one surface; the rest were ground on two or more surfaces. One specimen was pitted, suggesting use as an anvil, while another may have been used as a nutting stone, for it has a deep central depression. Some smaller fragments known from the site may have been originally parts of grinding stones.

The raw materials out of which handstones were made could not be identified easily without costly thin-sectioning. However, several different stones seem to have been used in their manufacture.

Figure 15/9: a-e. Bar or cylindrical manos; f-i. ovoid handstones.

2. Angular handstones (four specimens). These may have been more rectangular originally. In fact, one may be a reused metate leg, while another may have been used as an anvil. All of the specimens have only one ground edge. Measurements are not included because of the fragmentary nature of the specimens.

IV. Cobble Tools

Cobbles not clearly modified, except in minor ways, were selected according to their size and shape to make such tools as hammerstones (except for those made of reused celts), pebble polishers, anvils, and pounding-mashing stones. Many of these tools are made from stones similar to those found now on the beach at Isla Palenque.

A. Hammerstones (fig. 15/10)

Hammerstones vary greatly in shape. Most are end-battered, with only a few showing wear all around the edges.

Hammers were no doubt used for chipping and pecking stone. The part used (such as a tip) is more restricted than the broadly flattened ends of the pounding-mashing stones. Thus, hammerstones were apparently being selected for their narrower, pointed ends. They are also small enough to be held in one hand. The use varies from light, just barely noticeable, to heavy, where the shape of the cobble's surface appears changed. Edge-used hammers with central depressions are good examples of heavy use. Their original irregular shape was smoothed out through use, while their surfaces show irregularities and roughened surfaces.

Most hammers are made of compact dense stone that breaks down slowly. The lighter the wear the more variable the materials out of which they were made. A few siltstone ones could only have been very lightly used.

B. Pebble Polishers or Polished Pebbles (fig. 15/13 b-d)

A number of small stones from IS-3 were probably used for polishing pottery or for burnishing polished celt surfaces. They are 3 cm or bigger in size and are of brown- or greenstone with quartz inclusions. Although it is difficult to tell which pebbles were actually used, as very few show striation marks, they must in any case have been carried inland from the beach.

C. Pounding-Mashing Stones (fig. 15/11 g-i)

These large, fine-grained cobbles, which are battered at one or both ends, tend to be thick ovals in cross section. A depression near the center of one surface may indicate that some specimens were used as nutting stones, as anvils, or even as special pounding stones with thumb-holding depressions to prevent the hand from slipping. The ends seem to be gradually worn away, being broad and flat, unlike the pointed ends of hammers. Pounding-mashing stones are also bigger and heavier than most hammers, presumably because they were used differently. A few may have been used for grinding, as they are unnaturally smoothed. In some the edges exhibit pitting, battering, or faceting. One artifact is partially fire-cracked.

D. Anvils (fig. 15/11 d-f)

Cobbles and boulders with irregularly pitted surfaces were probably used as supports during stone tool manufacture. Some of these anvils must

Figure 15/10: a-f. Hammerstones; g-k. celts reused as hammers.

have undoubtedly been employed in bipolar flaking, a technique responsible for producing between a quarter and a half of the chipping debris at the site. The size of the anvils varies considerably, as do their shapes.

Many anvils show marks of battering on the ends, indicating that they were also used as hammers. Pitting is frequently found on the center of the surface, probably as a reflection of use with a bipolar core.

V. Worked Cobbles

These tools were made on cobbles modified somewhat before being used.

A. Nutting Stones (fig. 15/11 a-c)

These were usually made of a soft green siltstone like the one used for notched and grooved stones described below, only nutting stones are generally much larger and thicker. They have small holes in the center of one or two surfaces where a palm fruit kernel or nut could be placed and cracked with a light blow from another stone. Because siltstone will crack if pounded hard, the force used to open nuts or other food could not have been very great. The holes range from being rather shallow (about 1 mm) up to 8 mm deep. Some are quite wide (as much as 4.5 x 4.5 cm). The holes were apparently made by gouging with a sharp tool. A piece of flint worked nicely when used on this kind of stone in the laboratory, producing holes much like those on the excavated specimens from the site.

Figure 15/11: a-c. Nutting stones; d-f. anvils; g-i. pounding/mashing stones.

Often the area around the small holes is pitted and some nutting stones have battered edges. Some of the larger nutting stones are very thick, resembling thick bricks. Not all are large and bricklike, however. Some are quite small and irregular, others are oval, and still others are loaf shaped. A few nutting stones have split at the point where a hole occurred, suggesting that repeated blows, or even a single hard blow, split the stone in two. Occasionally nutting stones show some evidence of notching.

A number of pounding-mashing stones also show pitting in the center of one surface. Even though some are much larger than nutting stones, they are often found close enough to the latter to have been used with them, perhaps as the pounding stone for the nut.

Figure 15/12: a-d. Grooved stones; e-k. notched stones.

B. Notched Stones (fig. 15/12 e-k)

They are the largest category (192 specimens) of complete artifacts recovered from the site. The majority are made of green siltstone, though some are made of a somewhat denser, grayish-white stone. Their function seems to have been to weigh down nets or lines used in fishing.

Beach pebbles chosen to be flaked on the edges in order to form notches varied tremendously in shape. The notches themselves vary from slight indentations to deep scars extending onto the surfaces and part way around the pebble. They may be symmetrically placed on opposite sides of the artifact, or placed diagonally at different heights. A few specimens are notched on only one edge, while others are notched on three edges.

Many notched stones show evidence of having been roughly battered, probably as a result of their use as weights. It is unlikely that they could have served as hammerstones since the materials out of which they are made tend to crack and crumble easily if used with very much force. A few (four) specimens have holes in the center of their surfaces, as if they had also been used as nutting stones.

C. Grooved Stones (fig. 15/12 a-d)

These are small pebbles (22 specimens) with one or more incised grooves encircling them in the midsection. Most are very small, almost ovoid. Only a few resemble the notched stones in the larger size and irregularity of shape. A few of the grooves are as wide as 3 mm, but most are quite narrow. Some are continuous, others not. In some cases grooving is found on only one surface. The narrower grooves are found on smaller specimens, while the broader, bandlike marks, occur on larger stones. Almost all were made of the same green siltstone used for the notched stones. Whether or not they were used for the same purposes is difficult to say.

Figure 15/13: a. Whetstone; b-d. pebble polishers; e-h. rasps.

VI.   Miscellaneous Stones

This category includes rasps, whetstones, fragments of sculpture, as well as assorted beach cobbles showing no obvious wear but having been brought to the site from a distance of almost a mile.

A. Rasps (fig. 15/13 e-h)

Seven rasps, also called sandstone saws, were found at the site. They may have been used for cutting shell. The only complete specimen is 11.8 cm long, 4 cm wide, and 0.6 cm thick. It has almost parallel sides, and it is beveled on both surfaces, on each side. The edges resemble those of a worn emery board or file, with a sloping band that is hardly noticeable at one end, but gradually broadens out as it goes down the length of the artifact. The other specimens are sections of rasps showing wear patterns similar to the complete specimen, although none shows use on both sides of two edges. Two specimens are waterworn. They may have been ground prior to use or the bevels could have resulted simply from use. Rasps were made from some kind of lightweight and somewhat grainy sandstone.

B. Whetstones (fig. 15/13 a)

Only two specimens were found. One is concave on all four sides, as well as on one end, and is made of lightweight coarse stone. It was probably used with water and sand as an abrasive to resharpen slightly blunted celts, or celts in final stages of manufacture. It measures 5.3 x 5.3 x 3.4 cm and weighs 4.8 oz. The other, a fragment, seems originally to have been part of a much larger slab. One end is smoothed and has what appears to be a polish on it. The thicker end, like the reverse surface, is somewhat rough. It is made of a greenstone that is probably found naturally in tabular form.

A similar stone was chosen in the laboratory to conduct a celt grinding experiment. The slab was submerged in water, coarse sand was sprinkled on it to act as an abrasive agent, and the celt was rubbed back and forth across the surface. The smoothed and polished surface that was formed on the experimental whetstone duplicates the one on the excavated fragment.

C. Sculptural Fragments

Five detached fragments of sculpture, as well as part of a large metate with a lug on one end, were found in the excavations. Four of these specimens are made of a fine-grained greenstone similar to the one used for notched stones.

D. Beach Cobbles

Several hundred cobbles with no apparent use marks were recovered in the excavations. Presumably, they were hauled to the site from the beaches on the island. Their use remains unknown.

RAW MATERIALS

Material is one of the most important factors in determining how a stone was used. The type of material puts certain constraints on the use of the stone. For example, a piece of siltstone (quartz and mica) does not work well as a hammer for use on chalcedony. The chalcedony is harder and it is likely to break the hammer, rather than the reverse. However, the siltstone will work well as a hammer for cracking palm nuts. Similarly, an implement destined for heavy use, such as a celt, is usually made of a tough resilient stone.

At Isla Palenque some artifacts, for example manos and metates, were made on only one kind of material (an igneous rock) while others, such as hammers, were made of several different materials. An igneous rock was also used for tools such as pounding-mashing stones, handstones, hammers, anvils, and most celts. Metamorphic rock was used for some celts and some hammers. Metaigneous rock was used for notched and grooved stones, and nutting stones. Sedimentary rock was used for rasps. Both metamorphic milky quartz and sedimentary chalcedonies were used for chipped stone artifacts. Both these materials fracture concoidally and both give strong, sharp edges. Some andesite may have also been used.

Celts tend to be of hard, dense, and durable stones like andesites, diorites, rhyolites, and basalts. When polished, these stones hold up well under repeated blows from being used as cutting and perhaps planing instruments. However, the evidence indicates that they eventually wore down and/or broke, and were discarded. Thin sections were made from three celts at IS-3 and are described in Shelton Einhaus (ms. 1976, pp. 68–69).

Another specimen, one of the notched stone fragments, was also thin-sectioned. It is a volcanic tuff with fragments of mica, feldspar, clay, and quartz.

Pounding-mashing stones are heavy, dense stones, often very fine-grained, that do not seem to crack easily. Their strength was a necessary prerequisite for the repeated pounding and mashing action that has been attributed to them. The broad, flatly battered ends are evidence that the stone wears away evenly with this kind of usage, rather than chipping and breaking as lighter stones might do.

Anvils were also made of similar materials, but in some cases less fine-grained and dense stones were used.

Grinding stones or handstones, like manos and metates, were made of brittle stones, having the "self-sharpening" characteristics referred to previously in the artifact descriptions. A likely candidate is an andesite with large phenocrysts in a soft matrix.

The igneous materials out of which notched and grooved stones and nutting stones were made can be easily marked with a sharp implement such as a sharply chipped chalcedony flake; thus these stones could be quickly and easily shaped with such a tool. The light blows required for breaking palm nuts would not shatter the material as rapidly as hammer usage would.

Rasps were made of what appears to be slabs of water-smoothed sandstone, a material that is light and can be easily shaped by use, or so it seems. The small whetstone is a stone with larger phenocrysts, coarser than rasps in appearance.

William H. Bishop (ms. 1961) notes that lithic materials from the area around the city of David, and from the dikes farther north, are of igneous origin. Bishop also notes that on the mainland, in the area around San

Lorenzo, there are mountains of igneous material. Either of these sources could have supplied the materials for the IS-3 tools made of igneous stone.

The principal chipped stone materials — metamorphic quartz and sedimentary chalcedonies, particularly a green variety — were apparently available on or near the island. However, the red and yellow-brown jasper used in making trifacial points was not found locally; but it is known to occur both in the highlands of Chiriqui and in the central provinces and may have come from either region.

Celt materials probably came from mainland quarries or from gravels in major stream valleys. Beach cobbles as large as the pounding-mashing stones or anvils are not found now on Isla Palenque. Thus, large cobbles, like celt materials, may have been imported to the island. The igneous rocks used for manos and metates were not observed on the island and almost certainly came from the mainland, although the exact location of their source is not known.

Many of the materials used for hammers, and for grooved and notched stones, are available on the beach at IS-3 and probably on other nearby islands.

Thus, it seems clear that a wide variety of stone is represented in the tools found at this site and it is likely to have come from several different areas of Panama. The majority of the stone, however, is of volcanic origin.

TOOL REPLICATION AND WEAR STUDY

A number of experiments were carried out in an attempt to solve some of the questions posed by the artifacts recovered from IS-3. Some experiments were done early on as an aid to formulating a tool typology. These experiments involved method of manufacture and possible uses for the various artifacts.

A celt with a chipped bit from the surface of IS-3 was resharpened in order to observe the manufacturing and resharpening marks resulting from pecking and grinding the surface. This pointed up necessary revisions in existing descriptions of pecking hammers from this site. Since the celts are made of very hard, dense materials, only materials as hard or harder could have been used to peck them (e.g., broken celts and pebbles). Softer, oblong stones, previously classified as pecking hammers, would have crumbled rather than powdering the celt surface. By pecking the chipped bit with a hard stone hammer and then grinding the celt on a whetstone, using wet sand as an abrasive, it was possible to produce a surface resembling the polished ones on the excavated samples. Resharpening is a slow process; in the experiment it took approximately three hours to repair a small area of damage on a slightly blunted celt.

Experiments were also carried out to observe the results of tool use. The tool with the resharpened bit was hand-held and used as a plane. After two hundred strokes of this use, striations were visible microscopically. A pear-shaped celt from IS-3 with a sharp bit was also used to sever the head of a duck, following Lothrop's (1937) suggestion that such celts were used for butchering. For the experiment the tool was hand-held and the extended bit was used with both rotating and chopping motions.

Materials like those out of which the manos and metates were made were not obtained for experimentation. However, manos and metates are regularly used now by the Guaymí (Bort and Young, personal communication). Other evidence of grinding found on cobbles from IS-3 was thought to result from grinding foods and plants other than maize.

A large, dense anvil stone with a smooth and slightly hollowed surface was used in the lab in experiments involving the grinding of root crops. A cobble from IS-3 was used to mash and pulverize several manioc tubers. The edge of the cobble proved useful for smashing the tuber lengthwise, along its long fibers, while the smaller end of the ovoid stone was more useful for pulverizing the fleshy root. The ovoid stone used in the lab showed flattening of the end, much like the excavated pounding-mashing stones. The edge showed a slight facet, resulting from processing several pounds of manioc. Similar edge wear was noted on a few of the excavated tools. We do not mean to imply that manioc was the only foodstuff mashed or ground by these cobbles, or even that manioc was necessarily processed in this manner. A number of other food items could have been prepared by mashing and pounding. For example, Bort reports (personal communication) that pepper corns, garlic, and coffee are ground by modern Guaymí with stone manos and metates. These are all post-Contact additions to the diet, but presumably native foods would have been similarly processed in the past. Today Guaymí also make *chichas* out of mashed and chewed green corn (Young 1971, p. 205), or out of the peach palm which has been boiled, pitted, peeled, and pulped on a metate (J. Bort, personal communication, 1975).

Attempts to replicate line sinkers were also carried out in the lab. A small green siltstone pebble from the site was etched with a sharp flake of jasper to produce a groove around the stone. Going over and over the groove several times with the jasper flake rapidly produced a stone very similar to the grooved artifacts. The same piece of soft siltstone was also used to replicate a nutting stone, although it is somewhat smaller than the nutting stones from IS-3. The same sharp pointed jasper flake was used to hollow out a depression in the center of one surface, using a back and forth and a circular motion. Within five minutes a hole much like those on nutting stones was produced. A larger pebble of greenstone was also chosen to make a nutting stone replica, but it proved more resistant as it was much harder, and the work progressed more slowly.

We were particularly interested to know whether breaking down various kinds of stone on an anvil using bipolar flaking techniques would produce a large number of what I have suggested were grater chips at this site. One or two such flakes did result when a large chalcedony core was broken down in this manner. However, it is not clear whether all of those in the excavated assemblage from IS-3 were produced as by-products or as desired results of the bipolar technique. There are several small cores known from the excavation which could provide only small flakes, suggesting that such flakes were being intentionally produced, if not for grater insets then for some other as yet undetermined use.

Other experiments with chipped stone involved the production and use of trifacial points like those excavated at the IS-3 site. The most satisfactory technique employed was first to produce thick blades as blanks and then to trim these by steep unifacial retouch, using small pointed hammerstones with an anvil rest. Alternatively, a bifacially flaked ridge was made on a thin core, then removed by a blow in much the same manner as detaching a burin spall. The minimal retouch necessary to form the point and tang of the implement was done with a small pointed hammerstone on an anvil rest. A number of these points were socket hafted into the tips of hollow reeds which were then surrounded with tar and wound with cord, for use as drills (Emmert, personal communication). Microscopic examination of the trifacial points in our sample showed wear suggesting such a use in the form of smoothed-out flake scars near the tip, and somewhat crushed, snapped off, or chipped tips. Some smoothing of flake scars just behind the widened area of the tip could also indicate hafting.

SUMMARY

The stone tools recovered from La Pitahaya (IS-3) show a variety of manufacturing techniques. The techniques frequently employed were percussion flaking, pecking, grinding, polishing, and grooving. The majority of the chipped stone tools are quite simple and their manufacture required little skill, with the notable exceptions of trifacial points and blades, which would have required skill on the part of the maker. However, these tools are comparatively rare. The scarcity of chalcedony chipping debris of the same material raises the possibility that the points were not actually produced at the site, but were in fact, manufactured elsewhere and imported. The same types of points and blades are known from other areas of Panama.

The problem of which finished objects were being imported to the site is also raised by the stone sculpture and basalt columns found at the site. A very small number of chisels was recovered in the collections, suggesting the possibility that the sculpture was carved in situ. However, the materials used for the sculpture, as well as for the polished stone tools, manos, metates, blades, and possibly some of the trifacial points, were imported to the site. Hence, some of these objects were probably manufactured elsewhere, then imported.

Clearly, some of the artifacts found at the site required skilled workmanship. This is true for chipped stone as well as for polished tools such as celts, adzes, and chisels. Ethnographic descriptions and experiments with pecking, grinding, and polishing show this to be a long process requiring expertise. A bad blow can split a tool on which considerable effort has been expended. Cooke's recent work in central Panama (Cooke 1978) suggests that some stone workers were indeed specialists, although we have no way of knowing if this was true at Isla Palenque as well, as none of the burials found there contained stone-making kits.

The bipolar technique commonly employed in chipped stone working at Isla Palenque was known as early as preceramic times in the rock shelters of western Panama (section 3.5); hence, it does not represent a new technique at the much more recent IS-3 site.

CONCLUSIONS: TOOL USES AND IMPLICATIONS FOR SUBSISTENCE

The large number of metates and manos found at IS-3 suggests a heavy reliance on maize agriculture. Other tools thought to have been used in food processing and procurement are pounding-mashing stones, nutting stones, and both notched and grooved stones. Of these the notched stones are by far the most numerous. In turn, nutting stones are more numerous than pounding-mashing stones. Nutting stones may have been used for cracking nuts of the corozo palm thought by C.E. Smith (section 10.5) to have been probably under cultivation at IS-3. Pounding-mashing stones were probably used for crushing seeds, root crops, and/or spices of some kind.

Changes in the frequency of cobble tools in different layers may be particularly important in making inferences about subsistence, as nutting stones, pounding-mashing stones, and edge-used cobbles increase significantly through time. The evidence for metates and manos is not so clear, but in trench I, the most rich in artifacts, there does appear to be an increase in these artifacts in the top layers A and B. This evidence may indicate increased food-processing activities in response to increased population at the site. The diversity of food-processing tools in the top levels suggests a diversity of food resources, among these a growing use of nuts and root crops. Some of the stone tools at the site are indirect but essential parts of subsistence pursuits. For example, celts were probably used in land clearance or for other woodworking tasks like cutting wood for house posts, canoes, and for hafting other stone tools as well.

To conclude, tools are an indispensable part of all human cultural activities. Because they preserve well, they often make up a major segment of the archaeological materials recoverable from a site. The tools from IS-3 have provided valuable information about the activities of the prehistoric inhabitants at the site. However, many problems concerning the pattern of tool distribution are left unanswered, in large part due to the nature of the sample. Five of the eight trenches were placed on the highest parts of the site, on mounds built up by refuse accumulation. The absence of tools in trench VI probably indicates a specialized area of some kind. Trench I had the greatest density of tools and probably was built up by garbage accumulation. No house floors or workshop areas were located in the excavations with the possible exception of trench I, blocks 2 and 3, whose tool density may indicate a specialized area. It is hoped that additional excavations aimed at finding such specialized areas can be carried out at IS-3 sometime in the future.

Lithic Assemblages from the Aguacate Peninsula

A.J. RANERE AND E.J. ROSENTHAL

INTRODUCTION

In 1969 and 1970, excavations were conducted at several archaeological localities on the Aguacate Peninsula in the Atlantic province of Bocas del Toro, Panama (section 5.0 and report no. 6). Four of these shell-midden localities (a,b,c, and d) appeared to belong to a single dispersed hamlet designated as the Cerro Brujo (CA-3) site. A fifth spot, CA-2, belonged to a different hamlet 4½ kilometers away. The CA-3 localities are approximately one kilometer from the coast and occupy hilltops and ridges. The four midden localities which constitute CA-2 are found in similar topographic positions. Excavations were most extensive at locality CA-3a, where 118 square meters of deposits were removed. Additional excavations were undertaken at CA-3b (18 square meters), CA-3c (4 square meters), CA-3d (6 square meters) and CA-2a (12 square meters). The depth of the archaeological deposits varied from nearly 100 centimeters in the deeper middens to less than 20 centimeters in nonmidden habitation areas.

All the localities investigated are quite small, the largest (CA-3a) measuring 22 by 36 meters. All consist of "shell middens" or kitchen dumps and open spaces where, presumably, houses and outside activity areas were located. The major occupation of the sites — phase 2 or the Bocas phase — has been dated to the tenth century A.D., based on five radiocarbon dates from the Cerro Brujo site (section 7.7). An earlier occupation — phase 1 or the Aguacate phase — occurs at three of the four Cerro Brujo localities and has been dated to ca. A.D. 600. Faunal and floral remains suggest that these hamlets were populated by tropical forest agriculturalists who also hunted terrestrial fauna and, at least during the last occupation, made rather extensive use of marine resources.

Excavations at the Aguacate Peninsula sites produced 273 pieces of stone which had been modified by man (table 1). A number of other stone specimens, while showing no evidence of modification, were of materials foreign to the sites and were, therefore, carried in by the occupants. Of the modified stone specimens, 150 can be considered tools. The rest are either waste flakes from manufacturing processes or use flakes accidently removed from tools.

The stone artifacts from the Aguacate Peninsula were preliminarily analyzed and described after the 1970 field season by Rosenthal (1970). They were reexamined in 1975 and compared with the collections from La Pitahaya and Volcan by Rosenthal and Shelton Einhaus. Finally, the collections were reanalyzed by Ranere in 1978. In presenting the tool descriptions

TABLE 1 THE DISTRIBUTION OF STONE TOOLS AND FLAKES FROM THE AGUACATE PENINSULA SITES

	Bifacial cores	Bidirectional cores	Tanged blades	Miscellaneous blades	Flake blades	Used flakes	Stemmed unifacial points	Axes	Type A celts	Type B celts	Type C celts	Celt butts	Chisels	Adzes	Hammerstones	Pestles	Handstones	Miscellaneous	Totals (tools)	Flakes
CA-3a (I)	2					2			2	3			1						6	9
CA-3a (II)			12	6	5		1	1	11	34	2	4	8	3	3	2		3	99	65
CA-3b (I)																			0	1
CA-3b (II)			1	2	1				4	6		1	1				1		17	7
CA-3c																			0	
CA-3d										1									1	4
CA-2	1	2	2	1		2			1	6		1	1	3	2		1	5	28	31
Total	3	2	15	9	6	4	1	1	18	50	2	6	11	6	5	2	2	8	151	117

we have utilized a typology that is essentially descriptive. The typology was established in collaboration with Shelton Einhaus and Sheets in an attempt to keep the type definitions constant over the range of sites described in this volume. Thus, Type A celts from CA-3, IS-3, and BU-17 all have the same characteristics and the same type descriptions.

Primary tool categories were based on the final method of manufacture (cf. Einhaus 1976; this volume, section 8.0). Size, shape, and evidence of use served to subdivide further the primary categories. Those tools that were not manufactured, but were simply rocks used as found, were classified according to use modification and inferred function. A complicating factor in the classification was the fact that many of the stone tools served more than one purpose, or more frequently, served several purposes sequentially in their respective histories. Thus, for example, a tool originally manufactured as a celt almost inevitably was used as a hammer after its useful life as a celt was over. It might then (or instead) be used as a core for detachment of flakes. These flakes could subsequently be retouched or used as cutting, scraping, or piercing tools. In our classification, a tool is considered a celt regardless of whether it had also been used as a hammer or core, since the final method of *manufacture* was grinding and polishing. A flake tool was classified as such regardless of whether it was struck from an unmodified core, or from a core which had once been a celt, since the tool was *manufactured* by flaking. In both cases, the final manufacturing process (polishing for the celt, flaking for the flake tool) determined the primary category for the tool. Each specimen appears only once in the artifact descriptions. Where multiple use was present, it is indicated in the type descriptions.

THE CHIPPED STONE INDUSTRY

Two quite distinctive flaking patterns are represented in the Aguacate Peninsula assemblages. One is similar to what Sheets (1975) has called a household or cottage industry. Flakes were removed in a rather irregular fashion so that neither the flakes nor the cores display much patterning. In the Aguacate Peninsula assemblages, these flakes were removed by hammerstones without any preparation of the core platform surface. Usually the blow was struck well back from the platform edge.

In contrast, a number of chipped stone artifacts were made on skillfully manufactured blades. No blade cores were recovered in any of the Aguacate Peninsula sites (a point of some significance) but the manufacturing techniques can be reconstructed by examining the blades themselves. The regularity of the blades requires that they were made from prepared cores (perhaps polyhedral). Each blade usually has one or two dorsal ridges running its length, indicating successful removal of at least two or three blades prior to its own removal. The blades have little curvature, suggesting that an anvil or support was used for the core during blade detachment. The platforms have been minimally prepared prior to blade detachment by removal of the platform overhang. The point of impact occurs well back from the platform edge. The absence of crushing at the point of impact, the diffuse bulb of force, and the lack of *éraillure* flakes are consistent with either the use of a soft hammerstone or a punch. At any rate, the blades were clearly not made by pressure or by a hard hammer. These blades were the product of a skilled craftsman — a specialist — unlike the irregular flakes discussed previously, which could have been removed by anyone.

The lack of blade cores and the lack of debitage which would result from core preparation are strong indications that the blades were not manufactured at either the CA-3 or CA-2 sites. The bifacial, bidirectional, and irregular cores found at the sites and the irregular nature of nonblade flakes suggest that the blades were not made elsewhere by the Aguacate inhabitants and brought home either. Mistakes in flake removal resulting in step or hinge fractures, crushed platforms, and multiple bulbs of force attest to the rather low level of proficiency in stone knapping at the sites, and is inconsistent with the skill exhibited in the manufacturing of blades elsewhere. We should also note here that the source of raw material used for blade production lies well beyond the Aguacate Peninsula. Although some of the material might have been picked up as cobbles or pebbles along major rivers draining the central Cordillera (indeed, the two pebble cores from CA-2 are likely to have been from this source), larger blocks of raw material needed to manufacture blades were more likely to have come from farther inland, nearer the headwaters of these rivers, or perhaps from the southern side of the continental divide where extensive quarry/workshop sites are known. (We hasten to point out that very little is known about the distribution of lithic sources on the heavily forested, lightly occupied northern side of the divide.)

Most of the blades were modified for hafting by chipping a tang at one end (usually proximal). The tools were then hafted in a socket in much the same manner as we haft, or put handles on, files. These hafted blades have been used for a variety of purposes, sometimes with and sometimes without further modification. From an analysis of the microwear patterns we have inferred these tool functions as having included drilling, perforating, sawing, scraping, and slicing. These patterns, visible under a stereoscopic microscope (6x to 50x), were compared with wear patterns experimentally produced where possible (see blade descriptions for details).

The blades without tangs, and the flakes modified and/or used as tools, served many of the same functions as the hafted blades, with the exception of drilling and sawing. However, wear patterns for perforating, scraping, and slicing were visible using a stereoscopic microscope (6x to 50x).

THE GROUND AND POLISHED STONE INDUSTRY

Ground and polished stone tools dominated the Bocas assemblages. These tools, at their best, were very well made indeed. Where determining the manufacturing sequence was possible, the first step in making one of these tools was to percussion flake the block of raw material into the desired shape. Then a pecking hammer was used on the surface of the tool in order to even out the flake scar irregularities and to complete the shaping of the entire tool except for the bit. Next, the whole tool, or just the bit end, would be ground and polished with finer and finer grades of abrasives (probably sand and/or sandstones). Finally, the bit would be honed, and all or part of the tool's surface would be burnished with a hard pebble. There were deviations from this ideal sequence. Occasionally grinding would commence directly after flaking the implements; this was more likely to occur in smaller specimens — adze blades, chisels, and small celts — than in larger ones. Also, the final burnishing of the tool was often eliminated.

Clearly, the initial shaping of the tool preforms by flaking was not carried out at any of the sites examined. Only a very small number of flakes (123 in total) was recovered from the Aguacate excavations, and only 31 of those *could* have been manufacturing debris from original celt preforming, as 12 flakes were of chalcedony (a material not used for ground and polished implements) and the other 80 had polished surfaces indicating that they were struck from already completed tools. Now, in one celt-resharpening experiment that one of us (Ranere) conducted, we collected all flaking debris resulting from the reworking of the bit end of a damaged celt by hard hammer percussion flaking. Of the 48 flakes collected (with maximum diameters between 5 and 40 mm), 34 exhibited a portion of the original polished surface of the celt, while 14 of the flakes showed no evidence of having been removed from a celt. Thus, 29 percent of the flakes (14 out of 48) in the experimental situation could not be categorized as celt reshaping flakes even though they were. A similar percentage (29 percent) of nonchalcedony flakes from the Aguacate Peninsula assemblages could not be classified as celt resharpening flakes either. The experimental results thus suggest that all 31 of the excavated flakes could well have come from finished celts, from portions that did not retain the polished surface. In any event, it seems obvious that very little percussion flaking was carried out at the excavated sites, and that which was carried out was directed mainly at resharpening or reworking already manufactured (and presumably damaged) celts.

In contrast to percussion flaking, pecking must have been a major tool-shaping technique employed by the site inhabitants. Of the 69 celts recovered, 36 (and one large chisel) had been recycled as pecking hammers. These had broad, smooth hammering facets, either at both ends, or as on several specimens, completely encircling the perimeter. Other damaged celts have hammering facets on one end only. Four additional pecking hammers were recovered which were not originally celts. Thus, more than fifty tools at the sites saw moderate to very heavy use as pecking hammers.

Two alternative, though not mutually exclusive, explanations for the heavy use of pecking hammers can be suggested. First, the inhabitants could have been carrying in, or importing, flaked celt preforms for final shaping on site by pecking and grinding. Since sources of raw material for celts were at some distance from the sites, there may have been some incentive to reduce the weight of the specimens to be transported. There is abundant evidence for such "roughing out" of celt preforms at highland quarry/workshop sites on the Pacific side of the divide. On the other hand, the celts from the Aguacate Peninsula sites which were clearly reworked from damaged celts were not done with anything approaching the skill displayed in the original celt-manufacturing process. This leads us to suspect that not one of the inhabitants of the sites (or at least of CA-3, where our sample is reasonably large) was a skilled celt maker capable of shaping a roughed-out preform. Thus, the hypothetical life of a celt at one of the Aguacate sites would involve one or more major reshaping episodes accomplished by flaking and/or pecking. Major reworking would have been necessary if edge-damage was too extensive to be corrected by grinding on a whetstone. In the absence of skilled stone knappers, most of the reworking would have had to be done by pecking, thereby accounting for the large numbers of pecking hammers recovered from the excavations.

In summary, our interpretations of the lithic technology lead us to believe that most of the ground and polished stone implements were not manufactured at CA-3 or CA-2, but at quarry/workshop sites (probably) in the highlands. Furthermore, the Aguacate peoples did not go to the quarry stations either to manufacture tools, as all evidence points to their being unskilled stone knappers. It is much more likely that "outside" skilled craftsmen produced finished celts, adzes, and chisels at quarry/workshop sites and exchanged them with the Aguacate groups. These tools would then be repaired and recycled as long as possible in the hamlets of the Aguacate Peninsula where the tough, dense rocks suitable for manufacturing celts, adzes, and chisels, and for use as hammers, were unavailable. Since they require less skill than knapping, pecking and grinding were the major techniques used in the hamlets to work stone.

DESCRIPTION OF ARTIFACTS

Measuring artifacts proved to be a dilemma since so many of them were broken or extensively reworked. Where dimensions of objects could be confidently estimated, they are presented in the artifact descriptions in parentheses to distinguish them from actual measurements. If no estimate was possible, a question mark was used. Thus, a celt with dimensions listed as ? x (42) x 25 mm had a known maximum thickness of 25 mm, an estimated maximum width of 42 mm, and an unknown length.

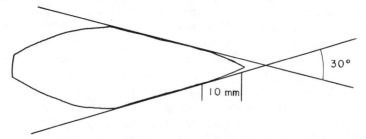

Figure 16/1: Method employed in the measurement of edge-angles for polished stone implements.

Measuring the edge angles of the bit portion of stone tools is always a difficult procedure. The Aguacate samples were particularly worrisome since very few bits were left unaltered. We measured all edge angles by arbitrarily drawing tangents to the surface of bit faces 10 mm back from the edge (see fig. 16/1) and rounding off to the nearest 5°. The measurement was taken at the center of the bit where possible.

I. Chipped Stone

A. Cores

1. Bifacial cores. Three cores have flakes removed around their entire perimeter from both faces. Two are made on celt remnants (1 basalt, 1 andesite), and the third on a chalcedony pebble (some of the weathered cortex is still present). Dimensions for the two cores made on celts and the chalcedony core are 55 x 48 x 27 mm, 48 x 32 x 17 mm, and 38 x 27 x 20 mm, respectively. The chalcedony core came from CA-3 (phase 1), the larger of the two celt cores from CA-2, and the smaller celt core from CA-3c (phase 2).

2. Bidirectional cores. Two cores from CA-2 have flakes removed from opposite ends of one face. On both, the other face retains the thick weathered cortex of the chalcedony pebbles on which the cores were made. The cores may have been flaked using a bipolar technique; that is, they may have been placed on an anvil for support while being struck with a hammerstone. Dimensions are 38 x 33 x 17 mm for one core and 39 x 28 x 18 mm for the other.

In addition to the above core types, we should note that four celts have been flaked in a manner suggesting they were being used as cores. It is possible, however, that the flaking represents an attempt to rework the celts for resharpening. All are Type B celts: three from CA-3a (phase 2) and one from CA-2 (see Type B celt descriptions).

B. Blades

1. Tanged blades (fig. 16/2 e-n). These tools, represented by 15 specimens, are long blades modified by steep bifacial or unifacial retouch at one end (normally the proximal or platform end) in order to form a stem or tang. Wear polish on the tangs is concentrated at the shoulder where the tang widens, presumably as a result of the friction between the tang and its socket haft.

The working ends of these tools have been modified and used in a variety of ways. On most specimens a tip or point has been formed by steep edge retouch on the dorsal face, sometimes accompanied by slight retouching of the ventral face to straighten out the tip. On two of three thick blades (the cross sections are nearly equilateral triangles) the dorsal ridge is unifacially retouched for a distance of 31 and 12 mm back from the tip (the third thick blade has the tip missing). One specimen has a concave working edge formed by unifacial retouch at the distal end. Usually, one or both lateral edges display unifacial retouch on the dorsal face. However, bifacial retouch also occurs, and some specimens display no purposeful lateral retouch at all.

Figure 16/2: a-d. Miscellaneous blades; e-n. tanged blades.

Wear patterns are as varied as the modifications described above. The most commonly observed pattern is for use polish to show along one or both lateral edges. In one case, striations running parallel to a unifacially retouched edge, within 5 mm of it, are visible on the polished surface. These striations imply that the tool was used in a back and forth or sawing fashion. On these specimens, wear polish is often visible on high areas of the dorsal surface (e.g., along the dorsal ridges) and occasionally on the ventral surface as well. Most such tools appear to have been used for cutting or slicing soft materials (meat and/or plant foods, for example). On lateral edges with steep unifacial retouch, wear polish is restricted to the edge or extends onto the ventral surface. Use flakes and edge crushing are characteristic of these steep-angled edges. Such edges appear to have served a scraping or planing function on a hard unyielding material like wood. On the tips of the complete thick specimens, rounded wear facets occur along both lateral edges and the dorsal ridge. The curvature of the facets and the lack of wear polish on the nonprotruding surfaces near the tip indicate that these tools were used to drill a hard substance like wood or shell.

Many of the specimens were used for more than one purpose. Special note should be made here of one tool (fig. 16/2 g) showing three distinct uses. One edge of this tanged blade, which had bifacial retouch and light wear polish, was apparently used for cutting soft materials. The opposite edge was formed by steep unifacial retouch and had heavy wear polish along the edge and extending onto the ventral surface. This edge was probably used to scrape wood or some equally resistant material. Finally, a narrow chisel-like bit (now badly damaged) had been purposefully formed by grinding and polishing the tip of the blade; the manufacturing striations are clearly visible on the polished facets. The third function for this tool, then, was as a chisel for use in light woodworking tasks. We suspect that the largest of the tanged blades also had ground and polished bits, although no portion of them was found intact. The large use flakes that were "peeled" back from the tip were probably produced because the hafted tool had been subjected to heavy battering in woodworking activities. (See the description of *chisels on blades* for somewhat similar specimens.)

Dimensions of the largest complete specimen are 130 x 21 x 20 mm and of the smallest, 63 x 22 x 7 mm; the median is 77 x 31 x 9 mm. The blades are all made on fine- to medium-grained igneous rocks. Twelve specimens were found at CA-3a (phase 2), one at CA-3b (phase 2), and two at CA-2.

2. Miscellaneous blades (fig. 16/2 a-d). This category, represented by nine specimens, includes blades clearly not modified for hafting by the production of a tang, and blade fragments for which the presence or absence of a tang could not be determined. The two complete specimens show use polish on the tips. The smaller of the two shows steep unifacial retouch on the dorsal face along one edge and on the ventral face along the other edge. Retouch and use polish occur on some but not all of the remaining blade fragments. Seven of the blades are made of fine-grained igneous rock (basalt and andesite); two are chalcedony. Only four specimens have platforms intact. In all cases, the platform overhang has been removed. The

platform was struck well back from the edge (4 to 11 mm) with a soft blunt hammerstone, or alternately, a punch was set well back from the edge. These blades, as well as those which were tanged (and therefore had the platform removed or altered beyond recognition) are very regular in form. They have either one or two dorsal ridges. Most are quite straight. These blades are clearly the product of a skilled craftsman.

Dimensions for the two complete specimens are 79 x 21 x 7 mm and 67 x 15 x 5 mm. Five blades came from CA-3a (phase 2), two from CA-3b (phase 2), and one from CA-2.

C. Flakes

1. Flake blades are represented by six specimens. These fragments are at least twice as long as they are wide, and were detached with the direction of force paralleling the long axis (thereby satisfying a minimal definition of blade). However, they were clearly not struck from prepared cores and should probably be considered fortuitous. Three blades were manufactured by using the side of a celt as the guiding ridge for detachment. One of the blades (59 x 22 x 11 mm) has use flakes and wear polish along one edge extending from the tip to a point midway between the base and the tip. Neither of the other specimens, one complete (54 x 23 x 12 mm) and one fragmentary, showed any signs of use.

Two other flake blades (55 x 23 x 5 mm and 50 x 24 x 5 mm) had small use flakes removed along the lateral edges (primarily from the dorsal surface) and show wear polish along both edges as well. On one, the wear polish extends onto the dorsal ridges and onto the high spots along compression rings on the ventral surface.

The three flake blades made on celts are medium-grained igneous rocks. The other three specimens are fine-grained igneous rocks.

2. Used flakes are represented by four specimens. One chalcedony flake (44 x 28 x 14 mm) from CA-3a (phase 2) shows retouch flakes and slight wear polish along one edge. A second chalcedony flake (25 x 23 x 8 mm) from CA-3a (phase 2) shows unifacial retouch flakes along one edge, but no traces of wear polish. An andesite flake (24 x 24 x 5 mm) from CA-2 had uniform use flakes removed from a concave working edge. A second chalcedony flake from CA-2, removed from a small pebble (the dorsal surface still retains the original cortex), has a tip formed by steep retouch primarily on the dorsal surface. The very tip has been damaged by the removal of a small (2 mm) use flake. Wear polish is visible behind this flake scar, along both edges, for a distance of 5 mm. The small flake (34 x 25 x 10 mm) appears to have been used as a graver or perforator.

3. Waste flakes. A total of 123 flakes was recovered from CA-2 and CA-3 localities which show no modification by design or by use after detachment. Eighty of these flakes retain a ground and/or polished surface on their dorsal face, indicating that they were removed (either purposefully or accidentally) from celts or from other ground and polished tools. An additional 31 flakes are made of the same material — igneous rocks of various descriptions — and can be reasonably considered celt flakes as well, even

though they do not retain any portion of a polished surface. We are left with only 12 flakes of chalcedony that are clearly not the product of breaking down celts. Of the flakes which retain portions of the celts' surfaces, 11 are from the bit, 23 are from some section other than the bit, and 46 cannot be categorized beyond saying that they came from celts.

The flakes were distributed as follows: 65 from CA-3a (phase 2), nine from CA-3a (phase 1), seven from CA-3b (phase 2), one from CA-3b (phase 2), four from CA-3d, 31 from CA-2, and six with no provenience.

D. A Stemmed Unifacial Point

This artifact was manufactured by trimming a flat andesite flake using steep unifacial retouch. The tool was probably *not* used as a projectile point since it is asymmetrical and has very blunted edges left by the steep retouch. The very tip (2–3 mm) of the tool has been snapped off, and wear polish is present on the edges to a point 10 mm back from the broken tip. This suggests that the tool was used as a graver or perforator. Dimensions of the specimen are 39 x 22 x 5 mm. It was recovered from CA-3a (phase 2).

II. Ground and Polished Stone

A. An Axe (fig. 16/3 e)

A single specimen was recovered from phase 2 contexts at CA-3a. A constriction (it cannot really be called a groove) just in front of the butt end distinguishes this ground and polished tool from all the others. The axe is 99 mm in length, 57 mm at the maximum width just behind the bit, 39 mm wide at the constriction, and 36 mm wide at the butt end. Maximum thickness on either side of the constriction is 29 mm, while the constriction itself is 27 mm thick. The bit is no longer intact, but an edge angle of ca. 55° can be reconstructed. The surface of the axe has been badly pitted, as if pecking of the tool was done in an attempt to resharpen it. The tool has remnants of a polished surface immediately in front of the constriction. Shaping of the constriction and the butt was by pecking. The butt end is heavily battered.

B. Celts

1. Type A (fig. 16/3 a-d) consisted of 18 celts or celt fragments complete enough to be placed in this category. The bit edge of these celts continues back along the side of the celt in a smooth curve so that the cutting edge forms a semicircle and extends from one side of the celt to the other. Behind the bit, the celts narrow to a butt which is round to oval in cross section. Type A celts are also called pear-shaped celts. The butts of these celts are shaped by flaking and usually not altered further, although some specimens are pecked. Above the butt end, the surface of the celt is completely polished except for the occasional deep flake scar which is not completely obliterated. On a few specimens it seems clear that the celts were initially flaked and then ground and polished without any pecking. The bits are all biconvex in cross section.

Figure 16/3: a-d. Celt Type A; e. axe; f-l. celt Type B; m. celt Type C.

Ten of the 18 specimens have been very extensively modified and used as pecking hammers. Only one specimen is complete, the smallest of the group (53 x 43 x 15 mm), and it appears to be the reworked butt half of a once much longer celt (the estimated original length is 83 mm). The edge angle of its bit is 40°. The largest celt for which dimensions can be reconstructed measures (193) x (100) x 39 mm. The bit for this specimen was missing. The only medium-sized specimen for which the dimensions could be reconstructed measured (142) x 78 x 29 mm (the bit is too battered for an edge angle measurement). A different medium-sized celt fragment had a bit edge angle of 50°.

The celts were made from a variety of igneous rocks (e.g., basalt, andesite, and granite). They were recovered from the following contexts: two in CA-3a (phase 1), eleven in CA-3a (phase 2), four in CA-3b (phase 2), and one in CA-2.

2. Type B (fig. 16/3 f-l) consisted of 50 specimens with straight sides tapered from front to back. The bit is only gently curved, and makes a

well-defined angle with the sides of the celt (cf. description of Type A celts). The celts are ground and polished over the entire surface. Characteristically, they have three facets on each face, making them hexagonal in cross section. Not one of the 50 specimens is complete, 25 have been utilized as pecking hammers; that is, they have broad, battered facets on both ends. Most of the other celts show on one end signs of use as hammering or pounding tools. Three appear to have been used as cores since large flakes have been removed from one or two edges. On one specimen, the edges have been rounded and ground smooth, from the midpoint of the bit, back along both sides to a point half way to the butt end.

Where retained, the original surface of the celts is always ground and polished. Presumably, the celts were intially flaked, then pecked into shape before the final grinding and polishing took place. Those celts which were reworked to function as celts were fashioned by some percussion flaking and much pecking.

The largest celt for which dimensions could be reconstructed measured (155) x (70) x 31 mm. The smallest celt has a reconstructed size of (75) x 29 x 18 mm. The bit edge angle for this small celt was 35°. The three other small Type B celts had edge angles of 40° (two specimens) and 45°. The reconstructed size of a medium-sized celt is (95) x 43 x 25 mm. The only medium-sized type B celt with a bit intact had an edge angle of 50° (specimen measured ? x 52 x 25 mm). These celts were made from a variety of igneous rocks (e.g., basalt, andesite, dacite, and granite). The smaller celts are made of very fine-grained materials. Type B celts were recovered in the following contexts: 34 in CA-3a (phase 2), three in CA-3a (phase 1), six in CA-3b (phase 2), one in CA-3d (phase 2), and six in CA-2.

3. Type C (fig. 16/3 m). Two small celts from CA-3a (phase 2) have flaring bits and incurvate sides. Both have been resharpened. In fact, one may have been made from the base of a Type A celt. They appear to have been flaked into shape, then ground and polished primarily at the bit end. The two measure 67 x 47 x 20 mm (bit angle 45°) and 58 (80) x 44 x 13 mm (bit angle 40°), respectively. Both are made of fine-grained igneous rock.

4. Butt of large celt. The shape of this fragment is similar to that of Type B celt butts. However, it has only traces of polishing. Some pecking has been done, particularly along the edges, but the flake scars from the initial shaping are still visible. The fragment measures 69 x 49 x 39 mm and is made of andesite. It was recovered from CA-3a (phase 2).

C. *Adzes (fig. 16/4 a-e)*

Six small adzes were made on the ends of blades. Only the bits have been ground and polished. The specimens are plano-convex (actually plano-diamond) in cross section, the ventral surface of the blade forming the flat side of the adze. On the five specimens which retain bits, the edge angles vary between 35° and 50°.

Dimensions of the two most complete specimens are 72 x 22 x 14 mm and 55 x 24 x 10 mm. All are made of fine-grained igneous rocks. Three are from CA-3a (phase 2) and three are from CA-2.

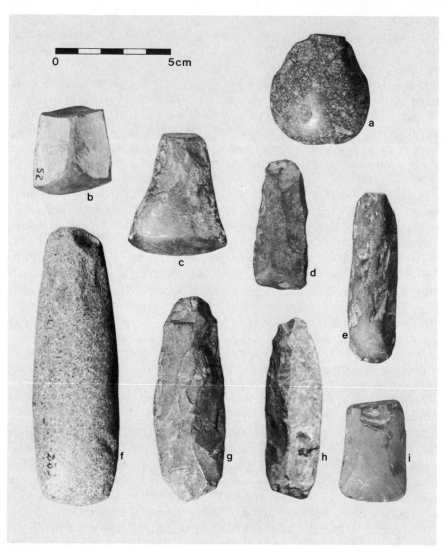

Figure 16/4: a-e. Adzes; f-i. chisels.

D. Chisels (fig. 16/4 f-i)

1. Large chisels are represented by four specimens. A large (117 x 37 x 25 mm, bit missing) ground and polished stone artifact appears to have been initially made as a chisel. The attributes closely parallel those for Type B celts except that this specimen is much narrower proportionally than any of the Type B celts, and the sides are subparallel. It has seen secondary use as a pecking hammer, so that the bit is completely destroyed. The specimen was recovered from CA-3b (phase 2) and is made of andesite. Three fragments of ground and polished tools may also be parts of chisels. One is a completely polished butt end fragment, oval in cross section and tapered to a blunt

point (? x 24 x 15 mm). It comes from CA-3a (phase 2) and it is made from a fine-grained igneous rock. The second fragment comes from a tool midsection (? x 27 x 16 mm); it is diamond-shaped in cross section and completely polished. It also comes from CA-3a (phase 2) and is made from a fine-grained igneous rock. The final chisel fragment has been heavily battered on both ends from secondary use as a pecking hammer (? x 27 x 17 mm). It is diamond-shaped in cross section, with a polished surface that does not completely obliterate the flake scars left from the initial manufacturing of the implement. It was recovered from CA-3a (phase 2) and is made from fine-grained basalt.

2. Medium chisels. Four nearly whole specimens have been flaked into form, then partially ground and polished (no pecking is in evidence). They have parallel sides, diamond-shaped cross sections, and are nearly as thick as they are wide. Only the bit and the high spots on the bit end of the chisels are polished. The dimensions of the four specimens are 109 (140) x 39 x 26 mm, 85 (110) x 30 x 19 mm, 79 (115) x 31 x 20 mm, and 75(105) x 24 x 17 mm. No bits were retained for edge angle measurements. All were made of fine-grained igneous rocks. Three came from CA-3a (phase 2) and one from CA-3b (phase 2).

3. Chisels on blades. Three blades have distal ends modified by grinding and polishing to form small chisel bits. Polishing occurs on both dorsal and ventral surfaces back 5 to 10 mm from the bit, then extends back along the dorsal ridge another 10 mm in one case, and nearly the entire length of the specimen in another. The latter specimen has retouch flakes removed along both sides, and a constricted base or tang for hafting. It measures 64 x 22 x 6 mm. Dimensions for the other chisels are 87 x 18 x 10 and 57 x 16 x 17. All are made of fine-grained igneous rocks. One specimen came from CA-3a (phase 1), one from CA-3b (phase 2), and one from CA-2. (One multipurpose tool placed in the category of tanged blade had a ground and polished chisel bit, and perhaps another did as well. See description for tanged blades.)

E. *Miscellaneous Ground and Polished Stone Implements*

1. Butt fragments. Not enough of the butt ends are present to assign these five fragments to a more specific tool category. However, they are probably fragments of either Type A celts or medium-sized chisels. All are bifacially flaked. In addition, three have been polished in small areas. All are biconvex to diamond-shaped in cross section. All are made of igneous rock. Three are from CA-3a (phase 2), one from CA-3b (phase 2), and one from CA-2.

2. Reworked celt flake. The dorsal surface of this flake retains the polished surface of the celt from which it was struck. In addition, the ventral surface and distal edge have been polished. The flake measures 40 x 27 x 5 mm and is shaped like a truncated isosceles triangle. The base of the triangle is damaged, perhaps through use as a chisel. The flake is made of granite and was recovered from CA-3a (phase 1/2).

III. Miscellaneous Stone Tools (fig. 16/5)

A. Whetstones

Two specimens were recovered from CA-2. Both are tabular and have four concave working surfaces. The larger one (51 x 43 x 18 mm) is a medium fine-grained sandstone which in cross section looks like a parallelogram. The smaller specimen (31 x 18 x 12 mm) is a very fine-grained sandstone and rectangular in cross section. Striations running parallel to the long axis of the tools are visible on all working surfaces of both tools. The curvature of these working surfaces suggests that the whetstones were used on chisels, adzes, and small celts only.

B. Polished Pebble

A quartz pebble from CA-2 has a highly polished surface with visible parallel striations. The wear pattern exactly duplicates that of a quartzite pebble used by one of us (Ranere) in polishing the surface and honing the bit of experimentally made celts.

C. Battered and Polished Cobble

A long, three-sided cobble with hammering facets on both ends and along the entire length of the three edges was recovered from CA-3a (phase 2). One of its three faces is unaltered, one is ground and lightly polished, and the third is heavily polished. The tool was presumably used in the pecking and polishing stages of celt manufacturing. It measured 92 x 31 x 28 mm and was made of andesite.

D. Hammerstones

Five small cobbles have been modified by hammering on one or both ends. Three specimens exhibit heavy use, the other two only light use. Three are of igneous materials, two are of quartzite. Dimensions of the tools are 93 x 52 x 23 mm, 82 x 33 x 32 mm, 75 x 49 x 33 mm, 59 x 40 x 28 mm, and 91 x 45 x 44 mm. Three are from CA-3a (phase 2) and two are from CA-2. (We should note that 10 Type A celts, 25 Type B celts, two large chisels, and one polished and battered cobble exhibited heavy use as hammers (fig. 16/6). In addition, most of the remaining celts showed some use as hammers.)

E. Anvil

One sandstone cobble from CA-2 has a series of small depressions gouged out from one surface. It appears to have been used as an anvil in percussion flaking. Its dimensions are 91 x 55 x 42 mm.

F. Cobble Pestles

Two specimens, both rather large, were recovered with pounding wear facets on both ends. One elongated igneous cobble measured 151 x 83 x 72 mm; the other, a pear-shaped cobble of dacite, measured 148 x 85 x 73 mm. Both were recovered from CA-3a (phase 2).

Figure 16/5: Tools presumably used in the manufacture of ground and polished stone implements: a. pebble polisher; b,c. whetstones of fine- and medium-grained sandstone, respectively; d. three-sided cobble polisher.

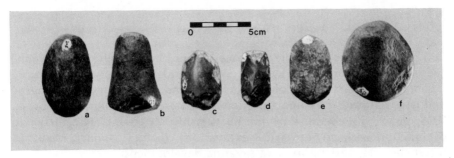

Figure 16/6: Celts reused as hammers.

G. Handstones

Two large cobbles may have been used as grinding implements. One is a flat oval cobble which appears to have ground facets on both flat sides, although heavy weathering of the limestone makes this difficult to determine. It measures 152 x 79 x 52 mm and comes from CA-3b (phase 2). The other handstone is a somewhat irregular elongated cobble of dacite (141 x 77 x 59 mm) which has a possible grinding surface. Both ends have seen light pounding, suggesting that this tool may have also served as a pestle. It came from CA-2.

H. Cylindrical Cobble

This heavily weathered dacite cobble from CA-3a (phase 2) is nearly square in cross section. Striations visible on one face parallel to the long axis of the cobble may indicate it was used as a whetstone.

A number of unmodified cobbles and pebbles were also recovered from the Aguacate localities. Although they showed no sign of use (weathering may have obscured patterns once present), they were undoubtedly brought onto the site for some purpose or another. Rounded cobbles and pebbles were not part of the natural sediments at any of the sites.

I. Notched Stone

A small oval igneous pebble from CA-2 has two notches pecked into opposite sides. It may have functioned as a net or line weight. Its dimensions are 46 x 33 x 16 mm.

Report Number 17

Sediment Analysis of a Core from Isla Palenque

G. J. WEST

INTRODUCTION

On viewing tropical Middle America one is immediately struck by the presence of large areas of open land covered with savanna type vegetation. Upon further examination one finds that in most cases these areas are by and large controlled by human activities related to agriculture (Budowski 1956, pp. 23–33). Because of this relationship an attempt was made, in conjunction with archaeological excavations, to find a pollen record of forest clearing, agriculture, and savanna development.

To obtain a pollen record, coring was done with a modified Livingston piston sampler. With this device, a series of core slugs each about a meter long can be taken to a depth of 8 to 10 meters depending on the nature of the sediments. Attempts were made to core many areas, but only a few proved successful. Cores that were recovered come mainly from coastal swamps on both the Pacific and Caribbean sides of western Panama. The sediments of one of those cores from Isla Palenque is reported below. The core is from the edge of a small estuary, some 100–150 meters away from La Pitahaya (IS-3) site (fig. 17/1).

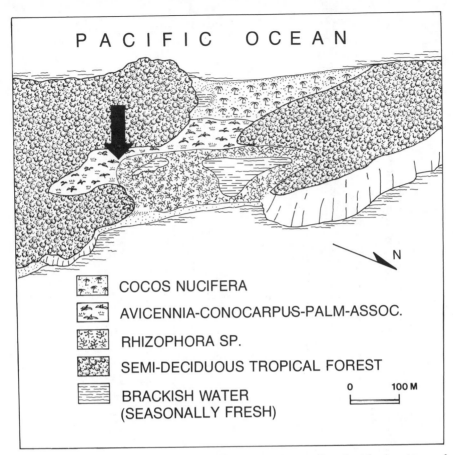

PACIFIC OCEAN

N

	COCOS NUCIFERA
	AVICENNIA-CONOCARPUS-PALM-ASSOC.
	RHIZOPHORA SP.
	SEMI-DECIDUOUS TROPICAL FOREST
	BRACKISH WATER (SEASONALLY FRESH)

0   100 M

Figure 17/1: Sketch map of Isla Palenque showing location of ancient freshwater pond. The arrow points to the core site. Original sketch by J. West.

POLLEN DATA

Preliminary pollen analysis of the core shows changes in relative pollen frequencies of grasses, chenoams, composites, and forest elements that suggest possible human induced vegetational changes (report no. 18). Other pollen frequency changes may reflect environmental factors such as a changing water table, substrate, or water chemistry. Other types of approaches such as sediment analysis may clarify these changes (table 1).

Although interpretations from one core are obviously limited, the following model is suggested as one possibility. It seems quite probable that conditions much like the present existed, except that the estuary was larger and has subsequently been filled in. The area is a small basin that has had rather continuous deposition, although the rate may have varied. With the exception of the shell and coral sand, the size of the sediments suggests a low energy environment such as one would expect to find in the central portions of a ponded body of water (J.L. Richardson 1969, pp. 78–93). On the other

TABLE 1   CORE LOG FROM ISLA PALENQUE (IS-3)

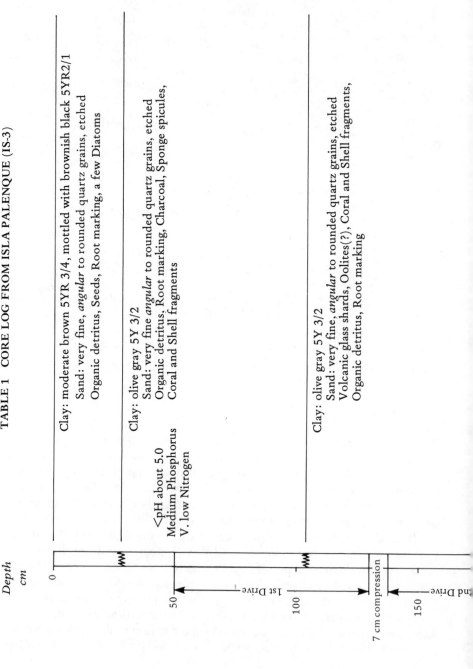

Depth
cm

Clay: moderate brown 5YR 3/4, mottled with brownish black 5YR2/1
Sand: very fine, *angular* to rounded quartz grains, etched
Organic detritus, Seeds, Root marking, a few Diatoms

Clay: olive gray 5Y 3/2
Sand: very fine *angular* to rounded quartz grains, etched
Organic detritus, Root marking, Charcoal, Sponge spicules,
Coral and Shell fragments

<pH about 5.0
Medium Phosphorus
V. low Nitrogen

Clay: olive gray 5Y 3/2
Sand: very fine, *angular* to rounded quartz grains, etched
Volcanic glass shards, Oolites(?), Coral and Shell fragments,
Organic detritus, Root marking

0

50

1st Drive

100

7 cm compression

150

2nd Drive

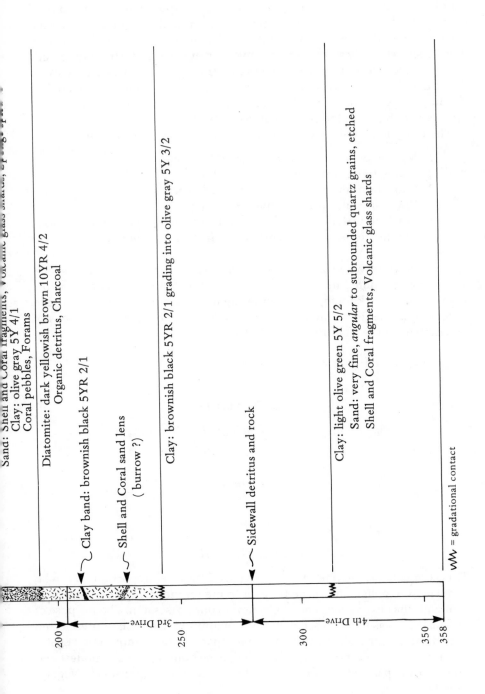

Sand: Shell and Coral fragments, volcanic glass shards, of stage 4/1 (?)

Clay: olive gray 5Y 4/1
Coral pebbles, Forams

Diatomite: dark yellowish brown 10YR 4/2
Organic detritus, Charcoal

Clay band: brownish black 5YR 2/1

Shell and Coral sand lens
(burrow ?)

Clay: brownish black 5YR 2/1 grading into olive gray 5Y 3/2

Sidewall detritus and rock

Clay: light olive green 5Y 5/2
Sand: very fine, *angular* to subrounded quartz grains, etched
Shell and Coral fragments, Volcanic glass shards

ᗺ = gradational contact

3rd Drive

4th Drive

200
250
300
350
358

hand the shell and coral sand suggest a short term high energy factor such as might be created by wave action. Presently, at the upper portions of the beach berm that separates the pond from the bay, similar shell and coral sands are found. A large wave(s) could have transported the shell and coral sand with clay, much like a turbidity current, into the basin. As suggested by the diatomite, the environment in the basin prior to the sand appears to have been relatively stable. The marine sand event appears to have considerably altered the environment, changing the water from fresh to brackish for a length of time until another high berm was established. Hence, a freshwater pond once existed at Palenque, probably at the time of occupation of the IS-3 site; the island suffers a shortage of fresh water now.

The environmental sequence appears to be something like this:

1. Marine or brackish water (light olive green clay)
2. Stable fresh water pond (diatomite)
3. Short term marine interval (shell and coral sand)
4. Brackish water (upper olive green clay)
5. Brackish water alternating to fresh seasonally; present conditions (moderate brown clay with a few freshwater diatoms)

This description would definitely help in explaining some of the vegetational changes noted in the pollen spectra. How long a period of time the core covers is not known, but considering the depositional rate reported in other tropical regions (Muller 1959, pp. 1–32), the core probably does not extend back more than two thousand years.

Report Number 18

The Identification of Selected Pollen Grains from a Core at Isla Palenque

K. H. CLARY

INTRODUCTION

This core is the same one that was analyzed by West (report no. 17), who extracted the pollen and turned it over to me for mounting and identification with the aid of a reference collection in our possession. The purpose of my analysis was to try to see if any one of approximately sixty preselected pollens from economic plants and/or trees that constitute important vegetational markers occurred in the core. Hence the objectives were modest and aimed principally at problems of subsistence and/or man-made vegetational changes.

The economic pollens selected for this exercise were, among others, those of *Manihot esculenta* (cassava), *Zea mays* (maize), *Persea americana* (avocado), *Cocos nucifera* (coconut), *Solanum* sp. (potato), *Phaseolus* sp. (common and lima beans), *Nicotiana* sp. (tobacco), *Capsicum annuum* (red pepper), *Lycopersicon esculentum* (tomato), *Carica papaya* (papaya), *Theobroma cacao* (cacao), *Ipomoea batatas* (sweet potato), *Gossypium* sp. (cotton) and *Sechium edule* (chayote).

Some pollens belonging to well-known trees were also selected in order to reconstruct the composition of the vegetation surrounding the site.

POLLENS IDENTIFIED FROM THE CORE SAMPLES

0–20 cm: Annonaceae

24–26 cm: Bombacaceae- *Pachira aquatica, Bombacopsis sessilis*

Cyperaceae sp.

Zea mays

Fern spores (cf. Bartlett and Barghoorn 1973, pp. 254, 255)

Annonaceae

48–50 cm: Fern spores dominant, with very little pollen

78–80 cm: Gramineae sp.

Leguminosae- *Calliandra ?*

Gr. Insert sed. 1 (Van der Hammen 1973, p. 80)

Palmae

143–144 cm: Sample is too dense with plant debris and charcoal to work with.

221–225 cm: *Hibiscus* sp.

Fern spores

Zea mays

344–355 cm: *Manihot esculenta*

Zea mays

Palmae

Gr. Insert. sed. 1 (Van der Hammen ibid.)

COMMENTS

The core contained pollen of two important cultivars (fig. 18/1): maize (*Zea mays*) and manioc (*Manihot esculenta*) in the bottom level. Maize pollen also occurred on the top level, suggesting that this plant possibly was important all throughout the occupation of the IS-3 site. This pollen may have come from fields on Palenque itself, at some distance from the occupational area.

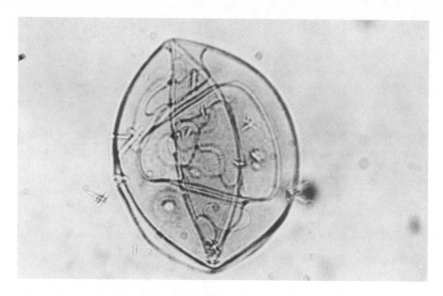

a

b

Figure 18/1: Pollen grains under magnification: a. Zea mays (Gramineae); size 95 u diameter; magnification 40x; description, Monoporate, operculate. b. Manihot esculentum (Euphorbiaceae); size 189 u diameter; magnification 40x; description, Polyforate (note "pegs," triangular in surface view, encircling foveolid areas).

Unfortunately, there was no datable material present in the core, but we may suggest that the oldest levels are coterminous with the initial occupation of IS-3 at A.D. 600 or a few centuries before.

Other pollens are from important tropical trees. The Annonaceae or Annona family includes such species as custard apple ("anón"), sugar apple ("chirimoya"), and soursop ("guanábana"). The Bombacaceae or Bombax family has among its members the silk-cotton tree ("bongo").

Pollens of rushes or hedges of the Cyperaceae family and assorted tropical grasses that grow around the border of swamps are also represented.

The Palmae family is also present but, unfortunately, it was impossible to identify the particular species occurring in the core.

Report Number 19

Marañon: A Report of Ethnographic Research Among the Bocas Guaymí

P. D. YOUNG

INTRODUCTION

Marañon is located along the Bocas del Toro coast on a narrow, irregular bifurcate ridge jutting out from the higher hills to the south and surrounded on three sides by tidal swamp (fig. 19/1). The ridge is estimated to be only 100–150 feet above sea level. This community was chosen for a brief ethnographic survey because in terms of its size, dispersal of dwellings, geographical location, and general environmental conditions it displayed striking parallels to what was known of prehistoric sites in the near vicinity, especially that of Cerro Brujo.

The data contained in this report were collected from March 20 to April 15, 1970. The three weeks were spent as follows: one week in Bocas town and (daily) at the Cerro Brujo archaeological site; one week in Chiriqui revisiting the Guaymí in San Felix district in order to collect comparative data; and one week in the Bocas Guaymí hamlet of Marañon, located near the shore of the Chiriqui Lagoon on the mainland not far from the island town of Bocas. Part of one day was spent in an aerial survey of this area as well as of nearby Cerro Brujo, the Valiente Peninsula, and the Cricamola river valley.

Marañon is one of a handful of small hamlets and isolated homesteads that represent the recolonization by Guaymí of this part of the Bocas coastline. The lands the community occupies and those its residents farm in the foothills inland from it were formerly part of an extensive, now abandoned cacao plantation.

The initial establishment of Marañon occurred approximately thirty years ago, according to its residents, some of whom are original settlers. This clearly represents a reoccupation of lands that were once a part of the territory of the Guaymí and their ancestors, a point easily substantiated by both archaeological and historical evidence. Most of the migrants who have settled and are settling in Marañon and the surrounding area come from hamlets located in Bocas del Toro, along the heavily Guaymí-populated Cricamola drainage system to the east. More and better farmland was given consistently as the primary reason for leaving the Cricamola.

Travel to nearby communities and to various hamlets along the Rio Cricamola is accomplished by means of dugout canoes skillfully maneuvered through the coastal waters. Frequent inclement weather restricts such travel. Only one man in Marañon owns an outboard motor (six horsepower) and he stated that, with the motor, the trip from Marañon to the Cricamola takes approximately four hours. No estimate of paddling time is available. There is an overland trail connecting Marañon with a nearby Guaymí hamlet, but apparently it is seldomly used. It was described by some residents as partially submerged and frequently impassable, and by others as nonexistent.

The Marañon Guaymí speak a dialect of *ŋawbére*, a Chibchan language. A lexicon of about 200 words, plus several phrases and sentences that I collected and compared with linguistic data I had gathered previously among the Guaymí of Chiriqui, revealed only slight dialectical differences at the phonological level. (It is known, however, that there are some slight variations in word usage and meaning between Bocas and Chiriqui Guaymí.) Such things as terms for kinsmen, body parts, and foodstuffs were identical in form and meaning; further confirmation of the fact that there is no linguistic division of the Guaymí into a northern Bocas group and a southern Chiriqui group (cf. Wassén 1952; Young 1971, pp. 20–21).

In 1970, Marañon consisted of six family houses spread out along the top of the ridge, and one structure (d in fig. 19/1) which served as a church, a community gathering place, and a temporary abode for visitors from the surrounding area when either space or close kinsmen were not available in the occupied houses. It is this normally unoccupied structure that housed me during my stay in the community. This communal meetinghouse was constructed through the labors of the entire community, but its ownership is claimed by the man who, in 1970, was the religious leader of Marañon, and who conducted nightly religious meetings in the building during my stay.

Figure 19/1: Aerial photograph of Marañon, a Bocas Guaymí hamlet on the Aguacate Peninsula: a. boathouse; b. household; c. household; d. meeting house; e. household; f. household; g. chicken house; h. household; i. tidal swamp; j. household; k. swampy ground; l. Quebrada Marañon. Distance between e and h is about 48 meters; between h and j about 41 meters. In terms of the categories of the Guaymí kinship system, and stating the matter as economically as possible, the relationships among household heads are as follows: The wives of the heads of households b, f, h, and j are "sisters" and the head of household c is their "brother." The female head of household e is the "mother" of this group of "siblings." (For Guaymí kinship terms and their glosses, see Young 1971, pp. 140-148.)

Four of the six occupied houses are similar in construction to houses b and j of figure 19/1; house 19/1b is also shown in figure 19/2. Similar Guaymí houses are common along other parts of the coast and along the lower and middle course of the Rio Cricamola, although this house type represents a departure from the more traditional large, circular dwelling with no partitioned rooms, examples of which can still be seen along the Rio Cricamola. The other two houses in Marañon (fig. 19/1 c, d) represent a further departure from the traditional style in that they incorporate plank construction (fig. 19/3). Perhaps the most noticeable difference in style when comparing Guaymí dwellings in Bocas del Toro with those in Chiriqui is the Bocas Guaymí practice of elevating the house on posts. This may represent an adaptation in some places to the almost everpresent mud resulting from the almost everpresent rain, but it is more likely an adaptation to the keeping of pigs which are much more common in Bocas del Toro than in Chiriqui (Gordon 1969, p. 42). Archaeological evidence does not reveal the exact type of house construction that existed in precontact times.

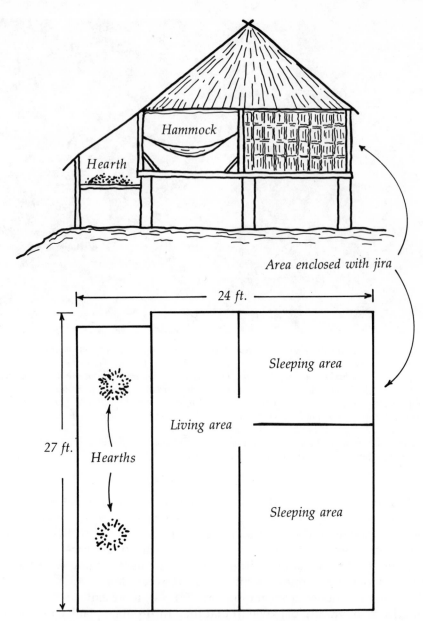

Figure 19/2: Sketch of a typical house in the Marañon community.

The present residents of Marañon are almost all related to one another by traceable ties of consanguinity and affinity. My major informant, whom I will hereafter refer to as Francisco, insisted that the women in the community are his wife, his mother, and his sisters (ŋwae, which in the Guaymí kinship terminological system includes cousins), and the men are his brothers-in-law. The fact that the residence arrangement after marriage appears to be uxorilocality in five of the six households is apparently due to

Figure 19/3: Nontraditional Marañon house incorporating plank construction.

specifics of the history of settlement of the community rather than to an ideological shift from postmarital virilocality to uxorilocality among this portion of the Guaymí population. Francisco's father (social father, on the basis of genealogical data) apparently founded the community and Francisco's "sisters" came to live here with their husbands due to the availability of suitable farmland and its relative scarcity in the Cricamola region from which they came. The greater proximity of the community to the United Brands banana plantations was probably another factor influencing migration, considering that most of the men in Marañon work for the company.

SUBSISTENCE ACTIVITIES

Wild pigs, rabbits, monkeys, paca (*Cuniculus paca*), deer, various birds, and various wild cats are all hunted by the Marañon inhabitants, and all but the last mentioned are definitely used as food. Tapir was formerly hunted in the vicinity of Marañon but, according to informants, there are no longer any left to hunt; most likely they are still present but scarce. A lack of ammunition due to recurrent governmental restrictions on its sale has made hunting difficult for the people of Marañon. Apparently no one in the community uses the bow and arrow (I saw none in use and none in the houses during my stay.)

Fish, shellfish, and lobsters are all used as food, but everyone insisted that these resources were much more plentiful twenty years ago (that is, twenty years before 1970) than they are today. Their explanation for the obvious decline in marine resources was that many people (especially non-Guaymí) now use boats with outboard motors to fish.

Cattle, pigs, chickens, ducks, dogs, parrots, and goats shared the community with the people during my stay, and all but dogs at one time or another become ingredients in the human diet, as occasionally do the products of some of these (milk and eggs). I did not attempt to count these animals since I suspected that their numbers fluctuated considerably over relatively short periods of time. Suffice it to say that cattle were very few in number and there were only three goats, all belonging to one man. All of the domestic animals wandered freely through the community during the day.

The agricultural lands of Marañón lie mainly to the south (inland) of the settlement, less than an hour's walk from the community. This may not represent an upper limit with respect to travel time to suitable farmland, but the nearest solid ground beyond that adjacent to the community itself seems to be Cerro Brujo — and that apparently is too far away to be farmed by the residents of Marañón.

Swidden agriculture is the only method used, with axe, machete, and digging stick making up the tool kit. Attempts are made to burn fields after clearing, but this procedure is usually unsuccessful because of the lack of any true dry season in this part of Panama. Hence, slash-and-burn frequently gives way in this area to a variant we may call slash-and-rot. Work parties (juntas) organized by individuals are utilized in clearing the land and in planting. A junta for planting corn, used mostly to feed pigs, occurred during my stay in the community. People from Cerro Brujo and Sharks Hole came to participate with those of Marañón. This parallels the usual pattern on the Pacific slopes where individuals from nearby hamlets may provide labor for work parties. The workers are usually relatives of one sort or another of the host (patrón), but in some instances they are just friends. The provision of food and drink to the workers by the host also matched the Chiriqui pattern.

A wide variety of crops is planted by the people of Marañón. Plantings of root crops are made around the house sites as well as on agricultural lands surrounding the hamlet. It was reported that squash is planted with the corn, but I did not see instances of this. The main crops are presented in the order in which they were given to me: Bananas, taro (dasheen — Colacosia esculenta), plantains, sweet manioc, otoe (Xanthosoma sp.), yams, corn, rice, red beans (little), cacao, pejibaye, avocado, squash, oranges, mangoes, lemons, grapefruit, pigeon peas (very little), and small chili peppers. The people of Marañón formerly planted a substantial quantity of sugarcane in order to make strong chicha, but now they raise only a little for sweetening because their new religion (not that of Mama Chi, but possibly a derivative of it; Young 1975) does not permit them to consume alcoholic beverages.

FOOD PRESERVATION AND DIET

Otoe is said to last practically forever after removing the tubers from the ground; this corresponds exactly to what I was told in Chiriqui. Yams last up to one month if picked carefully — meaning that the skin of the tuber should not be scratched, bruised, cut, or broken; in Chiriqui I was told they may last up to two months under the same circumstances, possibly due to climatological differences. According to my Bocas and Chiriqui informants, sweet manioc, once it has been dug up, lasts two days at most before spoiling, but it can be kept for a week or two by reburying it. It should be noted that both the Guaymí and the rural campesinos generally harvest sweet manioc only as needed. They are well aware of the fact that it will last for a long time if simply left in the ground, although it is said to become tough and stringy if left for too long a time after the tubers reach maturity. *Dasheen* is said to last as long as *otoe* if picked carefully so that the skin of the tubers is not damaged. (My Chiriqui informants had no comment on this. They know what *dasheen* is but do not plant it.) Green bananas, it is said by the Marañon informant, do not last after peeling. He claimed that they spoil within a single day. When asked the same question, my major informant in Chiriqui said that green bananas last practically forever; and, indeed, I have eaten peeled green bananas that had been stored in a net bag for several days without having received any special preparation, and these showed no signs of deterioration or spoilage. It would appear that with all root crops, except *otoe*, it is necessary to take care not to damage the skin if they are to be stored for even a day or two before eating.

Beef and pork are dried in the sun or over a fire, and this can be done with chicken as well (but rarely is). The meat is salted if there is salt available. Fish can be dried and made into flour. They are first cooked over a fire, all of the large bones removed, and then the meat is placed in a large metal pot without water, cooked slowly and stirred almost constantly until dry and powdery. It is then stored in bottles. If fish are to be kept only a few days, they are simply salted and dried, either over a fire or in the sun.

It is at times when people are intending to spend several days away from home, for example, when they are planning to visit friends and relatives along the Rio Cricamola, that they prepare dried meat and fish flour to carry as provisions.

Francisco said that of the cultivars grown by the Guaymí of Marañon, the people eat bananas (usually picked green and boiled or baked) and *dasheen* more frequently than anything else, followed by sweet manioc and *otoe*, with yams occupying the third position of importance. He also mentioned that they eat a good deal of squash, but the fact that squash is seasonal, while bananas and root crops are not, is apparently the reason he did not include squash in the same scale of importance as the others.

A tabulation of the foodstuffs served at a total of twenty-four meals during my stay in Marañon (table 1), although it can hardly be considered representative of the yearly dietary intake, does tend to agree with Francisco's assessment of the foodstuffs most often consumed. (Due to lack of equipment, no quantitative data on dietary intake were collected.) It is evident that, in this limited sample, bananas and root crops are the major constituents of the diet.

By reference to the section on subsistence activities, one can easily determine that there is a much wider variety of food available to and presumably utilized by the Marañon Guaymí than is represented in the dietary intake sample of twenty-four meals. I believe, however, that the emphasis on green bananas and root crops displayed in this sample is fairly representative of the proportion of their diet that these foodstuffs constitute on a year-round basis.

SUMMARY

Marañon appears to be typical of coastal communities of the Bocas Guaymí in terms of its crop inventory and the relative frequency of different natural foods in the diet. It reflects the strong dependence in Bocas on various root crops and bananas and the relative unimportance of corn and beans, both dietary staples in Chiriqui. Contributions to the diet from hunting and fishing mirror the rapid decline in availability of these resources in recent years. Marañon depends much less on the pejibaye palm than do the Guaymí communities of the Cricamola drainage system and somewhat more on purchased foods due to the large number of its residents that work for wages.

TABLE 1 FOODSTUFFS CONSUMED IN MARAÑON AT TWENTY-FOUR MEALS DURING SIX CONSECUTIVE DAYS, MARCH 30 TO APRIL 5, 1970, IN ORDER OF FREQUENCY

Natural foods	Frequency	Purchased foods	Frequency
Bananas, green, boiled	14	Onions*	6
Dasheen	7	Salt	4
Sweet manioc	7	Spaghetti	4
Chocolate water with sugar	6	Peppercorns*	3
Chocolate water without sugar	5	Fried bread made from white wheat flour	2
Fish soup	4	Bread	1
Ripe banana soup	3	Canned sardines	1
Plantains, boiled	3	Chicken noodle soup	1
Otoe	2	Vegetable soup	1
Coconut	2	Garlic*	1
Chicken	2	Rice	1
Yams	1	Tomato paste	1
Wild greens	1		
Culantro leaves (herb)	1		
Ripe bananas	1		
Pejibaye	1		
Lemonade	1		
Fish, boiled	1		

*I supplied all of the peppercorns and garlic and about half of the onions. In Chiriqui, onions, black peppercorns, and garlic are well liked, but rarely purchased. The same seems to be true in Marañon.

Ecology and Subsistence on Opposite Sides
of the Talamancan Range

J. BORT

INTRODUCTION

The contemporary Guaymí population has been profoundly affected by 450 years of contact with the European world. During most of the historic period the area occupied by the Guaymí has been shrinking (Young 1971). This contraction has eliminated some ecological zones occupied in prehistoric times and possibly some subsistence strategies as well. The Guaymí on the Pacific slopes have very limited access to the resources of the sea. There are some indications in a number of rituals and legends that the sea figured prominently in their life in the past.

The Guaymí of today employ a combined agricultural system based on permanent cultivation of tree crops and shifting cultivation of root crops and seed crops. Inventories and relative importance of crops have been altered — in some cases drastically — since pre-Columbian times, but agricultural patterns and techniques appear to have remained relatively stable throughout the historic period. The agricultural techniques employed are essentially the same as those used by the Panamanian *campesinos*. Guzman (1956) indicates that the techniques employed by the latter were, in turn, adopted from the aboriginal populations as the Iberians began occupying the Isthmus.

Because of a number of historic changes, such as the introduction of new crops, metal tools, and domestic animals, and the increasing importance of cash cropping and wage labor, direct enthnographic analogies in subsistence patterns between the contemporary and the precontact situation are not possible. However, archaeological data indicate variation in resource utilization on opposite sides of the Isthmian cordillera in prehistoric times. This situation still applies, as the following description documents.

CLIMATE AND BASIC AGRICULTURAL PATTERNS

Bocas and Chiriqui differ most notably in the seasonality of rainfall (section 2.1). This difference in precipitation patterns affects patterns of natural vegetation and strongly influences agricultural techniques (fig. 20/1a, 1b).

In Chiriqui, common slash-and-burn techniques are used. Land is cleared from January through March, and the dried vegetation is burned in March or April before the rains begin. Proper timing produces a good burn and a clean ash bed high in nutrients. Burning of the fields is more critical than the actual seeding. If the fields are burned too soon and the rains come late, the seed will germinate and die for lack of moisture, and weedy

a

b

Figure 20/1: Guaymí hamlets: a. Marañon on the Bocas side; b. hamlet near Tole on the Chiriqui side.

vegetation will also sprout. If the rains start before the fields are burned, a very poor burn results and the crops seeded are deprived of a good ash bed.

Seeding for the wet season cycle is ideally timed so sufficient rainy weather still remains to supply the crop with adequate moisture. If seeding is done too soon, the crop does poorly because it receives excessive moisture. If seeded too late, it suffers under the drought conditions of the dry season. During the wet season cycle, vegetation is cut but not burned and seeding is done in the tangled slash.

In Bocas, cut vegetation will not dry adequately to permit a good burn because of insufficient successive dry days. The agricultural pattern is very similar to the wet season cycle in Chiriqui and has sometimes been characterized as slash-and-mulch. Crops are seeded in cut but unburned fields.

In both Bocas and Chiriqui similar adaptations in cropping patterns can be found with increasing elevation. A number of cultivars cannot be successfully exploited at higher elevations. This results in increasingly restricted crop inventories as one moves from the lowlands up to the continental divide.

There is no evidence of major climatological change in the Guaymí area during historic times. Hence, it is reasonable to infer that the hazards and risks faced by the contemporary Guaymí in their agricultural endeavors are similar to those faced by their pre-Columbian ancestors.

ECOLOGICAL DEGRADATION

Ravaged may be the best term to describe the landscape in the area of Chiriqui occupied by the Guaymí. Small areas of mature forest exist on the crest of the continental divide and possibly in a few other widely scattered spots in their territory, although I am unaware of any. Very little mature second growth exists anywhere in Chiriqui, but substantial forested tracts are found in the more thinly populated areas of Bocas.

The terrain throughout the area is very irregular. Crops must be planted on hillsides, some of which are so steep it is literally possible to fall out of a field. The entire area experiences heavy rainfall. These conditions are highly conducive to soil deterioration when the vegetation cover is removed or disturbed. Damage can be minimized if sufficient time is allowed for vegetation regrowth between cropping cycles, but long fallow periods are not always possible.

In Chiriqui the erosion and heavy exploitation of the land are obvious. During the dry season, savannas turn brown, making it possible to see at a glance the extensive areas covered by grass. Closer examination reveals areas where the topsoil on steep slopes has been eroded away and areas in which only small pockets of soil are scattered among sterile rocks.

Informants' accounts indicate that there was more mature vegetation in the past. The most obvious factor in this change is artificial creation of grasslands for pasture, a direct response to the cash economy in which the Guaymí have become increasingly involved. Pasture is often maintained by burning during the dry season. This exposes soil to direct insolation and rainfall each year with consequent detrimental effects.

The signs of land deterioration are less apparent in Bocas than in Chiriqui except along the Cricamola drainage where population densities are quite high. Since there is no dry season, the vegetation is always green. Cattle are not raised, so land is not converted to pasture. Since burning is not always possible, land may be deteriorating at a slower rate than in Chiriqui, but the land is deteriorating nevertheless.

The most serious factor contributing to ecological degradation is rapid population increase. The Guaymí population has been increasing at a rate of about 3 percent annually for several decades. This means ever larger quantities of food must be grown on a finite area of land. Population pressure in Chiriqui is more severe than in Bocas, but cultivable land is becoming scarce and unclaimed land nonexistent throughout the area occupied by the Guaymí.

The Guaymí cultivator's overriding concern is securing the best possible yield in a given year. Low local population densities allow the exclusive use of areas covered by mature vegetation. At higher levels of population pressure, areas of less advanced vegetation regrowth must be used, resulting in lower yields, a fact that is apparent to the Guaymí agriculturalist but beyond his control. Concerned with an adequate food supply, he cannot postpone use of a plot of land because it is not up to optimal conditions.

The long-term effect of this situation is disastrous. As population pressure increases there is greater use of areas of immature vegetation. Resulting lower yields necessitate the cropping of even larger areas. This means even less mature growth for the following cropping cycle, so that a still greater area must be cropped. On a year-to-year basis, this effect is barely perceptible but the long-term effect is obvious. Huge tracts of impoverished land are already visible throughout the mountains.

Shifting cultivation techniques are well adapted to situations of low population density and abundant land. They are not well adapted to situations of high population densities and scarce or low-quality land. Unfortunately, more extensive land use techniques are not available to the Guaymí and, even if available, would be extremely difficult to apply to these mountainous areas.

THE CHARACTERISTICS OF INDIVIDUAL CROPS

Corn (Zea mays) is a traditional staple in the Guaymí diet in both Chiriqui and Bocas but makes up a far larger proportion of the diet in Chiriqui.

In Chiriqui, at altitudes below 1,200 meters, large kernel corn is double cropped. The dry season crop is planted in fields which have been burned, and the wet season crop is broadcast seeded in fields which have been cut and partially cleared of brush, but not burned. The dry season crop is planted in April, weeded in June and July, and harvested from mid-August through September. The wet season crop is seeded in late September and harvested in February and March; it is not weeded. A single field is generally used for both dry and wet season crops and then abandoned for from six to twenty years, depending on the quality of the soil and speed of vegetation regeneration.

At altitudes above 1,200 meters in Chiriqui, small kernel (*morocho*) corn is used in addition to large kernel corn. *Morocho* corn is broadcast in cut, unburned fields in January and harvested in June and July. It is not weeded. Large kernel corn is seeded in March or April, weeded in June or July, and harvested in September. This crop is sometimes also broadcast sown in cut and unburned fields. The choice depends on the inclination of the cultivator and the amount of mist ("bajareque") blown over from the Bocas side of the cordillera during the dry season. If the mist is heavy, vegetation may be too moist for a good burn.

On the Bocas side, the altitudinal gradient and cultivation techniques are different. *Morocho* corn is used at all altitudes, fields are not burned, and corn is usually broadcast rather than planted.

At elevations over 1,200 meters a single crop of *morocho* corn is broadcast seeded in cut, unburned fields in December or January and harvested in June or July. It is not weeded. The crop requires three to four weeks longer to mature than the *morocho* crop in Chiriqui, probably because of a lower level of solar insolation due to the dense cloud cover. Between 600 and 1,200 meters in elevation, double broadcast seeding is possible. At times fields are used for one cropping cycle, and at times a field used in the previous cropping cycle is recut and reused. This depends on the quality of the land. Often it is easier to cut more mature growth than to deal with the vegetation that springs up in the tangle of an already cropped area. On the Bocas side, *morocho* corn is either planted or broadcast sown below elevations of 600 meters. Broadcasting is the more common practice, with planting being restricted to coastal areas. Some large kernel corn is also grown in these areas, but it is generally produced in very limited quantities and confined to areas below approximately 300 meters.

Rice (*Oryza sativa*), of course, is not a native American plant. The varieties currently in use by the Guaymí do not produce well at altitudes above 760 meters and not at all above 900 meters. Because of this, rice is not part of the subsistence inventory in much of the area occupied by the Guaymí. Nonetheless, it has become a preferred food among the Guaymí and large quantities are consumed. It is grown in some parts of Guaymí territory and is readily marketable in the towns of rural Panama.

At altitudes below 760 meters in Chiriqui, rice has become increasingly important in recent years. Sizable areas are still devoted to corn, but rice is replacing it as the major crop.

In Bocas, at altitudes below 600 meters, rice is also becoming increasingly important, but not to the same extent as in Chiriqui. Rice requires specialized cropping practices which require more labor than corn. On the Cricamola River, below 300 meters, the land is significantly less rugged than in higher areas and rice cultivation is less taxing. In areas such as this, rice is supplanting corn as the major seed crop, but these areas are still quite restricted.

In Chiriqui, beans (*Phaseolus* sp.) and Pigeon Peas (*Cajanas indicus*) are grown at all altitudes and constitute a major crop. At elevations below 760 meters, Pigeon Peas (an Old World domesticate) and small *primo* (*Phaseolus* sp.) beans are the most frequently used. At altitudes over 760 meters, the *Boquete* (a kidney bean, *Phaseolus* sp.) is the dominant type used, although *primo* beans are common.

Boquete and *primo* beans are broadcast sown in unburned cut fields during November and harvested in January and February. They are not weeded. Pigeon Peas are seeded on burned fields in March and April, weeded in July, and harvested in January through March.

At altitudes below 760 meters, relatively less emphasis is put on beans than at higher altitudes. As with corn, rice is supplanting beans below 760 meters elevation.

Beans are a very insignificant crop in Bocas. Since they require a distinct dry season in order to dry sufficiently to be stored, they are grown only as a garden vegetable and consumed as they mature. At most, a man will plant a couple of handfuls of purchased seed.

Otoe (*Xanthosoma* sp.) is the most widely distributed root crop among the Guaymí. It is produced in all areas in Bocas and Chiriqui. In areas below 900 meters, it is a relatively less important crop than at higher altitudes. At higher altitudes the variety of crops that can be exploited is more restricted; because *otoe* does well, it becomes a staple of equal or greater importance than corn. In the middle altitude range between 600 and 1,200 meters, it is seeded in modest quantity and provides a measure of security when other crops produce poorly. In the areas below 600 meters, where rice is a major crop, it is grown for dietary variety since manioc produces higher yields than *otoe* and is more extensively used.

Otoe is generally seeded from December through April and harvested from January through July of the following year, but it can be planted and harvested throughout the year.

Dasheen (*Colocasia esculenta*), a root crop similar to *otoe*, is a post-Columbian introduction. Among the Guaymí, its use appears to be restricted to the Caribbean coastal areas.

Only sweet manioc (*Manihot esculenta*) is used by the Guaymí and is primarily a low altitude crop. It will produce at altitudes of 900 meters in both Chiriqui and Bocas, but it does not do well over 760 meters; it does best below 300 meters. Manioc is generally planted from January through July and harvested in January through July of the following years, or it may be left to grow for two to three years. Weeding is generally done when a man is either harvesting or planting. As with *otoe*, it can be planted and harvested throughout the year.

Old World imports of the *Musa* spp. family (bananas and plantains) are a major source of starch in the Guaymí diet. In both Bocas and Chiriqui, bananas produce at all altitudes. The number of varieties that can be used at high altitudes is more restricted than at low altitudes, but the number of plants is equally large. Various informants refer to them as Guaymí "bread." Among the Guaymí it is a very rare day in which bananas are not included in at least one meal and more commonly are part of every meal. At times they may be virtually the only food available; hence they serve as an insurance food.

Plantains are restricted to altitudes below 900 meters and do best at very low altitudes. Because they produce high yields, they are used as a substitute for bananas at low altitudes, and they are marketed for cash by some individuals living near small towns.

In both Chiriqui and Bocas, the peach palm (*Guilielma gasipaes*) is, and probably was in pre-Hispanic times, an important food source (Johannssen 1966). It is important in Chiriqui because it is harvested between the harvests of other major crops, thus providing food when other supplies are short. This is particularly important if the yields from the wet season harvest are low. In Bocas the peach palm is a valuable source of protein and a major crop.

Peach palms produce up to an altitude of 1,000 meters, but production declines above 600 meters. They are planted a few at a time from year to year. Natural seeding also is frequent. Seeding occurs during the harvest period. Plants begin to produce in five years. The palm continues to grow throughout its life cycle and is usually toppled by the wind when it is fifteen to twenty years old, with an occasional palm surviving twenty-five years. The peach palm does best on relatively wet land. The areas along streams and river courses are preferred for plantations. They are also intermixed in banana plantations. Undergrowth is cleared from around the palm when it is harvested; that is all the maintenance required.

In Chiriqui the peach palm harvest begins in late May, with peak production coming in July and August. The harvest then tapers off rapidly, with a few palms producing until late September or early October. The harvest in Bocas begins in August and runs until December or early January. The peak period of harvesting is from late September through November.

In Chiriqui, the peach palm provides an often valuable source of food, especially when the corn and bean harvests are unsuccessful. In Bocas, it is a crucial food source. Beans are not available as a protein source, but the peach palm is an alternative. In Chiriqui, one finds small clusters of trees, while in Bocas large tracts of hundreds of palms are planted.

Also in Bocas, in contrast to Chiriqui, peach palm fruit is stored. A cylindrical pit is dug and lined with leaves. This pit is filled with fruit, and bunches of bananas are piled on top of the fruit. This is then covered with leaves, rocks, and poles to keep out animals. Fruit can be stored from four to six months by this method. Households typically store from 350 kg to 500 kg annually.

The preserved fruit is used in making *chicha* (a mildly fermented beverage) for human consumption and also to feed hogs. Hogs are the most important domestic animal in Bocas and peach palm fruit provides excellent feed. Without this food source, it is doubtful that the large hog population could be maintained.

In addition to the crops already mentioned, the Guaymí of both Bocas and Chiriqui employ a range of crops that can only be considered minor parts of the diet. Some are very seasonal and others provide a very small part of their dietary intake. It is possible that a few provide essential minerals or vitamins, but the data available are not adequate for such determinations. Some of the more common minor crops are oranges, mangoes, avocados, ñame, ñampi (both *Dioscorea* spp.), and cucurbits. A more comprehensive list can be found in Young (1971, pp. 62–65).

DOMESTIC ANIMALS

The most important animals to the Guaymí in Chiriqui are cattle. They are raised for both meat and sale, but are more important as a source of cash income than as food. Animals are sold to Latino cattle dealers in order to secure money with which to purchase a wide range of items that can be obtained only from the outside. Less often they are slaughtered for consumption.

In Bocas cattle are rare. Some animals are raised near the cordillera and herded over the mountains to the Chiriqui side for sale. This is restricted to the area very close to the divide, and the number of animals is very small. Pasture is difficult to maintain since burning is not possible, and constant work is required to maintain tracts large enough for grazing. No cattle are present between these high areas over 1,200 meters and the extreme lowland areas below 300 meters. Cattle are a relatively recent introduction in the lower Bocas areas and are concentrated on the floodplains of rivers.

Hogs are relatively unimportant in Chiriqui. They are raised in small numbers and sold to outside buyers, or slaughtered for meat. In Bocas, however, the hog is the major domestic animal and is raised in large numbers up to the altitudinal limit of peach palm cultivation. Above 1,000 meters, some hogs are raised but in substantially reduced numbers. Pigs are kept both for local consumption and external sale. *Cayucos* (dugout canoes), the only means of travel along the Bocas coast, are capable of transporting live hogs but will not handle cattle.

In Chiriqui, horses are the major form of transport throughout the mountains. Because of this, they are significant in facilitating economic interchange with the outside. In Bocas, there are no horses except for a very small number in coastal areas. The terrain is excessively wet and rugged for horses; hence, all transport must be by human porters in the higher areas and by *cayuco* in the navigable lower reaches of the rivers.

Chickens are found in greater number in Chiriqui than in Bocas, although they are common throughout the Guaymí area. In Chiriqui, they are the most consistently consumed source of animal protein. Information from Bocas is less secure, but it appears that chickens are a less important source of animal protein than in Chiriqui because of the large hog population. A chicken or two provides adequate meat for a household unit and does not require destroying a major cash resource (a cow or pig). Distribution of meat to nonresident relatives is not required, as is the case with larger animals. Chickens are also readily marketable on the outside at a good price and are easily transported.

Ducks and turkeys are also raised by the Guaymí, but in very small numbers compared to chickens.

HUNTING, GATHERING, AND FISHING

Wild plants and animals now constitute a small segment of the Guaymí diet. Some wild plants are used, but none is a major element in the diet. Wild animals are irregularly taken, even by the few individuals that consistently hunt. The majority of the animals are taken by men guarding their fields. Animal damage can be serious, and deer and wild pigs are the most troublesome. When beans and maize are still green, the deer will eat them; when maize ripens, the collared peccary eats it. Peccaries, as well as the caviomorph rodents, eat root crops. In the past, the Guaymí pole-fenced their root crops to keep animals away. They still guard their maize and beans from a little hut in which they often stay overnight to hunt. During the day they patrol their plots, which are located some distance away from their dwelling place, for signs of animal damage. Another way of hunting is to wait by a tree that is fruiting and shoot the animals that come to feed on it; baiting game from an ambush is also practiced.

Although hunting is a minor source of food now, informant accounts indicate that there was more game and more intensive hunting even in the recent past. A number of species have been exterminated or greatly reduced in the area within memory. The white-lipped peccary *(Tayassu pecari)*, howler monkey *(Alouatta villosa)*, tapir *(Tapirus bairdii)*, and giant anteater *(Mymecopheoa tridactyla)* are among the most notable. It appears that both hunting pressure and habitat destruction have accounted for this. In addition, brocket deer *(Mazama americana)* have become extremely rare, presumably for the same reasons.

Snares and dreadfalls have almost vanished from active use, but are remembered by informants. Bow and arrows are still used, but rather unskillfully for lack of practice. Most game now is taken with firearms, or with dogs during the day, although dogs trained to hunt are becoming rare.

In Chiriqui, where the level of the rivers varies dramatically with the season, fishing is relatively unimportant. The Guaymí are also cut off from the more productive lower reaches of the rivers. In spite of the low yield, people living conveniently close to rivers do fish. Techniques are generally restricted to hooks and lines and to harpoons for taking crayfish. The use of vegetable poisons in temporarily dammed streams, an important pre-Hispanic fishing technique, was still in evidence, though not particularly common, as late as the early 1960s (Young, personal communication). The rivers appear to be heavily overfished and in the recent past were dynamited to the point where fish populations were seriously depleted.

Although fewer in number, rivers in Bocas are larger and fluctuate less. In the high mountain areas, fishing is relatively unimportant, but it becomes better at lower altitudes where the rivers are larger and slower. In Bocas fish seines and harpoons are common, as are hooks and lines. The Bocas Guaymí living near the coast also obtain fish, shellfish, crustaceans, and turtles from the sea. These maritime resources were clearly much more important to the Guaymí in the past than they are today.

HAZARDS TO PRODUCTION AND THEIR MINIMIZATION

Cultivation and animal husbandry are uncertain undertakings throughout the mountains of western Panama. Unfavorable weather, animal and insect pests, plant and animal diseases, and illness or injury to productive household members can all mean disaster.

Of all the potential hazards, bad weather is of most concern. Rainfall patterns are not uniform throughout the mountains. Locations a couple of miles apart can vary five to ten days in the beginning and end of the rains, or one area can experience heavy rains while another will receive very light precipitation. In addition, high winds can knock down or desiccate crops during the dry season; corn and beans being the most vulnerable. Wind damage may vary dramatically over short distances.

Root and tree crop yields are less sensitive than seed crops to vicissitudes of the weather. An extended dry season will reduce yields, but a few days variation in the start and end of the rains is not as significant as it can be for seed crops. The risk of severe food shortage is reduced, but not eliminated, by combining seed, tree, and root crops. Even though productive fluctuations would tend to average out over a period of years, long-term averages do not help the individual household since surpluses from good years cannot be accumulated against bad years.

Traditional patterns of labor organizations can help reduce the high risk of a crop failure under such uncertain weather conditions. Fields are cleared by work parties (juntas) composed of any number of men, but typically involving between six and eighteen. Labor is reciprocal. The work of clearing fields rotates, with the bulk of the work being done on any one individual's plot in a single day.

During the wet season, seeding is done on the same day as the field is cleared. This practice spreads out the period over which the total crop in an area is seeded, insuring good crops from at least some of the fields since some will have been seeded during the optimal seeding period for that year.

The dry season clearing is done in advance of the rains in order to allow the cut vegetation to dry sufficiently for a good burn. Juntas are also utilized but they do not affect the timing of the burning and seeding. The decision to burn the fields and to seed crops is made by the individual cultivator based on his guess of when the rains will begin. These evaluations are far from uniform and the seeding period is spread over several weeks, with the same results as the wet season seeding pattern. The difference in resultant yields when seedings occur a week apart can be great.

Illness and injury to essential productive members of the household are additional threats. If a productive member of the household is ill during a critical part of the agricultural cycle, the consequences can be serious. Given all of the hazards involved, an individual Guaymí household operating independently could literally face starvation at times. However, no household exists independently. Kinship ties are extended and strong. Reciprocity among kinsmen is strongly developed and a strong sense of moral obligation to aid kinsmen exists.

The kinship system of the Guaymí is complex, as are the concomitant duties and obligations toward kinsmen. Detailed examination of the kinship system is not necessary here, but its importance must be noted. In addition to other functions, kinship provides a framework within which it is possible to minimize the impact that a capricious environment has on individual productivity. Each household is able to draw on the resources of others during periods of shortage. This effectively distributes the risk of economic disaster throughout a larger population aggregate.

SUMMARY

Differences in subsistence patterns between Bocas and Chiriqui were well summarized by one of my Guaymí friends who noted that in Chiriqui corn, beans, bananas, and cattle are the central elements, while in Bocas they are corn, peach palms, bananas, and pigs. He qualified this by specifying that in lower areas rice has impinged on the position of corn and, with increasing altitude, *otoe* gains in importance because corn yields decline and peach palms fail to produce.

These comments indicate some major differences and similarities. In Chiriqui, beans are a far more important crop than peach palms. The situation in Bocas is reversed. Cattle are important in Chiriqui and pigs are not. The reverse is again true in Bocas. In Chiriqui, rice has become an important crop at low altitudes. It is relatively less important in Bocas. Manioc loses importance and *otoe* gains importance with increasing altitude on both sides of the cordillera. Bananas are a major staple in all locations.

The entire history of contact with the outside world has involved changes in Guaymí socioeconomic conditions that have been responses to immediate circumstances, yet have shaped future forms of social, political, and economic organization. In many ways, the contemporary Guaymí must be considered a marginal population. They have been excluded from the more productive land of western Panama and relegated to land that is marginal for the application of modern agricultural technologies. They participate in an international economy, but in a subordinate position as unskilled laborers and producers of agrarian products. They must respond to external forces, but they are powerless to shape the method of their response to their advantage.

An interpretation of precontact adaptations to the physical environment based on ethnographic analogies to the contemporary Guaymí population must be made with care. The present population is adapted as much to the social and economic influences of the contemporary world as it is to the physical setting in which it lives.

Bibliography

Adames, Abdiel, P. Galindo, E. Méndez, E. Durán, N. Smythe, H. Wolda, N. Gale, T. Aitken, C. Myers, R. Ridgely, and D. Wilton

    1977   "Fauna Terrestre," in *Evaluación Ambiental y Efectos del Proyecto Hidroeléctrico Fortuna*, prepared for the Instituto de Recursos Hidraúlicos y Electrificación, Panama, by Abdiel J. Adames. *Lotería*, nos. 254–256, Appendix 3, pp. 221–264.

Alegría, Ricardo, H.B. Nicholson, and G.R. Willey

    1955   "The Archaic Tradition in Puerto Rico," *American Antiquity*, vol. 21, no. 2, pp. 113–121.

Alphonse, Ephraim S.

    1956   "Guaymí Grammar and Dictionary with Some Ethnological Notes," *Bureau of American Ethnology*, Bulletin no. 162.

Bahuchet, Serge

    1978   "Contraintes Ecologiques en Fôret Tropicale Humide: l'Exemple des Pygmèes Aka de la Lobaye (Empire Centrafricain)," communication préliminaire présentée au Colloque Internationale sur les Sociétés de Chasseurs-Cueilleurs, Paris, mimeographed, 7 pp.

Bailey, Liberty Hyde

    1933   "Certain Palms of Panama," *Gentes Herbarium*, vol. 3, pt. 2, pp. 33–116.
    1943a   "New Palms in Panama and Others," *Gentes Herbarium*, vol. 6, pt. 4, pp. 199–264.
    1943b   "Palmaceae. Cyclanthaceae," in Flora of Panama, *Annual Missouri Botanical Garden*, vol. 3, no. 3, pp. 327–403.
    1949   "Palms Uncertain and New," *Gentes Herbarium*, vol. 8, pp. 92–205.

Barth, Fredrik

    1956   "Indus and Swat Kohistan, An Ethnographic Survey," *Studies Honoring the Centennial of Universitete Etnografiske Museum*, vol. 2. Oslo.

Bartlett, Alexandra S., E.S. Barghoorn, and R. Berger

    1969   "Fossil Maize from Panama," *Science*, vol. 165, no. 3891, pp. 389–390.

Bartlett, Alexandra S., and E.S. Barghoorn

    1973   "Phytogeographic History of the Isthmus of Panama during the Past 12,000 Years (A History of Vegetation, Climate, and Sea-Level Change)," in *Vegetation and Vegetational History of Northern Latin America*, edited by A. Graham. Elsevier Scientific Publishing Company, pp. 203–299.

Basso, Ellen B.

    1973   *The Kalapalo Indians of Central Brazil*. Holt, Rinehart and Winston.

Bennett, Charles F.

    1968   *Human Influences on the Zoogeography of Panama*. Ibero-Americana, no. 51, University of California Press.

Binford, Lewis R.

    1962   "Archaeology as Anthropology," *American Antiquity*, vol. 28, no. 2, pp. 217–225.

1968   "Archeological Perspectives," in *New Perspectives in Archeology*, edited by S.R. Binford and L.R. Binford. Aldine Publishing Co., pp. 5–32.

1978   *Nunamiut Ethnoarchaeology*. Academic Press.

Bird, Junius B., and Richard G. Cooke

1974   "Excavaciones en la Cueva de los Ladrones, Distrito de La Pintada, Provincia de Coclé, Panamá," report submitted to the Patrimonio Histórico, Instituto Nacional de Cultura, Panamá, mimeographed, 58 pp.

1978   "The Occurrence in Panama of Two Types of Paleo-Indian Projectile Points," in *Early Man in America from a Circum-Pacific Perspective*, edited by Alan Lyle Bryan. Occasional Papers no. 1, of the Department of Anthropology, University of Alberta, pp. 263–272.

Bishop, William H.

1961   "A Summary of Field Notes and Personal Impressions of the Geology of a Portion of Southwestern Panama," typewritten manuscript, 31 pp.

Böhlke, James E., and C.C.G. Chaplin

1968   *Fishes of the Bahamas and Adjacent Tropical Waters*. The Academy of Natural Sciences of Philadelphia.

Bonham-Carter, G.F.

1966   "Fortran IV Program for Q-Mode Cluster Analysis of Nonquantitative Data Using IBM 7090/7094 Computers." Department of Geology, University of Toronto.

Bort, John Roger

1976   "Guaymí Innovators: A Case Study of Entrepreneurs in a Small Scale Society," Ph.D. dissertation, Department of Anthropology, University of Oregon.

Boserup, Ester

1965   *The Conditions of Agricultural Growth; The Economics of Agrarian Change under Population Pressure*. Aldine Publishing Co., Chicago.

Bryan, Alan Lyle

1978   "An Overview of Paleo-American Prehistory from a Circum-Pacific Perspective," in *Early Man in America*, edited by Alan Lyle Bryan. Occasional Papers no. 1, of the Department of Anthropology, University of Alberta, pp. 306–327.

Budowski, Gerardo

1956   "Tropical Savannas: A Sequence of Forest Felling and Repeated Burning," *Turrialba*, vols. 1–2, pp. 23–33.

Butler, B. Robert

1962   *Contributions to the Prehistory of the Columbia Plateau*. Occasional Papers of the Idaho State College Museum, no. 9.

Callen, E.O.

1967   "Analysis of Tehuacan Coprolites," in *The Prehistory of the Tehuacan Valley*, vol. 1, D.S. Byers, editor. Austin, University of Texas Press, pp. 261–289.

Carneiro, Robert L.

1961   "Slash and Burn Cultivation Among the Kuikuru and Its Implications for Cultural Development in the Amazon Basin," in *The Evolution of Horticultural Systems in Native South America: Causes and Consequences*, edited by J. Wilbert. Editorial Sucre, La Salle, Caracas, pp. 47–67.

1968   "The Transition from Hunting to Horticulture in the Amazon Basin," in *Proceedings of the 8th Congress of Anthropological and Ethnological Sciences*, pp. 244–248.

1970   "Hunting and Hunting Magic Among the Amahuaca of the Peruvian Montaña," *Ethnology*, vol. 9, no. 4, pp. 331–341.

1979 "Tree Felling with the Stone Axe; An Experiment Carried Out Among the Yanomamö Indians of Southern Venezuela," in *Ethnoarchaeology*, edited by Carol Kramer. Columbia University Press, pp. 21–58.

Casteel, R.W.

1974 "A Method for Estimation of Live Weight of Fish from the Size of Skeletal Elements," *American Antiquity*, vol. 39, no. 1, pp. 94–98.

Chagnon, Napoleon A.

1968 *Yanomamö, the Fierce People*. Holt, Rinehart and Winston.

Chagnon, Napoleon A., and R.B. Hames

1979 "Protein Deficiency and Tribal Warfare in Amazonia: New Data," *Science*, vol. 203, no. 4383, pp. 910–913.

Chaplin, Raymond E.

1971 *The Study of Animal Bones from Archaeological Sites*. Seminar Press.

Coe, Michael D., and Kent V. Flannery

1964 "Microenvironments and Mesoamerican Prehistory," *Science*, vol. 143, no. 3607, pp. 650–654.

Coles, John

1973 *Archaeology by Experiment*. Charles Scribners Sons.

Collier, Albert

1964 "The American Mediterranean," in *Handbook of Middle American Indians*, vol. I, edited by R. Wauchope and R.C. West. University of Texas Press, pp. 122–142.

Cooke, Richard G.

1972 "The Archaeology of the Western Coclé Province of Panama," Ph.D. thesis, London University, 2 vols.

1975 "Excavaciones Arqueológicas en el Sitio AG-3 (Sitio Sierra), Distrito de Aguadulce, Coclé, Panamá," preliminary report on the 1975 excavations on file at the Dirección de Patrimonio Histórico, Panamá, 12 pp.

1976a "Nuevos Análisis de Carbono-14 para Panamá, al Este de Chiriquí: Una Actualización de los Cambios Culturales Prehistóricos," *La Antigua*, Año Vo. no. 6, pp. 88–114.

1976b "Una Nueva Mirada a la Evolución de la Cerámica en las Provincias Centrales," in *Actas del IV Simposium Nacional de Antropología y Etnohistoria de Panamá*, Octubre 1973. Universidad de Panamá e Instituto Nacional de Cultura, pp. 307–365.

1976c "Panamá: Región Central," *Vínculos*, vol. 2, no. 1, pp. 122–140. Museo Nacional, San José, Costa Rica.

1977a "Recursos Arqueológicos," in *Evaluación Ambiental y Efectos del Proyecto Hidroeléctrico Fortuna*, prepared for the Instituto de Recursos Hidráulicos y Electrificación, Panama, by Abdiel J. Adames. *Lotería*, nos. 254–256, Appendix 7, pp. 399–467.

1977b "El Carpintero y el Hachero; Dos Artesanos del Panamá Prehistórico," *Revista Panameña de Antropología*, Año, 2, no. 2, pp. 48–77.

1978 "Maximizing a Valuable Resource: the White-tailed Deer in Prehistoric Central Panama," paper presented at the 43rd annual meeting of the Society for American Archaeology, Tucson, mimeographed, 17 pp.

Cooke, Richard G., and Marcela Camargo R.

1977 "Coclé y su Arqueología: Una Breve Historia Crítica," *La Antigua*, Año vi°, no. 9, pp. 115–172.

Coult, Allan D.

1968 "Uses and Abuses of Computers in Anthropology," in *Calcul et Formalisation dans les Sciences de L'Homme*, editions du Centre National de la Recherche Scientifique, Paris, pp. 21–29.

Cowgill, George L.

    1977   "The Trouble with Significance Tests and What We Can Do About It," *American Antiquity*, vol. 42, no. 3, pp. 350–368.

Crabtree, Donald E., and E.L. Davis

    1968   "Experimental Manufacture of Wooden Implements with Tools of Flaked Stone," *Science*, vol. 159, no. 3813, pp. 426–428.

Cruxent, J.M., and Irving Rouse

    1958   *An Archaeological Chronology of Venezuela*. Social Science Monographs IV, Pan American Union, Washington, D.C., 2 vols.

Dade, Philip L.

    1961   "The Provenience of Polychrome Pottery in Panama," *Ethnos*, vol. 26, no. 4, pp. 172–197.

Davis, Dave D.

    1975   "Patterns of Early Formative Subsistence in Southern Mesoamerica," *Man*, vol. 10, no. 1, pp. 41–59.

De Boer, Warren R.

    1975   "The Archaeological Evidence for Manioc Cultivation: a Cautionary Note," *American Antiquity*, vol. 40, no. 4, pp. 419–433.

Deevey, Edward Smith, L.J. Gralenski, and Väinö Hoffren

    1959   "Yale Natural Radiocarbon Measurements IV," *American Journal of Science, Radiocarbon Supplement*, vol. 1, pp. 142–172.

Demirmen, F.

    1967   "DNPLOT." Stanford University.

Drennan, Robert D.

    1976   *Fábrica San José and Middle Formative Society in the Valley of Oaxaca*. Memoirs of the Museum of Anthropology, University of Michigan, no. 8.

Durham, William H.

    1978   "The Coevolution of Human Biology and Culture," in *Human Behavior and Adaptation*, edited by N.B. Bones and V. Reynolds. Taylor and Francis, pp. 11–32.

Eggan, Frederick R.

    1954   "Social Anthropology and the Method of Controlled Comparison," *American Anthropologist*, vol. 56, no. 5, pp. 743–763.

Einhaus, Catherine Shelton

    1976   "A Technological and Functional Analysis of Stone Tools from Isla Palenque, Panama," M.A. thesis, Department of Anthropology, Temple University.

Espinosa Estrada, Jorge

    1977   *Excavaciones Arqueológicas en "El Bosque."* Instituto Geográfico Nacional, Managua, Informe no. 1.

Estadística Panameña

    1973   Meteorología, Serie L. Año XXXIV. Dirección de Estadística y Censo. Contraloría General de la República, Panamá.

    1975   Meteorología: Situación Física, sección 121. Dirección de Estadística y Censo, Contraloría General de la República, Panamá.

    1976   Meteorología: Situación Física, sección 121. Dirección de Estadística y Censo, Contraloría General de la República, Panamá.

Flannery, Kent V.

    1968a   "Archaeological Systems Theory and Early Mesoamerica," in *Anthropological Archeology in the Americas*, edited by B. Meggers. Anthropological Society of Washington, pp. 67–87.

1968b   "The Olmec and the Valley of Oaxaca: A Model for Inter-Regional Interactions in Formative Times," in *Dumbarton Oaks Conference on the Olmec*, edited by E.P. Benson. Dumbarton Oaks, pp. 79–117.

1972   "The Origins of the Village as a Settlement Type in Mesoamerica and the Near East: A Comparative Study," in *Man, Settlement and Urbanism*, edited by P.J. Ucko and D.W. Dimbleby. Gerald Duckworth and Co., pp. 23–53.

1973   "The Origins of Agriculture," *Annual Review of Anthropology*, vol. 2, pp. 271–310.

Flannery, Kent V., editor

1976   *The Early Mesoamerican Village*. Academic Press.

Franco, Fray Blas José

1882   "Noticias de los Indios del Departamento de Veraguas y Vocabulario de las Lenguas Guaymí, Norteño, Sabanero, y Dorasque," *Colección de Lingüística y Etnografía Americanas*, vol. 4.

Fried, Morton H.

1967   *The Evolution of Political Society; An Essay In Political Anthropology*. Random House.

Fry, Robert E.

1972   "Manually Operated Post-hole Diggers as Sampling Instruments," *American Antiquity*, vol. 37, no. 2, pp. 259–261.

Galinat, Walton C.

1969   "The Evolution Under Domestication of the Maize Ear: String Cob Maize," Massachusetts Agricultural Experiment Station *Bulletin*, 577, pp. 1–19.

1978   "The Evolution of String Cob Corn," *Maize Genetics Coop Newsletter*, vol. 52, p. 59.

Gazin, C. Lewis

1957   "Exploration for the Remains of Giant Ground Sloths in Panama," *Annual Report of the Board of Regents of the Smithsonian Institution*, Publication 4979, pp. 341–354.

Gentry, H.S.

1969   "Origin of the Common Bean, *Phaseolus vulgaris*," *Economic Botany*, vol. 23, pp. 55–69.

Glynn, Peter

1972   "Observations on the Ecology of the Caribbean and Pacific Coasts of Panama," in *The Panamic Biota: Some Observations Prior to a Sea-level Canal*, edited by Meredith L. Jones. Bulletin of the Biological Society of Washington, no. 2, pp. 13–30.

Gómez-Pompa, Arturo

1973   "Ecology of the Vegetation of Veracruz," in *Vegetation and Vegetational History of Northern Latin America*, edited by Alan Graham. Elsevier Scientific Publishing Company, pp. 73–147.

Goodyear, Richard, Víctor Martínez, and Juan B. del Rosario

1977   "Fauna Acuática," in *Evaluación Ambiental y Efectos del Proyecto Hidroeléctrico Fortuna*, prepared for the Instituto de Recursos Hidráulicos y Electrificación, Panama, by Abdiel J. Adames. *Lotería*, nos. 254–256, Appendix 4, pp. 265–334.

Gordon, B. Le Roy

1969   *Anthropogeography and Rainforest Ecology in Bocas del Toro Province, Panamá*. A report to the Department of Geography, University of California, 99 pp.

Gould, Richard A., Dorothy A. Koster, and Ann H.L. Sontz

1971   "The Lithic Assemblage of the Western Desert Aborigines of Australia," *American Antiquity*, vol. 36, no. 2, pp. 149–169.

Grant, U.J., W.H. Hatheway, D.H. Timothy, C. Cassalett-D., and L.M. Roberts

    1963   *Races of Maize in Venezuela.* National Academy of Sciences, National Research Council Publication 1136. Washington, D.C.

Grayson, Donald K.

    1973   "On the Methodology of Faunal Analysis," *American Antiquity*, vol. 38, no. 4, pp. 432–439.

    1978   "Minimum Numbers and Sample Size in Vertebrate Faunal Analysis," *American Antiquity*, vol. 43, no. 1, pp. 53–65.

Greenwood, Roberta S.

    1961   "Quantitative Analysis of Shells from a Site in Goleta, California," *American Antiquity*, vol. 26, no. 3, pt. 1, pp. 416–420.

Grobman, Alexander, W.W. Salhuana, and R. Sevilla, with P.C. Mangelsdorf

    1961   *Races of Maize in Peru; Their Origins, Evolution and Classification.* National Academy of Sciences, National Research Council, Publication 915. Washington, D.C.

Gruhn, Ruth, and Alan L. Bryan

    1977   "Los Tapiales: A Paleo-Indian Campsite in the Guatemalan Highlands," *Proceedings of the American Philosophical Society*, vol. 121, no. 3, pp. 235–273.

Guzmán, Louis E.

    1956   *Farming and Farmlands in Panama.* The University of Chicago Press.

Haberland, Wolfgang

    1957   "Excavations in Costa Rica and Panama," *Archaeology*, vol. 10, no. 4, pp. 258–263.

    1960   "Villalba, a Preliminary Report," *Panama Archaeologist*, vol. 3, pp. 9–21.

    1962   "The Scarified Ware and the Early Cultures of Chiriquí (Panama)," in *34th International Congress of Americanists*, Vienna, 1960, pp. 381–389.

Hall, Eugene Raymond, and Keith R. Kelson

    1959   *The Mammals of North America.* Ronald Press.

Hamblin, W.K., and J.D. Howard

    1967   *Physical Geology: Laboratory Manual*, Second Edition. Burgess Publishing Company.

Harris, David R.

    1969   "Agricultural Systems, Ecosystems and the Origins of Agriculture," in *The Domestication and Exploitation of Plants and Animals*, edited by P.J. Ucko and G.W. Dimbleby. Gerald Duckworth and Co., pp. 3–15.

    1972a   "The Origins of Agriculture in the Tropics," *American Scientist*, vol. 60, no. 2, pp. 180–193.

    1972b   "Swidden Systems and Settlement," in *Man, Settlement and Urbanism*, edited by P.J. Ucko, R. Tringham, and G.W. Dimbleby. Gerald Duckworth and Co., pp. 245–262.

    1977   "Alternative Pathways Toward Agriculture," in *Origins of Agriculture*, edited by C.A. Reed. Mouton, pp. 179–244.

    1978a   "Adaptation to a Tropical Rain-Forest Environment: Aboriginal Subsistence in Northeastern Queensland," in *Human Behavior and Adaptation*, edited by B.N. Jones and V. Reynolds. Symposia of the Society for the Study of Human Biology, vol. 18. Taylor and Francis, pp. 113–134.

    1978b   "Settling Down: An Evolutionary Model for the Transformation of Mobile Bands into Sedentary Communities," in *The Evolution of Social Systems*, edited by J. Friedman and M.J. Rowlands. The University of Pittsburgh Press, pp. 401–417.

    1979   "Continuities and Change in Tropical Savanna Environments," *Current Anthropology*, vol. 20, no. 2, pp. 394–397.

Harris, Peter O'B.

1976 "The Preceramic Period in Trinidad," in *Proceedings of the First Puerto Rican Symposium in Archaeology*, Report no. 1. Fundación Arqueológica, Antropológica e Histórica de Puerto Rico, San Juan, pp. 33–64.

Healy, Paul F.

1978 "Preliminary Report on the Paleoecology of the Selin Farm Site (H-CN-5), Department of Colon, Honduras," paper prepared for the 43rd annual meeting of the Society for American Archaeology, Tucson, 28 pp.

Helms, Mary W.

1978 "Coastal Adaptations as Contact Phenomena," in *Prehistoric Coastal Adaptations: The Economy and Ecology of Maritime Middle America*, edited by Barbara Stark and B. Voorhies. Academic Press, pp. 121–149.

Hester, Thomas R., and Robert F. Heizer

1972 "Problems in the Functional Interpretation of Artifacts: Scraper Planes from Mitla and Yagul, Oaxaca," *Miscellaneous Papers in Archeology*, University of California, Department of Anthropopology, Contribution no. 14, pp. 107–123.

Hilderbrand, Samuel F.

1938 "A New Catalogue of the Fresh-Water Fishes of Panama," *Fieldiana: Zoology*, vol. 22, no. 4.

Holdridge, Leslie R., and G. Budowski

1956 "Report on an Ecological Survey of the Republic of Panama," *Caribbean Forester*, vol. 17, pp. 92–110.

Holmberg, Allan R.

1950 *Nomads of the Long Bow: The Siriono of Eastern Bolivia.* Smithsonian Institution, Institute of Social Anthropology, Publication no. 10.

Holmes, William H.

1888 "Ancient Art of the Province of Chiriqui," Bureau of American Ethnology, *6th Annual Report*, pp. 31–187.

Howell, Nancy

1976 "The Population of the Dobe Area !Kung," in *Kalahari Hunter-Gatherers*, edited by R. Lee and I. De Vore. Harvard University Press, pp. 138–151.

Hubbell, Stephen P.

1979 "Tree Dispersion, Abundance, and Diversity in a Tropical Dry Forest," *Science*, vol. 203, no. 4387, pp. 1299–1309.

Hurt, Wesley R., Thomas van der Hammen, and Gonzalo Correal Urrego

1976 *The El Abra Rockshelters, Sabana de Bogotá, Colombia, South America.* Indiana University Museum, Occasional Papers and Monographs, no. 2.

Ichon, Alain

1968a "La Mission Archéologique Française au Panama," *Journal de la Société des Américanistes*, Musée de l'Homme, Paris, Tome 57, pp. 139–143.
1968b "Le Problème de la Ceramique de Barriles," *Boletín del Museo Chiricano*, no. 6, pp. 15–24.
1974 "L'Archeologie du Sud de la Péninsule d'Azuero, Panama," thèse presentée devant l'Université de Paris, 1973. Service de Reproduction des Thèses, Université de Lille III.

Iglesia, Ramón

1947 *Vida del Almirante Don Cristóbal Colón, by Hernando Colón.* Mexico.

Jackson, Jean

1975 "Recent Ethnography of Indigenous Northern Lowland South America," *Annual Review of Anthropology*, vol. 4, pp. 307–340.

Janzen, Daniel H.

1973   "Tropical Agroecosystems," *Science*, vol. 182, no. 4118, pp. 1212–1219.

Jennings, D.L.

1976   "Cassava," in *Evolution of Crop Plants*, edited by N.W. Simmonds. Longman, pp. 81–84.

Johannessen, Carl L.

1966   "Pejibayes in Commercial Production," *Turrialba*, vol. 16, no. 2, pp. 181–187.

Johnson, Frederick

1948   "The Caribbean Lowland Tribes: The Talamanca Division," in *Handbook of South American Indians*, vol. 4, edited by J.H. Steward. Bureau of American Ethnology, Bulletin 143, vol. 4, pp. 231–252.

Johnson, L. Lewis

1978   "A History of Flint-Knapping Experimentation, 1838–1976," *Current Anthropology*, vol. 19, no. 2, pp. 337–372.

Keeley, Lawrence H.

1974   "Technique and Methodology in Microwear Studies: A Critical Review," *World Archaeology*, vol. 5, no. 3, pp. 323–336.

1977   "The Functions of Paleolithic Flint Tools," *Scientific American*, vol. 237, no. 5, pp. 108–126.

Keeley, Lawrence H., and M.H. Newcomer

1977   "Microwear Analysis of Experimental Flint Tools: A Test Case," *Journal of Archaeological Science*, vol. 4, no. 1, pp. 29–62.

Keen, A. Myra

1958   *Sea Shells of Tropical West America: Marine Mollusks from Lower California to Colombia*. Stanford University Press.

Kottak, Conrad P.

1972   "A Cultural Adaptive Approach to Malagasy Political Organization," in *Social Change and Interaction*, edited by Edwin N. Wilmsen. Anthropological Papers no. 46, Museum of Anthropology, University of Michigan.

La Bastille, Anne

1972   "An Ecological Survey of the Proposed Volcano Baru National Park, Republic of Panama," a report to the Departamento de Servicio Forestal Renare, Ministerio de Agricultura y Ganadería, Panamá, project no. 42–1, 112 pp.

Ladd, John

1964   *Archaeological Investigations in Parita and Santa María Zones of Panama*. Smithsonian Institution, Bureau of American Ethnology, Bulletin 193.

Laming, Annette, and Jose Emperaire

1959   "A Jazida Jose Viera; Um Sitio Guarani e Pre-Ceramico do Onterior do Parana," *Arqueologia*, no. 1, Seccao L, pp. 1–142. Universidade do Parana.

Lange, Frederick W.

1971   "Northwestern Costa Rica: Pre-Columbian Circum-Caribbean Affiliations," *Folk*, vol. 13, pp. 43–64.

Lathrap, Donald W.

1968   "The 'Hunting' Economies of the Tropical Forest Zone of South America: An Attempt at Historical Perspective," in *Man the Hunter*, edited by Richard B. Lee and Irven De Vore. Aldine, pp. 23–29.

1970   *The Upper Amazon*. Ancient People and Places, vol. 70, General Editor: Glyn Daniel. Praeger.

1973   "The Antiquity and Importance of Long-Distance Trade Relationships in the Moist Tropics of Pre-Columbian South America," *World Archaeology*, vol. 5, no. 2, pp. 170–186.

Lathrap, Donald W., J.G. Marcos, and J.A. Zeidler

1977   "Real Alto: An Ancient Ceremonial Center," *Archaeology*, vol. 30, no. 1, pp. 3–13.

Lee, Richard B., and Irven DeVore

1976   *Kalahari Hunter-Gatherers, Studies of the !Kung San and their Neighbors.* Harvard University Press.

Lévi-Strauss, Claude

1950   "The Use of Wild Plants in Tropical South America," in *Handbook of South American Indians*, vol. 6, edited by J.H. Steward. Bureau of American Ethnology, Washington, D.C., pp. 465–486.

Lewis, Herbert

1968   "Typology and Process in Political Evolution," in *Essays on the Problem of Tribe*, edited by June Helm. Proceedings of the 1967 Annual Spring Meeting of the American Ethnological Society. The University of Washington Press, pp. 101–110.

Linares, Olga F.

1966   "La Cronología Arqueológica del Golfo de Chiriquí, Panamá," *XXXIV Congreso Internacional de Americanistas*, España, 1964. Actas y Memorias, vol. 1, pp. 405–414.

1968a   "Ceramic Phases for Chiriquí, Panama, and their Relationship to Neighboring Sequences," *American Antiquity*, vol. 33, no. 2, pp. 216–225.

1968b   "Cultural Chronology of the Gulf of Chiriquí, Panama," *Smithsonian Contributions in Anthropology*, vol. 8, pp. 1–119.

1970   "Patrones de Poblamiento Prehispánico Comparados con los Modernos en Bocas del Toro, Panamá," *Hombre y Cultura*, tomo 2, no. 1, pp. 56–67.

1971   "Técnicas en la Paleo-Arqueología del Oeste Panameño: El Proyecto NSF en Bocas del Toro y Chiriquí," *Actas del II Simposium Nacional de Antropología, Arqueología e Etnohistoria de Panamá*, Universidad de Panamá e Instituto Nacional de Cultura, pp. 257–289.

1976   " 'Garden Hunting' in the American Tropics," *Human Ecology*, vol. 4, no. 4, pp. 331–349.

1977a   "Adaptive Strategies in Western Panama," *World Archaeology*, vol. 8, no. 3, pp. 304–319.

1977b   *Ecology and the Arts in Ancient Panama.* Studies in Pre-Columbian Art and Archaeology, no. 17, Dumbarton Oaks.

1979   "What is Lower Central American Archaeology?" *Annual Reviews of Anthropology*, vol. 8, pp. 21–43.

Linares, Olga F., and Richard G. Cooke

1975   "Differential Exploitation of Lagoon-Estuary Systems in Ancient Panama," paper presented at the 40th annual meeting of the Society for American Archaeology, Dallas, 12 pp.

Linares, Olga F., and Anthony J. Ranere

1971   "Human Adaptations to the Tropical Forests of Western Panama," *Archaeology*, vol. 24, no. 4, pp. 346–355.

Linares, Olga F., P.D. Sheets, and E.J. Rosenthal

1975   "Prehistoric Agriculture in Tropical Highlands," *Science*, vol. 187, no. 4172, pp. 137–145.

Lothrop, Samuel K.

1937   *Coclé. An Archaeological Study of Central Panama, Part I.* Memoirs of the Peabody Museum of Archaeology and Ethnology, Harvard University, vol. 7.

1942   *Coclé. An Archaeological Study of Central Panama, Part II.* Memoirs of the Peabody Museum of Archaeology and Ethnology, Harvard University, vol. 8.

1950   *Archaeology of Southern Veraguas, Panama,* Memoirs of the Peabody Museum of Archaeology and Ethnology, Harvard University, vol. 9, no. 3.

1966   "Archaeology of Lower Central America," in *Handbook of Middle American Indians,* vol. 4, edited by R. Wauchope, G.F. Ekholm, and G.R. Willey. University of Texas Press, pp. 180–208.

Lowe, Gareth W.

1967   "Discussion. Appendix: Results of the 1965 Investigations at Altamira," in *Altamira and Padre Piedra, Early Preclassic Sites in Chiapas, Mexico,* by Dee F. Green and Gareth W. Lowe. New World Archaeological Foundation, Paper 20, pp. 53–130.

Lynch, Thomas F.

1974   "The Antiquity of Man in South America," *Quaternary Research,* vol. 4, no. 3, pp. 356–377.

1976   "The Entry and Postglacial Adaptation of Man in Andean South America," in *Habitats Humains Anterieurs a l'Holocene en Amerique.* Colloque 27, International Union of Prehistoric and Protohistoric Sciences, Ninth Congress, Nice, pp. 69–100.

MacArthur, Robert H.

1972   *Geographical Ecology: Patterns in the Distribution of Species.* Harper and Row.

MacCurdy, George C.

1911   *A Study of Chiriquian Antiquities.* Memoirs of the Connecticut Academy of Science, no. 3.

McEwen, J.M.

1946   "An Experiment with Primitive Maori Carving Tools," *Journal of the Polynesian Society,* vol. 55, pp. 111–116.

McGimsey, Charles R., III

1956   "Cerro Mangote: A Preceramic Site in Panama," *American Antiquity,* vol. 22, no. 2, pt. 1, pp. 151–161.

McGimsey, Charles R., III, M.B. Collins, and T.W. McKern

1966   "Cerro Mangote and its Population," paper presented at the 37th International Congress of Americanists, Mar del Plata, 29 pp.

MacNeish, R.S.

1972   "The Evolution of Community Patterns in the Tehuacán Valley of Mexico and Speculations About the Cultural Processes," in *Man, Settlement and Urbanism,* edited by P.J. Ucko, R. Tringham, and G.W. Dimbleby. Gerald Duckworth and Co., pp. 67–93.

MacNeish, R.S., T.C. Patterson, and D.L. Browman

1975   *The Central Peruvian Prehistoric Interaction Sphere.* Papers of the Robert S. Peabody Foundation for Archaeology, vol. 7.

Mangelsdorf, Paul C.

1974   *Corn: Its Origin, Evolution and Improvement.* Harvard University Press.

Mangelsdorf, Paul C., R.S. MacNeish, and W.C. Galinat

1967   "Prehistoric Wild and Cultivated Maize," in *The Prehistory of the Tehuacán Valley,* vol. 1. University of Texas Press, pp. 178–200.

Mangelsdorf, Paul C., R.S. MacNeish, and G.R. Willey

1964   "Origins of Agriculture in Mesoamerica," in *Handbook of Middle American Indians,* vol. 1, edited by R. Wauchope and R. West. Texas University Press, pp. 427–445.

Mangelsdorf, Paul C., and M.O. Sanoja

    1965   "Early Archaeological Maize from Venezuela," *Botanical Museum Leaflets*, Harvard University, vol. 21, pp. 105–112.

Martin, M. Kay

    1969   "South American Foragers: A Case Study in Cultural Devolution," *American Anthropologist*, vol. 71, no. 2, pp. 243–260.

Mason, J. Alden

    1942   "New Excavations at Sitio Conte, Coclé, Panama," Proceedings, Eighth American Scientific Congress, Washington, D.C., vol. 2, pp. 103–107.

May, Robert M.

    1973   *Stability and Complexity in Model Ecosystems.* Princeton University Press.

Meek, Seth E., and S.F. Hilderbrand

1923-1928   *The Marine Fishes of Panama.* Field Museum of Natural History, Zoological Series, vol. 15, 3 pts.: publication 215 (1923), publication 226 (1925), and publication 249 (1928).

Meggers, Betty J.

    1954   "Environmental Limitations on the Development of Culture," *American Anthropologist*, vol. 56, pp. 801–824.

    1971   *Amazonia: Man and Culture in a Counterfeit Paradise.* Aldine-Atherton.

Messer, Ellen

    1979   "Cultivation and Cognition: Plants and Archaeological Research Strategies," in *Ethnoarchaeology*, edited by C. Kramer. Columbia University Press, pp. 247–264.

Miller, Jr., T.O.

    1969   "Pre-historia de Regiao de Rio Claro, S.P.; Tradicoes em Divergentia," *Cuadernos Rioclarenses de Ciencias Humanas*, Faculdade de Filosofia, Ciencias e Letras de Rio Claro, Brazil, vol. 1, pp. 22–52.

Morehead, Warren K.

    1910   *The Stone Age in North America 1.* Houghton Mifflin.

Morey, Jr., Robert V.

    1970   "Ecology and Culture Change Among the Colombian Guahibo," Ph.D. dissertation, University of Pittsburgh.

Moser, Beverly

    1977   "A Study of Edge-Ground Cobbles as Tools Used in the Processing of Root Crops," typewritten manuscript, Department of Anthropology, Temple University.

Moynihan, Martin H.

    1971   "Successes and Failures of Tropical Mammals and Birds," *The American Naturalist*, vol. 105, no. 944, pp. 371–383.

    1976   *The New World Primates.* Princeton University Press.

Muller, J.

    1959   "Palynology of Recent Orinoco Delta and Shelf Sediments," *Micropaleontology*, vol. 5, no. 1, pp. 1–32.

Myers, Charles W.

    1969   "The Ecological Geography of Cloud Forest in Panama," *American Museum Novitates*, no. 2396.

    1972   "The Status of Herpetology in Panamá," in *The Panamic Biota: Some Observations Prior to a Sea-Level Canal*, edited by Meredith L. Jones. Bulletin of the Biological Society of Washington, no. 2, pp. 199–209.

Myers, Thomas P.

 1979 "Formative-Period Interaction Spheres in the Intermediate Area: Archaeology of Central America and Adjacent South America," in *Advances in Andean Archaeology*, edited by David L. Browman. Mouton, pp. 203–234.

Nietschmann, Bernard

 1973 *Between Land and Water; The Subsistence Ecology of the Miskito Indians, Eastern Nicaragua*. Seminar Press.

 1976 *Memorias de Arrecife Tortuga*. Banco de América, Nicaragua, Serie Geografía y Naturaleza, no. 2.

Odell, George Hamley

 1975 "Micro-Wear in Perspective: A Sympathetic Response to Lawrence H. Keeley," *World Archaeology*, vol. 7, no. 2, pp. 226–240.

Olsen, Stanley J.

 1964 *Mammal Remains from Archaeological Sites, Part 1, Southeastern and Southwestern United States*. Papers of Peabody Museum of Archaeology and Ethnology, Harvard University, vol. 61, no. 2.

Osborn, Alan J.

 1977a "Strandloopers, Mermaids, and Other Fairy Tales: Ecological Determinants of Marine Resource Utilization — The Peruvian Case," in *For Theory Building in Archaeology*, edited by L.R. Binford. Academic Press, pp. 157–205.

 1977b "Prehistoric Utilization of Marine Resource in Coastal Peru: How Much Do We Understand," paper presented at the 76th annual meeting of the American Anthropological Association, Houston, 35 pp.

Osgood, Cornelius

 1935 "The Archaeological Problem of Chiriquí," *American Anthropologist*, vol. 37, pp. 234–243.

Pearsall, Deborah M.

 1978 "Phytolith Analysis of Archaeological Soils: Evidence for Maize Cultivation in Formative Ecuador," *Science*, vol. 199, no. 4325, pp. 177–178.

Perlman, Melvin L.

 1977 "Comments on Explanation, and on Stability and Change," in *Explanation of Culture Change*, edited by J.N. Hill. University of New Mexico Press, pp. 319–333.

Peterson, Jean Treloggen

 1978 "Hunter-Gatherer/Farmer Exchange," *American Anthropologist*, vol. 80, no. 2, pp. 335–351.

Pickersgill, Barbara

 1969 "The Archaeological Record of Chili Peppers (*Capsicum* spp.) and the Sequence of Plant Domestication in Peru," *American Antiquity*, vol. 34, no. 1. pp. 54–61.

Pickersgill, Barbara, and C.B. Heiser, Jr.

 1977 "Origins and Distributions of Plants Domesticated in the New World Tropics," in *Origins of Agriculture*, edited by C.A. Reed. Mouton, pp. 803–835.

Pinart, Alphonse Louis

 1885 "Chiriqui. Bocas del Toro - Valle Miranda," *Bulletin de la Société de Géographie*, Ser. 7, vol. 16, pp. 433–453.

Piperno, Dolores R.

 1979 Phytolith Analysis of Archaeological Soils from Central Panama, M.A. thesis (manuscript), Temple University. Philadelphia.

Pires-Ferreira, Jane W., and Kent V. Flannery

   1976   "Ethnographic Models for Formative Exchange," in *The Early Mesoamerican Village*, edited by Kent V. Flannery. Academic Press, pp. 286–292.

Plog, Stephen

   1976   "Measurement of Prehistoric Interaction Between Communities," in *The Early Mesoamerican Village*, edited by Kent V. Flannery. Academic Press, pp. 255–272.

Porter, James W.

   1972   "Ecology and Species Diversity of Coral Reefs on Opposite Sides of the Isthmus of Panama," in *The Panamic Biota: Some Observations Prior to a Sea-Level Canal*, edited by Meredith L. Jones. Bulletin of the Biological Society of Washington, no. 2, pp. 89–116.

Porter, Duncan M.

   1973   "The Vegetation of Panama; A Review," in *Vegetation and Vegetational History of Northern Latin America*, edited by Alan Graham. Elsevier Scientific Publishing Company, pp. 167–201.

Randall, John E.

   1968   *Caribbean Reef Fishes*. T.F.H. Publications.

Ranere, Anthony J.

   1971   *Stratigraphy and Stone Tools from Meadow Canyon, Eastern Idaho*. Birch Creek Papers no. 4, Occasional Papers of the Idaho State University Museum, no. 27.
   1972a   "Early Human Adaptations to New World Tropical Forests: The View from Panama," Ph.D. dissertation, Department of Anthropology, University of California at Davis.
   1972b   "Ocupación Precerámica en las Tierras Altas de Chiriquí," translated by R.T. de Araúz, in *Actas del II Simposium Nacional de Antropología, Arqueología e Etnohistoria de Panama*, Abril 1971. Universidad de Panamá e Instituto Nacional de Cultura, pp. 197–207.
   1975   "Toolmaking and Tool Use Among the Preceramic Peoples of Panama," in *Lithic Technology: Making and Using Stone Tools*, edited by Earl Swanson. Mouton, pp. 173–209.

Ranere, Anthony J., and Pat Hansell

   1978   "Early Subsistence Patterns Along the Pacific Coast of Central Panama," in *Prehistoric Coastal Adaptations*, edited by Barbara L. Stark and Barbara Voorhies. Academic Press, pp. 43–59.

Ranere, Anthony J., and Richard L. McCarty

   1976   "Informe Preliminar Sobre la Excavación de un Sitio Precerámico en Coclé, Panamá," in *Actas del IV Simposium Nacional de Antropología, Arqueología, y Etnohistoria de Panamá*, Octubre 1973. Universidad de Panamá e Instituto Nacional de Cultura, pp. 483–493.

Rappaport, Roy A.

   1968   *Pigs for the Ancestors: Ritual in the Ecology of a New Guinea People*. Yale University Press.
   1978   "Maladaptation in Social Systems," in *The Evolution of Social Systems*, edited by J. Friedman and M.J. Rowlands. The University of Pittsburgh Press, pp. 49–71.

Rathje, William L.

   1972   "Praise the Gods and Pass the Metates: A Hypothesis of the Development of Lowland Rainforest Civilization in Mesoamerica," in *Contemporary Archaeology*, edited by M.P. Leone. Southern Illinois University Press, pp. 365–392.

Rebel, Thomas P., editor

   1974   *Sea Turtles and the Turtle Industry of the West Indies, Florida and the Gulf of Mexico*. University of Miami Press.

Reichel-Dolmatoff, Gerardo

1957　"Momil: A Formative Sequence from the Sinú Valley, Colombia," *American Antiquity*, vol. 22, pp. 226–234.

1965　*Colombia*. Ancient Peoples and Places, vol. 44, General Editor: Glyn Daniel. Praeger.

Richardson, J.L.

1969　"Former Lake-Level Fluctuations — Their Recognition and Interpretation," *Mitteilungen der Internationalen Vereinigung für Theoretische und Angewandte Limnologie*, vol. 17, pp. 78–93.

Richardson, James B., III

1973　"The Preceramic Sequence and the Pleistocene and Post-Pleistocene Climate of Northwest Peru," in *Human Variation*, edited by Donald Lathrap. Illinois Archaeological Survey, pp. 73–89.

1978　"Early Man on the Peruvian North Coast, Early Maritime Exploitation and the Pleistocene and Holocene Environment," in *Early Man in America*, edited by Alan Lyle Bryan. Occasional Papers no. 1, of the Department of Anthropology, University of Alberta, Edmonton: Archaeological Researches International, pp. 274–289.

Rivière, Peter

1969　*Marriage Among the Trio. A Principle of Social Organization*. Clarendon Press.

Roberts, L.M., U.J. Grant, R. Ramírez-E., W.H. Hatheway, and D.L. Smith with P.C. Mangelsdorf

1957　*Races of Maize in Colombia*. National Academy of Sciences, National Research Council, Washington, D.C., publication no. 510.

Robins, Richard C.

1972　"The State of Knowledge of the Coastal Fish Fauna of the Panamic Region Prior to the Construction of a Sea-Level Canal," in *The Panamic Biota: Some Observations Prior to a Sea-Level Canal*, edited by Meredith L. Jones. Bulletin of the Biological Society of Washington, no. 2, pp. 159–166.

Roosevelt, Anna

1977　"La Gruta: An Early Tropical Forest Community of the Middle Orinoco Basin," paper presented at the 42nd annual meeting of the Society for American Archaeology, New Orleans, 38 pp.

Rosenthal, E. Jane

1970　"Preliminary Analysis of the Stone Artifacts of Cerro Brujo, Site CA-3, Bocas del Toro, Panama," Senior thesis, Department of Anthropology, University of Pennsylvania.

1972　"Comments on the Groundstone of the El Hato-Cerro Punta (Upper Chiriqui Viejo) Region," typewritten manuscript.

1975　"Stone Artifacts at Cerro Brujo," typewritten manuscript.

Ross, Eric Barry

1978　"Food Taboos, Diet, and Hunting Strategy: The Adaptation to Animals in Amazon Cultural Ecology," *Current Anthropology*, vol. 19, no. 1, pp. 1–36.

Rouse, Irving

1939　"Conceptual Technique," in *Prehistory in Haiti: A Study in Method*, edited by I. Rouse. Yale University Publications in Anthropology, no. 21.

Rouse, Irving, and J.M. Cruxent

1963　*Venezuelan Archaeology*. Yale University Caribbean Series, no. 6.

Sackett, James R.

1973　"Style, Function, and Artifact Variability in Paleolithic Assemblages," in *The Explanation of Culture Change: Models in Prehistory*, C. Renfrew, editor. Gerald Duckworth and Co., pp. 317–325.

1977 "The Meaning of Style in Archaeology: A General Model," *American Antiquity*, vol. 42, no. 3, pp. 369–380.

Sahlins, Marshall D.

1958 *Social Stratification in Polynesia.* University of Washington Press.

Sanders, William T.

1978 "Commentary," in *Prehistoric Coastal Adaptations: The Economy and Ecology of Maritime Middle America*, edited by Barbara L. Stark and B. Voorhies. Academic Press, pp. 269–274.

Sauer, Carl O.

1959 "Age and Area of American Cultivated Plants," in *Actas del XXXIII Congreso Internacional de Americanistas*, vol. 1, pp. 215–229. San José, Costa Rica.
1966 *The Early Spanish Main.* University of California Press.
1969 *Agricultural Origins and Dispersals.* M.I.T. Press.

Schoenwetter, James

1974 "Pollen Records of Guila Naquits Cave," *American Antiquity*, vol. 39, no. 2, pp. 292–303.

Schulz, Evelyn

n.d. "Thin Section Analysis of Lithic Materials from Isla Palenque, Panama," typewritten manuscript.

Semenov, S.A.

1964 *Prehistoric Technology*, translated by M.W. Thompson. Adams and Dart.

Service, Elman

1962 *Primitive Social Organization: An Evolutionary Account.* Random House.

Sharp, Lauriston

1968 "Steel Axes for Stone Age Australians," in *Man in Adaptation, The Cultural Present*, edited by Yehudi A. Cohen. Aldine Publishing Co., pp. 82–93.

Sheets, Payson D.

1972 "Stone Tools from Volcan Project (NSF Gr-2846), Third Season," typewritten manuscript.
1975 "Behavioral Analysis and the Structure of a Prehistoric Industry," *Current Anthropology*, vol. 16, no. 3, pp. 369–391.

Siegel, Sidney

1956 *Nonparametric Statistics for the Behavioral Sciences.* McGraw-Hill.

Simmonds, N.W.

1976 *Evolution of Crop Plants.* Longman.

Simpson, George Gaylord

1949 *The Meaning of Evolution: A Study of the History of Life and of Its Significance for Man.* Yale University Press.

Simpson Vuilleumier, Beryl

1971 "Pleistocene Changes in the Flora and Fauna of South America," *Science*, vol. 173, no. 3999, pp. 771–780.

Sims, Cort

1971 "Edged Cobbles in the Pacific Northwest," *Tebiwa*, vol. 14, no. 2, pp. 21–38.

Siskind, Janet

1973 *To Hunt in the Morning.* Oxford University Press.

Smith, C. Earle, Jr.

    1967   "Plant Remains," in *The Prehistory of the Tehuacan Valley*, vol. 1, edited by D.S. Byers. University of Texas Press, pp. 220–255.

Smythe, Nicholas

    1978   *The Natural History of the Central American Agouti*. Smithsonian Contributions to Zoology, no. 257.

Snarskis, Michael J.

    1976   "Stratigraphic Excavations in the Eastern Lowlands of Costa Rica," *American Antiquity*, vol. 41, no. 3, pp. 342–353.

    1979   "Turrialba: A Paleo-Indian Quarry and Workshop Site in Eastern Costa Rica," *American Antiquity*, vol. 44, no. 1, pp. 125–138.

Sollberger, J.B., and L.W. Patterson

    1976   "The Myth of Biopolar Flaking Industries," *Newsletter of Lithic Technology*, vol. 5, no. 3, pp. 40–41.

Spang, Sara

    1976   "Excavations of a Prehistoric Village Site in Western Panama," M.A. thesis, Temple University.

Standley, Paul C.

    1928   *Flora of the Panama Canal Zone*. Contributions from the U.S. National Herbarium, vol. 27. Smithsonian Institution, Washington, D.C.

Stark, Barbara L., and Barbara Voorhies, editors

    1978   *Prehistoric Coastal Adaptations: The Economy and Ecology of Maritime Middle America*. Academic Press.

Stebbins, Robert Cyril

    1954   *Amphibians and Reptiles of Western North America*. McGraw-Hill.

Steward, Julian H.

    1938   *Basin-Plateau Aboriginal Sociopolitical Groups*. Smithsonian Institution Bureau of American Ethnology, Bulletin 120.

Steward, Julian H., and L.C. Faron

    1959   *Native Peoples of South America*. McGraw-Hill.

Stewart, Robert H.

    1978   "Preliminary Geography: El Volcan Region, Province of Chiriquí, Republic of Panama," typewritten manuscript, 36 pp.

Stirling, Matthew W.

    1950   "Exploring Ancient Panama by Helicopter," The National Geographic Magazine, vol. 97, no. 2, pp. 227–246.

Stirling, Matthew W., and Marion Stirling

    1964   "Archaeological Notes on Almirante Bay, Bocas del Toro, Panama," Anthropological Papers no. 72, Bureau of American Ethnology, Washington, D.C., pp. 255–284.

Stone, Doris Z.

    1949   *The Boruca of Costa Rica*. Papers of the Peabody Museum of American Archaeology and Ethnology, Harvard University, vol. 25, no. 2.

Stothert, Karen E.

    1976   "The Early Prehistory of the Sta. Elena Peninsula, Ecuador: Continuities Between Preceramic and Ceramic Cultures," in *Actas del XLI Congreso Internacional de Americanistas*, Mexico, vol. II.

1977   "Preceramic Adaptation and Trade in the Intermediate Area," paper presented at the 76th annual meeting of the American Anthropological Association, Houston, 19 pp.

Struever, Stuart

1968   "Flotation Techniques for the Recovery of Small-Scale Archaeological Remains," *American Antiquity*, vol. 33, no. 3, pp. 353–362.

Swanson, Earl H.

1972   *Birch Creek: Human Ecology in the Cool Desert of the Northern Rocky Mountains 9000 B.C. – A.D. 1850*. The Idaho State University Press.

Swanson, Earl H., editor

1975   *Lithic Technology: Making and Using Stone Tools*. World Anthropology. Mouton.

Swanson, Earl H., and Paul G. Sneed

1966   *The Archaeology of the Shoup Rockshelters in East Central Idaho*. Birch Creek Papers no. 3, Occasional Papers of the Idaho State University Museum, no. 17.

Terrell, John, Marilyn Miller, and Derek Roe, editors

1977   "Human Biogeography," *World Archaeology*, vol. 8, no. 3.

Terry, Robert A.

1956   *A Geological Reconnaissance of Panama*. Occasional Papers no. 23 of the California Academy of Sciences.

Tosi, Joseph A.

1971   *Inventariación y Demostraciones Forestales. Panamá. Zonas de Vida*. FO:SF/PAN 6. Informe Técnico 2, Programa de las Naciones Unidas para el Desarrollo.

Towle, Margaret A.

1961   *The Ethnobotany of Pre-Columbian Peru*. Aldine Publishing Company.

Townsend, William H.

1969   "Stone and Steel Tool Use in a New Guinea Society," *Ethnology*, vol. 8, no. 2, pp. 199–205.

Tringham, Ruth, Glenn Cooper, George Odell, Barbara Voytek, and Anne Whitman

1974   "Experimentation in the Formation of Edge Damage: A New Approach to Lithic Analysis," *Journal of Field Archaeology*, vol. 1, nos. 1/2, pp. 171–196.

True, D.L., and R.G. Matson

1970   "Cluster Analysis and Multidimensional Scaling of Archaeological Sites in Northern Chile," *Science*, vol. 169, no. 3951, pp. 1201–1203.

Turnbull, Colin

1965   *Wayward Servants: The Two Worlds of the African Pygmies*. Natural History Press.

Ufeldre, Fray Adrian de

1682   "Conquista de la Provincia del Guaymí . . .," in *Tesoros Verdaderos de las Indias*. N.A. Tunassio, vol. 3, ch. 1.

Van der Hammen, T.

1973   "The Quaternary of Colombia: Introduction to a Research Project and a Series of Publications," *Palaeogeography, Palaeoclimatology, Palaeoecology*, vol. 14, no. 1, pp. 1–7.

Van Geel, B., and T. Van der Hammen

1973   "Upper Quaternary Vegetational and Climatic Sequence of the Fuquene Area (Eastern Cordillera, Colombia)," *Palaeogeography, Palaeoclimatology, Palaeoecology*, vol. 14, no. 1, pp. 9–92.

Vavilov, N.I.

1951 "The Origin, Variation, Immunity, and Breeding of Cultivated Plants," translated by K. Starr Chester. *Chronica Botanica,* vol. 13, pp. 1–364.

Vermeij, Geeret J.

1978 *Biogeography and Adaptation: Patterns of Marine Life.* Harvard University Press.

Wagner, P.L.

1964 "Natural Vegetation of Middle America," in *Handbook of Middle American Indians,* vol. 1., edited by R. Wauchope and R. West. University of Texas Press, pp. 216–264.

Wagner, Erika

1967 *The Prehistory and Ethnohistory of the Carache Area in Western Venezuela.* Yale University Publications in Anthropology, no. 71.

Walker, Ernest P.

1968 *Mammals of the World,* second edition, vol. 2. Johns Hopkins Press.

Warmke, Germaine L., and R. Tucker Abbott

1962 *Caribbean Seashells.* Livingston Publishing Co.

Wassén, S. Henri

1952 "Some Remarks on the Divisions of the Guaymí Indians," in *Indian Tribes of Aboriginal America,* edited by Sol Tax. Selected Papers of the Twenty-ninth International Congress of Americanists. University of Chicago Press, pp. 271–280.

Wellhausen, E.J., A. Fuentes O., A. Hernández C., with P.C. Mangelsdorf

1957 *Races of Maize in Central America.* National Academy of Sciences, National Research Council Washington, Publication 511.

Wellhausen, E.J., L.M. Roberts, and E. Hernandez, with P.C. Mangelsdorf

1952 *Races of Maize in Mexico.* Bussey Institute, Harvard University.

Wilbert, Johannes

1976 "*Manicaria saccifera* and Its Cultural Significance Among the Warao Indians of Venezuela," *Botanical Museum Leaflets,* Harvard University, vol. 24, no. 10, pp. 275–335.

Willey, Gordon R.

1971 *An Introduction to American Archaeology, vol. 2: South America.* Prentice-Hall.

Willey, Gordon R., and C.R. McGimsey

1954 *The Monagrillo Culture of Panama.* Papers of the Peabody Museum, Harvard University, vol. 49, no. 2.

Willoughby, Charles C.

1907 "The Adze and the Ungrooved Axe of the New England Indians," *American Anthropologist,* vol. 9, pp. 296–306.

Wilmsen, Edwin N.

1968 "Functional Analysis of Flaked Stone Artifacts," *American Antiquity,* vol. 33, no. 2, pp. 156–161.

1970 *Lithic Analysis and Cultural Inference: A Paleo-Indian Case.* Anthropological Papers, no. 16, University of Arizona.

Woodring, W.P.

1966 "The Panama Land Bridge as a Sea Barrier," *Proceedings of the American Philosophical Society,* vol. 110, no. 6, pp. 425–433.

Young, Philip D.

    1970   "Notes on the Ethnohistorical Evidence for Structural Continuity in Guaymí
           Society," *Ethnohistory*, vol. 17, nos. 1–2, pp. 11–29.

    1971   *Ngawbe: Tradition and Change Among the Western Guaymí of Panama.* Illinois
           Studies in Anthropology, no. 7.

    1975   "Guaymí Nativism: Its Rise and Demise," in *Proceedings of the XLI International Congress of Americanists*, Mexico, vol. 3, pp. 93–101.

    1976   "The Expression of Harmony and Discord in a Guaymí Ritual: The Symbolic
           Meaning of Some Aspects of the *Balsería*," in *Frontier Adaptations in Lower Central America*, edited by Mary W. Helms and F.O. Loveland. Institute for the
           Study of Human Issues, Philadelphia, pp. 37–53.

Young, Philip D., and John R. Bort

    1976   "Edabáli: The Ritual Sibling Relationship Among the Western Guaymí," in
           Ritual and Symbol in Native Central America, edited by P.D. Young and J.
           Howe. University of Oregon Anthropological Papers, no. 9, pp. 77–90.

Zevallos Menendez, Carlos, W.C. Galinat, D.W. Lathrap, E.R. Leng, J.G. Marcos, and K.M.
Klumpp

    1977   "The San Pablo Corn Kernel and its Friends," *Science*, vol. 196, no. 4288, pp.
           385–389.

LIST OF CONTRIBUTORS

IRENE BORGOGNO
McNeil Laboratories
Fort Washington, Pennsylvania

JOHN BORT
Department of Sociology and
    Anthropology
East Carolina University
Greenville, North Carolina

KAREN H. CLARY
Laboratory for Ethnobotany
Department of Biology
University of New Mexico
Albuquerque, New Mexico

RICHARD G. COOKE
Smithsonian Tropical
    Research Institute
Balboa, Panama

BRUCE H. DAHLIN
Department of Anthropology
The Catholic University of America
Washington, D.C.

WALTON C. GALINAT
Suburban Experiment Station
University of Massachusetts
Waltham, Massachusetts

MARGARET O. KUDARAUSKAS
Cambridge, Massachusetts

OLGA F. LINARES
Smithsonian Tropical Research
    Institute
Balboa, Panama

ANTHONY J. RANERE
Department of Anthropology
Temple University
Philadelphia, Pennsylvania

E. JANE ROSENTHAL
Anthropology Department
California State University
Long Beach, California

PAYSON D. SHEETS
Department of Anthropology
University of Colorado
Boulder, Colorado

CATHERINE SHELTON
EINHAUS
Department of Anthropology
Temple University
Philadelphia, Pennsylvania

C. EARLE SMITH
Department of Anthropology
The University of Alabama
University, Alabama

SARA SPANG
Institute for the Future
Menlo Park, California

G. JAMES WEST
Department of Anthropology
University of California at Davis
Davis, California

RICHARD S. WHITE
Florence, New Jersey

ELIZABETH S. WING
The Florida State Museum
University of Florida
Gainesville, Florida

PHILIP D. YOUNG
Department of Anthropology
University of Oregon
Eugene, Oregon

529

Acknowledgments for Illustrations

Isabel de Obaldía: 7.0-2 to 7.0-5, 7.0-6, 7.0-9, 10.0-1 to 10.0-4, 13.0-1 to 13.0-19, 14.0-1, 14.0-2

Steve Gaber: 16/5

Walton C. Galinat: 10.0-11

María Luz de Jimenez: 9.0-1 to 9.0-3

L.M.K. (Peabody):   10/2, 10/3

Benjamin Linares: 10/1, 11/1, 12/1 to 12/3

Francisco E. Linares: 10.0-5b, 10.0-9, 7/6

Olga F. Linares: 4.0-1, 5.0-1, 5.0-3, 6.0-2, 6.0-3, 7.0-1, 10.0-5a, 10.0-10, 15.0-2, 15.0-4, 4/2, 6/5 to 6/8, 7/2, 14/2, 15/1-4, 15/6-13, 16/2-4, 16/6, 20/1b

Olga T. de Linares: 7.0-6

Richard McCarty: Front cover, 3.0-9 to 3.0-12, 10.0-8, 15.0-1, 15.0-3, 15.0-5, 15.0-6, 6/2, 6/3, 6/6, 7/3

Robert McNealy: 3.0-13, 3.0-14, 4.0-3, 9/7

Francine Mendel-Sheets   7.0-8, 8/4-9, 8/11-13, 9/1, 9/4, 9/8, 14/2-9

Martin H. Moynihan: Back cover, 12.0-1, 12.0-2

Anthony J. Ranere: 3.0-3, 3.0-5, 3.0-7, 5.0-4, 1/2, 1/3, 1/5, 6/1, 6/2, 8/3, 8/4, 8/6, 8/8-11

E. Jane Rosenthal: 1/1, 1/4, 1/6, 4/6, 5/2, 6/4, 7/4

Payson D. Sheets: 4/4

Catherine Shelton Einhaus: 15/1-7, 15/9-13

C. Earle Smith: 10.0-6, 10.0-7

Joan Snowden: 9/2, 9/3, 9/5, 9/6

Elizabeth Wahle: 5.0-2, 6.0-1, 7.0-1, 7.0-7, 2/1 - 4/1, 4/3, 4/5, 5/1, 5/2, 6/3, 7/1, 7/3, 7/4, 7/5, 17/1, 19/2

Lynn Wigglesworth: 3.0-1, 3.0-4, 3.0-6, 8/1, 8/2, 16/1

Philip D. Young: 10/1, 19/3, 20/1a